Southampton - London
M3
A33
M25   junction 15

D1464684

Southampton - London
M3
A33

M25   junction 15

Town & city maps of Britain

Contents

This atlas lists towns and cities geographically starting in the south, progressing northwards.

Key to map pages	2
Key to map symbols	3
Road maps (8.7 miles to 1 inch)	4-35
Plymouth urban map	36
Bournemouth urban map	37
Southampton & Portsmouth urban map	38-39
Swansea urban map	40
Cardiff & Newport urban map	41
Bristol urban map	42
Milton Keynes urban map	43
London motorway map	44-45
London urban maps	46-53
London central maps	54-61
Birmingham motorway map	62-63
West Midlands urban map	64-65
Birmingham central map	66-67
Coventry urban map	68
Leicester urban map	69
Derby & Nottingham urban map	70-71
Stoke-on-Trent urban map	72
Sheffield urban map	73
Merseyside urban map	74-75
Liverpool central map	76-77
Manchester motorway map	78-79
Greater Manchester urban map	80-81
Manchester central map	82-83
Leeds & Bradford urban map	84-85
Leeds central map	86-87
Newcastle upon Tyne urban map	88
Edinburgh urban map	89
Glasgow urban map	90-91
Glasgow central map	92-93
Town & city centre plans	94-121
Index for road maps	122-129
Index for urban & central city maps	130-172
Distance chart	173
Motorway services information	174-175
Drivers' websites	176

Published by Collins
An imprint of HarperCollins*Publishers*
77-85 Fulham Palace Road, Hammersmith, London W6 8JB
www.collins.co.uk

Copyright © HarperCollins*Publishers* Ltd 2004
Collins® is a registered trademark of HarperCollins*Publishers* Limited
Mapping generated from Collins Bartholomew digital databases

Printed and bound in China by Imago.

ISBN 0 00 719204 5   Imp 001   RC11859   BDB

e-mail: roadcheck@harpercollins.co.uk

Key to map pages

Town and city centre plans

Aberdeen	94
Bath	94
Blackpool	95
Bournemouth	95
Bradford	96
Brighton	96
Bristol	97
Cambridge	97
Canterbury	98
Cardiff	98
Carlisle	99
Cheltenham	99
Chester	100
Coventry	100
Derby	101
Dover	101
Dundee	102
Durham	102
Eastbourne	103
Edinburgh	103
Exeter	104
Folkestone	104
Gloucester	105
Guildford	105
Harrogate	106
Hastings	106
Hereford	107
Inverness	107
Kingston upon Hull	108
Leicester	108
Lincoln	109
Middlesbrough	109
Milton Keynes	110
Newcastle upon Tyne	110
Norwich	111
Nottingham	111
Oxford	112
Perth	112
Plymouth	113
Portsmouth	113
Reading	114
Salisbury	114
Sheffield	115
Southampton	115
Stoke-on-Trent	116
Stratford-upon-Avon	116
Sunderland	117
Swansea	117
Swindon	118
Torquay	118
Watford	119
Weston-super-Mare	119
Winchester	120
Windsor	120
Worcester	121
York	121

Central city maps

Birmingham	66-67
Glasgow	92-93
Leeds	86-87
Liverpool	76-77
London	54-61
Manchester	82-83

Urban maps

Birmingham	65
Bournemouth	37
Bradford	84
Bristol	42
Cardiff	41
Coventry	68
Derby	70
Edinburgh	89
Glasgow	90-91
Greater Manchester	80-81
Leeds	85
Leicester	69
Liverpool	74
London	46-53
Manchester	81
Merseyside	74-75
Milton Keynes	43
Newcastle upon Tyne	88
Newport	41
Nottingham	71
Plymouth	36
Portsmouth	39
Sheffield	73
Southampton	38
Stoke-on-Trent	72
Swansea	40
West Midlands	64-65

Motorway maps

Birmingham	62-63
Greater London	44-45
Greater Manchester	78-79
London	44-45
Manchester	78-79
West Midlands	62-63

Legend:
- LONDON — Central city maps
- Oxford — Town & city centre plans
- Urban maps
- Motorway maps
- 4-5 — Road maps

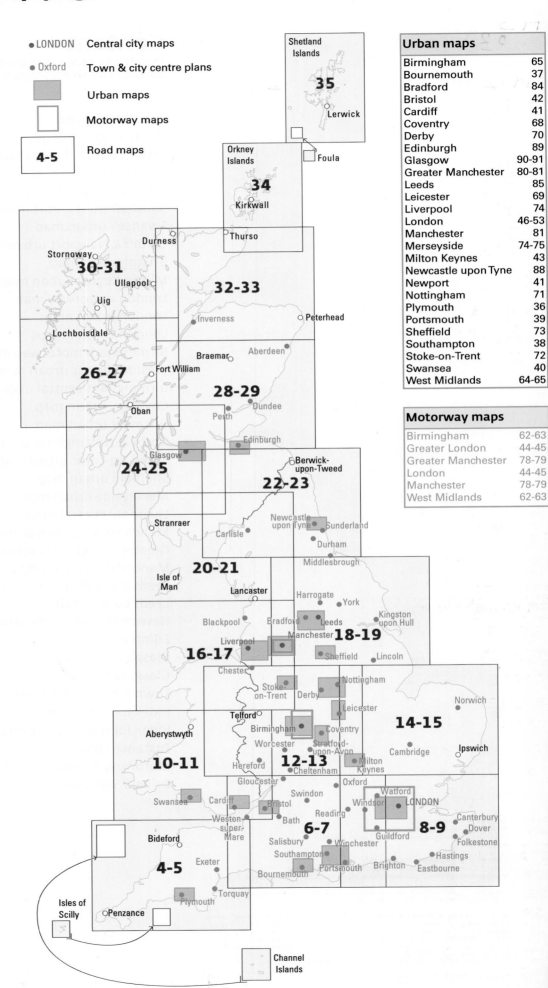

Road maps

Pages 4-35

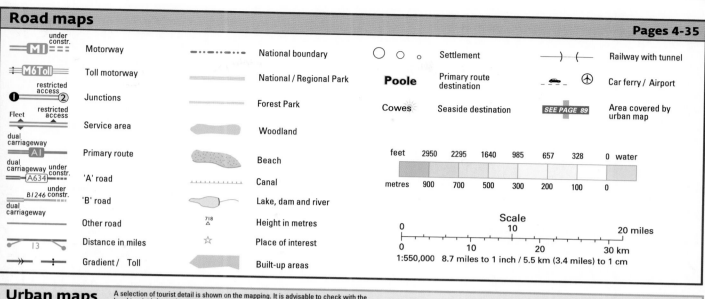

Motorway (under constr.)	National boundary	Settlement
Toll motorway (M6Toll)	National / Regional Park	Poole — Primary route destination
Junctions (restricted access)	Forest Park	Cowes — Seaside destination
Service area (Fleet, restricted access)	Woodland	SEE PAGE 89 — Area covered by urban map
Primary route (A1, dual carriageway)	Beach	Railway with tunnel
'A' road (A634, dual carriageway under constr.)	Canal	Car ferry / Airport
'B' road (B1246, under constr. dual carriageway)	Lake, dam and river	
Other road	Height in metres (718)	
Distance in miles (13)	Place of interest	
Gradient / Toll	Built-up areas	

feet 2950 2295 1640 985 657 328 0 water
metres 900 700 500 300 200 100 0

Scale
0 — 10 — 20 miles
0 — 10 — 20 — 30 km
1:550,000 8.7 miles to 1 inch / 5.5 km (3.4 miles) to 1 cm

Urban maps

A selection of tourist detail is shown on the mapping. It is advisable to check with the local tourist information centre regarding opening times and facilities available.

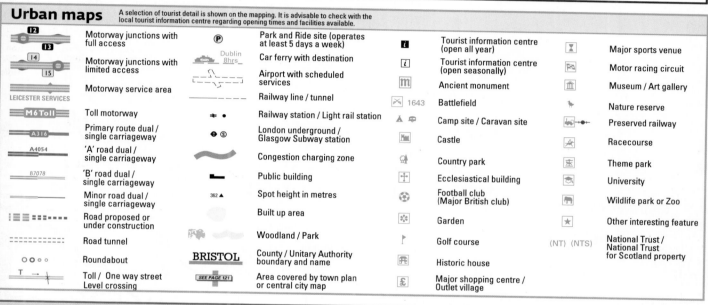

Motorway junctions with full access	Park and Ride site (operates at least 5 days a week)	Tourist information centre (open all year)	Major sports venue
Motorway junctions with limited access	Car ferry with destination (Dublin 8hrs)	Tourist information centre (open seasonally)	Motor racing circuit
Motorway service area (LEICESTER SERVICES)	Airport with scheduled services	Ancient monument	Museum / Art gallery
Toll motorway (M6Toll)	Railway line / tunnel	Battlefield (1643)	Nature reserve
Primary route dual / single carriageway (A316)	Railway station / Light rail station	Camp site / Caravan site	Preserved railway
'A' road dual / single carriageway (A4054)	London underground / Glasgow Subway station	Castle	Racecourse
'B' road dual / single carriageway (B7078)	Congestion charging zone	Country park	Theme park
Minor road dual / single carriageway	Public building	Ecclesiastical building	University
Road proposed or under construction	Spot height in metres (362)	Football club (Major British club)	Wildlife park or Zoo
Road tunnel	Built up area	Garden	Other interesting feature
Roundabout	Woodland / Park	Golf course	National Trust / National Trust for Scotland property (NT) (NTS)
Toll / One way street Level crossing	County / Unitary Authority boundary and name (BRISTOL)	Historic house	
	Area covered by town plan or central city map (SEE PAGE 121)	Major shopping centre / Outlet village	

Central city maps

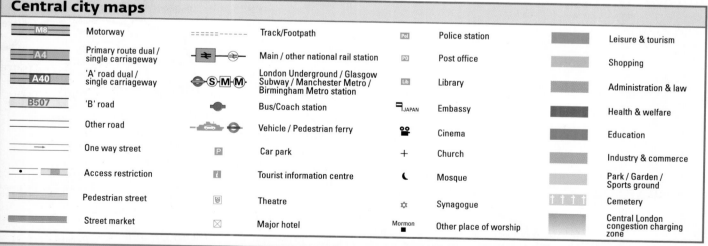

Motorway (M8)	Track/Footpath	Police station (Pol)	Leisure & tourism
Primary route dual / single carriageway (A4)	Main / other national rail station	Post office (PO)	Shopping
'A' road dual / single carriageway (A40)	London Underground / Glasgow Subway / Manchester Metro / Birmingham Metro station (S M M)	Library (Lib)	Administration & law
'B' road (B507)	Bus/Coach station	Embassy (JAPAN)	Health & welfare
Other road	Vehicle / Pedestrian ferry	Cinema	Education
One way street	Car park (P)	Church	Industry & commerce
Access restriction	Tourist information centre	Mosque	Park / Garden / Sports ground
Pedestrian street	Theatre	Synagogue	Cemetery
Street market	Major hotel	Other place of worship (Mormon)	Central London congestion charging zone

Town and city centre plans

Pages 94-121

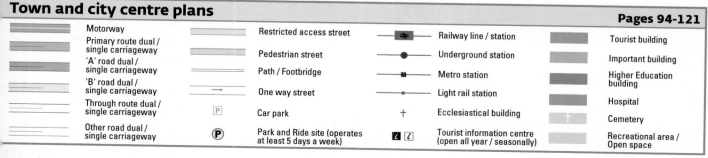

Motorway	Restricted access street	Railway line / station	Tourist building
Primary route dual / single carriageway	Pedestrian street	Underground station	Important building
'A' road dual / single carriageway	Path / Footbridge	Metro station	Higher Education building
'B' road dual / single carriageway	One way street	Light rail station	Hospital
Through route dual / single carriageway	Car park (P)	Ecclesiastical building	Cemetery
Other road dual / single carriageway	Park and Ride site (operates at least 5 days a week) (P)	Tourist information centre (open all year / seasonally)	Recreational area / Open space

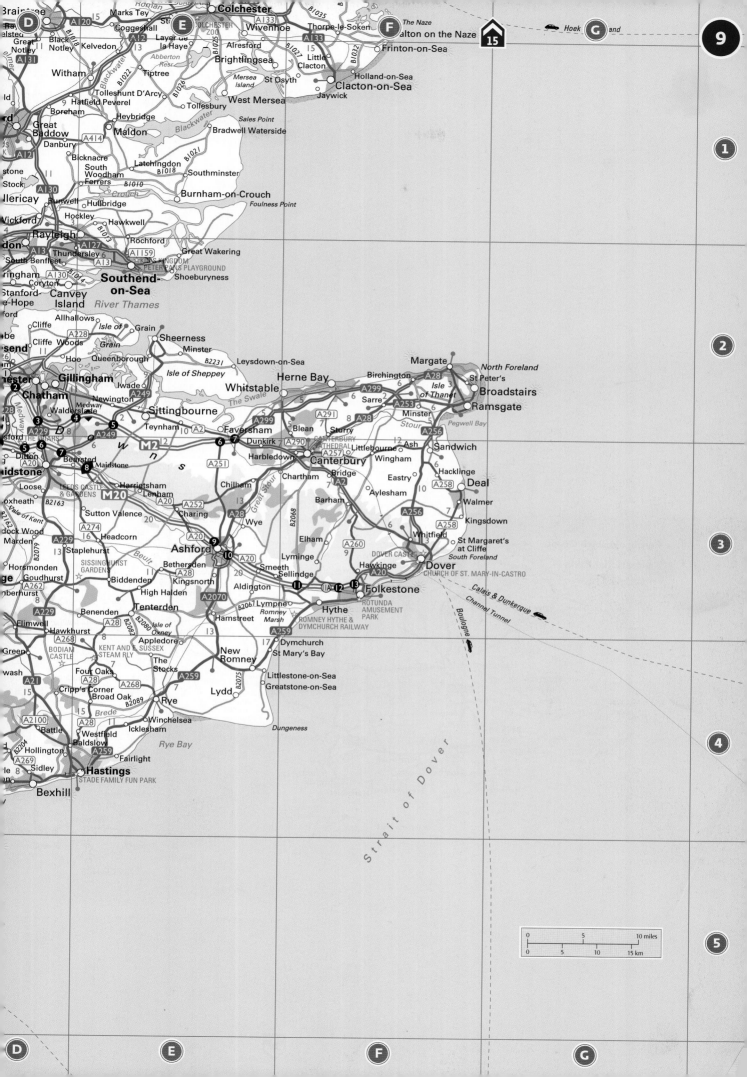

A   B   16   C   D

Barmouth
Barmouth Bay
(Bae B

Llwyn

Llangelynnin

Tywyn

A4

Aberd

Bor

C a r d i g a n   B a y

(B a e

C e r e d i g i o n)

Aberystwy

Llanbadarn
Fawr

1

0   5   10 miles
0   5   10   15 km

A487

Lla

Llanrhystud
16
Llanon
B4577   Cross Inn
B4576

2

Aberaeron

New Quay   7   A482

Llanarth
A486   A487   B4342   13

Aeron   B4337

Llangranog

Plwmp   Synod Inn   Temple
Bar

Talgarreg   A482

Lampeter

Aberporth   A487
15

B4334

Penrhiw-pal

Ffostrasol

A486   A475   12

B4333

Horeb   A485

Llanybydder

Llanfihangel ar-arth

Cardigan
St Dogmaels

A484   B4570   10

Newcastle
Emlyn   Llandysul

Llangeler   6

Pencader   5   13

Llansa

B4582
18
Newport   B4329   Eglwyswrw

Dinas
Head

Strumble
Head

Goodwick

A487   Fishguard
B4313

Scleddau

Letterston

Crymych

Mynydd Preseli

Greenway

Maenclochog   A478

Trelech   Brechfa

Cynwyl Elfed

Newport Bay   B4333

Cynin   21

Taf

B4329

B4313

A485   A4310   15

Pembrokeshire Coast

National Park

St David's Head

BISHOP'S PALACE
St David's   Solva
A487

A487   Camrose
16

Ramsey
Island

St Bride's
Bay

Solva
A487   A4330   15   SCOLTON
MANOR
C. PARK
LLYS-Y-FRAN
RESERVOIR
& PARK

Llandissilio

Clynderwen   Meidrim   10

Llanegwad

Carmarthen
A40   Llanarthne

Llangunnor   NATIONAL
BOTANIC
GARDEN
OF WALES

A485

B4310   15

Skomer
Island

Skokholm
Island

Rosslare

St Ann's Head

Broad Haven

Haverfordwest
A40   OAKWOOD
LEISURE PARK
B4341   A4076   4
Johnston
3   Llangwm

Dale

Milford
Haven   A477   8

Pembroke
Dock   Neyland
PEMBROKE CASTLE
GREAT WEDLOCK
DINOSAUR EXPERIENCE

Angle

Hundleton

Castlemartin   B4319

Linney
Head

CANASTON
CENTRE 2000

A4075

A477

Narberth
Templeton
A478
FOLLY
FARM
Kilgetty

Saundersfoot

Whitland
A4328   13

St Clears
A477   Llanddowror

Red Roses
Laugharne
(Lacharn)
Pendine
(Pentywyn)
St Ishmael

Carmarthen
Bay

Llangwm

Whitford Point

Llanddarog
A48   16
Llangendeirne
Drefach

Llansteffan   19   Pontyberem

B4312   Tywi

A484   A4306   B4317

Kidwelly
(Cydwelly)

Pembrey
(Pen-Bre)
PEMBREY C. PARK

LLANELLI
COASTAL
PARK

Trimsaran   A476

Burry Port

Llanelli

LLANELLI
Burry Inlet

A48   A476   49
M4   48
6

Amma

A47   A48

Llannon

Gorseinon

Loughor

Crofty

Dunvant

Ki

Gower   SEE PAGE 40

Llanrhidian   B4295

Rhossili
A41 18   Bishopston   The Mum

Worms Head

Port Eynon

Cork

Oakwood
A40
11

Broad Haven   B4327

Dinas
Head

Clynderwen
Whitland

A4066
A477   5
A4318
Tenby
Penally

Manorbier

Caldey
Island

Pembroke
A4139
Freshwater
East

St Govan's Head

MA
IND

3

4

5

A   B   4   C   D

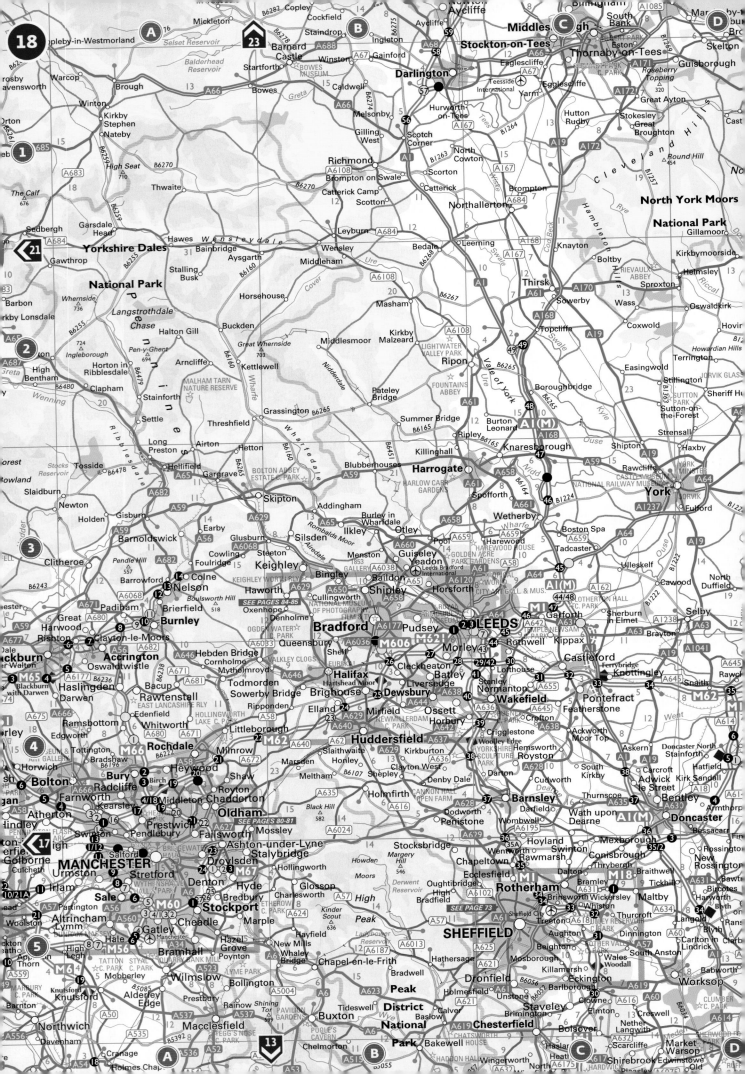

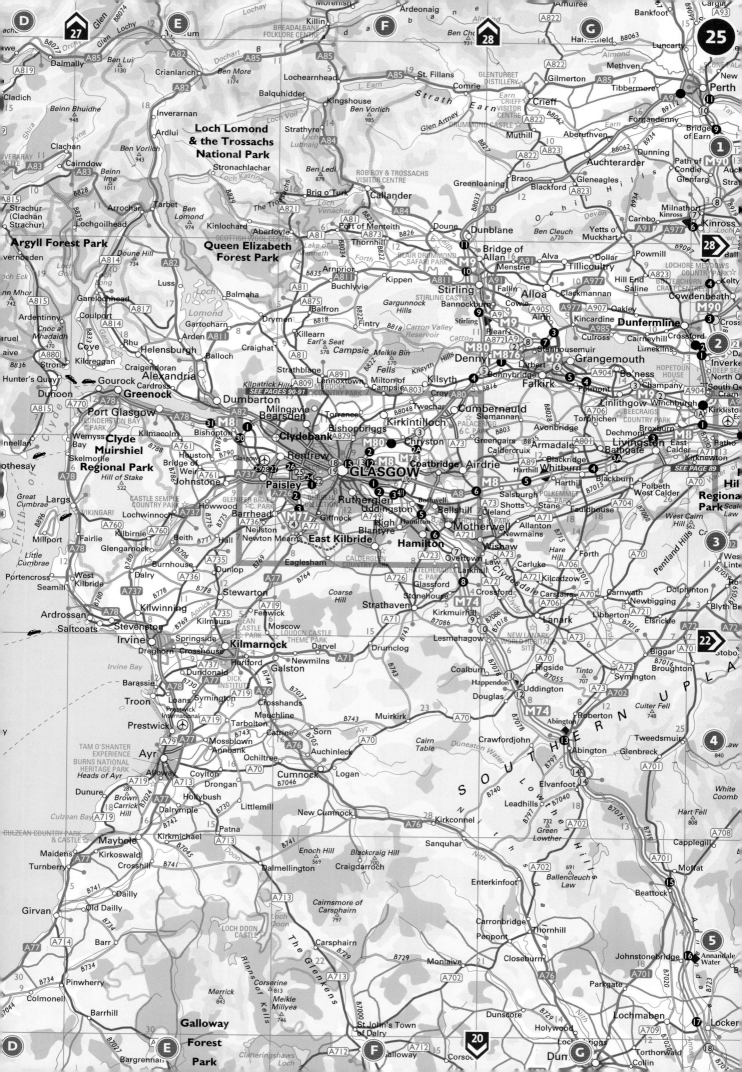

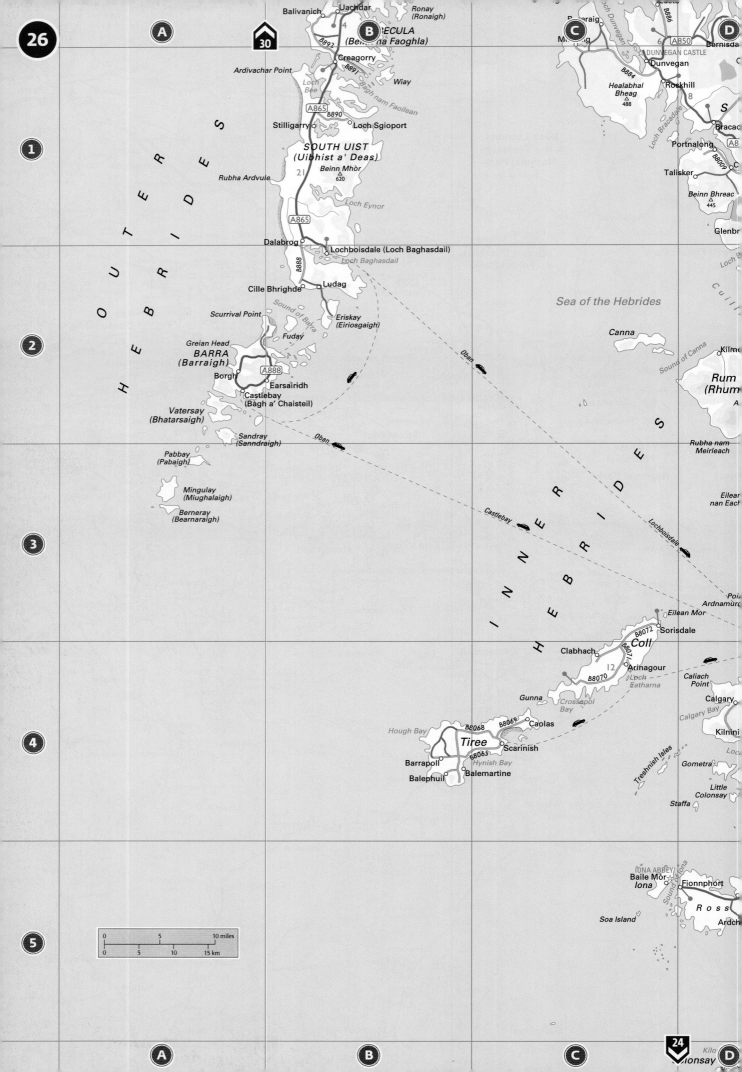

A **B** **C** **D**

0   5   10 miles
0   5   10   15 km

1

2

Arnol

Barv

Shawbost

Bragar

A858

ISLE

(Eile

Carloway

Beinn
Mholach
△
292

Tolastadh
a'Chaolais

Storno
(Steornabh

Breascleit

Miavaig

Great
Bernera

A858

Timsgearraidh

Crùlabhig

Callanish

Gearraidh na h-Aibhne

B8059

Achadh
Mòr

13

A859

12

Loch
Suainaval

Einacleit

B8011

Breanais

Mealisval
△
574

Balallan

Cearsiac

B8060

Mealasta
Island

NORTH HARRIS
(Ceann a Tuath na Hearadh)

Airidh
a'Bhruaich

Loch
Resort

Loch
Langavat

21

Scarp

Tirga Mòr
679

A859

Beinn
Mhòr
△
572

Loch S

Huisinis

3

Gasker

Clisham
799

A859

Loch
Claidh

Abhainnsuidhe

B887

Loch
Bhrollum

Taransay
(Taransaigh)

Aird
Asaig

Tarbert
(An Tairbeart)

A859

Kyles Scalpay

Scalpay
(Eilean Scalpaigh)

Toe Head

25

**SOUTH
HARRIS**
*(Ceann a Deas
na Hearadh)*

4

Shillay

A859

Northton

Pabbay

Loch
Langavat

Leverburgh

Rubha Hun

Sound of Pabbay

Rodel

Boreray

Berneray
*(Eilean
Bhearnaraigh)*

Renish Point

Port nan Long

Griminis Point

Vallay

A8

Balgown

Sollas

B893

Baile Mhartainn

NORTH UIST
(Uibhist a' Tuath)

A865

Ceann a'Bhàigh

8

Lochmaddy
(Loch na Madadh)

Vaternish Point

Idrigi

5

A865

A867

Loch
Euphoirt

Ben Geary
△
284

Monach Islands
(Heisker Islands)

Saighdinis

9

Dunvegan Head

Loch
Snizort

Baleshare

Ronay
(Ronaigh)

Loreraig

Lusta

B886

Balivanich

Uachdar

Miloyaig

6

A850

Bernisda

4

BENBECULA
(Beinn na Faoghla)

B892

DUNVEGAN CASTLE

14

A **26** **B** **C** **D**

Ardivachar Point

Crea
B891

B884

Dunvegan

Wiay

1

Cape
Wrath

Whiten
Head

Durness

A838

Portnacon

Kyle of Durness

19   Cranstackie
802

Kinlochbervie   B801
Loch
Inchard   Achriesgill
A838
Rhiconich   Foinaven
915

Loch Laxford

Handa
Island

Laxford
Bridge   Arkle
787

Scourie   Ben Stack
721   Loch
Stack

A894   Achfary

Eddrachillis
Bay   25   Kylestrome

Point of
Stoer   Drumbeg   B869   Unapool

Clashnessie   Quinag
808   Glas
Bheinn
776

Stoer
Clachtoll   10
B869   A837   A894   9

Lochinver   Loch Assynt   Inchnadamph

Rubha
Coigeach   Inverkirkaig   Suilven
731   Canisp
846

Enard
Bay   A837

Loch
Sionascaig   Cul
Mor
849

Stac Pollaidh
613   Ledmore

Achiltibuie   Loch
Lurgainn   Elphin

Summer
Isles   A835   17   A837   18

Culnacraig   Stornoway   Isle
Martin

Greenstone Point   Beinn
Ghobhlach
635   Ardmair   Oykel Bridge

Rubha Reidh   Gruinard
Bay   42   Little Loch Broom   Ullapool   Meall Liath
Choire
548

Cove   Laide   Coast   Badcaul   Leckmelm

Melvaig   Aultbea   An Teallach
1062   Inverlael   12

B8021   A832   A835   Beinn Dearg
1084

Poolewe   INVEREWE
GARDENS   Loch na
Sealga   CORRIESHALLOCH
GORGE

Gairloch   Fionn Loch   Mullach Coire
Mhic Fhearchair
1019   Sgurr Mor
1110

Port Henderson   B8056   20

Red Point   Slioch
980   Aultguish Inn

Talladale   A832   18   W E S T E R

Culnacnock   BEINN EIGHE
NATURE RESERVE   R O S S   Grudie   Garve

Lower
Diabaig   Beinn Alligin
985   Kinlochewe   9   Achnasheen   A832   Strathpeffer
Contin

Fearnmore   Liathach
1054   16   A896   Sgurr a'Mhuilinn
879   Marybank

Inveralligan   Torridon   Conon
Bridge

Shieldaig   Sgorr Ruadh
960   18   A890   27

Brochel   A896   Beinn Bhan
896   Balnacra   Sgurr a'Chaorachain   Beauly

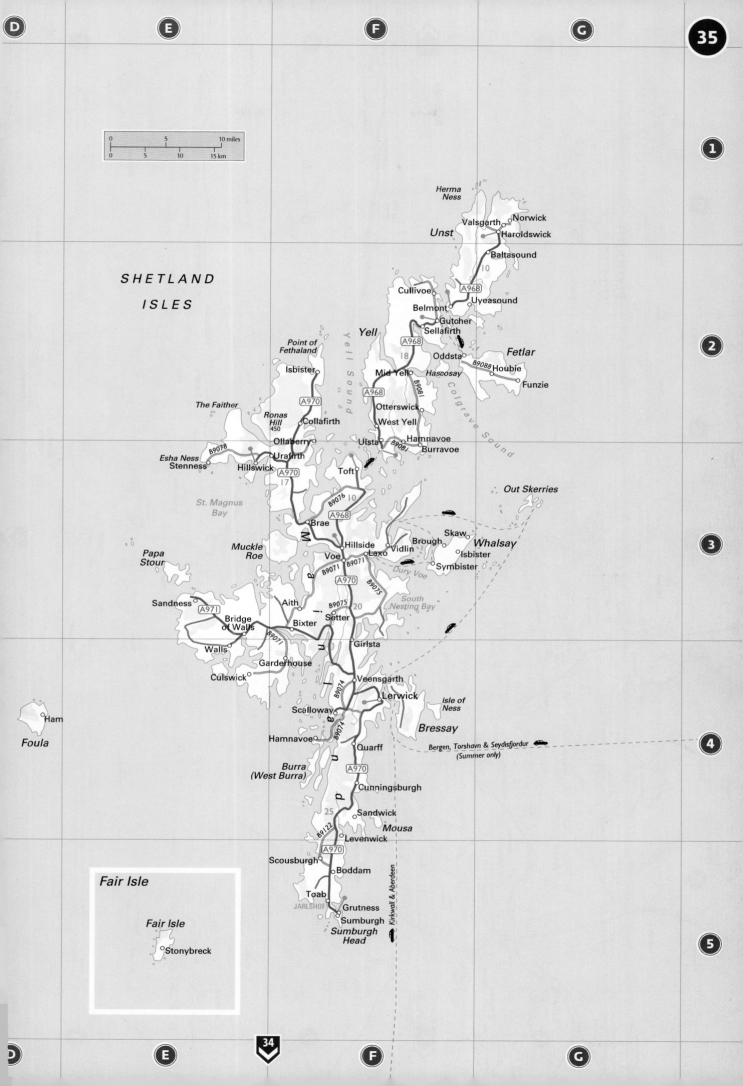

1

SHETLAND ISLES

Herma
Ness

Unst

Valsgarth   Norwick
  Haroldswick

Baltasound

10

Cullivoe   A968

Belmont   Uyeasound

Yell   Gutcher
Sellafirth

A968

Point of
Fethaland

Fetlar

2

Isbister

18   Oddsta   B9088   Houbie

Mid Yell   *Hascosay*

The Faither

Funzie

Ronas
Hill   Collafirth
450

Otterswick

A970   *Yell Sound*

West Yell

Ollaberry

B9081

Hamnavoe

Esha Ness   B9078   Urafirth

Ulsta   B9081   Burravoe

Stenness   Hillswick

Toft

A970

17

3

*St. Magnus
Bay*   B9076   10

Out Skerries

A968

Brae

*Papa
Stour*   *Muckle
Roe*

Hillside   Vidlin   Brough   Skaw

Voe   Laxo   *Whalsay*

B9071   B9071   *Dury Voe*   Isbister

A970   Symbister

B9075

Sandness   Aith   B9075   20   *South
Nesting Bay*

A971

Bridge
of Walls   Bixter   Setter

Walls   B9071   Girlsta

Garderhouse

Culswick   B9074   Veensgarth

Ham

Lerwick

Foula   Scalloway   *Isle of
Ness*

Bressay

Hamnavoe   B9074

Quarff   Bergen, Torshavn & Seydisfjordur   4
  (Summer only)

*Burra
(West Burra)*   A970

Cunningsburgh

25   Sandwick   *Mousa*

B9122   Levenwick

Scousburgh   A970

Boddam

Toab

JARLSHOF   Grutness

Sumburgh

*Sumburgh
Head*

Kirkwall & Aberdeen

5

Fair Isle

Fair Isle

Stonybreck

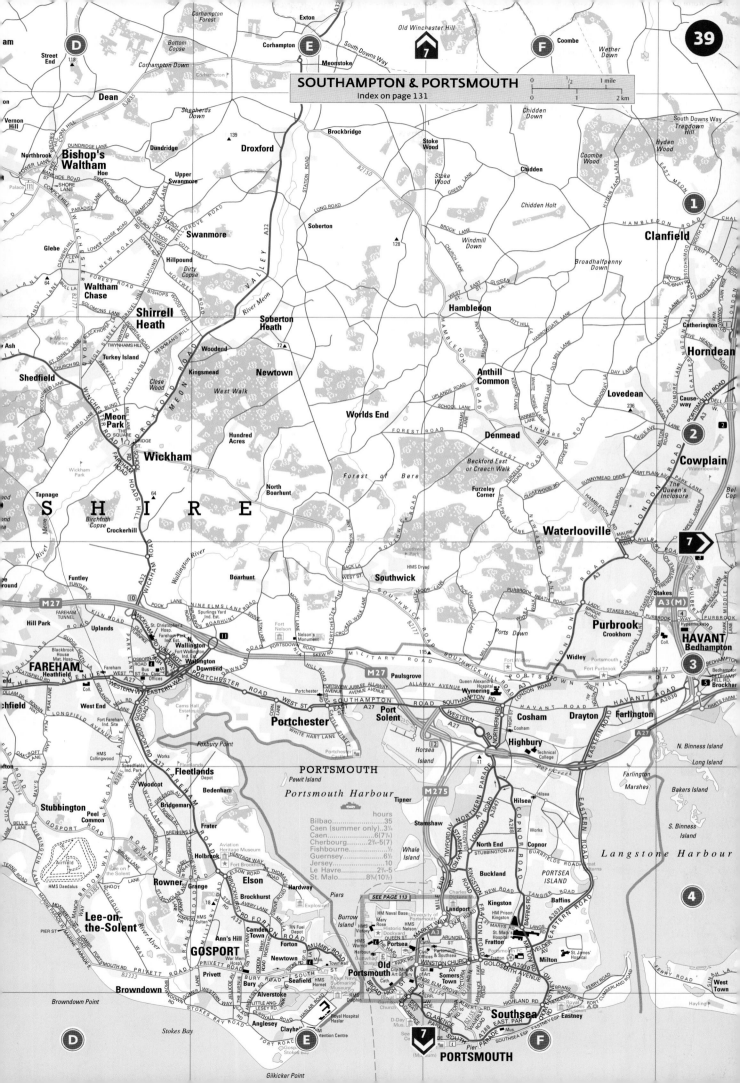

SOUTHAMPTON & PORTSMOUTH
Index on page 131

0   ½   1 mile
0   1   2 km

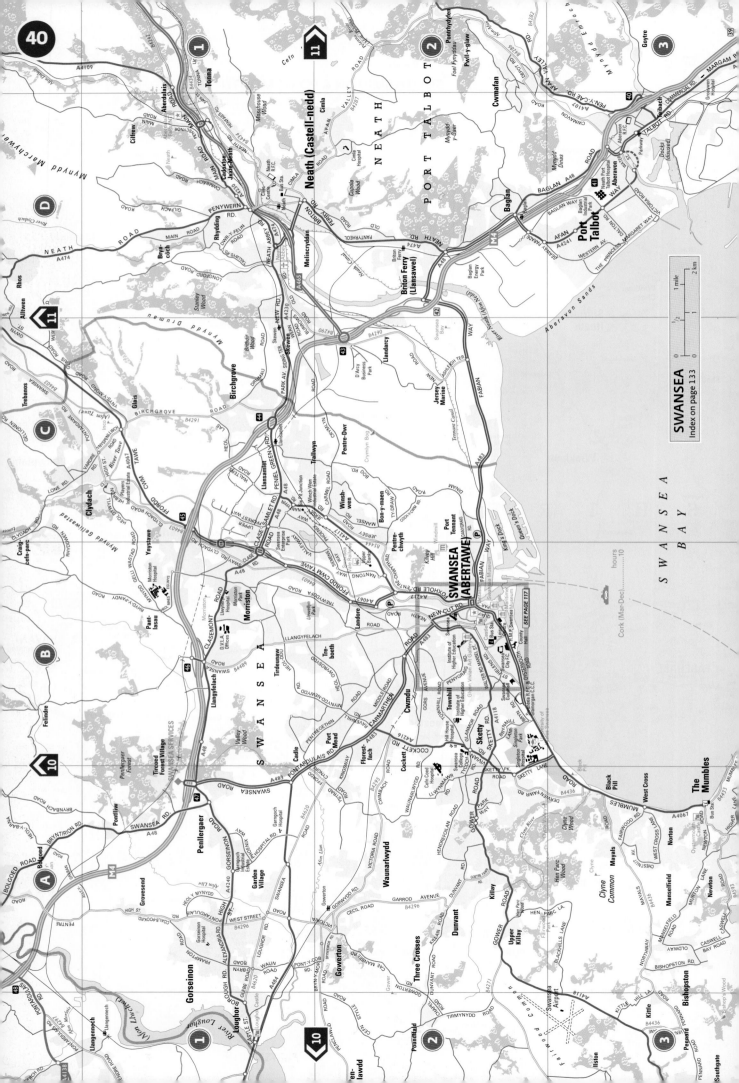

CARDIFF & NEWPORT
Index on page 133

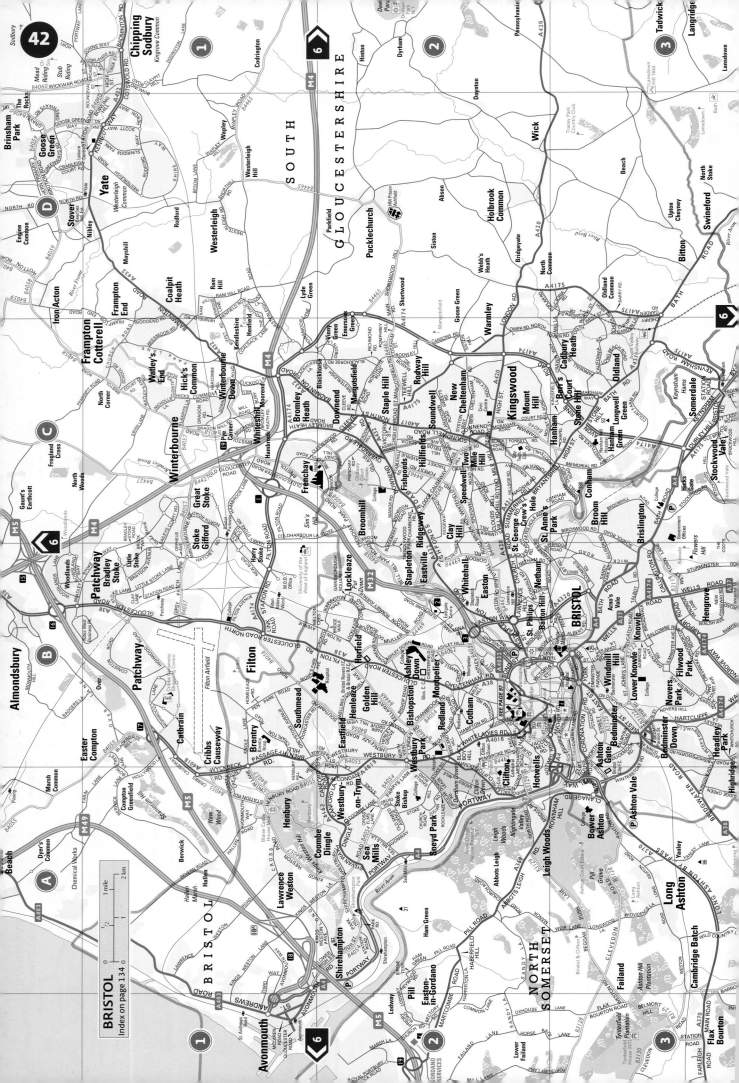

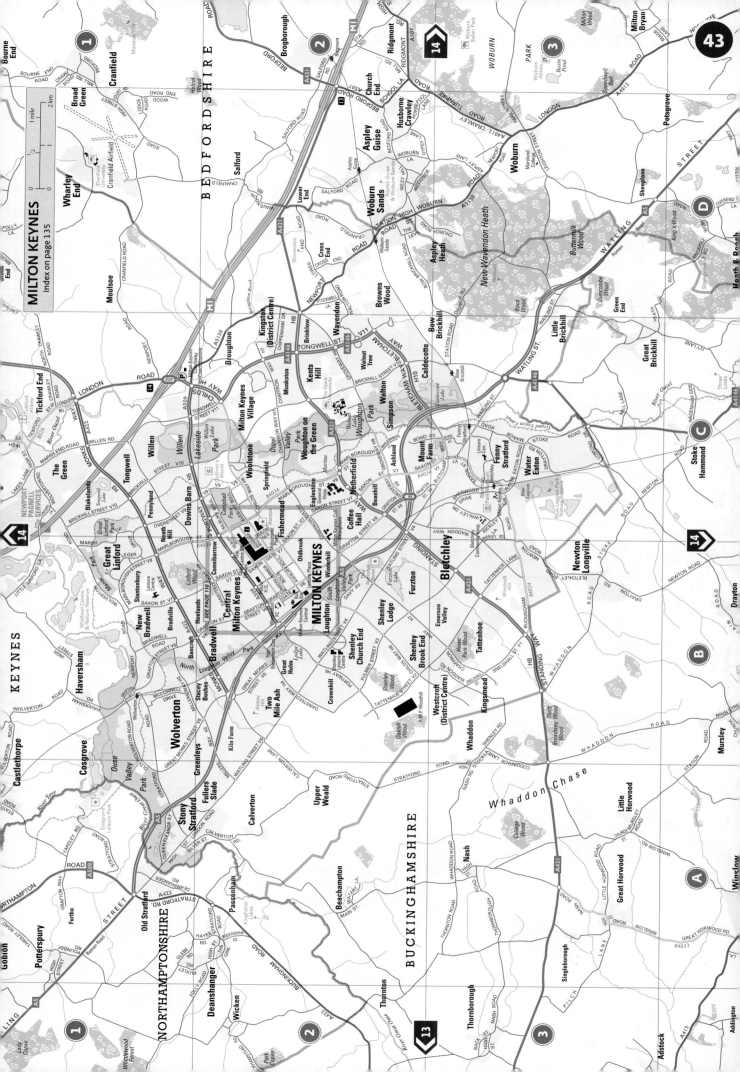

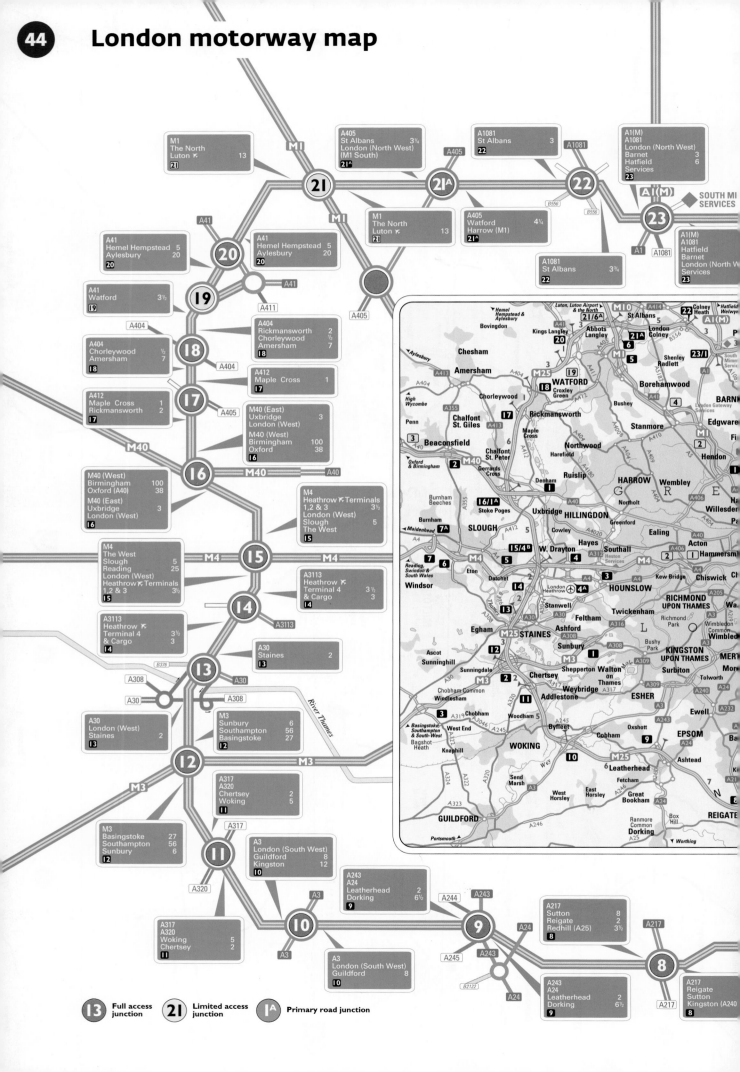

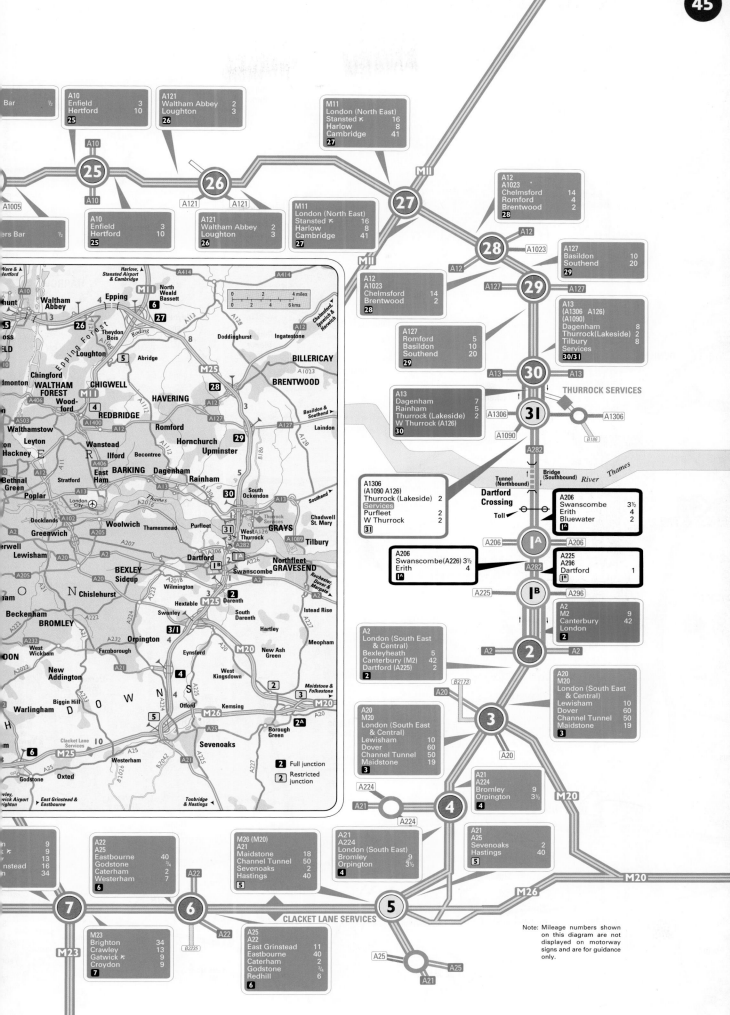

Bar ½

A10	
Enfield	3
Hertford	10
25	

A121	
Waltham Abbey	2
Loughton	3
26	

M11	
London (North East)	
Stansted ✈	16
Harlow	8
Cambridge	41
27	

A12	
A1023	
Chelmsford	14
Romford	4
Brentwood	2
28	

A1005

A10	
Enfield	3
Hertford	10
25	

A121	
Waltham Abbey	2
Loughton	3
26	

M11	
London (North East)	
Stansted ✈	16
Harlow	8
Cambridge	41
27	

A127	
Basildon	10
Southend	20
29	

A12	
A1023	
Chelmsford	14
Brentwood	2
28	

A127	
Romford	5
Basildon	10
Southend	20
29	

A13	
(A1306 A126)	
(A1090)	
Dagenham	8
Thurrock(Lakeside)	2
Tilbury	8
Services	
30/31	

A13	
Dagenham	7
Rainham	5
Thurrock (Lakeside)	2
W Thurrock (A126)	
30	

THURROCK SERVICES

A1306	
(A1090 A126)	
Thurrock (Lakeside)	2
Services	
Purfleet	2
W Thurrock	2
31	

Tunnel (Northbound) Bridge (Southbound) *River Thames*

Dartford Crossing

Toll ◄

A206	
Swanscombe	3½
Erith	4
Bluewater	2
1ᴬ	

A206	
Swanscombe(A226)	3½
Erith	4
1ᴬ	

A225	
A296	
Dartford	1
1ᴮ	

A2	
M2	9
Canterbury	42
London	
2	

A2	
London (South East & Central)	
Bexleyheath	5
Canterbury (M2)	42
Dartford (A225)	2
2	

A20	
M20	
London (South East & Central)	
Lewisham	10
Dover	60
Channel Tunnel	50
Maidstone	19
3	

A20	
M20	
London (South East & Central)	
Lewisham	10
Dover	60
Channel Tunnel	50
Maidstone	19
3	

A21	
A224	
Bromley	9
Orpington	3½
4	

A21	
A224	
London (South East)	
Bromley	9
Orpington	3½
4	

A21	
A25	
Sevenoaks	2
Hastings	40
5	

Inset map labels:

Ware & Hertford

Harlow, Stansted Airport & Cambridge

Waltham Abbey · North Weald Bassett · Epping · **M11** · **6** · **27**

Theydon Bois · Roding · Doddinghurst · Ingatestone · A414 · A414 · A12 · A128 · A113

Chelmsford, Ipswich & Harwich

0   2   4 miles
0   2   4   6 kms

WALTHAM FOREST · CHIGWELL · Loughton · Abridge · **M25** · **28** · BILLERICAY · BRENTWOOD

Chingford · Woodford · **4** · REDBRIDGE · HAVERING · Romford · Basildon & Southend · Laindon

Walthamstow · Leyton · Hackney · Wanstead · Ilford · Hornchurch · Upmerster · **29**

Stratford · Poplar · London City ✈ · BARKING · Dagenham · Rainham · South Ockendon · Chadwell St. Mary

Docklands · Greenwich · Woolwich · Thamesmead · Purfleet · Thurrock Services · **31** · West Thurrock · GRAYS · Tilbury

Lewisham · **30** · **31** · **282** · Dartford · **1ᴮ** · **2ᴬ** · Northfleet · GRAVESEND · Swanscombe · Rochester, Dover & Margate

BEXLEY · Sidcup · Wilmington · **M25** · Darenth · **2**

Chislehurst · Hextable · Swanley · South Darenth · Hartley · Istead Rise

Beckenham · BROMLEY · **3/1** · Orpington · Farnborough · Eynsford · West Kingsdown · New Ash Green · Meopham

New Addington · **4** · West Kingsdown · Otford · Kemsing · Maidstone & Folkestone · **3** · **M20**

Warlingham · Biggin Hill · D O W N S · **5** · **M26** · **2ᴬ**

Clacket Lane Services · **M25** · **6** · Westerham · Borough Green · Sevenoaks

Godstone · Oxted · A25 · B2026 · A21 · A225

Crawley, Gatwick Airport & Brighton · East Grinstead & Eastbourne · Tonbridge & Hastings

2 Full junction
2 Restricted junction

A22	
A25	
Eastbourne	40
Godstone	¾
Caterham	2
Westerham	7
6	

M26 (M20)	
A21	
Maidstone	18
Channel Tunnel	50
Sevenoaks	2
Hastings	40
5	

CLACKET LANE SERVICES

M23	
Brighton	34
Crawley	13
Gatwick ✈	9
Croydon	9
7	

A25	
A22	
East Grinstead	11
Eastbourne	40
Caterham	2
Godstone	¾
Redhill	6
6	

(left partial box):
	9
	9
	13
nstead	16
	34

Note: Mileage numbers shown on this diagram are not displayed on motorway signs and are for guidance only.

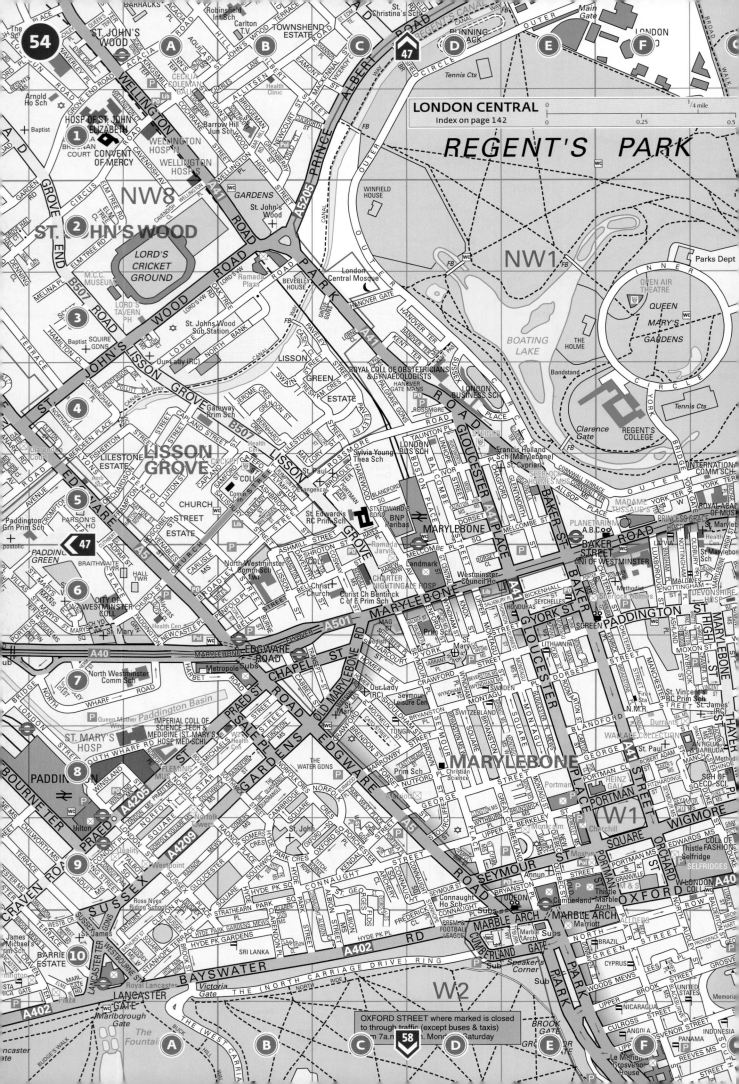

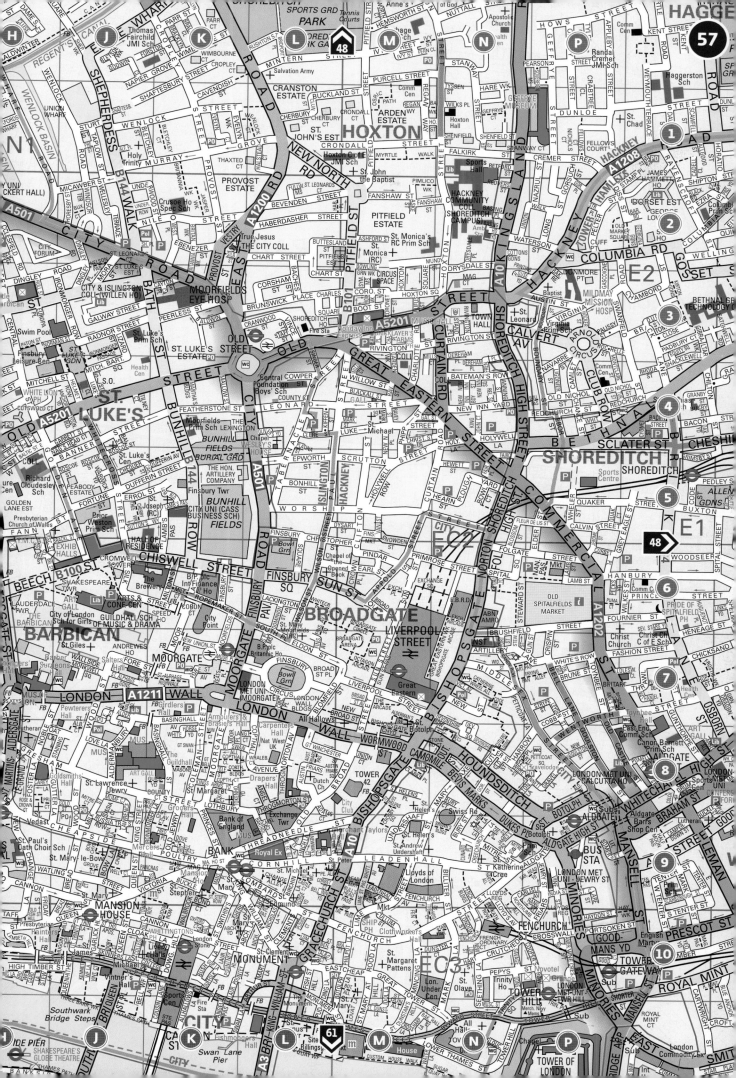

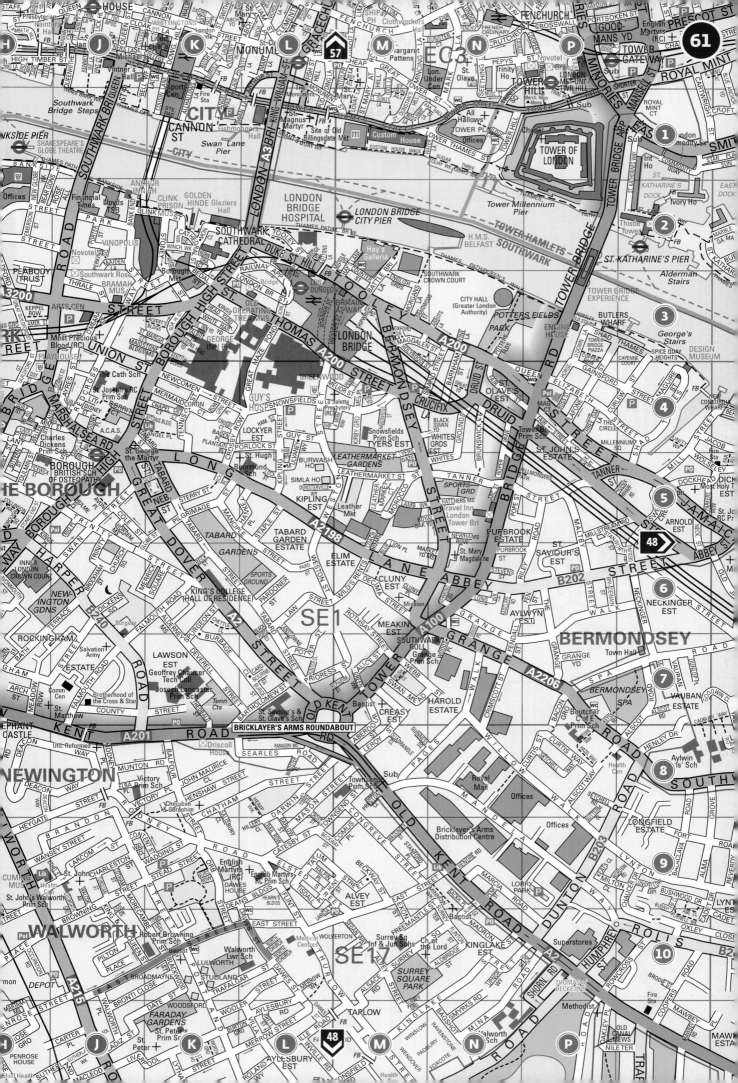

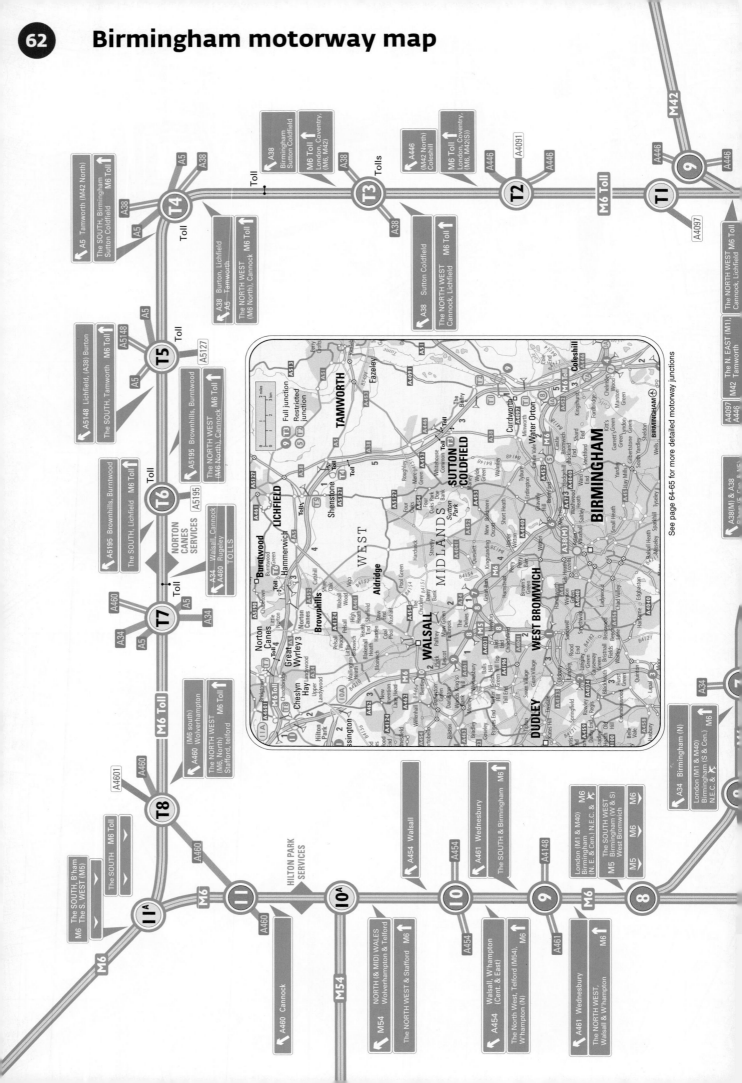

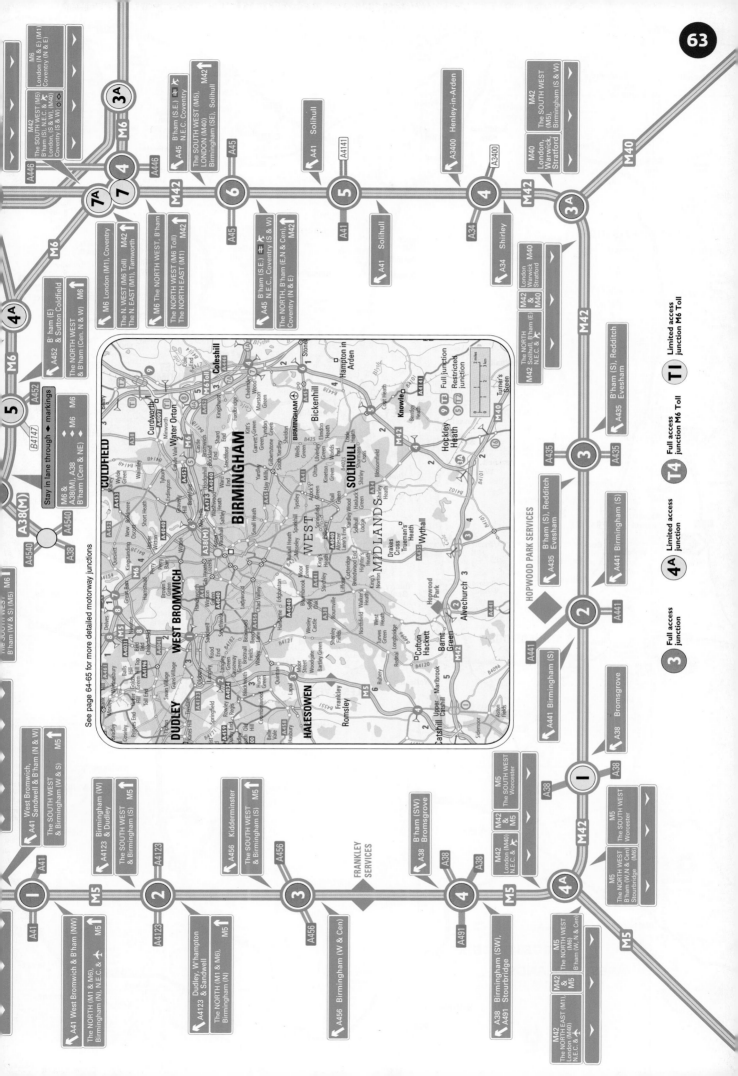

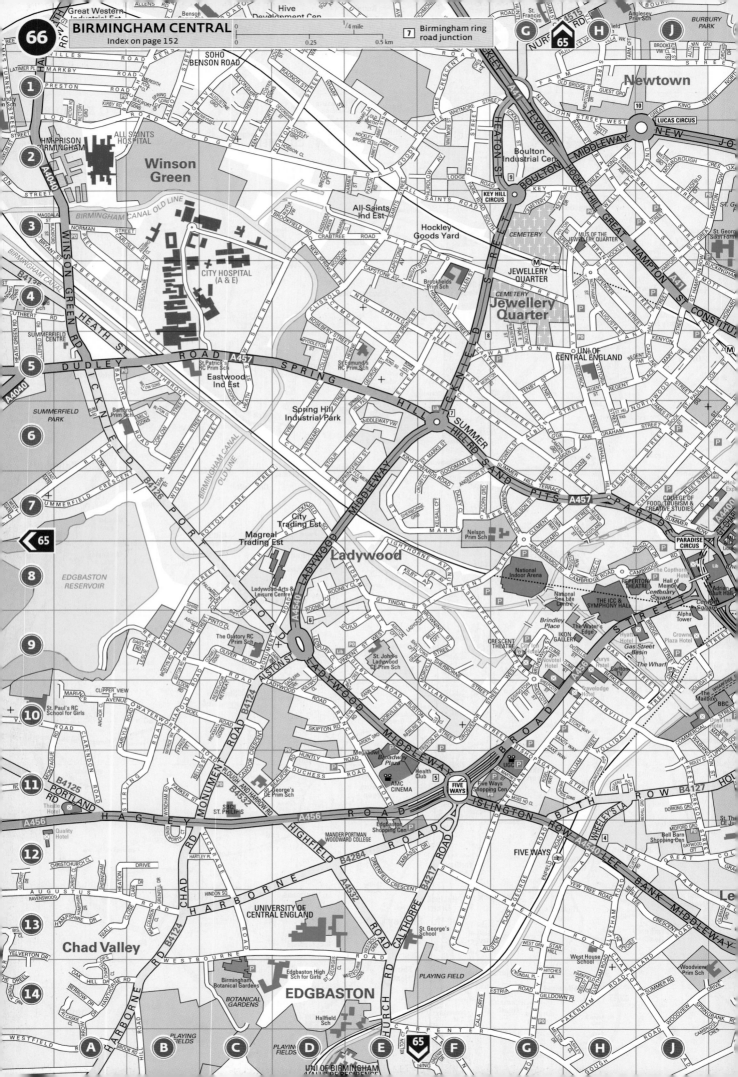

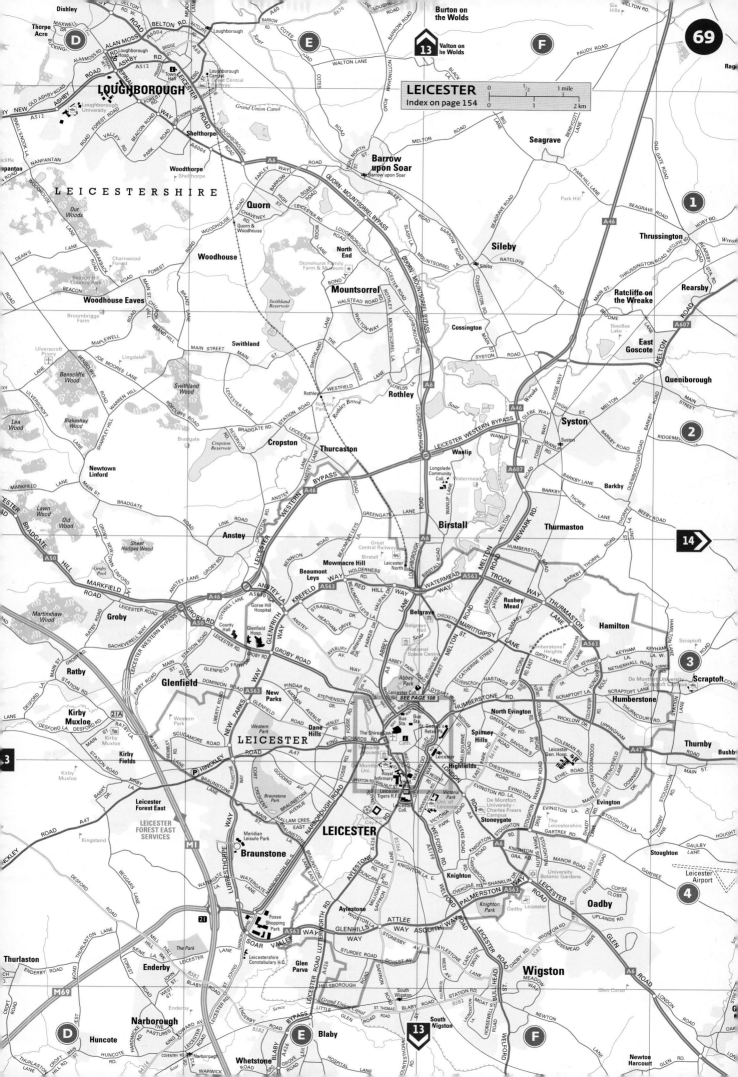

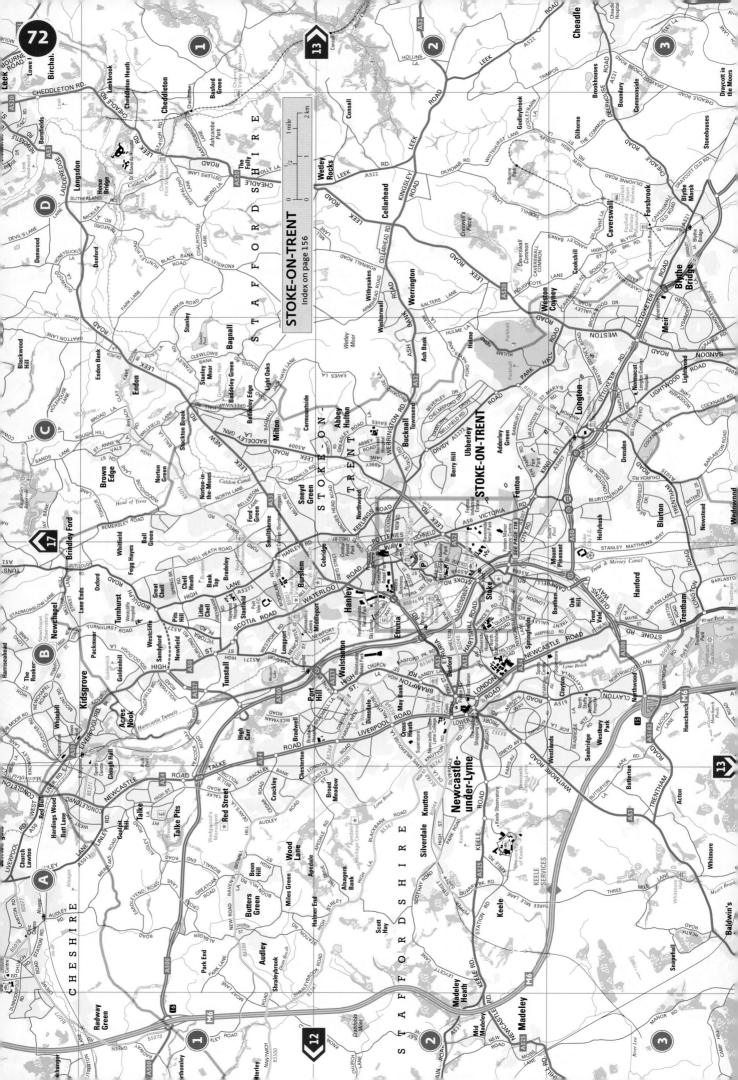

STOKE-ON-TRENT
Index on page 156

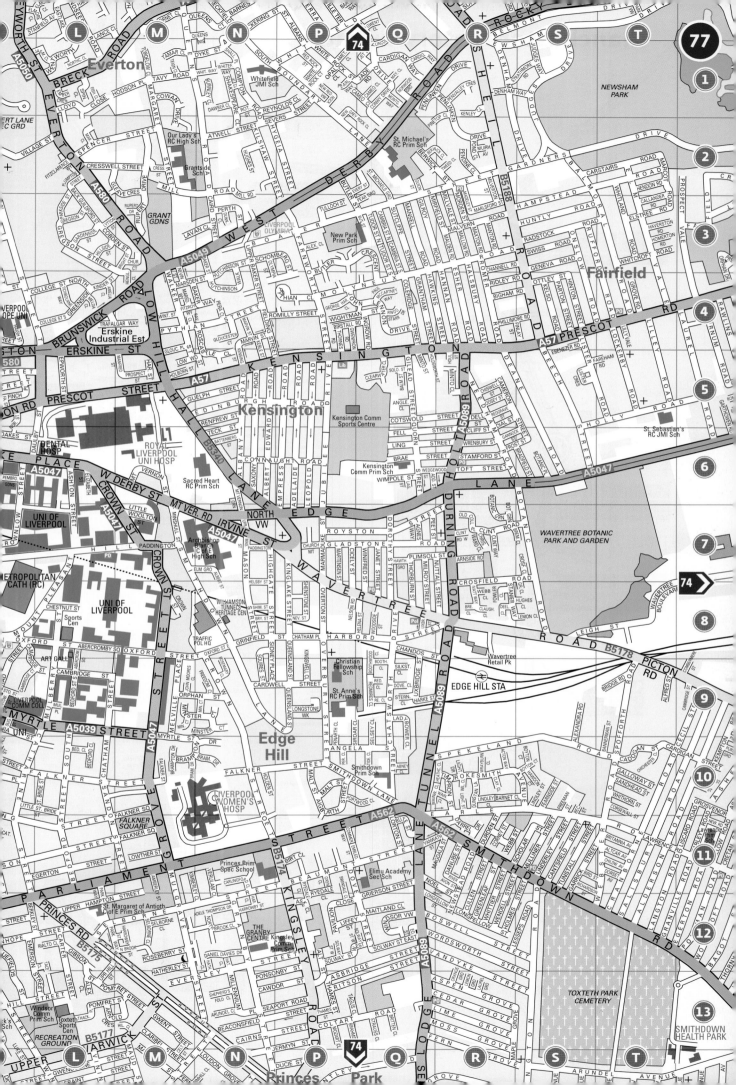

Manchester motorway map

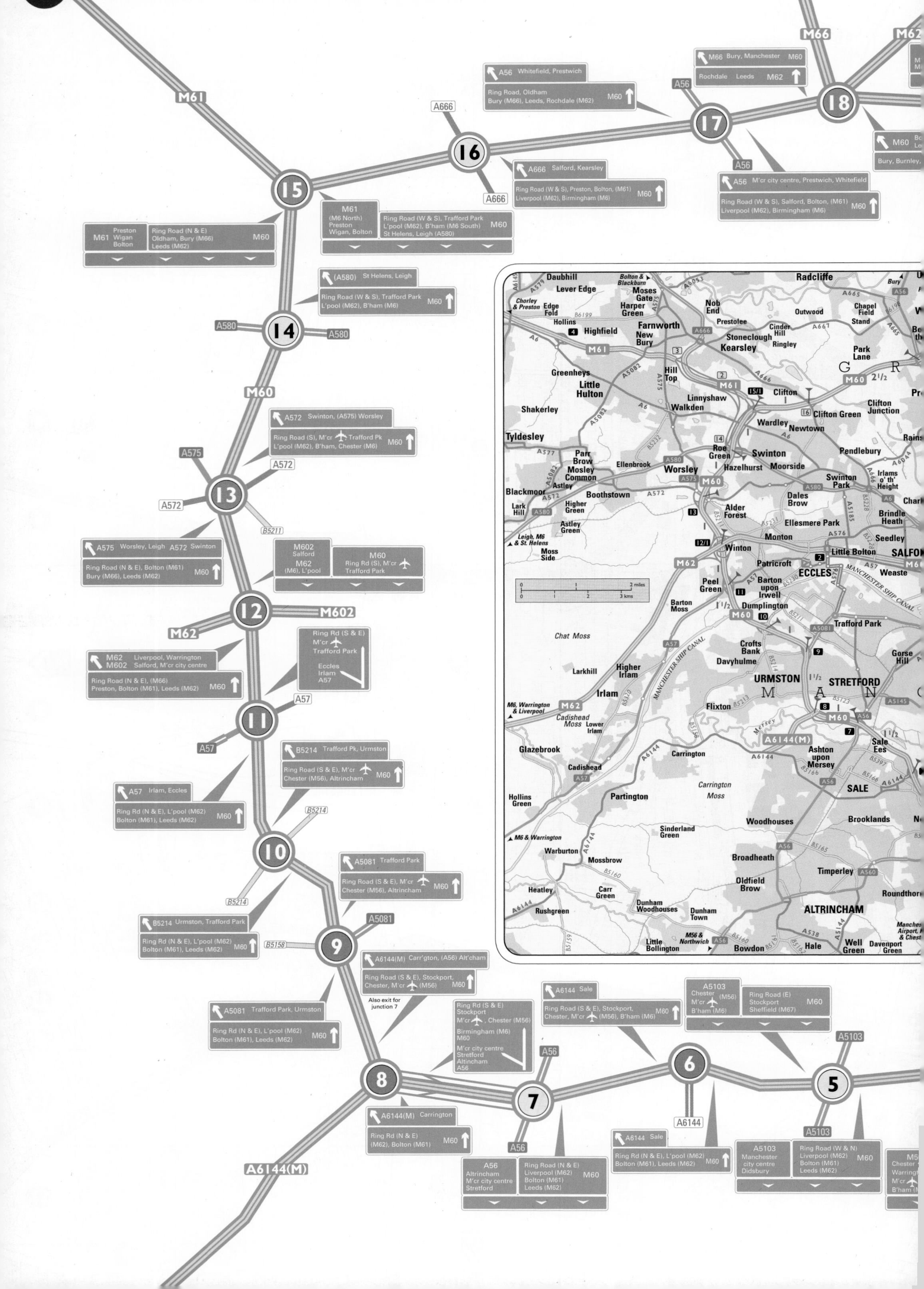

M61

A56 Whitefield, Prestwich
Ring Road, Oldham
Bury (M66), Leeds, Rochdale (M62) **M60**

M66 Bury, Manchester **M60**
Rochdale Leeds **M62**

A56

A666

M60 B
Bury, Burnley,

18

17

16

15

A666 Salford, Kearsley
Ring Road (W & S), Preston, Bolton, (M61)
Liverpool (M62), Birmingham (M6) **M60**

A666

A56 M'cr city centre, Prestwich, Whitefield
Ring Road (W & S), Salford, Bolton, (M61)
Liverpool (M62), Birmingham (M6) **M60**

M61 Preston Wigan Bolton
Ring Road (N & E) Oldham, Bury (M66), Leeds (M62) **M60**

M61 (M6 North) Preston Wigan, Bolton
Ring Road (W & S), Trafford Park
L'pool (M62), B'ham (M6 South)
St Helens, Leigh (A580) **M60**

(A580) St Helens, Leigh
Ring Road (W & S), Trafford Park
L'pool (M62), B'ham (M6) **M60**

A580 **14** **A580**

M60

A572 Swinton, (A575) Worsley
Ring Road (S), M'cr ✈ Trafford Pk
L'pool (M62), B'ham, Chester (M6) **M60**

A575 **A572**

A572 **13**

B5211

A575 Worsley, Leigh **A572** Swinton
Ring Road (N & E), Bolton (M61)
Bury (M66), Leeds (M62) **M60**

M602 Salford
M62 (M6), L'pool
M60 Ring Rd (S), M'cr ✈ Trafford Park

12 **M602**

M62

M62 Liverpool, Warrington
M602 Salford, M'cr city centre
Ring Road (N & E), (M66)
Preston, Bolton (M61), Leeds (M62) **M60**

Ring Rd (S & E) M'cr ✈ Trafford Park
Eccles Irlam A57

A57

11

A57

B5214 Trafford Pk, Urmston
Ring Road (S & E), M'cr ✈
Chester (M56), Altrincham **M60**

A57 Irlam, Eccles
Ring Rd (N & E), L'pool (M62)
Bolton (M61), Leeds (M62) **M60**

B5214

10

A5081 Trafford Park
Ring Road (S & E), M'cr ✈
Chester (M56), Altrincham **M60**

B5214

A5081

B5214 Urmston, Trafford Park
Ring Rd (N & E), L'pool (M62)
Bolton (M61), Leeds (M62) **M60**

B5158

9

A6144(M) Carr'gton, (A56) Alt'cham
Ring Road (S & E), Stockport,
Chester, M'cr ✈ (M56)

Also exit for junction 7

A5081 Trafford Park, Urmston
Ring Rd (N & E), L'pool (M62)
Bolton (M61), Leeds (M62) **M60**

Ring Rd (S & E) Stockport
M'cr ✈, Chester M56
Birmingham (M6)
M60
M'cr city centre
Stretford
Altrincham
A56

A6144 Sale
Ring Road (S & E), Stockport,
Chester, M'cr ✈ (M56), B'ham (M6) **M60**

A5103 Chester (M56)
B'ham (M6)
Ring Road (E) Stockport Sheffield (M67) **M60**

A5103

8

7

6

5

A6144(M) Carrington
Ring Rd (N & E)
(M62), Bolton (M61) **M60**

A56

A6144

A6144 Sale
Ring Rd (N & E), L'pool (M62)
Bolton (M61), Leeds (M62) **M60**

A5103 Manchester city centre Didsbury

A5103 Ring Road (W & N) Liverpool (M62) Bolton (M61) Leeds (M62) **M60**

M5
Chester
Warring
M'cr ✈
B'ham (

A56 Altrincham M'cr city centre Stretford

A6144(M)

Inset map labels

A61 Daubhill, Lever Edge, Moses Gate, Radcliffe, Bury
Chorley & Preston, Edge Fold, Hollins, Highfield, Harper Green, Farnworth, New Bury, Stoneclough, Kearsley, Ringley, Cinder Hill, Outwood, Chapel Field, Stand
Greenheys, Little Hulton, Hill Top, Linnyshaw, Walkden, Clifton, Clifton Green, Clifton Junction, Wardley, Newtown, Pendlebury
Shakerley, Tyldesley, Parr Brow, Mosley Common, Ellenbrook, Worsley, Swinton, Hazelhurst, Moorside, Swinton Park, Irlams o' th' Height
Blackmoor, Astley, Boothstown, Higher Green, Alder Forest, Monton, Dales Brow, Ellesmere Park, Brindle Heath, Seedley
Lark Hill, Astley Green, Leigh, M6 & St Helens, Moss Side, Winton, Patricroft, Eccles, Little Bolton, Salford, Weaste
Chat Moss, Peel Green, Barton upon Irwell, Dumplington, Trafford Park
Larkhill, Higher Irlam, Irlam, Crofts Bank, Davyhulme, Gorse Hill
M6 Warrington & Liverpool, Cadishead Moss, Lower Irlam, Flixton, Urmston, Stretford
Glazebrook, Carrington, Ashton upon Mersey, Sale, Sale Ees
Cadishead, Hollins Green, Partington, Carrington Moss, Broadheath, Brooklands
Warburton, Mossbrow, Woodhouses, Timperley, Roundthorn
M6 & Warrington, Sinderland Green, Oldfield Brow, Altrincham
Heatley, Rushgreen, Carr Green, Dunham Woodhouses, Dunham Town, Hale, Well Green, Davenport Green, Manchester Airport & Chest
Little Bollington, M56 & Northwich, Bowdon

Manchester Ship Canal

0 ... 2 miles / 0 ... 3 kms

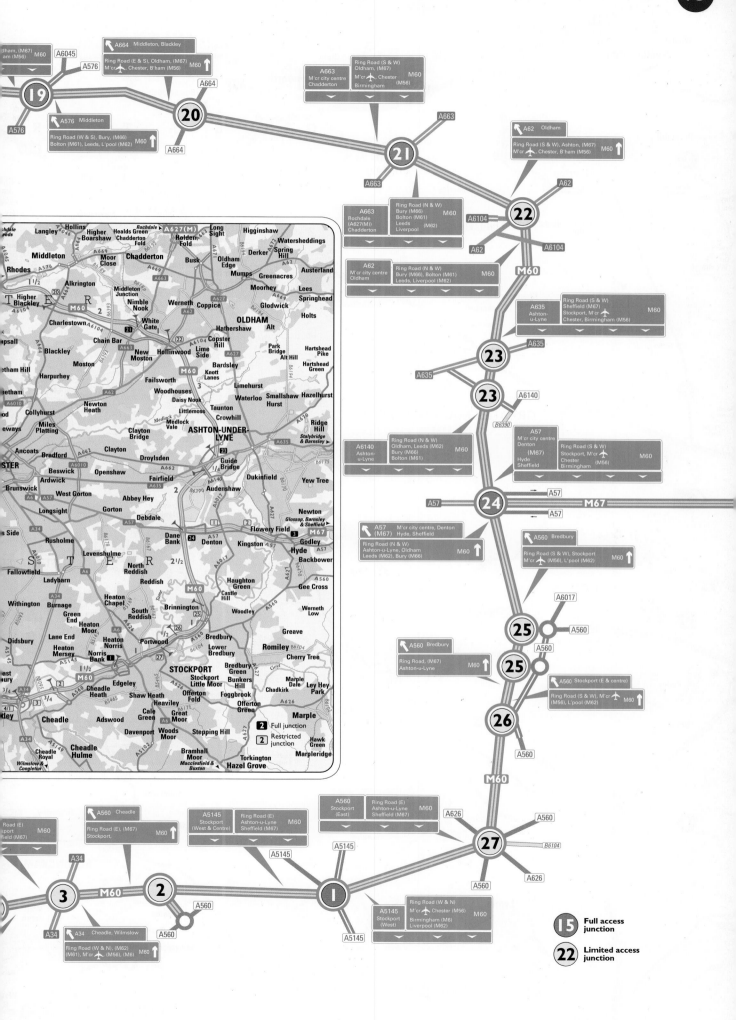

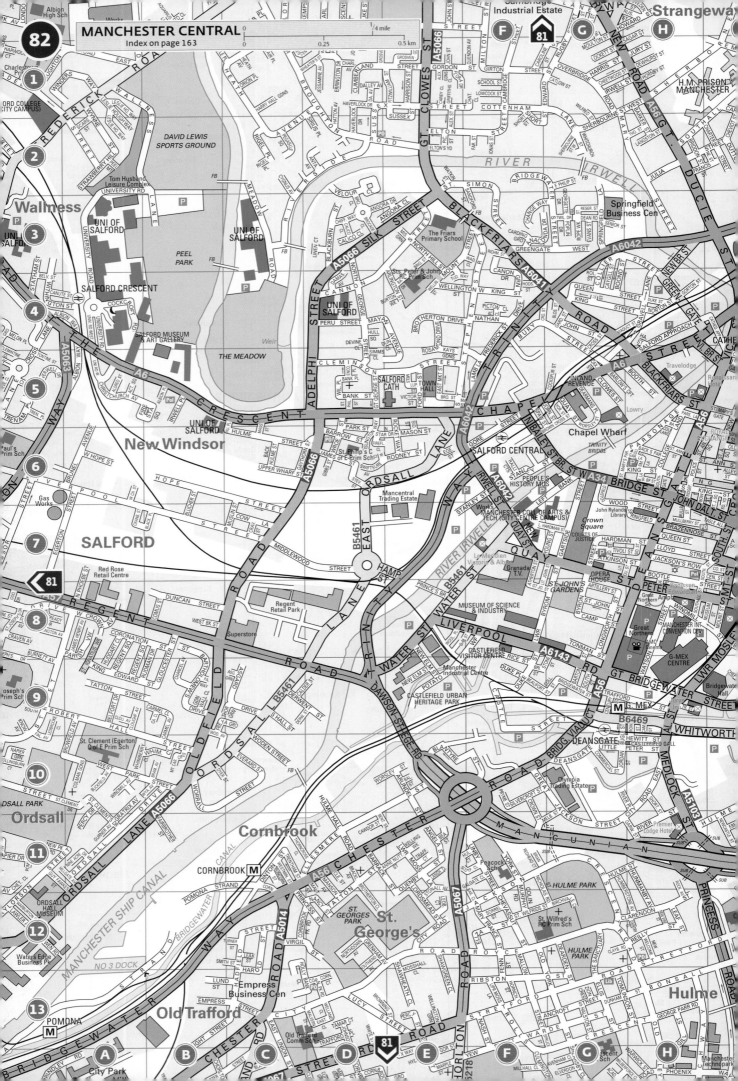

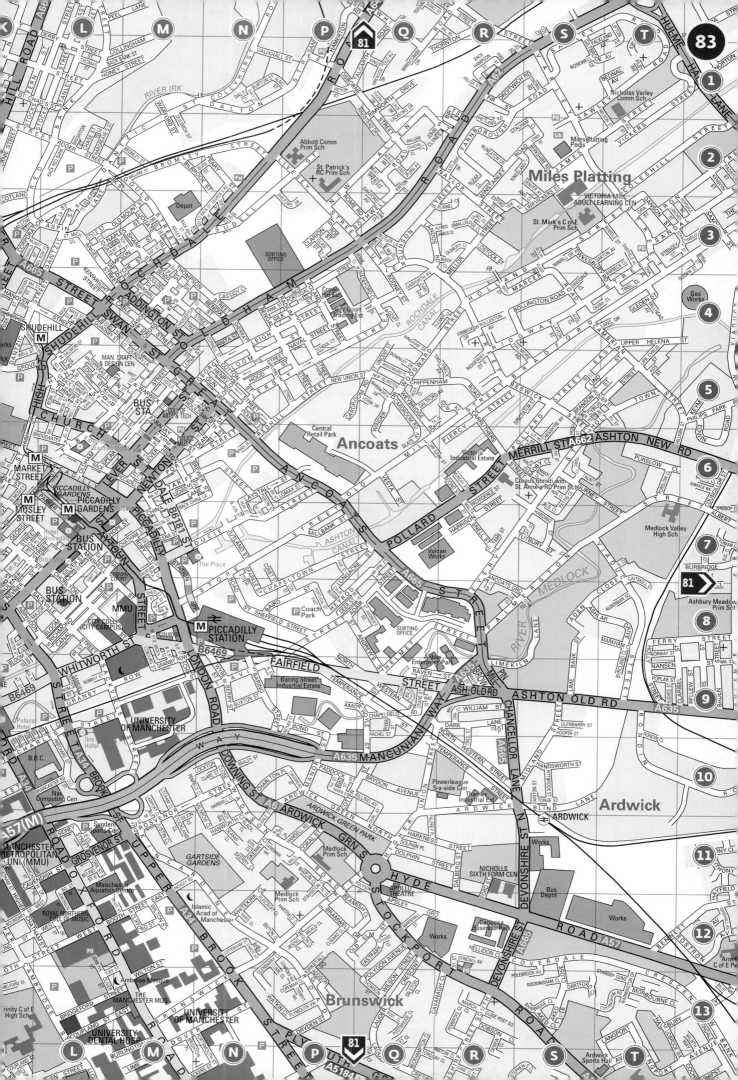

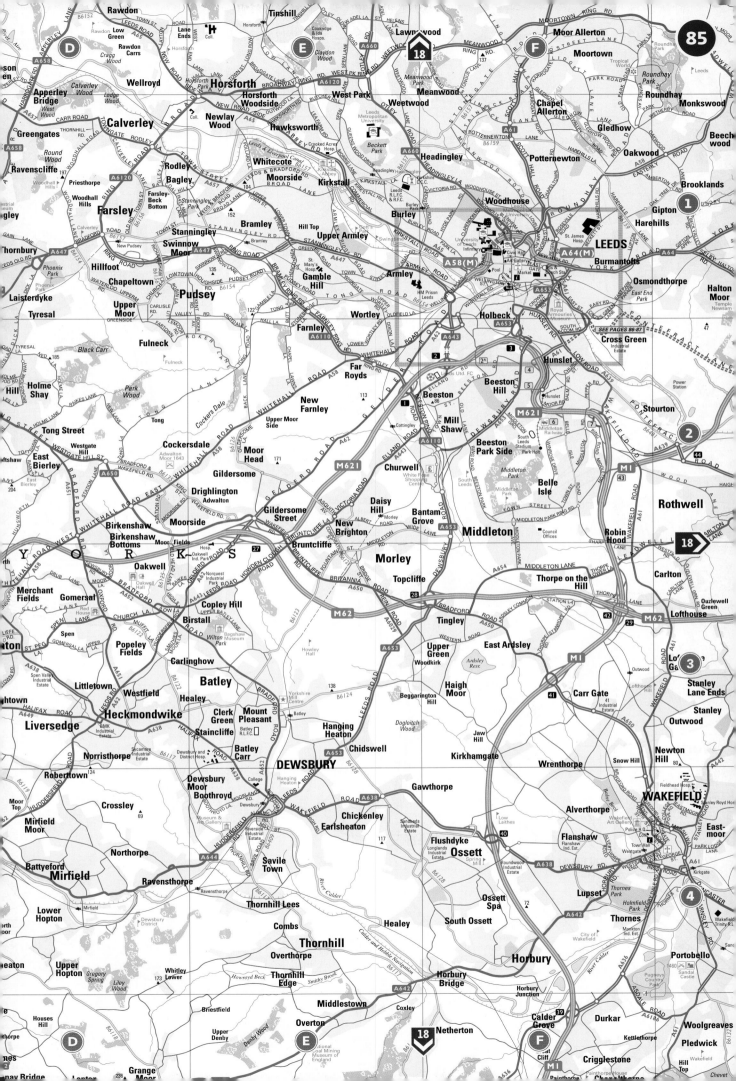

LEEDS CENTRAL
Index on page 167

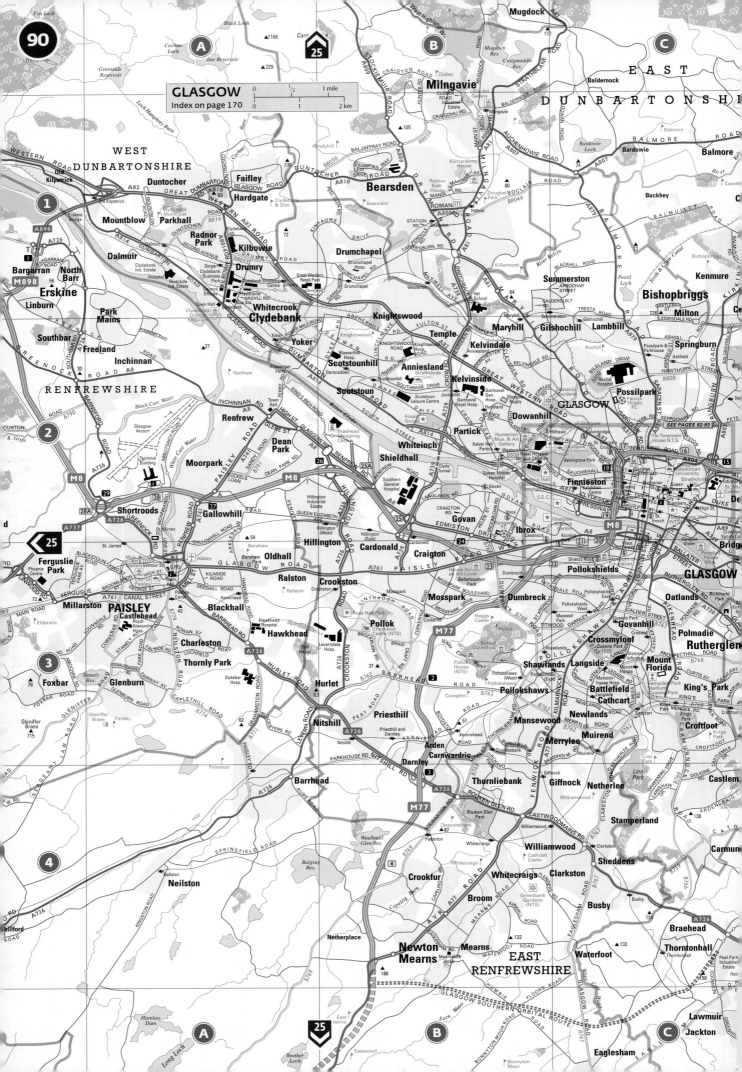

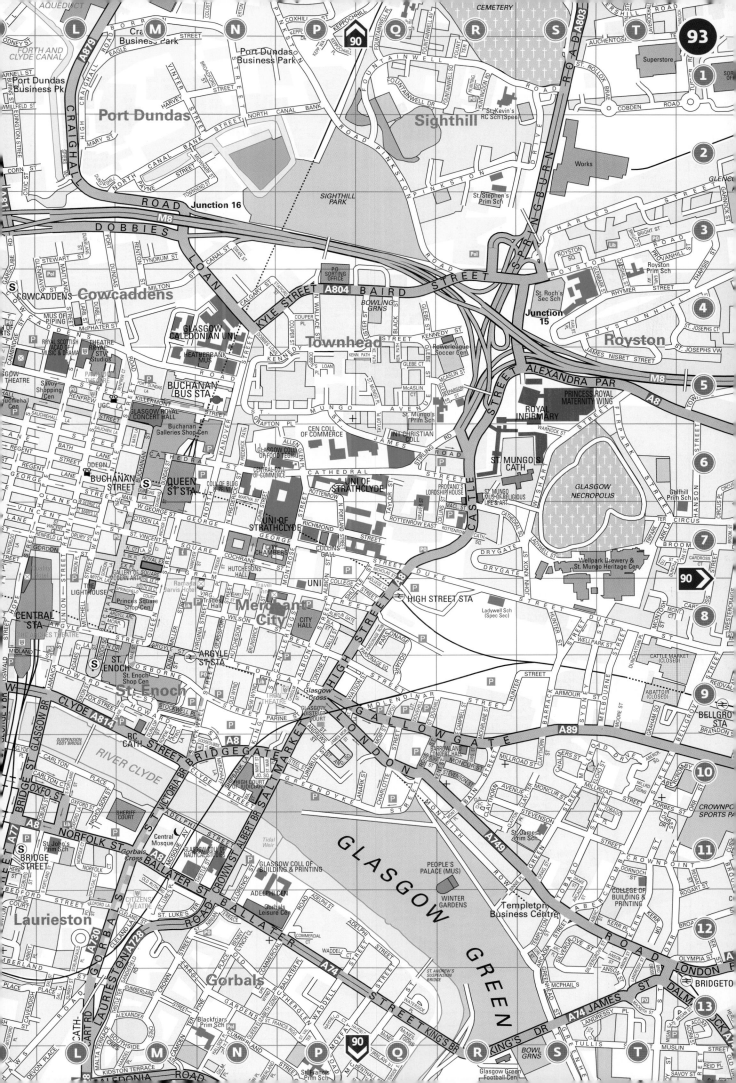

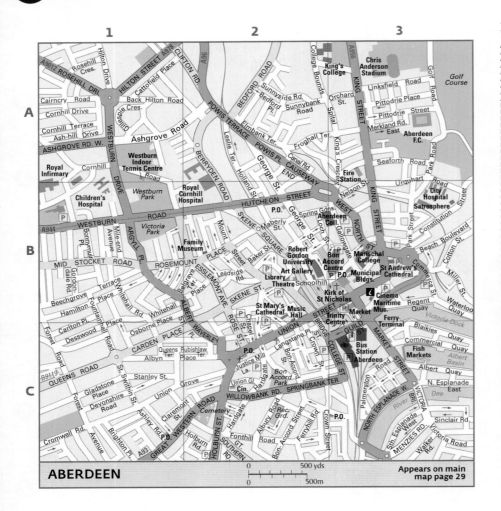

ABERDEEN

Appears on main map page 29

0	500 yds
0	500m

Tourist Information Centre: 23 Union Street
Tel: 01224 288828

Albert Quay	C3	Hutcheon Street	B2	
Albert Street	B2	Justice Mill Lane	C2	
Albury Road	C2	King's Crescent	A3	
Albyn Place	C1	King Street	A3	
Argyll Place	B1	Langstane Place	C2	
Ashgrove Road	A1	Leadside Road	B2	
Ashgrove Road West	A1	Leslie Terrace	A2	
Ash-hill Drive	A1	Linksfield Road	A3	
Ashley Road	C1	Loch Street	B2	
Back Hilton Road	A1	Maberly Street	B2	
Baker Street	B2	Market Street	C3	
Beach Boulevard	B3	Menzies Road	C3	
Bedford Place	A2	Merkland Road East	A3	
Bedford Road	A2	Mid Stocket Road	B1	
Beechgrove Terrace	B1	Mile-end Avenue	B1	
Belgrave Terrace	B1	Miller Street	B3	
Berryden Road	A2	Mount Street	B2	
Blaikie's Quay	C3	Nelson Street	B3	
Bon-Accord Street	C2	North Esplanade East	C3	
Bonnymuir Place	B1	North Esplanade West	C3	
Bridge Street	B2	Orchard Street	A3	
Brighton Place	C1	Osborne Place	C1	
Cairncry Road	A1	Palmerston Road	C2	
Canal Road	A2	Park Road	A3	
Carden Place	C1	Park Street	B3	
Carlton Place	C1	Pittodrie Place	A3	
Cattofield Place	A1	Pittodrie Street	A3	
Causewayend	A2	Powis Place	A2	
Chapel Street	B2	Powis Terrace	A2	
Claremont Street	C1	Queens Road	C1	
Clifton Road	A1	Queens Terrace	C1	
College Bounds	A2	Regent Quay	B3	
College Street	C3	Rosehill Crescent	A1	
Commerce Street	B3	Rosehill Drive	A1	
Commercial Quay	C3	Rosemount Place	B1	
Constitution Street	B3	Rose Street	B2	
Cornhill Drive	A1	Rubislaw Terrace	C2	
Cornhill Road	A1	St. Swithin Street	C1	
Cornhill Terrace	A1	Schoolhill	B2	
Cotton Street	B3	Seaforth Road	A3	
Cromwell Road	C1	Sinclair Road	C3	
Crown Street	C2	Skene Square	B2	
Desswood Place	C1	Skene Street	B2	
Devonshire Road	C1	South Esplanade West	C3	
Elmbank Terrace	A2	Spital	A3	
Esslemont Avenue	B2	Springbank Terrace	C2	
Ferryhill Road	C2	Spring Gardens	B2	
Fonthill Road	C1	Stanley Street	C1	
Forest Road	C1	Sunnybank Road	A2	
Forest Avenue	C1	Sunnyside Road	A2	
Fountainhall Road	B1	Union Glen	C1	
Froghall Terrace	A2	Union Grove	C1	
Gallowgate	B3	Union Street	C2	
George Street	A2	Urquhart Road	B3	
Gillespie Crescent	A1	Victoria Bridge	C3	
Gladstone Place	C1	Victoria Road	C3	
Golf Road	A3	Walker Road	C3	
Gordondale Road	B1	Waterloo Quay	B3	
Great Southern Road	C2	Waverley Place	C2	
Great Western Road	C1	Westburn Drive	A1	
Guild Street	C3	Westburn Road	A1	
Hamilton Place	B1	West North Street	B3	
Hardgate	C2	Whitehall Place	B1	
Hilton Drive	A1	Whitehall Road	B1	
Hilton Street	A1	Willowbank Road	C2	
Holburn Road	C2			
Holburn Street	C2			
Holland Street	A2			

BATH

Appears on main map page 6

0	200 yds
0	200m

Tourist Information Centre: Abbey Chambers, Abbey Churchyard
Tel: 0906 711 2000 (Premium Rate)

Ambury	C1	Pulteney Road	B3	
Archway Street	C3	Queen Street	B1	
Argyle Street	B2	Quiet Street	A1	
Avon Street	B1	Rossiter Road	C2	
Barton Street	B1	St. James's Parade	B1	
Bath Street	B2	St. John's Road	A2	
Bathwick Hill	A3	St. Marks Road	C3	
Beau Street	B2	Sawclose	B1	
Bennett Street	A1	Southgate Street	C2	
Bridge Street	B2	Spring Crescent	C3	
Broad Quay	C1	Stall Street	B2	
Broad Street	A2	Sutton Street	A3	
Broadway	C3	Sydney Place	A3	
Brock Street	A1	The Circus	A1	
Chapel Row	B1	Union Street	B2	
Charles Street	B1	Upper Borough Walls	A2	
Charlotte Street	A1	Walcot Street	A2	
Cheap Street	B2	Wells Road	C1	
Claverton Street	C2	Westgate Buildings	B1	
Corn Street	C1	Westgate Street	B1	
Daniel Street	A3	Wood Street	A1	
Darlington Street	A3	York Street	B2	
Dorchester Street	C2			
Edward Street	A3			
Excelsior Street	C3			
Ferry Lane	B3			
Gay Street	A1			
George Street	A1			
Grand Parade	B2			
Great Pulteney Street	A3			
Green Park Road	B1			
Green Street	A2			
Grove Street	A2			
Henrietta Gardens	A3			
Henrietta Mews	A3			
Henrietta Road	A2			
Henrietta Street	A2			
Henry Street	B2			
High Street	B2			
Holloway	C1			
James Street West	B1			
John Street	A1			
Kingsmead East	B1			
Lansdown Road	A2			
Laura Place	A2			
Lime Grove	B3			
Lime Grove Gardens	B3			
Lower Borough Walls	B2			
Lower Bristol Road	C1			
Magdalen Avenue	C1			
Manvers Street	C2			
Milk Street	B1			
Milsom Street	A2			
Monmouth Place	A1			
Monmouth Street	B1			
Newark Street	C2			
New Bond Street	B2			
New King Street	B1			
New Orchard Street	B2			
New Street	B1			
North Parade	B2			
North Parade Road	B3			
Old King Street	A1			
Orange Grove	B2			
Paragon	A2			
Pierrepont Street	B2			
Pulteney Crescent	C3			
Pulteney Mews	A3			

Tourist Information Centre: 1 Clifton Street
Tel: 01253 478222

Abingdon Street	B1	Market Street	B1
Adelaide Street	B1	Mather Street	A3
Albert Road	C1	Mere Road	B3
Ascot Road	A3	Milbourne Street	B2
Ashburton Road	A1	Mount Street	A1
Ashton Road	C2	New Bonny Street	C1
Bank Hey Street	B1	Newcastle Avenue	B3
Banks Street	A1	Newton Drive	B3
Beech Avenue	B3	Oxford Road	B2
Birchway Avenue	A3	Palatine Road	C2
Bonny Street	C1	Park Road	C2
Boothley Road	A2	Peter Street	B2
Breck Road	C3	Pleasant Street	A1
Bryan Road	B3	Portland Road	C3
Buchanan Street	B2	Princess Parade	B1
Butler Street	A2	Promenade	A1/C1
Caunce Street	B2/A3	Queens Square	B1
Cecil Street	A2	Queen Street	B1
Central Drive	C1	Rathlyn Avenue	A3
Chapel Street	C1	Reads Avenue	C2
Charles Street	B2	Regent Road	B2
Charnley Road	C1	Ribble Road	C2
Church Street	B2	Ripon Road	C2
Clifford Road	A1	St. Albans Road	C3
Clifton Street	B1	Salisbury Road	C3
Clinton Avenue	C2	Seasiders Way	C1
Cocker Square	A1	Selbourne Road	A2
Cocker Street	A1	Somerset Avenue	C3
Coleridge Road	A2	South King Street	B2
Collingwood Avenue	A3	Stirling Road	A3
Cookson Street	B2	Talbot Road	B1/A2
Coopers Way	A2	Talbot Square	B1
Coronation Street	C1	Topping Street	B1
Corporation Street	B1	Victory Road	A2
Cumberland Avenue	C3	Wayman Road	B3
Deansgate	B1	West Park Drive	B3
Devonshire Road	A2	Westmorland Avenue	C3
Devonshire Square	B3	Whitegate Drive	B3/C3
Dickson Road	A1	Woodland Grove	C3
Egerton Road	A1	Woolman Road	C2
Elizabeth Street	A2	Yates Street	A1
Exchange Street	A1		
Forest Gate	B3		
Gainsborough Road	C2		
George Street	B2/A2		
Gloucester Avenue	C3		
Gorse Road	C3		
Gorton Street	A2		
Granville Road	B2		
Grosvenor Street	B2		
High Street	A1		
Hollywood Avenue	B3		
Hornby Road	C1		
Hounds Hill	C1		
King Street	B1		
Knowsley Avenue	C3		
Larbreck Avenue	A3		
Laycock Gate	A3		
Layton Road	A3		
Leamington Road	B2		
Leicester Road	B2		
Lincoln Road	B2		
Liverpool Road	B2		
London Road	A3		
Lord Street	A1		
Manchester Road	A3		
Manor Road	C3		

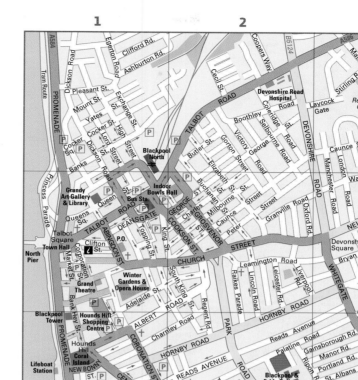

BLACKPOOL

0   300 yds
0   300m

Appears on main
map page 21

Tourist Information Centre: Westover Road
Tel: 0906 802 0234 (Premium Rate)

Ascham Road	A3	Wessex Way	B1/A3
Avenue Road	B1	West Cliff Promenade	C1
Bath Road	C2	West Cliff Road	C1
Beechey Road	A3	West Hill Road	C1
Bennett Road	A3	West Overcliff Drive	C1
Bourne Avenue	B1	West Promenade	C1
Braidley Road	B2	Westover Road	C2
Branksome Wood Road	B1	Wimborne Road	B2
Cavendish Road	A2		
Central Drive	A1		
Charminster Road	A2		
Christchurch Road	B3		
Cotlands	B3		
Dean Park Road	B2		
Dunbar Road	A2		
Durley Chine Road	C1		
Durley Chine Road South	C1		
Durley Road	C1		
East Avenue	A1		
East Overcliff Drive	C3		
Elgin Road	A1		
Exeter Road	C2		
Gervis Place	C2		
Gervis Road	C3		
Grove Road	C3		
Hinton Road	C2		
Holdenhurst Road	B3		
Knyveton Road	B3		
Lansdowne Road	A2		
Leven Avenue	A1		
Little Forest Road	A1		
Lowther Road	A3		
Madeira Road	B2		
Malmesbury Park Road	A3		
Manor Road	A3		
Methuen Road	A3		
Meyrick Road	B3		
Milton Road	A2		
Old Christchurch Road	B2		
Ophir Road	A3		
Oxford Road	B3		
Pier Approach	C2		
Poole Hill	C1		
Portchester Road	A3		
Priory Road	C1		
Queen's Road	B1		
Richmond Hill	B2		
Russell Cotes Road	C2		
St. Augustin's Road	A2		
St. Anthony's Road	A2		
St. Leonard's Road	A3		
St. Michael's Road	C1		
St. Pauls' Road	B3		
St. Peter's Road	B2		
St. Stephen's Road	B1		
St. Swithin's Road	B3		
St. Swithun's Road South	B3		
St. Valerie Road	A2		
St. Winifred's Road	A2		
Stewart Road	A3		
Surrey Road	B1		
The Lansdowne	B3		
The Square	B2		
The Triangle	B1		
Tregonwell Road	C1		
Undercliff Drive	C3		
Wellington Road	A2		

BOURNEMOUTH

0   400 yds
0   400m

Appears on urban
map page 37

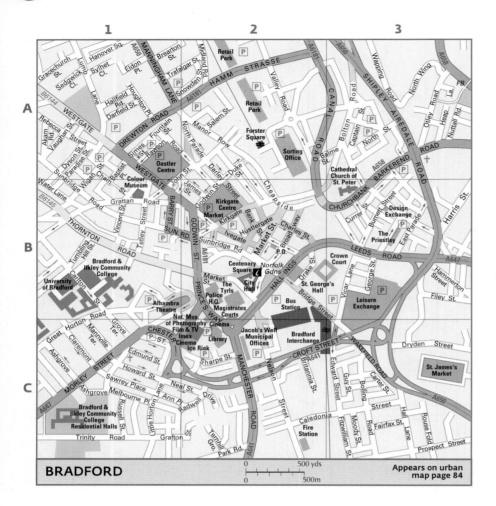

BRADFORD

0   500 yds
0   500m

Appears on urban
map page 84

Tourist Information Centre: City Hall, Centenary Square
Tel: 01274 753678

Akam Road	A1	Lumb Lane	A1
Ann Place	C1	Manchester Road	C2
Ashgrove	C1	Manningham Lane	A1
Balme Street	A2	Mannville Terrace	C1
Bank Street	B2	Manor Row	A2
Baptist Place	A1	Market Street	B2
Barkerend Road	A3	Melbourne Place	C1
Barry Street	B1	Midland Road	A1
Bolling Road	C3	Moody Street	C2
Bolton Road	A3	Morley Street	C1
Brearton Street	A1	Neal Street	C1
Bridge Street	B2	Nelson Street	C2
Britannia Street	C2	North Parade	A2
Broadway	B2	North Street	A3
Burnett Street	B3	North Wing	A3
Caledonia Street	C2	Nuttall Road	A3
Canal Road	A2	Otley Road	A3
Captain Street	A3	Paradise Street	A1
Carlton Street	B1	Park Road	C2
Carter Street	C3	Prince's Way	B2
Chain Street	A1	Prospect Street	C3
Charles Street	B2	Radwell Drive	C1
Cheapside	B2	Rawson Road	A1
Chester Street	C1	Rebecca Street	A1
Churchbank	B3	Rouse Fold	C3
Claremont	C1	Russell Street	C1
Croft Street	C2	Salem Street	A1
Currer Street	B3	Sawrey Place	C1
Darfield Street	A1	Sedgwick Close	A1
Darley Street	A2	Sharpe Street	C2
Drake Street	B2	Shipley Airedale Road	A3
Drewton Road	A1	Simes Street	A1
Dryden Street	C3	Snowden Street	A1
Duke Street	A2	Sunbridge Road	A1
Dyson Street	A1	Sylhet Close	A1
East Parade	B3	Ternhill Grove	C2
Edmund Street	C1	Tetley Street	B1
Edward Street	C3	Thornton Road	A1
Eldon Place	A1	Trafalgar Street	A1
Fairfax Street	C3	Trinity Road	C1
Filey Street	B3	Tumbling Hill Street	B1
Fitzwilliam Street	C3	Valley Road	A2
Fountain Street	A1	Vaughan Street	A1
George Street	B3	Vicar Lane	B3
Godwin Street	B2	Vincent Street	B1
Gracechurch Street	A1	Wakefield Road	C3
Grafton Street	C1	Wapping Road	A3
Grattan Road	B1	Water Lane	B1
Great Horton Road	C1	Westgate	A1
Grove Terrace	C1	Wigan Street	B1
Guy Street	C3		
Hall Ings	B2		
Hall Lane	C3		
Hallfield Road	A1		
Hamm Strasse	A2		
Hammerton Street	B3		
Hanover Square	A1		
Harris Street	B3		
Heap Lane	A3		
Houghton Place	A1		
Howard Street	C1		
Hustlergate	B2		
Ivegate	B2		
James Street	B2		
John Street	B1		
Kirkgate	B2		
Leeds Road	B3		
Little Horton Lane	C1		

BRIGHTON

0   200 yds
0   200m

Appears on main
map page 8

Tourist Information Centre: 10 Bartholomew Square
Tel: 0906 711 2255 (Premium Rate)

Addison Road	A1	Sussex Street	B3
Albion Hill	B3	Terminus Road	B2
Beaconsfield Road	A2	The Lanes	C2
Brunswick Square	B1	The Upper Drive	A1
Buckingham Place	A2	Trafalgar Street	B2
Buckingham Road	B2	Union Road	A3
Carlton Hill	B3	Upper Lewes Road	A3
Cheapside	B2	Upper North Street	B1
Church Street	B2	Viaduct Road	A2
Churchill Square	C2	Victoria Road	B1
Clifton Hill	B1	Waterloo Street	B1
Clyde Road	A2	Wellington Road	A3
Davigdor Road	A1	West Drive	B3
Ditchling Rise	A2	West Street	C2
Ditchling Road	A3	Western Road	B1
Dyke Road	B2	Wilbury Crescent	A1
Dyke Road Drive	A2	York Avenue	B1
Edward Street	C3	York Place	B3
Elm Grove	A3		
Florence Road	A2		
Freshfield Road	C3		
Furze Hill	B1		
Gloucester Road	B2		
Grand Junction Road	C2		
Hamilton Road	A2		
Hanover Street	B3		
Highdown Road	A1		
Holland Road	B1		
Hollingdean Road	A3		
Howard Place	A2		
Islingword Road	A3		
John Street	B3		
King's Road	C1		
Lansdowne Road	B1		
Lewes Road	A3		
London Road	A2		
Lyndhurst Road	A1		
Madeira Drive	C3		
Marine Parade	C3		
Montefiore Road	A1		
Montpelier Road	B1		
New England Road	A2		
New England Street	A2		
Nizells Avenue	A1		
Norfolk Terrace	B1		
North Road	B2		
North Street	B2		
Old Shoreham Road	A1		
Old Steine	C3		
Park Crescent Terrace	A3		
Park Street	B3		
Port Hall Road	A1		
Preston Circus	A2		
Preston Road	A2		
Preston Street	C1		
Prince's Crescent	A3		
Queen's Park Road	B3		
Queen's Road	B2		
Richmond Place	B3		
Richmond Road	A3		
Richmond Street	B3		
Richmond Terrace	B3		
St. James's Street	C3		
Somerhill Road	B1		
Southover Street	B3		
Springfield Road	A2		
Stafford Road	A1		
Stanford Road	A2		

Tourist Information Centre: The Annexe, Wildscreen Walk, Harbourside Tel: 0906 711 2191 (Premium Rate)

Alfred Hill A1
Anchor Road C1
Avon Street B3
Baldwin Street B1
Bath Road C3
Bond Street A2
Bridge Street B2
Bristol Bridge B2
Broadmead A2
Broad Quay B1
Broad Street B2
Broad Weir A3
Canon's Road C1
Canon's Way C1
Castle Street B3
Charles Street A2
Cheese Lane B3
Christmas Steps A1
Church Lane B3
College Green B1
Colston Avenue B1
Colston Street B1
Corn Street B1
Counterslip B2
Dale Street A3
Eugene Street A1
Fairfax Street A2
Frogmore Street B1
Harbour Way C1
High Street B2
Horfield Road A1
Houlton Street A3
John Street B2
King Street B1
Lewins Mead A1
Lower Castle Street A3
Lower Maudlin Street A2
Marlborough Street A2
Marsh Street B1
Merchant Street A2
Nelson Street A2
Newfoundland Street A3
Newgate B2
New Street A2
North Street A2
Old Bread Street B3
Old Market Street B3
Park Row B1
Park Street B1
Passage Street B3
Penn Street A3
Perry Road B1
Pipe Lane B1
Portwall Lane C2
Prewett Street C2
Prince Street C1
Prince Street Bridge C1
Queen Charlotte Street B2
Queen Square C1
Queen Street B3
Redcliff Backs C2
Redcliffe Bridge C2
Redcliffe Parade C2
Redcliff Hill C2
Redcliff Mead Lane C3
Redcliff Street B2
Redcross Street A3
River Street A3

Rupert Street A1
St. Michael's Hill A1
St. Nicholas Street B2
St. Thomas Street B2
Small Street B1
Somerset Street C3
Southwell Street A1
Station Approach Road C3
Straight Street B3
Surrey Street A3
Temple Back B3
Temple Gate C3
Temple Street B2
Temple Way C3
Terrell Street A1
The Grove C1
The Haymarket A2
The Horsefair A2
Thomas Lane B2
Trenchard Street B1
Tyndall Avenue A1
Union Street A2
Unity Street B1
Unity Street B3
Upper Maudlin Street A1
Victoria Street B2
Wapping Road C1
Water Lane B3
Wellington Road A3
Welsh Back B2
Wilder Street A2
Wine Street B2

Tourist Information Centre: Wheeler Street Tel: 0870 225 4900

Adam and Eve Street B3
Alpha Road A2
Aylestone Road A3
Barton Road C1
Bateman Street C2
Belvoir Road A3
Brookside C2
Burleigh Street B3
Carlyle Road A2
Castle Street A1
Chesterton Lane A2
Chesterton Road A2
Clarendon Street B3
De Freville Avenue A3
Devonshire Road C3
Downing Street B2
East Road B3
Eden Street B3
Elizabeth Way A3
Emmanuel Road B2
Fen Causeway, The C1
Glisson Road C3
Gonville Place C3
Granchester Street C1
Grange Road B1
Gresham Road C3
Hamilton Road A3
Harvey Road C3
Hills Road C3
Humberstone Road A3
Huntingdon Road A1
Jesus Lane B2
King's Parade B2
King Street B2
Lensfield Road C2
Madingley Road A1
Magdalene Bridge Street A2
Maids Causeway B3
Market Street B2
Mawson Road C3
Millington Road C1
Mill Road C3
Montague Road A3
Newmarket Road B3
Newnham Road C1
Norfolk Street B3
Panton Street C2
Parker Street B2
Park Parade A2
Parkside B3
Park Terrace B2
Pembroke Street B2
Queen's Road B1
Regent Street B2
Regent Terrace B2
St. Andrew's Street B2
St. Barnabas Road C3
St. John's Street B2
St. Matthew's Street B3
St. Paul's Road C3
Searce Street A1
Sidgwick Avenue C1
Sidney Street B2
Silver Street C1
Station Road C3
Storey's Way A1
Tenison Road C3
Tennis Court Road B2

Trinity Street B2
Trumpington Road C2
Trumpington Street C2
Union Road C2
Victoria Avenue A2
Victoria Road A2
West Road B1

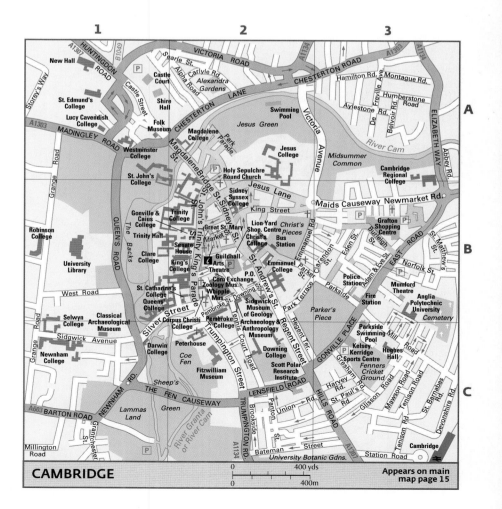

BRISTOL — Appears on urban map page 42

0 300 yds
0 300m

CAMBRIDGE — Appears on main map page 15

0 400 yds
0 400m

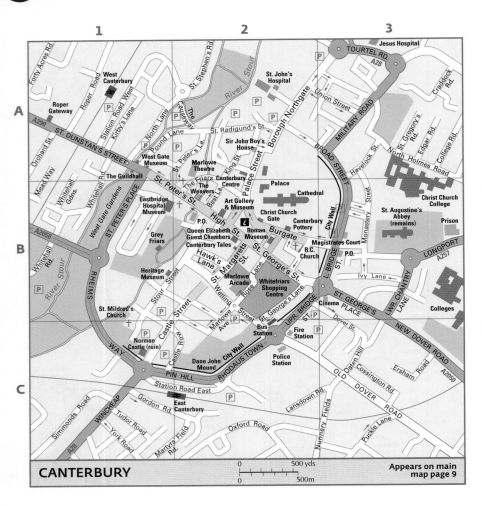

CANTERBURY

0   500 yds
0   500m

Appears on main
map page 9

Tourist Information Centre: 12/13 Sun Street, The Buttermarket
Tel: 01227 378100

Best Lane	B2	Whitehall Road	B1
Borough Northgate	A2	Wincheap	C1
Broad Street	A3	York Road	C1
Burgate	B2		
Castle Row	C1		
Castle Street	C1		
College Road	A3		
Cossington Road	C3		
Craddock Road	B3		
Dover Street	A3		
Edgar Road	A3		
Ersham Road	C3		
Forty Acres Road	A1		
Gordon Road	C1		
Havelock Street	A3		
Hawk's Lane	B2		
High Street	B2		
Ivy Lane	B3		
King Street	A2		
Kirby's Lane	A1		
Lansdown Road	C2		
Longport	B3		
Lower Bridge Street	B3		
Lower Chantry Lane	B3		
Marlowe Avenue	C2		
Martyrs' Field Road	C1		
Mead Way	B1		
Military Road	A3		
Monastery Street	B3		
New Dover Road	C3		
North Holmes Road	A3		
North Lane	A1		
Nunnery Fields	C3		
Oaten Hill	C3		
Old Dover Road	C3		
Orchard Street	A1		
Oxford Road	C2		
Palace Street	B2		
Pin Hill	C1		
Pound Lane	A1		
Puckle Lane	C3		
Rheims Way	B1		
Rhodaus Town	C2		
Roper Road	A1		
Rose Lane	B2		
St. Dunstan's Street	A1		
St. George's Lane	B2		
St. George's Place	B3		
St. George's Street	B2		
St. Gregory's Road	A3		
St. Margarets Street	B2		
St. Peter's Lane	A2		
St. Peter's Place	B1		
St. Peter's Street	A1		
St. Radigund's Street	A2		
St. Stephen's Road	A2		
Simmonds Road	C1		
Station Road East	C1		
Station Road West	A1		
Stour Street	B1		
The Causeway	A2		
The Friar's	B2		
Tourtel Road	A3		
Tudor Road	C1		
Union Street	A3		
Upper Bridge Street	C2		
Watling Street	B2		
Whitehall Gardens	B1		

CARDIFF

0   200 yds
0   200m

Appears on urban
map page 41

Tourist Information Centre: Cardiff Visitor Centre, 16 Wood St
Tel: 029 2022 7281

Adam Street	C3	Museum Avenue	A2
Albany Road	A3	Neville Street	B1
Allerton Street	C1	Newport Road	B3
Arran Place	A3	Newport Road Lane	B3
Arran Street	A3	Ninian Park Road	C1
Basil Place	A2	North Road	A1
Bedford Street	A3	Oxford Lane	B3
Boulevard de Nantes	B2	Park Grove	B2
Bridge Street	C2	Park Place	A2
Brook Street	B1	Park Street	C2
Bute Street	C2	Partridge Road	A3
Bute Terrace	C2	Penarth Road	C2
Castle Street	B1	Pendyris Street	C1
Cathays Terrace	A2	Pitman Street	B1
Cathedral Road	B1	Planet Street	B3
Celerity Drive	C3	Queen Street	B2
Central Link	C3	Rhymney Street	A2
Charles Street	B2	Richard Street	A2
Churchill Way	B3	Richmond Road	A3
City Road	A3	Ryder Street	B1
Clare Road	C1	St. Mary Street	C2
Clare Street	B1	St. Peters Street	B3
Claude Road	A3	Salisbury Road	A2
Coburn Street	A2	Schooner Way	C3
College Road	B2	Senghennydd Road	A2
Colum Road	A1	Stafford Road	C1
Corbett Road	A2	Strathnairn Street	A3
Cornwall Street	C1	Stuttgarter Strasse	B2
Cottrell Road	A3	Taffs Mead Embankment	C2
Cowbridge Road East	B1	Talbot Street	B1
Craddock Street	C1	Thesiger Street	A2
Craiglee Drive	C3	The Parade	B3
Croft Street	A3	The Walk	A3
Crwys Road	A2	Tudor Street	C1
Cyfartha Street	A3	Tyndall Street	C3
De Burgh Street	B1	Wedmore Road	C1
Despenser Street	C1	Wells Street	C1
Duke Street	B2	West Grove	B3
Dumfries Place	B3	Westgate Street	B2
Ellen Street	C3	Windsor Place	B2
Elm Street	A3	Windsor Road	B3
Fanny Street	A2	Wood Street	C2
Fitzhamon Embankment	C1	Woodville Road	A2
Flora Street	A2	Wordsworth Avenue	C3
Glossop Road	B3	Working Street	B2
Gordon Road	A3	Wyeverne Road	A2
Greyfriars Road	B2		
Hamilton Street	B1		
Harriet Street	A2		
Herbert Street	C3		
High Street	B2		
Hirwain Street	A2		
Keppoch Street	A3		
Kingsway	B2		
Lewis Street	B1		
Longcross Street	B3		
Maindy Road	A1		
Mardy Street	C1		
Mark Street	B1		
Merches Gardens	C1		
Merthyr Street	A2		
Meteor Street	B3		
Mill Lane	C2		
Minny Street	A2		
Miskin Street	A2		
Moira Place	B3		
Moira Terrace	B3		
Moy Road	A3		

Tourist Information Centre: Old Town Hall, Green Market
Tel: 01228 625600

Abbey Street	B2
Aglionby Street	B3
Albion Street	C3
Alexander Street	C3
Alfred Street	B3
Ashley Street	B1
Bank Street	B2
Bassenthwaite Street	C1
Bedford Road	C1
Botchergate	C2
Brampton Road	A2
Bridge Lane	B1
Bridge Street	B1
Broad Street	B3
Brook Street	C3
Brunswick Street	B3
Byron Street	B1
Caldcotes	B1
Carlton Gardens	A2
Castle Street	B2
Castle Way	B2
Cavendish Terrace	A2
Cecil Street	B3
Charlotte Street	C2
Chatsworth Square	B3
Chiswick Street	B3
Church Lane	A2
Church Road	A2
Church Street	B1
Clifton Street	C1
Close Street	C3
Collingwood Street	C2
Colville Street	C1
Crown Street	C2
Currock Road	C2
Currock Street	C2
Dale Street	C2
Denton Street	C2
Dunmail Drive	C1
East Dale Street	C2
East Norfolk Street	C2
Eden Bridge	A2
Edward Street	C3
Elm Street	C2
English Street	B2
Etterby Street	A2
Finkle Street	B2
Fisher Street	B2
Fusehill Street	C3
Georgian Way	B2
Goschen Road	C1
Graham Street	C2
Granville Road	B1
Greta Avenue	C1
Grey Street	C3
Hardwicke Circus	A2
Hart Street	B3
Hartington Place	B3
Howard Place	B3
Infirmary Street	B1
James Street	C2
John Street	B1
Junction Street	B1
Kendal Street	B1
King Street	C3
Lancaster Street	C3
Lime Street	C2
Lindon Street	C3

Lismore Place	B3
Lismore Street	B3
London Road	C3
Lonsdale	B2
Lorne Crescent	C2
Lorne Street	C2
Lowther Street	B2
Marlborough Gardens	A2
Mary Street	B2
Metcalfe Street	C2
Milbourne Street	B2
Morton Street	B1
Myddleton Street	B3
Nelson Street	C1
Norfolk Road	C1
Norfolk Street	C1
Peel Street	B1
Petteril Street	B3
Port Road	B2
Portland Place	C3
Rickergate	B2
Rigg Street	B1
River Street	B3
Robert Street	C2
Rome Street	C2
Rydal Street	C3
St. George's Crescent	A2
St. James Road	C1
St. Nicholas Street	C3
Scawfell Road	C1
Scotch Street	B2
Scotland Road	A2
Shaddongate	B1
Silloth Street	B1
Skiddaw Road	C1
Spencer Street	B3
Stanhope Road	B1
Strand Road	B3
Sybil Street	C3
Tait Street	C3
Talbot Road	C1
Trafalgar Street	C2
Viaduct Estate Road	B2
Victoria Place	B3
Victoria Viaduct	C2
Warwick Road	B2
Warwick Square	B3
Water Street	C2
Weardale Road	C1
West Tower Street	B2
West Walls	B2
Westmorland Street	C2
Wigton Road	B1
Willow Holme Road	A1

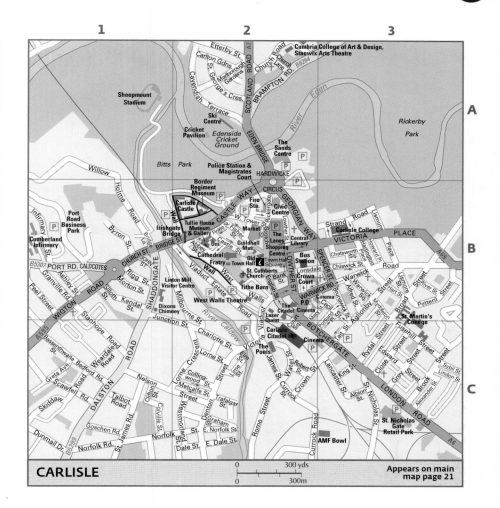

CARLISLE

0   300 yds
0   300m

Appears on main map page 21

Tourist Information Centre: 77 The Promenade
Tel: 01242 522878

Albany Road	C1
Albert Road	A3
Albion Street	B2
All Saints Road	B3
Andover Road	C1
Arle Avenue	A1
Ashford Road	C1
Bath Parade	B2
Bath Road	C2
Bayshill Road	B1
Berkeley Street	B2
Brunswick Street	A2
Carlton Street	B3
Central Cross Drive	A3
Christchurch Road	B1
Churchill Drive	C3
Clarence Road	A2
College Lawn	C2
College Road	C2
Douro Road	B1
Dunnally Street	A2
Eldon Road	B3
Evesham Road	A3
Fairview Road	B3
Folly Lane	A2
Gloucester Road	B1
Grafton Road	C1
Hale's Road	C3
Hanover Street	A2
Hayward's Road	C3
Henrietta Street	B2
Hewlett Road	B3
High Street	A2
Honeybourne Way	B1
Hudson Street	A2
Imperial Square	B2
Keynsham Road	C2
King Alfred Way	C3
King's Road	B3
Lansdown Crescent	C1
Lansdown Road	C1
London Road	C3
Lypiatt Road	C1
Malvern Road	B1
Market Street	A1
Marle Hill Parade	A2
Marle Hill Road	A2
Millbrook Street	A1
Montpellier Spa Road	B2
Montpellier Street	C1
Montpellier Terrace	C1
Montpellier Walk	C1
New Street	A2
North Place	B2
North Street	B2
Old Bath Road	C3
Oriel Road	B2
Overton Road	B1
Painswick Road	C1
Parabola Road	B1
Park Place	C1
Park Street	A1
Pittville Circus	A3
Pittville Circus Road	A3
Pittville Lawn	A3
Portland Street	B2
Prestbury Road	A3
Princes Road	C1

Priory Street	C3
Promenade	B2
Rodney Road	B2
Rosehill Street	C3
Royal Well Road	B2
St. George's Place	B2
St. George's Road	B1
St. James Street	B2
St. Johns Avenue	B2
St. Margaret's Road	A2
St. Paul's Road	A2
St. Paul's Street North	A2
St. Paul's Street South	A2
St. Stephen's Road	C1
Sandford Mill Road	C3
Sandford Road	C2
Sherborne Street	B3
Southgate Drive	C3
Strickland Road	C3
Suffolk Place	C1
Suffolk Road	C1
Sun Street	A1
Swindon Road	A1
Sydenham Road	B3
Sydenham Villas Road	C3
Tewkesbury Road	A1
Thirlestaine Road	C2
Tivoli Road	C1
Tivoli Street	C1
Townsend Street	A1
Vittoria Walk	C2
Wellington Road	A3
West Drive	A2
Western Road	B1
Whaddon Road	A3
Winchcombe Street	B2
Windsor Street	A3

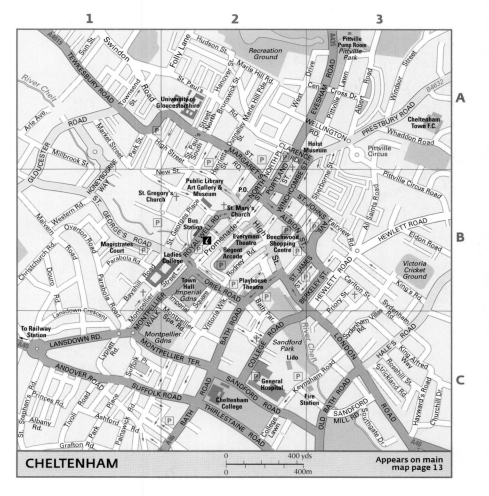

CHELTENHAM

0   400 yds
0   400m

Appears on main map page 13

CHESTER

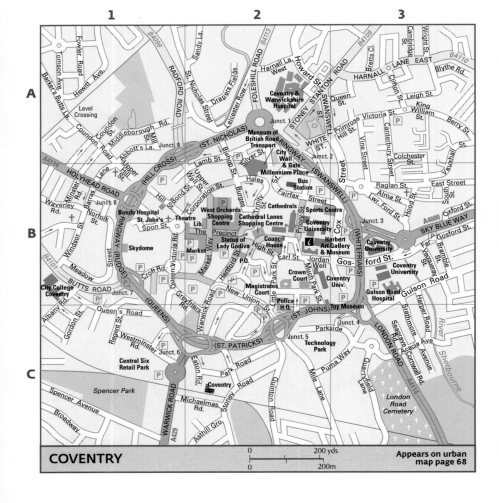

Tourist Information Centre: Town Hall, Northgate Street
Tel: 01244 402111

Bath Street	B3	Queen Street	B2
Bedward Row	B1	Raymond Street	A1
Black Diamond Street	A2	Russel Street	B3
Black Friars	C1	St. Anne Street	A2
Bold Square	B2	St. George's Crescent	C3
Boughton	B3	St. John's Road	C3
Bouverie Street	A1	St. John Street	B2
Bridge Street	B2	St. Martins Way	A1
Brook Street	A2	St. Oswalds Way	A1
Canal Street	A1	St. Werburgh Street	B2
Castle Drive	C1	Seller Street	B3
Charles Street	A2	Sibell Street	A3
Cheyney Road	A1	Souter's Lane	C2
Chichester Street	A1	Stanley Street	B1
City Road	B3	Station Road	A3
City Walls Road	B1	Steam Mill Street	B3
Commonhall Street	B1	Talbot Street	A2
Cornwall Street	A2	The Bars	B3
Crewe Street	A3	The Groves	C2
Cuppin Street	C1	Trafford Street	A2
Dee Hills Park	B3	Union Street	B2
Dee Lane	B3	Upper Northgate Street	A1
Deva Terrace	B3	Vicar's Lane	B2
Duke Street	C2	Victoria Crescent	C3
Eastgate Street	B2	Victoria Place	B2
Edinburgh Way	C3	Victoria Road	A1
Egerton Grove	A2	Walker Street	A3
Elizabeth Crescent	C3	Walpole Street	A1
Foregate Street	B2	Walter Street	A2
Forest Street	B2	Watergate Street	B1
Francis Street	A3	Water Tower Street	B1
Frodsham Street	B2	Weaver Street	B1
Garden Lane	A1	White Friars	C1
George Street	A2	York Street	B2
Gloucester Street	A2		
Grey Friars	C1		
Grosvenor Park Terrace	B3		
Grosvenor Road	C1		
Grosvenor Street	C1		
Handbridge	C2		
Hoole Road	A2		
Hoole Way	A2		
Hunter Street	B1		
King Street	B1		
Leadworks Lane	B3		
Lightfoot Street	A3		
Louise Street	A1		
Love Street	B2		
Lower Bridge Street	C2		
Lower Park Road	C3		
Mill Street	B3		
Milton Street	A2		
Newgate Street	B2		
Nicholas Street	B1		
Nicholas Street Mews	B1		
Northern Pathway	C3		
Northgate Avenue	A2		
Northgate Street	B1		
Nun's Road	C1		
Old Dee Bridge	C2		
Pepper Street	C2		
Phillip Street	A3		
Prince's Avenue	A3		
Princess Street	B1		
Queen's Avenue	A3		
Queen's Drive	C3		
Queen's Park Road	C2		
Queen's Road	A3		

Appears on main map page 17

Scale: 0 — 500 yds / 0 — 500m

COVENTRY

Tourist Information Centre: Bayley Lane
Tel: 024 7622 7264

Abbott's Lane	A1	Oxford Street	B3
Acacia Avenue	C3	Park Road	C2
Albany Road	C1	Parkside	C2
Alma Street	B3	Primrose Hill Street	A3
Asthill Grove	C2	Priory Street	B2
Barker's Butts Lane	A1	Puma Way	C2
Barras Lane	B1	Quarryfield Lane	C3
Berry Street	A3	Queen's Road	C1
Bishop Street	A2	Queen Street	A3
Blythe Road	A3	Queen Victoria Road	B1
Bond Street	B1	Quinton Road	C2
Bramble Street	B3	Radford Road	A1
Bretts Close	A3	Raglan Street	B3
Broadway	C1	Regent Street	C1
Burges	B2	Ringway Hill Cross	B1
Butts Road	B1	Ringway Queens	B1
Cambridge Street	A3	Ringway Rudge	B1
Canterbury Street	A3	Ringway St. Johns	B2
Clifton Street	A3	Ringway St. Nicholas	A2
Colchester Street	A3	Ringway St. Patricks	C2
Cornwall Road	C3	Ringway Swanswell	B3
Corporation Street	B2	Ringway Whitefriars	B3
Coundon Road	A1	St. Nicholas Street	A2
Coundon Street	A1	Sandy Lane	A2
Cox Street	B3	Seagrave Road	C3
Croft Road	B1	Silver Street	B2
Drapers Fields	A2	Sky Blue Way	B3
Earl Street	B2	South Street	B3
East Street	B3	Spencer Avenue	C1
Eaton Road	C2	Spon Street	B1
Fairfax Street	B2	Srathmore Avenue	C3
Far Gosford Street	B3	Stoney Road	C2
Foleshill Road	A2	Stoney Stanton Road	A2
Fowler Road	A1	Swanswell Street	A2
Gordon Street	C1	The Precinct	B2
Gosford Street	B3	Tomson Avenue	A1
Greyfriars Road	B1	Trinity Street	B2
Gulson Road	B3	Upper Hill Street	B1
Hales Street	B2	Upper Well Street	B2
Harnall Lane East	A3	Vauxhall Street	B3
Harnall Lane West	A2	Vecquexey Street	A3
Harper Road	B3	Victoria Street	A3
Harper Street	B2	Vine Street	B3
Hertford Street	B2	Warwick Road	C1
Hewitt Avenue	A1	Waveley Road	B1
High Street	B2	Westminster Road	C1
Hill Street	B1	White Street	A2
Holyhead Road	B1	Windsor Street	B1
Hood Street	B3	Wright Street	A3
Howard Street	A2		
Jordan Well	B2		
King William Street	A3		
Lamb Street	B2		
Leicester Row	A2		
Leigh Street	A3		
Little Park Street	C2		
London Road	C3		
Lower Ford Street	B3		
Market Way	B2		
Meadow Street	B1		
Michaelmas Road	C1		
Middleborough Road	A1		
Mile Lane	C2		
Mill Street	A1		
Minster Road	B1		
Much Park Street	B2		
New Union Street	B2		
Norfolk Street	B1		

Appears on urban map page 68

Scale: 0 — 200 yds / 0 — 200m

Tourist Information Centre: Assembly Rooms, Market Place
Tel: 01332 255802

Abbey Street	C1	Railway Terrace	C3
Agard Street	A1	Sacheverel Street	C1
Albert Street	B2	Saddlergate	B2
Arthur Street	A1	St. Alkmunds Way	A2
Babington Lane	C1	St. Helen's Street	A1
Bath Street	A2	St. James Street	A1
Becket Street	B1	St. Mary's Gate	B1
Bold Lane	B1	St. Mary's Wharf Road	A3
Bradshaw Way	C2	St. Peter's Churchyard	C2
Bridge Street	A1	St. Peter's Street	B2
Brook Street	A1	Siddals Road	C3
Burton Road	C1	Sir Frank Whittle Road	A3
Calvert Street	C3	Sitwell Street	C2
Canal Street	C3	Stafford Street	B1
Cathedral Road	B1	Station Approach	B3
City Road	A2	Stockbrook Street	C1
Clarke Street	B3	Stores Road	A3
Copeland Street	C2	The Strand	B1
Cornmarket	B2	Traffic Street	C2
Corporation Street	B2	Trinity Street	C2
Cranmer Road	B3	Victoria Street	B1
Crompton Street	C1	Wardwick	B1
Curzon Street	B1	West Avenue	A1
Darley Lane	A2	Willow Row	B1
Derwent Street	B2	Wilmot Street	C1
Drewry Lane	B1	Wilson Street	C1
Duffield Road	A1	Wolfa Street	C1
Duke Street	A2	Woods Lane	C1
Dunton Close	B3		
Eastgate	B3		
East Street	B2		
Edward Street	A1		
Exeter Street	B2		
Ford Street	B1		
Forester Street	C1		
Fox Street	A2		
Friar Gate	B1		
Friary Street	B1		
Full Street	B2		
Garden Street	A1		
Gerard Street	C1		
Gower Street	C2		
Green Lane	C1		
Grey Street	C1		
Handyside Street	A2		
Harcourt Street	C1		
Iron Gate	B2		
John Street	C3		
Kedleston Street	A1		
King Street	A1		
Leopold Street	C1		
Liversage Street	C2		
Lodge Lane	A1		
London Road	C2		
Macklin Street	B1		
Mansfield Road	A2		
Market Place	B2		
Meadow Road	B2		
Monk Street	C1		
Morledge	B2		
Normanton Road	C1		
North Parade	A2		
North Street	A1		
Nottingham Road	B3		
Osmaston Road	C2		
Parker Street	A1		
Pride Parkway	C3		
Queen Street	A2		

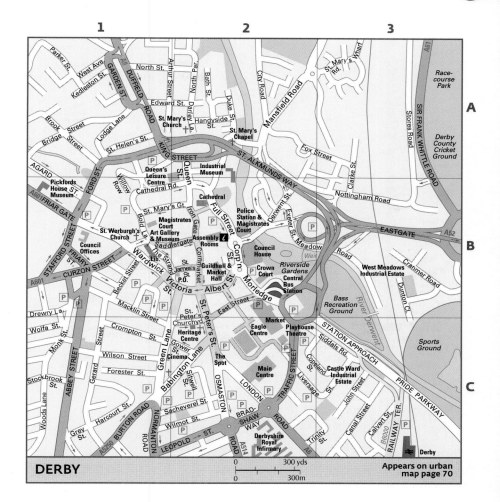

DERBY

Appears on urban map page 70

Tourist Information Centre: The Old Town Gaol, Biggin Street
Tel: 01304 205108

Astor Avenue	B1
Barton Road	A1
Beaconsfield Avenue	A1
Beaconsfield Road	A1
Belgrave Road	B1
Biggin Street	B2
Bridge Street	B2
Brookfield Avenue	A1
Buckland Avenue	A1
Cannon Street	B2
Canons Gate Road	B2
Castle Avenue	A2
Castle Hill Road	B2
Castle Street	B2
Cherry Tree Avenue	A1
Citadel Road	C1
Clarendon Place	B1
Clarendon Street	B1
Connaught Road	A2
Coombe Valley Road	B1
Dover Road	A3
Durham Hill	B2
Eaton Road	B1
Edred Road	B1
Elms Vale Road	B1
Folkestone Road	B1
Frith Road	A2
Godwyne Road	B2
Green Lane	A1
Guston Road	A2
Heathfield Avenue	A1
High Street	B2
Hillside Road	A1
Jubilee Way	A3
Ladywell	B2
Limekiln Street	C2
London Road	A1
Longfield Road	B1
Maison Dieu Road	B2
Marine Parade	B2
Mayfield Avenue	A1
Military Road	B2
Mount Road	C1
Napier Road	A1
Noah's Ark Road	B1
Northbourne Avenue	B1
North Military Road	B1
Old Charlton Road	A2
Old Folkestone Road	C1
Oswald Road	A1
Park Avenue	A2
Pencester Road	B2
Priory Hill	B1
St. Radigund's Road	A1
Salisbury Road	A2
Snargate Street	C2
South Road	B1
Stanhope Road	A2
The Viaduct	C2
Tower Street	B1
Townwall Street	B2
Union Street	C2
Upper Road	A3
York Street	B2

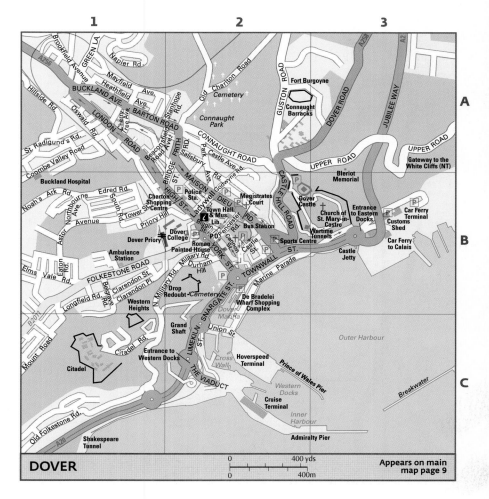

DOVER

Appears on main map page 9

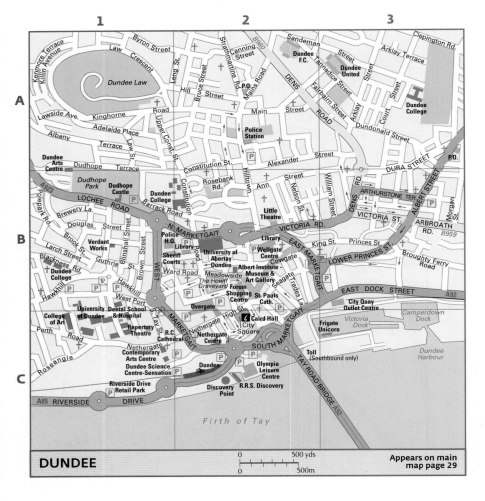

DUNDEE

Appears on main map page 29

Tourist Information Centre: 21 Castle Street
Tel: 01382 527527

Adelaide Place	A1	Tannadice Street	A2
Albany Terrace	A1	Tay Road Bridge	C2
Albert Street	B3	Trades Lane	B2
Alexander Street	A2	Upper Constitution Street	A1
Ann Street	B2	Victoria Road	B2
Arbroath Road	B3	Victoria Street	B3
Arklay Street	A3	Ward Road	B1
Arklay Terrace	A3	West Marketgait	B1
Arthurstone Terrace	B3	West Port	B1
Barrack Road	B1	William Street	B3
Blackness Road	B1		
Blinshall Street	B1		
Brewery Lane	B1		
Brook Street	B1		
Broughty Ferry Road	B3		
Brown Street	B1		
Bruce Street	A1		
Byron Street	A1		
Canning Street	A2		
City Square	C2		
Clepington Road	A3		
Constitution Road	B2		
Constitution Street	A2		
Court Street	A3		
Cowgate Street	B2		
Dens Road	A2		
Douglas Street	B1		
Dudhope Street	A1		
Dudhope Terrace	A1		
Dundonald Street	A3		
Dura Street	B3		
East Dock Street	B3		
East Marketgait	B2		
Fairbairn Street	A2		
Guthrie Street	B1		
Hawkhill	B1		
High Street	C2		
Hill Street	A2		
Hilltown	A2		
Kenmore Terrace	A1		
Killin Avenue	A1		
Kinghorne Road	A1		
King Street	B2		
Larch Street	B1		
Law Crescent	A1		
Lawside Avenue	A1		
Law Street	A1		
Leng Street	A1		
Lochee Road	B1		
Lower Princes Street	B3		
Mains Road	A2		
Main Street	A2		
Meadowside	B2		
Morgan Street	B3		
Nelson Street	B2		
Nethergate	C1		
North Marketgait	B1		
Perth Road	C1		
Polepark Road	B1		
Princes Street	B3		
Riverside Drive	C1		
Roseangle	C1		
Rosebank Road	B2		
Sandeman Street	A2		
Seagate	B2		
South Marketgait	C2		
South Tay Street	C1		
Strathmartine Road	A2		

DURHAM

Appears on main map page 23

Tourist Information Centre: 2 Millennium Place
Tel: 0191 384 3720

Aykley Heads	A1
Church Street	C2
Clay Lane	C1
Claypath	B2
Crossgate	B2
Crossgate Peth	C1
Darlington Road	C1
Dryburn Road	A1
Durham Road	A1
Fieldhouse Lane	A1
Framwelgate	B2
Framwelgate Peth	A2
Framwelgate Waterside	B2
Gilesgate	B3
Great North Road	A1
Green Lane	B3
Grove Street	C2
Hallgarth Street	C3
Hawthorn Terrace	B1
Leazes Road	B2
Margery Lane	C2
Market Place	B2
Millburngate Bridge	B2
Newcastle Road	A1
New Elvet	B2
North Bailey	B2
North End	A1
North Road	B2
Old Elvet	B3
Pity Me Bypass	A1
Potters Bank	C1
Quarryheads Lane	C2
Providence Row	B2
Redhills Lane	B1
St. Monica Grove	B1
Sidegate	B2
Silver Street	B2
South Bailey	C2
South Road	C2
South Street	C2
Southfield Way	A1
Stockton Road	C2
Sutton Street	B2
The Avenue	C1
Toll House Road	B1
Western Hill	B1
Whinney Hill	C3
Whitesmocks	A1

Tourist Information Centre: 3 Cornfield Road
Tel: 01323 411400

Arlington Road	B1
Arundel Road	A2
Ashford Road	B2/B3
Avondale Road	A3
Bedfordwell Road	A2
Belmore Road	A3
Blackwater Road	C2
Borough Lane	A1
Bourne Street	B3
Carew Road	A1/A2
Carlisle Road	C1
Cavendish Avenue	A3
Cavendish Place	B3
College Road	C2
Commercial Road	B2
Compton Place Road	B1
Compton Street	C2
Cornfield Terrace	B2
Denton Road	C1
Devonshire Place	B2
Dittons Road	B1
Dursley Road	B3
Enys Road	A2
Eversfield Road	A2
Fairfield Road	C1
Firle Road	A3
Furness Road	C2
Gaudick Road	C1
Gilbert Road	A3
Gildredge Road	B2
Gorringe Road	A2
Grand Parade	C3
Grange Road	C2
Grassington Road	C2
Grove Road	B2
Hartfield Road	A2
Hartington Place	B3
High Street	A1
Hyde Gardens	B2
King Edward's Parade	C2
Langney Road	B3
Lewes Road	A2
Marine Parade	B3
Mark Lane	B2
Meads Road	C1
Melbourne Road	A3
Mill Gap Road	A1
Mill Road	A1
Moat Croft Road	A1
Moy Avenue	A3
Ratton Road	A1
Royal Parade	B3
Saffrons Park	C1
Saffrons Road	B1
St. Anne's Road	A1
St. Leonard's Road	B2
Seaside	B3
Seaside Road	B3
Selwyn Road	A1
Silverdale Road	C2
South Street	B2
Southfields Road	B1
Station Parade	B2
Susan's Road	B3
Sydney Road	B3
Terminus Road	B2
The Avenue	B2
The Goffs	A1
Trinity Trees	B3
Upper Avenue	A2
Upperton Lane	B2
Upperton Road	A1
Watts Lane	A1
Whitley Road	A1
Willingdon Road	A1
Winchcombe Road	A3

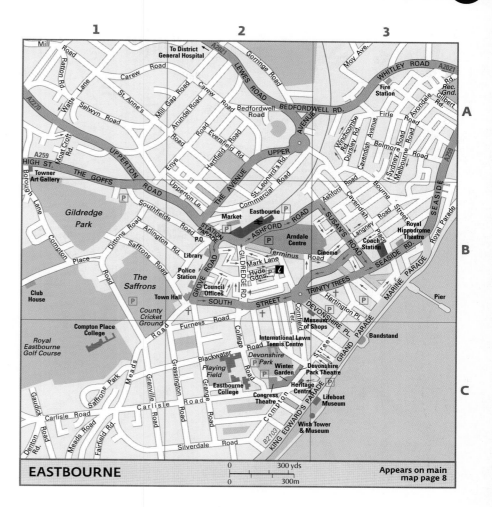

EASTBOURNE

Appears on main map page 8

Tourist Information Centre: Edinburgh & Scotland Information Centre, 3 Princes Street Tel: 0131 473 3800

Abbey Hill	A3
Abercromby Place	A2
Albany Street	A2
Alva Street	B1
Ann Street	A1
Arden Street	C2
Atholl Crescent	B1
Bellevue	A2
Bread Street	B1
Brougham Street	C1
Broughton Street	A2
Brunswick Road	A3
Bruntsfield Place	C1
Buccleuch Place	C2
Buccleuch Street	C3
Calton Road	B3
Canongate	B3
Castle Street	A1
Castle Terrace	B1
Causewayside	C3
Chalmers Street	C2
Chambers Street	B2
Charlotte Square	B1
Clerk Street	C3
Coates Crescent	B1
Cowgate	B2
Cumberland Street	A1
Dalkeith Road	C3
Dean Terrace	A1
Doune Terrace	A1
Dumbiedykes Road	B3
Dundas Street	A1
Easter Road	A3
East London Street	A2
East Market Street	B2
East Preston Street	C3
Elgin Street	A3
Eyre Place	A2
Fettes Row	A1
Fountainbridge	C1
Frederick Street	A1
Gardners Crescent	B1
George IV Bridge	B2
George Square	C2
George Street	B1
Gilmore Place	C1
Gloucester Lane	A1
Grassmarket	B2
Great King Street	A1
Grove Street	B1
Hamilton Place	A1
Hanover Street	A2
Hatton Place	C2
Henderson Row	A1
Heriot Row	A1
High Riggs	B1
High Street	B2
Hill Street	A1
Hillside Crescent	A3
Holyrood Park Road	C3
Holyrood Road	B3
Home Street	C1
Howe Street	A1
India Street	A1
Jamaica Street	A1
Johnston Terrace	B1
Lauriston Gardens	C2
Lauriston Place	B2
Lawnmarket	B2
Leamington Terrace	C1
Leith Street	A2
Leith Walk	A3
Leven Street	C1
London Road	A3
London Street	A2
Lothian Road	B1
Marchmont Road	C2
Marchmont Crescent	C2
Market Street	B2
Melville Drive	C2
Melville Street	B1
Melville Terrace	C2
Montgomery Street	A3
Montpelier Park	C1
Moray Place	A1
Morrison Street	B1
Nicolson Street	B2
North Bridge	A2
Northumberland Street	A1
Pleasance	B3
Potterrow	B2
Princes Street	B1
Queen's Drive	B3
Queensferry Street	B1
Queen Street	A1
Raeburn Place	A1
Regent Road	A3
Regent Terrace	A3
Rose Street	B1
Royal Circus	A1
Royal Terrace	A3
St. Andrew's Square	A2
St. Leonards Street	C3
St. Stephen Street	A1
Salisbury Road	C3
Sciennes Road	C2
Scotland Street	A2
Shandwick Place	B1
South Bridge	B2
The Mound	B2
Thistle Street	A2
Union Street	A2
Viewforth	C1
Viewcraig Gardens	B3
Warrender Park Terrace	C1
Warrender Park Road	C1
Waterloo Place	A2
Waverley Bridge	B2
West Approach Road	B1
West Port	B1
Whitehouse Loan	C1
Young Street	A1
York Place	A2

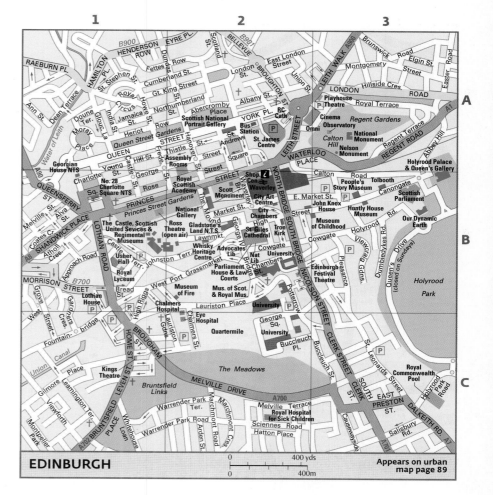

EDINBURGH

Appears on urban map page 89

EXETER

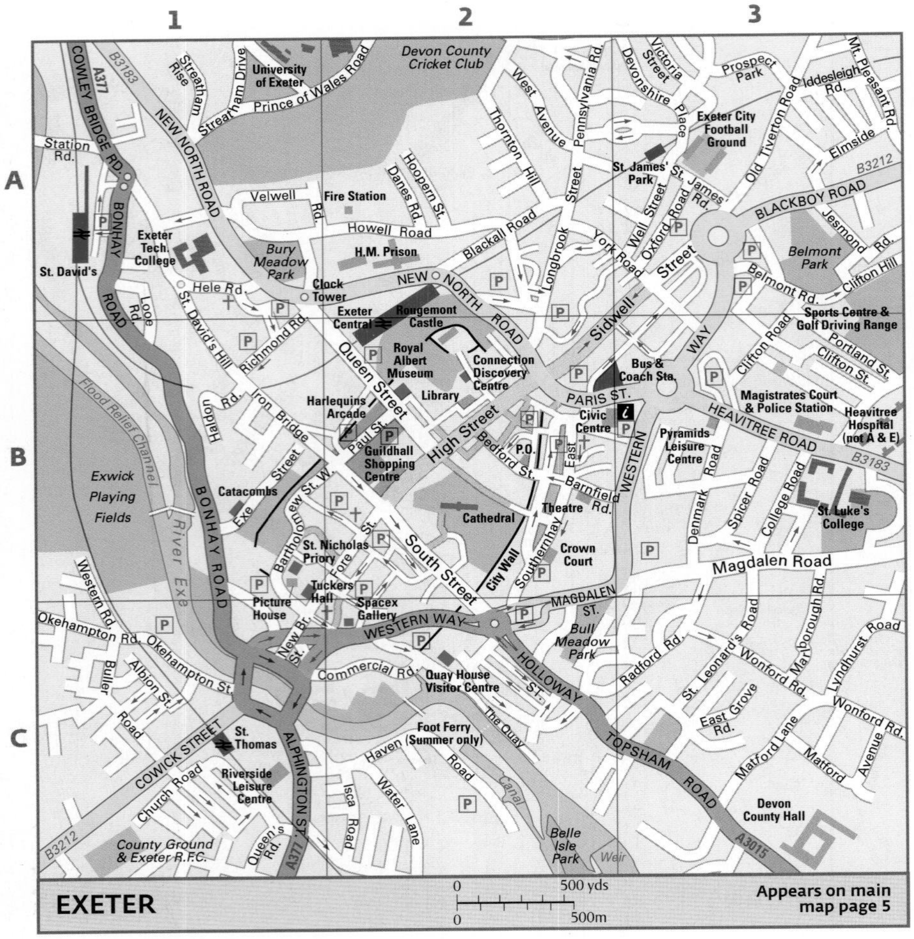

Tourist Information Centre: Civic Centre, Paris Street
Tel: 01392 265700

Appears on main map page 5

FOLKESTONE

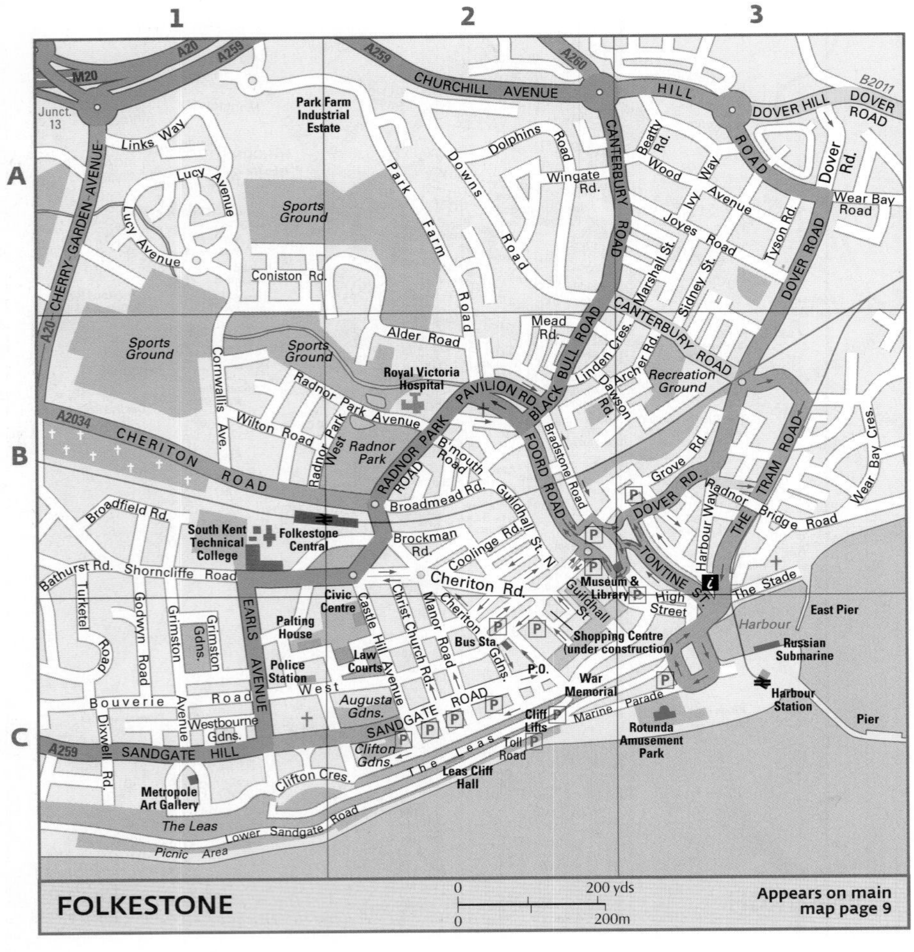

Tourist Information Centre: Harbour Street
Tel: 01303 258594

Appears on main map page 9

Tourist Information Centre: 28 Southgate Street
Tel: 01452 421188

Adelaide Street	C2
Alexandra Road	A2
Alfred Street	B3
Alma Place	C1
Alvin Street	A2
Archdeacon Street	A1
Argyll Road	A3
Askwith Road	C3
Barnwood Road	A3
Barton Street	B2
Black Dog Way	A2
Bristol Road	C1
Brunswick Road	B2
Bruton Way	B2
Calton Road	C2
Cecil Road	C1
Cheltenham Road	A3
Churchill Road	C1
Conduit Street	C2
Coney Hill Road	C3
Dean's Way	A2
Denmark Road	A2
Derby Road	B2
Estcourt Road	A2
Eastern Avenue	C3
Eastgate Street	B2
Frampton Road	C1
Gouda Way	A1
Great Western Road	B2
Greyfriars	B2
Hatherley Road	C2
Heathville Road	A2
Henry Road	A2
High Street	C2
Hopewell Street	C2
Horton Road	B3
Howard Street	C2
India Road	B3
King Edward's Avenue	C2
Kingsholm Road	A2
Lansdown Road	A2
Linden Road	C1
Llanthony Road	B1
London Road	A2
Lower Westgate Street	A1
Marlborough Road	C3
Merevale Road	A3
Metz Way	B2
Midland Road	C2
Millbrook Street	B2
Myers Road	B3
Northgate Street	B2
Oxford Road	A2
Oxstalls Lane	A3
Painswick Road	C3
Park Road	B2
Parkend Road	C2
Pitt Street	A2
Quay Street	B1
Regent Street	C2
Robinson Road	C1
Ryecroft Street	C2
St. Ann Way	C1
St. Oswald's Road	A1
Secunda Way	C1
Severn Road	B1
Seymour Road	C1
Southgate Street	B1
Spa Road	B1
Stanley Road	C2
Station Road	B2
Stroud Road	C1
The Quay	B1
Tredworth Road	C2
Trier Way	C1
Upton Street	C3
Vicarage Road	C3
Victoria Street	B2
Wellington Street	B2
Westgate Street	A1
Weston Road	C1
Wheatstone Road	C2
Willow Avenue	C3
Worcester Street	A2

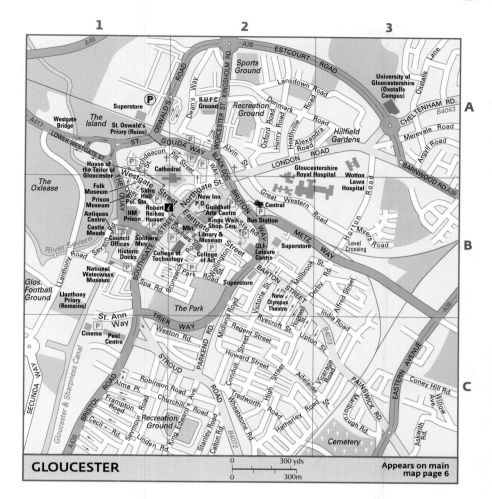

GLOUCESTER

0 — 300 yds
0 — 300m

Appears on main map page 6

Tourist Information Centre: 14 Tunsgate
Tel: 01483 444333

Abbot Road	C3
Artillery Road	A2
Artillery Terrace	A2
Bedford Road	A2
Bridge Street	B2
Bright Hill	B3
Bury Fields	C2
Bury Street	C2
Castle Hill	C3
Castle Square	B3
Castle Street	B2
Chertsey Street	A3
Cheselden Road	B3
Commercial Road	B2
Dapdune Road	A2
Dapdune Wharf	A2
Dene Road	A3
Denmark Road	A3
Denzil Road	B1
Drummond Road	A2
Eagle Road	A3
Eastgate Gardens	A3
Farnham Road	B1
Flower Walk	C2
Fort Road	C3
Friary Bridge	B2
Friary Street	B2
Genyn Road	B1
Guildford Park Avenue	A1
Guildford Park Road	B1
Harvey Road	B3
Haydon Place	A2
High Street	B2/B3
Laundry Road	C2
Lawn Road	B2
Leap Lane	B2
Leas Road	A2
Ludlow Road	B1
Market Street	B2
Martyr Road	B2
Mary Road	A2
Millbrook	C2
Millmead	B2
Millmead Terrace	B2
Mount Pleasant	C1
Nightingale Road	A3
North Street	B2
Onslow Road	A3
Onslow Street	B2
Pannells Court	B3
Park Road	A2
Park Street	B2
Pewley Hill	B3
Portsmouth Road	C2
Quarry Street	B2
Rookwood Court	C1
Sand Terrace	A2
Semaphore Road	C3
South Hill	B3
Springfield Road	A3
Station Approach	A3
Station View	A1
Stoke Road	A3
Swan Lane	B2
Sydenham Road	B3
The Bars	B2
The Mount	C1
Victoria Road	A3
Walnut Tree Close	A1
Warwicks	C3
Wharf Road	A2
Wherwell Road	B1
Wodeland Avenue	C1
Woodbridge Road	A2
York Road	A2

GUILDFORD

0 — 400 yds
0 — 400m

Appears on main map page 7

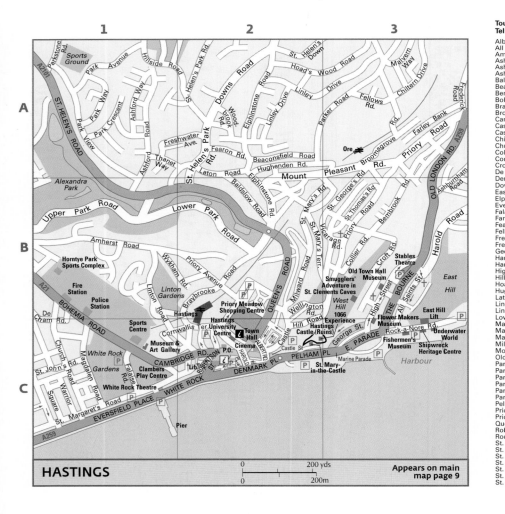

HARROGATE

Appears on main map page 18

Tourist Information Centre: Royal Baths Assembly Rooms, Crescent Road   Tel: 01423 537300

Ainsty Road	A3	Regent Street	A3
Albert Street	B2	Regent Terrace	A3
Alexandra Road	A2	Ripon Road	A1
Arthington Avenue	B2	Robert Street	C2
Beech Grove	C1	St. James Drive	C3
Belford Road	B2	St. Mary's Walk	C1
Bower Road	A2	Skipton Road	A3
Bower Street	B2	South Park Road	C2
Cambridge Street	B2	Springfield Avenue	A1
Cavendish Avenue	C3	Spring Grove	A1
Chelmsford Road	B2	Spring Mount	A1
Cheltenham Mount	A2	Station Avenue	B2
Chudleigh Road	A3	Station Parade	B2
Clarence Drive	B1	Stray Rein	C2
Claro Road	A3	Stray Walk	C3
Cold Bath Road	C1	Studley Road	A2
Commercial Street	A2	Swan Road	B1
Coppice Drive	A1	The Grove	A3
Cornwall Road	B1	Tower Street	C2
Crescent Gardens	B1	Trinity Road	C2
Dragon Avenue	A2	Valley Drive	B1
Dragon Parade	A2	Victoria Avenue	B2
Dragon Road	A2	Victoria Road	C1
Duchy Road	A1	West End Avenue	C1
East Parade	B2	West Park	B2
East Park Road	B2	Woodside	C2
Franklin Mount	A2	York Place	C2
Franklin Road	A2	York Road	B1
Gascoigne Crescent	A3		
Glebe Avenue	B1		
Glebe Road	C1		
Grove Park Terrace	A3		
Grove Road	A2		
Harcourt Drive	B3		
Harcourt Road	A3		
Heywood Road	C1		
Hollins Road	A1		
Homestead Road	B2		
James Street	B2		
Kent Road	A1		
King's Road	B1		
Knaresborough Road	B3		
Lancaster Road	C1		
Leeds Road	C2		
Lime Grove	A3		
Lime Street	A3		
Mayfield Grove	A2		
Montpellier Hill	B1		
Montpellier Street	B1		
Mowbray Square	A3		
North Park Road	B3		
Oatlands Drive	C3		
Otley Road	C1		
Oxford Street	B2		
Park Chase	A3		
Park Drive	C2		
Park Parade	B3		
Park Road	C1		
Park View	B2		
Parliament Street	B1		
Princes Villa Road	B2		
Providence Terrace	A2		
Queen Parade	B3		
Queen's Road	C1		
Raglan Street	B2		
Regent Avenue	A3		
Regent Grove	A3		
Regent Parade	A3		

HASTINGS

Appears on main map page 9

Tourist Information Centre: Queens Square, Priory Meadow   Tel: 01424 781111

Albert Road	C2	St. Mary's Terrace	B2
All Saints Street	B3	St. Thomas's Road	B1
Amherst Road	B1	Thanet Way	A1
Ashburnham Road	B3	The Bourne	B3
Ashford Road	A1	Upper Park Road	B1
Ashford Way	A1	Vicarage Road	B2
Baldslow Road	B2	Warrior Square	C1
Beaconsfield Road	A2	Wellington Road	B2
Bembrook Road	B3	White Rock	C1
Bohemia Road	B1	Woodbrook Road	A2
Braybrooke Road	B2	Wykeham Road	B1
Broomsgrove Road	A3		
Cambridge Road	C1		
Castle Hill Road	C2		
Castle Street	C2		
Chiltern Drive	A3		
Church Road	C1		
Collier Road	B3		
Cornwallis Terrace	C1		
Croft Road	B3		
De Cham Road	C1		
Denmark Place	C2		
Downs Road	A2		
East Parade	C3		
Elphinstone Road	A2		
Eversfield Place	C1		
Falaise Road	C1		
Farley Bank	A3		
Fearon Road	A2		
Fellows Road	A3		
Frederick Road	A3		
Freshwater Avenue	A1		
George Street	C3		
Harold Place	C2		
Harold Road	B3		
High Street	B3		
Hillside Road	A1		
Hoad's Wood Road	A2		
Hughenden Road	A2		
Laton Road	A2		
Linley Drive	A2		
Linton Road	B1		
Lower Park Road	B1		
Magdalen Road	C1		
Malvern Way	A3		
Marine Parade	C3		
Milward Road	B2		
Mount Pleasant Road	A2		
Old London Road	B3		
Park Avenue	A1		
Park Crescent	A1		
Park View	A1		
Park Way	A1		
Parker Road	A2		
Parkstone Road	A1		
Pelham Place	C2		
Priory Avenue	B2		
Priory Road	B3		
Queen's Road	B2		
Robertson Street	C2		
Rock-a-Nore Road	C3		
St. George's Road	B3		
St. Helen's Down	A2		
St. Helen's Park Road	B2		
St. Helen's Road	A1		
St. John's Road	C1		
St. Margaret's Road	C1		
St. Mary's Road	B2		

Hereford Inverness

Tourist Information Centre: 1 King Street
Tel: 01432 268430

Aubrey Street	B2	Victoria Street	B1
Barrs Court Road	A3	West Street	B2
Barton Road	B1	Widemarsh Street	B2
Barton Yard	B1	Wye Street	C2
Bath Street	B3		
Belmont Avenue	C1		
Berrington Street	B2		
Bewell Street	B2		
Blackfriars Street	A2		
Blueschool Street	A2		
Brewers Passage	B2		
Bridge Street	B2		
Broad Street	B2		
Canonmoor Street	A1		
Cantilupe Street	B3		
Castle Street	B2		
Catherine Street	A2		
Central Avenue	B3		
Church Street	B2		
Commercial Road	A3		
Commercial Street	B2		
Coningsby Street	A2		
East Street	B2		
Edgar Street	A2		
Eign Gate	B2		
Eign Street	B1		
Ferrers Street	B2		
Friars Street	B1		
Fryzer Court	B2		
Gaol Street	B3		
Green Street	C3		
Grenfell Road	C3		
Greyfriars Avenue	C1		
Greyfriars Bridge	B2		
Grove Road	C3		
Harold Street	C3		
High Street	B2		
High Town	B2		
King Street	B2		
Kyrle Street	B3		
Maylord Street	B2		
Mill Street	C3		
Monkmoor Street	A3		
Moorfield Street	A2		
Moor Street	A2		
Mostyn Street	A1		
Nelson Street	C3		
Newmarket Street	A2		
Park Street	C3		
Penhaligon Way	A1		
Plough Lane	A1		
Portland Street	A1		
Quay Street	B2		
Ryeland Street	B1		
St. Guthiac Street	B3		
St. James Road	C3		
St. Martin's Avenue	C2		
St. Martin's Street	C2		
St. Owen Street	B3		
Station Approach	A3		
Station Road	B1		
Stonebow Road	A3		
Symonds Street	B3		
The Atrium	A2		
Turner Street	C3		
Union Street	B2		
Union Walk	A3		
Vaughan Street	B3		

Tourist Information Centre: Castle Wynd
Tel: 0845 2255121

Abban Street	A1	Muirfield Road	C3
Academy Street	B2	Nelson Street	A1
Alexander Place	B2	Ness Bank	C2
Anderson Street	A2	Ness Bridge	B2
Ardconnel Street	C2	Ness Walk	C2
Ardconnel Terrace	B3	Old Edinburgh Road	C2
Ardross Place	B2	Park Road	C1
Ardross Street	C1	Perceval Road	B1
Argyle Street	C3	Planefield Road	B1
Argyle Terrace	C3	Queensgate	B2
Attadale Road	B1	Rangemore Road	B1
Bank Street	B2	Riverside Street	A2
Baron Taylor's Street	B2	Ross Avenue	B1
Benula Road	A1	Shore Street	A2
Bishop's Road	C1	Smith Avenue	C1
Bridge Street	B2	Southside Place	C3
Broadstone Park	C3	Southside Road	C3
Bruce Gardens	C1	Stephens Street	B3
Burnett Road	A3	Strother's Lane	B2
Carse Road	A1	Telford Road	A1
Castle Road	B2	Telford Street	A1
Castle Street	B2	Tomnahurich Street	C1
Celt Street	B1	Union Road	C3
Chapel Street	A2	Union Street	B2
Charles Street	B3	View Place	C2
Church Street	B2	Walker Road	A2
Columba Road	C1	Waterloo Bridge	A2
Crown Avenue	B3	Wells Street	B2
Crown Circus	B3	Young Street	B2
Crown Road	B3		
Crown Street	C3		
Culduthel Road	C2		
Denny Street	C3		
Dochfour Drive	C1		
Douglas Row	A2		
Duffy Drive	C2		
Dunabban Road	A1		
Duncraig Street	B1		
Eastgate	B3		
Fairfield Road	B1		
Friars Bridge	A1		
Friars Lane	B2		
Friars Street	B2		
Gilbert Street	A1		
Glebe Street	A2		
Glen Urquhart Road	C1		
Grant Street	A1		
Greig Street	B1		
Harbour Road	A2		
Harrowden Road	A1		
Haugh Road	C2		
High Street	B2		
Hill Street	B3		
Hontly Place	A1		
Huntly Street	B1		
Innes Street	A2		
Kenneth Street	B1		
Kingsmills Road	B3		
King Street	B1		
Leys Drive	C3		
Lindsay Avenue	C1		
Lochalsh Road	A1		
Longman Road	A2		
Maxwell Drive	C1		
Mayfield Road	C2		
Midmills Road	B3		
Millburn Road	B3		
Montague Row	B1		

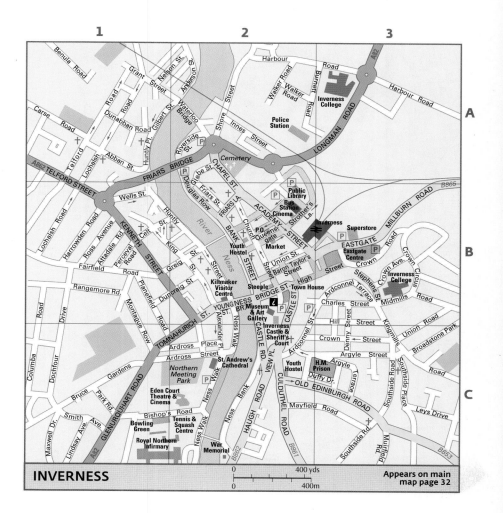

HEREFORD

INVERNESS

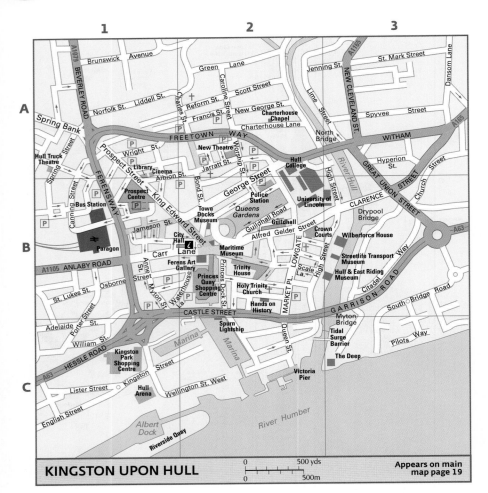

KINGSTON UPON HULL

1 2 3

A B C

0 ____ 500 yds
0 ____ 500m

Appears on main map page 19

Tourist Information Centre: 1 Paragon Street
Tel: 01482 223559

Adelaide Street	C1
Albion Street	B1
Alfred Gelder Street	B2
Anlaby Road	B1
Anne Street	B1
Beverley Road	A1
Bond Street	B2
Brunswick Avenue	A1
Canning Street	B1
Caroline Street	A2
Carr Lane	B1
Castle Street	B2
Charles Street	A2
Charterhouse Lane	A2
Church Street	B3
Citadel Way	B3
Clarence Street	B3
Cleveland Street	A3
Dansom Lane	A3
English Street	C1
Ferensway	A1
Francis Street	A2
Freetown Way	A1
Garrison Road	B3
George Street	B2
Great Union Street	A3
Green Lane	A2
Guildhall Road	B2
Hessle Road	C1
High Street	A3
Hyperion Street	A3
Jameson Street	B1
Jarratt Street	A2
Jenning Street	A2
King Edward Street	B1
Kingston Street	C1
Liddell Street	A1
Lime Street	A2
Lister Street	C1
Lowgate	B2
Market Place	B2
Myton Street	B1
New Cleveland Street	A3
New George Street	A2
Norfolk Street	A1
North Bridge	A2
Osborne Street	B1
Pilots Way	C3
Porter Street	C1
Princes Dock Street	B2
Prospect Street	A1
Queen Street	C2
Reform Street	A2
St. Lukes Street	B1
St. Mark Street	A3
Scale Lane	B2
Scott Street	A2
Scott Street Bridge	A2
South Bridge Road	B3
Spring Bank	A1
Spring Street	B1
Spyvee Street	A3
Waterhouse Lane	B1
Wellington Street West	C1
William Street	C1
Witham	A3
Worship Street	A2
Wright Street	A1

LEICESTER

1 2 3

A B C

0 ____ 200 yds
0 ____ 200m

Appears on urban map page 69

Tourist Information Centre: 7-9 Every Street, Town Hall Square
Tel: 0906 294 1113 (Premium Rate)

Abbey Street	A2	Market Street	B2
Albion Street	B2	Mill Lane	C1
All Saints Road	B1	Millstone Lane	B2
Aylestone Road	C2	Montreal Road	A3
Bassett Street	A1	Morledge Street	B3
Bath Lane	B1	Narborough Road	C1
Bedford Street North	A3	Narborough Road North	B1
Belgrave Gate	A2	Nelson Street	C2
Bell Lane	A3	Newarke Close	C1
Belvoir Street	B2	Newarke Street	B2
Braunstone Gate	B1	Northgate Street	A1
Burgess Street	A2	Ottawa Road	A3
Burleys Way	A2	Oxford Street	B2
Byron Street	A2	Pasture Lane	A1
Cank Street	B2	Peacock Lane	B2
Castle Street	B1	Pocklingtons Walk	B2
Charles Street	B3	Prebend Street	C3
Christow Street	A3	Princess Road East	C3
Church Gate	A2	Pringle Street	A1
Clarence Street	A2	Queen Street	B3
Clyde Street	A3	Regent Road	C2
College Street	B3	Regent Street	C3
Colton Street	B3	Repton Street	A1
Conduit Street	B3	Rutland Street	B3
Crafton Street East	A3	Samuel Street	B3
Cravan Street	A1	Sanvey Gate	A1
De Montfort Street	C3	Saxby Street	C3
Deacon Street	C2	Slater Street	A1
Dryden Street	A2	Soar Lane	A1
Duns Lane	B1	South Albion Street	B3
Dunton Street	A1	Southampton Street	B3
Eastern Boulevard	C1	Sparkenhoe Street	B3
Friar Lane	B2	St. George Street	B3
Friday Street	A2	St. George's Way	B3
Frog Island	A1	St. John's Street	A2
Gallowtree Gate	B2	St. Margaret's Way	A1
Gaul Street	C1	St. Matthew's Way	A3
Glebe Street	B3	St. Nicholas Circle	B1
Gotham Street	C3	St. Peter's Lane	A2
Granby Street	B2	Swain Street	B3
Grange Lane	C2	Swan Street	A1
Grasmere Street	C1	Taylor Road	A3
Great Central Street	A1	Thames Street	A2
Halford Street	B2	The Gateway	C1
Havelock Street	C2	The Newarke	B1
Haymarket	A2	Tower Street	C2
High Street	B2	Tudor Road	A1
Highcross Street	A1	Ullswater Street	C1
Hobart Street	B3	University Road	C3
Horsfair Street	B2	Upperton Road	C1
Humberstone Gate	B2	Vaughan Way	A1
Humberstone Road	A3	Vestry Street	B3
Infirmary Road	C2	Walnut Street	C1
Jarrom Street	C1	Waterloo Way	C2
Jarvis Street	B1	Welford Road	B2
Kamloops Crescent	A3	Wellington Street	B2
Kent Street	A3	West Street	C2
King Richard's Road	B1	Western Boulevard	C1
King Street	B2	Western Road	C1
Lancaster Road	C2	Wharf Street	A3
Lee Street	A2	Wharf Street North	A3
Lincoln Street	B3	Wilberforce Road	C1
London Road	C3	Windermere Street	C1
Loseby Lane	B2	Woodboy Street	A3
Lower Brown Street	B2	Yeoman Street	B2
Manitoba Road	A3	York Road	B2
Mansfield Street	A2		
Market Place South	B2		

Tourist Information Centre: 9 Castle Hill
Tel: 01522 873213

Alexandra Terrace	B1
Baggholme Road	B3
Bailgate	A2
Beaumont Fee	B2
Beevor Street	C1
Brayford Way	C1
Brayford Wharf North	B1
Broadgate	B2
Broadway	A2
Bruce Road	A3
Burton Road	A1
Canwick Road	C2
Carholme Road	B1
Carline Road	A1
Carr Street	B1
Cheviot Street	B3
Church Lane	A2
Clasketgate	B2
Croft Street	B2
Cross Street	C2
Curle Avenue	A3
Drury Lane	B2
East Gate	B2
Firth Road	C1
George Street	C3
Great Northern Terrace	C2
Greetwell Close	A3
Greetwell Road	B3
Gresham Street	B1
Hampton Street	B1
Harvey Street	B1
High Street	C2
John Street	B3
Langworthgate	A2
Lee Road	A3
Lindum Road	B2
Lindum Terrace	B3
Long Leys Road	A1
Mainwaring Road	A3
Mill Road	A1
Milman Road	B3
Monks Road	B3
Monson Street	C2
Moor Street	B1
Mount Street	A1
Nettleham Road	A2
Newland	B1
Newland Street West	B1
Newport	A2
Northgate	A2
Orchard Street	B1
Pelham Bridge	C2
Portland Street	C2
Portland Street	C2
Pottergate	B2
Queensway	A3
Rasen Lane	A2
Richmond Road	B1
Ripon Street	C2
Rope Walk	C1
Rosemary Lane	B2
Ruskin Avenue	A3
Saltergate	B2
Sewell Road	B3
Silver Street	B2
Sincil Bank	C2
Spa Road	C3
St. Anne's Road	B3
St. Giles Avenue	A3
St. Mark Street	C2
St. Mary's Street	C2
St. Rumbold Street	B2
Stamp End	C3
Steep Hill	B2
The Avenue	B1
Tritton Road	C1
Union Row	B2
Upper Lindum Street	B3
Upper Long Leys Road	A1
Vere Street	A2
Vine Street	B3
Waterside North	C2
Waterside South	C2
West Parade	B1
Westgate	A2
Wigford Way	B2
Wilson Street	A1
Winn Street	B3
Wragby Road	B3
Yarborough Road	A1

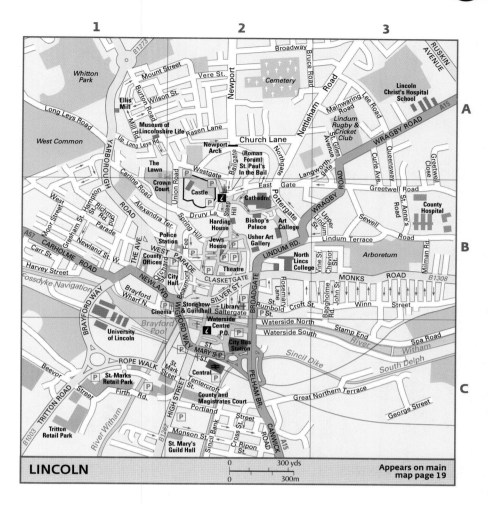

Tourist Information Centre: 99-101 Albert Road
Tel: 01642 358086

Abingdon Road	B2
Aire Street	B1
Albert Road	A2
Ayresome Green Lane	B1
Ayresome Street	B1
Beech Grove Road	C2
Belle Vue Grove	C3
Bishopton Road	C2
Borough Road	A2/C3
Breckon Hill Road	B3
Bridge Street East	A2
Bridge Street West	A2
Burlam Road	C1
Cambridge Road	C1
Cannon Park Way	A1
Cannon Street	A1
Cargo Fleet Road	A3
Chipchase Road	C1
Clairville Road	B2
Clive Road	B1
Corporation Road	A2
Crescent Road	B1
Cumberland Road	C2
Deepdale Avenue	C2
Derwent Street	A1
Dockside Road	A2/A3
Douglas Street	B3
Eastbourne Road	C2
Emerson Avenue	C2
Forty Foot Road	A1
Grange Road	A2
Granville Road	B2
Gresham Road	B1
Harford Street	B1
Harrow Road	C1
Hartington Road	A1
Heywood Street	B1
Highfield Road	C3
Holwick Road	A1
Hutton Road	B3
Ingram Road	B3
Keith Road	C2
Lansdowne Road	B3
Linthorpe Road	C2
Longford Street	B1
Longlands Road	B3
Marsh Street	A1
Marton Burn Road	C2
Marton Road	B3/C3
Newport Road	A1/A2
North Ormesby Road	A3
Nut Lane	B3
Orchard Road	C1
Overdale Road	C3
Oxford Road	C1
Park Lane	B2
Park Road North	B2
Park Road South	B2
Park Vale Road	B2
Parliament Road	B1
Portman Street	B2
Princes Road	B1
Reeth Road	C1
Riverside Park Road	A1
Rockliffe Road	C1
Roman Road	C1
Roseberry Road	B3
Saltwells Road	B3
Scotts Road	A3
Sheperdson Way	A3
Snowdon Road	A2
Southfield Road	B2
Southwell Road	C2
St. Barnabas Road	B1
Surrey Street	B1
Sycamore Road	C2
The Avenue	C2
The Crescent	C1
The Vale	C2
Thornfield Road	C1
Union Street	B1
Valley Road	C2
Victoria Road	B2
Victoria Street	A1
Westbourne Grove	B3
Westbourne Road	C1
Westminster Road	C2
Wilson Street	A2
Woodlands Road	B2

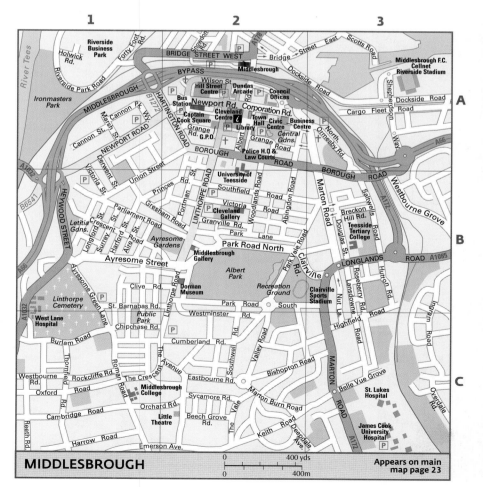

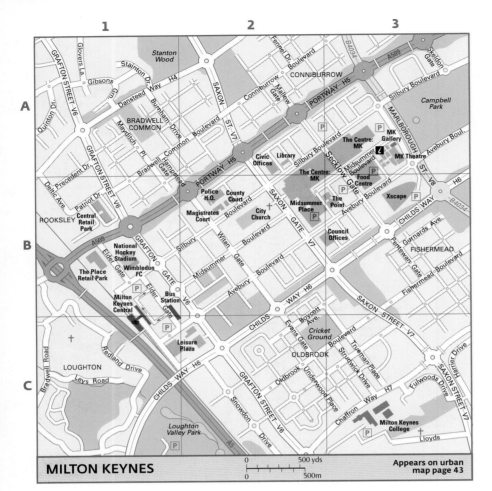

MILTON KEYNES

Appears on urban map page 43

Tourist Information Centre: Margaret Powell Square, 890 Midsummer Boulevard Tel: 01908 558300

Avebury Boulevard	B2/A3
Boycott Avenue	C2
Bradwell Common Boulevard	A1
Bradwell Road	C1
Burnham Drive	A1
Chaffron Way	C3
Childs Way	C1/B3
Conniburrow Boulevard	A2
Dansteed Way	A1
Deltic Avenue	B1
Elder Gate	B1
Evans Gate	C2
Fennel Drive	A2
Fishermead Boulevard	B3
Fulwoods Drive	C3
Gibsons Green	A1
Glovers Lane	A1
Grafton Gate	B1
Grafton Street	A1/C2
Gurnards Avenue	B3
Hampstead Gate	A1
Harrier Drive	C3
Leys Road	C1
Lloyds	C3
Mallow Gate	A2
Marlborough Street	A3
Mayditch Place	A1
Midsummer Boulevard	B2/A3
Oldbrook Boulevard	C2
Patriot Drive	B1
Pentewan Gate	B3
Portway	B2/A3
Precedent Drive	A1
Quinton Drive	A1
Redland Drive	C1
Saxon Gate	B2
Saxon Street	A2/C3
Secklow Gate	A3
Silbury Boulevard	B2/A3
Skeldon Gate	A3
Snowdon Drive	C2
Stainton Drive	A1
Strudwick Drive	C3
Trueman Place	C2
Underwood Place	C3
Witan Gate	B2

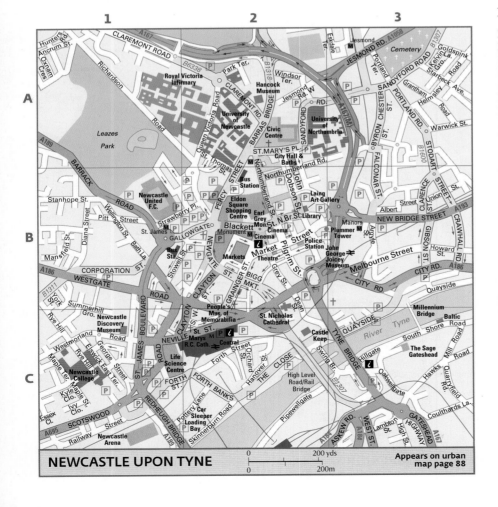

NEWCASTLE UPON TYNE

Appears on urban map page 88

Tourist Information Centre: 132 Grainger Street Tel: 0191 277 8000

Albert Street	B3	Portland Terrace	A3
Ancrum Street	A1	Pottery Lane	C1
Argyle Street	B3	Quarryfield Road	C3
Askew Road	C3	Quayside	C3
Barrack Road	A1	Queen Victoria Road	A2
Barras Bridge	A2	Railway Street	C1
Bath Lane	B1	Redheugh Bridge	C1
Bigg Market	B2	Richardson Road	A1
Blackett Street	B2	Rye Hill	C1
Byron Street	A3	St. James Boulevard	C1
Chester Street	A3	St. Mary's Place	A2
City Road	B3	St. Thomas Street	A2
Claremont Road	A2	Sandyford Road	A2/A3
Clarence Street	B3	Scotswood Road	C1
Clayton Street	B2	Skinnerburn Road	C2
Clayton Street West	C1	South Shore Road	C3
Corporation Street	B1	Stanhope Street	B1
Coulthards Lane	C3	Starbeck Avenue	A3
Crawhall Road	B3	Stodart Street	A3
Dean Street	B2	Stowell Street	B1
Diana Street	B1	Strawberry Place	B1
Elswick East Terrace	C1	Summerhill Grove	B1
Eskdale Terrace	A3	Swing Bridge	C2
Essex Close	C1	The Close	C2
Falconar Street	A3	Tyne Bridge	C3
Forth Banks	C2	Union Street	B3
Forth Street	C1	Warwick Street	A3
Gallowgate	B1	Wellington Street	B1
Gateshead Highway	C3	West Street	C3
George Street	C1	Westgate Road	B1
Gibson Street	B3	Westmorland Road	C1
Grainger Street	B2	Windsor Terrace	A2
Grantham Road	A3	York Street	B1
Grey Street	B2		
Hanover Street	C2		
Hawks Road	C3		
Helmsley Road	A3		
High Street	C3		
Hillgate	C3		
Howard Street	B3		
Hunters Road	A1		
Ivy Close	C1		
Jesmond Road	A3		
Jesmond Road West	A2		
John Dobson Street	B2		
Kelvin Grove	A3		
Kyle Close	C1		
Lambton Street	C3		
Mansfield Street	B1		
Maple Street	C1		
Maple Terrace	C1		
Market Street	B2		
Melbourne Street	B3		
Mill Road	C3		
Neville Street	C1		
New Bridge Street	B3		
Newgate Street	B2		
Northumberland Road	A3		
Northumberland Street	A2		
Oakwellgate	C3		
Orchard Street	C2		
Oxnam Crescent	A1		
Park Terrace	A2		
Percy Street	B2		
Pilgrim Street	B2		
Pipewellgate	C2		
Pitt Street	B1		
Portland Road	A3		

Tourist Information Centre: The Forum, Millennium Plain
Tel: 0870 225 4830

Albion Way	C3	Recorder Road	B3
All Saints Green	C2	Red Lion Street	B2
Ashby Street	C2	Riverside	C3
Bakers Road	A1	Riverside Road	B3
Bank Plain	B2	Rosary Road	B3
Barker Street	A1	Rose Lane	B2
Barn Road	B1	Rouen Road	C2
Barrack Street	A2	Rupert Street	C1
Bedford Street	B2	Russell Street	A1
Ber Street	C2	St. Andrew's Street	A2
Bethel Street	B1	St. Augustine's Street	A1
Bishopbridge Road	B3	St. Benedict's Street	A2
Bishopgate	B3	St. Crispin's Road	A1
Botolph Street	A2	St. Faiths Lane	B2
Brazen Gate	C2	St. George's Street	A2
Britannia Road	A3	St. Giles Street	B1
Brunswick Road	C1	St. James Close	A3
Bullclose Road	A2	St. Leonards Road	B3
Canary Way	C3	St. Martin's Road	A1
Carrow Hill	C3	St. Stephen's Road	C1
Carrow Road	C3	St. Stephen's Street	C1
Castle Meadow	B2	Silver Road	A2
Chapel Field Road	B1	Silver Street	A2
Chapelfield North	B1	Southwell Road	C2
City Road	C2	Surrey Street	C2
Clarence Road	C3	Sussex Street	A1
Colegate	A2	Theatre Street	B1
Coslany Street	B1	Thorn Lane	C2
Cowgate	A2	Thorpe Road	B3
Dereham Road	A1	Tombland	B2
Duke Street	A2	Trinity Street	C1
Earlham Road	B1	Trory Street	C1
Edward Street	A2	Union Street	C1
Elm Hill	B2	Unthank Road	C1
Fishergate	A2	Vauxhall Street	C1
Gas Hill	A3	Victoria Street	C1
Grapes Hill	B1	Wensum Street	A2
Grove Avenue	C1	Wessex Street	C1
Grove Road	C1	Westwick Street	A1
Grove Walk	C1	Wherry Road	C3
Gurney Road	A3	Whitefriars	A2
Hall Road	C2	Wodehouse Street	A2
Hardy Road	C3	York Street	C1
Heathgate	A3		
Heigham Street	A1		
Horns Lane	C2		
Ipswich Road	C1		
Ketts Hill	A3		
King Street	C2		
Koblenz Avenue	C3		
Lothian Street	A1		
Lower Clarence Road	B3		
Magdalen Street	A2		
Magpie Road	A2		
Market Avenue	B2		
Marlborough Road	A2		
Mountergate	B2		
Mousehold Street	A3		
Newmarket Road	C1		
Newmarket Street	C1		
Oak Street	A1		
Orchard Street	A1		
Palace Street	B2		
Pitt Street	A2		
Pottergate	B1		
Prince of Wales Road	B2		
Queens Road	C2		
Rampant Horse Street	B2		

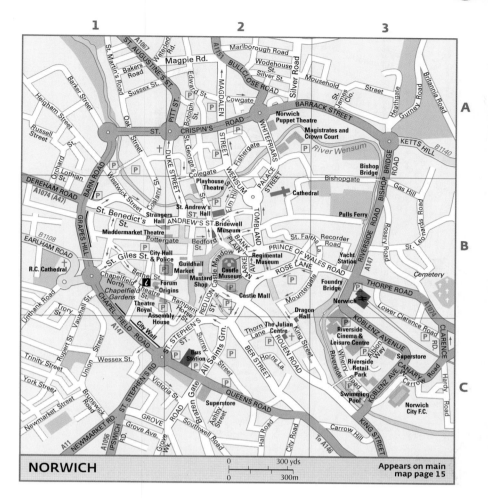

NORWICH

0 — 300 yds
0 — 300m

Appears on main map page 15

Tourist Information Centre: 1-4 Smithy Row
Tel: 0115 915 5330

Abbotsford Drive	A2	Market Street	B2
Albert Street	B2	Middle Pavement	B2
Angel Row	B1	Milton Street	A2
Barker Gate	B3	Mount Street	B1
Bath Street	A3	North Church Street	A2
Beacon Hill Rise	A3	North Sherwood Street	A2
Bellar Gate	B3	Park Row	B1
Belward Street	B3	Park Terrace	B1
Bridlesmith Gate	B2	Park Valley	B1
Broad Street	B2	Peel Street	A1
Brook Street	A3	Pelham Street	B2
Burton Street	A1	Pennyfoot Street	B3
Canal Street	C2	Peveril Drive	C1
Carlton Street	B2	Pilcher Gate	B2
Carrington Street	C2	Plantagenet Street	A3
Castle Boulevard	C1	Popham Street	C2
Castle Gate	B2	Poplar Street	B3
Castle Meadow Road	C1	Queens Road	C2
Castle Road	C1	Queen Street	B2
Chapel Bar	B1	Regent Street	B1
Chaucer Street	A1	Robin Hood Street	A3
Cheapside	B2	Roden Street	A3
City Link	C3	St. Ann's Well Road	A3
Clarendon Street	A1	St. James Street	B1
Cliff Road	C2	St. Mary's Gate	B2
Clumber Street	B2	St. Peter's Gate	B2
College Street	B1	Shakespeare Street	A1
Collin Street	C2	Shelton Street	A2
Cranbrook Street	B3	Smithy Row	B2
Cromwell Street	A1	Sneinton Road	B3
Curzon Street	A2	South Parade	B2
Derby Road	B1	South Sherwood Street	A2
Dryden Street	A1	Southwell Road	B2
Fisher Gate	B3	Station Street	C2
Fishpond Drive	C1	Stoney Street	B2
Fletcher Gate	B2	Talbot Street	A1
Forman Street	B2	The Great Northern Close	C3
Friar Lane	B1	The Rope Walk	B1
Gedling Street	B3	Union Road	A2
George Street	B2	Upper Parliament Street	B1
Gill Street	A1	Victoria Street	B2
Glasshouse Street	A2	Warser Gate	B2
Goldsmith Street	A1	Waverley Street	A1
Goose Gate	B3	Wheeler Gate	B2
Hamilton Drive	C1	Wilford Street	C1
Hampden Street	A1	Wollaton Street	B1
Handel Street	B3	Woolpack Lane	B3
Heathcote Street	B2		
High Pavement	B2		
Hockley	B3		
Hollowstone	B3		
Hope Drive	C1		
Huntingdon Drive	B1		
Huntingdon Street	A2		
Instow Rise	A3		
Kent Street	A2		
King Edward Street	B2		
King Street	B2		
Lamartine Street	A3		
Lenton Road	C1		
Lincoln Street	B2		
Lister Gate	C2		
London Road	C3		
Low Pavement	B2		
Lower Parliament Street	B2		
Maid Marian Way	B1		
Mansfield Road	A2		
Manvers Street	B3		

NOTTINGHAM

0 — 400 yds
0 — 400m

Appears on urban map page 71

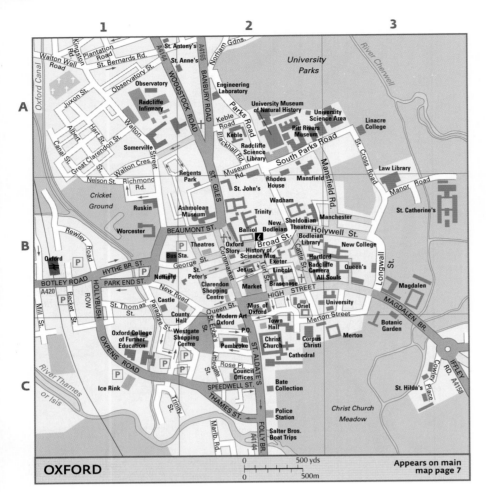

OXFORD

0   500 yds
0   500m

Appears on main
map page 7

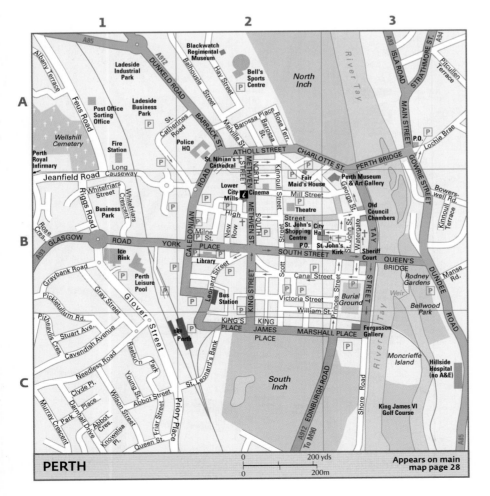

PERTH

0   200 yds
0   200m

Appears on main
map page 28

Tourist Information Centre: Island House, 9 The Barbican
Tel: 01752 264849

Alexandra Road	A3	Notte Street	C2
Alma Road	A1	Oxford Street	B1
Armada Street	B3	Pentillie Road	A2
Armada Way	B2	Ponsonby Road	A1
Ashford Road	A3	Princess Street	C2
Barbican Approach	C3	Queen's Road	A3
Beaumont Road	B3	Royal Parade	B2
Beechwood Avenue	A2	Salisbury Road	B3
Belgrave Road	A3	Saltash Road	A1
Bretonside	B2	Seaton Avenue	A2
Buckwell Street	C2	Seymour Avenue	B3
Camden Street	B2	Southside Street	C2
Cattledown Road	C3	Stoke Road	B1
Cecil Street	B1	Stuart Road	A1
Central Park Avenue	A1	Sutton Road	B3
Charles Street	B2	Sydney Street	B1
Citadel Road	C1	Teats Hill Road	C3
Clarence Place	B1	The Crescent	C1
Cliff Road	C1	Tothill Avenue	B3
Clifton Place	A2	Tothill Road	B3
Clovelly Road	C3	Union Street	B1
Cobourg Street	B2	Vauxhall Street	C2
Coleridge Road	A3	West Hoe Road	C1
Connaught Avenue	A3	Western Approach	B1
Cornwall Street	B2	Whittington Street	A1
Dale Road	A2	Wilton Street	B1
De-La-Hay Avenue	A1	Wyndham Street	B1
Desborough Road	B3		
Drake Circus	B2		
East Street	C1		
Eastlake Street	B2		
Ebrington Street	B2		
Elliot Street	C1		
Embankment Road	B3		
Exeter Street	B2		
Ford Park Road	A2		
Furzehill Road	A3		
Gdynia Way	C3		
Glen Park Avenue	A2		
Grand Parade	C1		
Greenbank Avenue	B3		
Greenbank Road	A3		
Grenville Road	B3		
Harwell Street	B1		
Hill Park Crescent	A2		
Hoe Road	C2		
Houndiscombe Road	A2		
James Street	B2		
King Street	B1		
Knighton Road	B3		
Lipson Hill	A3		
Lipson Road	B3		
Lisson Grove	A3		
Lockyer Street	C2		
Looe Street	B2		
Madeira Road	C2		
Manor Road	B1		
Martin Street	C1		
Mayflower Street	B2		
Millbay Road	C1		
Mount Gould Road	A3		
Mutley Plain	A2		
New George Street	B1		
North Cross	B2		
North Hill	B2		
North Road East	B2		
North Road West	B2		
North Street	B2		

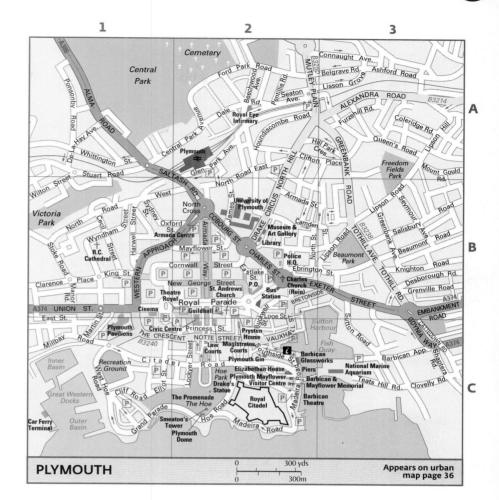

PLYMOUTH

0   300 yds
0   300m

Appears on urban
map page 36

Tourist Information Centre: The Hard
Tel: 023 9282 6722

Albany Road	C3	Queen Street	B1
Albert Grove	C3	Raglan Street	B3
Alfred Road	B2	Railway View	B3
Anglesea Road	B2	St. Andrews Road	C3
Arundel Street	B3	St. Edward's Road	C2
Astley Street	C2	St. George's Road	B1
Bailey's Road	C3	St. James Road	C2
Bellevue Terrace	C2	St. James Street	B2
Belmont Street	C3	St. Paul's Road	C2
Bishop Street	A1	St. Thomas's Street	C1
Blackfriars Road	B3	Somers Road	B3
Bradford Road	B3	Southsea Terrace	C2
Britain Street	B1	Station Road	B3
Broad Street	C1	Stone Street	C2
Burnaby Road	B2	Sultan Road	A3
Cambridge Road	C2	Sussex Street	C2
Canal Walk	B3	The Hard	B1
Castle Road	C2	Turner Road	A3
Church Road	A3	Unicorn Road	A2
Church Street	A3	Upper Arundel Street	B3
Clarendon Street	A3	Victoria Road North	C3
College Street	B1	Warblington Street	C1
Commercial Road	B2	Watts Road	A3
Cottage Grove	C3	White Hart Road	C1
Crasswell Street	A3	Wingfield Street	A3
Cross Street	A1	Winston Churchill Avenue	B2
Cumberland Street	A1	York Place	B2
Duke Crescent	A3		
Edinburgh Road	B2		
Eldon Street	C2		
Elm Grove	C3		
Flathouse Road	A3		
Fyning Street	A3		
Green Road	C2		
Greetham Street	B3		
Grosvenor Street	C3		
Grove Road South	C3		
Gunwharf Road	C1		
Hampshire Terrace	C2		
Havant Street	B1		
High Street	C1		
Holbrook Road	A3		
Hope Street	A2		
Hyde Park Road	B3		
Isambard Brunel Road	B2		
Kent Road	C2		
Kent Street	A1		
King Charles Street	C1		
King's Road	C2		
King's Terrace	C2		
King Street	C2		
Lake Road	A3		
Landport Terrace	C2		
Lombard Street	C1		
Margate Road	C3		
Market Way	A2		
Melbourne Place	B2		
Museum Road	C2		
Nelson Road	A3		
Norfolk Street	C2		
Northam Street	B3		
Outram Road	C3		
Pain's Road	C3		
Paradise Street	A3		
Park Road	B2		
Pembroke Road	C1		
Penny Street	C1		
Queen's Crescent	C3		

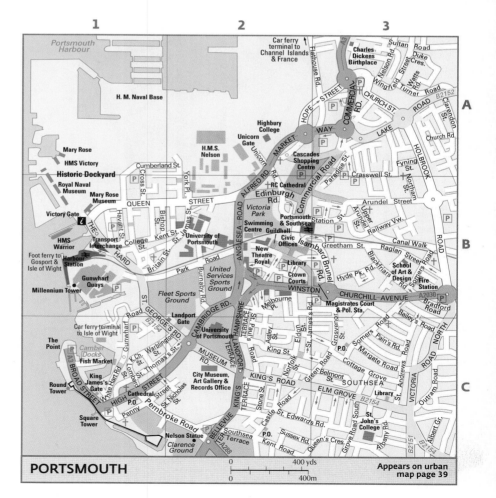

PORTSMOUTH

0   400 yds
0   400m

Appears on urban
map page 39

READING

Scale: 0 — 500 yds / 0 — 500m

Appears on main map page 7

Tourist Information Centre: Church House, Chain Street
Tel: 0118 956 6226

Addington Road	C3	London Street	B2
Addison Road	A1	Lower Henley Road	A3
Alexandra Road	B3	Mill Road	A3
Allcroft Road	C3	Milford Road	A1
Alpine Street	C2	Milman Road	C2
Amersham Road	A3	Minster Street	B2
Amity Road	B1	Morgan Road	C2
Ardler Road	A2	Napier Road	B2
Ashley Road	C1	Orts Road	B2
Audley Street	B1	Oxford Road	B1
Baker Street	B1	Pell Street	B2
Basingstoke Road	C2	Portman Road	A1
Bath Road	C1	Priest Hill	A2
Bedford Road	B1	Prospect Street *Caversham*	A2
Berkeley Avenue	C1	Prospect Street *Reading*	B1
Blagrave Street	B2	Queen's Road *Caversham*	A2
Blenheim Road	B3	Queen's Road *Reading*	B2
Briant's Avenue	A3	Redlands Road	C3
Bridge Street	B2	Richfield Avenue	A1
Broad Street	B2	Rose Kiln Lane	C1
Cardiff Road	A1	Russell Street	B1
Castle Hill	B1	St. Anne's Road	A3
Castle Street	B2	St. John's Road	A3
Catherine Street	B1	St. Mary's Butts	B2
Caversham Road	B2	St. Peters Avenue	A1
Chatham Street	B1	St. Saviours Road	C1
Cheapside	B2	Silver Street	C2
Cholmeley Road	B3	South Street	C2
Christchurch Road	C2	Southampton Street	C2
Church Road	A1	South View Road	A2
Church Street	A2	Star Road	A3
Coley Avenue	C1	Station Hill	B2
Coley Place	B1	Station Road	A2
Cow Lane	A1	Swansea Road	A2
Craven Road	B3	Tessa Road	A2
Crown Place	B3	The Warren	A2
Crown Street	C2	Tilehurst Road	B1
Cumberland Road	B3	Upper Redlands Road	C3
Curzon Street	B1	Vastern Road	A2
De Beauvoir Road	B3	Waldeck Street	C2
Donnington Road	B3	Waterloo Road	C2
Duke Street	B2	Wensley Road	C1
East Street	B2	Western Elms Avenue	B1
Eldon Road	B3	Westfield Road	A2
Eldon Terrace	B3	West Street	B2
Elgar Road	C2	Whitley Street	C2
Elgar Road South	C2	Wolsey Road	A2
Elmhurst Road	C3	York Road	A2
Erleigh Road	B3		
Fobney Street	B2		
Forbury Road	B2		
Friar Street	B2		
Gas Work Road	C2		
George Street *Caversham*	A2		
George Street *Reading*	B1		
Gosbrook Road	A2		
Gower Street	B1		
Great Knollys Street	B1		
Greyfriars Road	B2		
Hemdean Road	A2		
Hill Street	C2		
Holybrook Road	C1		
Kenavon Drive	B3		
Kendrick Road	C2		
King's Road *Caversham*	A2		
King's Road *Reading*	B2		
Lesford Road	C1		
London Road	B3		

SALISBURY

Scale: 0 — 200 yds / 0 — 200m

Appears on main map page 6

Tourist Information Centre: Fish Row
Tel: 01722 334956

Albany Road	A2	Southampton Road	C3
Ashley Road	A1	Swaynes Close	A2
Avon Terrace	A1	Tollgate Road	B3
Barnard Street	B3	Trinity Street	B3
Bedwin Street	A2	Wain-a-long Road	A3
Belle Vue Road	A2	West Walk	C2
Bishops Walk	C2	Wilton Road	A1
Blackfriars Way	C3	Winchester Street	B2
Blue Boar Row	B2	Windsor Road	B1
Bourne Avenue	A3	Wyndham Road	A2
Bourne Hill	A3	York Road	A1
Bridge Street	B2		
Brown Street	B2		
Butcher Row	B2		
Carmelite Way	C2		
Castle Street	A2		
Catherine Street	B2		
Chipper Lane	B2		
Churchfields Road	B1		
Churchill Way East	B3		
Churchill Way North	A2		
Churchill Way South	C2		
Churchill Way West	A1		
Clifton Road	A1		
College Street	A3		
Crane Bridge Road	B1		
Crane Street	B2		
De Vaux Place	C2		
Devizes Road	A1		
Elm Grove Road	B3		
Endless Street	A2		
Estcourt Road	A3		
Exeter Street	C2		
Fairview Road	A3		
Fisherton Street	B1		
Fowlers Hill	B3		
Fowlers Road	B3		
Friary Lane	C3		
Gas Lane	A1		
Gigant Street	B3		
Greencroft Street	A3		
Hamilton Road	A2		
High Street	B2		
Ivy Street	B2		
Kelsey Road	A3		
Laverstock Road	B3		
Manor Road	A3		
Marsh Lane	A1		
Meadow Road	A1		
Milford Hill	B3		
Milford Street	B2		
Mill Road	B1		
Millstream Approach	A2		
Minster Street	B2		
New Canal	B2		
New Street	B2		
North Walk	C2		
Park Street	A3		
Queens Road	A2		
Rampart Road	B3		
Rollestone Street	B2		
St. Ann Street	C3		
St. John's Street	B2		
St. Marks Road	A2		
St. Paul's Road	A1		
Salt Lane	B2		
Scots Lane	B2		
Silver Street	B2		

Sheffield Southampton

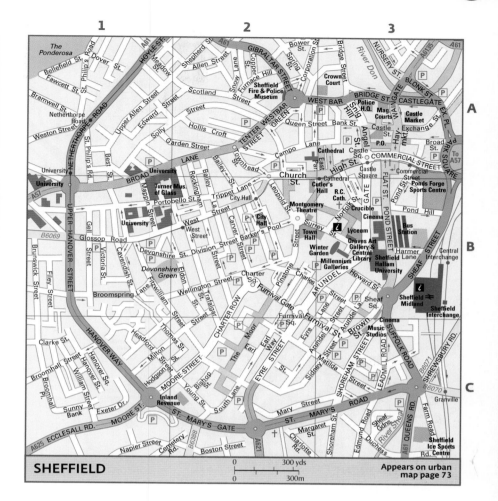

115

Tourist Information Centre: 1 Tudor Square
Tel: 0114 221 1900

Allen Street	A2	Hanover Square	C1
Angel Street	A3	Hanover Street	C1
Arundel Gate	B2	Hanover Way	C1
Arundel Lane	C3	Harmer Lane	B3
Arundel Street	C2	Haymarket	A3
Bailey Lane	A2	Headford Street	C1
Bailey Street	A2	High Street	A3
Bank Street	A3	Hodgson Street	C1
Barker's Pool	B2	Hollis Croft	A2
Bellefield Street	A1	Howard Street	B3
Best Street	A1	Hoyle Street	A1
Bishop Street	C2	Leadmill Road	C3
Blonk Street	A3	Leopold Street	B2
Boston Street	C2	Mappin Street	B1
Bower Street	A2	Margaret Street	C2
Bramwell Street	A1	Mary Street	C2
Bridge Street	A3	Matilda Street	C3
Broad Lane	B1	Meadow Street	A1
Broad Street	A3	Milton Street	C1
Broomhall Street	C1	Moore Street	C1
Broomhall Place	C1	Napier Street	C1
Broomspring Lane	B1	Netherthorpe Road	A1
Brown Street	C3	Norfolk Street	B3
Brunswick Street	B1	Nursery Street	A3
Campo Lane	A2	Pinstone Street	B2
Carver Street	B2	Pond Hill	B3
Castle Square	A3	Pond Hill	B3
Castle Street	A3	Pond Street	B3
Castlegate	A3	Portobello Street	B1
Cavendish Street	B1	Queen Street	A2
Cemetery Road	C1	Queens Road	C3
Charles Street	B2/B3	Rockingham Street	B2
Charlotte Road	C2	St. Mary's Gate	C2
Charter Row	C2	St. Mary's Road	C2
Charter Square	B2	St. Philip's Road	A1
Church Street	A2	Scotland Street	A2
Clarke Street	C1	Sheaf Gardens	C3
Commercial Street	A3	Sheaf Square	B3
Copper Street	A2	Sheaf Street	B3
Corporation Street	A2	Shepherd Street	A2
Devonshire Street	B1	Shoreham Street	C3
Division Street	B2	Shrewsbury Road	C3
Dover Street	A1	Sidney Street	C2
Duchess Road	C3	Snig Hill	A3
Earl Street	C2	Snow Lane	A2
Earl Way	C2	Solly Street	A1
East Parade	A3	South Lane	C2
Ecclesall Road	C1	Spring Street	A2
Edmund Road	C3	Suffolk Road	C3
Edward Street	A1	Sunny Bank	C1
Eldon Street	B2	Surrey Street	B2
Exchange Street	A3	Tenter Street	A2
Exeter Drive	C1	The Moor	C1
Eyre Lane	C2	Thomas Street	C1
Eyre Street	C2	Townhead Street	A2
Farm Road	C3	Trafalgar Street	B2
Fawcett Street	A1	Trippet Lane	A2
Filey Street	B1	Upper Allen Street	A1
Fitzwilliam Street	B1	Upper Hanover Street	B1
Flat Street	A3	Victoria Street	B1
Furnace Hill	A2	Waingate	A3
Furnival Gate	B2	Wellington Street	B2
Furnival Square	B2	West Bar	A2
Furnival Street	B2	West Street	B1
Garden Street	A1	Westbar Green	A2
Gell Street	B1	Weston Street	A1
Gibraltar Street	A2	William Street	C1
Glossop Road	B1	Young Street	C2

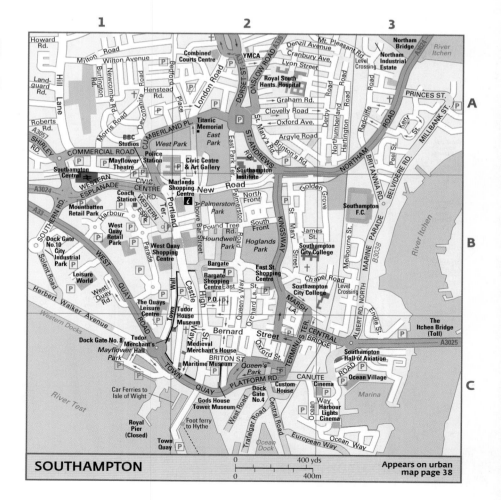

Tourist Information Centre: 9 Civic Centre Road
Tel: 023 8083 3333

Above Bar Street	B2	Roberts Road	A1
Albert Road North	C3	St. Andrews Road	A2
Argyle Road	A2	St. Mary's Road	A2
Bedford Place	A1	St. Mary Street	B2
Belvidere Road	B3	Shirley Road	A1
Bernard Street	C2	Solent Road	B1
Brintons Road	A2	Southern Road	B1
Britannia Road	A3	South Front	B2
Briton Street	C2	Terminus Terrace	C2
Burlington Road	A1	Town Quay	C1
Canute Road	C2	Trafalgar Road	C2
Castle Way	B2	West Quay Road	B1
Central Bridge	C2	West Road	C2
Central Road	C2	Western Esplanade	B1
Chapel Road	B2	Wilton Avenue	A1
Civic Centre Road	B1		
Clovelly Road	A2		
Commercial Road	A1		
Cranbury Avenue	A2		
Cumberland Place	A1		
Denzil Avenue	A2		
Derby Road	A3		
Devonshire Road	A1		
Dorset Street	A2		
East Park Terrace	A2		
East Street	B2		
Endle Street	B3		
European Way	C2		
Golden Grove	B2		
Graham Road	A2		
Harbour Parade	B1		
Hartington Road	A3		
Henstead Road	A1		
Herbert Walker Avenue	B1		
High Street	B2		
Hill Lane	A1		
Howard Road	A1		
James Street	B2		
Kent Street	A3		
Kingsway	B2		
Landguard Road	A1		
London Road	A2		
Lyon Street	A2		
Marine Parade	B3		
Marsh Lane	B2		
Melbourne Street	B3		
Millbank Street	A3		
Milton Road	A1		
Morris Road	A1		
Mount Pleasant Road	A3		
Newcombe Road	A1		
New Road	B2		
Northam Road	A3		
North Front	A2		
Northumberland Road	A3		
Ocean Way	C2		
Onslow Road	A2		
Orchard Lane	C2		
Oxford Avenue	A2		
Oxford Street	C2		
Palmerston Road	B2		
Peel Street	A3		
Platform Road	C2		
Portland Terrace	B1		
Pound Tree Road	B2		
Princes Street	A3		
Queen's Way	C2		
Radcliffe Road	A3		

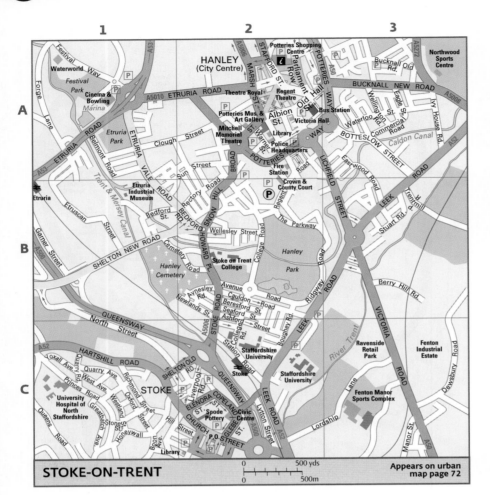

STOKE-ON-TRENT

Appears on urban
map page 72

Tourist Information Centre: Potteries Shopping Cen,
Quadrant Rd Tel: 01782 236000

Albion Street	A2	Station Road	C2
Ashford Street	B2	Stoke	C2
Avenue Road	B2	Stoke Road	C2
Aynsley Road	B2	Stone Street	C1
Bedford Road	B2	Stuart Road	B3
Bedford Street	B1	Sun Street	A2
Belmont Road	A1	The Parkway	B2
Beresford Street	B2	Trentham Road	B3
Berry Hill Road	B3	Victoria Road	B2
Boon Avenue	C1	Warner Street	A3
Botteslow Street	A3	Waterloo Street	A3
Boughey Road	C2	Wellesley Street	B2
Broad Street	A2	Wellington Road	A3
Bucknall New Road	A3	West Avenue	C1
Bucknall Old Road	A3	Westland Street	C1
Cauldon Road	B2	Yoxall Avenue	C1
Cemetery Road	B1		
Church Street	C2		
Clough Street	A1		
College Road	B2		
Commercial Road	A3		
Copeland Street	C2		
Dewsbury Road	C3		
Eagle Street	A3		
Eastwood Road	A3		
Elenora Street	C2		
Etruria Road	A1		
Etruria Vale Road	A1		
Etruscan Street	B1		
Festival Way	A1		
Forge Lane	A1		
Garner Street	B1		
Glebe Street	C2		
Greatbatch Avenue	C1		
Hanley	A2		
Hartshill Road	C1		
Hill Street	C1		
Honeywall	C1		
Howard Place	B2		
Ivy House Road	A3		
Leek Road	C2		
Lichfield Street	A3		
Liverpool Road	C2		
Lordship Lane	C2		
Lytton Street	C2		
Manor Street	C3		
Marsh Street	A2		
Newlands Street	B2		
North Street	B1		
Old Hall Street	A2		
Oxford Street	C1		
Parliament Row	A2		
Potteries Way	A2		
Potters Way	A3		
Prince's Road	C1		
Quarry Avenue	C1		
Quarry Road	C1		
Queen's Road	C1		
Queensway	B1		
Rectory Road	B2		
Regent Road	B2		
Richmond Street	C1		
Ridgway Road	B2		
Seaford Street	B2		
Shelton New Road	B1		
Shelton Old Road	C1		
Snow Hill	B2		
Stafford Street	A2		

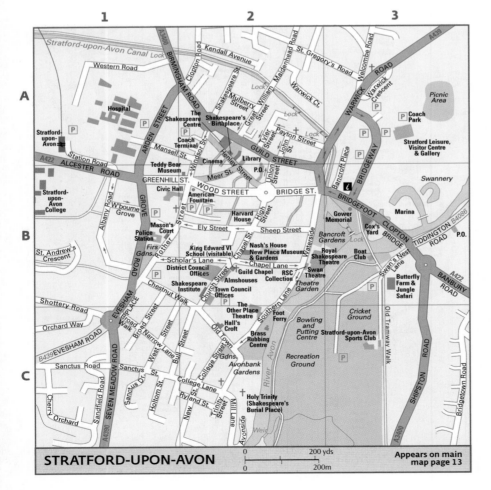

STRATFORD-UPON-AVON

Appears on main
map page 13

Tourist Information Centre: Bridgefoot
Tel: 0870 160 7930

Albany Road	B1	Warwick Crescent	A3
Alcester Road	A1	Warwick Road	A3
Arden Street	C2	Waterside	B2
Avonside	A3	Welcombe Road	A3
Banbury Road	B3	Westbourne Grove	B1
Bancroft Place	B3	Western Road	A1
Birmingham Road	A1	West Street	C1
Bridgefoot	B3	Windsor Street	B2
Bridge Street	B2	Wood Street	B2
Bridgeway	B3		
Bridgetown Road	C3		
Broad Street	C1		
Broad Walk	C1		
Bull Street	C1		
Chapel Lane	B2		
Chapel Street	B2		
Cherry Orchard	C1		
Chestnut Walk	B1		
Church Street	B2		
Clopton Bridge	B3		
Clopton Road	A2		
College Lane	C2		
College Street	C2		
Ely Street	B2		
Evesham Place	C1		
Evesham Road	C1		
Great William Street	A2		
Greenhill Street	B1		
Grove Road	B1		
Guild Street	A2		
Henley Street	A2		
High Street	B2		
Holtom Street	C1		
John Street	A2		
Kendall Avenue	A2		
Maidenhead Road	A2		
Mansell Street	A1		
Meer Street	B2		
Mill Lane	C2		
Mulberry Street	A2		
Narrow Lane	C1		
New Street	C2		
Old Town	C2		
Old Tramway Walk	C3		
Orchard Way	C1		
Payton Street	A2		
Rother Street	B1		
Ryland Street	C2		
St. Andrews Crescent	B1		
St. Gregory's Road	A2		
Sanctus Drive	C1		
Sanctus Road	C1		
Sanctus Street	C1		
Sandfield Road	C1		
Scholar's Lane	B1		
Shakespeare Street	A2		
Sheep Street	B2		
Shipston Road	C3		
Shottery Road	B1		
Seven Meadow Road	C1		
Southern Lane	C2		
Station Road	A1		
Swan's Nest Lane	B3		
Tiddington Road	B3		
Trinity Street	C2		
Tyler Street	A2		
Union Street	B2		
Warwick Court	A2		

Tourist Information Centre: 50 Fawcett Street
Tel: 0191 553 2000

Addison Street	C3	Lime Street	B1
Aiskell Street	B1	Livingstone Road	B2
Argyle Street	C2	Lumley Road	B1
Ashwood Street	C1	Matamba Terrace	B1
Azalea Terace South	C2	Milburn Street	B1
Barnes Park Road	C1	Millennium Way	A2
Barrack Street	A3	Moor Terrace	B3
Beach Street	B1	Mount Road	C1
Beechwood Terrace	C1	Mowbray Road	C2
Belvedere Road	C2	New Durham Road	C1
Black Road	A2	Newcastle Road	A2
Borough Road	B2/B3	North Bridge Street	B2
Bramwell Road	C3	Otto Terrace	C1
Brougham Street	B2	Pallion New Road	B1
Burdon Road	C2	Park Lane	B2
Burn Park Road	C1	Park Road	C2
Burnaby Street	C1	Peel Street	C2
Burnville Road	C1	Prospect Row	B3
Carol Street	B1	Queens Road	A1
Chatsworth Street	C1	Raby Road	B1
Chaytor Grove	B3	Railway Row	B1
Chester Road	B1	Roker Avenue	A2/A3
Chester Street	B1	Rosalie Terrace	C3
Church Street North	A2	Ryhope Road	C2
Cleveland Road	C1	St. Albans Street	C3
Commercial Road	C3	St. Leonards Street	C3
Cooper Street	A3	St. Marks Road	B1
Coronation Street	B3	St. Mary's Way	B2
Corporation Road	C3	St. Michaels Way	B2
Cousin Street	B3	St. Peter's Way	A3
Cromwell Street	B1	Salem Road	C3
Crowtree Road	B2	Salem Street	C3
Crozier Street	A2	Salisbury Street	B2
Dame Dorothy Street	A2	Sans Street	B2
Deptford Road	B1	Selbourne Street	A2
Deptford Terrace	A1	Silksworth Row	B1
Durham Road	C1	Sorley Street	B1
Easington Street	A2	Southwick Road	A2
Eden House Road	C1	Southwick Road	A2
Eglinton Street	A2	Stockton Road	C2
Enderby Road	B1	Suffolk Street	C3
Farringdon Row	A1	Sunderland Road	A1
Forster Street	A3	Swan Street	A2
Fox Street	C1	Tatham Street	B3
Fulwell Road	A2	The Cedars	C2
General Graham Street	C1	The Cloisters	C2
Gladstone Street	A2	The Parade	C3
Gray Road	C2/C3	The Quadrant	B3
Hanover Place	A1	The Royalty	B1
Hartington Street	A3	Thornholme Road	C1
Hartley Street	B3	Thornhill Park	C2
Hastings Street	C3	Toward Road	B2/C3
Hay Street	A2	Tower Street	C3
Hendon Road	B3	Tower Street West	C3
Hendon Valley Road	C3	Trimdon Street	B1
High Street East	B3	Tunstall Road	C2
High Street West	B2	Tunstall Vale	C2
Holmeside	B2	Vaux Brewery Way	A2
Horatio Street	A3	Villette Road	C3
Hurstwood Road	C1	Vine Place	B2
Hutton Street	C1	Wallace Street	A2
Hylton Road	B1	West Lawn	C2
Hylton Street	B1	West Wear Street	B2
Jackson Street	C1	Western Hill	B1
James William Street	B3	Wharncliffe Street	B1
Kenton Grove	A2	White House Road	C3
Kier Hardy Way	A1	Woodbine Street	B3
King's Place	B1	Wreath Quay Road	A2
Lawrence Street	B3		

Tourist Information Centre: Westway
Tel: 01792 468321

Aberdyberthi Street	A3	Neath Road	A3
Albert Row	C2	New Cut Road	B3
Alexandra Road	B2	New Orchard Street	A2
Argyle Street	C1	Nicander Parade	B1
Baptist Well Place	A2	Norfolk Street	B1
Baptist Well Street	A2	North Hill Road	A2
Beach Street	C1	Orchard Street	B2
Belgrave Lane	C1	Oystermouth Road	C1
Belle Vue Way	B2	Page Street	B2
Berw Road	A1	Pant-y-Celyn Road	B1
Berwick Terrace	A2	Park Terrace	A2
Bond Street	C1	Pedrog Terrace	A1
Brooklands Terrace	B1	Penlan Crescent	B1
Brunswick Street	C1	Pentre Guinea Road	A3
Brynmor Crescent	C1	Pen-y-Craig Road	A1
Brynmor Road	C1	Picton Terrace	B2
Burrows Place	C3	Powys Avenue	A1
Cambrian Place	C3	Princess Way	B2
Carig Crescent	A1	Quay Parade	B3
Carlton Terrace	B2	Rhondda Street	B1
Carmarthen Road	A2	Rose Hill	B1
Castle Street	B2	St. Elmo Avenue	A3
Clarence Terrace	C2	St. Helen's Avenue	C1
Colbourne Terrace	A2	St. Helen's Road	C1
Constitution Hill	B1	St. Mary Street	B2
Creidiol Road	A1	Singleton Street	B2
Cromwell Street	B1	Somerset Place	C3
Cwm Road	A3	South Guildhall Road	C1
De La Beche Street	B2	Strand	B3
Delhi Street	B3	Taliesyn Road	B1
Dyfatty Street	A2	Tan-y-Marian Road	B1
Dyfed Avenue	B1	Tegid Road	A1
Earl Street	A3	Teilo Crescent	A1
East Burrows Road	C3	Terrace Road	B1
Eigen Crescent	A1	The Kingsway	B2
Emlyn Road	A1	Townhill Road	A1
Fabian Way	B3	Trawler Road	C2
Ffynone Drive	B1	Villiers Street	A3
Ffynone Road	B1	Vincent Street	C1
Foxhole Road	A3	Walter Road	C1
Glamorgan Street	C2	Watkin Street	B2
Gors Avenue	A1	Waun-Wen Road	A2
Granagwen Road	A2	Wellington Street	C2
Grove Place	B2	West Way	C2
Gwent Road	A1	Westbury Street	C1
Gwili Terrace	A1	Western Street	C1
Hanover Street	B1	William Street	C2
Heathfield	B2	Windmill Terrace	A3
Hewson Street	B1	York Street	C3
High Street	B2		
High View	A1		
Islwyn Road	A1		
Kilvey Road	A3		
Kilvey Terrace	B3		
King Edward's Road	B1		
King's Road	B3		
Llangyfelach Road	A2		
Long Ridge	A2		
Lower Oxford Street	C1		
Mackworth Street	B3		
Maesteg Street	A3		
Mansel Street	B1		
Mayhill Road	A1		
Milton Terrace	B2		
Morris Lane	B3		
Mount Pleasant	B2		
Mumbles Road	C1		

SUNDERLAND

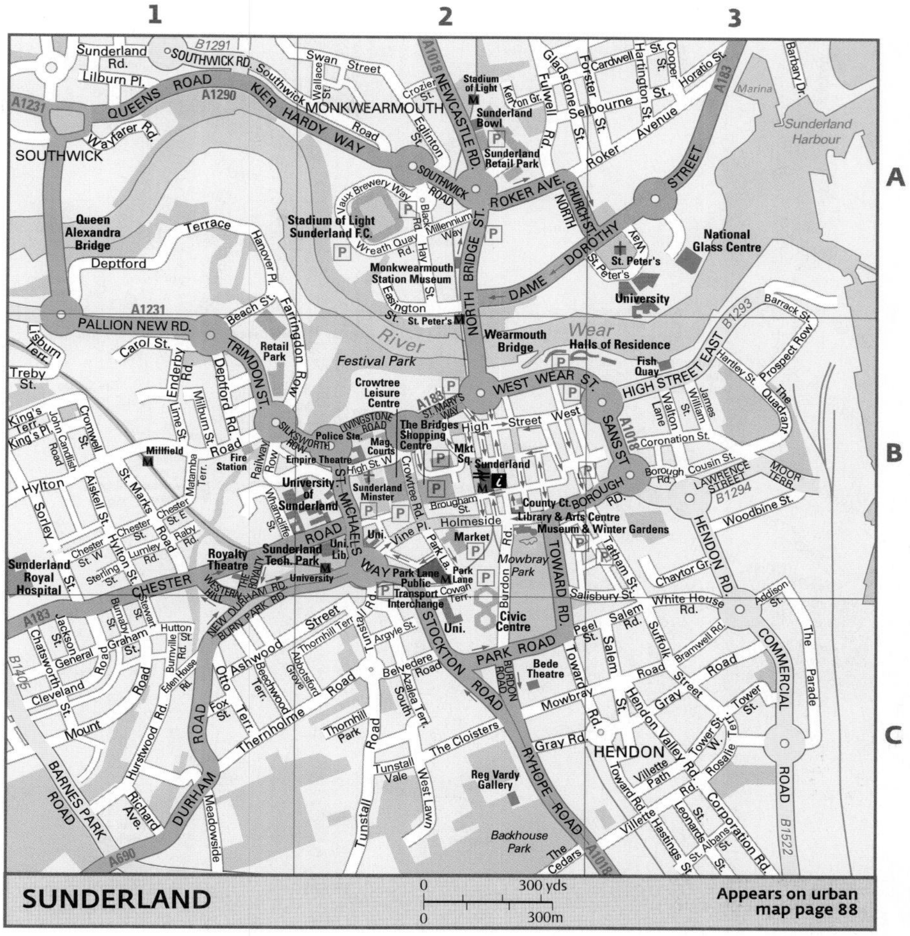

0 300 yds
0 300m

Appears on urban map page 88

SWANSEA

0 400 yds
0 400m

Appears on urban map page 40

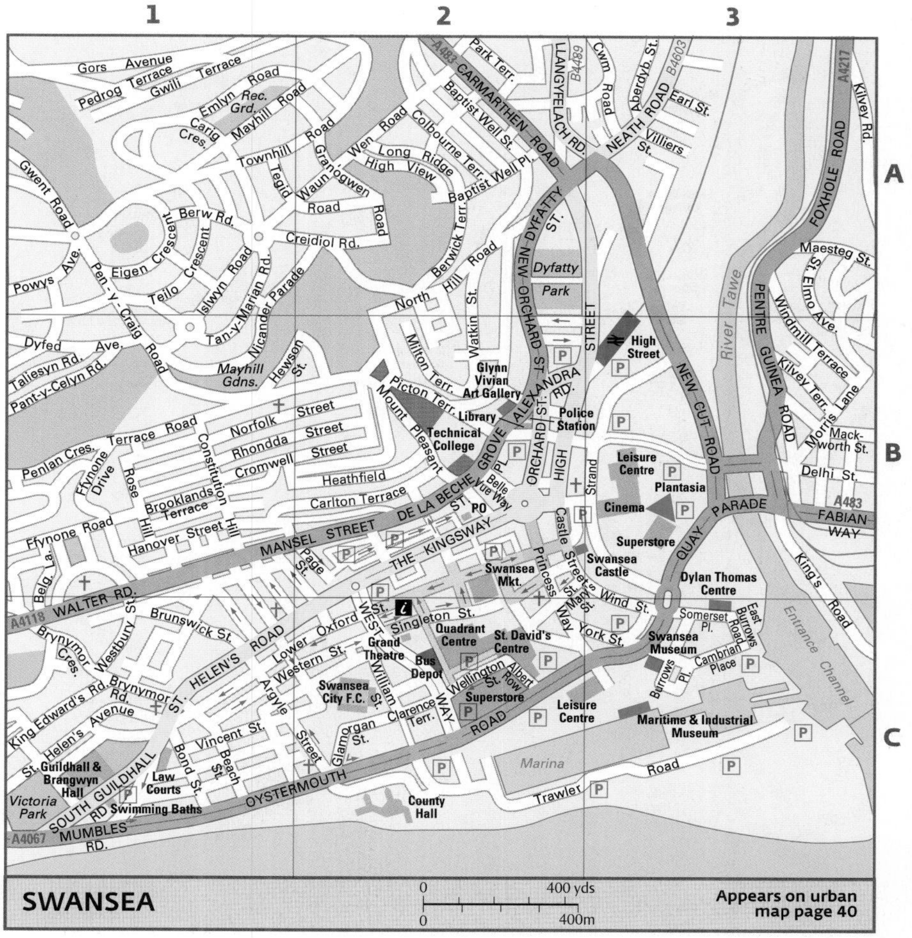

SWINDON

Tourist Information Centre: 37 Regent Street
Tel: 01793 530328

Appears on main map page 6

TORQUAY

Tourist Information Centre: Vaughan Parade
Tel: 01803 297428

Appears on main map page 5

Tourist Information Centre: Town Hall, Market Place, St. Albans
Tel: 0870 225 4870

Addiscombe Road	B1
Albert Road North	A1
Albert Road South	A1
Aynho Street	C1
Banbury Street	C1
Beechen Grove	A1/B3
Brightwell Road	C1
Brocklesbury Close	A3
Bushey Hall Road	B3
Cardiff Road	C2
Cassio Road	B1
Chester Road	B1
Church Street	B2
Clarendon Road	A2
Clifton Road	C1
Cross Street	A2
Dalton Way	C3
Durban Road East	B1
Ebury Road	A3
Estcourt Road	A2
Exchange Road	B1
Farraline Road	C1
Fearnley Street	B1
George Street	B2
Harwoods Road	C1
Hempsted Road	A1
High Street	A1/B2
King Street	B2
Lady's Close	B2
Lammas Road	C2
Liverpool Road	C1
Loates Lane	B2
Lord Street	B2
Lower High Street	B3
Market Street	B1
May Cottages	C2
Merton Road	B1
Muriel Avenue	C2
New Road	C3
New Street	B2
Park Avenue	A3
Park Avenue	B1
Queens Road	A2/B2
Radlett Road	A3
Rickmansworth Road	B1
Rosslyn Road	A1
Shaftesbury Road	A3
Souldern Street	C1
St. James Road	C2
St. Johns Road	A1
St. Pauls Way	A3
Stephenson Way	B3
Sutton Road	A2
The Avenue	A1
The Broadway	B2
The Hornets	C1
The Parade	A1
Upton Road	B1
Vicarage Road	C1/B2
Water Lane	B3
Waterfields Way	B3
Watford Field Road	C2
Wellstones	B2
Whippendell Road	B1
Wiggenhall Road	C2
Willow Lane	C1

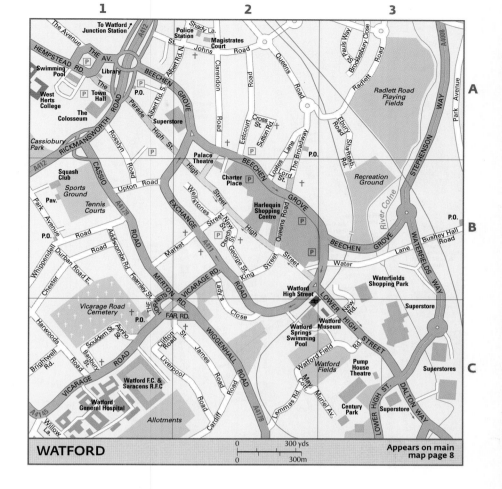

WATFORD   0   300 yds / 0   300m   Appears on main map page 8

Tourist Information Centre: Beach Lawns
Tel: 01934 888800

Addicote Road	C2	Swiss Road	B3
Albert Avenue	C2	The Centre	B2
Alexandra Parade	B2	Trewartha Park	A3
Alfred Street	B2	Upper Church Road	A1
All Saints Road	A2	Walliscote Road	C2
Amberey Road	C3	Waterloo Street Boulevard	B2
Arundell Road	A2	Whitecross Road	C2
Ashcombe Gardens	A3	Winterstoke Road	C3
Ashcombe Road	B3		
Atlantic Road	A1		
Baker Street	B2		
Beach Road	C2		
Beaconsfield Road	B2		
Birnbeck Road	A1		
Brendon Avenue	A3		
Bridge Road	B3		
Brighton Road	C2		
Bristol Road	A2		
Carlton Street	B2		
Cecil Road	A2		
Clarence Road North	C2		
Clarendon Road	B3		
Clevedon Road	C2		
Clifton Road	C2		
Drove Road	C3		
Earlham Grove	B3		
Ellenborough Park North	C2		
Ellenborough Park South	C2		
Exeter Road	C2		
George Street	B2		
Gerard Road	A2		
Grove Park Road	A2		
High Street	B2		
Highbury Road	A1		
Hildesheim Bridge	B2		
Hill Road	A3		
Jubilee Road	B2		
Kenn Close	C3		
Kensington Road	C3		
Knightstone Road	A1		
Langford Road	B3		
Lewisham Grove	B3		
Locking Road	B3		
Lower Bristol Road	A3		
Lower Church Road	A1		
Manor Road	A3		
Marchfields Way	C3		
Marine Parade	C2		
Meadow Street	B2		
Milton Road	B3		
Montpelier	A2		
Neva Road	B2		
Norfolk Road	C3		
Oxford Street	B2		
Queen's Road	A2		
Rectors Way	C3		
Regent Street	B2		
Ridgeway Avenue	C2		
Royal Crescent	A1		
St. Paul's Road	C2		
Sandford Road	B3		
Severn Road	C2		
Shrubbery Road	A1		
South Road	A1		
Southside	A2		
Stafford Road	B3		
Station Road	B2		
Sunnyside Road	C2		

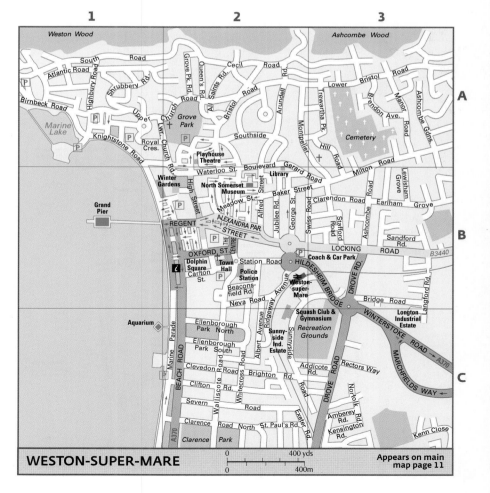

WESTON-SUPER-MARE   0   400 yds / 0   400m   Appears on main map page 11

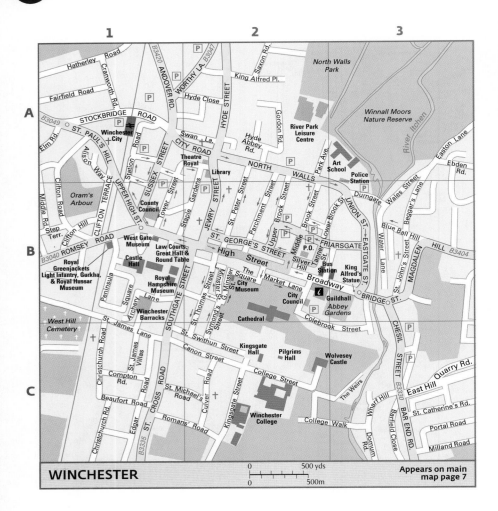

WINCHESTER

0 _____ 500 yds
0 _____ 500m

Appears on main
map page 7

Tourist Information Centre: Guildhall, The Broadway
Tel: 01962 840500

Alison Way	A1
Andover Road	A1
Archery Lane	B1
Bar End Road	C3
Barfield Close	C3
Beaufort Road	C1
Beggar's Lane	B3
Blue Ball Hill	B3
Bridge Stret	B3
Broadway	B2
Canon Street	C2
Chesil Street	C3
Christchurch Road	C1
City Road	A1
Clifton Hill	B1
Clifton Road	A1
Clifton Terrace	B1
Colebrook Street	B2
College Street	C2
College Walk	C2
Compton Road	C1
Cranworth Road	A1
Culver Road	C2
Domum Road	C3
Durngate	B3
East Hill	C3
Eastgate Street	B3
Easton Lane	A3
Ebden Road	A3
Edgar Road	C1
Elm Road	A1
Fairfield Road	A1
Friarsgate	B2
Gordon Road	A2
Great Minster Street	B2
Hatherley Road	A1
High Street	B2
Hyde Abbey Road	A2
Hyde Close	A2
Hyde Street	A2
Jewry Street	B2
King Alfred Place	A2
Kingsgate Street	C2
Little Minster Street	B2
Lower Brook Street	B2
Magdalen Hill	B3
Market Lane	B2
Middle Brook Street	B2
Middle Road	B1
Milland Road	C3
North Walls	A1
Parchment Street	B2
Park Avenue	A2
Peninsula Square	B1
Portal Road	C3
Quarry Road	C3
Romans' Road	C1
Romsey Road	B1
St. Catherine's Road	C3
St. Cross Road	C1
St. George's Street	B2
St. James Lane	B1
St. James Villas	C1
St. John's Street	B3
St. Michael's Road	C1
St. Paul's Hill	A1
St. Peter Street	B2
St. Swithun Street	C2

St. Thomas Street	C2
Saxon Road	A2
Silver Hill	B2
Southgate Street	C1
Staple Gardens	B2
Station Road	A1
Step Terrace	B1
Stockbridge Road	A1
Sussex Street	B1
Swan Lane	A2
Symond's Street	C2
Tanner Street	B2
The Square	B2
Tower Street	B1
Union Street	B3
Upper Brook Street	B2
Upper High Street	B1
Wales Street	B3
Water Lane	B3
Wharf Hill	C3
Worthy Lane	A1

WINDSOR

0 _____ 200 yds
0 _____ 200m

Appears on main
map page 8

Tourist Information Centre: 24 High Street
Tel: 01753 743900

Adelaide Square	C3
Albert Street	B1
Alexandra Road	C2
Alma Road	B2/C2
Arthur Road	B2
Barry Avenue	A2
Bexley Street	B2
Bolton Avenue	C2
Bolton Crescent	C2
Bolton Road	C2
Bulkeley Avenue	C1
Castle Hill	B3
Charles Street	B2
Clarence Road	B1
Clarence Street	B2
College Crescent	C1
Dagmar Road	B2
Datchet Road	A3
Frances Road	C2
Goslar Way	B1
Goswell Road	B2
Green Lane	B1
Grove Road	B2
Helston Lane	B1
High Street (Eton)	A2
High Street (Windsor)	B3
Imperial Road	C1
King Edward VII Avenue	A3
Kings Road	C3
Meadow Lane	A2
Mill Lane	A1
Osborne Road	C2
Oxford Road	B2
Park Street	B3
Parsonage Lane	B1
Peascod Street	B2
Peel Close	C1
Princess Avenue	C1
Romney Lock Road	A3
St. Leonards Road	C2
St. Marks Road	B2
Sheet Street	B3
South Meadow Lane	A2
Springfield Road	C1
Stovell Road	A1
Thames Street	A3
The Long Walk	C3
Upcroft	C1
Vansittart Road	B2
Victoria Street	B2
Victor Road	C2
Westmead	C1
Windsor & Eton Relief Road	B1
York Avenue	C1
York Road	C1

Tourist Information Centre: The Guildhall, High Street
Tel: 01905 726311

Albany Terrace	A1	Shrub Hill Road	B3
Albert Road	C3	Sidbury	C2
Angel Place	B1	Southfield Street	A2
Angel Street	B2	Spring Hill	B3
Arboretum Road	A2	Stanley Road	C3
Back Lane South	A1	Tallow Hill	B3
Bath Road	C2	Tennis Walk	A1
Bridge Street	B1	The Butts	B1
Britannia Road	A1	The Cross	B2
Britannia Square	A1	The Moors	A1
Broad Street	B1	The Shambles	B2
Carden Street	C2	The Tything	A1
Castle Street	B1	Tolladine Road	A3
Charles Street	C2	Trinity Street	B2
Chestnut Street	A2	Upper Tything	A1
Chestnut Walk	A2	Vincent Road	C3
City Walls Road	B2	Washington Street	A2
Cole Hill	C3	Westbury Street	A2
College Street	C2	Wyld's Lane	C3
Compton Road	C3		
Copenhagen Street	C1		
Croft Road	B1		
Deansway	B1		
Dent Close	C3		
Dolday	B1		
Farrier Street	B1		
Foregate Street	B1		
Fort Royal Hill	C3		
Foundry Street	C2		
Friar Street	C2		
George Street	B3		
Grand Stand Road	B1		
High Street	B2		
Hill Street	B3		
Hylton Road	B1		
Infirmary Walk	B1		
Kleve Walk	C2		
Lansdowne Crescent	A2		
Lansdowne Walk	A3		
London Road	C2		
Loves Grove	A1		
Lowesmoor	B2		
Lowesmoor Place	B2		
Midland Road	C3		
Moor Street	A1		
Newport Street	B1		
New Road	C1		
New Street	B2		
Northfield Street	A2		
North Quay	B1		
Padmore Street	B2		
Park Street	C2		
Park Street	C3		
Pheasant Street	B2		
Pump Street	C2		
Rainbow Hill	A2		
Richmond Hill	C3		
St. Martin's Gate	B2		
St. Mary's Street	A1		
St. Oswalds Road	A1		
St. Paul's Street	B2		
Sansome Street	B2		
Sansome Walk	A2		
Severn Street	C2		
Severn Terrace	A1		
Shaw Street	B1		
Sherriff Street	A3		
Shrub Hill	B3		

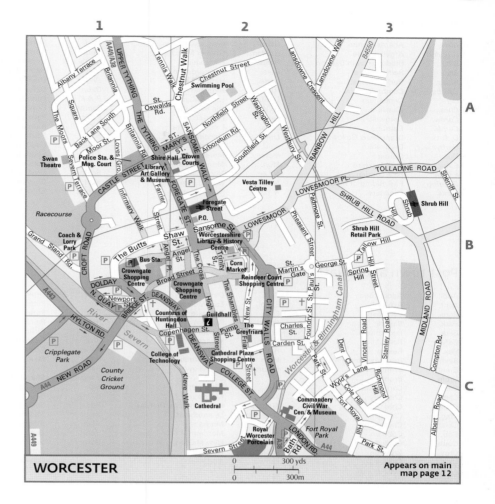

WORCESTER

Appears on main map page 12

Tourist Information Centre: De Grey Rooms, Exhibition Square
Tel: 01904 621756

Abbey Street	A1	Park Street	C1
Albermarle Road	C1	Penley's Grove Street	A2
Aldwark	B2	Petergate	B2
Barbican Road	C3	Piccadilly	B2
Bishopthorpe Road	C2	Queen Street	B1
Bishopgate Street	C2	Rougier Street	B1
Blossom Street	C1	St. Andrewgate	B2
Bootham	A1	St. John Street	A2
Bootham Crescent	A1	St. Maurice's Road	B2
Bridge Street	B2	St. Olave's Road	A1
Bull Lane	A3/B3	Scarcroft Hill	C1
Burton Stone Lane	A1	Scarcroft Road	C1
Cemetery Road	C3	Shambles	B2
Charlotte Street	B3	Sixth Avenue	A3
Church Street	B2	Skeldergate	B2
Clarence Street	A2	Southlands Road	C1
Clifford Street	B2	Station Road	B1
Clifton	A1	Terry Avenue	C2
Coney Street	B2	The Avenue	A1
Dale Street	C1	The Mount	C1
Dalton Terrace	C1	The Stonebow	B2
Dodsworth Avenue	A3	Thorpe Street	C1
East Parade	A3	Tower Street	B2
Eldon Street	A2	Vine Street	C2
Fairfax Street	C2	Walmgate	B2
Fifth Avenue	A3	Water End	A1
Fishergate	C2	Watson Street	C1
Foss Bank	B3	Wellington Street	C3
Fossgate	B2	Westminster Road	A1
Foss Islands Road	B3	Wigginton Road	A2
Fourth Avenue	B3		
Gillygate	A2		
Goodramgate	B2		
Grange Garth	C2		
Grosvenor Road	A1		
Grosvenor Terrace	A1		
Hallfield Road	B3		
Haxby Road	A2		
Heslington Road	C3		
Heworth Green	A3		
Holgate Road	C1		
Hope Street	C2		
Huntington Road	A3		
Irwin Avenue	A3		
James Street	B2		
Kent Street	C3		
Lawrence Street	C3		
Layerthorpe	B3		
Leeman Road	B1		
Lendal	B2		
Longfield Terrace	B1		
Lord Mayor's Walk	A2		
Lowther Street	A2		
Malton Road	A3		
Marygate	B1		
Maurices Road	B2		
Micklegate	B1		
Monkgate	B2		
Moss Street	C1		
Mount Vale	C1		
Museum Street	B2		
Navigation Road	B3		
North Street	B2		
Nunnery Lane	C1		
Nunthorpe Road	C1		
Ousegate	B2		
Paragon Street	C2		
Park Grove	A2		

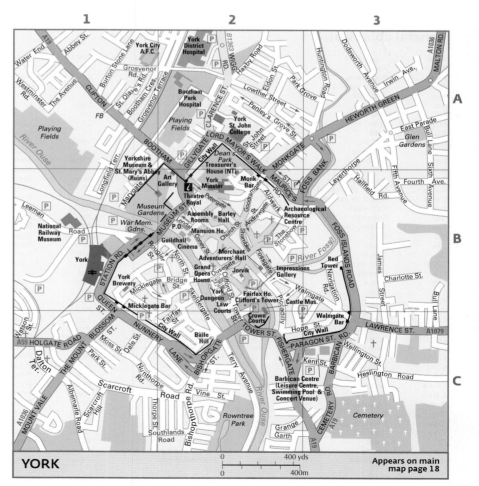

YORK

Appears on main map page 18

Administrative abbreviations

Aber.	Aberdeenshire	Glos.	Gloucestershire	Norf.	Norfolk	Som.	Somerset
Arg. & B.	Argyll & Bute	Gt.Man.	Greater Manchester	Northants.	Northamptonshire	Staffs.	Staffordshire
B'burn.	Blackburn with Darwen	Hants.	Hampshire	Northumb.	Northumberland	Stir.	Stirling
Beds.	Bedfordshire	Here.	Herefordshire	Notts.	Nottinghamshire	Suff.	Suffolk
Bucks.	Buckinghamshire	Herts.	Hertfordshire	Ork.	Orkney	Surr.	Surrey
Cambs.	Cambridgeshire	High.	Highland	Oxon.	Oxfordshire	T. & W.	Tyne & Wear
Cere.	Ceredigion	I.o.M.	Isle of Man	P. & K.	Perth & Kinross	Tel. & W.	Telford & Wrekin
Ches.	Cheshire	I.o.W.	Isle of Wight	Pembs.	Pembrokeshire	V. of Glam.	Vale of Glamorgan
Cornw.	Cornwall	Lancs.	Lancashire	Peter.	Peterborough	W'ham	Wokingham
Cumb.	Cumbria	Leics.	Leicestershire	R.C.T.	Rhondda Cynon Taff	W.Isles	Western Isles
D. & G.	Dumfries & Galloway	Lincs.	Lincolnshire	S.Ayr.	South Ayrshire		(Na h-Eileanan an Iar)
Derbys.	Derbyshire	Med.	Medway	S.Glos.	South Gloucestershire	W.Loth.	West Lothian
Dur.	Durham	Mersey.	Merseyside	S.Lan.	South Lanarkshire	W.Suss.	West Sussex
E.Ayr.	East Ayrshire	Mon.	Monmouthshire	S.Yorks.	South Yorkshire	W.Yorks.	West Yorkshire
E.Loth.	East Lothian	N.Lan.	North Lanarkshire	Sc.Bord.	Scottish Borders	Wilts.	Wiltshire
E.Riding	East Riding of Yorkshire	N.Lincs.	North Lincolnshire	Shet.	Shetland	Worcs.	Worcestershire
Flints.	Flintshire	N.Yorks.	North Yorkshire	Shrop.	Shropshire	Wrex.	Wrexham

Post town abbreviations

Add.	Addlestone	Dart.	Dartford	Orp.	Orpington	Tedd.	Teddington
Ashf.	Ashford	E.Mol.	East Molesey	Pnr.	Pinner	T.Ditt.	Thames Ditton
Bans.	Banstead	Edg.	Edgware	Pur.	Purley	Th.Hth.	Thornton Heath
Bark.	Barking	Felt.	Feltham	Rain.	Rainham	Twick.	Twickenham
Beck.	Beckenham	Grnf.	Greenford	Rich.	Richmond	Uxb.	Uxbridge
Belv.	Belvedere	Hmptn.	Hampton	Rick.	Rickmansworth	Wall.	Wallington
Bex.	Bexley	Har.	Harrow	Rom.	Romford	Walt.	Walton-on-Thames
Bexh.	Bexleyheath	Horn.	Hornchurch	Ruis.	Ruislip	Warl.	Warlingham
Brent.	Brentford	Houns.	Hounslow	Sev.	Sevenoaks	Well.	Welling
Brom.	Bromley	Ilf.	Ilford	Shep.	Shepperton	Wem.	Wembley
Cars.	Carshalton	Islw.	Isleworth	Sid.	Sidcup	W.Byf.	West Byfleet
Cher.	Chertsey	Kes.	Keston	S.Croy.	South Croydon	West Dr.	West Drayton
Chess.	Chessington	Kings.T.	Kingston upon Thames	Sthl.	Southall	W.Mol.	West Molesey
Chig.	Chigwell	Lthd.	Leatherhead	Stai.	Staines	W.Wick.	West Wickham
Chis.	Chislehurst	Mitch.	Mitcham	Stan.	Stanmore	West.	Westerham
Cob.	Cobham	Mord.	Morden	Sun.	Sunbury-on-Thames	Wey.	Weybridge
Couls.	Coulsdon	N.Mal.	New Malden	Surb.	Surbiton	Wok.	Woking
Croy.	Croydon	Nthlt.	Northolt	Sutt.	Sutton	Wdf.Grn.	Woodford Green
Dag.	Dagenham	Nthwd.	Northwood	Swan.	Swanley	Wor.Pk.	Worcester Park

General abbreviations

Acad	Academy	Dep	Depot	JMI	Junior Mixed	Rec	Recreation
All	Alley	Dept	Department		& Infant(s)	Rehab	Rehabilitation
Allot	Allotments	Dev	Development	Jun	Junior	Res	Reservoir, Residence
Amb	Ambulance	Dr	Drive	Junct	Junction	Ri	Rise
App	Approach	Dws	Dwellings	La	Lane	S	South
Arc	Arcade	E	East	Las	Lanes	SM	Secondary Mixed
Av	Avenue	Ed	Education, Educational	Lib	Library	Sch	School
Bdy	Broadway	Elec	Electricity	Ln	Loan	Schs	Schools
Bk	Bank	Embk	Embankment	Lo	Lodge	Sec	Secondary
Bldg	Building	Est	Estate	Lwr	Lower	Sen	Senior
Bldgs	Buildings	Ex	Exchange	Mag	Magistrates	Shop	Shopping
Blvd	Boulevard	Exhib	Exhibition	Mans	Mansions	Spec	Special
Bowl	Bowling	FB	Footbridge	Med	Medical, Medicine	Sq	Square
Br	Bridge	FC	Football Club	Mem	Memorial	St	Street
C of E	Church of England	Fld	Field	Mid	Middle	St.	Saint
C of S	Church of Scotland	Flds	Fields	Mkt	Market	Sta	Station
Cath	Cathedral	Fm	Farm	Mkts	Markets	Sts	Streets
Cem	Cemetery	GM	Grant Maintained	Ms	Mews	Sub	Subway
Cen	Central, Centre	Gall	Gallery	Mt	Mount	Swim	Swimming
Cft	Croft	Gar	Garage	Mus	Museum	TA	Territorial Army
Cfts	Crofts	Gdn	Garden	N	North	TH	Town Hall
Ch	Church	Gdns	Gardens	NHS	National Health Service	Tech	Technical, Technology
Chyd	Churchyard	Gen	General	NT	National Trust	Tenn	Tennis
Cin	Cinema	Govt	Government	Nat	National	Ter	Terrace
Circ	Circus	Gra	Grange	Nurs	Nursery	Thea	Theatre
Cl	Close	Grad	Graduate	PH	Public House	Trd	Trading
Co	County	Gram	Grammar	PO	Post Office	Twr	Tower
Coll	College	Grd	Ground	PRU	Pupil Referral Unit	Twrs	Towers
Comb	Combined	Grds	Grounds	Par	Parade	Uni	University
Comm	Community	Grn	Green	Pas	Passage	Upr	Upper
Comp	Comprehensive	Grns	Greens	Pav	Pavilion	VA	Voluntary Aided
Conf	Conference	Gro	Grove	Pk	Park	VC	Voluntary Controlled
Cont	Continuing	Gros	Groves	Pl	Place	Vil	Villas
Conv	Convent	Gt	Great	Pol	Police	Vil	Villa
Cor	Corner	HQ	Headquarters	Poly	Polytechnic	Vw	View
Coron	Coroners	Ho	House	Prec	Precinct	W	West
Cors	Corners	Hos	Houses	Prep	Preparatory	Wd	Wood
Cotts	Cottages	Hosp	Hospital	Prim	Primary	Wds	Woods
Cov	Covered	Hts	Heights	Prom	Promenade	Wf	Wharf
Crem	Crematorium	Ind	Industrial	Pt	Point	Wk	Walk
Cres	Crescent	Indep	Independent	Quad	Quadrant	Wks	Works
Ct	Court	Inf	Infant(s)	RC	Roman Catholic	Yd	Yard
Cts	Courts	Int	International	Rd	Road		
Ctyd	Courtyard	JM	Junior Mixed	Rds	Roads		

A

Abbeytown 21 E2
Abbots Bromley 13 E2
Abbotsbury 6 B5
Aberaeron 10 C2
Aberaman 11 E4
Aberavon 11 D5
Abercanaid 11 E4
Aberchirder 33 E4
Abercynon 11 E4
Aberdare 11 E4
Aberdaron 16 A5
Aberdeen 29 F1
Aberdeen Airport 29 F1
Aberdour 28 D5
Aberdyfi 10 D1
Aberfeldy 28 C3
Aberffraw 16 B4
Aberfoyle 28 B4
Abergavenny 11 F4
Abergele 16 D3
Abergynolwyn 11 D1
Aberkenfig 11 E5
Aberlady 29 E5
Aberlemno 29 E3
Aberlour 33 D5
Abernethy 28 D4
Aberporth 10 C2
Abersoch 16 B5
Abersychan 11 F4
Abertillery 11 F4
Aberuthven 28 C4
Aberystwyth 10 D1
Abhainnsuidhe 30 C4
Abingdon 7 E1
Abington 25 G4
Aboyne 29 E1
Abram 17 F2
Accrington 18 A4
Achadh Mòr 30 D3
Achahoish 24 C2
Acharacle 27 E3
Achavanich 32 D1
Achfary 31 G2
Achiltibuie 31 F4
Achintee 27 F1
Achnacroish 27 E4
Achnasheen 31 F5
Achosnich 26 D3
Achriesgill 31 G2
Ackworth Moor Top 18 C4
Acle 15 G2
Acomb 23 D4
Adderbury 13 F5
Addingham 18 B3
Addlestone 8 B2
Adlington 17 F2
Adwick le Street 18 C4
Ainsdale 17 E2
Aintree 17 E3
Aird Asaig 30 C4
Aird of Sleat 27 D2
Airdrie 25 F3
Airidh a'Bhruaich 30 C3
Airth 25 G2
Airton 18 A3
Aith *Ork.* 34 B3
Aith *Shet.* 35 F3
Akeld 23 D2
Albrighton 12 D3
Alcester 13 E4
Aldbourne 7 D2
Aldbrough 19 F3
Aldeburgh 15 G4
Aldenham 8 B1
Alderbury 7 D4
Alderholt 6 D4
Alderley Edge 18 A5
Aldershot 8 A3
Aldingham 21 E5
Aldington 9 E3
Aldridge 13 E3
Alexandria 25 E2
Alford *Aber.* 29 E1
Alford *Lincs.* 19 F5
Alfreton 13 F1
Allanton 25 G3
Allendale Town 22 D4
Allenheads 23 D5
Allhallows 9 E2
Allnabad 31 G2
Alloa 25 G2
Allonby 21 D3
Alloway 25 E4
Almondsbury 6 B2
Alness 32 B4
Alnmouth 23 E2
Alnwick 23 E2
Alresford 15 E5
Alrewas 13 E2
Alsager 12 D1
Alston 22 D5
Altnafeadh 27 G4
Altnaharra 32 B2
Alton *Hants.* 8 A3
Alton *Staffs.* 13 E1
Altrincham 18 A5
Alva 25 G2
Alvechurch 13 E4
Alveley 12 D3
Alves 32 D4
Alveston 6 B2
Alvie 28 C1
Alyth 28 D3
Ambergate 13 F1
Amble 23 E3
Amblecote 13 D3
Ambleside 21 E4
Ambrosden 8 A1
Amersham 8 B1
Amesbury 7 D3
Amlwch 16 B3
Ammanford 10 D4
Ampthill 14 B5
Amulree 28 C3
Ancaster 14 B1
Ancroft 23 D1
Ancrum 22 C2
Andover 7 E3
Andreas 20 B4
Angle 10 A4
Angmering 8 B4
Anlaby 19 E4
Annan 21 E2
Annbank 25 E4
Annfield Plain 23 E4
Anstey 13 F3
Anstruther 29 E4
An Tairbeart 30 C4
Aoradh 24 A3
Appleby-in-
Westmorland 21 F3
Appleby Magna 13 F2
Applecross 27 E1
Appledore *Devon* 5 D1
Appledore *Kent* 9 E4
Appleton Thorn 17 F3
Appley Bridge 17 F2
Arbirlot 29 E3
Arbroath 29 E3
Ardchiavaig 26 D5
Arden 25 E2
Ardentinny 25 D2
Ardeonaig 28 B3
Ardersier 32 B4
Ardfern 27 E5
Ardgay 32 B3
Ardleigh 15 E5
Ardlui 27 G5
Ardlussa 24 C2
Ardmair 31 F4
Ardminish 24 C3
Ardmolich 27 E3
Ardrishaig 24 C2
Ardrossan 25 E3
Ardtalnaig 28 B3
Ardtoe 27 E3
Ardvasar 27 E2
Arinagour 26 C4
Arisaig 27 E3
Armadale 25 G3
Armitage 13 E2
Armthorpe 18 D4
Arncliffe 21 G5
Arnisdale 27 E2
Arnol 30 D2
Arnold 13 F1
Arnprior 25 F2
Arrochar 27 G5
Arundel 8 B4
Ascot 8 B2
Asfordby 13 G2
Ash *Kent* 9 F3
Ash *Surr.* 8 A3
Ashbourne 13 E1
Ashburton 5 E4
Ashbury 7 D2
Ashby de la Zouch 13 F2
Ashchurch 13 D5
Ashcott 6 B3
Ashford *Kent* 9 E3
Ashford *Surr.* 8 B2
Ashington 23 E3
Ashkirk 22 C2
Ashley 15 D4
Ashton 17 F4
Ashton-in-Makerfield 17 F3
Ashton-under-Lyne 18 A5
Ashurst *Hants.* 7 E4
Ashurst *Kent* 8 D3
Ashwick 6 B3
Askern 18 C4
Aspatria 21 E3
Aston Clinton 8 A1
Aston on Trent 13 F2
Astwood Bank 13 E4
Atherington 5 E2
Atherstone 13 F3
Atherton 17 F2
Attadale 27 F1
Attleborough 15 E3
Attlebridge 15 F2
Auchallater 28 D2
Auchenblae 29 F2
Auchenbreck 24 D2
Auchencairn 20 D2
Auchencrow 22 D1
Auchindrain 27 F5
Auchinleck 25 F4
Auchmull 29 E2
Auchnagatt 33 F5
Aucholzie 29 D1
Auchterarder 28 C4
Auchtermuchty 28 D4
Auchtertool 28 D5
Audlem 17 F4
Audley 12 D1
Aughton *Lancs.* 17 E2
Aughton *S.Yorks.* 18 C5
Auldearn 32 C4
Aultbea 31 E4
Aultguish Inn 31 G5
Aveley 8 D2
Aviemore 28 C1
Avoch 32 B4
Avonbridge 25 G2
Avonmouth 6 B2
Awre 6 C1
Awsworth 13 F1
Axminster 6 A5
Aycliffe 23 E5
Aylesbury 8 A1
Aylesford 9 D3
Aylesham 9 F3
Aylsham 15 F2
Ayr 25 E4
Aysgarth 18 B2

B

Babworth 18 D5
Backaland 34 B2
Backwell 6 B2
Bacup 18 A4
Badcaul 31 F4
Badenscoth 33 E5
Badlipster 32 D1
Badsey 13 E5
Bàgh a' Chaisteil 26 A2
Bagillt 17 E3
Baglan 11 D4
Bagshot 8 B2
Baildon 18 B3
Baile Mhartainn 30 B5
Baile Mòr 26 C5
Bainbridge 21 G4
Bainton 19 E3
Bakewell 13 E1
Bala 16 D5
Balallan 30 C3
Balbeggie 28 D4
Balblair 32 B4
Balcombe 8 C3
Balderton 13 G1
Baldock 14 C5
Baldslow 9 D4
Balemartine 26 B4
Balephuil 26 B4
Balfour 34 B3
Balfron 25 F2
Balgown 30 D5
Balgray 29 E3
Balintore 32 C4
Balivanich 30 B5
Ballabeg 20 B5
Ballachulish 27 F4
Ballantrae 25 D5
Ballasalla 20 B5
Ballater 29 D1
Ballaugh 20 B4
Ballingry 28 D5
Ballinluig 28 C3
Ballintuim 28 D3
Balloch 25 E2
Ballochroy 24 C3
Ballygrant 24 B3
Balmacara 27 E1
Balmaha 25 E2
Balmedie 29 F1
Balnacra 27 F1
Balnahard 27 D4
Balnapaling 32 B4
Balquhidder 28 B4
Baltasound 35 G2
Balvicar 27 E5
Bamburgh 23 E2
Bampton *Devon* 5 F2
Bampton *Oxon.* 7 E1
Banbury 13 F5
Banchory 29 F1
Banff 33 E4
Bangor 16 C3
Banham 15 E3
Bankfoot 28 C3
Bannockburn 25 G2
Banstead 8 C3
Banwell 6 A3
Barassie 25 E4
Barbaraville 32 B4
Barbon 21 F5
Barby 13 F4
Bardney 14 B1
Bardsea 21 E5
Bargoed 11 F4
Bargrennan 20 B2
Barham 9 F3
Bar Hill 14 C4
Barkston 14 B1
Barkway 14 C5
Barlaston 13 D2
Barlborough 18 C5
Barley 14 C5
Barmouth 16 C5
Barnard Castle 18 B1
Barningham 15 E4
Barnoldswick 18 A3
Barnsley 18 C4
Barnstaple 5 E1
Barnton 17 F3
Barr 25 E5
Barrapoll 26 B4
Barrhead 25 F3
Barrhill 25 E5
Barrock 34 A4
Barrowford 18 A3
Barrow-in-Furness 21 E5
Barrow upon Humber 19 E4
Barrow upon Soar 13 F2
Barry 11 F5
Barton 17 F1
Barton-le-Clay 14 B5
Barton-under-
Needwood 13 E2
Barton-upon-Humber 19 E4
Barvas 30 D2
Baschurch 12 C2
Basildon 9 D2
Basingstoke 8 A3
Baslow 18 B5
Bassingham 14 B1
Bath 6 C2
Batheaston 6 C2
Bathford 6 C2
Bathgate 25 G3
Batley 18 B4
Battle 9 D4
Bawdeswell 15 E2
Bawdsey 15 F5
Bawtry 18 D5
Baycliff 21 E5
Bayston Hill 12 C3
Beaconsfield 8 B1
Beadnell 23 E2
Beaminster 6 B4
Bearsden 25 F2
Bearsted 9 D3
Beattock 25 G5
Beauly 32 B5
Beaumaris 16 C3
Bebington 17 E3
Beccles 15 G3
Beckingham 19 D5
Bedale 18 B2
Beddau 11 E5
Beddgelert 16 C4
Beddingham 8 C4
Bedford 14 B5
Bedlington 23 E3
Bedwas 11 F5
Bedworth 13 F3
Beeford 19 E3
Beer 6 A5
Beeston 13 F2
Beighton 18 C5
Beith 25 E3
Belbroughton 13 D4
Belford 23 E2
Bellingham 22 D3
Bellshill 25 F3
Belmont 35 F2
Belper 13 F1
Belsay 23 E4
Bembridge 8 A5
Bempton 19 E2
Benenden 9 E3
Benllech 16 C3
Benson 8 A1
Bentley 18 C4
Bere Alston 5 D4
Bere Ferrers 5 D4
Bere Regis 6 C5
Berinsfield 7 E1
Berkeley 6 B1
Berkhamsted 8 B1
Berkswell 13 E4
Bernisdale 30 D5
Berriedale 32 D2
Berrow 6 A3
Bersham 17 E4
Berwick-upon-Tweed 23 D1
Bessacarr 18 D4
Bethersden 9 E3
Bethesda 16 C4
Bettyhill 32 B1
Betws-y-coed 16 C4
Beverley 19 E3
Bewdley 12 D4
Bexhill 9 D4
Bibury 6 D1
Bicester 13 F5
Bickleigh (Plymouth)
Devon 5 E4
Bickleigh (Tiverton)
Devon 5 F2
Bicknacre 9 D1
Biddenden 9 E3
Biddulph 13 D1
Bideford 5 D2
Bidford-on-Avon 13 E4
Bigbury-on-Sea 5 E4
Biggar 25 G4
Biggin Hill 8 C3
Biggleswade 14 B5
Bilbster 33 D1
Billericay 9 D1
Billinge 17 F2
Billingham 23 F5
Billinghay 14 B1
Billingshurst 8 B4
Billockby 15 G2
Billy Row 23 E5
Bilston 22 B1
Bilton 19 E3
Bimbister 34 A3
Binbrook 19 F5
Binfield 8 A2
Bingham 13 G2
Bingley 18 B3
Birchgrove 11 D4
Birchington 9 F2
Bircotes 18 D5
Birkenhead 17 E3
Birmingham 13 E3
Birmingham Airport 13 E3
Birsay 34 A3
Birstall 13 F3
Birtley 23 E4
Bishop Auckland 23 E5
Bishopbriggs 25 F3
Bishop's Castle 12 B3
Bishop's Cleeve 13 D5
Bishop's Hull 6 A4
Bishop's Itchington 13 F4
Bishop's Lydeard 6 A4
Bishop's Stortford 14 C5
Bishop's Tawton 5 E1
Bishopston 10 D5
Bishop's Waltham 7 E4
Bishopton 25 E2
Bisley 6 C1
Bitton 6 B2
Bixter 35 F3
Blaby 13 F3
Black Bourton 7 D1
Blackburn *Aber.* 29 F1
Blackburn *B'burn.* 17 F2
Blackburn *W.Loth.* 25 G3
Blackford 28 C4
Blackhall Colliery 23 F5
Blacklunans 28 D2
Blackmoor Gate 5 E1
Black Notley 15 D5
Blackpool 17 E1
Blackpool Airport 17 E1
Blackridge 25 G3
Blackwaterfoot 24 D4
Blackwood 11 F4
Blaenau Ffestiniog 16 C4
Blaenavon 11 F4
Blaengarw 11 E4
Blaengwrach 11 E4
Blagdon 6 B3
Blaich 27 F3
Blaina 11 F4
Blair Atholl 28 C2
Blairgowrie 28 D3
Blakeney *Glos.* 6 B1
Blakeney *Norf.* 15 E1
Blandford Forum 6 C4
Blaydon 23 E4
Blean 9 F2
Bletchley 13 G5
Blewbury 7 E2
Blisworth 13 G4
Blockley 13 E5
Bloxham 13 F5
Blubberhouses 18 B3
Blyth *Northumb.* 23 F3
Blyth *Notts.* 18 D5
Blyth Bridge 22 B1
Blyton 19 D5
Boath 32 B4
Boat of Garten 28 C1
Boddam *Aber.* 33 G5
Boddam *Shet.* 35 F5
Bodelwyddan 17 D3
Bodenham 12 C4
Bodicote 13 F5
Bodmin 4 C4
Bogniebrae 33 E5
Bognor Regis 8 B5
Boldon 23 F4
Boldre 7 E5
Bollington 18 A5
Bolnhurst 14 B4
Bolsover 18 C5
Boltby 18 C2
Bolton *E.Loth.* 29 E5
Bolton *Gt.Man.* 18 A4
Bolton-le-Sands 21 F5
Bolventor 4 C3
Bonar Bridge 32 B3
Bonawe 27 F4
Bonawe Quarries 27 F4
Bonchester Bridge 22 C2
Bo'ness 25 G2
Bonjedward 22 C2
Bonnybridge 25 G2
Bonnyrigg 22 B1
Bonvilston 11 E5
Bootle *Cumb.* 21 E5
Bootle *Mersey.* 17 E3
Boreham 9 D1
Borehamwood 8 B1
Boreland 22 B3
Boreraig 30 C5
Borgh 26 A2
Borgue *D. & G.* 20 C3
Borgue *High.* 32 D2
Boroughbridge 18 C2
Borough Green 8 D3
Borrowash 13 F2
Borrowdale 21 E4
Borth 10 D1
Borve 26 D1
Bosbury 12 C5
Boscastle 4 C3
Bosham 8 A4
Boston 14 C1
Boston Spa 18 C3
Botesdale 15 E4
Bothel 21 E3
Bothenhampton 6 B5
Bottesford *Leics.* 13 G2
Bottesford *N.Lincs.* 19 E4
Boughton 13 G1
Bourne 14 B2
Bourne End 8 A2
Bournemouth 6 D5
Bournemouth Airport 6 D5
Bournmoor 23 F4
Bourton 6 C3
Bourton-on-the-Water 13 E5
Bovey Tracey 5 F3
Bow 34 A4
Bowburn 23 F5
Bowes 21 G4
Bowmore 24 B3
Bowness-on-Solway 21 E2
Bowness-on-
Windermere 21 F4
Box 6 C2
Bozeat 14 B4
Braaid 20 B5
Bracadale 26 D1
Bracebridge Heath 14 B1
Brackley 13 F5
Bracknell 8 A2
Braco 28 C4
Bracora 27 E2
Bradford 18 B3
Bradford-on-Avon 6 C2
Brading 8 A5
Bradninch 5 F2
Bradpole 6 B5
Bradshaw 18 A4
Bradwell *Derbys.* 18 B5
Bradwell *Norf.* 15 G3
Bradwell Waterside 9 E1
Brae 35 F3
Braeantra 32 B4
Braemar 28 D1
Bragar 30 C2
Brailsford 13 E1
Braintree 15 D5
Braithwaite 21 E3
Braithwell 18 C5
Bramford 15 F5
Bramhall 18 A5
Bramley 18 C5
Brampton *Cambs.* 14 C4
Brampton *Cumb.* 21 F2
Brampton *Suff.* 15 G3
Brancaster 15 D1
Brandesburton 19 E3
Brandon *Dur.* 23 E5
Brandon *Suff.* 15 D3
Branston 14 B1
Brantham 15 F5
Bratton 6 C3
Braunston 13 F4
Braunstone 13 F3
Braunton 5 D1
Bray 8 B2
Brayton 18 D3
Breage 4 B5
Breakish 27 E1
Bream 6 B1
Breanais 30 B3
Breascleit 30 C3
Breaston 13 F2
Brechfa 10 D3
Brechin 29 E2
Brecon 11 E3
Bredbury 18 A5
Bredon 13 D5
Brentwood 8 D1
Bretton 17 E4
Brewood 13 D3
Bridge 9 F3
Bridgend *Angus* 29 E2
Bridgend (Islay)
Arg. & B. 24 B3
Bridgend (Lochgilphead)
Arg. & B. 24 C2
Bridgend *Bridgend* 11 E5
Bridgend *Moray* 33 D5
Bridge of Allan 25 F2
Bridge of Balgie 28 B3
Bridge of Cally 28 D3
Bridge of Craigisla 28 D3
Bridge of Don 29 F1
Bridge of Dun 29 E3
Bridge of Dye 29 E2
Bridge of Earn 28 D4
Bridge of Orchy 27 G4
Bridge of Walls 35 E3
Bridge of Weir 25 E3
Bridgnorth 12 D3
Bridgwater 6 A3
Bridlington 19 E2
Bridport 6 B5
Brierfield 18 A3
Brigg 19 E4
Brigham 21 D3
Brighouse 18 B4
Brighstone 7 E5
Brightlingsea 9 E1
Brighton 8 C4
Brig o'Turk 28 B4
Brigstock 14 B3
Brimington 18 C5
Brinian 34 B3
Brinsley 13 F1

Brinsworth 18 C5
Bristol 6 B2
Bristol International Airport 6 B2
Briston 15 E2
Briton Ferry 11 D4
Brixham 5 F4
Brixworth 13 G4
Broadclyst 5 F3
Broadford 27 E1
Broad Haven 10 A4
Broadheath 12 C4
Broadmayne 6 C5
Broad Oak 9 E4
Broadstairs 9 F2
Broadway 13 E5
Broadwey 6 B5
Broadwindsor 6 B4
Brochel 27 D1
Brockenhurst 7 E4
Brockworth 6 C1
Brodick 24 D4
Bromham *Beds.* 14 B4
Bromham *Wilts.* 6 C2
Brompton 18 C1
Brompton on Swale 18 B1
Bromsgrove 13 D4
Bromyard 12 C4
Bronaber 16 C5
Brooke 15 F3
Brookmans Park 8 C1
Broomfield 9 D1
Brora 32 C3
Broseley 12 C3
Brotton 23 G5
Brough *Cumb.* 21 G4
Brough *E.Riding* 19 E4
Brough *High.* 34 A4
Brough *Shet.* 35 F4
Broughton *Flints.* 17 E4
Broughton *N.Lincs.* 19 E4
Broughton *Northants.* 13 G4
Broughton *Sc.Bord.* 22 B2
Broughton Astley 13 F3
Broughton in Furness 21 E5
Broughtown 34 B2
Broughty Ferry 29 E3
Brownhills 13 E3
Broxburn 25 G2
Brundall 15 F3
Brundish 15 F4
Bruton 6 B3
Brynamman 11 D4
Brynford 17 E3
Brynmawr 11 F4
Bubwith 18 D3
Buchlyvie 25 F2
Buckden *Cambs.* 14 B4
Buckden *N.Yorks.* 21 G5
Buckfastleigh 5 E4
Buckhaven 29 D5
Buckie 33 E4
Buckingham 13 G5
Bucklebury 7 E2
Buckley 17 E4
Bucksburn 29 F1
Bude 4 D2
Budleigh Salterton 5 F3
Bugbrooke 13 G4
Builth Wells 11 E2
Buldoo 32 C1
Bulford 7 D3
Bulkington 13 F3
Bulmer Tye 15 E5
Bunessan 26 D5
Bungay 15 F3
Buntingford 14 C5
Burbage 7 D2
Bures 15 E5
Burford 7 D1
Burgess Hill 8 C4
Burgh by Sands 21 E2
Burghead 32 D4
Burghfield Common 8 A2
Burghill 12 C5
Burgh le Marsh 14 C1
Burley 7 D4
Burley in Wharfdale 18 B3
Burness 34 B2
Burnham 8 B2
Burnham Market 15 E1
Burnham-on-Crouch 9 E1
Burnham-on-Sea 6 A3
Burnhouse 25 E3
Burniston 19 E1
Burnley 18 A3
Burnmouth 23 D1
Burnopfield 23 E4
Burntisland 28 D5
Burntwood Green 13 E3
Burravoe 35 F2
Burrelton 28 D3
Burry Port 10 C4
Burscough 17 F2
Burscough Bridge 17 F2
Bursledon 7 E4
Burton Bradstock 6 B5
Burton-in-Kendal 21 F5
Burton Joyce 13 G1
Burton Latimer 14 B4
Burton Leonard 18 C2
Burton upon Stather 19 D4
Burton upon Trent 13 E2
Burwardsley 17 F4
Burwarton 12 C3
Burwash 9 D4
Burwell 14 D4
Burwick 34 B4
Bury 18 A4
Bury St. Edmunds 15 E4
Bushey 8 B1
Buttermere 21 E4
Butterwick 19 E2
Buxted 8 C4
Buxton 18 B5
Byfield 13 F4
Byfleet 8 B2
Bylchau 17 D4

C

Caerau 11 F5
Caergwrle 17 E4
Caerhun 16 C3
Caerleon 11 F4
Caernarfon 16 B4
Caerphilly 11 F5
Caerwent 6 B1
Cairnbaan 24 C2
Cairndow 27 F5
Cairneyhill 25 G2
Cairnryan 20 A2
Caister-on-Sea 15 G2
Caistor 19 E4
Caldbeck 21 E3
Caldecott 13 G3
Caldercruix 25 G3
Caldicot 6 B2
Caldwell 18 B1
Calfsound 34 B2
Calgary 26 D4
Callander 28 B4
Callanish 30 C3
Callington 5 D4
Calne 6 C2
Calver 18 B5
Calverton 13 G1
Calvine 28 C2
Cam 6 C1
Camasnacroise 27 E4
Camberley 8 A2
Camborne 4 B4
Cambridge 14 C4
Cambridge Airport 14 C4
Camelford 4 C3
Campbeltown 24 C4
Camptown 22 C2
Camrose 10 B4
Cannich 27 G1
Cannington 6 A3
Cannock 13 D2
Canonbie 21 E2
Canterbury 9 F3
Canton 11 F5
Canvey Island 9 D2
Caolas 26 C4
Capel 8 B3
Capel Curig 16 C4
Capel St. Mary 15 E5
Cappercleuch 22 B2
Capplegill 22 B3
Caputh 28 C3
Carbost (Loch Harport) *High.* 26 D1
Carbost (Loch Snizort Beag) *High.* 26 D1
Carcroft 18 C4
Cardenden 28 D5
Cardiff 11 F5
Cardiff International Airport 11 E5
Cardigan 10 B3
Cardross 25 E2
Cargenbridge 21 D2
Cargill 28 D3
Carlisle 21 F2
Carlops 22 B1
Carloway 30 C2
Carlton 13 G1
Carlton Colville 15 G3
Carlton in Lindrick 18 C5
Carlton-on-Trent 13 G1
Carluke 25 G3
Carmarthen 10 C4
Carmyllie 29 E3
Carnbee 29 E4
Carnbo 28 C4
Carnforth 21 F5
Carno 11 E1
Carnoustie 29 E3
Carnwath 25 G3
Carradale 24 C4
Carrbridge 32 C5
Carronbridge 25 G5
Carsaig 27 D5
Carsluith 20 B2
Carsphairn 25 F5
Carstairs 25 G3
Carterton 7 D1
Cartmel 21 E5
Castlebay 26 A2
Castle Bromwich 13 E3
Castle Carrock 21 F2
Castle Cary 6 B3
Castle Donington 13 F2
Castle Douglas 20 C2
Castleford 18 C4
Castle Kennedy 20 A2
Castlemartin 10 B4
Castleside 23 E5
Castleton 18 D1
Castletown *High.* 32 D1
Castletown *I.o.M.* 20 B5
Caterham 8 C3
Caton 21 F5
Catrine 25 F4
Catshill 13 D4
Catterick 18 B1
Catterick Camp 18 B1
Caverswall 13 D1
Cawdor 32 C4
Cawood 18 C3
Cawston 15 F2
Caythorpe 14 B1
Cayton 19 E2
Ceann a' Bhàigh 30 B5
Cearsiadar 30 D3
Cefn-mawr 17 E4
Ceres 29 D4
Cerrigydrudion 17 D4
Chadderton 18 A4
Chagford 5 E3
Chailey 8 C4
Chalfont St. Giles 8 B1
Chalford 6 C1
Chalgrove 8 A1
Champany 25 G2
Chapel-en-le-Frith 18 B5
Chapel St. Leonards 19 G5
Chapeltown 18 C5
Chard 6 A4
Chardstock 6 A4
Charfield 6 C1
Charing 9 E3
Charlbury 7 E1
Charlestown 29 F1
Charlesworth 18 B5
Charlton *Hants.* 7 E3
Charlton *Wilts.* 6 C2
Charlton Kings 13 D5
Charlwood 8 C3
Charminster 6 B5
Charmouth 6 A5
Chartham 9 F3
Chatham 9 D2
Chatteris 14 C3
Chatton 23 E2
Cheadle *Gt.Man.* 18 A5
Cheadle *Staffs.* 13 E1
Checkley 13 E2
Chedburgh 15 D4
Cheddar 6 B3
Cheddleton 13 D1
Chelmorton 13 E1
Chelmsford 9 D1
Cheltenham 13 D5
Chepstow 6 B1
Cheriton 7 E4
Chertsey 8 B2
Chesham 8 B1
Cheshunt 8 C1
Chester 17 F4
Chesterfield 18 C5
Chester-le-Street 23 E4
Chesters 22 C2
Chew Magna 6 B2
Chichester 8 A4
Chickerell 6 B5
Chiddingfold 8 B3
Chieveley 7 E2
Chigwell 8 C1
Chilcompton 6 B3
Childrey 7 E2
Chilham 9 E3
Chilton 23 E5
Chingford 8 C1
Chinnor 8 A1
Chippenham 6 C2
Chipping Campden 13 E5
Chipping Norton 13 F5
Chipping Ongar 8 D1
Chipping Sodbury 6 C2
Chirbury 12 B3
Chirk 17 E5
Chirnside 23 D1
Chiseldon 7 D2
Chopwell 23 E4
Chorley 17 F2
Chorleywood 8 B1
Christchurch 7 D5
Christon Bank 23 E2
Chryston 25 F2
Chudleigh 5 F3
Chulmleigh 5 E2
Church Aston 12 D2
Churchdown 13 D5
Church Lawton 12 D1
Church Stretton 12 C3
Cilcain 17 E4
Cille Bhrighde 26 B2
Cinderford 6 B1
Cirencester 6 D1
Clabhach 26 C4
Clachan (Kintyre) *Arg. & B.* 24 C3
Clachan (Loch Fyne) *Arg. & B.* 27 F5
Clachan (Raasay) *High.* 27 D1
Clachan of Glendaruel 24 D2
Clachtoll 31 F3
Clackmannan 25 G2
Clacton-on-Sea 9 F1
Cladich 27 F5
Claggan 27 E4
Clanfield 7 D1
Claonaig 24 C3
Clapham *Beds.* 14 B4
Clapham *N.Yorks.* 21 G5
Clarborough 18 D5
Clare 15 D5
Clashmore 32 B3
Clashnessie 31 F3
Clavering 14 C5
Clay Cross 13 F1
Claydon 15 F5
Claypole 13 G1
Clayton 8 C4
Clayton-le-Moors 18 A3
Clayton-le-Woods 17 F2
Clayton West 18 B4
Cleadale 27 D3
Cleadon 23 F4
Cleat 34 B4
Cleator Moor 21 D4
Cleckheaton 18 B4
Cleehill 12 C4
Cleethorpes 19 F4
Clehonger 12 C5
Cleland 25 F3
Clenchwarton 14 D2
Clent 13 D4
Cleobury Mortimer 12 C4
Clestrain 34 A3
Clevedon 6 B2
Cleveleys 17 E1
Cliffe 9 D2
Cliffe Woods 9 D2
Clitheroe 18 A3
Closeburn 25 G5
Cloughton 19 E1
Clova 29 D2
Clovelly 4 D2
Clovenfords 22 C2
Clovullin 27 F3
Clowne 18 C5
Clun 12 B3
Clunes 27 F3
Clutton 6 B3
Clydach 11 D4
Clydach Vale 11 E4
Clydebank 25 F3
Clynderwen 10 B4
Clyro 12 B5
Coalburn 25 G4
Coalville 13 F2
Coast 31 F4
Coatbridge 25 F3
Cobham 8 B3
Cock Bridge 29 D1
Cockburnspath 29 F5
Cockenzie & Port Seton 29 E5
Cockerham 17 F1
Cockermouth 21 E3
Cockett 10 D4
Cockfield 23 E5
Coddenham 15 F4
Coddington 13 G1
Codicote 8 C1
Codnor 13 F1
Codsall 13 D3
Coggeshall 15 E5
Colchester 15 E5
Colden Common 7 E4
Coldingham 23 D1
Coldstream 22 D2
Coleford 6 B1
Colehill 6 D4
Coleshill 13 E3
Colintraive 24 D2
Collafirth 35 F2
Collieston 33 G5
Collin 21 D2
Collingham 13 G1
Colmonell 25 D5
Colnabaichin 29 D1
Colnbrook 8 B2
Colne 18 A3
Colney Heath 8 C1
Colquhar 22 B1
Colsterworth 14 B2
Coltishall 15 F2
Colwich 13 E2
Colwick 13 G1
Colwyn Bay 16 D3
Colyford 6 A5
Colyton 6 A5
Combe Martin 5 E1
Comberton 14 C4
Combe St. Nicholas 6 A4
Comrie 28 B4
Congdon's Shop 4 D3
Congleton 13 D1
Congresbury 6 B2
Coningsby 14 C1
Conisbrough 18 C5
Coniston 21 E4
Connah's Quay 17 E4
Connel 27 F4
Conon Bridge 32 B4
Consett 23 E4
Constantine 4 B5
Contin 31 G5
Conwy 16 C3
Cookham 8 A2
Cookley 12 D3
Coombe Bissett 6 D4
Copley 23 E5
Copplestone 5 E2
Coppull 17 F2
Copythorne 7 E4
Corbridge 23 D4
Corby 13 G3
Corfe Castle 6 C5
Corfe Mullen 6 C5
Cornhill 33 E4
Cornhill-on-Tweed 23 D2
Cornholme 18 A4
Corpach 27 F3
Corrie 24 D3
Corringham 9 D2
Corsham 6 C2
Corsock 20 C2
Corton 15 G3
Corwen 17 D4
Coryton 9 D2
Cosby 13 F3
Coshieville 28 B3
Cotgrave 13 G2
Cottenham 14 C4
Cottesmore 14 B2
Cottingham *E.Riding* 19 E3
Cottingham *Northants.* 13 G3
Coulport 25 E2
Coundon 23 E5
Coupar Angus 28 D3
Cove *Arg. & B.* 25 E2
Cove *High.* 31 E4
Cove Bay 29 F1
Coventry 13 F4
Coverack 4 B5
Cowbit 14 C2
Cowbridge 11 E5
Cowdenbeath 28 D5
Cowes 7 E5
Cowfold 8 C4
Cowie 25 G2
Cowling 18 A3
Cowshill 23 D5
Coxheath 9 D3
Coxwold 18 C2
Coychurch 11 E5
Coylton 25 E4
Coylumbridge 28 C1
Cradley 12 D5
Craichie 29 E3
Craig 27 F1
Craigandaive 24 D2
Craigdarroch 25 F5
Craigellachie 33 D5
Craigendoran 25 E2
Craighat 25 E2
Craignure 27 E4
Crail 29 E4
Cramlington 23 E4
Cramond 28 D5
Cranage 12 D1
Cranfield 14 B5
Cranleigh 8 B3
Cranshaws 22 C1
Cranwell 14 B1
Crask Inn 32 B2
Craster 23 E2
Crathie 29 D1
Craven Arms 12 C3
Crawfordjohn 25 G4
Crawley 8 C3
Creagorry 26 B1
Credenhill 12 C5
Crediton 5 F2
Creetown 20 B2
Cregneash 20 A5
Creswell 18 C5
Crewe 12 D1
Crewkerne 6 B4
Crianlarich 27 G5
Criccieth 16 B5
Crickhowell 11 F4
Cricklade 6 D1
Crieff 28 C4
Crigglestone 18 C4
Crimond 33 G4
Crinan 24 C2
Cringleford 15 F3
Cripp's Corner 9 D4
Crocketford 20 D2
Croeserw 11 E4
Crofton 18 C4
Crofty 10 D4
Cromarty 32 B4
Cromer 15 F1
Cromford 13 E1
Cromhall 6 B1
Crondall 8 A3
Crook 23 E5
Crookham 23 D2
Crosbost 30 D3
Crosby *Mersey.* 17 E3
Crosby *N.Lincs.* 19 D4
Crosby Ravensworth 21 F4
Crossaig 24 C3
Crosscanonby 21 D3
Crossford *Fife* 25 G2
Crossford *S.Lan.* 25 G3
Crossgates *Fife* 28 D5
Crossgates *Powys* 11 E2
Crosshands 25 E4
Crosshill 25 E5
Crosshouse 25 E4
Cross Inn 10 D2
Crossmichael 20 C2
Crossway 11 E2
Croston 17 F2
Croughton 13 F5
Crowborough 8 D3
Crow Hill 12 C5
Crowland 14 C2
Crowle 19 D4
Crowthorne 8 A2
Croy *High.* 32 B5
Croy *N.Lan.* 25 F2
Croyde 5 D1
Cruden Bay 33 G5
Crùlabhig 30 C3
Crumlin 11 F4
Crymych 10 B3
Crynant 11 D4
Cubbington 13 F4
Cuckfield 8 C4
Cuddington 17 F3
Cudworth 18 C4
Cuffley 8 C1
Culbokie 32 B4
Culcheth 17 F3
Culdrain 33 E5
Cullen 33 E4
Cullicudden 32 B4
Cullingworth 18 B3
Cullipool 27 E5
Cullivoe 35 F2
Cullompton 5 F2
Culmstock 5 F2
Culnacraig 31 F4
Culnaknock 31 D5
Culross 25 G2
Culswick 35 E4
Cults 29 F1
Cumbernauld 25 F2
Cuminestown 33 F4
Cumnock 25 F4
Cumnor 7 E1
Cunningsburgh 35 F4
Cupar 29 D4
Curry Rivel 6 A4
Cwm 11 F4
Cwmafan 11 D4
Cwmbrân 11 F4
Cwmllynfell 11 D4
Cydwelli 10 C4
Cymmer 11 E4
Cynghordy 11 E3
Cynwyl Elfed 10 C3

D

Dacre 21 F3
Dailly 25 E5
Dairsie 29 E4
Dalabrog 26 B1
Dalbeattie 20 D2
Dalby 20 B5
Dale 10 A4
Dalgety Bay 28 D5
Dalham 15 D4
Dalkeith 22 B1
Dallas 32 D4
Dalmally 27 F5
Dalmellington 25 E5
Dalnavie 32 B4
Dalry 25 E3
Dalrymple 25 E4
Dalston 21 E2
Dalton 18 C5
Dalton-in-Furness 21 E5
Dalwhinnie 28 B2
Damerham 6 D4
Danbury 9 D1
Danby 18 D1
Danehill 8 C4
Darfield 18 C4
Darlington 18 B1
Darra 33 F5
Dartford 8 D2
Dartington 5 E4
Dartmeet 5 E3
Dartmouth 5 F4
Darton 18 C4
Darvel 25 F4
Darwen 17 F2
Dava 32 C5
Davenham 17 F3
Daventry 13 F4
Daviot 32 B5
Dawlish 5 F3
Deal 9 F3
Dearham 21 D3
Debenham 15 F4
Dechmont 25 G2
Deddington 13 F5
Dedham 15 E5
Deeping St. James 14 B3
Deeping St. Nicholas 14 C2
Deganwy 16 C3
Delabole 4 C3
Delamere 17 F4
Denbigh 17 D4
Denby Dale 18 B4
Denham 8 B2
Denholm 22 C2
Denholme 18 B3
Denmead 8 A4
Dennington 15 F4
Denny 25 G2
Denton 18 A5
Denver 14 D3
Derby 13 F2
Dereham 15 E2
Dersingham 15 D2
Dervaig 26 D4
Desborough 13 G3
Devil's Bridge 11 D2
Devizes 6 D2
Dewsbury 18 B4
Dhoon 20 B5
Dibden 7 E4
Didcot 7 E2
Dinas Powys 11 F5
Dingwall 32 B4
Dinnet 29 E1
Dinnington 18 C5
Dippen 24 C4
Dirleton 29 E5
Diss 15 F3
Distington 21 D3
Ditton 9 D3
Dobwalls 4 D4
Dochgarroch 32 B5
Docking 15 D2
Doddington 23 D2
Dodington 6 C2
Dodworth 18 C4
Dogdyke 14 C1
Dolanog 17 D5
Dolbenmaen 16 C4
Dolfor 12 B3
Dolgarrog 16 C4

Place	Ref
Dolgellau	16 C5
Dollar	25 G2
Dolphinton	22 B1
Doncaster	18 C4
Donington	14 C2
Donnington	12 C3
Dorchester	6 B5
Dordon	13 E3
Dores	32 B5
Dorking	8 B3
Dornie	27 E1
Dornoch	32 B3
Dougarie	24 C4
Douglas *I.o.M.*	20 B5
Douglas *S.Lan.*	25 G4
Douglastown	29 E3
Dounby	34 A3
Doune	28 B4
Dounreay	32 C1
Dover	9 F3
Doveridge	13 E2
Dowally	28 C3
Downham Market	14 D3
Downton	7 D4
Dowsby	14 B2
Drayton *Norf.*	15 F2
Drayton *Oxon.*	7 E1
Drefach	10 D4
Dreghorn	25 E4
Drem	29 E5
Driffield	19 E3
Drimnin	27 D4
Droitwich	13 D4
Dronfield	18 C5
Drongan	25 E4
Droylsden	18 A5
Druid	17 D4
Druimdrishaig	24 C2
Drumbeg	31 F3
Drumclog	25 F4
Drumlithie	29 F2
Drummore	20 A3
Drumnadrochit	32 B5
Drybrook	6 B1
Drymen	25 E2
Duddo	23 D1
Dudley	13 D3
Duffield	13 F1
Dufftown	33 D5
Duirinish	27 E1
Dullingham	14 D4
Dulnain Bridge	32 C5
Dulverton	5 F2
Dumbarton	25 E2
Dumfries	21 D2
Dunbar	29 E5
Dunbeath	32 D2
Dunblane	28 B4
Dunchurch	13 F4
Dundee	29 E3
Dundonald	25 E4
Dundreggan	27 G2
Dundrennan	20 C3
Dunecht	29 F1
Dunfermline	25 G2
Dunholme	19 E5
Dunkeld	28 C3
Dunkirk	9 E3
Dunlop	25 E3
Dunnet	34 A4
Dunning	28 C4
Dunoon	25 D2
Dunragit	20 A2
Duns	22 D1
Dunscore	25 G5
Dunstable	14 B5
Dunster	5 F1
Dunure	25 E4
Dunvant	10 D4
Dunvegan	26 C1
Durham	23 E5
Durness	31 G2
Durrington	7 D3
Dursley	6 C1
Dyce	29 F1
Dyke	32 C4
Dykehead	29 D2
Dymchurch	9 E4
Dymock	12 D5
Dyserth	17 D3
E	
Eaglescliffe	18 C1
Eaglesfield	21 E2
Eaglesham	25 F3
Earby	18 A3
Eardisley	12 B5
Earith	14 C4
Earls Barton	13 G4
Earls Colne	15 E5
Earl Shilton	13 F3
Earlston	22 C2
Earl Stonham	15 F4
Earsairidh	26 B2
Easdale	27 E5
Easebourne	8 A4
Easington *Dur.*	23 F5
Easington *E.Riding*	19 F4
Easington Colliery	23 F5
Easingwold	18 C2
East Bergholt	15 E5
Eastbourne	8 D5
East Bridgford	13 G1
East Calder	25 G3
East Dereham	15 E2
Eastfield	19 E2
Eastgate	23 D5
East Goscote	13 G2
East Grinstead	8 C3
East Hanney	7 E1
East Harling	15 E3
East Haven	29 E3
East Horsley	8 B3
East Huntspill	6 A3
East Keal	14 C1
East Kilbride	25 F3
East Leake	13 F2
East Linton	29 E5
East Malling	9 D3
East Markham	18 D5
Eastoft	19 D4
Easton	6 B5
Easton-in-Gordano	6 B5
Easton on the Hill	14 B3
East Preston	8 B4
East Retford	18 D5
Eastriggs	21 E2
Eastry	9 F3
East Wemyss	29 D5
East Wittering	8 A5
Eastwood	13 F1
Eaton Socon	14 B4
Ebbw Vale	11 F4
Ecclaw	22 D1
Ecclefechan	21 E2
Eccles	22 D1
Ecclesfield	18 C5
Eccleshall	12 D2
Eccleston	17 F2
Echt	29 F1
Eckford	22 D2
Eckington *Derbys.*	18 C5
Eckington *Worcs.*	13 D5
Edderton	32 B3
Eddleston	22 B1
Edenbridge	8 C3
Edenfield	18 A4
Edgworth	18 A4
Edinburgh	29 D5
Edinburgh Airport	28 C5
Edlingham	23 E3
Edmundbyers	23 E4
Edwinstowe	13 G1
Edzell	29 E2
Egglescliffe	18 C1
Egham	8 B2
Eglingham	23 E2
Eglwys Fach	11 D1
Eglwyswrw	10 B3
Egremont	21 D4
Egton	19 D1
Einacleit	30 C3
Elgin	32 C4
Elgol	27 D2
Elham	9 F3
Elie	29 E4
Elland	18 B4
Ellesmere	17 E5
Ellesmere Port	17 E3
Ellingham	23 E2
Ellington	23 E3
Ellon	33 F5
Elloughton	19 E4
Elm	14 C3
Elmswell	15 E4
Elmton	18 C5
Elphin	31 G3
Elsdon	23 D3
Elsrickle	25 G3
Elstead	8 B3
Elstree	8 B1
Elswick	17 F1
Elton *Cambs.*	14 B3
Elton *Ches.*	17 F3
Elvanfoot	25 G4
Elvington	18 D3
Ely *Cambs.*	14 D4
Ely *Cardiff*	11 F5
Embleton	23 E2
Emsworth	8 A4
Enderby	13 F3
Endon	13 D1
Enstone	13 F5
Enterkinfoot	25 G5
Eoropaidh	31 D2
Epping	8 C1
Epsom	8 C2
Epworth	19 D4
Eriboll	31 G2
Eriswell	15 D4
Errogie	32 B5
Errol	28 D4
Esher	8 B2
Esh Winning	23 E5
Eskdalemuir	22 B3
Eston	18 C1
Eton	8 B2
Etteridge	28 B1
Ettington	13 E5
Ettrick	22 B2
Ettrickbridge	22 B2
Euxton	17 F2
Evanton	32 B4
Evercreech	6 B3
Evesham	13 E5
Ewell	8 C2
Ewhurst	8 B3
Exebridge	5 F2
Exeter	5 F3
Exminster	5 F3
Exmouth	5 F3
Eye *Peter.*	14 C3
Eye *Suff.*	15 F4
Eyemouth	23 D1
Eynsford	8 D2
Eynsham	7 E1
F	
Failsworth	18 A4
Fairford	6 D1
Fairlie	25 E3
Fairlight	9 E4
Fair Oak	7 E4
Fakenham	15 E2
Falkirk	25 G2
Falkland	29 D4
Fallin	25 G2
Falmouth	4 B5
Falstone	22 D3
Fareham	7 E4
Faringdon	7 D1
Farington	17 F2
Farmborough	6 B2
Farnborough	8 A3
Farndon	13 G1
Farnham	8 A3
Farnham Royal	8 B2
Farnsfield	13 G1
Farnworth	18 A4
Farr	32 B5
Fauldhouse	25 G3
Faversham	9 E2
Fawley	7 E4
Fazeley	13 E3
Fearnhead	17 F3
Fearnmore	31 E5
Featherstone *Staffs.*	13 D3
Featherstone *W.Yorks.*	18 C4
Felindre	12 B3
Felixstowe	15 F5
Felling	23 E4
Felsted	15 D5
Felton	23 E3
Feltwell	15 D3
Feniton	6 A5
Fenstanton	14 C4
Fenwick *E.Ayr.*	25 E3
Fenwick *Northumb.*	23 E1
Feochaig	24 C4
Feolin Ferry	24 B3
Fern	29 E2
Ferndale	11 E4
Ferndown	6 D4
Ferness	32 C5
Fernhill Heath	13 D4
Fernhurst	8 A4
Ferryden	29 F3
Ferryhill	23 E5
Feshiebridge	28 C1
Fettercairn	29 E2
Ffestiniog	16 C4
Ffostrasol	10 C3
Filey	19 E2
Fillongley	13 E3
Filton	6 B2
Fimber	19 D2
Finavon	29 E3
Finchampstead	8 A2
Finchingfield	15 D5
Findern	13 F2
Findhorn	32 C4
Findochty	33 E4
Findon	8 B4
Finedon	14 B4
Finningham	15 E4
Finningley	18 D5
Finnygaud	33 E4
Finstown	34 A3
Fintry	25 F2
Fionnphort	26 D5
Fishburn	23 F5
Fishguard	10 B3
Fishnish	27 E4
Fiunary	27 E4
Five Oaks	4 B3
Flackwell Heath	8 A2
Flamborough	19 F2
Fleet	8 A3
Fleetwood	17 E1
Flempton	15 E4
Flimby	21 D3
Flimwell	9 D3
Flint	17 E3
Flitwick	14 B5
Flodden	23 D2
Flookburgh	21 E5
Fochabers	33 D4
Folkestone	9 F3
Folkingham	14 B2
Folly Gate	5 E3
Ford *Arg. & B.*	27 E5
Ford *Northumb.*	23 D2
Fordham	14 D4
Fordingbridge	6 D4
Fordoun	29 F2
Fordyce	33 E4
Forest Row	8 C3
Forfar	29 E3
Forgandenny	28 C4
Forgie	33 D4
Formby	17 E2
Forres	32 C4
Forsbrook	13 D1
Forsinard	32 C1
Fort Augustus	27 G2
Forth	25 G3
Fortingall	28 B3
Fortrose	32 B4
Fortuneswell	6 B5
Fort William	27 F3
Fotherby	19 F5
Foulden	23 D1
Foulridge	18 A3
Four Elms	8 C3
Four Marks	8 A3
Four Oaks	9 E4
Fowey	4 C4
Fownhope	12 C5
Foxdale	20 B5
Foyers	27 G1
Framfield	8 C4
Framlingham	15 F4
Frampton Cotterell	6 B2
Frampton on Severn	6 C1
Frankley	13 D3
Fraserburgh	33 F4
Freckleton	17 F2
Fremington	5 E1
Freshwater	7 E5
Freshwater East	10 B4
Fressingfield	15 F4
Freswick	33 D1
Freuchie	29 D4
Fridaythorpe	19 D3
Frimley	8 A3
Frinton-on-Sea	9 F1
Friockheim	29 E3
Frithelstock Stone	5 D2
Frizington	21 D4
Frodsham	17 F3
Frogmore	8 A3
Frome	6 C3
Fulbourn	14 D4
Fulford *Staffs.*	13 D2
Fulford *York*	18 D3
Fulham	8 C2
Fulwood	17 F1
Funzie	35 G2
Furnace	27 F5
Fyfield	8 D1
Fyvie	33 F5
G	
Gaer	12 B5
Gainford	18 B1
Gainsborough	19 D5
Gairloch	31 E5
Galashiels	22 C2
Galmisdale	27 D3
Galston	25 F4
Gamlingay	14 C4
Gardenstown	33 F4
Garderhouse	35 F4
Garelochhead	25 E2
Garforth	18 C3
Gargrave	18 A3
Garsdale Head	21 G4
Garstang	17 F1
Garth	11 E3
Garthmyl	12 B3
Gartocharn	25 E2
Garvald	29 E5
Garvamore	28 B1
Garvard	24 B2
Garve	31 G5
Gatehouse of Fleet	20 C2
Gateshead	23 E4
Gatley	18 A5
Gatwick (London) Airport	8 C3
Gawthrop	21 F5
Gayton	15 D2
Gearraidh na h-Aibhne	30 C3
Geddington	13 G3
Gedney	14 C2
Gelligaer	11 F4
Georgeham	5 D1
Gerrards Cross	8 B2
Giffnock	25 F3
Gifford	29 E5
Gilberdyke	19 D4
Gillamoor	18 D1
Gillingham *Dorset*	6 C4
Gillingham *Med.*	9 D2
Gilling West	18 B1
Gilmerton	28 C4
Gilsland	21 F2
Gilston	22 C1
Gilwern	11 F4
Girlsta	35 F3
Girvan	25 D5
Gisburn	18 A3
Glamis	29 D3
Glanaman	11 D4
Glanton	23 E2
Glasbury	12 B5
Glasgow	25 F3
Glasgow Airport	25 E3
Glasgow Prestwick International Airport	25 E4
Glassford	25 F3
Glastonbury	6 B3
Glemsford	15 E5
Glenbarr	24 C4
Glenbeg	27 D3
Glenborrodale	27 E3
Glenbrittle	26 D1
Glencaple	21 D2
Glencarse	28 D4
Glencoe	27 F4
Gleneagles	28 C4
Glenegedale	24 B3
Glenelg	27 E2
Glenfield	13 F3
Glenfinnan	27 F3
Glengarnock	25 E3
Glenkindie	29 E1
Glenluce	20 A2
Glenrothes	29 D4
Glen Vine	20 B5
Glinton	14 B3
Glossop	18 B5
Gloucester	6 C1
Glusburn	18 B3
Glyn Ceiriog	17 E5
Glyncorrwg	11 E4
Glyn-Neath	11 E4
Gnosall	12 D2
Gobowen	17 E5
Godalming	8 B3
Godmanchester	14 C4
Godstone	8 C3
Golborne	17 F3
Goldcliff	11 F5
Golden Pot	8 A3
Golspie	32 C3
Goodwick	10 B3
Goole	18 D4
Goonhavern	4 B4
Gordon	22 C1
Gorebridge	22 B1
Gorey	4 B3
Goring	8 A2
Gorseinon	10 D4
Gosberton	14 C2
Gosfield	15 D5
Gosforth *Cumb.*	21 D4
Gosforth *T. & W.*	23 E4
Gosport	8 A5
Gotham	13 F2
Goudhurst	9 D3
Gourdon	29 F2
Goxhill	19 E4
Grabhair	30 D3
Grain	9 E2
Grampound	4 C4
Grandtully	28 C3
Grangemouth	25 G2
Grange-over-Sands	21 F5
Grantham	14 B2
Grantown-on-Spey	32 C5
Grantshouse	22 D1
Grasmere	21 E4
Grassington	18 B2
Gravesend	8 D2
Grayrigg	21 F4
Grays	8 D2
Grayshott	8 A3
Greasby	17 E3
Great Ayton	18 C1
Great Baddow	9 D1
Great Barton	15 E4
Great Bircham	15 D2
Great Broughton	18 C1
Great Clifton	21 D3
Great Cornard	15 E5
Great Dunmow	14 D5
Great Eccleston	17 F1
Great Ellingham	15 E3
Great Glen	13 G3
Great Gonerby	13 G2
Great Gransden	14 C4
Greatham	8 A3
Great Harwood	18 A3
Great Horkesley	15 E5
Great Linford	13 G5
Great Malvern	12 D5
Great Marton	17 E1
Great Missenden	8 A1
Great Notley	15 D5
Great Ponton	14 B2
Great Salkeld	21 F3
Great Sampford	14 D5
Great Sankey	17 F3
Great Shelford	14 C4
Great Torrington	5 E2
Great Wakering	9 E2
Great Wyrley	13 D3
Great Yarmouth	15 G3
Great Yeldham	15 D5
Greengairs	25 F2
Greenham	7 E2
Greenhead	21 F2
Greenigo	34 B3
Greenlaw	22 D1
Greenloaning	28 C4
Greenock	25 E2
Greenodd	21 E5
Greenway	10 B3
Gresford	17 E4
Gress	31 D2
Gretna	21 E2
Greystoke	21 F3
Grimoldby	19 F5
Grimsby	19 F4
Grimston	15 D2
Gringley on the Hill	18 D5
Gritley	34 B3
Grizebeck	21 E5
Grove	7 E1
Grudie	31 G5
Grutness	35 F5
Guernsey Airport	4 A2
Guide Post	23 E3
Guildford	8 B3
Guildtown	28 C3
Guisborough	18 D1
Guiseley	18 B3
Guist	15 E2
Gullane	29 E5
Gunness	19 D4
Gunnislake	5 D3
Gurnos	11 D4
Gutcher	35 F2
Gwaun-Cae-Gurwen	11 D4
Gwithian	4 A4
Gwytherin	16 D4
H	
Hackleton	13 G4
Hacklinge	9 F3
Hackness	19 E1
Haddenham	14 C4
Haddington	29 E5
Haddiscoe	15 G3
Hadleigh	15 E5
Hadley	12 C2
Hagley *Here.*	11 F5
Hagley *Worcs.*	13 D3
Hailsham	8 D4
Hale	18 A5
Hales	15 F3
Halesowen	13 D3
Halesworth	15 F4
Halewood	17 F3
Halifax	18 B4
Halkirk	32 D1
Halkyn	17 E3
Hall	25 E3
Halland	8 D4
Hallow	12 D4
Hallworthy	4 C3
Halstead	15 E5
Halton Gill	21 G5
Haltwhistle	22 D4
Halwell	5 E4
Ham	35 D4
Hamble-le-Rice	7 E4
Hambleton	17 E1
Hamilton	25 F3
Hamnavoe (Mainland) *Shet.*	35 F4
Hamnavoe (Yell) *Shet.*	35 F2
Hampreston	6 D5
Hamstreet	9 E3
Handsacre	13 E2
Hanham	6 B2
Hanley Castle	12 D5
Hanwood	12 C3
Happisburgh	15 F2
Harbledown	9 F3
Harbost	31 D2
Harbury	13 F4
Hardingstone	13 G4
Hardwicke	6 C1
Harefield	8 B1
Hare Street	14 C5
Harewood	18 C3
Harlech	16 C5
Harleston	15 F3
Harlington	14 B5
Harlow	8 C1
Harmston	14 B1
Haroldswick	35 G1
Harpenden	8 B1
Harpole	13 G4
Harrietfield	28 C3
Harrietsham	9 E3
Harrogate	18 C3
Harston	14 C4
Hartfield	8 C3
Harthill	25 G3
Hartland	4 D2
Hartlebury	12 D4
Hartlepool	23 F5
Hartley	8 D2
Hartley Wintney	8 A3
Hartpury	12 D5
Hartshill	13 F3
Hartshorne	13 F2
Harvington	13 E5
Harwell	7 E1
Harwich	15 F5
Harworth	18 D5
Hasland	13 F1
Haslemere	8 B3
Haslingden	18 A4
Hassendean	22 C2
Hastings	9 E4
Haswell	23 F5
Hatfield *Herts.*	8 C1
Hatfield *S.Yorks.*	18 D4
Hatfield Broad Oak	8 D1
Hatfield Peverel	9 D1
Hatherleigh	5 E2
Hathern	13 F2
Hathersage	18 B5
Hatton *Aber.*	33 G5
Hatton *Derbys.*	13 E2
Haugh of Urr	20 D2
Haughton	13 D2
Havant	8 A4
Haverfordwest	10 B4
Haverhill	15 D5
Hawarden	17 E4
Hawes	21 G5
Hawick	22 C2
Hawkhurst	9 D3
Hawkinge	9 F3
Hawkshead	21 E4
Hawkwell	9 E1
Hawley	8 A3
Haworth	18 B3
Haxby	18 D3
Haxey	19 D5
Haydock	17 F3
Haydon Bridge	22 D4
Haydon Wick	6 D2
Hayfield	18 B5
Hayle	4 A5
Hay-on-Wye	12 B5
Hayton	19 D3

Haywards Heath	8	C4
Hazel Grove	18	A5
Hazlemere	8	A1
Heacham	15	D2
Headcorn	9	E3
Headley	8	A3
Healeyfield	23	E5
Healing	19	F4
Heanor	13	F1
Heath	13	F1
Heathfield	8	D4
Heathrow (London) Airport	8	B2
Hebburn	23	F4
Hebden Bridge	18	A4
Heckington	14	B1
Hedge End	7	E4
Hedon	19	E4
Heighington	14	B1
Helensburgh	25	E2
Helhoughton	15	E2
Hellifield	18	A3
Helmsdale	32	C2
Helmsley	18	D2
Helpringham	14	B1
Helsby	17	F3
Helston	4	B5
Hemel Hempstead	8	B1
Hemingford Grey	14	C4
Hempnall	15	F3
Hempstead	14	D5
Hemsby	15	G2
Hemsworth	18	C4
Hemyock	6	A4
Hendon	8	C2
Henfield	8	C4
Hengoed	11	F4
Henley-in-Arden	13	E4
Henley-on-Thames	8	A2
Henlow	14	B5
Henstridge	6	C4
Hereford	12	C5
Heriot	22	B1
Herne Bay	9	F2
Herstmonceux	8	D4
Herston	34	B4
Hertford	8	C1
Heswall	17	E3
Hethersett	15	F3
Hetton	18	A3
Hetton-le-Hole	23	F5
Hexham	23	D4
Hextable	8	D2
Heybridge	9	E1
Heysham	21	F5
Heywood	18	A4
Hibaldstow	19	E4
Higham	9	D2
Higham Ferrers	14	B4
Highampton	5	D2
High Bentham	21	F5
High Blantyre	25	F3
High Bradfield	18	B5
Highbridge	6	A3
Highclere	7	E2
Higher Walton	17	F2
High Etherley	23	E5
High Garrett	15	D5
High Halden	9	E3
High Hawsker	19	E1
High Hesket	21	F3
High Legh	18	A5
Highley	12	D3
High Lorton	21	E3
Highnam	6	C1
Highworth	7	D1
High Wycombe	8	A1
Hildenborough	8	D3
Hilgay	14	D3
Hill End	25	G2
Hill of Fearn	32	C4
Hillside Angus	29	F2
Hillside Shet.	35	F3
Hillswick	35	E3
Hilperton	6	C3
Hilton	13	E2
Hinckley	13	F3
Hinderwell	19	D1
Hindhead	8	A3
Hindley	17	F2
Hindon	6	C3
Hingham	15	E3
Hirwaun	11	E4
Histon	14	C4
Hitchin	14	B5
Hockley	9	E1
Hockley Heath	13	E4
Hoddesdon	8	C1
Hodnet	12	C2
Hogsthorpe	19	G5
Holbeach	14	C2
Holbrook	15	F5
Holden	18	A3
Holland-on-Sea	9	F1
Hollington	9	D4
Hollingworth	18	A5
Hollybush E.Ayr.	25	E4
Hollybush Worcs.	12	D5
Holme-on-Spalding-Moor	19	D3
Holmes Chapel	12	D1
Holmesfield	18	C5
Holmfirth	18	B4
Holsworthy	4	D2
Holt Norf.	15	E2
Holt Wilts.	6	C2
Holt Wrex.	17	F4
Holyhead	16	B3
Holywell	17	E3
Holywood	25	G5
Homersfield	15	F3
Honiton	6	A4
Honley	18	B4
Hoo	9	D2
Hook E.Riding	19	D4
Hook Hants.	8	A3
Hook Norton	13	F5
Hope	17	E4
Hopeman	32	D4
Hopton Norf.	15	G3
Hopton Suff.	15	E4
Horam	8	D4
Horbling	14	B2
Horbury	18	B4
Horden	23	F5
Horeb	10	C3
Horley	8	C3
Hornby	21	F5
Horncastle	14	C1
Horndean	8	A4
Horning	15	F2
Hornsea	19	F3
Horrabridge	5	E4
Horringer	15	E4
Horsehouse	18	B2
Horsford	15	F2
Horsforth	18	B3
Horsham	8	B3
Horsmonden	9	D3
Horstead	15	F2
Horton Heath	7	E4
Horton in Ribblesdale	21	G5
Horwich	17	F2
Houbie	35	G2
Houghton le Spring	23	F4
Houghton Regis	14	B5
Houndslow	22	C1
Houston	25	E3
Houton	34	A3
Hove	8	C4
Hoveton	15	F2
Hovingham	18	D2
Howden	19	D4
Howwood	25	E3
Hoylake	17	E3
Hoyland	18	C4
Hucknall	13	F1
Huddersfield	18	B4
Huggate	19	D3
Hugh Town	4	C5
Huish Episcopi	6	B4
Huisinis	30	B3
Hull	19	E4
Hullavington	6	C2
Hullbridge	9	E1
Humberside International Airport	19	E4
Humberston	19	F4
Humbie	22	C1
Hundleby	14	C1
Hundleton	10	B4
Hungerford	7	E2
Hunmanby	19	E2
Hunstanton	15	D1
Hunter's Quay	25	D2
Huntingdon	14	C4
Huntly	33	E5
Hurlford	25	E4
Hursley	7	E3
Hurst Green	9	D4
Hurstpierpoint	8	C4
Hurstbourne Tarrant	7	E3
Hurworth-on-Tees	18	C1
Husbands Bosworth	13	G3
Huttoft	19	G5
Hutton Cranswick	19	E3
Hutton Rudby	18	C1
Huyton	17	F3
Hyde	18	A5
Hythe Hants.	7	E4
Hythe Kent	9	F3

I

Ibstock	13	F2
Icklesham	9	E4
Icklingham	15	D4
Idrigil	30	D5
Ilchester	6	B4
Ilford	8	C2
Ilfracombe	5	E1
Ilkeston	13	F1
Ilkley	18	B3
Ilminster	6	A4
Immingham	19	E4
Inchbare	29	E2
Inchnadamph	31	G3
Inchture	29	D4
Ingatestone	9	D1
Ingleton Dur.	23	E5
Ingleton N.Yorks.	21	F5
Inglewhite	17	F1
Ingoldmells	14	D1
Inkberrow	13	E4
Innellan	25	D3
Innerleithen	22	B2
Insch	33	E5
Inveralligan	31	E5
Inverallochy	33	G4
Inveraray	27	F5
Inverarity	29	E3
Inverarnan	27	G5
Inverbervie	29	F2
Invercassley	31	G4
Invercharnan	27	F4
Inverey	28	C2
Invergarry	27	G2
Invergordon	32	B4
Inverinan	27	F5
Inverkeilor	29	E3
Inverkeithing	28	D5
Inverkirkaig	31	F3
Inverlael	31	F4
Invermoriston	27	G2
Inverneil	24	C2
Inverness	32	B5
Invernoaden	25	D2
Inverurie	33	F5
Ipplepen	5	F4
Ipstones	13	E1
Ipswich	15	F5
Irchester	14	B4
Irlam	18	A5
Ironbridge	12	C3
Irthlingborough	14	B4
Irvine	25	E4
Isbister (Mainland) Shet.	35	F2
Isbister (Whalsay) Shet.	35	F3
Isleham	14	D4
Isle of Man Airport	20	B5
Isle of Whithorn	20	B3
Iver	8	B2
Ivinghoe	8	B1
Ivybridge	5	E4
Iwade	9	E2
Ixworth	15	E4

J

Jarrow	23	F4
Jaywick	9	F1
Jedburgh	22	C2
Jemimaville	32	B4
Jersey Airport	4	B3
John o' Groats	34	A4
Johnston	10	B4
Johnstone	25	E3
Johnstonebridge	25	G5

K

Kames	24	D2
Kearsley	18	A4
Kedington	15	D5
Keelby	19	E4
Keele	12	D1
Kegworth	13	F2
Keighley	18	B3
Keillmore	24	C2
Keiss	33	D1
Keith	33	E4
Kellas Angus	29	E3
Kellas Moray	32	D4
Kelso	22	D2
Kelty	28	D5
Kelvedon	9	E1
Kelvedon Hatch	8	D1
Kemnay	29	F1
Kempsey	13	D5
Kempston	14	B5
Kendal	21	F4
Kenilworth	13	E4
Kenmore	28	B3
Kennacraig	24	C3
Kennethmont	33	E5
Kennington	7	E1
Kennoway	29	D4
Kensaleyre	30	D5
Kensworth	8	B1
Kentallen	27	F4
Kenton	5	F4
Kesgrave	15	F5
Kessingland	15	G3
Keswick	21	E3
Kettering	13	G4
Kettletoft	34	B2
Kettlewell	21	G5
Ketton	14	B3
Kewstoke	11	F5
Keyingham	19	F4
Keymer	8	C4
Keynsham	6	B2
Keyworth	13	G2
Kibworth Harcourt	13	G3
Kidderminster	12	D4
Kidlington	7	E1
Kidsgrove	12	D1
Kidwelly	10	C4
Kielder	22	C3
Kilberry	24	C3
Kilbirnie	25	E3
Kilburn	13	F1
Kilcadzow	25	G3
Kilchattan	25	D3
Kilchenzie	24	C4
Kilchiaran	24	A3
Kilchoan	26	C4
Kilchoman	24	A3
Kilchrenan	27	F5
Kilconquhar	29	E4
Kilcreggan	25	E2
Kildonan Lodge	32	C2
Kildrummy	29	E1
Kilfinan	24	D2
Kilgetty	10	B4
Kilham E.Riding	19	E2
Kilham Northumb.	22	D2
Kilkhampton	4	D2
Killamarsh	18	C5
Killay	10	D4
Killean	24	C3
Killearn	25	F2
Killichonan	28	B3
Killiecrankie	28	C2
Killin	28	B3
Killinghall	18	B3
Killingworth	23	E4
Killundine	27	D4
Kilmacolm	25	E3
Kilmalieu	27	E4
Kilmaluag	30	D5
Kilmarnock	25	E4
Kilmartin	24	C2
Kilmaurs	25	E3
Kilmelford	27	E5
Kilmington	6	A5
Kilmory Arg. & B.	24	C2
Kilmory (Rum) High.	26	D2
Kilninian	26	D4
Kilninver	27	E5
Kiloran	24	B2
Kilrenny	29	E4
Kilsyth	25	F2
Kilwinning	25	E3
Kimberley Norf.	15	E3
Kimberley Notts.	13	F1
Kimbolton	14	B4
Kimpton	8	B1
Kinbrace	32	C2
Kincardine	25	G2
Kincardine O'Neil	29	E1
Kincraig	28	C1
Kingarth	25	D3
Kinghorn	29	D5
Kinglassie	28	D5
Kingsbarns	29	E4
Kingsbridge	5	E4
Kingsbury	13	E3
Kingsbury Episcopi	6	B4
Kingsclere	7	E3
Kingsdown	9	F3
Kingshouse	28	B4
Kingskerswell	5	F4
Kings Langley	8	B1
Kingsley Ches.	17	F3
Kingsley Staffs.	13	E1
King's Lynn	14	D2
Kingsnorth	9	E3
King's Sutton	13	F5
Kingsteignton	5	F3
Kingsthorne	12	C5
Kingston	33	D4
Kingston Bagpuize	7	E1
Kingstone	12	C5
Kingston Seymour	11	F5
Kingston upon Hull	19	E4
Kingswear	5	F4
Kingswood S.Glos.	6	B2
Kingswood Surr.	8	C3
Kings Worthy	7	E3
Kington	12	B4
Kingussie	28	B1
Kinloch	26	D2
Kinlochard	27	G5
Kinlochbervie	31	G2
Kinlocheil	27	F3
Kinlochewe	31	F5
Kinloch Hourn	27	F2
Kinlochleven	27	F3
Kinloch Rannoch	28	B3
Kinloss	32	C4
Kinmel Bay	17	D3
Kinross	28	D4
Kintbury	7	E2
Kintore	29	F1
Kintour	24	B3
Kintra	24	B3
Kinver	12	D3
Kippax	18	C3
Kippen	25	F2
Kirby Muxloe	13	F3
Kirkbean	21	D2
Kirkbride	21	E2
Kirkburton	18	B4
Kirkby	17	F3
Kirkby in Ashfield	13	F1
Kirkby Lonsdale	21	F5
Kirkby Malzeard	18	B2
Kirkbymoorside	18	D2
Kirkby Stephen	21	G4
Kirkcaldy	29	D5
Kirkcolm	20	A2
Kirkconnel	25	F4
Kirkcowan	20	B2
Kirkcudbright	20	C2
Kirkham	17	F1
Kirkinner	20	B2
Kirkintilloch	25	F2
Kirkliston	25	G2
Kirk Michael I.o.M.	20	B4
Kirkmichael P. & K.	28	C2
Kirkmichael S.Ayr.	25	E5
Kirkmuirhill	25	F3
Kirknewton Northumb.	23	D2
Kirknewton W.Loth.	22	B1
Kirkoswald Cumb.	21	F3
Kirkoswald S.Ayr.	25	E5
Kirkpatrick Durham	20	C2
Kirkpatrick-Fleming	21	E2
Kirk Sandall	18	D4
Kirkton	21	E2
Kirkton of Culsalmond	33	E5
Kirkton of Durris	29	F1
Kirkton of Glenisla	28	D2
Kirkton of Kingoldrum	29	D3
Kirkton of Menmuir	29	E2
Kirkton of Skene	29	F1
Kirktown of Auchterless	33	F5
Kirktown of Deskford	33	E4
Kirkwall	34	B3
Kirk Yetholm	22	D2
Kirriemuir	29	D3
Kirtlington	7	E1
Kirton Lincs.	14	C2
Kirton Suff.	15	F5
Kirton in Lindsey	19	E5
Knaresborough	18	C3
Knayton	18	C2
Knebworth	8	C1
Knighton	12	B4
Knock	27	D4
Knockandhu	32	D5
Knottingley	18	C4
Knowle	13	E4
Knucklas	12	B4
Knutsford	18	A5
Kyleakin	27	E1
Kyle of Lochalsh	27	E1
Kylerhea	27	E1
Kyles Scalpay	30	C4
Kylestrome	31	G3

L

Laceby	19	F4
Lacock	6	C2
Ladybank	29	D4
Ladykirk	23	D1
Ladysford	33	F4
Lagg	24	D4
Laggan (Invergarry) High.	27	G2
Laggan (Newtonmore) High.	28	B1
Lagganulva	27	D4
Laide	31	E4
Lairg	32	B3
Lakenheath	15	D3
Laleston	11	E5
Lamberhurst	9	D3
Lambourn	7	E2
Lamlash	24	D4
Lampeter	10	D3
Lamport	13	G4
Lanark	25	G3
Lancaster	21	F5
Lanchester	23	E5
Landore	11	D4
Lane End	8	A1
Langford	14	B5
Langham	13	G2
Langholm	22	B3
Langold	18	C5
Langport	6	B4
Langtoft	19	E2
Langwathby	21	F3
Lanivet	4	C4
Lapworth	13	E4
Larbert	25	G2
Largoward	29	E4
Largs	25	E3
Larkhall	25	F3
Larkhill	6	D3
Larling	15	E3
Latchingdon	9	E1
Latheron	32	D2
Latheronwheel	32	D2
Lauder	22	C1
Laugharne	10	C4
Launceston	4	D3
Laurencekirk	29	F2
Laurieston	20	C2
Lavenham	15	E5
Law	25	G3
Lawers	28	B3
Lawford	15	E5
Laxey	20	B5
Laxford Bridge	31	G2
Laxo	35	F3
Layer de la Haye	9	E1
Lazonby	21	F3
Leadburn	22	B1
Leadenham	14	B1
Leadgate	23	E4
Leadhills	25	G4
Leamington Spa	13	F4
Leasingham	14	B1
Leatherhead	8	B3
Leavening	19	D2
Lechlade	7	D1
Leckhampton	6	C1
Leckmelm	31	F4
Ledaig	27	F4
Ledbury	12	D5
Ledmore	31	G3
Lee	17	F1
Leeds	18	B3
Leeds Bradford International Airport	18	B3
Leedstown	4	B5
Leek	13	D1
Leeming	18	B2
Lee Moor	5	E4
Lee-on-the-Solent	7	E4
Leicester	13	F3
Leigh	17	F2
Leighton Buzzard	8	B1
Leiston	15	G4
Leith	29	D5
Lenham	9	E3
Lennoxtown	25	F2
Leominster	12	C4
Lerwick	35	F4
Leslie	28	D4
Lesmahagow	25	G4
Leswalt	20	A2
Letchworth Garden City	14	C5
Letheringsett	15	E2
Letterston	10	B3
Leuchars	29	E4
Leumrabhagh	30	D3
Leven E.Riding	19	E3
Leven Fife	29	D4
Levenwick	35	F4
Leverburgh	30	C4
Lewes	8	C4
Leyburn	18	B1
Leyland	17	F2
Leysdown-on-Sea	9	E2
Lhanbryde	33	D4
Libberton	25	G3
Lichfield	13	E3
Lightwater	8	B2
Lilleshall	12	D2
Lilliesleaf	22	C2
Limekilns	25	G2
Lincoln	19	E5
Lindfield	8	C4
Lindores	29	D4
Linford	9	D2
Lingfield	8	C3
Linksness	34	A3
Linlithgow	25	G2
Linsidemore	32	B3
Linton	14	D4
Liphook	8	A3
Liskeard	4	D4
Liss	8	A4
Liswerry	11	F5
Litherland	17	E3
Littleborough	18	A4
Littlebourne	9	F3
Little Clacton	9	F1
Little Common	8	D4
Littledean	6	B1
Little Downham	14	D3
Little Eaton	13	F1
Littlehampton	8	B4
Littlemill E.Ayr.	25	E4
Littlemill High.	32	C4
Little Missenden	8	B1
Littlemore	7	E1
Little Oakley	15	F5
Little Paxton	14	B4
Little Plumstead	15	F2
Littleport	14	D3
Littlestone-on-Sea	9	E4
Liverpool	17	E3
Liverpool John Lennon Airport	17	F3
Liversedge	18	B4
Livingston	25	G3
Lizard	4	B5
Llanaelhaearn	16	B4
Llanarth	11	F4
Llanarthney	10	D4
Llanbadarn Fawr	10	D1
Llanbadrig	16	B3
Llanbedr	16	B4
Llanbedrog	16	B5
Llanberis	16	C4
Llanbister	12	B4
Llanblethian	11	E5
Llanddarog	10	D4
Llanddeiniolen	16	C4
Llandderfel	17	D5
Llanddowror	10	C4
Llandeilo	10	D4
Llandinam	11	E1
Llandissilio	10	B3
Llandovery	11	D3
Llandrillo	17	D5
Llandrindod Wells	11	E2
Llandudno	16	C3
Llandwrog	16	B4
Llandybie	10	D4
Llandysul	10	C3
Llanegwad	10	D3
Llanelli	10	D4
Llanelltyd	16	C5
Llanelly	11	F4
Llanelwy	17	D3
Llanerch-y-medd	16	B3
Llanfaelog	16	B3
Llanfair Caereinion	12	B3
Llanfairfechan	16	C3
Llanfairpwllgwyngyll	16	C3
Llanfair Talhaiarn	16	D3
Llanfihangel ar-arth	10	C3
Llanfyllin	17	E5
Llanfynydd	17	E4
Llangadfan	17	D5
Llangadog	10	D3
Llangefni	16	B3
Llangeler	10	C3
Llangelynin	10	D1
Llangendeirne	10	C4
Llangernyw	16	D4
Llangoed	16	C3
Llangollen	17	E4
Llangranog	10	C2
Llangunnor	10	C3
Llangurig	11	E2
Llangwm	10	B4
Llangynidr	11	F4
Llanharan	11	E5
Llanhilleth	11	F4
Llanidloes	11	E2
Llanilar	10	D2
Llanishen	11	F5
Llanllwchaiarn	12	B3
Llanllyfni	16	B4
Llannon	10	D2
Llanrhaeadr-ym-Mochnant	17	E5
Llanrhidian	10	D4
Llanrhystud	10	D2
Llanrug	16	C4
Llanrumney	11	F5
Llanrwst	16	C4
Llansamlet	11	D4

Llansanffraid Glan Conwy 16 D3
Llansannan 16 D4
Llansawel 10 D3
Llansteffan 10 C4
Llanthony 12 B5
Llantilio Pertholey 11 F4
Llantrisant *Mon.* 11 F4
Llantrisant *R.C.T.* 11 E5
Llantwit Major 11 E5
Llanuwchllyn 16 D5
Llanwddyn 17 D5
Llanwnda 16 B4
Llanwnog 11 E1
Llanwrda 11 D3
Llanwrtyd Wells 11 E3
Llanybydder 10 D3
Llanynghenedl 16 B3
Llanystumdwy 16 B5
Lledrod 10 D2
Loanhead 22 B1
Loans 25 E4
Lochailort 27 E3
Lochaline 27 E4
Lochans 20 A2
Locharbriggs 25 G5
Lochawe 27 F5
Loch Baghasdail 26 B2
Lochboisdale 26 B2
Lochcarron 27 E1
Lochdon 27 E4
Lochearnhead 28 B4
Lochend 32 B5
Lochgelly 28 D5
Lochgilphead 24 C2
Lochgoilhead 27 G5
Lochinver 31 F3
Lochmaben 25 G5
Lochmaddy 30 B5
Loch na Madadh 30 B5
Lochranza 24 D3
Loch Sgioport 26 B1
Lochwinnoch 25 E3
Lockerbie 22 B3
Locking 6 A3
Locks Heath 7 E4
Lockton 19 D1
Loddiswell 5 E4
Loddon 15 F3
Lofthouse 18 C4
Loftus 18 D1
Logan 25 F4
Loggerheads 12 D2
London 8 C2
London Colney 8 B1
London Gatwick Airport 8 C3
London Heathrow Airport 8 B2
London Luton Airport 8 B1
London Stansted Airport 14 D5
Long Ashton 6 B2
Long Bennington 13 G1
Longbenton 23 E4
Longbridge Deverill 6 C3
Long Buckby 13 G4
Long Compton 13 E5
Long Crendon 8 A1
Longdon 13 E2
Long Eaton 13 F2
Longforgan 29 D4
Longframlington 23 E3
Long Hanborough 7 E1
Longhope *Glos.* 6 B1
Longhope *Ork.* 34 A4
Longhorsley 23 E3
Longhoughton 23 E2
Long Itchington 13 F4
Long Lawford 13 F4
Longmanhill 33 F4
Long Melford 15 E5
Longmorn 32 D4
Longniddry 29 E5
Long Preston 18 A3
Longside 33 G5
Long Stratton 15 F3
Long Sutton *Lincs.* 14 C2
Long Sutton *Som.* 6 B4
Longton 17 F2
Longtown 21 E2
Looe 4 D4
Loose 9 D3
Lopcombe Corner 7 D3
Loscoe 13 F1
Lossiemouth 32 D4
Lostwithiel 4 C4
Loth 34 B2
Lothmore 32 C2
Loughborough 13 F2
Loughor 10 D4
Loughton 8 C1
Louth 19 F5
Lowdham 13 G1
Lower Beeding 8 C4
Lower Cam 6 C1
Lower Diabaig 31 E5
Lower Killeyan 24 A3
Lowestoft 15 G3
Loweswater 21 E3
Lowick 23 E2
Low Street 15 F2
Ludag 26 B2
Ludgershall 7 D3
Ludgvan 4 A5
Ludlow 12 C4
Luib 27 D1
Lumphanan 29 E1

Luncarty 28 C4
Lundin Links 29 E4
Luss 25 E2
Lusta 30 C5
Luton 14 B5
Luton (London) Airport 8 B1
Lutterworth 13 F3
Luxulyan 4 C4
Lybster 32 D2
Lydd 9 E4
Lydd Airport 9 E4
Lydford 5 E3
Lydiate 17 E2
Lydney 6 B1
Lyme Regis 6 A5
Lyminge 9 F3
Lymington 7 E5
Lymm 17 F3
Lympne 9 F3
Lympstone 5 F3
Lyndhurst 7 E4
Lynemore 32 C5
Lynemouth 23 E3
Lyne of Skene 29 F1
Lyness 34 A4
Lynmouth 5 E1
Lynton 5 E1
Lytchett Matravers 6 C5
Lytchett Minster 6 C5
Lytham St. Anne's 17 E2

M
Mablethorpe 19 G5
Macclesfield 18 A5
Macduff 33 F4
Macharioch 24 C5
Machen 11 F5
Machrihanish 24 C4
Machynlleth 11 D1
Macmerry 29 E5
Madeley 12 D1
Madley 12 C5
Madron 4 A5
Maenclochog 10 B3
Maentwrog 16 C4
Maerdy 11 E4
Maesteg 11 E4
Maghull 17 E2
Maiden Bradley 6 C3
Maidenhead 8 A2
Maiden Newton 6 B5
Maidens 25 E5
Maidstone 9 D3
Maldon 9 E1
Mallaig 27 E2
Mallwyd 16 D5
Malmesbury 6 C2
Malpas *Ches.* 17 F4
Malpas *Newport* 11 F4
Maltby 18 C5
Maltby le Marsh 19 F5
Malton 19 D2
Malvern Link 12 D5
Manby 19 F5
Mancetter 13 F3
Manchester 18 A5
Manchester Airport 18 A5
Manea 14 C3
Mangotsfield 6 B2
Manningtree 15 F5
Manorbier 10 B4
Mansfield 13 F1
Mansfield Woodhouse 13 F1
Manston 6 C4
Marazion 4 A5
March 14 C3
Marchwiel 17 E4
Marden 9 D3
Mareham le Fen 14 C1
Maresfield 8 C4
Margam 11 D5
Margate 9 F2
Marham 15 D3
Mark 6 A3
Market Bosworth 13 F3
Market Deeping 14 B2
Market Drayton 12 C2
Market Harborough 13 G3
Market Lavington 6 D3
Market Rasen 19 E5
Market Warsop 13 F1
Market Weighton 19 D3
Markfield 13 F2
Markinch 29 D4
Marks Tey 15 E5
Markyate 8 B1
Marlborough 7 D2
Marldon 5 F4
Marlow 8 A2
Marnhull 6 C4
Marple 18 A5
Marsden 18 B4
Marshfield 6 C2
Marske-by-the-Sea 23 G5
Marston 7 E1
Marston Magna 6 B4
Marston Moretaine 14 B5
Martham 15 G2
Martlesham 15 F5
Martley 12 D4
Martock 6 B4
Marybank 31 G5
Marykirk 29 E2
Marypark 32 D5
Maryport 21 D3
Marywell 29 E1

Masham 18 B2
Matlock 13 F1
Matlock Bath 13 E1
Mauchline 25 F4
Maud 33 F5
Maughold 20 B4
Maybole 25 E5
Mayfield 13 E1
Mealsgate 21 E3
Meare 6 B3
Measham 13 F2
Medstead 8 A3
Meidrim 10 C3
Meigle 29 D3
Meikle Kilmory 25 D3
Meikleour 28 D3
Melbourn 14 C5
Melbourne 13 F2
Melksham 6 C2
Melmerby 21 F3
Melrose 22 C2
Melsonby 18 B1
Meltham 18 B4
Melton 15 F4
Melton Mowbray 13 G2
Melvaig 31 E4
Melvich 32 C1
Memsie 33 F4
Menai Bridge 16 C3
Menston 18 B3
Menstrie 25 G2
Mere 6 C3
Meriden 13 E3
Merthyr Tydfil 11 E4
Messingham 19 D4
Metfield 15 F3
Metheringham 14 B1
Methlick 33 F5
Methven 28 C4
Methwold 15 D3
Mevagissey 4 C4
Mexborough 18 C5
Mey 34 A4
Miavaig 30 C3
Mickleton *Dur.* 23 D5
Mickleton *Glos.* 13 E5
Mid Ardlaw 33 F4
Midbea 34 B2
Middle Barton 13 F5
Middleham 18 B2
Middlemarsh 6 B4
Middle Rasen 19 E5
Middlesbrough 23 F5
Middlesmoor 18 B2
Middleton *Gt.Man.* 18 A4
Middleton *Norf.* 15 D2
Middleton Cheney 13 F5
Middleton-in-Teesdale 23 D5
Middleton-on-Sea 8 B5
Middleton-on-the-Wolds 19 E3
Middleton Stoney 13 F5
Middlewich 12 D1
Midhurst 8 A4
Midlem 22 C2
Midsomer Norton 6 B3
Mid Yell 35 F2
Milborne Port 6 B4
Milborne St. Andrew 6 C5
Mildenhall 15 D4
Mile End 15 E5
Milfield 23 D2
Milford 8 B3
Milford Haven 10 B4
Milford on Sea 7 D5
Millbrook 5 D4
Millhouse 24 D2
Millom 21 E5
Millport 25 D3
Milltown of Rothiemay 33 E5
Milnathort 28 D4
Milngavie 25 F2
Milnrow 18 A4
Milnthorpe 21 F5
Milovaig 30 C5
Milton *High.* 27 G1
Milton *P. & K.* 28 C3
Milton Keynes 13 G5
Milton of Campsie 25 F2
Milverton 6 A4
Minard 24 D2
Minchinhampton 6 C1
Minehead 5 F1
Minera 17 E4
Minnigaff 20 B2
Minster (Sheppey) *Kent* 9 E2
Minster (Thanet) *Kent* 9 F2
Minsterley 12 B3
Mintlaw 33 G5
Mirfield 18 B4
Misterton 19 D5
Mitcheldean 6 B1
Mobberley 18 A5
Modbury 5 E4
Moelfre 16 C3
Moffat 25 G3
Mold 17 E4
Molescroft 19 E3
Moniaive 25 F5
Monifieth 29 E3
Monimail 29 D4
Monkokehampton 5 E2
Monks Eleigh 15 E5
Monmouth 6 B1
Monreith 20 B3
Montgomery 12 B3
Montrose 29 F3

Moorends 18 D4
Morar 27 E2
Morebattle 22 D2
Morecambe 21 F5
Morenish 28 B3
Moresby 21 D3
Moreton 17 E3
Moretonhampstead 5 E3
Moreton-in-Marsh 13 E5
Morfa Nefyn 16 B4
Morley 18 B4
Morpeth 23 E3
Morriston 11 D4
Mortehoe 5 D1
Mortimer's Cross 12 C4
Morton (Bourne) *Lincs.* 14 B2
Morton (Gainsborough) *Lincs.* 19 D5
Morville 12 C3
Mosborough 18 C5
Moscow 25 E3
Mossat 29 E1
Mossblown 25 E4
Mossley 18 A4
Mosstodloch 33 D4
Motherwell 25 F3
Moulsecoomb 8 C4
Moulton *Lincs.* 14 C2
Moulton *Suff.* 15 D4
Mountain Ash 11 E4
Mountbenger 22 B2
Mountsorrel 13 F2
Moy 32 B5
Muchalls 29 F1
Much Wenlock 12 C3
Muirdrum 29 E3
Muirhead 29 D3
Muirkirk 25 F4
Muir of Fowlis 29 E1
Muir of Ord 32 B4
Mulbarton 15 F3
Mulben 33 D4
Mullion 4 B5
Mundesley 15 F2
Mundford 15 D3
Munlochy 32 B4
Murton 23 F5
Musbury 6 A5
Musselburgh 29 D5
Muthill 28 C4
Mybster 32 D1
Mytholmroyd 18 B4

N
Nailsea 6 B2
Nailsworth 6 C1
Nairn 32 C4
Nantwich 17 F4
Nantyglo 11 F4
Narberth 10 B4
Narborough *Leics.* 13 F3
Narborough *Norf.* 15 D2
Nateby 21 G4
Nazeing 8 C1
Near Sawrey 21 E4
Neath 11 D4
Necton 15 E3
Needham Market 15 E4
Needingworth 14 C4
Nefyn 16 B4
Neilston 25 E3
Nelson 18 A3
Nenthead 22 D5
Neston 17 E3
Nether Langwith 18 C5
Netherley 29 F1
Nether Stowey 6 A3
Netherton 23 D3
Nethy Bridge 32 C5
Nettlebed 8 A2
Nettleham 19 E5
New Abbey 21 D2
New Aberdour 33 F4
New Addington 8 C2
New Alresford 7 E3
Newark-on-Trent 13 G1
New Ash Green 8 D2
Newbiggin-by-the-Sea 23 F3
Newbigging 25 G3
Newbold Verdon 13 F3
Newborough 14 C3
Newbridge 11 F4
Newburgh *Aber.* 33 F5
Newburgh *Fife* 28 D4
Newburn 23 E4
Newbury 7 E2
Newby Bridge 21 E5
New Byth 33 F4
Newcastle 12 B3
Newcastle Emlyn 10 C3
Newcastle International Airport 23 E4
Newcastleton 22 C3
Newcastle-under-Lyme 13 D1
Newcastle upon Tyne 23 E4
New Cumnock 25 F4
New Deer 33 F5
Newent 12 D5
New Galloway 20 C2
Newhaven 8 C4
Newick 8 C4
Newington 9 E2
New Leeds 33 F4
New Luce 20 A2
Newlyn 4 A5
Newmachar 29 F1

Newmains 25 G3
Newmarket *Suff.* 14 D4
Newmarket *W.Isles* 30 D3
Newmill 33 E4
New Mills 18 A5
Newmilns 25 F4
New Milton 7 D5
New Mistley 15 F5
Newnham 6 B1
New Pitsligo 33 F4
Newport *Essex* 14 D5
Newport *High.* 32 D2
Newport *I.o.W.* 7 E5
Newport *Pembs.* 10 B3
Newport *Tel. & W.* 12 D2
Newport-on-Tay 29 E4
Newport Pagnell 13 G5
New Quay *Cere.* 10 C2
Newquay *Cornw.* 4 B4
New Radnor 12 B4
New Romney 9 E4
New Rossington 18 D5
Newton *Arg. & B.* 24 D2
Newton *Lancs.* 17 F1
Newton Abbot 5 F3
Newton Aycliffe 23 E5
Newton Ferrers 5 E4
Newtonhill 29 F1
Newton-le-Willows 17 F3
Newton Mearns 25 F3
Newtonmore 28 B1
Newton Poppleford 5 F3
Newton St. Cyres 5 F3
Newton Stewart 20 B2
Newtown *Here.* 12 C5
Newtown *Powys* 12 B3
Newtown St. Boswells 22 C2
New Tredegar 11 F4
Newtyle 29 D3
Neyland 10 B4
Ninemile Bar 20 D2
Ninfield 9 D4
Nisbet 22 C2
Norham 23 D1
Normanton 18 C4
Northallerton 18 C1
Northam 5 D2
Northampton 13 G4
North Baddesley 7 E4
North Ballachulish 27 F3
North Berwick 29 E5
North Cave 19 D3
North Cheriton 6 B4
North Cowton 18 B1
North Dell 31 D2
North Duffield 18 D3
North Elmham 15 E2
North Ferriby 19 E4
Northfleet 8 D2
North Grimston 19 D2
North Hykeham 14 B1
Northill 14 B5
North Kessock 32 B5
Northleach 6 D1
North Leigh 7 E1
North Middleton 22 B1
North Molton 5 E2
North Queensferry 28 D5
North Shields 23 F4
North Somercotes 19 F5
North Sunderland 23 E2
North Thoresby 19 F5
Northton 30 B4
North Walsham 15 F2
North Weald Bassett 8 C1
Northwich 17 F3
North Wingfield 13 F1
Northwood 7 E5
Norton *N.Yorks.* 19 D2
Norton *Suff.* 15 E4
Norton Canes 13 E3
Norton Fitzwarren 6 A4
Norwich 15 F3
Norwich Airport 15 F2
Norwick 35 G1
Nottingham 13 F1
Nottingham East Midlands Airport 13 F2
Nuneaton 13 F3

O
Oadby 13 G3
Oakdale 11 F4
Oakengates 12 C2
Oakham 13 G3
Oakley *Bucks.* 8 A1
Oakley *Fife* 25 G2
Oakley *Hants.* 7 E3
Oban 27 E5
Ochiltree 25 F4
Ockbrook 13 F2
Ockle 27 D3
Ockley 8 C3
Oddsta 35 F2
Odiham 8 A3
Ogmore 11 E4
Ogmore Vale 11 E4
Okehampton 5 E3
Oldbury 13 D3
Old Clipstone 13 G1
Old Colwyn 16 D3
Old Dailly 25 E5
Old Felixstowe 15 F5
Oldham 18 A4
Oldland 6 B2
Old Leake 14 C1
Oldmeldrum 33 F5
Old Town 21 F5

Olgrinmore 32 C1
Ollaberry 35 F2
Ollerton 13 G1
Olney 13 G4
Olveston 6 B2
Ombersley 12 D4
Onchan 20 B5
Onich 27 F3
Orford 15 G5
Ormesby St. Margaret 15 G2
Ormiston 22 C1
Ormskirk 17 F2
Orpington 8 C2
Orrell 17 F2
Orton 21 F4
Orton Longueville 14 B3
Oskaig 27 D1
Ossett 18 B4
Oswaldkirk 18 D2
Oswaldtwistle 18 A4
Oswestry 17 E5
Otford 8 D3
Otley *Suff.* 15 F4
Otley *W.Yorks.* 18 B3
Otterburn 23 D3
Otter Ferry 24 D2
Otterswick 35 F2
Ottery St. Mary 5 F3
Oughtibridge 18 C5
Oulton 15 G3
Oundle 14 B3
Outwell 14 D3
Overbister 34 B2
Overseal 13 E2
Overton *Hants.* 7 E3
Overton *Wrex.* 17 E4
Overtown 25 G3
Over Wallop 7 D3
Oxenhope 18 B3
Oxford 7 E1
Oxnam 22 C2
Oxshott 8 B2
Oxted 8 C3
Oxton 22 C1
Oykel Bridge 31 G4

P
Padbury 13 G5
Paddock Wood 9 D3
Padiham 18 A3
Padstow 4 C3
Paignton 5 F4
Painswick 6 C1
Paisley 25 E3
Palnackie 20 D2
Pandy 12 B5
Pangbourne 8 A2
Pant-y-dwr 11 E2
Papworth Everard 14 C4
Par 4 C4
Parbold 17 F2
Parkgate 25 G5
Partington 18 A5
Partney 14 C1
Parton 21 D3
Patchway 6 B2
Pateley Bridge 18 B2
Path of Condie 28 C4
Patna 25 E4
Patrick 20 B5
Patrington 19 F4
Patterdale 21 E4
Paulton 6 B3
Paxton 23 D1
Peacehaven 8 C4
Peasedown St. John 6 C3
Peebles 22 B1
Peel 20 B5
Pegswood 23 E3
Peinchorran 27 D1
Pelsall 13 E3
Pelynt 4 D4
Pembrey 10 C4
Pembridge 12 B4
Pembroke 10 B4
Pembroke Dock 10 B4
Pembury 8 D3
Penally 10 B4
Penarth 11 F5
Pencader 10 C3
Pencaitland 22 C1
Pencoed 11 E5
Pendeen 4 A5
Pendine 10 C4
Pendlebury 18 A4
Penicuik 22 B1
Peninver 24 C4
Penistone 18 B4
Penkridge 13 D2
Penley 12 C2
Penmaenmawr 16 C3
Pennyghael 27 D5
Penpont 25 G5
Penrhiw-pal 10 C3
Penrhyn Bay 16 D3
Penrhyndeudraeth 16 C5
Penrith 21 F3
Penryn 4 B5
Pensilva 4 D4
Pentir 16 C4
Pentraeth 16 C4
Pentre 11 E4
Pentrefoelas 16 D4
Penwortham 17 F2
Penybont 12 B4
Pen-y-bont-fawr 17 D5
Penygraig 11 E4

Place	Map	Grid
Penygroes	16	B4
Penywaun	11	E4
Penzance	4	A5
Perranporth	4	B4
Pershore	13	D5
Perth	28	D4
Peterborough	14	B3
Peterculter	29	F1
Peterhead	33	G5
Peterlee	23	F5
Petersfield	8	A4
Petworth	8	B4
Pevensey	8	D4
Pewsey	7	D2
Pickering	19	D2
Piddletrenthide	6	C5
Pierowall	34	B2
Pilgrims Hatch	8	D1
Pilling	17	F1
Pilning	6	B2
Pimperne	6	C4
Pinchbeck	14	C2
Pinhoe	5	F3
Pinwherry	25	D5
Pirbright	8	B3
Pirnmill	24	C3
Pitagowan	28	C2
Pitlochry	28	C3
Pitmedden	33	F5
Pitscottie	29	E4
Pitt	7	E4
Pittentrail	32	B3
Pittenweem	29	E4
Plean	25	G2
Pleasley	13	F1
Plwmp	10	C2
Plymouth	5	D4
Plymouth City Airport	5	E4
Plympton	5	E4
Plymstock	5	E4
Pocklington	19	D3
Polbeth	25	G3
Polegate	8	D4
Polesworth	13	E3
Polloch	27	E3
Polmont	25	G2
Polperro	4	D4
Polwarth	22	D1
Pondersbridge	14	C3
Pontardawe	11	D4
Pontarddulais	10	D4
Pontefract	18	C4
Ponteland	23	E4
Pontesbury	12	C3
Pontllanfraith	11	F4
Pontrhydfendigaid	11	D2
Pontrilas	12	B5
Pontyberem	10	D4
Pontycymer	11	E4
Pontypool	11	F4
Pontypridd	11	E5
Pool	18	B3
Poole	6	D5
Poolewe	31	E4
Pooley Bridge	21	F3
Porlock	5	F1
Port Appin	27	F4
Port Askaig	24	B3
Port Bannatyne	25	D3
Portchester	8	A4
Port Driseach	24	D2
Port Ellen	24	B3
Portencross	25	D3
Port Erin	20	B5
Portesham	6	B5
Port Eynon	10	C5
Port Glasgow	25	E2
Porth	11	E4
Porthcawl	11	E5
Port Henderson	31	E5
Porthleven	4	B5
Porthmadog	16	C5
Portishead	6	B2
Portknockie	33	E4
Portlethen	29	F1
Port Logan	20	A3
Portmahomack	32	C3
Portnacon	31	G2
Portnacroish	27	F4
Portnaguran	31	D3
Portnahaven	24	A3
Portnalong	26	D1
Port nan Long	30	B5
Port Ness	31	D2
Port of Menteith	28	B4
Portpatrick	20	A2
Portreath	4	B4
Portree	27	D1
Port St. Mary	20	B5
Portsmouth	8	A5
Portsoy	33	E4
Port Talbot	11	D4
Port William	20	B3
Potterne	6	C3
Potters Bar	8	C1
Potton	14	C5
Poulton-le-Fylde	17	E1
Powburn	23	E2
Powick	12	D4
Powmill	25	G2
Poynton	18	A5
Prees	12	C2
Preesall	17	E1
Prescot	17	F2
Prestatyn	17	D3
Prestbury *Ches.*	18	A5
Prestbury *Glos.*	13	D5
Presteigne	12	B4
Preston *Dorset*	6	C5
Preston *E.Riding*	19	E3
Preston *Lancs.*	17	F2
Preston *Sc.Bord.*	22	D1
Prestonpans	29	D5
Prestwich	18	A4
Prestwick	25	E4
Prestwick (Glasgow) International Airport	25	E4
Prestwood	8	A1
Princes Risborough	8	A1
Princethorpe	13	F4
Princetown	5	E3
Probus	4	B4
Prudhoe	23	E4
Puddletown	6	C5
Pudsey	18	B3
Pulborough	8	B4
Pumsaint	11	D3
Purfleet	8	D2
Purleigh	8	D1
Purley	8	C2
Purley on Thames	8	A2
Purton	6	D2
Pwllheli	16	B5
Pyle	11	E5

Q

Place	Map	Grid
Quarff	35	F4
Quedgeley	6	C1
Queenborough	9	E2
Queensbury	18	B3
Queensferry	17	E4
Queniborough	13	G2
Quernmore	21	F5

R

Place	Map	Grid
Rackheath	15	F2
Radcliffe	18	A4
Radcliffe on Trent	13	G2
Radford Semele	13	F4
Radlett	8	B1
Radstock	6	B3
Rafford	32	C4
Raglan	6	B1
Rainford	17	F2
Rainhill	17	F3
Rainow	18	A5
Rainworth	13	F1
Rait	28	D4
Rampside	21	E5
Ramsbottom	18	A4
Ramsbury	7	D2
Ramsey *Cambs.*	14	C3
Ramsey *I.o.M.*	20	B4
Ramsey St. Mary's	14	C3
Ramsgate	9	F2
Ranskill	18	D5
Rathillet	29	D4
Ratho	28	D5
Rattray	28	D3
Raunds	14	B4
Ravenglass	21	D4
Ravenshead	13	F1
Rawcliffe *E.Riding*	18	D4
Rawcliffe *York*	18	C3
Rawmarsh	18	C5
Rawtenstall	18	A4
Rayleigh	9	E1
Rayne	15	D5
Reading	8	A2
Reay	32	C1
Redbourn	8	B1
Redcar	23	G5
Redcastle	32	B5
Redcliff Bay	6	B2
Redditch	13	E4
Redford	29	E3
Redhill	8	C3
Redlynch	7	D4
Red Point	31	E5
Red Roses	10	C4
Redruth	4	B4
Reepham	15	E2
Reigate	8	C3
Reiss	33	D1
Renfrew	25	F3
Rennington	23	E2
Repton	13	F2
Rescobie	29	E3
Resolven	11	E4
Reston	23	D1
Retford	18	D5
Reydon	15	G4
Rhayader	11	E2
Rhiconich	31	G2
Rhoose	11	E5
Rhos	11	D4
Rhoslлanerchrugog	17	E4
Rhôs-on-Sea	16	D3
Rhossili	10	C5
Rhu	25	E2
Rhuddlan	17	D3
Rhyl	17	D3
Rhymney	11	F4
Rhynie	33	E5
Ribchester	17	F1
Richmond	18	B1
Rickarton	29	F2
Rickinghall	15	E4
Rickmansworth	8	B1
Riding Mill	23	E4
Rigside	25	G4
Ringford	20	C2
Ringmer	8	C4
Ringwood	7	D4
Ripley *Derbys.*	13	F1
Ripley *N.Yorks.*	18	B2
Ripon	18	C2
Ripple	13	D5
Ripponden	18	B4
Risca	11	F4
Rishton	18	A3
Risley	13	F2
Roade	13	G4
Roadside	32	D1
Roadside of Kinneff	29	F2
Roath	11	F5
Roberton *S.Lan.*	25	G4
Roberton *Sc.Bord.*	22	C2
Robin Hood's Bay	19	E1
Rocester	13	E2
Rochdale	18	A4
Roche	4	C4
Rochester *Med.*	8	D2
Rochester *Northumb.*	22	D3
Rochford	9	E1
Rock	12	D4
Rockcliffe	20	D2
Rockingham	13	G3
Rode Heath	12	D1
Rodel	30	C4
Rodney Stoke	6	B3
Rogart	32	B3
Rogate	8	A4
Rogerstone	11	F5
Romannobridge	22	B1
Romford	8	D2
Romsey	7	E4
Romsley	13	D3
Ropley	8	A3
Ropsley	14	B2
Rosedale Abbey	18	D1
Rosehearty	33	F4
Rosemarkie	32	B4
Rosewell	22	B1
Roshven	27	E3
Roskhill	26	C1
Roslin	22	B1
Rossett	17	E4
Rossington	18	D5
Ross-on-Wye	12	C5
Rothbury	23	E3
Rotherfield	8	D4
Rotherham	18	C5
Rothes	33	D5
Rothesay	25	D3
Rothiesholm	34	B3
Rothley	13	F2
Rothwell *Northants.*	13	G3
Rothwell *W.Yorks.*	18	C4
Rottingdean	8	C4
Roughton	15	F2
Roundway	6	D2
Rowde	6	C2
Rowhedge	23	E4
Rowlands Gill	23	E4
Roxton	14	B4
Royal Leamington Spa	13	F4
Royal Tunbridge Wells	8	D3
Roybridge	27	G3
Roydon	8	D1
Royston *Herts.*	14	C5
Royston *S.Yorks.*	18	C4
Royton	18	A4
Ruabon	17	E4
Ruardean	6	B1
Ruddington	13	F2
Rudgwick	8	B3
Rudston	19	E2
Rufford	17	F2
Rugby	13	F4
Rugeley	13	E2
Rumney	11	F5
Runcorn	17	F3
Runwell	9	D1
Rushall	13	E3
Rushden	14	B4
Rushmere St. Andrew	15	F5
Ruskington	14	B1
Ruspidge	6	B1
Rustington	8	B4
Rutherglen	25	F3
Ruthin	17	E4
Ruyton-XI-Towns	17	E5
Ryde	7	E5
Rye	9	E4
Ryhall	14	B2

S

Place	Map	Grid
Sacriston	23	E5
Saddell	24	C4
Saffron Walden	14	D5
Saham Toney	15	E3
Saighdinis	30	B5
St. Abbs	23	D1
St. Agnes	4	B4
St. Albans	8	B1
St. Andrews	29	E4
St. Anne	4	B1
St. Asaph	17	D3
St. Athan	11	E5
St. Austell	4	C4
St. Bees	21	D4
St. Brelade	4	B3
St. Briavels	6	B1
St. Brides Major	11	E5
St. Buryan	4	A5
St. Clears	10	C4
St. Columb Major	4	C4
St. Combs	33	G4
St. Cyrus	29	F2
St. David's	10	A3
St. Day	4	B4
St. Dennis	4	C4
St. Dogmaels	10	B3
St. Endellion	4	C3
St. Enoder	4	B4
St. Fergus	33	G4
St. Fillans	28	B4
St. Germans	5	D4
St. Helens	17	F3
St. Helier	4	B3
St. Ishmael	10	C4
St. Ive	5	D4
St. Ives *Cambs.*	14	C4
St. Ives *Cornw.*	4	A4
St. John	4	B3
St. John's Chapel	23	D5
St. John's Town of Dalry	25	F5
St. Just	4	A5
St. Just in Roseland	4	B5
St. Keverne	4	B5
St. Leonards	6	D4
St. Margaret's at Cliffe	9	F3
St. Margaret's Hope	34	B4
St. Martin	4	A2
St. Martin's	17	E5
St. Mary Bourne	7	E3
St. Mary's	34	B3
St. Mary's Bay	9	E4
St. Mawes	4	B5
St. Merryn	4	B3
St. Monans	29	E4
St. Neots	14	B4
St. Osyth	9	F1
St. Peter Port	4	A2
St. Peter's	9	F2
St. Sampson	4	A2
St. Stephen	4	C4
St. Teath	4	C3
Salcombe	5	E5
Sale	18	A5
Salen *Arg. & B.*	27	D4
Salen *High.*	27	E3
Salford	18	A5
Salfords	8	C3
Salhouse	15	F2
Saline	25	G2
Salisbury	6	D3
Salsburgh	25	G3
Saltash	5	D4
Saltburn-by-the-Sea	23	G5
Saltcoats	25	E3
Saltdean	8	C4
Saltford	6	B2
Saltney	17	E4
Sanaigmore	24	A3
Sandbach	12	D1
Sandgarth	34	B3
Sandhead	20	A2
Sandhurst	8	A2
Sandiacre	13	F2
Sandness	35	E3
Sandown	7	E5
Sandplace	4	D4
Sandridge	8	B1
Sandsend	19	D1
Sandwich	9	F3
Sandwick	35	F4
Sandy	14	B5
Sandygate	20	B4
Sanquhar	25	F5
Sapcote	13	F3
Sarre	9	F2
Satley	23	E5
Saundersfoot	10	B4
Sawbridgeworth	8	C1
Sawston	14	C5
Sawtry	14	B3
Saxilby	19	D5
Saxmundham	15	F4
Saxthorpe	15	F2
Scalasaig	24	B2
Scalby	19	E2
Scalloway	35	F4
Scampton	19	E5
Scapa	34	B3
Scarborough	19	E2
Scarcliffe	13	F1
Scarinish	26	C4
Scarisbrick	17	E2
Scleddau	10	B3
Scole	15	F4
Scone	28	D4
Sconser	27	D1
Scorton	18	B1
Scotch Corner	18	B1
Scotter	19	D4
Scotton	18	B1
Scourie	31	F2
Scousburgh	35	F5
Scrabster	32	C1
Scraptoft	13	G3
Scremerston	23	E1
Scunthorpe	19	D4
Seaford	8	C5
Seaham	23	F5
Seahouses	23	E2
Seamer	19	E2
Seamill	25	D3
Seascale	21	D4
Seaton *Cumb.*	21	D3
Seaton *Devon*	6	A5
Seaton Delaval	23	F4
Seaton Sluice	23	F4
Sedbergh	21	F4
Sedgebrook	13	G2
Sedgefield	23	F5
Sedgley	13	D3
Seend	6	C2
Seghill	23	E4
Seighford	13	D2
Selattyn	17	E5
Selby	18	D3
Selkirk	22	C2
Sellafield	21	D4
Sellafirth	35	F2
Sellindge	9	E3
Selsey	8	A5
Selston	13	F1
Send	8	B3
Sennen	4	A5
Sennybridge	11	E3
Setter	35	F3
Settle	21	G5
Sevenoaks	8	D3
Seven Sisters	11	E4
Severn Beach	6	B2
Sgiogarstaigh	31	D2
Shaftesbury	6	C4
Shalfleet	7	E5
Shalford	8	B3
Shanklin	7	E5
Shap	21	F4
Sharpness	6	B1
Shavington	17	F4
Shaw	18	A4
Shawbost	30	C2
Sheering	8	D1
Sheerness	9	E2
Sheffield	18	C5
Sheffield City Airport	18	C5
Shefford	14	B5
Shelf	18	B4
Shelford	14	B5
Shenstone	13	E3
Shepley	18	B4
Shepperton	8	B2
Shepshed	13	F2
Shepton Mallet	6	B3
Sherborne	4	A5
Sherborne St. John	8	A3
Sherburn	23	F5
Sherburn in Elmet	18	C3
Shere	8	B3
Sheriffhales	12	D2
Sheriff Hutton	18	D2
Sheringham	15	F1
Sherston	6	C2
Shevington	17	F2
Shiel Bridge	27	F2
Shieldaig	31	E5
Shifnal	12	D3
Shilbottle	23	E3
Shildon	23	E5
Shinfield	8	A2
Shinness Lodge	32	B2
Shiplake	8	A2
Shipley	18	B3
Shipston on Stour	13	E5
Shipton *N.Yorks.*	18	C3
Shipton *Shrop.*	12	C3
Shipton-under-Wychwood	7	D1
Shirebrook	13	F1
Shiremoor	23	F4
Shirenewton	6	B1
Shirland	13	F1
Shoeburyness	9	E2
Shoreham	9	F3
Shoreham-by-Sea	8	C4
Shotley Gate	15	F5
Shotton	17	E4
Shotts	25	G3
Shrewsbury	12	C2
Shrewton	6	D3
Shrivenham	7	D2
Sible Hedingham	15	D5
Sibsey	14	C1
Sidbury	6	A5
Sidcup	8	C2
Sidford	6	A5
Sidley	9	D4
Sidmouth	6	A5
Sigglesthorne	19	E3
Sileby	13	G2
Silloth	21	E2
Silsden	18	B3
Silsoe	14	B5
Silverdale	21	F5
Silverstone	13	G5
Silverton	5	F2
Simonsbath	5	E1
Sittingbourne	9	E2
Siulaisiadar	31	D3
Skaill (East Coast) *Ork.*	34	B3
Skaill (West Coast) *Ork.*	34	A3
Skaw	35	F3
Skegness	14	D1
Skelmersdale	17	F2
Skelmorlie	25	D3
Skelton	18	D1
Skelwick	34	B2
Skenfrith	12	C5
Skerray	32	B1
Skipness	24	D3
Skipsea	19	E3
Skipton	18	A3
Skirlaugh	19	E3
Slaidburn	18	A3
Slaithwaite	18	B4
Slamannan	25	G2
Sleaford	14	B1
Sledmere	19	E2
Sleights	19	D1
Sligachan	27	D1
Slinfold	8	B3
Slough	8	B2
Smailholm	22	C2
Smalley	13	F1
Smeeth	9	E3
Smethwick	13	E3
Snainton	19	E2
Snaith	18	D4
Snettisham	15	D2
Snitterfield	13	E4
Snodland	9	D2
Soham	14	D4
Solihull	13	E4
Sollas	30	B5
Solva	10	A3
Somercotes	13	F1
Somersham	14	C4
Somerton	6	B4
Sompting	8	B4
Sonning Common	8	A2
Sorbie	20	B3
Sorisdale	26	C3
Sorn	25	F4
Southam	6	C4
Southampton	7	E4
Southampton Airport	7	E4
South Anston	18	C5
South Bank	23	F5
South Benfleet	9	D2
Southborough	8	D3
Southbourne	8	A4
South Brent	5	E4
South Cave	19	E3
South Chard	6	A4
Southdean	22	C3
Southend	24	C5
Southend-on-Sea	9	E2
Southery	14	D3
Southgate	8	C1
South Harting	8	A4
South Hetton	23	F5
South Kelsey	19	E5
South Kirkby	18	C4
South Leverton	19	D5
South Lopham	15	E3
Southminster	9	E1
South Molton	5	E2
South Normanton	13	F1
South Ockendon	8	D2
South Oxhey	8	B1
South Petherton	6	B4
Southport	17	E2
South Queensferry	28	D5
South Shields	23	F4
Southwell	13	G1
Southwick	6	C3
Southwold	15	G4
South Woodham Ferrers	9	E1
South Wootton	14	D2
Sowerby	18	C2
Sowerby Bridge	18	B4
Spalding	14	C2
Spean Bridge	27	G3
Speen	7	E2
Spennymoor	23	E5
Spey Bay	33	D4
Spilsby	14	C1
Spinningdale	32	B3
Spittal	32	D1
Spittal of Glenshee	28	D2
Spixworth	15	F2
Spofforth	18	C3
Springholm	20	D2
Springside	25	E4
Sproatley	19	E3
Sprowston	15	F2
Sproxton	18	D2
Stadhampton	8	A1
Staffin	31	D5
Stafford	13	D2
Staindrop	23	E5
Staines	8	B2
Stainforth *N.Yorks.*	21	G5
Stainforth *S.Yorks.*	18	D4
Staintondale	19	E1
Stalbridge	6	C4
Stalham	15	F2
Stalling Busk	21	G5
Stalybridge	18	A5
Stamford	14	B3
Stamfordham	23	E4
Standish	17	F2
Standon	14	C5
Stane	25	G3
Stanford-le-Hope	9	D2
Stanhoe	15	E2
Stanhope	23	D5
Stanley *Dur.*	23	E4
Stanley *P. & K.*	28	D3
Stanley *W.Yorks.*	18	C4
Stannington	23	E4
Stansted (London) Airport	14	D5
Stansted Mountfitchet	14	D5
Stanton	15	E4
Stanway	15	E5
Stapleford	13	F2
Staplehurst	9	D3
Starcross	5	F3
Startforth	18	B1
Staunton	12	D5
Staveley	18	B1
Staxton	19	E2
Steeple Claydon	13	G5
Steeton	18	B3
Stenhousemuir	25	G2
Stenness	35	E3
Stenton	29	E5
Steornabhagh	30	D3
Stevenage	14	C5
Stevenston	25	E3
Stewarton	25	E3
Steyning	8	B4
Stibb Cross	5	D2
Stichill	22	D2
Stickney	14	C1
Stilligarry	26	B1
Stillington	18	C2
Stilton	14	B3

Stirling 25 F2
Stobo 22 B2
Stock 9 D1
Stockbridge 7 E3
Stockport 18 A5
Stocksbridge 18 B5
Stocksfield 23 E4
Stockton Heath 17 F3
Stockton-on-Tees 23 F5
Stoer 31 F3
Stoke Albany 13 G3
Stoke Ash 15 F4
Stoke-by-Nayland 15 E5
Stoke Holy Cross 15 F3
Stoke Mandeville 8 A1
Stokenchurch 8 A1
Stokenham 5 F4
Stoke-on-Trent 13 D1
Stoke Poges 8 B2
Stoke Prior 13 D4
Stokesay 12 C3
Stokesley 18 C1
Stone *Glos.* 6 B1
Stone *Kent* 8 D2
Stone *Staffs.* 13 D2
Stonehaven 29 F2
Stonehouse *Glos.* 6 C1
Stonehouse *S.Lan.* 25 F3
Stoneykirk 20 A2
Stoneybreck 35 E5
Stony Stratford 13 G5
Stornoway 30 D3
Storrington 8 B4
Stotfold 14 C5
Stourbridge 13 D3
Stourport-on-Severn 12 D4
Stow 22 C1
Stowmarket 15 E4
Stow-on-the-Wold 13 E5
Strachan 29 E1
Strachur 27 F5
Stradbroke 15 F4
Stradishall 15 D4
Stradsett 15 D3
Straloch 28 C2
Stranraer 20 A2
Stratford-upon-Avon 13 E4
Strathaven 25 F3
Strathblane 25 F2
Strathdon 29 D1
Strathmiglo 28 D4
Strathpeffer 31 G5
Strathy 32 C1
Strathyre 28 B4
Stratton 4 D2
Stratton St. Margaret 7 D2
Streatley 7 E2
Street 6 B3
Strensall 18 D2
Stretford 18 A5
Stretham 14 D4
Stretton 13 E2
Strichen 33 F4
Stromeferry 27 E1
Stromness 34 A3
Stronachlachar 27 G5
Strone 25 D2
Strontian 27 E3
Stroud 6 C1
Stuartfield 33 F5
Studley 13 E4
Sturminster Newton 6 C4
Sturry 9 F2
Sturton le Steeple 19 D5
Sudbury *Derbys.* 13 E2
Sudbury *Suff.* 15 E5
Sully 11 F5
Sumburgh 35 F5
Summer Bridge 18 B2
Sunbury 8 B2
Sunderland 23 F4
Sunninghill 8 B2
Surfleet 14 C2
Sutterton 14 C2
Sutton 14 C4
Sutton Bridge 14 C2
Sutton Coldfield 13 E3
Sutton Courtenay 7 E1
Sutton in Ashfield 13 F1
Sutton-on-the-Forest 18 C2
Sutton on Trent 13 G1
Sutton Valence 9 E3
Swadlincote 13 F2
Swaffham 15 E3
Swanage 6 D5
Swanland 19 E4
Swanley 8 D2
Swanscombe 8 D2
Swansea 11 D4
Swanton Morley 15 E2
Sway 7 D5
Swindon 7 D2
Swindon Village 13 D5
Swinefleet 19 D4
Swinton *Gt.Man.* 18 A4
Swinton *S.Yorks.* 18 C5
Swinton *Sc.Bord.* 22 D1
Symbister 35 F3
Symington *S.Ayr.* 25 E4
Symington *S.Lan.* 25 G4
Synod Inn 10 C2
Syre 32 B1
Syston 13 G2

T
Tadcaster 18 C3
Tadley 8 A2
Taffs Well 11 F5
Tain 32 B3

Takeley 14 D5
Talgarreg 10 C2
Talgarth 12 B5
Taliesin 11 D1
Talisker 26 D1
Talladale 31 F5
Tamworth 13 E3
Tannadice 29 E3
Tansley 13 F1
Tarbert (Jura) *Arg. & B.* 24 C2
Tarbert (Kintyre) *Arg. & B.* 24 C3
Tarbert *W.Isles* 30 C4
Tarbet 27 G5
Tarbolton 25 E4
Tarfside 29 E2
Tarleton 17 F2
Tarporley 17 F4
Tarrel 32 C3
Tarves 33 F5
Tarvin 17 F4
Tattershall 14 C1
Taunton 6 A4
Taverham 15 F2
Tavistock 5 D3
Tayinloan 24 C3
Taynuilt 27 F4
Tayport 29 E4
Tayvallich 24 C2
Teangue 27 E2
Tebay 21 F4
Teesside International Airport 18 C1
Teignmouth 5 F3
Telford 12 C3
Temple Bar 10 D2
Temple Sowerby 21 F3
Templeton 10 B4
Tenbury Wells 12 C4
Tenby 10 B4
Tenterden 9 E3
Terrington 18 D2
Terrington St. Clement 14 D2
Tetbury 6 C1
Tetford 19 F5
Tetney 19 F4
Teviothead 22 C3
Tewkesbury 13 D5
Teynham 9 E2
Thame 8 A1
Thatcham 7 E2
Thaxted 14 D5
Theale 8 A2
The Mumbles 10 D5
The Stocks 9 E4
Thetford 15 E3
Thirsk 18 C2
Thornaby-on-Tees 18 C1
Thornbury 6 B2
Thorne 18 D4
Thorney 14 C3
Thorngumbald 19 F4
Thornhill *D. & G.* 25 G5
Thornhill *Stir.* 28 B4
Thornley 23 F5
Thornton *Fife* 29 D5
Thornton *Lancs.* 17 E1
Thornton *Mersey.* 17 E2
Thornton-le-Dale 19 D2
Thorpe-le-Soken 15 F5
Thorpe Market 15 F2
Thorpeness 15 G4
Thorpe on the Hill 13 G1
Thorpe St. Andrew 15 F3
Thrapston 14 B4
Threlkeld 21 E3
Threshfield 21 G5
Thropton 23 E3
Thrumster 33 D1
Thrupp 6 C1
Thrybergh 18 C5
Thundersley 9 D2
Thurcroft 18 C5
Thurlby 14 B2
Thurmaston 13 G3
Thurnscoe 18 C4
Thursby 21 E2
Thurso 32 D1
Thurton 15 F3
Thwaite 21 G4
Tibbermore 28 C4
Tibshelf 13 F1
Ticehurst 9 D3
Ticknall 13 F2
Tidenham 6 B1
Tideswell 18 B5
Tidworth 7 D3
Tighnabruaich 24 D2
Tilbury 8 D2
Tilehurst 8 A2
Tillicoultry 25 G2
Tillyfourie 29 E1
Tilston 17 F4
Timsbury 6 B3
Timsgearraidh 30 C3
Tingewick 13 G5
Tingwall 34 B3
Tintagel 4 C3
Tintern Parva 6 B1
Tiptree 9 E1
Tisbury 6 C4
Tiverton 5 F2
Toab 35 F5
Tobermory 27 D4
Toberonochy 27 E5
Toddington *Beds.* 14 B5
Toddington *Glos.* 13 E5
Todmorden 18 A4

Toft 35 F3
Togston 23 E3
Tolastadh a'Chaolais 30 C3
Tolastadh 31 D2
Tollesbury 9 E1
Tolleshunt D'Arcy 9 E1
Toll of Birness 33 G5
Tomatin 32 C5
Tomich 32 B4
Tomintoul 28 D1
Tomnavoulin 32 D5
Tonbridge 8 D3
Tongland 20 C2
Tongue 32 B1
Tonna 11 D4
Tonyrefail 11 E5
Topcliffe 18 C2
Topsham 5 F3
Tore 32 B4
Tormore 24 D4
Torphichen 25 G2
Torphins 29 E1
Torpoint 5 D4
Torquay 5 F4
Torrance 25 F2
Torridon 31 F5
Torrin 27 D1
Torthorwald 21 D2
Torver 21 E4
Toscaig 27 E1
Tosside 18 A3
Totland 7 E5
Totnes 5 F4
Tottington 18 A4
Totton 7 E4
Towcester 13 G5
Tow Law 23 E5
Townhead of Greenlaw 20 C2
Town Yetholm 22 D2
Towyn 17 D3
Trawsfynydd 16 C5
Trecastle 11 E3
Tredegar 11 F4
Tredington 13 E5
Treeton 18 C5
Trefaldwyn 12 B3
Trefeglwys 11 E1
Trefriw 16 C4
Trefynwy 6 B1
Tregaron 11 D2
Tregony 4 C4
Tregynon 11 E1
Treharris 11 E4
Treherbert 11 E4
Trelech 10 C3
Trelleck 6 B1
Tremadog 16 C4
Trenance 4 B4
Treorchy 11 E4
Tressait 28 C2
Tretower 12 B5
Trimdon 23 F5
Trimsaran 10 C4
Tring 8 B1
Trinity 29 E2
Trochry 28 C3
Troedyrhiw 11 E4
Troon 25 E4
Troutbeck 21 F4
Troutbeck Bridge 21 F4
Trowbridge 6 C3
Trumpington 14 C4
Truro 4 B4
Tudweiliog 16 B5
Tummel Bridge 28 B3
Tunga 30 D3
Tunstall 15 F4
Tunbridge Wells 8 D3
Turnberry 25 E5
Turners Hill 8 C3
Turriff 33 F4
Tutbury 13 F2
Tutshill 6 B1
Tuxford 18 D5
Twatt 34 A3
Twechar 25 F2
Tweedmouth 23 D1
Tweedsmuir 25 G4
Twyford *Hants.* 7 E4
Twyford *W'ham* 8 A2
Twynholm 20 C2
Twyning 13 D5
Tyndrum 27 G4
Tynemouth 23 F4
Tythegston 11 E5
Tywardreath 4 C4
Tywyn 10 D1

U
Uachdar 30 B5
Uckfield 8 C4
Uddingston 25 F3
Uddington 25 G4
Uffculme 5 F2
Uig 30 D5
Ulbster 33 D1
Ulceby 19 E4
Ulgham 23 E3
Ullapool 31 F4
Ulleskelf 18 C3
Ulpha 21 E4
Ulsta 35 F2
Ulverston 21 E5
Umberleigh 5 E2
Unapool 31 G3
Undy 6 B2
Unstone 18 C5

Upavon 6 D3
Up Holland 17 F2
Uplyme 6 A5
Upper Clatford 7 E3
Upper Heyford 13 F5
Upper Knockando 32 D5
Upper Tean 13 E2
Uppingham 13 G3
Upton *Ches.* 17 F4
Upton *Dorset* 6 C5
Upton St. Leonards 6 C1
Upton upon Severn 12 D5
Urafirth 35 F3
Urmston 18 A5
Ushaw Moor 23 E5
Usk 11 F4
Uttoxeter 13 E2
Uxbridge 8 B2
Uyeasound 35 F2

V
Valley 16 B3
Valsgarth 35 G1
Veensgarth 35 F4
Ventnor 7 E5
Verwood 6 D4
Vickerstown 21 E5
Vidlin 35 F3
Virginia Water 8 B2
Voe 35 F3

W
Waddesdon 8 A1
Waddington 14 B1
Wadebridge 4 C3
Wadhurst 8 D3
Wainfleet All Saints 14 C1
Wainhouse Corner 4 C3
Wakefield 18 C4
Walberswick 15 G4
Walderslade 9 D2
Wales 18 C5
Wallasey 17 E3
Wallingford 8 A2
Walls 34 E4
Wallsend 23 F4
Walmer 9 F3
Walsall 13 E3
Waltham 19 F4
Waltham Abbey 8 C1
Waltham on the Wolds 13 G2
Walton-le-Dale 17 F2
Walton on the Naze 15 F5
Wantage 7 E2
Warboys 14 C4
Warcop 21 G4
Wardington 13 F5
Ware 8 C1
Wareham 6 C5
Wargrave 8 A2
Wark 23 D4
Warkworth 23 E3
Warlingham 8 C3
Warmington 13 F5
Warminster 6 C3
Warrington 17 F3
Warslow 13 E1
Warton 21 F5
Warwick 13 E4
Warwick Bridge 21 F2
Wasbister 34 A2
Washingborough 19 E5
Washington 23 F4
Wass 18 C2
Watchet 5 F1
Watchgate 21 F4
Waterbeach 14 C4
Waterbeck 21 E2
Waterlooville 8 A4
Water Orton 13 E3
Watford 8 B1
Wath upon Dearne 18 C4
Watlington 8 A1
Watten 32 D1
Watton 15 E3
Watton-at-Stone 8 C1
Weaverham 17 F3
Wedmore 6 B3
Wednesbury 13 D3
Weedon Bec 13 G4
Weem 28 C3
Weldon 14 B3
Wellesbourne 13 E4
Wellingborough 13 G4
Wellington *Som.* 6 A4
Wellington *Tel. & W.* 12 C2
Wells 6 B3
Wells-next-the-Sea 15 E1
Welney 14 D3
Welshpool 12 B3
Welton 19 E5
Welwyn 8 C1
Welwyn Garden City 8 C1
Wem 12 C2
Wembdon 6 A3
Wemyss Bay 25 D3
Wendens Ambo 14 D5
Wendover 8 A1
Wendron 4 B5
Wensley 18 B1
Wentworth 18 C5
Weobley 12 B4
Wereham 15 D3
West Auckland 23 E5
West Bergholt 15 E5
West Bridgford 13 F2
West Bromwich 13 E3
Westbury 6 C3

West Calder 25 G3
West Coker 6 B4
Westcott 8 B3
Westerdale 32 D1
Westergate 8 B4
Westerham 8 C3
Westfield 9 E4
Westgate 23 D5
West Grinstead 8 B4
West Haddon 13 G4
West Harptree 6 B3
Westhill *Aber.* 29 F1
West Hill *Devon* 5 F3
West Kilbride 25 E3
West Kirby 17 E3
West Knapton 19 D2
West Lavington 6 D3
Westleton 15 G4
West Linton 22 B1
West Lulworth 6 C5
West Malling 9 D3
West Meon 8 A4
West Mersea 9 E1
West Monkton 6 A4
West Moors 6 D4
Westness 34 A3
Westnewton 21 E3
Weston *Dorset* 6 B5
Weston *Staffs.* 13 D2
Weston-super-Mare 11 F5
Westonzoyland 6 A3
Westruther 22 C1
West Somerton 15 G2
West Tarbert 24 C3
Westward Ho! 5 D2
West Winch 14 D2
West Wycombe 8 A1
West Yell 35 F2
Wetheral 21 F2
Wetherby 18 C3
Weybridge 8 B2
Weymouth 6 B5
Whaley Bridge 18 B5
Whalton 23 E3
Whaplode 14 C2
Whauphill 20 B3
Wheatley Hill 23 F5
Wheaton Aston 13 D2
Wheddon Cross 5 F1
Wherwell 7 E3
Whickham 23 E4
Whiddon Down 5 E3
Whimple 5 F3
Whiston 18 C5
Whitburn 25 G3
Whitby 19 D1
Whitchurch *Bucks.* 13 G5
Whitchurch *Cardiff* 11 F5
Whitchurch *Hants.* 7 E3
Whitchurch *Shrop.* 17 F4
Whitecraig 29 D5
Whitehall 34 B3
Whitehaven 21 D4
Whitehill 8 A3
Whitehills 33 E4
Whiterashes 33 F5
Whitfield 9 F3
Whithorn 20 B3
Whiting Bay 24 D4
Whitland 10 C4
Whitley Bay 23 F4
Whitnash 13 F4
Whitstable 9 F2
Whittingham 23 E2
Whittington 17 E5
Whittlesey 14 C3
Whitworth 18 A4
Wick *High.* 33 D1
Wick *S.Glos.* 6 C2
Wick *V. of Glam.* 11 E5
Wick *W.Suss.* 8 B4
Wickersley 18 C5
Wickford 9 D1
Wickham 7 E4
Wickham Market 15 F4
Wickwar 6 C2
Widecombe in the Moor 5 E3
Widford 8 C1
Widnes 17 F3
Wigan 17 F2
Wigmore 12 C4
Wigston 13 G3
Wigton 21 E3
Wigtown 20 B2
Willaston 17 E3
Willingdon 8 D4
Willingham 14 C4
Willington *Derbys.* 13 E2
Willington *Dur.* 23 E5
Williton 5 F1
Willoughby 19 F5
Wilmington 8 D2
Wilmslow 18 A5
Wilton 6 D3
Wimblington 14 C3
Wimborne Minster 6 D4
Wincanton 6 C4
Winchburgh 25 G2
Winchcombe 13 E5
Winchelsea 9 E4
Winchester 7 E4
Windermere 21 F4
Windsor 8 B2
Windygates 29 D4
Winford 6 B2
Wing 13 G5
Wingate 23 F5
Wingerworth 13 F1
Wingham 9 F3

Winkfield 8 B2
Winkleigh 5 E2
Winnersh 8 A2
Winscombe 6 B3
Winsford 17 F4
Winsley 6 C2
Winslow 13 G5
Winston 18 B1
Winterbourne 6 B2
Winterbourne Abbas 6 B5
Winterton 19 E4
Winton 21 G4
Winwick 14 B3
Wirksworth 13 E1
Wisbech 14 C3
Wishaw 25 F3
Wistanstow 12 C3
Wistaston 17 F4
Witham 9 E1
Witheridge 5 F2
Withernsea 19 F4
Witley 8 B3
Witney 7 E1
Wittering 14 B3
Witton Gilbert 23 E5
Wiveliscombe 5 F2
Wivenhoe 15 E5
Woburn 14 B5
Woburn Sands 14 B5
Woking 8 B3
Wokingham 8 A2
Wold Newton 19 E2
Wollaston 14 B4
Wolston 13 F4
Wolverhampton 13 D3
Wolverley 12 D4
Wolverton 13 G5
Wombourne 13 D3
Wombwell 18 C4
Wooburn 8 B2
Woodborough 13 G1
Woodbridge 15 F5
Woodcote 8 A2
Woodhall Spa 14 B1
Woodingdean 8 C4
Woodland 23 E5
Woodley 8 A2
Woodmansey 19 E3
Woodplumpton 17 F1
Woodstock 7 E1
Woodton 15 F3
Woodville 13 F2
Wool 6 C5
Woolacombe 5 D1
Wooler 23 D2
Woolston 17 F3
Wootton 14 B5
Wootton Bassett 6 D2
Worcester 12 D4
Worfield 12 D3
Workington 21 D3
Worksop 18 C5
Wormit 29 D4
Worplesdon 8 B3
Worth 8 C3
Worthing 8 B4
Wotton-under-Edge 6 C1
Woughton on the Green 13 G5
Wragby 19 E5
Wrangle 14 C1
Wrea Green 17 E1
Wrelton 19 D2
Wrexham 17 E4
Wrington 6 B2
Writtle 9 D1
Wroughton 6 D2
Wyberton 14 C1
Wye 9 E3
Wylye 6 D3
Wymondham *Leics.* 13 G2
Wymondham *Norf.* 15 F3
Wyre Piddle 13 D5
Wythall 13 E4

Y
Yapton 8 B4
Yarm 18 C1
Yarmouth 7 E5
Yarnton 7 E1
Yarrow 22 B2
Yate 6 C2
Yateley 8 A2
Yatton 6 B2
Yaxley 14 B3
Y Drenewydd 12 B3
Yeadon 18 B3
Yealmpton 5 E4
Yeovil 6 B4
Yeovilton 6 B4
Yetts o' Muckhart 28 C4
Ynysddu 11 F4
York 18 D3
Youlgreave 13 E1
Yoxall 13 E2
Yoxford 15 F4
Ysbyty Ystwyth 11 D2
Ystalyfera 11 D4
Ystrad 11 E4
Ystradgynlais 11 D4

Z
Zennor 4 A5

Index to urban & central city maps

This index lists towns and cities geographically starting in the south, progressing northwards. The same order is used for the maps in the atlas. Street and place names are shown for each area. **Bold** entries refer to place names.

BIRMINGHAM CENTRAL	152	GREATER MANCHESTER URBAN	161	MILTON KEYNES URBAN	135
BIRMINGHAM URBAN	150	LEEDS CENTRAL	167	NEWCASTLE UPON TYNE URBAN	168
BOURNEMOUTH URBAN	130	LEEDS URBAN	165	NEWPORT URBAN	133
BRADFORD URBAN	165	LEICESTER URBAN	154	NOTTINGHAM URBAN	154
BRISTOL URBAN	134	LIVERPOOL CENTRAL	159	PLYMOUTH URBAN	130
CARDIFF URBAN	133	LIVERPOOL URBAN	158	PORTSMOUTH URBAN	131
COVENTRY URBAN	153	LONDON CENTRAL	142	SHEFFIELD URBAN	157
DERBY URBAN	154	LONDON URBAN	136	SOUTHAMPTON URBAN	131
EDINBURGH URBAN	169	MANCHESTER CENTRAL	163	STOKE-ON-TRENT URBAN	156
GLASGOW CENTRAL	171	MANCHESTER URBAN	161	SWANSEA URBAN	133
GLASGOW URBAN	170	MERSEYSIDE URBAN	158	WEST MIDLANDS URBAN	150

PLYMOUTH URBAN page 36

Albert Rd	A2	Crownhill Rd	A1	Haye Rd	C2	**Membland**	C3
Allern La	A1	Culver Way	B1	**Hemerdon**	C1	Merafield Rd	C2
Alma Rd	A2	Dean Hill	B2	Hemerdon La	C1	Milford La	A1
Anderton	A2	Delamere Rd	B1	**Heybrook Bay**	B3	Miller Way	B1
Antony Rd	A2	Derriford Rd	B1	Hoe Rd	A2	Molesworth Rd	A2
Bampton Rd	B1	**Devonport**	A2	**Holbeton**	D3	**Mothecombe**	D3
Barne Barton	A1	Devonport Rd	A2	**Hollacombe Hill**	C3	**Mount Gould**	B2
Barne Rd	A1	**Down Thomas**	B3	Holland Rd	C2	**Mount Wise**	A2
Battisborough Cross	D3	**Drakeland Corner**	C1	Honicknowe La	A1	**Mutley**	B2
Beacon Pk Rd	A1	Dunnet Rd	B1	**Honicknowle**	A1	Newnham Rd	C1
Beaumont Rd	B2	**Dunstone**	D3	**Hooe**	B2	New Pk Rd	D2
Beech Rd	D2	Durnford St	A2	Hooe Hill	B2	New Rd (Cawsand)	A3
Billacombe	B2	**Efford**	B2	Hooe La	B3	New Rd (Lutton)	D1
Billacombe Rd	B2	Efford La	B2	Hooe Rd	B2	**Newton Ferrers**	C3
Blandford Rd	B2	Efford Rd	B2	Hunsdown Rd	D2	North Hill	B2
Blunts La	B1	**Eggbuckland**	B1	**Insworke**	A2	North Prospect Rd	A1
Bodmin Rd	A1	Eggbuckland Rd	B2	**Keyham**	A2	North Rd (Saltash)	A1
Bond St	D1	**Elburton**	C2	**Kingsand**	A3	North Rd (Torpoint)	A2
Bridgend	C3	Elburton Rd	B2	**Kings Tamerton**	A1	North Rd E	B2
Brixton	C2	Embankment Rd	B2	**Kitley**	C3	North Rd W	A2
Budshead Rd	A1	**Ernesettle**	A1	**Knighton**	C3	**Noss Mayo**	C3
Cadleigh	D2	Ernesettle La	A1	**Laira**	B2	Novorossisk Rd	B1
Cadleigh Park	D2	**Estover**	B1	**Landulph**	A1	Old Laira Rd	B2
Carbeile Rd	A2	**Ford**	A2	**Langage**	C2	Orchard Hill	D2
Cattedown	B2	**Ford (Holbeton)**	D3	Larkham La	C2	**Oreston**	B2
Cawsand	A3	Forder Valley Rd	B1	**Lee Mill Bridge**	D2	Oreston Rd	B2
Chaddlewood	C2	Ford Pk Rd	B2	**Lee Moor**	C1	Outland Rd	A2
Chittleburn Hill	C2	Ford Rd (Wembury)	B3	**Leigham**	B1	Park Av	A2
Church Hill	B1	Ford Rd (Yealmpton)	D3	**Lipson**	B2	Parkway, The	B1
Church Rd		Fore St (Holbeton)	D3	Lipson Rd	B2	Parsonage Rd	C3
(Plymstock)	B2	Fore St (Yealmpton)	D3	Lodge La	C2	Pemros Rd	A1
Church Rd		Fort Austin Av	B1	**Longbridge**	B1	**Pennycross**	B1
(Wembury)	B3	Furzehatt Rd	B2	Longbridge Rd	B1	**Peverell**	B2
Cittaford Rd	B1	Gabber La	B3	Looseleigh La	B1	Peveril Pk Rd	B1
Colebrook	C2	Galva Rd	C1	Lucas La	C1	Pike Rd	B2
Colesdown Hill	B2	**Glenholt**	B1	**Lutton**	D1	Plymbridge Rd	B1
Collard La	C1	Glen Rd	C2	**Mainstone**	B1	Plymbridge Rd	
Combe	C2	**Goosewell**	B2	Maker La	A2	(Plympton)	C1
Compton	B2	Goosewell Rd	B2	**Manadon**	B1	**Plymouth**	A2
Cornwood	D1	Greenbank Rd	B2	**Mannamead**	B2	Plymouth City	
Cornwood Rd	D2	Green Pk Rd	B2	Mannamead Rd	B2	Airport	B1
Crabtree	B2	**Ham**	A1	Market St	D2	Plymouth Rd	B2
Cremyll	A2	Ham Dr	A1	**Marsh Mills**	B2	**Plympton**	C2
Crownhill	B1	**Hartley**	B1	**Maryfield**	A2	Plympton Bypass	B2

Plymstock	B2	Torr La	B1
Plymstock Rd	B2	Train Rd	C3
Pomphlett	B2	**Turnchapel**	B2
Pomphlett Rd	B2	Underhay	C3
Powisland Dr	B1	Underlane	
Rame	A3	(Plympton)	C2
Renney Rd	B3	Underlane	
Ridge Rd	C2	(Plymstock)	B2
Ridgeway	C2	**Underwood**	C2
Roborough La	A1	Union St	A2
Royal Navy Av	A2	**Venton**	D2
Saint Budeaux	A1	Victoria Rd	A1
Saint Judes	B2	**Wearde**	A1
St. Levan Rd	A2	**Wembury**	C3
St. Peters Rd	B1	Wembury Rd	B2
Saltash Rd	A2	Western App	A2
Sandy Rd	C2	**Westlake**	D2
Seymour Rd	B2	**Weston Mill**	A1
Sherford Rd	C2	Weston Pk Rd	B1
Southdown	A2	**West Park**	A1
Southdown Rd	A2	West Pk Hill	C1
Southway	B1	**Whitleigh**	A1
Southway Dr	B1	**Widewell**	B1
Sparkwell	D1	Widey Hill	C3
Spriddlestone	C3	Widey La	B1
Springfield Rd	C2	**Wilcove**	A2
Spring Rd	B3	Wolseley Rd	A1
Staddiscombe	B3	Wolverwood La	C2
Staddiscombe Rd	B3	**Woodford**	C1
Staddon La	B3	Woodford Av	B2
Stamps Hill	C2	**Woolwell**	B1
Stanborough Rd	B2	Woolwell Rd	B1
Station Rd	A1	**Worston**	D2
Steer Pt Rd	C3	**Worswell**	C3
Stoke	A2	**Wotter**	C1
Stoke Rd	C3	**Yealmbridge**	D2
Stonehouse	A2	**Yealmpton**	D2
Tamar Br	A1	Yealm Rd	C3
Tamerton Foliot	A1	**Yondertown**	D1
Tamerton Foliot Rd	B1		
Taunton Av	A1		
Tavistock Rd	B1		
Torpoint	A2		
Torr	D3		

BOURNEMOUTH URBAN page 37

Abbot Rd	C3	Bath Rd	C3	Bridge St	D3	**Charminster**	C3
Abbott St	A1	**Bearwod**	B2	Broadmoor Rd	A2	Charminster Rd	C3
Adastral Rd	A3	Beechbank Av	A3	**Broadstone**	A2	Chesildene Dr	C2
Albert Rd	B3	Belle Vw Rd	D3	Broadstone Way	A3	Chessel Av	C3
Alder Rd	B3	**Bisterne**	D1	Broadway	D3	**Christchurch**	D3
Alma Rd	C3	Blandford Rd	A3	Broadway La	C2	Christchurch	
Alumhurst Rd	B3	Bloxworth Rd	B3	**Broom Hill**	B1	Bypass	D3
Ameysford Rd	B1	Bockhampton Rd	D2	Burley Rd	D2	Christchurch Rd	C3
Anna La	D1	**Boscombe**	C3	**Burton**	D2	Christchurch Rd	
Arne Av	B3	Boscombe		Burts Hill	A1	(Hurn)	C1
Arrowsmith Rd	A2	Overcliffe Dr	C3	Cabot La	A3	Christchurch Rd	
Ashington La	A2	Boundary La	C1	Canford Bottom	B1	(Kingston)	D1
Ashley	D1	Boundary Rd	B3	Canford Cliffs Rd	B3	Christchurch Rd	
Ashley Heath	C1	**Bournemouth**	C3	**Canford Heath**	A2	(West Parley)	C2
Ashley Rd	C3	Bournemouth		Canford Heath Rd	A2	Churchill Rd	B3
Ashley Rd		Int Airport	C2	Canford Magna	B2	Church La	C2
(Poole)	B3	Bournemouth Rd	B3	Canford Way	B2	Church Rd	D3
Avenue, The	B3	Bracken Rd	B1	Carbery Av	D3	Church Rd	
Avon	D2	**Branksome**	B3	Castle La E	C3	(Ferndown)	B1
Avon Causeway	D2	**Branksome Park**	B3	Castle La W	C2	**Clapgate**	A1
Barrack Rd	D3	Branksome Wd Rd	B3	Central Dr	C3	Clarendon Rd	A2

Cobham Rd	B1	Dudsbury Rd	B2
Colehill	A1	Dunyeats Rd	B2
Colehill La	A1	East Dr	B3
Coles Av	A3	**East End**	A2
Columbia Rd	B2	**East Howe**	B2
Compton Av	B3	East Howe La	B2
Corfe Mullen	A2	East Overcliffe Dr	C3
Cowgrove	A1	East Way	C3
Cowgrove Rd	A1	**Fairmile**	D3
Coy Pond Rd	B3	Fairmile Rd	D3
Cranborne Rd	A1	**Ferndown**	B1
Cranleigh Rd	D3	Fernside Rd	A3
Creekmore La	A3	Fleets La	A3
Crow	D1	Footners La	D2
Dale Valley Rd	A3	Foxbury Rd	C1
De Havilland Way	D3	Furzehill	A1
Derritt La	D2	Glenferness Av	B3
Dogdean	A1	Glenmoor Rd	B1
Dorchester Rd	A3	Golf Links Rd	C2
Dorset Way	A3	Grand Av	D3
Dudsbury	B2	**Grange Estate**	C1

Name	Ref	Name	Ref
Gravel Hill	A2	Kitchener Cres	A3
Green Rd	C3	Knights Rd	B2
Grove, The	D3	Lake Rd	A3
Ham La	B2	Lancaster Dr	A2
Hampreston	**B2**	**Langham**	**B2**
Hamworthy	**A3**	Leicester Rd	B3
Harewood Av	C3	Leigh Rd	A1
Hart's Rd	B1	Leybourne Av	B2
Hawthorn Rd	D2	**Lilliput**	**B3**
Hayes La	B1	Lilliput Rd	B3
Herbert Av	B3	Lindsay Rd	B3
Higher Blandford Rd	A2	Links Rd	B3
Highfield Rd	A2	Lions La	C1
Hillside Rd	A2	**Littledown**	**C3**
Hill View	**A2**	Longfield Rd	A3
Holdenhurst	**C2**	**Longfleet**	**A3**
Holdenhurst Rd	C3	Long La	A1
Holdenhurst Rd (Holdenhurst)	C2	Longmeadow La	A3
Holes Bay Rd	A3	Lonnen Rd	B1
Holloway Av	B2	Lower Blandford Rd	C3
Holt	**B1**	Lowther Rd	C3
Holt La	A1	Lyndhurst Rd	D2
Holt Rd	B1	Magna Rd	B2
Hunt Rd	D3	Malvern Rd	C2
Hurn	**C2**	Matchams La	C2
Hurn Ct La	C2	**Merley**	**A2**
Hurn Rd (Christchurch)	D2	Merley La	A2
Hurn Rd (Matchams)	C1	Merley Pk Rd	A2
Iford La	D3	Merriefield Av	A2
Jumpers Common	**D3**	Middlehill Rd	A1
Jumpers Rd	D3	Mill La	C2
King John Av	B2	**Moordown**	**C2**
Kingston	**D1**	Moorlands Rd	B1
Kinson	**B2**	Mudeford	D3
Kinson Rd	B3	Mudeford La	D3
		Muscliffe La	C2
		New Rd	C2
		Newtown	**B3**
		Northleigh La	A1

Name	Ref	Name	Ref
Northmead Dr	A3	Richmond Pk Av	C3
North Ripley	**D1**	Ringwood Rd	B3
North Rd	B3	Ringwood Rd (Avon)	D2
Nuffield Rd	A3	**Ripley**	**D2**
Oakdale	**A3**	Ripon Rd	C3
Oakley Hill	A2	River Way	D3
Oakley La	A2	Roman Rd	A2
Old Wareham Rd	B3	Rossmore Rd	B3
Pamphill	**A1**	Rowlands Hill	A1
Parkstone	**B3**	**St. Leonards**	**C1**
Parkstone Rd	A3	St. Osmunds Rd	B3
Parkwood Rd	C3	Salisbury Rd	D2
Parley Cross	**C2**	Sandbanks Rd	B3
Parley La	C2	Sandcotes Rd	B3
Penn Hill Av	B3	Sandy La	C1
Petersfield Rd	C3	Sea Rd	C3
Petersham La	A1	Sherborn Cres	A3
Pilford Heath Rd	B1	**Shirley**	**D2**
Pilford La	B1	**Sleight**	**A2**
Pinehurst Rd	C1	Smugglers La	A1
Pinesprings Dr	A2	**Somerford**	**D3**
Pond Head	B1	Somerford Rd	D3
Poole	**A3**	Sopers La	A3
Poole La	B2	**Sopley**	**D2**
Poole Rd	B3	**Southbourne**	**D3**
Poole Rd (Poole)	B3	Southbourne Coast Rd	D3
Poole Rd (Upton)	A3	Southbourne Overcliffe Dr	D3
Poole Rd (Wimborne Minster)	A1	Southbourne Rd	C3
Pound La	A3	Southcote Rd	C3
Preston La	D2	South Kinson Dr	B2
Priestley Rd	B3	Springdale Rd	A2
Purewell	D3	**Stanbridge**	**A1**
Purewell Cross Rd	D3	Stanpit	D3
Quay, The	A3	**Stapehill**	**B1**
Queen Anne Dr	A2	Stapehill Rd	B2
Queen's Pk Av	C3	Station Rd	B1
Redhill Av	C2		
Redhill Dr	C2		

Name	Ref	Name	Ref
Sterte Rd	A3	West Moors Rd (Three Legged Cross)	B1
Stone La	A1	**West Parley**	**C2**
Stony La	D2	West Quay Rd	A3
Stour Rd	D3	West Rd	D2
Stourvale Rd	C3	**West Southbourne**	**D3**
Surrey Rd	B3	West St	A3
Tadden	**A1**	West Way	C2
Talbot Av	C3	West Way (Broadstone)	A2
Tatnam Rd	A3	Whitelegg Way	C2
Thickett's Cross	**C1**	**Wick**	**D3**
Throop	**C2**	Wick La	D3
Throop Rd	C2	**Wimborne Minster**	**A1**
Turbary Pk Av	B2	Wimborne Rd	C3
Turlin Rd	A3	Wimborne Rd (Colehill)	A1
Uddens Dr	B1	Wimborne Rd (East End)	A2
Uplands Rd	C1	Wimborne Rd (Kinson)	B2
Upton	**A3**	Wimborne Rd (Poole)	A3
Upton Rd	A3	Wimborne Rd E	B1
Victoria Rd	B1	Wimborne Rd W	B1
Vine Hill	A1	Winston Av	B3
Wallisdown	**B3**	**Winton**	**C3**
Wallisdown Rd	B2	Woodlands Av	A3
Waterditch Rd	D2	Woolsbridge Rd	C1
Waterloo	**A3**	Yarrow Rd	B3
Waterloo Rd (Corfe Mullen)	A2	Yeomans Rd	C2
Waterloo Rd (Poole)	A3	York Rd	A2
Wayside Rd	C1		
Wentworth Av	C3		
Wessex Way	B3		
Westbourne	**B3**		
West Cliff Rd	B3		
Western Av	B3		
Western Rd	B3		
West Howe	**B2**		
West Moors	**B1**		
West Moors Rd (Ferndown)	B1		

SOUTHAMPTON & PORTSMOUTH URBAN pages 38-39

Name	Ref	Name	Ref
Abbey Hill	B2	Bitterne Rd E	B2
Abshot	**C3**	Bitterne Rd W	B2
Abshot Rd	C3	**Blackfield**	**A4**
Alan Drayton Way	B1	Blackfield Rd	B4
Albert Rd N	A2	Blackhorse La	D2
Aldermoor	**A1**	Blind La (Horton Heath)	C1
Aldermoor Rd	A1	Blind La (Meon Park)	D2
Allaway Av	E3	Blundell La	C2
Allington La	B1	**Boarhunt**	**E3**
Anglesea Rd	A1	Boarhunt Rd	E3
Anmore Rd	F2	**Boorley Green**	**C2**
Ann's Hill	**E4**	**Botany Bay**	**B2**
Ann's Hill Rd	E4	**Botley**	**C2**
Anthill Common	**F2**	Botley Rd (Bishop's Waltham)	D1
Applemore	**A3**	Botley Rd (Burridge)	C2
Archer's Rd	A2	Botley Rd (Fair Oak)	C1
Archery Rd	B2	Botley Rd (Hedge End)	B1
Arundel St	F4	Botley Rd (Park Gate)	C3
Ashlett	**B4**	Botley Rd (Swanwick)	C2
Ashlett Rd	B4	Botley Rd (Woolston)	B2
Ashton	**D1**	Bournemouth Rd	A1
Athelston Rd	B3	Bowden La	A1
Avenue, The (Fareham)	D3	Bransbury Rd	F4
Avenue, The (Southampton)	A1	Brewers La	D4
Avery La	E4	**Bridgemary**	**D4**
Back La	E3	Bridge Rd	B2
Baffins	**F4**	Bridge Rd (Bursledon)	C2
Baffins Rd	F4	Bridge Rd (Park Gate)	C3
Bailey's Hard	**A4**	Bridge St (Titchfield)	D3
Banister's Park	**A2**	Bridge St (Wickham)	D2
Bank St	D1	Broad Oak	C2
Barbe Baker Av	B1	Broad St	E4
Barnes La	C3	Broadway La	F2
Bassett	**A1**	**Brockbridge**	**E1**
Bassett Av	A1	**Brockhurst**	**E4**
Bassett Green	**A1**	Brockhurst Rd	E4
Bassett Grn Rd	A1	Brook La (Botley)	C2
Beaulieu Rd	A3	Brook La (Hambledon)	F1
Bedenham	**E4**	Brook La (Locks Heath)	C3
Bedford Place	**A2**	Brook La (Warsash)	C3
Beeches Hill	D1	Broom Way	D4
Bell's La	D4	**Browndown**	**D4**
Bernard St	A2	Browndown Rd	D4
Bevois Mount	**A2**	**Brownwich**	**C4**
Bevois Town	**A2**		
Bevois Valley Rd	A2		
Biddenfield La	D2		
Bishopstoke	**B1**		
Bishopstoke Rd	B1		
Bishop's Waltham	**D1**		
Bishops Wd Rd	D1		
Bitterne	**B2**		
Bitterne Park	**B1**		

Name	Ref	Name	Ref
Brune La	D4	Church La (Botley)	C2
Bubb La	C1	Church La (Bursledon)	B2
Buckland	**F4**	Church La (Curdridge)	C2
Bucklers Hard	**A4**	Church La (Fawley)	B4
Bullar Rd	B2	Church La (Hambledon)	F1
Bull La	D1	Church La (Southampton)	A1
Burgess Rd	A1	Church La (Swanmore)	D1
Burgoyne Rd	B2	Church Rd (Locks Heath)	C3
Burnetts La	B1	Church Rd (Shedfield)	D2
Burridge	**C2**	Church Rd (Swanmore)	D1
Burridge Rd	C2	**Clanfield**	**F1**
Burrfields Rd	F4	Claypits La	A3
Bursledon	**B2**	Clewers Hill	D1
Bursledon Rd (Hedge End)	C2	Clewers La	D1
Bursledon Rd (Southampton)	B2	Cliff Rd	C4
Bury	**E4**	Closewood Rd	F2
Bury Rd	E4	Coach Hill	C3
Butlocks Heath	**B2**	Cobden Av	B2
Buttsash	**A3**	Cobden Br	B2
Buttsash La	A3	College Rd	F3
Butts Br Hill	A3	Common La (Southwick)	E3
Butts Rd	B2	Common La (Titchfield)	C3
Cadland Rd	A3	**Copnor**	**F4**
Calcot Hill	C1	Copnor Rd	F4
Calshot	**B4**	Coppice Hill	D1
Cambridge Rd	D4	Copse La	B3
Camden Town	**E4**	Corbett Rd	B2
Canute Rd	A2	Cornaway La	E3
Carisbrooke Rd	D4	Corn Hill	D1
Castle St	E3	**Cosham**	**F3**
Catisfield	**D3**	Cott St	D1
Catisfield Rd	D3	**Coxford**	**A1**
Chalk Hill	B2	Coxford Drove	A1
Chapel La (Blackfield)	B4	Coxford Rd	A1
Chapel La (Curdridge)	C2	**Crabthorne**	**D4**
Chapel Rd (Swanmore)	D1	Cracknore Hard La	A2
Chapel Rd (West End)	B1	**Crockerhill**	**D2**
Charles Watts Way	B2	**Crofton**	**D4**
Cherque Way	D4	Crofton La	D4
Chestnut Av	A1	Crooked Wk La	E3
Chidden	**F1**	**Crookhorn**	**F3**
Chilling	**C3**	Crookhorn La	F3
Chilworth	**A1**	**Crosshouse**	**A2**
Chilworth Old Village	**A1**	Crows Nest La	C2
Chilworth Old Village	A1	Cuckoo La	D4
Chilworth Rd	A1		
Church Hill	B1		

Name	Ref	Name	Ref
Cumberland Pl.	A2	Fawley Rd (Buttsash)	A3
Curbridge	**C2**	Fawley Rd (Fawley)	B4
Curdridge	**C2**	Ferry Rd	F4
Curdridge La	D1	Firtree La	B1
Day La	F2	Fishers Hill	D3
Deacon Rd	B2	**Fleetend**	**C3**
Dean	**D1**	Fleet End Rd	C3
Denmead	**F2**	**Fleetlands**	**D4**
Derby Rd	B1	Fontley La	D3
Dibden	**A3**	Forest Hills Dr	B1
Dibden Purlieu	**A3**	Forest Rd (Denmead)	F2
Dibles Rd	C3	Forest Rd (Waltham Chase)	D1
Dodds La	D1	**Forton**	**E4**
Dodwell La	C2	Forton Rd	E4
Dorset St	A2	**Fourposts**	**A2**
Downend	**E3**	**Frater**	**E4**
Downend Rd	E3	**Fratton**	**F4**
Drayton	**F3**	Fratton Rd	F4
Droxford	**E1**	**Freemantle**	**A2**
Droxford Rd	D2	Free St	D1
Drummond Rd	C1	Frith La	D2
Dundridge	**C1**	**Frostlane**	**A3**
Dundridge La	D1	Frost La	A3
Durley	**C1**	**Funtley**	**D3**
Eagle Av	F2	Funtley Rd	D3
Eaglehurst	**B4**	**Furzeley Corner**	**F2**
Eastern Rd (Hilsea)	F4	Furzeley Rd	F2
Eastern Way	D3	**Gilbury Hard**	**A4**
Eastleigh	**B1**	Gladys Av	F4
Eastleigh Rd (Fair Oak)	C1	**Glebe**	**D1**
East St (Fareham)	D3	Glidden La	F1
East St (Hambledon)	F1	Goldsmith Av	F4
East St (Portchester)	E3	Gordon Rd	E4
East St (Titchfield)	D3	Gorselands Way	D4
Edneys La	F2	**Gosport**	**E4**
Elm Gro	F4	Gosport Rd (Fareham)	D3
Elson	**E4**	Gosport Rd (Stubbington)	D4
Elson Rd	E4	**Grange**	**E4**
Exbury	**A4**	Grange La	D4
Exbury Rd	A4	Grange Rd (Gosport)	D4
Fair Oak	**C1**	Grange Rd (Hedge End)	C2
Fair Oak Rd	B1	Grange Rd (Netley Abbey)	B3
Fareham	**D3**	Gravel Hill	D1
Fareham Rd (Fleetlands)	D4	**Great Posbrook**	**C3**
Fareham Rd (Wickham)	D2	Greenaway La	C3
Farlington	**F3**	Green La (Hamble-le-Rice)	B3
Farlington Av	F3		
Fawcett Rd	F4		
Fawley	**B4**		

Name	Ref
Green La (Hambledon)	F1
Gregson Av	D4
Grove Rd	E4
Gudge Heath La	D3
Hambledon	F1
Hambledon Rd (Clanfield)	F1
Hambledon Rd (Hambledon)	F2
Hambledon Rd (Waterlooville)	F2
Hamble La (Bursledon)	B3
Hamble La (Hamble-le-Rice)	B3
Hamble-le-Rice	B3
Hampton Hill	D1
Hampton La	B4
Hampton Park	A1
Hard, The	E4
Hardley	A3
Hardway	E4
Harefield	B2
Harrowgate La	F2
Hart Plain Av	F2
Havant Rd (Cosham)	F3
Havant Rd (Farlington)	F3
Heathfield	D3
Heath Ho La	C2
Heath Rd	C3
Hedge End	C2
Heritage Way	E4
Highbury	F3
Highfield	A1
Highfield Av	A1
Highfield La	A1
Highlands Rd	D3
High St (Beaulieu)	A4
High St (Botley)	C2
High St (Bursledon)	B2
High St (Cosham)	F3
High St (Fareham)	D3
High St (Hamble-le-Rice)	B3
High St (Lee-on-the-Solent)	D4
High St (Old Portsmouth)	E4
High St (Shirrell Heath)	D2
High St (Titchfield)	D3
High St (West End)	B1
Hightown	B2
Hillgrove Rd	D1
Hill Head (Fareham)	C3
Hillhead (Fawley)	B4
Hill La	A1
Hill Park	D3
Hillpound	D1
Hillpound Rd	D1
Hill Rd	E3
Hill Top	A4
Hilsea	F4
Hinkler Rd	B2
Hoads Hill	D2
Hobb La	C2
Hoe	D1
Hoe Rd	D1
Holbrook	E4
Holbury	A4
Holbury Drove	A4
Hollam Dr	D3
Holmesland La	C2
Holywell Rd	D1
Hook	C3
Hook La	C3
Hook Park	C3
Horton Heath	C1
Hospital Rd	D2
Hound	B3
Hound Rd	B3
Hound Way	B3
Howard Rd	A2
Hulbert Rd	F2
Hundred Acres	E2
Hunt's Pond Rd	C3
Hyden Fm La	F1
Hythe	A3
Hythe Bypass	A3
Hythe Rd	A2
Inhams La	F2
Inner Av	A2
Itchen	B2
Itchen Br	A2
Jones La	A3
Jubilee Av	E3
Kanes Hill	B2
Kathleen Rd	B2
Keeping	A4
Kew La	B2
Kidmore La	F2
Kiln Rd	D3
King's Copse Av	C2
Kingsmead	D2
Kings Rd	E4
Kingston	F4
Kingston Rd	F4
Kingsway	A2
Kitnocks	C2
Kitnocks Hill	C2
Knowle La	C1
Ladybridge Rd	F3
Lake Rd	F4
Landport	F4
Lands End Rd	C2
Langdown	A3
Langdown Lawn	A3
Langley	B4
Langstone Rd	F4
Lee Ground	D3
Lee-on-the-Solent	D4
Lepe Rd	B4
Little Abshot Rd	C3
Little Holbury	A3
Little Posbrook	C3
Locke Rd	C2
Lockhams Rd	D2
Locks Heath	C3
Lock's Rd	C3
Lockswood Rd	C3
Lodge Rd	A2
London Rd (Portsmouth)	F4
London Rd (Purbrook)	F3
London Rd (Southampton)	A2
London Rd (Waterlooville)	F2
Longacres	C3
Long Common	C1
Long Common	C1
Longcopse	B4
Longfield Av	D3
Long La (Bursledon)	B2
Long La (Holbury)	A3
Lord's Hill	A1
Lord's Hill Way	A1
Lordswood	A1
Lordswood Rd	A1
Lovedean	F2
Lovedean La	F2
Lower Chase Rd	D1
Lower Ch Rd	C3
Lower Exbury	A4
Lower La	C2
Lower Northam Rd	C2
Lower Swanwick	C3
Lowford	B2
Lowford Hill	B2
Maddoxford La	C1
Main Rd (Hythe)	A3
Main Rd (Marchwood)	A2
Manor Way	D4
Mansbridge Rd	B1
Marchwood	A2
Marine Par	A2
Marine Par E	D4
Marine Par W	D4
Market Way	E4
Marsh La (Fawley)	B4
Marsh La (Southampton)	A2
Maunsell Way	C1
Maurepas Way	F2
Maybray King Way	B2
May's La	D4
Meggeson Av	B1
Meon	C4
Meon Park	D4
Meon Rd (Hill Head)	C4
Meon Rd (Meon)	C4
Merry Oak	B2
Merry Oak Rd	B2
Midanbury	B1
Middle Rd	B2
Mile End Rd	F4
Military Rd (Gosport)	E4
Military Rd (Paulsgrove)	E3
Millbrook	A2
Millbrook Rd	A2
Mill Hill	C2
Mill La (Fareham)	D3
Mill La (Gosport)	E4
Mill La (Wickham)	D2
Mill La (Wymering)	F2
Mill Rd (Denmead)	F2
Mill Rd (Fareham)	D3
Milton	F4
Milton Rd (Portsmouth)	F4
Milton Rd (Waterlooville)	F2
Montserrat Rd	D4
Monument La	E3
Moorgreen	B1
Moorgreen Rd	B1
Moorhill Rd	B2
Mortimers La	C1
Mountbatten Way	C3
Mousehole La	B2
Mumby Rd	E4
Nelson La	E3
Netley Abbey	B3
Newgate La	D4
Newlands La	F2
Newlands Rd	B4
Newmans Hill	D2
New Rd (Hythe)	A3
New Rd (Portsmouth)	F4
New Rd (Waltham Chase)	D1
Newtown (Bishop's Waltham)	D1
Newtown (Gosport)	E4
Newtown (Locks Heath)	C3
Newtown (Soberton Heath)	E2
Newtown (Southampton)	A2
Newtown (Woolston)	B2
Newtown Rd (Warsash)	C3
Newtown Rd (Woolston)	B2
Nimrod Dr	D4
Nine Elms La	E3
Nobes Av	D4
Northam	A2
Northam Br	A2
Northam Rd	A2
North Boarhunt	E2
Northbrook	D1
North End	F4
Northern Par	F4
Northern Rd	F3
North La	A3
North Stoneham	B1
N. Wallington	D3
Oakcroft La	D3
Oakhill	C2
Oakley Rd	A2
Old Mill La	F2
Old Netley	B2
Old Portsmouth	E4
Old Shirley	A1
Old St	D4
Old Turnpike	D3
Olive Rd	A1
Onslow Rd	A2
Osborn Rd	D3
Otterwood	A4
Outlands La	C2
Ower	B4
Palace La	A4
Paradise La	D1
Park Gate	C3
Park La (Fareham)	D3
Park La (Holbury)	A4
Park Rd	E4
Park St	A2
Passfield Av	B1
Paulsgrove	E3
Payne's Rd	A2
Peak La	D3
Peartree Av	B2
Peartree Green	B2
Peel Common	D4
Peters Rd	C3
Pier St	D4
Pigeon Ho La	F3
Pitt Hill La	F2
Pitymoor La	E3
Platform Rd	A2
Pleasant View	B2
Polygon	A2
Pook La	D3
Portchester	E3
Portchester La	E3
Portchester Rd	E3
Portsdown Hill Rd	F3
Portsdown Rd	E3
Portsea	E4
Portsmouth Rd (Lee-on-the-Solent)	D4
Portsmouth Rd (Woolston)	B2
Port Solent	E3
Portsview Av	E3
Portswood	A1
Portswood Rd	A1
Posbrook La	C3
Pound Rd	B2
Pricketts Hill	D1
Primate Rd	C3
Princes St	A2
Privett	E4
Privett Rd	D4
Providence Hill	B2
Purbrook	F3
Purbrook Heath Rd	F3
Purbrook Way	F3
Pylands La	C2
Pylehill	C1
Quay, The	B3
Queen St	E4
Quob La	B1
Raymond Rd	A2
Redbridge Hill	A1
Redlands La	D3
Regent's Pk Rd	A2
Riverside	B1
Rollestone Rd	A4
Romsey Rd	A1
Roughdown	A4
Rowan Way	D3
Row Ash	D2
Rowner	D4
Rowner La	D4
Rowner Rd	D4
Rownhams	A1
Rownhams La (North Baddeley)	A1
Rownhams La (Rownhams)	A1
Rownhams Rd	A1
Rownhams Rd N	A1
Ruby Rd	B2
Rushmere La	F2
St. Anne's La	D2
St. Denys	A2
St. Deny's Rd	A1
St. James Rd	A1
St. John's Rd	B2
St. John's St	A3
St. Margarets La	C3
St. Marys Rd	F4
St. Nicholas Av	D4
St. Thomas's Rd	E4
Salterns Rd	D4
Sandy La (Bishopstoke)	C1
Sandy La (Waltham Chase)	D2
Sarisbury	C3
Satchell La	B3
School La (Denmead)	F2
School La (Hamble-le-Rice)	B3
School Rd (Bursledon)	B2
School Rd (Fawley)	B4
School Rd (Wickham)	D2
Seafield	E4
Segensworth Rd	C3
Shaftesbury Av	A1
Shamblehurst La N	C1
Shedfield	D2
Sheepwash La	F2
Shirley	A2
Shirley High St	A2
Shirley Park	A2
Shirley Rd	A2
Shirley Warren	A1
Shirrell Heath	D1
Sholing	B2
Sholing Common	B2
Sholing Rd (Merry Oak)	B2
Sholing Rd (Sholing)	B2
Shoot La	D4
Shop La	B2
Shore La	D1
Shore Rd (Hythe)	A3
Shore Rd (Warsash)	C3
Skew Rd	E3
Soake Rd	F2
Soberton	E1
Soberton Heath	E2
Solent Breezes	C4
Solomons La	D1
Somerset Av	B2
Somers Town	F4
Southampton Rd (Eastleigh)	B1
Southampton Rd (Hythe)	A3
Southampton Rd (Locks Heath)	C3
Southampton Rd (Park Gate)	C3
Southampton Rd (Portchester)	E3
Southampton Rd (Wymering)	F3
South St (Gosport)	E4
South St (Hythe)	A3
South St (Titchfield)	D3
Southwick	E3
Southwick Hill Rd	F3
Southwick Rd (Southwick, North)	E3
Southwick Rd (Southwick, South)	E3
Spring Gdn La	E4
Spring Rd (Itchen)	B2
Spring Rd (Merry Oak)	B2
Spurlings Rd	E3
Square, The	D2
Stakes Hill Rd	F3
Stakes Rd	F3
Stamshaw	E4
Stamshaw Rd	F4
Station Hill	C2
Station Rd (Bursledon)	C2
Station Rd (Gosport)	E4
Station Rd (Netley Abbey)	B3
Station Rd (Portchester)	E3
Station Rd (Sholing)	B2
Station Rd (Soberton)	E1
Stoke Rd	E4
Stoke Wood	F1
Stoneham La (Eastleigh)	B1
Stoneham La (Swaythling)	B1
Stonehills	B4
Stubbington	D4
Stubbington Av	F4
Stubbington La	D4
Summer La	A4
Sunnymead Dr	F2
Swanmore	D1
Swanmore Rd	D1
Swanwick	C2
Swanwick La	C2
Swaythling	B1
Swaythling Rd	B1
Swivelton La	E3
Tangier Rd	F4
Tanners La	F2
Tapnage	D2
Tebourba Way	A2
Thornhill	B2
Thornhill Park	B2
Thornhill Pk Rd	B2
Tichborne Way	D4
Tipner	E4
Titchfield	D3
Titchfield Common	C3
Titchfield Haven	C4
Titchfield La	D2
Titchfield Park	D3
Titchfield Rd	D3
Tollbar Way	B1
Townhill Park	B1
Townhill Way	B2
Town Quay	A2
Triangle La	C4
Tukes Rd	D4
Turkey Island	D2
Turnpike Way	B1
Twyford Av	F4
Twynhams Hill	D2
University Rd	A1
Uplands	D3
Uplands Rd	B2
Upper Deacon Rd	B2
Upper Northam Rd	B2
Upper Shirley	A1
Upper Swanmore	D1
Velder Av	B2
Vernon Hill	D1
Vicarage La (Curdridge)	C2
Vicarage La (Swanmore)	D1
Victoria Rd (Netley Abbey)	B3
Victoria Rd (Woolston)	B2
Victoria Rd N	F4
Wallington	D3
Wallington Way	D3
Waltham Chase	D1
Wangfield La	C1
Warburton Rd	B2
Warren Av	A1
Warsash	C3
Warsash Rd	C3
Waterloo Rd	A2
Waterlooville	F2
Welbeck Av	A1
West Common	B4
West Common Rd	B4
West End (Fareham)	D3
West End (Southampton)	B2
West End Rd (Bitterne)	B2
West End Rd (Hightown)	B2
West End Rd (West End)	B2
Western Esplanade	A2
Western Rd	F3
Western Way	D3
Weston	B2
Weston Common	B2
Weston Gro Rd	B2
Weston La	B2
Weston Par	B2
West Quay Rd	A2
West St (Fareham)	D3
West St (Hambledon)	F1
West St (Hythe)	A3
West St (Portchester)	E3
West St (Southwick)	E3
West St (Titchfield)	C3
Westwood Park	A2
White Hart La	B2
White Horse La	F2
Whiteley	C2
Whiteley La	C3
Whitworth Rd	E4
Wickham	D2
Wickham Rd (Crocker Hill)	D3
Wickham Rd (Uplands)	D3
Wide La	B1
Widley	F3
Widley Wk	F3
Wildern	C2
Wildern La	C2
Winchester Rd (Bassett Green)	A1
Winchester Rd (Lower Upham)	C1
Winchester Rd (Shirley)	A1
Winchester Rd (Waltham Chase)	D1
Winchester Rd (Wickham)	D2
Winston Churchill Av	F4
Wintershill	C1
Winters Rd	D2
Witts Hill	D2
Woodcot	D4
Woodend	E2
Woodhouse La	C2
Woodmill La	B1
Woolston	B2
Woolston Rd	B2
Worlds End	D2
Wych La	D4
Wymering	F3

SWANSEA URBAN page 40

Name	Ref	Name	Ref	Name	Ref
Aberavon	D3	**Clydach**	C1	Hebron Rd	C1
Aberdulais	D1	Clydach Rd	B1	Hendrefoilan Rd	A2
Afan Valley Rd	D2	Coalbrook Rd	A1	Henfaes Rd	D1
Afan Way	D3	Coch-y-Cwm Rd	C2	Hen Parc La	A2
Alexandria Rd	A1	**Cockett**	B2	Heol-ddu	B1
Ashleigh Ter	C2	Cockett Rd	B2	Heol Dywyll	B1
Baglan	D2	Commercial Rd	D3	Heol Gwyrosydd	B2
Baglan Rd	D2	Crymlyn Rd	C2	Heol Las	C1
Baglan Way	D3	Cwmavon Rd	D3	Heol Maes Eglwys	B1
Birchgrove	C1	Cwmbach Rd	A2	Heol y Mynydd	A1
Birchgrove Rd	C1	Cwmbach Rd		Higher La	A3
Bishopston	A3	(Cadoxton-		High St (Clydach)	C1
Bishopston Rd	A3	Juxta-Neath)	D1	High St (Gorseinon)	A1
Blackhills La	A3	**Cwmdu**	B2	High St (Grovesend)	A1
Black Pill	A3	Dalton Rd	D3	Hospital Rd	A1
Bog La	C2	Danygraig Rd	C2	**Jersey Marine**	C2
Bon-y-maen	C2	Derwen Fawr Rd	A3	Jersey Rd	C2
Briton Ferry		Dinam Rd	C2	Killan Rd	A2
(Llansawel)	D2	Drumau Rd	C1	**Killay**	A2
Briton Ferry Rd	D2	**Dunvant**	A2	Kingsway	A2
Bryn-côch	D1	Dunvant Rd	A2	**Landore**	B2
Brynmill La	B2	Dwr-y-Felin Rd	D1	**Llandarcy**	C2
Bryn Rd	B2	Fabian Way	B2	**Llangyfelach**	B1
Bryn Rd		Fairwood Rd	A3	Llangyfelach Rd	B1
(Gorseinon)	A1	Fford Cwm Tawe	B2	**Llansamlet**	C1
Bryn-y-mor Rd	A2	Fford Cynore	A2	Llwynmawr Rd	A2
Burrows Rd	C1	**Fforest-fach**	B2	Longford Rd	D1
Cadle	B1	Foxhole Rd	B2	Loughor Rd	A1
Cadoxton-Juxta-		Frampton Rd	A1	Main Rd (Bryn-côch)	D1
Neath	D1	**Garden Village**	A1	Main Rd (Cadoxton-	
Cae Mansel Rd	A2	Garrod Av	A2	Juxta-Neath)	D1
Camarthen Rd	B2	Gilfach Rd	D1	Main Rd (Cilfrew)	D1
Carmel Rd	C2	**Glais**	C1	**Manselfield**	A3
Caswell Bay Rd	A3	Glanmor Rd	B2	Manselfield Rd	A3
Caswell Rd	A3	Goetre Fawr Rd	A2	Mansel Rd	C2
Cecil Rd	A2	Gors Av	B2	Mansel St	B2
Chestnut Av	A3	**Gorseinon**	A1	**Mayals**	A3
Cilfrew	D1	Gorseinon Rd	A1	Mayals Rd	A3
Cimla	D2	Gorwydd Rd	A2	**Melincryddan**	D1
Cimla Rd	D1	Gower Rd	A2	Middle Rd	B2
Clasemont Rd	B1	**Gowerton**	A2	**Morriston**	B1
Clase Rd	B1	**Grovesend**	A1	**Mumbles, The**	A3

Name	Ref	Name	Ref	Name	Ref
Mumbles Rd	A3	Phoenix Way		**Three Crosses**	A2
Murton La	A3	(Gorseinon)	A1	**Tircoed Forest**	
Mynydd Gelli		Plunch La	A3	**Village**	B1
Wastad Rd	B1	Pontardawe Rd	C1	**Tirdeunaw**	B1
Mynydd-Newydd Rd	B2	Pontardulais Rd	A1	**Townhill**	B2
Nantong Way	B2	Pontardulais Rd		Townhill Rd	B2
Nantyffin Rd	C1	(Gorseinon)	A1	**Trallwyn**	C1
Neath Abbey Rd	D1	**Pontlliw**	A1	**Tre-boeth**	B2
Neath		Pont-y-Cob Rd	A1	Trewyddfa Rd	B2
(Castell-nedd)	D2	**Port Mead**	B2	Tycoch Rd	A2
Neath Rd	B2	**Port Talbot**	D3	Ty-Draw Rd	C2
Neath Rd		**Port Tennant**	C2	Upper Fforest Way	C1
(Briton Ferry)	D2	Princess Margaret		**Upper Killay**	A2
Neath Rd (Tonna)	D1	Way, The	D3	Valley Way	B1
New Cut Rd	B2	Quay Par	B2	Vardre Rd	C1
New Rd		Ravenhill Rd	B2	Victoria Rd	
(Jersey Marine)	C2	**Rhydding**	D1	(Gowerton)	A2
New Rd (Skewen)	C1	Rhyd-y-Pandy Rd	B1	Victoria Rd	
Newton	A3	St. Helens Rd	B2	(Port Talbot)	D3
Newton Rd	A3	Samlet Rd	C1	Victoria Rd	
Northway	A3	Seaway Par	D3	(Waunarlwydd)	A2
Norton	A3	Siding Ter	C1	Vivian Rd	B2
Old Rd (Neath)	D2	Siemens Way	B2	Walter Rd	B2
Old Rd (Skewen)	D1	**Sketty**	B2	Walters Rd	C1
Oldway	A3	Sketty La	A2	Water St	D3
Oystermouth Rd	B2	Sketty Pk Rd	A2	**Waunarlwydd**	A2
Pant-lasau	B1	Sketty Rd	B2	Waunarlwydd Rd	A2
Pantyrheol	D2	**Skewen**	C1	Waun Rd	A1
Park Av	C1	**Swansea**		Wern Rd	C1
Park St	D1	**(Abertawe)**	B2	**West Cross**	A3
Park Way	A2	Swansea Rd		West Cross La	A3
Peniel Grn Rd	C1	(Gorseinon)	A1	Western Av	D3
Penllergaer	A1	Swansea Rd		**Winsh-wen**	C2
Penscynor	D1	(Llangyfelach)	B1	Ynyspenllwch Rd	C1
Pentre-chwth	B2	Swansea Rd		**Ynystawe**	B1
Pentre-chwyth Rd	B2	(Penllergaer)	A1	Ynys-y-Mond Rd	C1
Pentre-Dwr	C2	Swansea Rd		Ystrad Rd	A2
Pentregethin Rd	B1	(Pontlliw)	A1		
Pen-y-Cae Rd	D3	Sway Rd	B1		
Penygraig Rd	B2	**Taibach**	D3		
Penywern Rd	D1	Taillwyd Rd	D1		
Phoenix Way	C2	Talbot Rd	D3		

CARDIFF & NEWPORT URBAN page 41

Name	Ref	Name	Ref	Name	Ref
Aberthaw Rd	D1	**Caledfryn**	A1	Coryton	A2
Adam St	B3	**Canton**	A3	Cowbridge Rd E	A3
Addison Way	B1	Capelgwilym Rd	A2	Cowbridge Rd W	A3
Albany Rd	B3	Cardiff Rd		**Craig-y-Rhacca**	B1
Alexandra Rd	D1	(Caerphilly)	A1	**Crindau**	D1
Allensbank Rd	A3	Cardiff Rd (Llandaff)	A3	Croescadarn Rd	B2
Allt-yr-yn	D1	Cardiff Rd (Newport)	D1	Cromwell Rd	D1
Allt-yr-yn Av	D1	**Castle Park**	A1	Crown Way	A3
Allt-yr-yn Vw	D1	**Castleton**	C2	Crwys Rd	A3
Almond Dr	B2	**Cathays**	A3	Cwm La	C1
Amroth Rd	A3	Cathays Ter	A3	**Cyncoed**	B3
Bach Rd	A3	Cathedral Rd	A3	Cyn Coed Rd	B2
Barnardtown	D1	**Cefn**	C1	Cypress Dr	C2
Barrack Hill	D1	Cefn Coed Rd	B3	**Danygraig**	B1
Barrack Hill	D1	Cefn Rd	C1	Docks Way	D2
Bassaleg	C1	Cefn Wk	C1	**Draethen**	B1
Bassaleg Rd	D1	Celyn Av	B3	Druidstone Rd	B2
Beaufort Rd	D1	Chargot Rd	A3	Duckpool Rd	D1
Bedwas	A1	**Chatham**	B1	**Duffryn**	D2
Bedwas Rd	A1	Chatham Rd	B1	Duffryn Dr	D2
Beechwood	D1	Chepstow Rd	D1	Duffryn Link	C2
Beechwood Rd	D1	Cherry Orchard Rd	A2	Duffryn Way	D2
Began	B2	**Christchurch**	D1	Eastern Av	A3
Began Rd	B2	Christchurch Rd	D1	East Tyndall St	B3
Bettws	C1	Churchill Pk	A1	Elm Dr	C1
Bettws Hill	C1	Church Rd		**Ely**	A3
Bettws La	D1	(Llandaff North)	A3	Ely Rd	A3
Beulah Rd	A2	Church Rd		**Energlyn**	A1
Birchgrove	A3	(Pentwyn)	B2	Excalibur Dr	A2
Blacktown	C2	Church St	A1	Fairoak Rd	A3
Blackweir	A3	Circle Way E	B3	**Fairwater**	A3
Bridge Rd (Llandaff)	A3	Circle Way W	B3	Fairwater Rd	A3
Bridge Rd (Pentwyn)	B2	City Rd	B3	Fidlas Rd	A2
Bridge St	A3	Claude Rd	B3	Fields Pk Rd	D1
Broad St	A3	Clifton St	B3	Fields Rd	D1
Broadstreet		Clive Rd	A3	Forge Rd	
Common	C3	**Coedkernew**	C2	(Bassaleg)	C1
Broadway	B3	Coed-y-brain	A1	Forge Rd	
Bryn Celyn Rd	B2	Colchester Av	B3	(Nant-y-ceisiad)	B1
Brynglas	D1	College Rd	A3	**Gabalfa**	A3
Brynhyfryd	A1	Colum Rd	A3	Gabalfa Av	A3
Caerau Rd	D1	Commercial Rd		**Gaer**	D1
Caerleon Rd	D1	(Nant-y-ceisiad)	B1	**Garth**	C1
Caerphilly	A1	Commercial Rd		Garth Vw	A1
Caerphilly Rd		(Newport)	D1	Gelli Av	C1
(Birchgrove)	A2	Commercial St	B1	George St	D1
Caerphilly Rd (Garth)	C1	Corporation Rd	D1	**Glasllwch**	D1

Name	Ref	Name	Ref	Name	Ref
Glenfields	A1	**Llandaff**	A3	Newton	C3
Glyn Coed Rd	B2	**Llandaff North**	A3	Ninian Pk Rd	A3
Greenacre	A1	Llandaff Rd	A3	Ninian Rd	B3
Green La	D2	**Llanedeyrn**	B3	Northern Av	A3
Greenway	A1	Llanedeyrn Dr	B3	North Rd	A3
Greenway Rd	B3	Llanedeyrn Rd	B3	Oakfield St	B3
Groes Rd	C1	**Llanfabon**	A1	Ocean Way	B3
Groeswen Dr	A1	**Llanishen**	A2	**Ochrwyth**	B1
Gwern Rhuddi	B2	**Llanrumney**	B3	Old Ch Rd	A3
Heath	A3	Lon-y-llyn	A1	Old Rudry Rd	A1
Heath Pk Av	A3	**Lower Machen**	B1	Pandymawr Rd	A1
Heathwood Rd	A3	Ludlow St	A1	Pant	A3
Henllys La	C1	**Machen**	B1	**Pantmawr**	A2
Heol Aneurin	A1	Mackintosh Pl	B3	Pantmawr Rd	A2
Heol Don	A3	**Maendy**	A3	**Parc**	A2
Heol Hir	A2	**Maes-glas**	D1	Park Rd	A3
Heol Las	A2	Maes Y Coed Rd	A3	Pencarn La	C2
Heol Llanishen Fach	A2	Maindy Rd	A3	Pencarn Way	C2
Heol Pont Cwcw	D2	**Malpas**	D1	Pencisely Rd	A3
Heol Pwllypant	A1	Manor Way	A3	Pendwyallt Rd	A2
Heol Uchaf	A2	Marlborough Rd	B3	Penhally Rd	A3
Heol y Delyn	A2	**Marshfield**	C2	Penhill Rd	A3
Heol-y-deri	A2	Melbourne Way	C1	Penllwyn La	B1
High Cross	C1	**Mendalgief**	D1	**Pentre-poeth**	C1
Highcross La	C1	Mendalgief Rd	D1	Pentre-poeth Rd	C1
Highcross Rd	C1	Merthyr Rd	A3	**Pentwyn**	B2
Highfields	A1	**Michaelston-y-Fedw**	C2	Pentwyn Dr	B2
High St	D1	Mill Rd (Caerphilly)	A1	Pentwyn Rd	B2
Hillside Ter	A1	Mill Rd (Llanishen)	A2	**Pen-y-Lan**	B3
Hollybush Rd	B3	Monnow Way	C1	Pen-y-Lan Rd	
Holly Rd	C1	Moorland Rd	B3	(Pen-y-Lan)	B3
Kelston Rd	A3	Morgan Way	D2	Pen-y-Lan Rd	
Kimb Rd	B3	**Morningtown**		(Pentre-poeth)	C1
Kingsway	D1	**Meadows**	A1	**Penyrheol**	A1
Lake Rd E	B3	Mountain Rd	A1	**Peterstone**	
Lake Rd W	A3	Muirton Rd	B3	**Wentlooge**	C3
Lambourne Way	D1	**Mynachdy**	A3	**Pillgwenlly**	D1
Lamby Way	B3	Nantgarw Rd	A1	Plas Mawr Rd	A3
Lansbury Park	A1	**Nant-y-ceisiad**	B1	**Pontcanna**	A3
Lansdowne Rd	A3	Nash Rd	D1	**Pontprennau**	B2
Lawrence Hill	D1	Newport Rd		Pontygwindy Rd	A1
Lewis Rd	B3	(Pontymister)	C1	**Pontymister**	B1
Lighthouse Rd	D2	Newport Rd		Pwll Melin Rd	A3
Lisvane	A2	(Rumney)	B3	**Pwllypant**	A1
Lisvane Rd	A2	Newport Rd		**Pye Corner**	C1
Liswerry	D1	(Trethomas)	A1	Queens Hill	D1
Llanbradach	A1	New Rd	B3	**Rhiwbina**	A2

Rhiwbina Hill	A2
Rhiwderin	**C1**
Rhyd Y Penau Rd	B2
Richmond Rd	B3
Ridgeway	**D1**
Ridgeway	D1
Ridgeway Av	D1
Risca Rd (Glasllwch)	D1
Risca Rd (Rogerstone)	C1
Riverside	**A3**
Roath	**B3**
Roath Park	**B3**
Rogerstone	**C1**
Romilly Cres	A3
Rover Way	B3
Rudry	**B1**
Rumney	**B3**
St. Brides Wentlooge	**C2**
St. Cenydd Rd	A1
St. Julians	**D1**
St. Julians Rd	D1
St. Martins Rd	A1
St. Mellons	**C2**
St. Mellons Rd	B2
Sanquhar St	B3
Seawall Rd	B3
Somerton	**D1**
Somerton Rd	D1
Southern Way	B3
Splott	**B3**
Splott Rd	B3
Spytty Rd	D1
Standard St	A1
Station Rd (Llandaff North)	A3
Station Rd (Llanishen)	A2
Station Ter	A1
Stelvio	**D1**
Stephenson St	D1
Stow Hill	D1
Stow Pk Av	D1
Summerhill Maindee	**D1**
Templeton Av	A2
Thornhill (Caerphilly)	**A2**
Thornhill (Cardiff)	**A2**
Thornhill Rd	A2
Tongwynlais	**A2**
Traston Rd	D1
Trecenydd	**A1**
Tregwilym Rd	C1
Tremorfa	**B3**
Trethomas	**A1**
Trowbridge	**B3**
Trowbridge Rd	B3
Tweedsmuir Rd	B3
Ty-draw Rd (Pen-y-Lan)	B3
Ty Draw Rd (Pontprennau)	B2
Ty Glas Av	A2
Ty Glas Rd	A2
Ty Isaf	A1
Tyndall St	B3
Tyn Y Parc Rd	A3
Tyr Winch Rd	B2
Ty-Sign	**C1**
Ty Wern Rd	A3
Uskmouth	**D2**
Uskway	D1
Vaendre Cl	C2
Van	**A1**
Van Rd	A1
Waterhall Rd	A3
Waterloo	**B1**
Waterloo Rd	B3
Watford Park	**A2**
Watford Rd	A2
Wedal Rd	A3
Wellington St	A3
Wenallt Rd	A2
Wentloog	**B3**
Wentloog Rd	B3
Western Av (Cardiff)	A3
Western Av (Glasllwch)	C1
Western Valley Rd	C1
Wharf Rd	D1
Whitchurch	**A3**
Whitchurch Rd	A3
Willowbrook Dr	B2
Windsor Rd	A3
Wyndham Cres	A3

BRISTOL URBAN page 42

Abbots Leigh	**A2**
Abbots Leigh Rd	A2
Abbots Rd	C3
Abson	**D2**
Acacia Rd	C2
Airport Rd	B3
Albert Rd (Keynsham)	C3
Albert Rd (St. Philips)	B3
Allison Rd	B3
Anchor Rd	B3
Arley Hill	B2
Arno's Vale	**B3**
Ashley Down	**B2**
Ashley Down Rd	B2
Ashley Hill	B2
Ashley Rd	B2
Ashton Gate	**B3**
Ashton Rd (Ashton Gate)	A3
Ashton Rd (Bower Ashton)	A3
Ashton Vale	**A3**
Avondale Rd	B2
Avonmouth Way (Avonmouth)	A1
Avonmouth Way (Henbury)	A1
Avon Ring Rd	C3
Avon St	B2
Avonway	A2
Axbridge Rd	B3
Badminton Rd (Coalpit Heath)	C1
Badminton Rd (Downend)	C2
Baileys Ct Rd	C1
Bamfield	B3
Barrow Common	**A3**
Barrow Gurney	**A3**
Barrow St	A3
Barr's Court	**C3**
Barry Rd	D3
Barton Hill	**B2**
Bath Hill	C3
Bath Rd (Arno's Vale)	B3
Bath Rd (Bitton)	D3
Bath Rd (Brislington)	C3
Bath Rd (Keynsham)	C3
Bath Rd (Longwell Green)	C3
Beach	**D3**
Beckspoll Rd	C2
Bedminster	**B3**
Bedminster Down	**B3**
Bedminster Down Rd	B3
Bedminster Par	B3
Bedminster Rd	B3
Beesmoor Rd	C1
Begbrook Pk	C2
Beggar Bush La	A3
Bell Hill Pk Rd	B2
Bell Hill Rd	C2
Berwick	**A1**
Berwick La	A1
Besom La	D1
Birchwood Rd	C3
Bishop Rd	B2
Bishopston	**B2**
Bishopsworth	**B3**
Bishopsworth Rd	B3
Bitton	**D3**
Blackberry Hill	C2
Black Boy Hill	B2
Blackhorse Hill	B1
Blackhorse La	C1
Black Horse Rd	C2
Blackhorse Rd (Mangotsfield)	C2
Blacksworth Rd	B2
Bloomfield Rd	B3
Bond St	B2
Bonnington Wk	B2
Bower Ashton	**A3**
Bowling Hill	D1
Bowstreet La	A1
Bradley Stoke	**B1**
Bradley Stoke Rd	C1
Bradley Stoke Way	B1
Braydon Av	B1
Brentry	**B1**
Brentry Hill	B1
Bridge Rd	A2
Bridge Valley Rd	A2
Bridge Wk	B2
Bridgeyate	**D2**
Bridgwater Rd	A3
Brislington	**C3**
Bristol Rd (Keynsham)	C3
Bristol Rd (Whitchurch)	B3
Bristol Rd (Winterbourne)	C1
Broad St	C2
Broadwalk	B3
Bromley Heath	**C1**
Bromley Heath Rd (Bromley Heath)	C2
Bromley Heath Rd (Whiteshill)	C1
Brook Rd	C2
Brook Way	B1
Broom Hill	B2
Broomhill (Bristol, North)	**C2**
Broom Hill (Bristol, South)	**C3**
Broomhill Rd	C3
Brunel Way	A3
Bryantshill	C2
Bury Hill	C1
Cadbury Heath	**C3**
California Rd	C3
Callington Rd	B3
Cambridge Batch	**A3**
Canford Rd	A2
Carsons Rd	C2
Cassell Rd	C2
Catbrain	**B1**
Channons Hill	C2
Chapel Rd	C3
Charlton Rd (Brentry)	B1
Charlton Rd (Keynsham)	C3
Charlton Rd (Kingswood)	C2
Cheltenham Rd	B2
Cherry Gdn La	C3
Cherry Gdn Rd	D3
Chesterfield Rd	B2
Church Rd (Abbots Leigh)	A2
Church Rd (Bishopsworth)	A3
Church Rd (Frampton Cotterell)	C1
Church Rd (St. George)	B2
Church Rd (Stoke Bishop)	A2
Church Rd (Stoke Gifford)	C1
Circular Rd	A2
City Rd	B2
Clanage Rd	A3
Clarence Rd	B3
Clay Hill	**C2**
Clay La	B1
Cleeve Hill	C2
Cleeve Rd	C2
Cleevewood Rd	C1
Clevedon Rd	A3
Clift Ho Rd	A3
Clifton	**A2**
Clifton Down	A2
Clifton Down Rd	A2
Cloisters Rd	C1
Clouds Hill Rd	C2
Coalpit Heath	**D1**
Coalsack La	C1
Coldharbour La	C1
Conham	**C3**
Conham Rd	C3
Coniston Rd	B1
Constable Rd	B2
Cooks La	D1
Coombe Dingle	**A2**
Coombe La	A2
Coots, The	B3
Coronation Rd	B3
Cossham St	C2
Cotham	**B2**
Cotham Rd	B2
Cotswold Rd	D1
Court Fm Rd	C3
Court Rd (Frampton Cotterell)	C1
Court Rd (Kingswood)	C2
Cranbrook Rd	B2
Craven Way	C3
Craydon Rd	B3
Creswicke Rd	B3
Crew's Hole	**C2**
Crews Hole Rd	C2
Cribbs Causeway	**B1**
Cribbs Causeway	A1
Cromwell Rd	B2
Croombes Hill	C2
Cross Elms La	A2
Crow La	A1
Cuckoo La	C1
Cumberland Rd	B3
Daventry Rd	B3
Dibden La	C2
Dingle Rd	A2
Doncaster Rd	B1
Dovercourt Rd	B2
Downend	**C2**
Downend	C2
Downend Rd (Fishponds)	C2
Downend Rd (Horfield)	B2
Down Leaze	A2
Down Rd	C1
Doynton	**D2**
Dragon Mill Rd	C1
Dragon Rd	C1
Druid Hill	A2
Duckmoor Rd	B3
Durley Hill	C3
Easter Compton	**B1**
Eastfield	**B2**
Easton	**B2**
Easton-in-Gordano	**A2**
Easton Rd	B2
Easton Way	B2
East St	B3
Eastville	**B2**
Eirene Ter	A2
Emersons Green	**C2**
Failand	**A3**
Falcondale Rd	A2
Farm La	A1
Feeder Rd	B3
Fenchay	**C1**
Filton	**B1**
Filton Av (Filton)	B1
Filton Av (Horfield)	B2
Filton Rd (Hambrook)	C1
Filton Rd (Horfield)	B2
Filton Rd (Stoke Gifford)	B1
Filwood Park	**B3**
Fishponds	**C2**
Fishponds Rd	B2
Flaxpits La	C1
Footshill Rd	C2
Forest Rd (Fishponds)	C2
Forest Rd (Kingswood)	C2
Fortfield Rd	B3
Four Acres	A3
Frampton Cotterell	**C1**
Frampton End	**D1**
Frampton End Rd	C1
Frenchay Hill	C2
Frenchay Pk Rd	B2
Frenchay Rd	C2
Furber Rd	C2
Gainsborough Sq	B2
Gill Av	C2
Gipsy Patch La	B1
Glenfrome Rd	B2
Gloucester Rd (Bishopston)	B2
Gloucester Rd (Patchway)	B1
Gloucester Rd N	B1
Golden Hill	**B2**
Goose Green	**D2**
Gordon Rd	B2
Great Stoke	**C1**
Greystoke Av	A2
Haberfield Hill	A2
Hallen	**A1**
Hallen Rd	A1
Hambreak	**C1**
Hambrook La	C1
Ham Green	**A2**
Ham Grn	A2
Hampton Rd	B2
Hanham	**C3**
Hanham Green	**C3**
Hanham Rd	C2
Happerton La	A2
Harcombe Hill	C1
Hareclive Rd	B3
Harry Stoke	**B1**
Harry Stoke Rd	C1
Hartcliffe	**B3**
Hartcliffe Way	B3
Hatchet Rd	B1
Headley La	B3
Headley Park	**B3**
Henbury	**A1**
Henbury Hill	A1
Henbury Rd	A1
Henfield	**C1**
Henfield Rd	C1
Hengrove	**B3**
Hengrove La	B3
Hengrove Park	**B3**
Hengrove Way	B3
Henleaze	**B2**
Henleaze Rd	B2
Henley Gro	B2
Heron Way	D1
Heywood	A2
Hick's Common	**C1**
Hicks Common Rd	C1
Highridge	**A3**
Highridge Grn	A3
High St (Hanham)	C3
High St (Keynsham)	C3
High St (Kingswood)	C2
High St (Shirehampton)	A2
High St (Staple Hill)	C2
High St (Westbury-on-Trym)	B2
Highwood La	B1
Highwood Rd	B1
Hill Ch Rd	C3
Hillfields	**C2**
Hill Flds Av	C2
Hillside Rd	C2
Hill Vw	C2
Holbrook Common	**D2**
Hollows, The	C1
Holly Hill	C2
Hollywood La	A1
Homeleaze Rd	B1
Horfield	**B2**
Hotwell Rd	A2
Hotwells	**A2**
Howard Rd	B2
Howsmoor La	C1
Ilminster Av	B3
Inns Ct Av	B3
Jacob's Wells Rd	B2
James St	B2
Julian Rd	A2
Kellaway Av	B2
Kendleshire	**C1**
Kennedy Way	D1
Keynsham By-pass	C3
Keynsham Rd	C3
Kingsfield La	C3
Kingshead La	A3
Kingsland Rd	B3
Kingsway	C2
Kings Weston Av	A2
Kings Weston La	A1
Kings Weston Rd	A2
Kingswood	**C2**
Knole La	B1
Knowle	**B3**
Ladies Mile	A2
Lansdown Rd	C2
Lawrence Hill	B2
Lawrence Weston	**A1**
Lawrence Weston Rd	A1
Leigh Woods	**A2**
Leinster Av	B3
Lindon Rd	B2
Link Rd (Filton)	B1
Link Rd (Yate)	D1
Little Stoke	**B1**
Little Stoke La	B1
Lockleaze	**C2**
Lockleaze Rd	C2
Lodge Causeway	C2
Lodge Hill	C2
Lodge Rd	C2
London Rd	C2
Long Ashton	**A3**
Long Ashton By-pass	A3
Long Ashton Rd	A3
Long Beach Rd	C3
Long Cross	A2
Longwell Green	**C3**
Longwood La	A3
Lower High St	A3
Lower Knowle	**B3**
Lyde Green	**D1**
Maggs La	B3
Main Rd	D2
Malago Rd	B3
Mangotsfield	**C2**
Mangotsfield Rd	C2
Manor Rd (Abbots Leigh)	A2
Manor Rd (Fishponds)	C2
Manor Rd (Mangotsfield)	C2
Marsham Way	C3
Marsh La	B2
Mayshill	**D1**
Melton Cres	B2
Memorial Rd	C3
Merchants Rd	A2
Midland Rd	B2
Mill La	A2
Mill Rd	C1
Mina Rd	B2
Monk's Pk Av	B1
Montpelier	**B2**
Moorend	**C1**
Moorend Rd	C1
Moravian Rd	C2
Mount Hill	**C2**
Mount Hill Rd	C2
Muller Rd	B2
Nagshead Hill	C2
Netham	**B2**
Netham Rd	B2
Newbridge Rd	B2
New Cheltenham	**C2**
New Cheltenham Rd	C2
New Fosseway Rd	B3
Newfoundland Way	B2

New Rd	B1	Passage Rd		St. Georges Rd	B2
Nibley	D1	(Brentry)	B1	St. John's La	B3
Nicholls La	C1	Passage Rd (Westbury-		St. Ladoc Rd	C3
North Common	D2	on-Trym)	B2	St. Luke's Rd	B3
North Corner	C1	Patchway	B1	St. Paul's Rd	B2
Northcote Rd	C2	Peache Rd	C2	St. Peter's Ri	B3
North Rd		Pembroke Rd	B2	Salcombe Rd	B3
(Leigh Woods)	A2	Pen Pk Rd	B1	Sandy La	A2
North Rd		Perrinpit Rd	C1	Sandy Pk Rd	B3
(Stoke Gifford)	C1	Pill	A2	Saville Rd	A2
North Stoke	D3	Pill Rd	A2	School Rd	
North St		Plummer's Hill	C2	(Brislington)	B3
(Bedminster)	B3	Pomphrey Hill	C2	School Rd (Frampton	
North St (Downend)	C2	Poplar Rd	D2	Cotterell)	C1
North St (Oldland		Portway	A2	School Rd (Oldland	
Common)	C3	Providence La	A3	Common)	C3
North Vw	B2	Pucklechurch	D2	Scott Way	D1
Novers Hill	B3	Pye Corner	C1	Sea Mills	A2
Novers La	B3	Queens Rd	B2	Sea Mills La	A2
Novers Park	B3	Ram Hill	D1	Serridge La	D1
Old Bristol Rd	C3	Ram Hill	D1	Severn Rd	A1
Old Gloucester Rd	C1	Ram Hill Rd	D1	Shaldon Rd	B2
Oldland	C3	Redcatche Rd	B3	Shirehampton	A2
Oldland Common	D3	Redland	B2	Shirehampton Rd	A2
Old Sneed Av	A2	Redland Hill	B2	Shire Way	D1
Orpheus Av	B1	Redland Rd	B2	Shorthill Rd	D1
Over	B1	Regent St	C2	Shortwood	D2
Over La	B1	Richmond Rd	C2	Shortwood Hill	D2
Overndale Rd	C2	Ridgeway	C2	Siston	D2
Ower Rd N	C2	Ridgeway La	B3	Siston Hill	C2
Palmyra Rd	B3	Ridgeway Rd	C2	Sneyd Park	A2
Parkfield	D2	Rockleaze	A2	Snowdon Rd	C2
Park Gro	B2	Rock Rd	C3	Somerdale	C3
Park Hill	B2	Rodford	D1	Soundwell	C2
Park La	C1	Rodford Way	D1	Soundwell Rd	C2
Park Rd (Keynsham)	C3	Rodway Hill	C2	Southmead	B1
Park Rd		Romney Av	B2	Southmead Rd	B2
(Shirehampton)	A2	Rosegreen Rd	B2	Speedwell	C2
Parkwall Rd	C3	Rownham Hill	A3	Speedwell Rd	C2
Parrys La	A2	Ruffet Rd	C1	Stackpool Rd	B3
Parson St	B3	St. Anne's Park	C2	Stannes Rd	B2
Parston St	B3	St. George	B2	Staple Hill	C2

Staplehill Rd	C2	Throgmorton Rd	B3	West St (Oldland	
Stapleton	B2	Tormarton Cres	A1	Common)	C3
Stapleton Rd	B2	Toronto Rd	B2	West St (St. Philips)	B2
Station Rd (Filton)	B1	Tower Rd S	C3	West Town La	B3
Station Rd		Trendlewood Pk	B2	West Vw Rd	C3
(Henbury)	A1	Two Mile Hill	C2	Wharne Cliffe Gdns	B3
Station Rd		Two Mile Hill	C2	Whitby Rd	B3
(Keynsham)	C3	Upper Weston	D3	Whitchurch La	B3
Station Rd		Upton Cheyney	D3	Whitchurch Rd	B3
(Patchway)	B1	Vale La	B3	Whitefield Rd	C2
Station Rd		Victoria St		Whitehall	B2
(Shirehampton)	A2	(Bristol)	B2	Whitehall Rd	B2
Station Rd (Yate)	D1	Victoria St		White Ladies Rd	B2
Stockwood	C3	(Staple Hill)	C2	Whiteshill	C1
Stockwood Hill	C3	Vinny Green	C2	Whiteway Rd	C2
Stockwood La	C3	Walsh Av	B3	Whittucks Rd	C3
Stockwood Rd	C3	Wapley	D1	Wick	D2
Stockwood Vale	C3	Wapley Hill	D1	Wick Rd	B3
Stoke Bishop	A2	Wapley Rd	D1	Wild Country La	A3
Stoke Gifford	B1	Warmley	C2	Windmill Hill	B3
Stoke Hill	A2	Watley's End	C1	Winterbourne	C1
Stoke La (Patchway)	B1	Watley's End Rd	C1	Winterbourne Down	C1
Stoke La (Stapleton)	C2	Webb's Heath	D2	Winterbourne Rd	B1
Stoke La (Westbury-		Weir La	A3	Winterstoke Rd	A3
on-Trym)	A2	Wellington Hill	B2	Withywood	A3
Stoke Rd	A2	Wells Rd	B3	Woodend Rd	C1
Stone Hill	C3	Wesbury Park	B2	Woodland Rd	B2
Stone Hill	C3	Westbury Hill	B2	Woodland Way	C2
Sturminster Rd	B3	Westbury La	A2	Wyckbeck Rd	A1
Summerhill Rd	C2	Westbury-on-Trym	A2	Yanley	A3
Sunridge Pk	D1	Westbury Rd	B2	Yanley La	A3
Swan La	C1	Westerleigh	D1	Yate	D1
Sweets Rd	C2	Westerleigh Hill	D1	York Rd	B3
Swineford	D3	Westerleigh Rd		Zetland Rd	B2
Sylvan Way	A2	(Mangotsfield)	C2		
Syston Way	C2	Westerleigh Rd			
Talbot Rd	B3	(Westerleigh)	D1		
Teewell Hill	C2	Westerleigh Rd			
Temple St	C3	(Yate)	D1		
Temple Way	B3	Weston Rd	A3		
Thicket Av	C2	West St			
Third Way	A1	(Bedminster)	B3		

MILTON KEYNES URBAN page 43

Some roads have H (for horizontal) and V (for vertical) road numbers.

Ashland	C2	Conniburrow	B2	Greenleys	B2
Aspley Guise	D2	Cosgrove	A1	Groveway H9	C2
Aspley Heath	D3	Court Rd	D1	Hanslope Rd	A1
Aspley La	D3	Cranfield Airfield	D1	Haversham	B1
Avebury Boul	C2	Cranfield Rd		Haversham Rd	B1
Bancroft	B1	(Moulsoe)	D1	Hayes Rd	A2
Beachampton	A2	Cranfield Rd		Heath Rd	C3
Beanhill	C2	(Salford)	D2	Heelands	B2
Bedford Rd	D2	Cranfield Rd		High St	
Blakelands	C1	(Woburn Sands)	D2	(Cranfield)	D1
Bletcham Way H10	C3	Crawley Rd		High St	
Bletchley	C3	(Cranfield)	D1	(Deanshanger)	A2
Bletchley Rd	B3	Crawley Rd		High St (Great	
Bond Av	C2	(Woburn)	D3	Horwood)	A3
Bow Brickhill	C3	Cross End	D2	High St	
Bow Brickhill Rd	C3	Cross End	D2	(Haversham)	B1
Bradville	B1	Crownhill	B2	High St (Nash)	A3
Bradwell	B2	Dansteed Way H4	B2	High St (Newport	
Bradwell Rd	B1	Davy Av	B2	Pagnell)	C1
Brickhill St V10	C1	Deanshanger	A2	High St	
Brinklow	C2	Deanshanger Rd	A1	(North Crawley)	D1
Brook End	D1	Downs Barn	C1	High St	
Brook End	D1	Drayton Rd		(Potterspury)	A1
Broughton	C2	(Newton Longville)	B3	High St (Stony	
Browns Wood	D2	Drayton Rd		Stratford)	A1
Buckingham Rd		(Water Eaton)	C3	High St (Whaddon)	A3
(Bletchley)	B3	Eaglestone	C2	High St	
Buckingham Rd		East End	D1	(Woburn Sands)	D2
(Deanshanger)	A2	Emerson Valley	B3	High St (Yardley	
Bullington End Rd	A1	Fenny Stratford	C3	Gobion)	A1
Caldecote	C2	Fishermead	C2	Horsepool La	D2
Calverton	A2	Folly La	D1	Husborne	
Calverton La	A2	Fullers Slade	A2	Crawley	D2
Calverton Rd	A2	Fulmer St V3	B2	Kents Hill	C2
Castlethorpe	A1	Furtho	A1	Kiln Farm	B2
Central Milton		Furzton	B2	Kingston	C2
Keynes	B2	Glebe Rd	A1	Lakes La	C1
Chaffron Way H7	C2	Grafton Gate V6	B2	Leighton St	D3
Childs Way H6	C2	Grafton St V6	B2	Leys, The	D2
Chippenham Dr	C2	Grafton Way	A1	Little Brickhill	D3
Church End	D2	Great Brickhill	C3	Little Horwood	A3
Church Rd (Bow		Great Holm	B2	Little Horwood Rd	A3
Brickhill)	D3	Great Horwood	A3	Little Linford	B1
Church Rd		Great Linford	B1	Little Linford La	A3
(Woburn Sands)	D3	Great Monks St V5	B1	Lodge Rd	D1
Church St	A3	Green, The	C1	Lomond Dr	C3
Coddimoor La	A3	Green, The	A2	London Rd	
Coffee Hall	C2	Green End	D3	(Newport Pagnell)	C1

London Rd		Northampton Rd	A1	Station Rd	
(Stony Stratford)	A1	North Crawley	D1	(Bow Brickhill)	C3
London Rd		North Crawley Rd	C1	Station Rd	
(Woburn)	D3	Oldbrook	B2	(Castlethorpe)	A1
Loughton	B2	Old Stratford	A1	Station Rd	
Lower End	D2	Old Wolverton Rd	A1	(Woburn Sands)	D2
Lower End Rd	D2	Overstreet V9	C1	Stock La	A3
McConnell Dr	B1	Park St	D3	Stockwell La	D2
Main St	A2	Passenham	A2	Stoke Rd (Bletchley)	C3
Manor Rd	C3	Pennyland	C1	Stoke Rd (Newton	
Marlborough St V8	C2	Portway H5	C2	Longville)	B3
Marsh Dr	B1	Potterspury	A1	Stony Stratford	A1
Marsh End Rd	C1	Pound La	D1	Stratford Rd	
Midsummer Boul	B2	Poundsfield Rd	A1	(Cosgrove)	A1
Millers Way H2	B1	Queen Eleanor St	A1	Stratford Rd	
Mill La	C3	Rickley La	C3	(Deanshanger)	A2
Milton Keynes	B2	St. Leger Dr	B1	Stratford Rd	
Milton Keynes		Salford	D2	(Whaddon)	A2
Village	C2	Salford Rd		Stratford Rd	
Monkston	C2	(Aspley Guise)	D2	(Wolverton)	A1
Monks Way	C1	Salford Rd		Tattenhoe	B3
Monks Way H3	B2	(Brogborough)	D2	Tattenhoe La	B3
Moorend Rd	A1	Saxon Gate V7	B2	Tattenhoe St V2	B2
Moulsoe	D1	Saxon St V7	B2	Thornborough Rd	A3
Mount Farm	C2	School La	D2	Thornton Rd	A3
Mursley Rd	A3	Secklow Gate	C2	Tickford End	C1
Nash	A3	Sheeplane	D3	Tickford St	C1
Nash Rd (Great		Shenley		Tongwell	C1
Horwood)	A3	Brook End	B2	Tongwell St V11	C1
Nash Rd		Shenley		Turnpike Rd	D3
(Whaddon)	A3	Church End	B2	Two Mile Ash	B2
Neath Hill	C1	Shenley Lodge	B2	Upper Weald	A2
Netherfield	C2	Shenley Rd		V9	C2
New Bradwell	B1	(Bletchley)	C3	Waddon Rd	B3
Newport Pagnell	C1	Shenley Rd		Waddon Way	C3
Newport Rd		(Whaddon)	B3	Walley Dr	C3
(Moulsoe)	C1	Sherington Rd	C1	Walnut Tree	C2
Newport Rd (New		Sherwood Dr	C3	Walton	C3
Bradwell)	B1	Silbury Boul	B2	Walton Rd	C3
Newport Rd		Silver St	A1	Water Eaton	C3
(Woburn)	D3	Simpson	C2	Water Eaton Rd	C3
Newport Rd		Singleborough	A3	Watery La	A2
(Woburn Sands)	D2	Snelshall St	B3	Watling St	
Newton Longville	B3	Snelshall St V1	B3	(Little Brickhill)	C3
Newton Rd		Springfield	C2	Watling St V4	B2
(Bletchley)	B3	Stacey Bushes	B2	Wavendon	C2
Newton Rd		Standing Way H8	B3	Wavendon Rd	D2
(Stoke Hammond)	C3	Stantonbury	B1	Westcroft	B3

Whaddon Rd (Nash) A3
Whaddon Rd (Newton Longville) B3
Winslow Rd A3
Whaddon B3
Whaddon Rd (Mursley) B3
Wharley End D1
Willen C1
Winterhill B2
Woburn D3
Woburn La D2
Woburn Rd D2
Woburn Sands D2
Wolverton B1
Wolverton Rd (Great Linford) B1
Wolverton Rd (Haversham) B1
Wood End Rd D1
Woodside D2
Woolstone C2
Woughton on the Green C2
Yardley Gobion A1
Yardley Rd (Cosgrove) A1
Yardley Rd (Yardley Gobion) A1

LONDON URBAN pages 46 to 53

Abbeville Rd SW4 52 A1
Abbey Rd, Bark. IG11 49 D2
Abbey Rd NW6; NW8 47 F3
Abbey Rd SE2; Belv. DA17 49 E4
Abbey St SE1 48 B4
Abbey Wood SE2 49 E4
Abbotsbury Rd, Mord. SM4 51 F3
Abbott Rd E14 48 C3
Abercorn Pl NW8 47 F3
Acacia Rd, Hmptn. TW12 50 C2
Academy Rd SE18 49 D4
Acre La, Cars. SM5; Wall. SM6 52 A3
Acre La SW2 52 A1
Acton W3 47 E3
Acton La NW10 47 E3
Acton La W3; W4 47 E4
Addington, Croy. CR0 52 C3
Addington Rd, S.Croy. CR2 52 B4
Addington Rd, W.Wick. BR4 52 C3
Addiscombe, Croy. CR0 52 A3
Addiscombe Rd, Croy. CR0 52 B3
Addlestone, Add. KT15 50 A3
Addlestone Moor, Add. KT15 50 A3
Adelaide Av SE4 52 C1
Adelaide Rd NW3 47 F2
Aerodrome Rd NW4; NW9 47 E1
Agincourt Rd NW3 47 F2
Akerman Rd SW9 48 A4
Albany Rd SE5 48 B4
Albany St NW1 48 A3
Albemarle Rd, Beck. BR3 52 C2
Albert Br Rd SW11 47 F4
Albert Rd, Rom. RM1 49 F1
Albert Rd E16 49 D3
Albert Rd N22 48 A1
Albion Rd, Bexh. DA6 53 F1
Albion Rd N16 48 B2
Aldborough Hatch, Ilf. IG2 49 E1
Aldborough Rd N, Ilf. IG2 49 E1
Aldborough Rd S, Ilf. IG3 49 E2
Alderney Av, Houns. TW5 46 C4
Aldersbrook E12 49 D2
Aldersbrook Rd E11; E12 49 D2
Alexandra Av, Har. HA2 46 C2
Alexandra Av W4 47 E4
Alexandra Pk Rd N10; N22 48 A1
Alexandra Rd, Epsom KT17 51 E4
Alexandra Rd SW19 51 F2
Alfreds Way (Barking Bypass), Bark. IG11 49 E3
Allenby Rd, Sthl. UB1 46 C3
All Saints Rd, Sutt. SM1 51 F3
All Souls Av NW10 47 E3
Alperton, Wem. HA0 47 D3
Alperton La, Grnf. UB6; Wem. HA0 47 D3
Ambleside Av, Walt. KT12 50 B3
Amhurst Pk N16 48 B2
Amhurst Rd N16 48 B2
Anerley SE20 52 B2
Anerley Hill SE19 52 B2
Anerley Rd SE19; SE20 52 B2
Anson Rd NW2 47 E2
Arbuthnot La, Bex. DA5 53 F1
Archway Rd N6; N19 47 F1
Argyle Rd W13; Grnf. UB6 47 D3
Arkwright Rd, S.Croy. CR2 52 B4
Armoury Way SW18 51 F1
Arnham Dr, Croy. CR0 52 C4
Arnsberg Way, Bexh. DA7 53 F1
Arthur Rd SW19 51 F2
Ashford, Ashf. TW15 50 A2
Ashford Rd, Ashf. TW15 50 B2
Ashford Rd, Felt. TW13 50 B2
Ashford Rd, Stai. TW18 50 A2
Ashgrove Rd, Brom. BR1 52 C2
Ashley Av, Epsom KT18 51 E4
Ashley Park, Walt. KT12 50 B3
Ashley Pk Rd, Walt. KT12 50 B3
Ashley Rd, Walt. KT12 50 B3
Askew Rd W12 47 E3
Aspen Way E14 48 C3

Avalon Rd, Orp. BR6 53 E3
Avenue, The (Claygate), Esher KT10 50 C3
Avenue, The, Hmptn. TW12 50 C2
Avenue, The (Hatch End), Pnr. HA5 46 C1
Avenue, The, Sun. TW16 50 B2
Avenue, The, Twick. TW1 51 D1
Avenue, The, Wem. HA9 47 D2
Avenue, The, Wor.Pk. KT4 51 E3
Avenue, The SW4 52 A1
Avenue, The W4 47 E4
Avenue Rd NW8 47 F2
Avery Hill SE9 53 D1
Avery Hill Rd SE9 53 E1
Avondale Rd, Brom. BR1 47 F1
Aylmer Rd N2 47 F1
Badgers Mount, Sev. TN14 53 F4
Balaam St E13 49 D3
Balaclava Rd, Surb. KT6 51 D3
Balham SW12 51 F1
Balham High Rd SW12; SW17 52 A1
Balham Hill SW12 52 A1
Ballards La N3; N12 47 F1
Ballards Rd, Dag. RM10 49 F3
Ballards Way, Croy. CR0; S.Croy. CR2 52 B4
Balls Pond Rd N1 48 B2
Balmoral Dr, Hayes UB4 46 B3
Banstead, Bans. SM7 51 F4
Banstead Rd, Bans. SM7; Epsom KT17 51 E4
Banstead Rd, Cars. SM5 51 F4
Banstead Rd S, Sutt. SM2 51 F4
Baring Rd SE12 53 D1
Baring St N1 48 B3
Barking, Bark. IG11 49 D2
Barking Rd E6; E13; E16 48 C3
Barkingside, Ilf. IG6 49 E1
Barlby Rd W10 47 E3
Barley La, Ilf. IG3; Rom. RM6 49 E2
Barnehurst, Bexh. DA7 49 F4
Barnes SW13 51 E1
Barnes High St SW13 47 E4
Barnes Wallis Dr, Wey. KT13 50 A4
Barnfield Wd Rd, Beck. BR3 52 C3
Barnsbury N1 48 A2
Barry Rd SE22 52 B1
Bartholomew Way, Swan. BR8 53 F2
Basildon Rd SE2 49 E4
Baston Rd, Brom. BR2 53 D3
Bath Rd, Hayes UB3; Houns. TW3, TW4, TW5, TW6; West Dr. UB7 46 B4
Bath Rd W4 47 E4
Battersea SW11 47 F4
Battersea Br Rd SW11 47 F4
Battersea Pk Rd SW8; SW11 47 F4
Battersea Ri SW11 51 F1
Bayswater W2 47 F3
Bayswater Rd W2 47 F3
Bear Rd, Felt. TW13 50 B2
Beavers La, Houns. TW4 46 B4
Beckenham, Beck. BR3 52 C2
Beckenham Hill Rd SE6; Beck. BR3 52 C2
Beckenham La, Brom. BR2 52 C2
Beckenham Rd, Beck. BR3 52 C2
Beckton E6 49 D3
Becontree, Dag. RM8 49 E2
Becontree Av, Dag. RM8 49 E2
Becontree Heath, Dag. RM8 49 F2
Beddington, Croy. CR0 52 A3
Beddington La, Croy. CR0 52 A3
Bedfont, Felt. TW13, TW14 50 B1
Bedfont Rd, Felt. TW13, TW14 50 B1

Bedfont Rd (Stanwell), Stai. TW19 50 A1
Bedford Hill SW12; SW16 52 A1
Bedford Park W4 47 E4
Bedford Rd SW4 52 A1
Bedonwell Rd, Bexh. DA7; Belv. DA17 49 F4
Beeches Av, Cars. SM5 51 F4
Beehive La, Ilf. IG1, IG4 49 D1
Belgrave Rd SW1 48 A4
Belgrave Sq SW1 48 A4
Bellegrove Rd, Well. DA16 49 E4
Bellevue Rd SW17 51 F1
Bell Green SE6 52 C1
Bell Grn SE26 52 C1
Bellingham SE6 52 C1
Bell La NW4 47 E1
Belmont, Har. HA3 47 D1
Belmont, Sutt. SM2 51 F4
Belmont Hill SE13 52 C1
Belmont Ri, Sutt. SM2 51 F4
Belmont Rd, Erith DA8 49 F4
Belmont Rd, Uxb. UB9 46 A2
Belmont Rd N15 48 B1
Belsize Park NW3 47 F2
Belsize Rd NW6 47 F3
Belvedere, Belv. DA17 49 F4
Belvedere Rd, Bexh. DA7 53 F1
Benhill Rd, Sutt. SM1 51 F3
Benhilton, Sutt. SM1 51 F3
Ben Jonson Rd E1 48 C3
Bennetsfield Rd, Uxb. UB11 46 A3
Bennetts Castle La, Dag. RM8 49 E2
Bensham La, Croy. CR0; Th.Hth. CR7 52 A3
Bentham Rd SE28 49 E3
Benton Rd, Ilf. IG1 49 E2
Beresford St SE18 49 D4
Berkshire Gdns N13 48 A1
Bermondsey SE1 48 B4
Berrylands, Surb. KT5 51 D3
Berry's Green, West. TN16 53 D4
Bessborough Rd, Har. HA1 46 C2
Bethnal Green E2 48 B3
Bethnal Grn Rd E1; E2 48 B3
Bethune Rd N16 48 B2
Between Sts, Cob. KT11 50 B4
Beulah Hill SE19 52 A2
Beverley Dr, Edg. HA8 47 D1
Beverley Rd, Dag. RM9 49 F2
Beverley Way (Kingston Bypass) SW20 51 E2
Bexley, Bex. DA5 53 E1
Bexleyheath, Bexh. DA6 53 F1
Bexley High St, Bex. DA5 53 F1
Bexley La, Sid. DA14 53 E2
Bexley Rd, Erith DA8 49 F4
Bexley Rd SE9 53 D1
Bickley, Brom. BR1 53 D2
Bickley Pk Rd, Brom. BR1 53 D2
Bickley Rd, Brom. BR1 53 D2
Biggin Hill, West. TN16 53 D4
Billet La, Rom. RM6 49 E1
Billet Rd E17 48 B1
Bilton Rd, Grnf. UB6 47 D3
Birchwood Rd, Dart. DA2; Swan. BR8 53 F2
Birdcage Wk SW1 48 A4
Bishops Av, The N2 47 F2
Bishops Br Rd W2 47 F3
Bishopsford Rd, Mord. SM4 51 F3
Bishopsgate EC2 48 B3
Bishops Way E2 48 C2
Bittacy Hill NW7 47 E1
Blackbrook La, Brom. BR1, BR2 53 D2
Blackfen, Sid. DA15 53 E1
Blackfen Rd, Sid. DA15 53 E1
Blackfriars Rd SE1 48 A3
Blackheath SE3 48 C4
Blackheath Park SE3 53 D1
Blackheath Hill SE10 48 C4
Blackhorse La E17 48 B1
Blackshaw Rd SW17 51 F2
Blackstock Rd N4; N5 48 A2
Blackwall La SE10 48 C4

Blackwall Tunnel E14 48 C3
Blake Hall Rd E11 49 D2
Blendon Rd, Bex. DA5 53 E1
Bloomsbury WC1 48 A3
Blossom Way, Uxb. UB10 46 A2
Bollo La W3; W4 47 D4
Bolters La, Bans. SM7 51 F4
Booth Rd NW9 47 E1
Bostall Hill SE2 49 E4
Boston Manor Rd, Brent. TW8 47 D4
Boston Rd W7 46 C4
Botwell Common Rd, Hayes UB3 46 B3
Botwell La, Hayes UB3 46 B3
Boundary Rd E13 49 D3
Boundary Rd E17 48 B1
Bounds Grn Rd N11; N22 48 A1
Bourne Rd, Bex. DA5; Dart. DA1 53 F1
Bourne Way, Brom. BR2 52 C3
Bow E3 48 C3
Bowes Rd, Walt. KT12 50 B3
Bow Rd E3 48 C3
Boxtree La, Har. HA3 46 C1
Boxtree Rd, Har. HA3 46 C1
Brady St E1 48 B3
Bramley Hill, S.Croy. CR2 52 A3
Brampton Rd SE2; Bexh. DA7 49 F4
Brantwood Rd N17 48 B1
Breakspear Rd, Ruis. HA4 46 A1
Breakspear Rd N, Uxb. UB9 46 A1
Breakspear Rd S, Uxb. UB9, UB10 46 A2
Brecknock Rd N7; N19 47 F2
Brentfield NW10 47 E2
Brentfield Rd NW10 47 E2
Brentford, Brent. TW8 47 D4
Brent St NW4 47 E1
Brick La E1; E2 48 B3
Bridge La NW11 47 F1
Bridge Rd, Cher. KT16 50 A3
Bridge Rd, E.Mol. KT8 50 C2
Bridge Rd, Epsom KT17 51 E4
Bridge Rd, Houns. TW3; Islw. TW7 50 C1
Bridge St, Walt. KT12 50 B3
Bridgewater Rd, Wem. HA0 47 D2
Bridle Rd, Pnr. HA5 46 B1
Brighton Rd, Add. KT15 50 A3
Brighton Rd, Bans. SM7 51 D3
Brigstock Rd, Th.Hth. CR7 52 A3
Brixton SW2 52 A1
Brixton Hill SW2 52 A1
Brixton Rd SW9 48 A4
Brixton Water La SW2 52 A1
Broad La, Hmptn. TW12 50 C2
Broad La N15 48 B1
Broadmead Rd, Wdf. Grn. IG8 49 D1
Broad Wk SE3 49 D4
Broadway, Bexh. DA6 53 F1
Broadway E15 48 C2
Broadway, The, Add. KT15 50 A4
Broadway, The, Grnf. UB6 46 C3
Broadway, The, Sthl. UB1 46 B3
Broadway, The, Stai. TW18 50 A2
Broadway, The, Sutt. SM3 51 E4
Broadway, The SW19 51 F2
Broadway, The SW20 51 E2
Broadway, The W5 47 D3
Brockley SE4 52 C1
Brockley Gro SE4 52 C1
Brockley Ri SE23 52 C1
Brockley Rd SE4 52 C1
Bromley, Brom. BR 53 D2
Bromley E3 48 C3
Bromley Common, Brom. BR2 53 D3
Bromley Common, Brom. BR2 53 D2
Bromley Hill, Brom. BR1 52 C2
Bromley La, Chis. BR7 53 E2

Bromley Rd, Beck. BR3; Brom. BR2 52 C2
Bromley Rd SE6; Brom. BR1 52 C1
Brompton SW3 47 F4
Brompton Rd SW1; SW3; SW7 47 F4
Brondesbury NW2 47 E2
Brondesbury Pk NW2; NW6 47 E2
Brondesbury Rd NW6 47 F3
Bronze Age Way, Belv. DA17; Erith DA8 49 F4
Brooklands, Wey. KT13 50 A4
Brooklands Rd, Wey. KT13 50 A4
Brookmill Rd SE8 48 C4
Brook St (Lessness Heath), Belv. DA17; Erith DA8 49 F4
Broom Rd, Tedd. TW11 51 D2
Broomwood Rd SW11 51 F1
Browells La, Felt. TW13 50 B1
Brownhill Rd SE6 52 C1
Browning Rd E12 49 D2
Brownlow Rd N11 48 A1
Bruce Gro N17 48 B1
Brunswick Rd W5 47 D3
Buckhold Rd SW18 51 F1
Bugsby's Way SE7; SE10 49 D4
Bunns La NW7 47 E1
Burdett Rd E3; E14 48 C3
Burdon La, Sutt. SM2 51 F4
Burges Rd E6 49 D2
Burgh Heath Rd, Epsom KT17 51 E4
Burlington La W4 47 E4
Burlington Rd, N.Mal. KT3 51 E2
Burns Av, Felt. TW14 50 B1
Burnt Ash Hill SE12 53 D1
Burnt Ash La, Brom. BR1 53 D2
Burnt Ash Rd SE12 52 C1
Burnt Oak, Edg. HA8 47 E1
Burnt Oak Bdy, Edg. HA8 47 D1
Burntwood La SW17 51 F1
Burrage Rd SE18 49 D4
Burwood Park, Walt. KT12 50 B3
Burwood Rd, Walt. KT12 50 B4
Bury St, Ruis. HA4 46 B1
Bushey Mead SW20 51 E2
Bushey Rd SW20 51 E2
Bush Rd E11 49 D2
Byfleet, W.Byf. KT14 50 A4
Byfleet Rd, Add. KT15 50 A4
Byfleet Rd, Cob. KT11 50 A4
Byron Rd, Har. HA3 46 C1
Cable St E1 48 B3
Cadbury Rd, Sun. TW16 50 B2
Cadlocks Hill, Sev. TN14 53 F4
Caledonian Rd N1; N7 48 A2
Calmont Rd, Brom. BR1 52 C2
Calverley Rd, Epsom KT17 51 E4
Camberwell SE5 48 B4
Camberwell Ch St SE5 48 B4
Camberwell New Rd SE5 48 A4
Camberwell Rd SE5 48 B4
Cambridge Heath Rd E1; E2 48 B3
Camden High St NW1 48 A3
Camden Rd N7; NW1 48 A2
Camden Town NW1 48 A2
Cameron Rd, Ilf. IG3 49 E2
Camphill Rd, W.Byf. KT14 50 A4
Camrose Av, Edg. HA8 47 D1
Canning Town E16 48 C3
Cannizaro Rd SW19 51 E2
Cannon Hill La SW20 51 E3
Cannon St Rd E1 48 B3
Canonbury Rd N1 48 A2
Canons Park, Edg. HA8 47 D1
Canterbury Rd, Croy. CR0 52 A3
Capel Rd E7; E12 49 D2
Capworth St E10 48 C2
Carlton Rd, Erith DA8 49 F4
Carlton Rd, S.Croy. CR2 52 B4
Carlyle Rd SE28 48 C2
Carpenters Rd E15 48 C2
Carr Rd, Nthlt. UB5 46 C2
Carshalton, Cars. SM5 53 D3

Entry	Page	Grid
Carshalton Beeches, Cars. SM5	51	F4
Carshalton on the Hill, Cars. SM5	52	A4
Carshalton Rd, Bans. SM7	51	F4
Carshalton Rd, Cars. SM5; Sutt. SM1	51	F3
Carshalton Rd, Mitch. CR4	52	A3
Cassland Rd E9	48	B2
Castelnau SW13	47	E4
Castelnau SW13	47	E4
Castlebar Hill W5	47	D3
Castlebar Rd W5	47	D3
Castle Fm Rd, Sev. TN14	53	F4
Catford SE6	52	C1
Catford Hill SE6	52	C1
Catford Rd SE6	52	C1
Cathall Rd E11	48	C2
Causeway, The, Felt. TW14	50	B1
Cavendish Rd SW12	52	A1
Cazenove Rd N16	48	B2
Cedars Rd SW4	52	A1
Cedars Rd W4	47	D4
Central Av, Houns. TW3	50	C1
Central Hill SE19	52	B2
Central Par, Croy. CR0	52	C4
Central Pk Rd E6	49	D3
Central Rd, Mord. SM4	51	F3
Central Rd, Wor.Pk. KT4	51	E3
Central Way SE28	49	E3
Centre Rd E7; E11	49	D2
Chadwell Heath, Rom. RM6	49	E1
Chadwell Heath La, Rom. RM6	49	E1
Chalk Fm Rd NW1	48	A2
Chamberlayne Rd NW10	47	E3
Charlton SE7	49	D4
Charlton Ch La SE7	49	D4
Charlton La, Shep. TW17	50	B2
Charlton Pk La SE7	49	D4
Charlton Pk Rd SE7	49	D4
Charlton Rd, Har. HA3	47	D1
Charlton Rd, Shep. TW17	50	B2
Charlton Rd SE3; SE7	49	D4
Charlton Way SE3	48	C4
Charter Rd, The, Wdf.Grn. IG8	48	C1
Charville La, Hayes UB4	46	B3
Chase, The, Stan. HA7	47	D1
Chase Cross, Rom. RM1	49	F1
Chase Cross Rd, Rom. RM5	49	F1
Chase Rd NW10; W3	47	E3
Cheam, Sutt. SM3	51	E4
Cheam Common Rd, Wor.Pk. KT4	51	E3
Cheam Rd, Epsom KT17; Sutt. SM2	51	E4
Cheam Rd, Sutt. SM1	51	F4
Cheapside EC2	48	B3
Chelsea SW3	47	F4
Chelsea Embk SW3	48	A4
Chelsfield, Orp. BR6	53	E3
Chelsfield Hill, Orp. BR6	53	E4
Chelsfield La, Orp. BR5, BR6	53	E3
Chelsfield La, Orp. BR6; Sev. TN14	53	F4
Chelsfield Rd, Orp. BR5	53	E3
Chepstow Rd W2	47	F3
Chequers La, Dag. RM9	49	F3
Cherry La, West Dr. UB7	46	A4
Cherry Tree La, Rain. RM13	49	F3
Chertsey Rd, Add. KT15	50	A3
Chertsey Rd, Felt. TW13; Sun. TW16	50	B2
Chertsey Rd, Shep. TW17	50	A3
Chertsey Rd, Twick. TW1, TW2	50	C1
Chessington, Chess. KT9	51	D4
Chessington Rd, Epsom KT17; KT19	51	D4
Cheyne Wk SW10	47	F4
Chichele Rd NW2	47	E2
Chigwell Rd, E18; Wdf.Grn. IG8	49	D1
Childs Hill NW2	47	F2
Chiltern Rd, Sutt. SM2	51	F4
Chinbrook Rd SE12	53	D1
Chingford Rd E4; E17	48	C1
Chipperfield Rd, Orp. BR5	53	E2
Chislehurst, Chis. BR7	53	D2
Chislehurst Rd, Brom. BR1; Chis. BR7	53	D2
Chislehurst Rd, Orp. BR5, BR6	53	E2
Chislehurst Rd, Sid. DA14	53	E2
Chislehurst West, Chis. BR7	53	D2
Chiswick W4	47	D4
Chiswick High Rd W4; Brent. TW8	47	D4
Chiswick La W4	47	E4
Choats Manor Way, Bark. IG11	49	F3
Choats Rd, Bark. IG11	49	E3
Chobham Rd E15	48	C2
Chrisp St E14	48	C3
Christchurch Av, Har. HA3	47	D1
Christ Ch Rd, Epsom KT19	51	D4
Christchurch Rd SW2	52	A1
Church Elm La, Dag. RM10	49	F2
Church End N3	47	F1
Church Gro, Kings.T. KT1	51	D2
Church Hill (Harefield), Uxb. UB9	46	A1
Church Hill Rd, Sutt. SM3	51	E3
Church La, Chess. KT9	51	D4
Church La, Dag. RM10	49	F2
Church La E11	48	C2
Church La NW9	47	E1
Church La SW17	52	A2
Church Rd, Add. KT15	50	A3
Church Rd, Ashf. TW15	50	A2
Church Rd, Bexh. DA7	53	F1
Church Rd, Epsom KT17	51	E4
Church Rd, Hayes UB3	46	B3
Church Rd (Heston), Houns.TW5	46	C4
Church Rd, Kes. BR2	53	D4
Church Rd, Mitch. CR4	51	F2
Church Rd, Nthlt. UB5	46	B3
Church Rd (Chelsfield), Orp. BR6	53	E4
Church Rd (Farnborough), Orp. BR6	53	E3
Church Rd (Halstead), Sev. TN14	53	F4
Church Rd (Crockenhill), Swan. BR8	53	F3
Church Rd (Cowley), Uxb. UB8	46	A3
Church Rd, Wor.Pk. KT4	51	E3
Church Rd E10	48	C2
Church Rd NW10	47	E2
Church Rd SE19	52	B2
Church Rd SW13	47	E4
Church Rd SW19	51	E2
Church Rd W7	46	C3
Church St, Cob. KT11	50	B4
Church St, Epsom KT17	51	E4
Church St, Hmptn. TW12	50	C2
Church St (Shoreham), Sev. TN14	53	F4
Church St, Walt. KT12	50	B3
Church St, Wey. KT13	50	A3
Church Way, S.Croy. CR2	52	B4
City Rd EC1	48	A3
Clandon Cl, Epsom KT17	51	E4
Clapham SW4	52	A1
Clapham Common N Side SW4	52	A1
Clapham Common S Side SW4	52	A1
Clapham Park SW4	52	A1
Clapham Pk Rd SW4	52	A1
Clapham Rd SW9	48	A4
Clapton Common E5	48	B2
Clapton Park E5	48	B2
Claremont La, Esher KT10	50	C3
Claremont Park, Esher KT10	50	C4
Claremont Rd, Surb. KT6	51	D3
Claremont Rd W9	51	E2
Clarence Av, N.Mal. KT3	51	E2
Clarence La SW15	51	E1
Clarendon Rd, Uxb. UB8	46	A3
Claygate, Esher KT10	50	C4
Clayhall, Ilf. IG5	49	D1
Clayhall Av, Ilf. IG5	49	D1
Clayton Rd, Chess. KT9	51	D3
Clayton Rd SE15	48	B4
Clerkenwell Rd EC1	48	A3
Cleveland Rd, Uxb. UB8	46	A3
Clifford Av SW14	51	D1
Clifton Gdns W9	47	F3
Clockhouse La, Ashf. TW15; Felt. TW14	50	A2
Clockhouse La, Rom. RM5	49	F1
Clyde Rd, Croy. CR0	52	B3
Cobham, Cob. KT11	50	B4
Cockerhurst Rd, Sev. TN14	53	F4
Coldblow, Bex. DA5	53	F1
Coldharbour La, Hayes UB3	46	B3
Coldharbour La SE5; SW9	52	A1
Colham Grn Rd, Uxb. UB8	46	A3
Colindale Av NW9	47	E1
Colindeep La NW4; NW9	47	E1
College Hill Rd, Har. HA3	46	C1
College Rd, Brom. BR1	53	D2
College Rd, Epsom KT17	51	E4
College Rd, Har. HA1	46	C1
College Rd, Swan. BR8	53	F2
College Rd SE19; SE21	52	B1
Collier Row, Rom. RM5	49	F1
Collier Row La, Rom. RM5	49	F1
Collier Row Rd, Rom. RM5	49	F1
Collier's Wood SW19	51	F2
Colney Hatch La N10; N11	47	F1
Colyers La, Erith DA8	49	F4
Commercial Rd, Stai. TW18	50	A2
Commercial Rd E1; E14	48	B3
Commercial St E1	48	B3
Commercial Way SE15	48	B4
Commonside, Kes. BR2	53	D3
Commonside E, Mitch. CR4	52	A2
Commonside W, Mitch. CR4	51	F2
Coningham Rd W12	47	E3
Connaught Rd E16	49	D3
Convent Rd, Ashf. TW15	50	A2
Cool Oak La NW9	47	E2
Coombe, Kings.T. KT2	51	E2
Coombe La, Croy. CR0	52	B3
Coombe La SW20	51	E2
Coombe La W, Kings.T. KT2	51	D2
Coombe Rd, Croy. CR0	52	B3
Coombe Rd, Kings.T. KT2	51	D2
Coombe Rd, N.Mal. KT3	51	E2
Copenhagen St N1	48	A3
Coppetts Rd N10	48	A1
Copse Hill SW20	51	E2
Copsem La, Esher KT10; Lthd. KT22	50	C4
Corkscrew Hill, W.Wick. BR4	52	C3
Coronation Rd NW10	47	D3
Cotswold Rd, Sutt. SM2	51	F4
Cottenham Pk Rd SW20	51	E2
Cottimore La, Walt. KT12	50	B3
Country Way, Felt. TW13; Sun. TW16	50	B2
Court Dr, Uxb. UB10	46	A3
Court Rd (Orpington Bypass), Orp. BR6	53	E3
Court Rd SE9	53	D1
Cowley, Uxb. UB8	46	A3
Cowley Mill Rd, Uxb. UB8	46	A3
Cowley Rd, Uxb. UB8	46	A3
Cox La, Chess. KT9	51	D3
Crab Hill, Beck. BR3	52	C2
Cranbrook, Ilf. IG1	49	D2
Cranbrook Rd, Ilf. IG1, IG2, IG6	49	D1
Cranford, Houns. TW5	46	B4
Cranford La, Hayes UB3	46	B4
Cranford La (Heston), Houns. TW5	46	B4
Cranley Gdns N10	48	A1
Cranmer Rd, Mitch. CR4	51	F2
Craven Gdns, Ilf. IG6	49	E1
Craven Pk NW10	47	E3
Cray Av, Orp. BR5	53	E3
Crayford, Dart. DA1	53	F1
Crayford Rd, Dart. DA1	53	F1
Crayford Way, Dart. DA1	53	F1
Cray Rd, Sid. DA14	53	E2
Cray Rd, Swan. BR8	53	F3
Creekmouth, Bark. IG11	49	E3
Creek Rd SE8; SE10	48	C4
Creighton Av N2; N10	47	F1
Cricklewood NW2	47	E2
Cricklewood La NW2	47	F2
Crockenhill, Swan. BR8	53	F3
Crockenhill Rd, Orp. BR5; Swan. BR8	53	E3
Crofton La, Orp. BR5, BR6	53	E3
Crofton Rd, Orp. BR6	53	D3
Croham Manor Rd, S.Croy. CR2	52	B4
Croham Rd, S.Croy. CR2	52	B3
Croham Valley Rd, S.Croy. CR2	52	B4
Cromwell Rd SW5; SW7	47	F4
Crook Log, Bexh. DA6	53	E1
Cross Deep, Twick. TW1	50	C1
Cross Rd, Rom. RM7	49	F1
Crossway SW20	51	E2
Crouch End N8	48	A1
Crouch Hall Rd N8	48	A2
Crouch Hill N4; N8	48	A1
Crow La, Rom. RM7	49	F2
Crown Dale SE19	52	B2
Crown La, Brom. BR2	53	D3
Crown La, Mord. SM4	51	F3
Crown La SW16	52	A2
Crown Rd, Twick. TW1	51	D1
Crowshott Av, Stan. HA7	47	D1
Croxted Rd SE21; SE24	52	B1
Croydon, Croy. CR0	52	B3
Croydon La, Bans. SM7	51	F4
Croydon Rd, Beck. BR3	52	C2
Croydon Rd, Brom. BR2; W.Wick. BR4	52	C3
Croydon Rd, Croy. CR0; Mitch. CR4	52	A3
Croydon Rd, Croy. CR0; Wall. SM6	52	A3
Croydon Rd SE20	52	B2
Crystal Palace Par SE19	52	B2
Crystal Palace Pk Rd SE26	52	B2
Cubitt Town E14	48	C4
Cuckoo Hill, Pnr. HA5	46	B1
Cuddington Way, Sutt. SM2	51	E4
Cudham, Sev. TN14	53	E4
Cudham La N, Orp. BR6; Sev. TN14	53	E4
Cudham Rd, Orp. BR6	53	D4
Culver Gro, Stan. HA7	47	D1
Currey Rd, Grnf. UB6	46	C2
Custom House E16	49	D3
Dagenham, Dag. RM9	49	F2
Dagenham Rd, Dag. RM10; Rom. RM7	49	F2
Dagenham Rd, Rain. RM13	49	F2
Dalston E8	48	B2
Dalston La E8	48	B2
Daltons Rd, Orp. BR6; Swan. BR8	53	F3
Dames Rd E7	49	D2
Danson La, Well. DA16	53	E1
Danson Rd, Bex. DA5; Bexh. DA6	53	E1
Dartford Rd, Bex. DA5	53	F1
Dartmouth Park NW5	48	A2
Dartmouth Pk Hill N19; NW5	48	A2
Dartmouth Rd SE23; SE26	52	B1
Dartnell Park, W.Byf. KT14	50	A4
Davidson Rd, Croy. CR0	52	B3
Dawes Rd SW6	47	F4
Dawley Rd, Hayes UB3	46	B3
Days La, Sid. DA15	53	E1
Deansbrook Rd, Edg. HA8	47	D1
Deans La, Edg. HA8	47	E1
Denham, Uxb. UB9	46	A2
Denmark Hill SE5	52	B1
Denning Av, Croy. CR0	52	A3
Deptford SE8	48	C4
Deptford Ch St SE8	48	C4
Derry Downs, Orp. BR5	53	E3
Devas St E3	48	C3
Devonshire Rd NW7	47	E1
Devonshire Rd SE23	52	B1
Devons Rd E3	48	C3
Ditton Hill, Surb. KT6	51	D3
Ditton Rd, Surb. KT6	51	D3
Dog Kennel Hill SE22	52	B1
Dollis Hill NW2	47	E2
Dollis Hill La NW2	47	E2
Dollis Rd N3; NW7	47	F1
Dormer's Wells, Sthl. UB1	46	C3
Dorset Rd SW19	51	F2
Dover Ho Rd SW15	51	E1
Downe, Orp. BR6	53	D4
Downe La, Kes. BR2	53	D4
Downe Rd, Kes. BR2	53	D4
Downe Rd, Sev. TN14	53	E4
Downham, Brom. BR1	52	C2
Downham Way, Brom. BR1	52	C2
Downhills Way N17	48	B1
Downs Ct Rd, Pur. CR8	52	A4
Downside Br Rd, Cob. KT11	50	B4
Downs Rd, Sutt. SM2	51	F4
Drakefell Rd SE4; SE14	52	B1
Draycott Av, Har. HA3	47	D1
Drayton Grn Rd W13	47	D3
Drayton Pk N5	48	A2
Drive, The, Ilf. IG1	49	D2
Drive, The, Mord. SM4	51	F3
Drury Way NW10	47	E2
Ducks Hill Rd, Nthwd. HA6; Ruis. HA4	46	A1
Dudden Hill La NW10	47	E2
Dukes Av, Rich. TW10; Kings.T. KT2	51	D2
Dulwich SE21	52	B1
Dulwich Common SE21; SE22	52	B1
Dulwich Rd SE24	52	A1
Dulwich Village SE21	52	B1
Dulwich Wd Pk SE19	52	B1
Dunton Rd SE1	48	B4
Durham Rd SW20	51	E2
Durnsford Rd N11	48	A1
Durnsford Rd SW19	51	F1
Ealing W5	47	D3
Ealing Grn W5	47	D3
Ealing Rd, Brent. TW8	47	D4
Ealing Rd, Wem. HA0	47	D2
Earls Ct Rd SW5; W8	47	F4
Earlsfield SW18	51	F1
Earlsfield Rd SW18	51	F1
East Acton W3	47	E3
East Av E12	49	D2
East Bedfont, Felt. TW14	50	B1
Eastbury Rd, Nthwd. HA6	46	B1
Eastcote, Pnr. HA5	46	B1
Eastcote La, Har. HA2	46	C2
Eastcote La, Nthlt. UB5	46	C2
Eastcote Rd, Pnr. HA5	46	B1
Eastcote Rd, Ruis. HA4	46	B2
Eastcote Village, Pnr. HA5	46	B1
East Cross Route E3	48	C2
East Dulwich SE22	52	B1
East Dulwich Gro SE22	52	B1
East Dulwich Rd SE15; SE22	52	B1
East End Rd N2; N3	47	F1
Eastern Av, Rom. RM1, RM2, RM3	49	D1
Eastern Av E11; Ilf. IG2, IG4	49	D1
Eastern Av E, Rom. RM1, RM2, RM3	49	E1
Eastern Av W, Rom. RM1, RM5, RM6, RM7	49	E1
Eastern Way SE2; SE28; Belv. DA17; Erith DA18	49	E4
East Ewell, Sutt. SM2	51	E4
East Ferry Rd E14	48	C4
East Finchley N2	47	F1
East Ham E6	49	D3
East Heath Rd NW3	47	F2
East Hill SW18	51	F1
East India Dock Rd E14	48	C3
East La, Wem. HA0	47	D2
East Molesey, E.Mol. KT8	50	C2
East Rd N1	48	B3
East Rochester Way SE9; Bex. DA5; Sid. DA15	53	E1
East Sheen SW14	51	E1
East St, Epsom KT17	51	E4
East St SE17	48	B4
Eastway E9; E10; E15	48	C2
East Wickham, Well. DA16	49	E4
Eastworth Rd, Cher. KT16	50	A3
Eaton Pk Rd, Cob. KT11	50	C4
Eaton Ri W5	47	D3
Eden Park, Beck. BR3	52	C3
Eden Pk Av, Beck. BR3	52	C2
Eden St, Kings.T. KT1	51	D2
Edgington Way, Sid. DA14	53	E2
Edgware Rd NW2	47	E2
Edgware Rd NW9	47	E1
Edgware Rd W2	47	F3
Effra Rd SW2	52	A1
Elder Rd SE27	52	B2
Elgar Av, Surb. KT5	51	D3
Elgin Av W9	47	F3
Ellesmere Rd W4	47	E4
Elm Av, Ruis. HA4	46	B2
Elmbridge Rd, Ilf. IG6	49	E1
Elmers End, Beck. BR3	52	C2
Elmers End Rd, SE20; Beck. BR3	52	B2
Elm Pk Rd, Pnr. HA5	46	B1
Elm Rd, Chess. KT9	51	D3
Elm Rd, Sid. DA14	53	E2
Elms Rd, Har. HA3	46	C1
Elmstead, Chis. BR7	53	D2
Elmstead La, Chis. BR7	53	D2
Elmwood Dr, Bex. DA5	53	F1
Eltham SE9	53	D1
Eltham High St SE9	53	D1
Eltham Hill SE9	53	D1
Eltham Rd SE9; SE12	53	D1
Embercourt Rd, T.Ditt. KT7	50	C3
Ember La, E.Mol. KT8; Esher KT10	50	C3
Emlyn Rd W12	47	E4
Emmanuel Rd SW12	52	A1
Empire Way, Wem. HA9	47	D2
Endymion Rd N4	48	A2
Englefield Rd N1	48	B2
Epsom, Epsom KT17	51	E4
Epsom Rd, Croy. CR0	52	A4
Epsom Rd, Epsom KT17	51	E4
Epsom Rd, Mord. SM4; Sutt. SM3	51	F3
Eriswell Rd, Walt. KT12	50	B4
Erith, Erith DA8	49	F4
Erith High St, Erith DA8	49	F4
Erith Rd, Bexh. DA7	53	F1
Erith Rd, Bexh. DA7; Erith DA8	49	F4
Esher, Esher KT10	50	C3
Esher Bypass, Cob. KT11; Esher KT10	50	C3
Esher Grn, Esher KT10	50	C3
Esher Pk Av, Esher KT10	50	C3
Esher Rd, E.Mol. KT8	50	C3
Esher Rd, Walt. KT12	50	C3
Essex Rd N1	48	A3
Euston Rd N1; NW1	48	A3
Evelina Rd SE15	48	B4
Evelyn Av, Ruis. HA4	46	B2
Evelyn Dr, Pnr. HA5	46	B1
Evelyn St SE8	48	C4
Ewell, Epsom KT17	51	E4
Ewell Bypass, Epsom KT17	51	E4

Ewell Rd (Long Ditton), Surb. KT6 51 D3
Ewell Rd, Sutt. SM3 51 E4
Eynsford Rd, Swan. BR8 53 F3
Eynsham Dr SE2 49 E4
Faggs Rd, Felt. TW14 50 B1
Fairchildes La, Warl. CR6 52 C4
Fairfield Rd E3 48 C3
Fairfield S, Kings.T. KT1 51 D2
Fairlop Rd, Ilf. IG6 49 D1
Fairmile, Cob. KT11 50 C4
Fairmile La, Cob. KT11 50 B4
Fairoak La, Chess. KT9; Lthd. KT22 50 C4
Fairway, The, Ruis. HA4 46 B2
Falcon Rd SW11 47 F4
Falconwood, Well. DA16 53 E1
Falling La, West Dr. UB7 46 A3
Falloden Way NW11 47 F1
Fanshawe Av, Bark. IG11 49 E2
Farleigh, Warl. CR6 52 C4
Farleigh Ct Rd, Warl. CR6 52 C4
Farley Rd, S.Croy. CR2 52 B4
Farm Rd, Mord. SM4 51 F3
Farnaby Rd, Brom. BR1, BR2 52 C2
Farnborough, Orp. BR6 53 E3
Farnborough Common, Orp. BR6 53 D3
Farnborough Hill, Orp. BR6 53 E3
Farnborough Way, Orp. BR6 53 E3
Featherbed La, Croy. CR0; Warl. CR6 52 C4
Feltham, Felt. TW13 50 B1
Felthambrook Way, Felt. TW13 50 B1
Felthamhill, Felt. TW13 50 B2
Feltham Hill Rd, Ashf. TW15 50 A2
Feltham Hill Rd, Felt. TW13 50 B2
Feltham Rd, Ashf. TW15 50 A2
Fentiman Rd SW8 48 A4
Fernhead Rd W9 47 F3
Fern La, Houns. TW5 46 C4
Ferry La, Rain. RM13 49 F3
Ferry La (Laleham), Stai. TW18 50 A2
Ferry La N17 48 B1
Ferry Rd SW13 47 E4
Field End Rd, Pnr. HA5; Ruis. HA4 46 B2
Filston La, Sev. TN14 53 F4
Finborough Rd SW10; SW17 47 F4
Finchley N3 47 F1
Finchley La NW4 47 E1
Finchley Rd NW2; NW3; NW8; NW11 47 F2
Finsbury EC1 48 A3
Fitzjohns Av NW3 47 F2
Fleece Rd, Surb. KT6 51 D3
Foots Cray, Sid. DA14 53 E2
Foots Cray La, Sid. DA14 53 E1
Footscray Rd SE9 53 D1
Fordbridge Rd, Ashf. TW15 50 A2
Fordbridge Rd, Shep. TW17; Sun. TW16 50 B3
Fordwater Rd, Cher. KT16 50 A3
Forestdale, Croy. CR0 52 C4
Forest Dr E12 49 D2
Foresters Dr, Wall. SM6 52 A4
Forest Hill SE23 52 B1
Forest Hill Rd SE22; SE23 52 B1
Forest La E7; E15 48 C2
Fore St, Pnr. HA5 46 B1
Fore St N9; N18 48 B1
Forest Ri E17 48 C1
Forest Rd, Rom. RM7 49 E1
Forest Rd, Sutt. SM3 51 F3
Forest Rd E17 48 B1
Fortess Rd NW5 48 A2
Fortis Grn N2; N10 47 F1
Fortune Grn Rd NW6 47 F2
Forty Av, Wem. HA9 47 D2
Forty La, Wem. HA9 47 D2
Fourth Av E12 49 D2
Foxgrove Rd, Beck. BR3 52 C2
Fox Hill, Kes. BR2 53 D3
Fox La, Kes. BR2 53 D3
Foxley La, Pur. CR8 52 A4
Frances St SE18 49 D4
Francis Rd E10 48 C2
Fraser Rd, Erith DA8 49 F4
Freemasons Rd E16 49 D3
Free Prae Rd, Cher. KT16 50 A3
French St, Sun. TW16 50 B2
Frith La NW7 47 F1
Fryent Way NW9 47 D1
Fulbourne Rd E17 48 C1
Fulham SW6 47 F4
Fulham Palace Rd SW6; W6 47 E4
Fulham Rd SW3; SW10 47 F4
Fulham Rd SW6 47 F4
Fullers Way N, Surb. KT6 51 D3
Fullwell Cross, Ilf. IG6 49 D1
Furzedown SW17 52 A2
Furzeground Way, Uxb. UB11 46 B3
Gale St, Dag. RM9 49 E2
Galpins Rd, Th.Hth. CR7 52 A2
Gander Grn La, Sutt. SM1, SM3 51 F3
Gants Hill, Ilf. IG2 49 D1
Gap Rd SW19 51 F2
Garfield Rd, Add. KT15 50 A3
Garnet St E1 48 B3
Garrad's Rd SW16 52 A1
Garratt La SW17; SW18 51 F1
Garrison La, Chess. KT9 51 D4
Garth Rd, Mord. SM4 51 E3
Gascoigne Rd, Bark. IG11 49 E3
Gaston Br Rd, Shep. TW17 50 B3
Gates Grn Rd, Kes. BR2; W.Wick. BR4 52 C3
Gellatly Rd SE14 48 B4
George V Av, Pnr. HA5 46 C1
George La E18 49 D1
George Rd, Kings.T. KT2 51 D2
George St, Croy. CR0 52 B3
George St, Rich. TW9 51 D1
Gervase Rd, Edg. HA8 47 E1
Giggs Hill Rd, T.Ditt. KT7 51 D3
Gillespie Rd N5 48 A2
Gipsy Hill SE19 52 B2
Gipsy Rd SE27 52 B2
Glebe Way, W.Wick. BR4 52 C3
Globe Rd E1; E2 48 B3
Gloucester Rd, Kings.T. KT1 51 D2
Gloucester Rd SW7 47 F4
Goat Rd, Mitch. CR4 51 F3
Goddard Rd, Beck. BR3 52 B2
Goddington, Orp. BR6 53 E3
Goddington La, Orp. BR6 53 E3
Goffers Rd SE3 48 C4
Golders Green NW11 47 F1
Golders Grn Rd NW11 47 F1
Goldhawk Rd W6; W12 47 E4
Goldsel Rd, Swan. BR8 53 F3
Goodmayes, Ilf. IG3 49 E2
Goodmayes La, Ilf. IG3 49 E2
Gordon Av, Stan. HA7 46 C1
Goswell Rd EC1 48 A3
Grafton Rd, Wor.Pk. KT4 51 E3
Grahame Pk Way NW7; NW9 47 E1
Graham Rd E8 48 B2
Grand Dep Rd SE18 49 D4
Grand Dr SW20 51 E2
Grange Hill, Chig. IG7 49 E1
Grange Rd E13 48 C3
Grange Rd SE1 48 B4
Grange Rd SE19; SE25; Th.Hth. CR7 52 B2
Gravel Hill, Bexh. DA6 53 F1
Gravel Hill, Croy. CR0 52 B4
Gray's Inn Rd WC1 48 A3
Great Cambridge Rd N9; N17; N18; Enf. EN1; Wal.Cr. EN8 48 B1
Great Cen Way NW10; Wem. HA9 47 E2
Great Chertsey Rd (Whitton), Felt. TW13 50 C1
Great Chertsey Rd W4 47 E4
Great Dover St SE1 48 B4
Great N Rd N2 47 F1
Great N Way NW4 47 E1
Great South-West Rd, Felt. TW14; Houns. TW4 50 B1
Great Western Rd W2; W9; W11 47 F3
Great W Rd, Brent. TW8; Houns. TW5; Islw. TW7 46 C4
Great W Rd W4; W6 47 E4
Green, The, Sid. DA14 53 E2
Green, The, Sthl. UB2 46 C4
Green, The, Twick. TW2 50 C1
Green, The, West Dr. UB7 46 A4
Green Ct Rd, Swan. BR8 53 F3
Greenford, Grnf. UB6 46 C3
Greenford Av W7 46 C3
Greenford Rd, Grnf. UB6; Sthl. UB1 46 C3
Greengate St E13 49 D3
Greenhill Way, Har. HA1 46 C1
Green La, Dag. RM8; Ilf. IG1, IG3 49 E2
Green La, Houns. TW4 50 B1
Green La, Mord. SM4 51 F3
Green La, Nthwd. HA6 46 B1
Green La, Shep. TW17 50 B3
Green La SE9; Chis. BR7 53 D1
Green La SW16 52 A2
Green Las N4; N8; N15; N16 48 A1
Green St, Sun. TW16 50 B2
Green St E7; E13 49 D2
Green Street Green, Orp. BR6 53 E4
Greenway, The, Uxb. UB8 46 A3
Greenwich SE10 48 C4
Greenwich High Rd SE10 48 C4
Greenwich S St SE10 48 C4
Green Wrythe La, Cars. SM5 51 F3
Gresham Dr, Rom. RM6 49 E1
Greyhound La SW16 52 A2
Griffin Rd SE18 49 E4
Grosvenor Pl SW1 48 A4
Grosvenor Rd N10 48 A1
Grosvenor Rd SW1 48 A4
Grove End Rd NW8 47 F3
Grove Grn Rd E11 48 C2
Grove La, Kings.T. KT1 51 D2
Grove La SE5 48 B4
Groveley Rd, Sun. TW16 50 B2
Grove Park SE12 53 D1
Grove Park W4 47 E4
Grove Pk Rd SE9 53 D1
Grove Rd, Mitch. CR4 52 A2
Grove Rd (Chadwell Heath), Rom. RM6 49 E2
Grove Rd E3 48 C3
Grove Rd E17 48 C1
Grove St SE8 48 C4
Grove Vale SE22 52 B1
Guilford St WC1 48 A3
Gunnersbury W4 47 D4
Gunnersbury Av W3; W4; W5 47 D3
Gunnersbury La W3 47 D4
Hackbridge, Wall. SM6 51 F3
Hackney E8 48 B2
Hackney Rd E2 48 B3
Hackney Wick E9 48 C2
Haggerston E2 48 B3
Ha-Ha Rd SE18 49 D4
Hainault Rd, Rom. RM5 49 F1
Hainault Rd (Chadwell Heath), Rom. RM6 49 E1
Hale End Rd E4; E17; Wdf.Grn. IG8 48 C1
Half Acre, Brent. TW8 47 D4
Half Moon La SE24 52 B1
Halfway St, Sid. DA15 53 E1
Haling Pk Rd, S.Croy. CR2 52 A3
Halliford Rd, Shep. TW17; Sun. TW16 50 B2
Hall Rd, Islw. TW7 50 C1
Halstead, Sev. TN14 53 F4
Halstead La, Sev. TN14 53 F4
Ham, Rich. TW10 51 D1
Ham Gate Av, Rich. TW10 51 D1
Hammersmith W6 47 E4
Hammersmith Gro W6 47 E4
Hammersmith Rd W6; W14 47 E4
Ham Pk Rd E7; E15 48 C2
Hampstead NW3 47 F2
Hampstead Garden Suburb N2 47 F1
Hampstead La N6; NW3 47 F2
Hampstead Rd NW1 48 A3
Hampton, Hmptn. TW12 50 C2
Hampton Ct Rd, E.Mol. KT8; Hmptn. TW12; Kings.T. KT1 50 C2
Hampton Ct Way, E.Mol. KT8; T.Ditt. KT7 50 C3
Hampton Hill, Hmptn. TW12 50 C2
Hampton Rd, Hmptn. TW12 50 C2
Hampton Rd, Twick. TW2 50 C1
Hampton Rd E, Felt. TW13 50 C2
Hampton Rd W, Felt. TW13 50 C1
Hampton Wick, Kings. T. KT1 51 D2
Ham St, Rich. TW10 51 D1
Hanger Hill, Wey. KT13 50 A4
Hanger La W5 47 D3
Hanwell W7 46 C3
Hanworth, Felt. TW13 50 C2
Hanworth Rd, Felt. TW13 50 B1
Hanworth Rd, Hmptn. TW12 50 C2
Hanworth Rd, Houns. TW3, TW4 50 C1
Harefield, Uxb. UB9 46 A1
Harefield Rd, Uxb. UB8 46 A2
Hare La, Esher KT10 50 C3
Harlesden NW10 47 E3
Harlesden Rd NW10 47 E3
Harlington, Hayes UB3 46 A4
Harlington Rd, Uxb. UB8 46 A3
Harlington Rd E, Felt. TW13, TW14 50 B1
Harlington Rd W, Felt. TW14 50 B1
Harmondsworth, West Dr. UB7 46 A4
Harmondsworth La, West Dr. UB7 46 A4
Harmondsworth Rd, West Dr. UB7 46 A4
Harold Rd E13 49 D3
Harold Rd SE19 52 B2
Harringay N8 48 A1
Harrow, Har. HA 46 C2
Harrow Manorway SE2 49 E4
Harrow on the Hill, Har. HA1 46 C2
Harrow Rd, Wem. HA0 47 D2
Harrow Rd (Tokyngton), Wem. HA9 47 D2
Harrow Rd E11 48 C2
Harrow Rd NW10; W9; W10 47 E3
Harrow Vw, Har. HA2, HA3 46 C1
Harrow Weald, Har. HA3 46 C1
Hartfield Rd SW19 51 F2
Hartland Way, Croy. CR0 52 C3
Harvil Rd, Uxb. UB9, UB10 46 A1
Harvist Rd NW6 47 E3
Hastings Rd, Brom. BR2 53 D3
Hatch End, Pnr. HA5 46 C1
Hatch La, West Dr. UB7 46 A4
Hatton, Felt. TW14 50 B1
Hatton Rd, Felt. TW14 50 B1
Haven Grn W5 47 D3
Havering Park, Rom. RM5 49 F1
Havering Rd, Rom. RM1 49 F1
Haverstock Hill NW3 47 F2
Hawkshill Way, Esher KT10 50 C4
Hawks Rd, Kings.T. KT1 51 D2
Hawstead La, Orp. BR6 53 F3
Haydons Rd SW19 51 F2
Hayes, Brom. BR2 53 D3
Hayes, Hayes UB3 46 B3
Hayes Bypass, Hayes UB3, UB4 46 B4
Hayes End, Hayes UB3 46 B3
Hayes La, Beck. BR3 52 C2
Hayes La, Brom. BR2 53 D3
Hayes Rd, Brom. BR2 53 D2
Hayes Rd, Sthl. UB2 46 B4
Hayes Town, Hayes UB3 46 B3
Hazelwood, Sev. TN14 53 E4
Headstone, Har. HA2 46 C1
Headstone La, Har. HA2, HA3 46 C1
Headstone Rd, Har. HA1 46 C1
Heathfield La, Chis. BR7 53 E2
Heathfield Rd, Kes. BR2 53 D3
Heathfield Ter W4 47 E4
Heath Rd, Houns. TW3 50 C1
Heath Rd, Twick. TW1, TW2 50 C1
Heath Rd, Wey. KT13 50 A3
Heath St NW3 47 F2
Heathway, Dag. RM9, RM10 49 F2
Hedgemans Rd, Dag. RM9 49 E2
Hendon NW4 47 E1
Hendon La N3 47 F1
Hendon Way NW2; NW4 47 E1
Hepworth Way, Walt. KT12 50 B3
Hercies Rd, Uxb. UB10 46 A2
Heriot Rd, Cher. KT16 50 A3
Hermitage Rd SE19 52 B2
Hermit Rd E16 48 C3
Hermon Hill E11; E18 49 D1
Herne Hill SE24 52 B1
Herne Hill SE24 52 B1
Hersham, Walt. KT12 50 B3
Hersham Bypass, Walt. KT12 50 B3
Heston, Houns. TW5 46 C4
Heston Rd, Houns. TW5 46 C4
Hewitts Rd, Orp. BR6 53 F4
Higham Hill E17 48 C1
Higham Hill Rd E17 48 C1
Highams Park E4 48 C1
Highbury N5 48 B2
Highbury Gro N5 48 A2
Highbury Pk N5 48 A2
Highgate N6 48 A1
Highgate High St N6 48 A2
Highgate Hill N6; N19 48 A2
Highgate Rd NW5 48 A2
Highgate W Hill N6 48 A2
High Holborn WC1 48 A3
High Rd, Har. HA3 46 C1
High Rd (Eastcote Village), Pnr. HA5 46 B1
High Rd, Rom. RM6 49 E2
High Rd (Ickenham), Uxb. UB10 46 A2
High Rd (Cowley), Uxb. UB8 46 A3
High Rd, Wem. HA0 47 D2
High Rd E18; Wdf.Grn. IG8 48 C1
High Rd N2; N12; N20 47 F1
High Rd N15 48 B1
High Rd N22 48 A1
High Rd NW10 47 E2
High Rd Leyton E10; E15 48 C2
High Rd Leytonstone E11; E15 48 C2
High St, Add. KT15 50 A3
High St, Beck. BR3 52 C2
High St, Brent. TW8 47 D4
High St, Brom. BR1 53 D2
High St, Cars. SM5 52 A3
High St, Chis. BR7 53 D2
High St, Cob. KT11 50 B4
High St, Croy. CR0 52 B3
High St (Ewell), Epsom KT17 51 E4
High St, Epsom KT19 51 E4
High St, Esher KT10 50 C3
High St, Felt. TW13 50 B1
High St, Hmptn. TW12 50 C2
High St (Wealdstone), Har. HA3 46 C1
High St (Harlington), Hayes UB3 46 B4
High St (Cranford), Houns. TW5 46 B4
High St, Ilf. IG6 49 E1
High St (Hampton Wick), Kings.T. KT1 51 D2
High St, N.Mal. KT3 51 E2
High St, Nthwd. HA6 46 B1
High St (St. Mary Cray), Orp. BR5 53 E3
High St, Orp. BR6 53 E3
High St (Chelsfield), Orp. BR6 53 E4
High St (Downe), Orp. BR6 53 D4
High St (Farnborough), Orp. BR6 53 E3
High St, Pnr. HA5 46 C1
High St, Ruis. HA4 46 B2
High St (Shoreham), Sev. TN14 53 F4
High St, Shep. TW17 50 A3
High St, Sthl. UB1 46 C3
High St (Stanwell), Stai. TW19 50 A1
High St, Sutt. SM1 51 F3
High St, Swan. BR8 53 F2
High St, Tedd. TW11 51 D2
High St, T.Ditt. KT7 51 D3
High St, Th.Hth. CR7 52 B2
High St (Whitton), Twick. TW2 50 C1
High St, Uxb. UB8 46 A2
High St (Cowley), Uxb. UB8 46 A3
High St, Walt. KT12 50 B3
High St (Yiewsley), West Dr. UB7 46 A3
High St, W.Wick. BR4 52 C3
High St, Wey. KT13 50 A3
High St E11 49 D1
High St E13 49 D3
High St E15 48 C3
High St N8 48 A1
High St NW10 47 E3
High St SE20 52 B2
High St SE25 52 B2
High St W3 47 D3
High St Colliers Wd SW19 51 F2
High St N E6; E12 49 D2
High St S E6 49 D3
High St Wimbledon SW19 51 E2
Highway, The, Orp. BR6 53 E3
Highway, The E1; E14 48 B3
Hillcross Av, Mord. SM4 51 F3
Hill End, Uxb. UB9 46 A1
Hill End Rd, Uxb. UB9 46 A1
Hillfoot Rd, Rom. RM5 49 F1
Hilliers La, Croy. CR0 52 A3
Hillingdon, Uxb. UB 46 A3
Hillingdon Hill, Uxb. UB10 46 A3
Hillingdon Rd, Uxb. UB10 46 A3
Hillreach SE18 49 D4
Hillside NW10 47 E2
Hillside Rd, Nthwd. HA6 46 B1
Hill Vw Rd, Orp. BR6 53 E3
Hinchley Wood, Esher KT10 51 D3
Hindmans Way, Dag. RM9 49 F3
Hither Green SE13 52 C1
Hither Grn La SE13 52 C1
Hockenden La, Swan. BR8 53 F2
Hoe St E17 48 C1
Hogarth La W4 47 E4
Hog Hill Rd, Rom. RM5 49 F1
Holborn WC2 48 A3

Holbrook Way, Brom. BR2 53 D3
Holders Hill Rd NW4; NW7 47 E1
Holland Pk Av W11 47 E4
Holland Rd W14 47 F4
Holloway N7 48 A2
Holloway La, West Dr. UB7 46 A4
Holloway Rd N7; N19 48 A2
Holly Bk Rd, W.Byf. KT14 50 A4
Holly Bk Rd, Wok. GU22 50 A4
Hollybush Hill E11 48 C1
Homerton High St E9 48 B2
Homerton Rd E9 48 C2
Homesdale Rd, Brom. BR1, BR2 53 D2
Honeycroft Hill, Uxb. UB10 46 A2
Honey Hill, Uxb. UB10 46 A2
Honeypot La NW9; Stan. HA7 47 D1
Honor Oak SE23 52 B1
Honor Oak Park SE4 52 C1
Honor Oak Pk SE23 52 B1
Hook Grn La, Dart. DA2 53 F1
Hook Rd, Epsom KT19 51 E4
Hook Rd, Surb. KT6 51 D3
Hornchurch Rd, Horn. RM11, RM12 49 F2
Hornfair Rd SE7 49 D4
Horn La W3 47 E3
Hornsey N8 48 A1
Hornsey La N6; N19 48 A2
Hornsey Ri N19 48 A2
Hornsey Rd N7; N19 48 A2
Horns Green, Sev. TN14 53 E4
Horns Rd, Ilf. IG2, IG6 49 E1
Horsenden La N, Grnf. UB6 46 C2
Horsenden La S, Grnf. UB6 47 D3
Horton, Epsom KT19 51 D4
Horton La, Epsom KT19 51 D4
Horton Rd (Stanwell Moor), Stai. TW19 50 A1
Horton Rd, West Dr. UB7 46 A3
Hospital Br Rd, Twick. TW2 50 C1
Hounslow, Houns. TW 50 C1
Hounslow Rd, Felt. TW13 50 B1
Hounslow Rd (Hanworth), Felt. TW13 50 B2
Hounslow West, Houns. TW4 50 B1
Howberry Rd, Edg. HA8; Stan. HA7 47 D1
Hoxton N1 48 B3
Hunters Rd, Chess. KT9 51 D3
Hurst La, E.Mol. KT8 50 C2
Hurst Rd, Bex. DA5; Sid. DA15 53 E1
Hurst Rd, E.Mol. KT8; W.Mol. KT8 50 C2
Hyde, The NW9 47 E1
Hyde Vale SE10 48 C4
Ickenham, Uxb. UB10 46 A2
Ickenham Rd, Ruis. HA4; Uxb. UB10 46 B2
Icklingham Rd, Cob. KT11 50 B4
Ilderton Rd SE15; SE16 48 B4
Ilford, Ilf. IG 49 E2
Ilford La, Ilf. IG1 49 D2
Imperial Dr, Har. HA2 46 C2
Island Fm Rd, W.Mol. KT8 50 C3
Isleworth, Islw. TW7 50 C1
Iver La, Iver SL0; Uxb. UB8 46 A3
Jackass La, Kes. BR2 53 D4
Jamaica Rd SE1; SE16 48 B4
Jerningham Rd SE14 48 C4
Jersey Rd, Houns. TW5; Islw. TW7 46 C4
Jewels Hill, West. TN16 53 D4
Joel St, Nthwd. HA6; Pnr. HA5 46 B1
John Ruskin St SE5 48 A4
John Wilson St SE18 49 D4
Joydens Wood, Bex. DA5 53 F2
Jubilee Way, Chess. KT9 51 D3
Judd St WC1 48 A3
Judge Heath La, Hayes UB3; Uxb. UB8 46 B3
Junction Rd, Rom. RM1 49 F1
Junction Rd N19 48 A2
Katherine Rd E6; E7 49 D2
Kendal Rd NW10 47 E2
Kenley Rd, Kings.T. KT1 51 D2
Kenmore Av, Har. HA3 47 D1
Kenmore Rd, Har. HA3 47 D1
Kennington SE11 48 A4
Kennington La SE11 48 A4
Kennington Pk Rd SE11 48 A4
Kennington Rd SE1; SE11 48 A4
Kensal Rise NW6 47 E3
Kensington W8 47 F4
Kensington Ch St W8 47 F3
Kensington High St W8; W14 47 F4
Kensington Pk Rd W11 47 F3
Kensington Rd SW7; W8 47 F4
Kent Gdns W13 47 D3
Kent Gate Way, Croy. CR0 52 C4
Kent Ho Rd SE26; Beck. BR3 52 B2
Kentish Town NW5 48 A2
Kentish Way, Brom. BR1 53 D2
Kenton, Har. HA3 47 D1
Kenton La (Belmont), Har. HA3 47 D1
Kenton La (Harrow Weald), Har. HA3 46 C1
Kenton Rd, Har. HA3 47 D1
Kent Rd, Orp. BR5 53 E3
Keston, Kes. BR2 53 D3
Kew, Rich. TW9 47 D4
Kew Br Rd, Brent. TW8 47 D4
Kew Rd, Rich. TW9 47 D4
Kidbrooke SE3 49 D4
Kidbrooke Pk Rd SE3 49 D4
Kilburn NW6 47 F3
Kilburn High Rd NW6 47 F2
Kilburn La W9; W10 47 F3
Kilburn Pk Rd NW6 47 F3
King Charles Rd, Surb. KT5 51 D3
King Harolds Way, Bexh. DA7 49 E4
King Henry's Dr, Croy. CR0 52 C4
King's Av SW4; SW12 52 A1
Kingsbury NW9 47 D1
Kingsbury Rd NW9 47 D1
King's Cross N1 48 A3
Kingsdowne Rd, Surb. KT6 51 D3
Kingsend, Ruis. HA4 46 B2
Kingsfield Av, Har. HA2 46 C1
Kings Highway SE18 49 E4
Kingshill Av, Hayes UB4; Nthlt. UB5 46 B3
Kingsland Rd E2; E8 48 B2
Kingsley Rd, Houns. TW3 46 C4
Kings Rd, Kings.T. KT2 51 D2
Kings Rd, Rich. TW10 51 D1
King's Rd SW1; SW3; SW6; SW10 47 F4
Kingston Bypass, Esher KT10; Surb. KT5, KT6 51 D3
Kingston Hill, Kings.T. KT2 51 D2
Kingston La, Uxb. UB8 46 A3
Kingston Rd, Ashf. TW15 50 A2
Kingston Rd, Epsom KT17, KT19; Surb. KT5; Wor.Pk. KT4 51 E3
Kingston Rd, Kings.T. KT1; N.Mal. KT3 51 D2
Kingston Rd, Tedd. TW11 51 D2
Kingston Rd SW15 51 E1
Kingston Rd SW20 51 E2
Kingston upon Thames, Kings.T. KT 51 D2
Kingston Vale SW15 51 E2
Kingston Vale SW15 51 E2
King St, Twick. TW1 51 D1
King St W6 47 E4
Kirkdale SE26 52 B1
Knee Hill SE2 49 E4
Kneller Rd, Twick. TW2 50 C1
Knightsbridge SW1; SW7 47 F4
Knights Hill SE27 52 A2
Knipp Hill, Cob. KT11 50 C4
Knockholt, Sev. TN14 53 E4
Knockholt Rd, Sev. TN14 53 F4
Ladbroke Gro W10; W11 47 F3
Ladygate La, Ruis. HA4 46 A1
Lady Margaret Rd, Sthl. UB1 46 C3
Ladywell SE13 52 C1
Ladywell Rd SE13 52 C1
Lake Ho Rd E11 49 D2
Lakeswood Rd, Orp. BR5 53 D3
Laleham, Stai. TW18 50 A2
Laleham Rd, Shep. TW17 50 A3
Lambeth SE1 48 A4
Lambeth Rd SE1; SE11 48 A4
Lammas La, Esher KT10 50 C3
Lamorbey, Sid. DA15 53 E1
Lampton, Houns. TW3 46 C4
Lampton Rd, Houns. TW3 50 C1
Langdale Dr, Hayes UB4 46 B3
Lansbury Dr, Hayes UB4 46 B3
Lansdowne Rd N17 48 B1
Lansdowne Way SW8 48 A4
Larden Rd W3 47 E4
Larkshall Rd E4 48 C1
Lascelles Av, Har. HA1 46 C2
Latchmere Rd, Kings.T. KT2 51 D2
Latchmere Rd SW11 47 F4
Lauriston Rd E9 48 B2
Lausanne Rd SE15 48 B4
Lavender Av, Mitch. CR4 51 F2
Lawrie Pk Rd SE26 52 B2
Layhams Rd, Kes. BR2; W.Wick. BR4 52 C3
Lea Bridge E5 48 B2
Lea Br Rd E5; E10; E17 48 B2
Leatherhead Rd, Chess. KT9 51 D4
Leatherhead Rd (Oxshott), Lthd. KT22 50 C4
Leaves Green, Kes. BR2 53 D4
Leaves Grn Rd, Kes. BR2 53 D4
Lee SE12 53 D1
Lee High Rd SE12; SE13 52 C1
Lee Rd SE3 52 C1
Leesons Hill, Chis. BR7; Orp. BR5 53 E2
Lees Rd, Uxb. UB8 46 A3
Lee Ter SE3; SE13 52 C1
Leigham Ct Rd SW16 52 A1
Leigh Hill Rd, Cob. KT11 50 B4
Leighton Rd NW5 48 A2
Lessness Heath, Belv. DA17 49 F4
Lever St EC1 48 B3
Lewisham SE13 52 C1
Lewisham High St SE13 52 C1
Lewisham Rd SE13 48 C4
Lewisham Way SE4; SE14 48 C4
Leydenhatch La, Swan. BR8 53 F2
Ley St, Ilf. IG1, IG2 49 E2
Leyton E11 48 C2
Leyton Cross Rd, Dart. DA2 53 F1
Leyton Grn Rd E10 48 C1
Leytonstone E11 48 C2
Lilford Rd SE5 48 A4
Lillie Rd SW6 47 E4
Limeharbour E14 48 C4
Limehouse E14 48 C3
Limpsfield Rd, S.Croy. CR2; Warl. CR6 52 B4
Lingfield Av, Kings.T. KT1 51 D2
Links Av, Mord. SM4 51 F2
Lisson Gro NW1; NW8 47 F3
Little Ealing W5 47 D4
Little Ealing La W5 47 D4
Little Heath SE7 49 D4
Littleheath La, Cob. KT11 50 C4
Little Ilford La E12 49 D2
Littleton, Shep. TW17 50 A2
Littleton La, Shep. TW17 50 A3
Little Woodcote La, Cars. SM5; Pur. CR8; Wall. SM6 52 A4
Littleworth Rd, Esher KT10 50 C3
Liverpool Rd N1; N7 48 A2
Loampit Hill SE13 48 C4
Loampit Vale SE13 48 C4
Locket Rd, Har. HA3 46 C1
Locks La, Mitch. CR4 52 A2
Lodge Av, Dag. RM8, RM9 49 E3
Lodge Hill SE2; Well. DA16 49 E4
Lodge La, Bex. DA5 53 E1
Lodge La, Croy. CR0 52 C4
Lodge La, Rom. RM5 49 F1
Logs Hill, Brom. BR1; Chis. BR7 53 D2
Lombard Rd SW11 47 F4
London La, Brom. BR1 52 C2
London Rd, Ashf. TW15; Felt. TW14; Stai. TW18 50 A1
London Rd, Brent. TW8; Houns. TW3; Islw. TW7 46 C4
London Rd, Brom. BR1 52 C2
London Rd, Croy. CR0; Th.Hth. CR7 52 A3
London Rd (Crayford), Dart. DA1 53 F1
London Rd, Epsom KT17; Sutt. SM3 51 E4
London Rd, Kings.T. KT2 51 D2
London Rd, Mitch. CR4 51 F2
London Rd, Mitch. CR4; Wall. SM6 52 A3
London Rd, Mord. SM4 51 F3
London Rd, Rom. RM6, RM7 49 F1
London Rd (Halstead), Sev. TN14 53 F4
London Rd, Swan. BR8 53 F2
London Rd, Twick. TW1 51 D1
London Rd SE23 52 B1
London Rd SW16 52 A2
London St, Cher. KT16 50 A3
Longbridge Rd, Bark. IG11; Dag. RM8 49 E2
Long Ditton, Surb. KT10 51 D3
Longdown La N, Epsom KT17 51 E4
Long Elmes, Har. HA3 46 C1
Longford, West Dr. UB7 46 A4
Long Gro Rd, Epsom KT19 51 D4
Longlands, Chis. BR7 53 D2
Longlands Rd, Sid. DA15 53 E1
Long La, Bexh. DA7 49 F4
Long La, Croy. CR0 52 B3
Long La (Stanwell), Stai. TW19 50 A1
Long La, Uxb. UB10 46 A3
Long La (Ickenham), Uxb. UB10 46 A2
Long La SE1 48 B4
Longleigh La SE2; Bexh. DA7 49 E4
Longley Rd SW17 51 F2
Long Rd SW4 52 A1
Longwalk Rd, Uxb. UB11 46 A3
Longwood Gdns, Ilf. IG5 49 D1
Lonsdale Av E6 49 D3
Lordship La N17; N22 48 A1
Lordship La SE22 52 B1
Lordship Pk N16 48 B2
Lothian Rd SW9 48 A4
Loughborough Rd SW9 48 A4
Lower Addiscombe Rd, Croy. CR0 52 B3
Lower Bedfords Rd, Rom. RM1 49 F1
Lower Boston Rd W7 46 C4
Lower Clapton E5 48 B2
Lower Clapton Rd E5 48 B2
Lower Feltham, Felt. TW13 50 B1
Lower Green, Esher KT10 50 C3
Lower Grn Rd, Esher KT10 50 C3
Lower Hampton Rd, Sun. TW16 50 B2
Lower Lea Crossing E14; E16 48 C3
Lower Morden La, Mord. SM4 51 F3
Lower Mortlake Rd, Rich. TW9 51 D1
Lower Richmond Rd SW14; Rich. TW9 51 D1
Lower Richmond Rd SW15 51 E1
Lower Rd, Belv. DA17; Erith DA8 49 F4
Lower Rd, Har. HA2 46 C2
Lower Rd SE16 48 B4
Lower Sunbury Rd, Hmptn. TW12 50 C2
Lower Sydenham SE26 52 B2
Lower Teddington Rd, Kings.T. KT1 51 D2
Lowlands Rd, Har. HA1 46 C2
Luxted Rd, Orp. BR6 53 D4
Lynwood Dr, Wor.Pk. KT4 51 E3
Lyttleton Rd N8 47 F1
Mackenzie Rd N7 48 A2
McLeod Rd SE2 49 E4
Madeley Rd W5 47 D3
Magdalen Rd SW18 51 F1
Magpie Hall La, Brom. BR2 53 D3
Maida Vale W9 47 F3
Maida Vale W9 47 F3
Maidstone Rd, Sid. DA14 53 E2
Maidstone Rd, Sid. DA14; Swan. BR8 53 F2
Main Rd, Orp. BR5 53 E2
Main Rd, Rom. RM1, RM2 49 F1
Main Rd, Sid. DA14 53 E1
Main Rd, Swan. BR8 53 F2
Main Rd, West. TN16 53 D4
Main St, Felt. TW13 50 B2
Major Rd E15 48 C2
Malden Rd, N.Mal. KT3; Wor.Pk. KT4 51 E3
Malden Rd, Sutt. SM3 51 E3
Malden Rd NW5 47 F2
Malden Rushett, Chess. KT9 51 D4
Malden Way, N.Mal. KT3 51 E3
Mall, The, Har. HA3 47 D1
Mall, The W5 47 D3
Malpas Rd SE4 52 C1
Manchester Rd E14 48 C4
Mandeville Rd, Nthlt. UB5 46 C2
Manor Fm Rd, Wem. HA0 47 D3
Manor La, Sun. TW16 50 B2
Manor Pk Rd, Chis. BR7 53 E2
Manor Pk Rd, W.Wick. BR4 52 C3
Manor Pk Rd NW10 47 E3
Manor Rd, Chig. IG7 49 D1
Manor Rd, Dart. DA1 53 F1
Manor Rd, Mitch. CR4 52 A2
Manor Rd, Rich. TW9 51 D1
Manor Rd, Wall. SM6 52 A3
Manor Rd E16 48 C3
Manor Rd N16 48 B2
Manor Rd N, Esher KT10; T.Ditt. KT7 50 C3
Manor Rd S, Esher KT10 50 C3
Mansfield Rd NW3 47 F2
Manygate La, Shep. TW17 50 B3
Mapesbury Rd NW2 47 F2
Maple Rd, Surb. KT6 51 D3
Mare St E8 48 B3
Market Rd N7 48 A2
Markhouse Rd E17 48 C1
Mark's Gate, Rom. RM6 49 F1
Marlborough Rd, Rom. RM7 49 F1
Marshgate La E15 48 C2
Marsh Rd, Pnr. HA5 46 C1
Marsh Wall E14 48 C4
Martindale Rd, Houns. TW4 50 C1
Martin Way SW20; Mord. SM4 51 F2
Marylebone NW1 47 F3
Marylebone Rd NW1 47 F3
Masons Hill, Brom. BR1 53 D2
Matthias Rd N16 48 B2
Mawney Rd, Rom. RM7 49 F1
Maxwell Rd, Nthwd. HA6 46 B1
Mayes Rd N22 48 A1
Mayfair W1 48 A3
Mayfield Av, Orp. BR6 53 E3
Mayfield Rd, S.Croy. CR2 52 B4
Mayow Rd SE23; SE26 52 B1
Mayplace Rd E, Bexh. DA7; Dart. DA1 53 F1
Mayplace Rd W, Bexh. DA7 53 F1
Maypole, Orp. BR6 53 F4
Maze Hill SE3; SE10 48 C4
Mead Way, Brom. BR2 52 C3
Melfort Rd, Th.Hth. CR7 52 A2
Merantun Way SW19 51 F2
Mercury Gdns, Rom. RM1 49 F1
Merrick Rd, Sthl. UB2 46 C4
Merton SW19 51 F2
Merton Rd SW18 51 F1
Merton Rd SW19 51 F2
Middle La N8 48 A1
Middle Pk Av SE9 53 D1
Middleton Rd, Cars. SM5; Mord. SM4 51 F3
Midfield Way, Orp. BR5 53 E2
Milbourne La, Esher KT10 50 C3
Mildmay Pk N1 48 B2
Mile End E1 48 B3
Mile End Rd E1; E3 48 C3
Miles La, Cob. KT11 50 C4
Milkwood Rd SE24 52 A1
Millbank SW1 48 A4
Mill Brook Rd, Orp. BR5 53 E2
Mill Hill Rd SW13 47 E4
Mill La (Chadwell Heath), Rom. RM6 49 F1
Mill La NW6 47 F2
Mill Rd, Epsom KT17 51 E4
Mill Rd, West Dr. UB7 46 A4
Millwall E14 48 C4
Mitcham, Mitch. CR4 51 F2
Mitcham La SW16 52 A2
Mitcham Rd, Croy. CR0 52 A3
Mitcham Rd SW17 51 F2
Mitchley Av, Pur. CR8; S.Croy. CR2 52 B4
Mitchley Hill, S.Croy. CR2 52 B4
Mogden La, Islw. TW7 50 C1
Molesey Pk Rd, E.Mol. KT8; W.Mol. KT8 50 C3
Molesey Rd, Walt. KT12; W.Mol. KT8 50 B3
Monks Orchard, Croy. CR0 52 B3
Monks Orchard Rd, Beck. BR3 52 C3
Monument Hill, Wey. KT13 50 A3
Monument Way N17 48 B1
Moorhall Rd, Uxb. UB9 46 A1
Moor La, Chess. KT9 51 D3
Morden, Mord. SM4 51 F2
Morden Hall Rd, Mord. SM4 51 F2
Morden Park, Mord. SM4 51 F3
Morden Rd, Mitch. CR4 51 F2
Morden Rd SW19 51 F2
More La, Esher KT10 50 C3
Morning La E9 48 B2
Mornington Rd, Grnf. UB6 46 C3
Mortimer Rd NW10 47 E3
Mortlake SW14 51 E1
Mortlake High St SW14 47 E4
Mortlake Rd, Ilf. IG1 49 E2
Mortlake Rd, Rich. TW9 47 D4
Mossford La, Ilf. IG6 49 D1
Mostyn Rd SW19 51 F2
Motspur Park, N.Mal. KT3 51 E3
Motspur Pk, N.Mal. KT3 51 E3
Mottingham SE9 53 D1
Mottingham La SE9; SE12 53 D1
Mottingham Rd SE9 53 D1
Mount Pleasant Rd N17 48 B1
Movers La, Bark. IG11 49 E3
Murchison Av, Bex. DA5 53 E1
Muswell Hill N10 48 A1

Muswell Hill N10 48 A1
Muswell Hill Rd N6; N10 48 A1
Nallhead Rd, Felt. TW13 50 B2
Nash La, Kes. BR2 53 D4
Nathan Way SE28 49 E4
Neasden NW2 47 E2
Neasden La NW10 47 E2
Nelson Rd, Houns. TW3, TW4; Twick. TW2 50 C1
Nelson Rd E4 48 C1
Nether St N3; N12 47 F1
New Addington, Croy. CR0 52 C4
New Barn Rd, Swan. BR8 53 F2
New Barn St E13 49 D3
New Beckenham, Beck. BR3 52 C2
New Bond St W1 48 A3
Newbury Park, Ilf. IG2 49 E1
New Charlton SE7 49 D4
New City Rd E13 49 D3
New Cross SE14 48 C4
New Cross Gate SE14 48 B4
New Cross Rd SE14 48 B4
New Eltham SE9 53 D1
Newham Way E6; E16 49 D3
New Haw, Add. KT15 50 A4
New Haw Rd, Add. KT15 50 A3
New Kings Rd SW6 47 F4
Newlands Pk SE26 52 B2
New Malden, N.Mal. KT3 51 E2
New N Rd, Ilf. IG6 49 E1
New N Rd N1 48 B2
New Plaistow Rd E15 48 C3
New Rd, Esher KT10 50 C3
New Rd, Felt. TW14 50 B1
New Rd, Rain. RM13 49 F3
New Rd, Shep. TW17 50 A2
New Rd, W.Mol. KT8 50 C2
New Rd E1 48 B3
New Rd Hill, Kes. BR2; Orp. BR6 53 D4
New Wanstead E11 48 C2
New Windsor St, Uxb. UB8 46 A2
New Years Grn La, Uxb. UB9 46 A1
New Zealand Av, Walt. KT12 50 B3
Nightingale La SW4; SW12 51 F1
Nightingale Pl SE18 49 D4
Nightingale Rd, Cars. SM5 51 F3
Nine Elms La SW8 48 A4
Noel Park N22 48 A1
Noel Rd W3 47 D3
Norbiton, Kings.T. KT2 51 E2
Norbury SW16 52 A2
Norbury Cres SW16 52 A2
Norbury Hill SW16 52 A2
North Acton Rd NW10 47 E3
Northborough Rd SW16 52 A2
North Cheam, Sutt. SM3 51 E3
Northcote, Croy. CR0 52 B3
Northcote Rd SW11 51 F1
North Cray, Sid. DA14 53 F1
North Cray Rd, Bex. DA5; Sid. DA14 53 F2
North End La, Orp. BR6 53 D4
Northend Rd, Dart. DA1; Erith DA8 49 F4
North End Rd NW11 47 F2
North End Rd SW6; W14 47 F4
Northern Perimeter Rd, Houns. TW6 46 A4
Northern Perimeter Rd W, Houns. TW6 46 A4
Northern Relief Rd, Bark. IG11 49 D2
Northey Av, Sutt. SM2 51 E4
Northfield Av W5; W13 47 D3
North Harrow, Har. HA2 46 C1
North Hill N6 48 A1
North Hillingdon, Uxb. UB10 46 B2
North Hyde, Sthl. UB2 46 C4
North Hyde Rd, Hayes UB3 46 B4
North Looe, Epsom KT17 51 E4
Northolt, Nthlt. UB5 46 C2
Northolt Rd, Har. HA2 46 C2
Northover, Brom. BR1 52 C1
North Pole La, Kes. BR2 52 C4
North Rd N6 48 A1
North Sheen, Rich. TW9 47 D4
North St, Cars. SM5 51 F3
North St, Rom. RM1 49 F1
North St SW4 52 A1
Northumberland Heath, Erith DA8 49 F4
North Wembley, Wem. HA0 47 D2

Northwold Rd E5; N16 48 B2
Northwood Hills, Nthwd. HA6 46 B1
Northwood Rd, Th.Hth. CR7 52 B2
Northwood Rd (Harefield), Uxb. UB9 46 A1
North Woolwich E16 49 D4
North Woolwich Rd E16 49 D3
Norwood SE19 52 B2
Norwood Green, Sthl. UB2 46 C4
Norwood High St SE27 52 B1
Norwood New Town SE19 52 A2
Norwood Rd, Sthl. UB2 46 C4
Norwood Rd SE24; SE27 52 A1
Notting Hill W11 47 F3
Notting Hill Gate W11 47 F3
Nunhead SE15 52 B1
Nunhead La SE15 52 B1
Nursery Rd, Sun. TW16 50 B2
Nuxley Rd, Belv. DA17 49 F4
Oak Av, Hmptn. TW12 50 C2
Oaken La, Esher KT10 50 C3
Oak Hill, Wdf.Grn. IG8 48 C1
Oaklands La, West. TN16 53 D4
Oakley Rd, Brom. BR2 53 D3
Oakley St SW3 47 F4
Oaks Rd, Croy. CR0 52 B3
Oakwood Av, Beck. BR3 52 C2
Oatlands Av, Wey. KT13 50 B3
Oatlands Chase, Wey. KT13 50 B3
Oatlands Dr, Wey. KT13 50 B3
Oatlands Park, Wey. KT13 50 B3
Okehampton Cres, Well. DA16 49 E4
Old Bexley, Bex. DA5 53 F1
Old Bexley La, Bex. DA5; Dart. DA1 53 F1
Old Brompton Rd SW5; SW7 47 F4
Oldchurch Rd, Rom. RM7 49 F2
Old Farleigh Rd, S.Croy. CR2; Warl. CR6 52 B4
Oldfield La N, Grnf. UB6 46 C3
Oldfields Rd, Sutt. SM1 51 F3
Old Ford E3 48 C3
Old Ford Rd E2; E3 48 B3
Old Hill, Chis. BR7 53 D2
Old Kent Rd SE1; SE15 48 B4
Old London Rd, Sev. TN14 53 F4
Old Malden, Wor.Pk. KT4 51 E3
Old Malden La, Wor.Pk. KT4 51 E3
Old Oak Common La NW10; W3 47 E3
Old Oak La NW10 47 E3
Old Oak Rd W3 47 E3
Old St EC1 48 B3
Old Town, Croy. CR0 52 A3
Old Town SW4 52 A1
Orchard Av, Croy. CR0 52 C2
Orchard Way, Beck. BR3; Croy. CR0 52 C2
Orpington, Orp. BR6 53 E3
Orpington Bypass, Orp. BR6; Sev. TN14 53 F4
Orpington Rd, Chis. BR7 53 E2
Ossulton Way N2 47 F1
Osterley, Islw. TW7 46 C4
Otford La, Sev. TN14 53 F4
Oval, The, Sid. DA15 53 E1
Oxford St W1 48 A3
Oxlow La, Dag. RM9, RM10 49 F2
Oxshott, Lthd. KT22 50 C4
Oyster La, W.Byf. KT14 50 A4
Paddington W2 47 F3
Page Heath La, Brom. BR1 53 D2
Page St NW7 47 E1
Paines La, Pnr. HA5 46 C1
Painters Rd, Ilf. IG2 49 E1
Pall Mall SW1 48 A3
Palmerston Rd N22 48 A1
Pampisford Rd, Pur. CR8; S.Croy. CR2 52 A4
Pancras Rd NW1 48 A3
Parchmore Rd, Th.Hth. CR7 52 B2
Parish La SE20 52 B2
Park Av, Ruis. HA4 46 B1
Park Av N22 48 A1
Park Av E, Epsom KT17 51 E4
Park Hill, Cars. SM5 51 F4
Parkhill Rd, Bex. DA5 53 F1
Park Hill Rd, Croy. CR0 52 B3
Parkhurst Rd N7 48 A2
Park La, Cars. SM5 51 F3
Park La, Croy. CR0 52 B3
Park La, Hayes UB4 46 B3
Park La, Houns. TW5 46 B4

Park La (Harefield), Uxb. UB9 46 A1
Park La, Wem. HA9 47 D2
Park La W1 48 A3
Park Langley, Beck. BR3 52 C3
Park Rd, Hmptn. TW12 50 C2
Park Rd, Hayes UB4 46 B3
Park Rd (Hampton Wick), Kings.T. KT1 51 D2
Park Rd, Kings.T. KT2 51 D2
Park Rd (Stanwell), Stai. TW19 50 A1
Park Rd, Tedd. TW11 50 C2
Park Rd, Uxb. UB8 46 A3
Park Rd, Warl. CR6 52 C4
Park Rd N8 48 A1
Park Rd NW1; NW8 47 F3
Park Royal NW10 47 D3
Park Royal Rd NW10; W3 47 E3
Parkside SW19 51 E1
Parkside Way, Har. HA2 46 C1
Park Vw Rd, Uxb. UB8 46 A3
Park Vw Rd, Well. DA16 53 E1
Parkway, Croy. CR0 52 C4
Parkway, The, Hayes UB3; Houns. TW4, TW5; Nthlt. UB5; Sthl. UB2 46 B3
Parnell Rd E3 48 C3
Parsloes Av, Dag. RM9 49 E2
Parsonage Manorway, Belv. DA17 49 F4
Parsons Green SW6 47 F4
Parson St NW4 47 E1
Parvis Rd, W.Byf. KT14 50 A4
Pawson's Rd, Croy. CR0 52 B3
Peckham SE15 48 B4
Peckham High St SE15 48 B4
Peckham Hill St SE15 48 B4
Peckham Pk Rd SE15 48 B4
Peckham Rd SE5; SE15 48 B4
Peckham Rye SE15; SE22 52 B1
Pembroke Rd, Ruis. HA4 46 B2
Pembury Rd E5 48 B2
Penge SE20 52 B2
Penge Rd SE20; SE25 52 B2
Penhill Rd, Bex. DA5 53 E1
Penrhyn Rd, Kings.T. KT1 51 D2
Pentonville Rd N1 48 A3
Percy Rd, Hmptn. TW12 50 C2
Percy Rd, Twick. TW2 50 C1
Perivale, Grnf. UB6 47 D3
Perry Hall Rd, Orp. BR6 53 E3
Perry Hill SE6 52 C1
Perry Ri SE23 52 C1
Perry St, Chis. BR7 53 E2
Perry St, Dart. DA1 53 F1
Perry Vale SE23 52 B1
Perth Rd, Ilf. IG2 49 D1
Petersham, Rich. TW10 51 D1
Petersham Rd, Rich. TW10 51 D1
Pettits La, Rom. RM1 49 F1
Pettits La N, Rom. RM1 49 F1
Petts Hill, Nthlt. UB5 46 C2
Petts Wood, Orp. BR5 53 E2
Petts Wd Rd, Orp. BR5 53 E3
Philip La N15 48 B1
Picardy Manorway, Belv. DA17 49 F4
Picardy Rd, Belv. DA17 49 F4
Piccadilly W1 48 A3
Pickhurst La, Brom. BR2; W.Wick. BR4 52 C3
Pield Heath Rd, Uxb. UB8 46 A3
Pimlico SW1 48 A4
Pimlico Rd SW1 48 A4
Pinner, Pnr. HA5 46 B1
Pinner Green, Pnr. HA5 46 B1
Pinner Hill Rd, Pnr. HA5 46 B1
Pinner Rd, Har. HA1 46 C1
Pinner Rd, Nthwd. HA6 46 C1
Pinner Rd, Pnr. HA5 46 C1
Pinner Vw, Har. HA1, HA2 46 C1
Pinnerwood Park, Pnr. HA5 46 B1
Pitfield St N1 48 B3
Pitshanger La W5 47 D3
Pixton Way, Croy. CR0 52 C4
Plaistow, Brom. BR1 52 C2
Plaistow E13 48 C3
Plaistow La, Brom. BR1 53 D2
Plaistow Rd E13; E15 48 C3
Plashet Gro E6 49 D3
Plashet Rd E13 49 D3
Plough La, Pur. CR8 52 A4
Plough La, Wall. SM6 52 A3
Plough La SW17; SW19 51 F2
Plough Way SE16 48 B4
Plumstead SE18 49 E4
Plumstead Common Rd SE18 49 D4
Plumstead High St SE18 49 E4
Plumstead Rd SE18 49 D4
Pole Hill Rd, Hayes UB4; Uxb. UB10 46 A3
Pomeroy St SE14 48 B4
Pool Rd, W.Mol. KT8 50 C3
Popes La W5 47 D4

Poplar E14 48 C3
Poplar High St E14 48 C3
Poplar Way, Felt. TW13 50 B1
Porters Av, Dag. RM8, RM9 49 E2
Portland Pl W1 48 A3
Portland Rd SE25 52 B2
Portmore Pk Rd, Wey. KT13 50 A3
Portsmouth Rd, Esher KT10; Kings.T. KT6; T.Ditt. KT7 50 C3
Pound La NW10 47 E2
Pound St, Cars. SM5 51 F3
Poverest Rd, Orp. BR5 53 E3
Powder Mill La, Twick. TW2 50 C1
Poynders Rd SW4 52 A1
Praed St W2 47 F3
Pratt's Bottom, Orp. BR6 53 E4
Preston Hill, Har. HA3 47 D2
Preston Rd, Har. HA3; Wem. HA9 47 D2
Prestons Rd E14 48 C3
Primrose Av, Rom. RM6 49 E2
Prince Albert Rd NW1; NW8 47 F3
Prince Imperial Rd, Chis. BR7 53 D2
Prince of Wales Rd SE3 53 D1
Prince Regent La E13; E16 49 D3
Priory La SW15 51 E1
Priory Rd N8 48 A1
Puddledock La, Dart. DA2 53 F2
Pump La, Hayes UB3 46 B3
Purley, Pur. CR8 52 A4
Purley Downs Rd, Pur. CR8; S.Croy. CR2 52 B4
Purley Way, Croy. CR0; Pur. CR8 52 A3
Pursley Rd NW7 47 E1
Putney SW15 51 E1
Putney Br Rd SW15; SW18 51 F1
Putney Heath SW15 51 E1
Putney Heath SW15 51 E1
Putney High St SW15 51 E1
Putney Hill SW15 51 E1
Putney Vale SW15 51 E1
Pyrford Rd, W.Byf. KT14; Wok. GU22 50 A4
Queen Anne Av, Brom. BR2 52 C2
Queensbridge Rd E2; E8 48 B2
Queensbury, Har. HA3 47 D1
Queens Dr W3; W5 47 D3
Queens Ride SW13; SW15 51 E1
Queen's Rd, Croy. CR0 52 A3
Queen's Rd, Erith DA8 49 F4
Queens Rd, Kings.T. KT2 51 D2
Queens Rd, Rich. TW10 51 D1
Queen's Rd, Tedd. TW11 50 C2
Queens Rd, Walt. KT12; Wey. KT13 50 B3
Queens Rd NW4 47 E1
Queens Rd SE14; SE15 48 B4
Queenstown Rd SW8 48 A4
Raeburn Av, Surb. KT5 51 D3
Railton Rd SE24 52 A1
Rainham Rd, Rain. RM13 49 F2
Rainham Rd N, Dag. RM10 49 F2
Rainham Rd S, Dag. RM10 49 F2
Ramsden, Orp. BR5 53 E3
Rancliffe Rd E6 49 D3
Randles La, Sev. TN14 53 E4
Ravensbourne Av, Beck. BR3; Brom. BR2 52 C2
Raymouth Rd SE16 48 B4
Rayners Lane, Har. HA2 46 C2
Rayners La, Har. HA2; Pnr. HA5 46 C1
Raynes Park SW20 51 E2
Rectory La, Sid. DA14 53 E2
Rectory La, Surb. KT6 51 D3
Rectory La SW17 52 A2
Rectory Pk, S.Croy. CR2 52 B4
Rectory Rd, Beck. BR3 52 C2
Rectory Rd N16 48 B2
Redbridge, Brom. BR1 49 D1
Redbridge La E, Ilf. IG4 49 D1
Redcliffe Gdns SW5; SW10 47 F4
Red Hill, Chis. BR7 53 D2
Redhill Rd, Cob. KT11 50 B4
Red Lion Rd, Surb. KT6 51 D3
Redmans La, Sev. TN14 53 F4
Redriff Rd SE16 48 B4
Reede Rd, Dag. RM10 49 F2
Regent's Park NW1 48 A3
Regents Pk Rd N3 47 F1
Regent St W1; SW1 48 A3
Reigate Av, Sutt. SM1 51 F3
Reigate Rd, Epsom KT17, KT18; Tad. KT20 51 E4
Renfree Way, Shep. TW17 50 A3
Repository Rd SE18 49 D4

Richmond, Rich. TW10 51 D1
Richmond Hill, Rich. TW10 51 D1
Richmond Rd, Kings.T. KT2 51 D2
Richmond Rd, Twick. TW1 51 D1
Rickmansworth Rd (Harefield), Uxb. UB9 46 A1
Riddlesdown Rd, Pur. CR8 52 B4
Ridge Rd, Sutt. SM3 51 F3
Ridgeway, The (North Harrow), Har. HA2 46 C1
Ridgway SW19 51 E1
Riefield Rd SE9 53 E1
Ripple Rd, Bark. IG11; Dag. RM9 49 E3
River Rd, Bark. IG11 49 E3
Riverside Dr, Rich. TW10 51 E1
Robin Hood Way (Kingston Bypass) SW15; SW20 51 E1
Robinsway, Walt. KT12 50 B3
Rochester Way SE3; SE9 53 D1
Rochester Way Relief Rd SE3; SE9 49 D4
Rock Hill, Orp. BR6 53 F4
Rockingham Rd, Uxb. UB8 46 A3
Rocks La SW13 51 E1
Roding La N, Wdf.Grn. IG8 49 D1
Rodney Rd, Walt. KT12 50 B3
Rodney Rd SE17 48 B4
Roe Grn NW9 47 E1
Roehampton SW15 51 E1
Roehampton La SW15 51 E1
Roehampton Vale SW15 51 E1
Rolls Rd SE1 48 B4
Roman Rd E2; E3 48 C3
Roman Way, Croy. CR0 52 A3
Romford, Rom. RM 49 F1
Romford Rd E7; E15 48 C3
Ron Leighton Way E6 49 D3
Rookery Rd, Orp. BR6 53 D4
Rosebery Av EC1 48 A3
Rosedale Rd, Epsom KT17 51 E4
Rosehill, Sutt. SM1 51 F3
Rose Hill, Sutt. SM1 51 F3
Rose La, Rom. RM6 49 F1
Rosslyn Hill NW3 47 F2
Rosslyn Rd NW3 47 F2
Rotherhithe SE16 48 B4
Rotherhithe New Rd SE16 48 B4
Rotherhithe Tunnel E1 48 B3
Roundway, The N17 48 B1
Rowan Rd SW16 52 A2
Row Town, Add. KT15 50 A4
Roxeth Grn Av, Har. HA2 46 C2
Roxeth Hill, Har. HA2 46 C2
Royal Albert Way E16 49 D3
Royal Docks Rd E6 49 D3
Royal Hosp Rd SW3 47 F4
Royal La, Uxb. UB8; West Dr. UB7 46 A3
Royston Pk Rd, Pnr. HA5 46 C1
Ruckholt Rd E10 48 C2
Ruislip, Ruis. HA4 46 B1
Ruislip Common, Ruis. HA4 46 B2
Ruislip Gardens, Ruis. HA4 46 B2
Ruislip Manor, Ruis. HA4 46 B2
Ruislip Rd, Grnf. UB6; Nthlt. UB5; Sthl. UB1 46 B3
Ruislip Rd E W7; W13; Grnf. UB6 46 C3
Rushett La, Chess. KT9; Epsom KT18 51 D4
Rushey Grn SE6 52 C1
Rush Green, Rom. RM7 49 F2
Rush Grn Rd, Rom. RM7 49 F2
Rushmore Hill, Orp. BR6; Sev. TN14 53 E4
Ruskin Rd, Cars. SM5 51 F3
Russell Rd N15 48 B1
Rydens, Walt. KT12 50 B3
Rydens Rd, Walt. KT12 50 B3
Rye La SE15 48 B4
St. Ann's Hill SW18 51 F1
St. Ann's Rd N15 48 B1
St. Davids Rd, Swan. BR8 53 F2
St. Dunstan's Hill, Sutt. SM1 51 F3
St. George's Av, Wey. KT13 50 A4
St. George's Hill, Wey. KT13 50 B4
St. Georges Rd E7 49 D2
St. Helier, Cars. SM5 51 F3
St. Helier Av, Mord. SM4 51 F3
St. James's Dr SW12; SW17 51 F1
St. James's Rd, Croy. CR0 52 B3
St. James's Rd SE1; SE16 48 B4
St. John's Rd SW11 51 F1
St. John's Rd, Islw. TW7 46 C4
St. Johns Rd, Uxb. UB8 46 A3
St. John's Wood NW8 47 F3
St. John's Wd Rd NW8 47 F3

St. Leonards Rd, T.Ditt. KT7 51 D3
St. Luke's EC1 **48 B3**
St. Margarets, Twick. TW1 **51 D1**
St. Margarets Rd, Twick. TW1 51 D1
St. Mary Cray, Orp. BR5 **53 E2**
St. Mary's Rd SW19 51 F2
St. Mary's Rd W5 47 D4
St. Mildreds Rd SE12 52 C1
St. Nicholas Way, Sutt. SM1 51 F3
St. Pancras WC1 **48 A3**
St. Paul's Cray, Orp. BR5 **53 E2**
St. Paul's Cray Rd, Chis. BR7 53 E2
St. Paul's Rd N1 48 A2
St. Paul's Rd E3; E14 48 C3
St. Pauls Wd Hill, Orp. BR5 53 E2
St. Peter's Rd, Croy. CR0 52 B3
St. Quintin Av W10 47 E3
St. Thomas' Dr, Pnr. HA5 46 C1
Salisbury Rd (Hounslow West), Houns. TW4 50 B1
Salmon St NW9 47 D2
Salt Box Hill, West. TN16 53 D4
Salter Rd SE16 48 B4
Salters Hill SE19 52 B2
Salusbury Rd NW6 47 F3
Sanders La NW7 47 E1
Sanderstead, S.Croy. CR2 **52 B4**
Sanderstead Hill, S.Croy. CR2 52 B4
Sanderstead Rd, S.Croy. CR2 52 B4
Sandown Av, Esher KT10 50 C3
Sandown Rd, Esher KT10 50 C3
Sands End SW6 **47 F4**
Sandycombe Rd, Rich. TW9 51 D1
Sandy La, Cob. KT11; Lthd. KT22 50 C4
Sandy La, Kings.T. KT1; Tedd. TW11 51 D2
Sandy La, Orp. BR5; Sid. DA14 53 E2
Sandy La, Rich. TW10 51 D1
Sandy La, Sutt. SM2 51 F4
Sandy La S, Wall. SM6 52 A4
Sanford St SE14 48 C4
School La, Add. KT15 50 A3
School Rd, Ashf. TW15 50 A2
Scotch Common W13 47 D3
Scotland Br Rd, Add. KT15 50 A4
Scotshall La, Warl. CR6 52 C4
Scotts La, Brom. BR2 52 C2
Scrubs La NW10; W10 47 E3
Selhurst SE25 **52 B3**
Selhurst Rd SE25 52 B3
Selsdon, S.Croy. CR2 **52 B4**
Selsdon Pk Rd, S.Croy. CR2 52 B4
Selsdon Rd, S.Croy. CR2 52 B3
Selwyn Av E4 48 C1
Seven Hills Rd, Cob. KT11; Walt. KT12 50 B4
Seven Kings, Ilf. IG3 **49 E2**
Sevenoaks Rd, Orp. BR6 53 E3
Sevenoaks Rd (Green Street Green), Orp. BR6 53 E4
Sevenoaks Way, Orp. BR5; Sid. DA14 53 E2
Seven Sisters Rd N4; N7; N15 48 A2
Shacklands Rd, Sev. TN14 53 F4
Shacklewell N16 **48 B2**
Shacklewell La E8 48 B2
Shadwell E1 **48 B3**
Shaftesbury Av, Har. HA2 46 C2
Sheen La SW14 51 E1
Sheen Rd, Rich. TW9 51 D1
Sheepbarn La, Warl. CR6 52 C4
Sheepcote La, Orp. BR5; Swan. BR8 53 F3
Sheepcote Rd, Har. HA1 46 C1
Sheep Wk, Shep. TW17 50 A3
Shepherdess Wk N1 48 B3
Shepherd's Bush W12 **47 E3**
Shepherds Bush Rd W6 47 E4
Shepherds Hill N6 48 A1
Shepiston La, Hayes UB3; West Dr. UB7 46 A4
Shepperton, Shep. TW17 **50 A3**
Shepperton Rd, Stai. TW18 50 A2
Shernhall St E17 48 C1
Sherwood Pk Av, Sid. DA15 53 E1
Sherwood Pk Rd, Mitch. CR4 52 A2
Shire La, Orp. BR6 53 D4
Shirland Rd W9 47 F3
Shirley, Croy. CR0 **52 C3**
Shirley Ch Rd, Croy. CR0 52 B3

Shirley Hills Rd, Croy. CR0 52 B3
Shirley Rd, Croy. CR0 52 B3
Shooter's Hill Rd SE3; SE10; SE18 48 C4
Shoot Up Hill NW2 47 F2
Shoreditch E1 **48 B3**
Shoreham, Sev. TN14 **53 F4**
Shoreham La, Sev. TN14 53 F4
Shortlands, Brom. BR1 **52 C2**
Shortlands Rd, Brom. BR2 52 C2
Short La, Stai. TW19 50 A1
Sidcup, Sid. DA14 **53 E2**
Sidcup Bypass, Chis. BR7; Orp. BR5; Sid. DA14 53 E2
Sidcup High St, Sid. DA14 53 E2
Sidcup Hill, Sid. DA14 53 E2
Sidcup Rd SE9; SE12 53 D1
Sidmouth Rd NW2 47 E2
Sidney Rd, Walt. KT12 50 B3
Sidney St E1 48 B3
Silverthorne Rd SW8 48 A4
Silvertown E16 **49 D4**
Silvertown Way E16 48 C3
Single Street, West. TN16 **53 D4**
Sipson, West Dr. UB7 **46 A4**
Sipson La, Hayes UB3; West Dr. UB7 46 A4
Sipson Rd, West Dr. UB7 46 A4
Skeet Hill La, Orp. BR5, BR6 53 F3
Skid Hill La, Warl. CR6 52 C4
Slade, The SE18 49 E4
Sloane St SW1 47 F4
Smitham Bottom La, Pur. CR8 52 A4
Smitham Downs Rd, Pur. CR8 52 A4
Snakes La E, Wdf.Grn. IG8 49 D1
Snakes La W, Wdf.Grn. IG8 49 D1
Snaresbrook E11 **49 D1**
Snaresbrook Rd E11 49 C1
Soho W1 **48 A3**
Somerset Rd, Sthl. UB1 46 C3
Somerville Rd, Rom. RM6 49 E1
Sopwith Dr, W.Byf. KT14; Wey. KT13 50 A4
South Acton W3 **47 D4**
Southall, Sthl. UB **46 B3**
Southall La, Houns. TW5; Sthl. UB2 46 B4
Southampton Way SE5 48 B4
South Beddington, Wall. SM6 **52 A4**
Southborough, Brom. BR2 **53 D3**
Southborough La, Brom. BR2 53 D3
Southborough Rd, Brom. BR1 53 D2
Southbourne Gdns, Ruis. HA4 46 B2
South Circular Rd SW2 52 A1
South Croxted Rd SE21 52 B1
South Croydon, S.Croy. CR2 **52 B4**
South Ealing Rd W5 47 D4
South Eden Pk Rd, Beck. BR3 52 C3
Southend SE6 **52 C2**
Southend La SE6; SE26 52 C2
Southend Rd, Beck. BR3 52 C2
Southend Rd, Wdf.Grn. IG8 49 D1
Southend Rd E4; E17; E18 48 C1
Southern Perimeter Rd, Houns. TW6 50 A1
Southfield Rd W4 47 E4
Southfields SW18 **51 F1**
Southgate Rd N1 48 B3
South Hampstead NW6 **47 F2**
South Harefield, Uxb. UB9 **46 A1**
South Harrow, Har. HA2 **46 C2**
South Hill Av, Har. HA1, HA2 46 C2
South Hornchurch, Rain. RM13 **49 F3**
South Lambeth SW8 **48 A4**
South Lambeth Rd SW8 48 A4
Southlands Rd, Brom. BR1, BR2 53 D2
South La, N.Mal. KT3 51 E2
South Lo Av, Mitch. CR4 52 A2
South Norwood SE25 **52 B2**
South Norwood Hill SE25 52 B2
Southover, Brom. BR1 53 D2
South Par W4 47 E4
South Pk Dr, Bark. IG11; Ilf. IG3 49 E2
South Rd, Erith DA8 49 F4
South Rd, Sthl. UB1 46 C4
South Ruislip, Ruis. HA4 **46 B2**
South St, Epsom KT18 51 E4

South St, Islw. TW7 51 D1
South Tottenham N15 **48 B2**
Southwark SE1 **48 B4**
Southwark Pk Rd SE16 48 B4
Southwark St SE1 48 A3
South Woodford E18 **48 C1**
South Woodford to Barking Relief Rd E11; E12; E18; Bark. IG11; Ilf. IG1 49 D1
Southwood La N6 48 A2
Spa Hill SE19 52 B2
Spaniards Rd NW3 47 F2
Spelthorne La, Ashf. TW15 50 B2
Spencer Pk SW18 51 F1
Spencer Rd, E.Mol. KT8 50 C3
Spout Hill, Croy. CR0 52 C3
Spring Grove, Islw. TW7 **46 C4**
Spring Gro Rd, Houns. TW3; Islw. TW7 46 C4
Spring La SE25 52 B3
Spur Rd, Orp. BR6 53 E3
Square, The, Hayes UB3 46 B4
Squires Br Rd, Shep. TW17 50 A2
Stafford Rd, Croy. CR0; Wall. SM6 52 A4
Stag La NW9 47 D1
Staines, Stai. TW18 **50 A1**
Staines Rd, Felt. TW14; Houns. TW3; TW4 50 B1
Staines Rd, Stai. TW18 50 A1
Staines Rd, Twick. TW2 50 C1
Staines Rd E, Sun. TW16 50 B2
Staines Rd W, Ashf. TW15; Sun. TW16 50 B2
Stamford Hill N16 **48 B2**
Stamford Hill N16 48 B2
Stamford St SE1 48 A3
Stanley Pk Rd, Cars. SM5; Wall. SM6 51 F4
Stanley Rd, Tedd. TW11; Twick. TW2 50 C2
Stansfeld Rd E6 49 D3
Stanstead Rd SE6; SE23 52 B1
Stanton Way SE26 52 C2
Stanwell, Stai. TW19 **50 A1**
Stanwell Moor Rd, Stai. TW19; West Dr. UB7 50 A1
Stanwell Rd, Ashf. TW15 50 A1
Stanwell Rd (East Bedfont), Felt. TW14 50 A1
Star & Garter Hill, Rich. TW10 51 D1
Station App, Ruis. HA4 46 B2
Station Av, Walt. KT12 50 B3
Station Rd, Add. KT15 50 A3
Station Rd (Crayford), Dart. DA1 53 F1
Station Rd, Edg. HA8 47 D1
Station Rd, Esher KT10 50 C3
Station Rd, Har. HA1 46 C1
Station Rd, Hayes UB3 46 B4
Station Rd (St. Mary Cray), Orp. BR5 53 E2
Station Rd, Orp. BR6 53 E3
Station Rd (Chadwell Heath), Rom. RM6 49 E2
Station Rd (Halstead), Sev. TN14 53 F4
Station Rd, Sid. DA15 53 E1
Station Rd, T.Ditt. KT7 50 C3
Station Rd (Cowley), Uxb. UB8 46 A3
Station Rd, West Dr. UB7 46 A4
Station Rd, W.Wick. BR4 52 C3
Station Rd E12 49 D2
Station Rd NW4 47 E1
Station Rd NW10 47 E2
Station Rd SW13 47 E4
Station Way, Sutt. SM3 51 F4
Stayton Rd, Sutt. SM1 51 F3
Steels La, Lthd. KT22 50 C4
Stephenson St E16 48 C3
Stepney E1 **48 B3**
Stepney Grn E1 48 B3
Stepney Way E1 48 B3
Steyne Rd W3 47 D3
Stoats Nest Rd, Couls. CR5 52 A4
Stockley Rd, West Dr. UB7; Uxb. UB8 46 A3
Stockwell SW9 52 A1
Stockwell Rd SW9 48 A4
Stoke Newington N16 **48 B2**
Stoke Newington Rd N16 48 B2
Stokesheath Rd, Lthd. KT22 50 C4
Stondon Pk SE23 52 C1
Stonebridge NW10 **47 D3**
Stonecot Hill, Sutt. SM3 51 F3
Stonehouse La, Sev. TN14 53 E4
Stoneleigh, Epsom KT17 **51 E3**
Stoneleigh Av, Wor.Pk. KT4 51 E3
Stone Pk Av, Beck. BR3 52 C2
Stopford Rd E13 49 D3

Strand WC2 48 A3
Stratford E15 **48 C2**
Strathyre Av SW16 52 A2
Strawberry Hill, Twick. TW1 **50 B1**
Strawberry Vale, Twick. TW1 51 D1
Streatfeild Rd, Har. HA3 47 D1
Streatham SW16 **52 A2**
Streatham Common N SW16 52 A2
Streatham High Rd SW16 52 A1
Streatham Hill SW2 **52 A1**
Streatham Hill SW2 52 A1
Streatham Park SW16 **52 A2**
Streatham Pl SW2 52 A1
Streatham Rd, Mitch. CR4 52 A2
Streatham Vale SW16 **52 A2**
Streatham Vale SW16 52 A2
Strone Rd E7; E12 49 D2
Stroud Green N4 **48 A2**
Stroud Grn Rd N4 48 A2
Sudbury, Wem. HA0 **47 D2**
Sudbury Hill, Har. HA1 46 C2
Sugden Rd, T.Ditt. KT7 51 D3
Summer La, Chis. BR7 53 D2
Summer Rd, E.Mol. KT8; T.Ditt. KT7 50 C3
Summers La N12 47 F1
Summerstown SW17 **51 F1**
Sunbury, Sun. TW16 50 B2
Sunbury Rd, Felt. TW13 50 B1
Sundridge, Sev. TN14 53 D2
Sunnyside Rd, Ilf. IG1 49 E2
Sunray Av SE24 52 B1
Surbiton, Surb. KT6 **51 D3**
Surbiton Hill Pk, Surb. KT5 51 D3
Surbiton Rd, Kings.T. KT1 51 D2
Surrey Canal Rd SE14; SE15 48 B4
Surrey Quays Rd SE16 48 B4
Sussex Gdns W2 47 F3
Sutton, Sutt. SM **51 F4**
Sutton Common Rd, Sutt. SM1, SM3 51 F3
Sutton La, Bans. SM7; Sutt. SM2 51 F4
Sutton La, Houns. TW3 50 C1
Swakeleys Rd, Uxb. UB10 46 A2
Swandon Way SW18 51 F1
Swan La, Dart. DA1 53 F1
Swanley, Swan. BR8 **53 F2**
Swanley Bypass, Sid. DA14; Swan. BR8 53 F2
Swanley La, Swan. BR8 53 F2
Swan Rd (Hanworth), Felt. TW13 50 C2
Swan Rd, West Dr. UB7 46 A4
Sweetcroft La, Uxb. UB10 46 A2
Sydenham SE26 **52 B2**
Sydenham Hill SE23; SE26 52 B1
Sydenham Rd SE26 52 B2
Sydney St SW3 47 F4
Syon La, Islw. TW7 46 C4
Tachbrook Rd, Felt. TW14 50 B1
Talgarth Rd W6; W14 47 E4
Tamworth La, Mitch. CR4 52 A2
Tamworth Rd, Croy. CR0 52 A3
Tatsfield, West. TN16 53 D4
Teddington, Tedd. TW11 **51 D2**
Teignmouth Gdns, Grnf. UB6 47 D3
Tennison Rd SE25 52 B2
Tentelow La, Sthl. UB2 46 C4
Terrace, The SW13 47 E4
Terrace, The, Walt. KT12 50 B3
Tetherdown N10 48 A1
Thames Ditton, T.Ditt. KT7 **50 C3**
Thamesmead SE28 **49 E3**
Thamesmead North SE28 **49 E3**
Thamesmead West SE18 **49 E4**
Thames Side, Cher. KT16; Stai. TW18 50 A2
Thames St, Sun. TW16 50 B2
Thames St, Walt. KT12 50 B3
Thicket Rd SE20 52 B2
Thorkhill Rd, T.Ditt. KT7 51 D3
Thornbury Rd, Islw. TW7 46 C4
Thorney, Iver SL0 **46 A4**
Thorney Mill Rd, Iver SL0; West Dr. UB7 46 A4
Thornton Av SW2 52 A1
Thornton Rd, Croy. CR0 52 A2
Thornton Heath, Th.Hth. CR7 **52 B2**
Thornton Rd, Croy. CR0; Th.Hth. CR7 52 A3
Throwley Way, Sutt. SM1 51 F3
Thurlow Pk Rd SE21 52 A1
Tokyngton, Wem. HA9 47 D2
Tollgate Rd E16 49 D3
Tollington Pk N4 48 A2
Tolworth, Surb. KT6 **51 D3**
Tomswood Hill, Ilf. IG6 49 D1
Tomswood Rd, Chig. IG7 49 D1

Tooting Bec Rd SW16; SW17 52 A1
Tooting Graveney SW17 **51 F2**
Tooting High St SW17 51 F2
Top Dartford Rd, Dart. DA2; Swan. BR8 53 F2
Torrington Rd, Ruis. HA4 46 B2
Tottenham N17 **48 B1**
Tottenham Hale N17 **48 B1**
Tottenham La N8 48 A1
Tower Br Rd SE1 48 B4
Towncourt La, Orp. BR5 53 E3
Town La, Stai. TW19 50 A1
Townley Rd, Bexh. DA6 53 F1
Trafalgar Av SE15 48 B4
Trafalgar Rd SE10 48 C4
Traps La, N.Mal. KT3 51 E2
Trinity Ri SW2 52 A1
Trinity Rd SW17; SW18 51 F1
Trott Rd N10 47 F1
Trundleys Rd SE8 48 B4
Tubbenden La, Orp. BR6 53 E3
Tudor Dr, Kings.T. KT2 51 D2
Tudor Way, Orp. BR5 53 E3
Tufnell Park N7 **48 A2**
Tufnell Pk Rd N7; N19 48 A2
Tulse Hill SE21 **52 B1**
Tulse Hill SW2 52 A1
Tunmarsh La E13 49 D3
Turnpike La N8 48 A1
Twickenham, Twick. TW **50 C1**
Twickenham Rd (Hanworth), Felt. TW13 50 C1
Twickenham Rd, Islw. TW7 51 D1
Twickenham Rd, Rich. TW9 51 D1
Twickenham Rd, Tedd. TW11 51 D2
Twyford Av W3 47 E2
Tylers Grn Rd, Swan. BR8 53 F3
Union Rd SW4; SW8 48 A4
Upper Brighton Rd, Surb. KT6 51 D3
Upper Clapton Rd E5 48 B2
Upper Elmers End, Beck. BR3 **52 C2**
Upper Elmers End Rd, Beck. BR3 52 C2
Upper Halliford, Shep. TW17 **50 B2**
Upper Halliford Rd, Shep. TW17 50 B2
Upper Ham Rd, Rich. TW10 51 D2
Upper Holloway N19 **48 A2**
Upper N St E14 48 C3
Upper Norwood SE19 **52 B2**
Upper Rainham Rd, Horn. RM12 49 F2
Upper Richmond Rd SW15 51 E1
Upper Richmond Rd W SW14; Rich. TW10 51 E1
Upper Rd E13 49 D2
Upper Selsdon Rd, S.Croy. CR2 52 B4
Upper Shirley Rd, Croy. CR0 52 B3
Upper St N1 48 A3
Upper Sunbury Rd, Hmptn. TW12 50 C2
Upper Sydenham SE26 **52 B2**
Upper Tooting SW17 **51 F1**
Upper Tooting Rd SW17 51 F2
Upper Tulse Hill SW2 52 A1
Upper Wickham La, Well. DA16 49 E4
Upton E7 **49 D2**
Upton La E7 49 D2
Upton Park E6 **49 D3**
Upton Rd, Bex. DA5; Bexh. DA6 53 F1
Uxbridge, Uxb. UB8 **46 A2**
Uxbridge Moor, Iver SL0 **46 A3**
Uxbridge Rd (Hanworth), Felt. TW13 50 B1
Uxbridge Rd, Hmptn. TW12 50 C2
Uxbridge Rd, Har. HA3; Pnr. HA5; Stan. HA7 46 B1
Uxbridge Rd, Hayes UB4 46 B3
Uxbridge Rd, Sthl. UB1 46 C3
Uxbridge Rd W3; W5 47 E2
Uxbridge Rd W12 47 E3
Vale, The NW11 47 F2
Vale, The W3 47 E3
Vallance Rd E1; E2 48 B3
Valley Rd, Brom. BR2 52 C2
Vanbrugh Pk SE3 48 C4
Vauxhall SE11 **48 A4**
Vauxhall Br Rd SW1 48 A4
Verdant La SE6 52 C1
Verdun Rd SW13 47 E4

Vicarage Cres SW11 47 F4
Vicarage La E15 48 C2
Vicarage Rd, Bex. DA5 53 F1
Vicarage Rd, Sun. TW16 50 B2
Vicarage Rd E10 48 C2
Victoria Dock Rd E16 49 D3
Victoria Pk Rd E9 48 B3
Victoria Rd, Rom. RM1 49 F1
Victoria Rd, Ruis. HA4 46 B2
Victoria Rd NW10; W3 47 E3
Victoria St SW1 48 A4
Village, The SE7 49 D4
Village Way, Beck. BR3 52 C2
Village Way, Pnr. HA5 46 C2
Village SE21 52 B1
Villiers Av, Surb. KT5 51 D3
Villiers La, Kings.T. KT1 51 D2
Vine La, Uxb. UB10 46 A2
Violet Rd E3 48 C3
Vivian Av NW4 47 E1
Waddon Rd, Croy. CR0 52 A3
Waddon Way, Croy. CR0 52 A4
Waldegrave Rd, Tedd.
   TW11; Twick. TW1 50 C1
Waldram Pk Rd SE23 52 B1
Wales Fm Rd W3 47 E3
Walham Green SW6 47 F4
Wallington, Wall. SM6 52 A3
Walm La NW2 47 E2
Walterton Rd W9 47 F3
Walthamstow E17 48 B2
Walton Br Rd, Shep. TW17 50 B3
Walton Rd, Shep. TW17 50 B3
Walton-on-Thames, Walt.
   KT12 50 B3
Walton Pk, Walt. KT12 50 B3
Walton Rd, E.Mol. KT8; Walt.
   KT12; W.Mol. KT8 50 B3
Walworth SE17 48 A4
Walworth Rd SE1; SE17 48 B4
Wandle Rd, Mord. SM4 51 F2
Wandsworth SW18 51 F1
Wandsworth Br Rd SW6 47 F4
Wandsworth High St
   SW18 51 F1
Wandsworth Rd SW8 52 A1
Wapping E1 48 B3
Wapping High St E1 48 B3
Warham Rd, S.Croy. CR2 52 B3
Warren Av, Brom. BR1 52 C2
Warren Av, Sutt. SM2 51 F4
Warren Av (Oxshott),
   Lthd. KT22 50 C4
Warren Rd, Kings.T. KT2 51 E2
Warren Rd, Orp. BR6 53 E3
Warwick Rd W14 47 F4
Waterden Rd E15 48 C2
Water La E15 48 C2
Waterloo Rd, Rom. RM7 49 F1
Waterloo Rd SE1 48 A3
Watermead Way N17 48 B1

Watford Rd, Nthwd. HA6 46 B1
Watling Av, Edg. HA8 47 E1
Watling St, Bexh. DA6 53 F1
Watts La, Chis. BR7 53 D2
Watts Rd, T.Ditt. KT7 51 D3
Waverley Cres SE18 49 E4
Waxwell La, Pnr. HA5 46 B1
Wealdstone, Har. HA3 47 D1
Weigall Rd SE12 53 D1
Weir Rd, Cher. KT16 50 A3
Wellesley Rd, Croy. CR0 52 B3
Wellesley Rd W4 47 D4
Well Hall Rd SE9 49 D4
Well Hill, Orp. BR6 53 F3
Well Hill, Orp. BR6 53 F3
Well Hill Rd, Sev. TN14 53 F4
Welling, Well. DA16 53 E1
Welling High St, Well.
   DA16 53 E1
Wellington Av, Sid. DA15 53 E1
Wellington Rd, Hmptn.
   TW12 50 C2
Wellington Rd NW8 47 F3
Wellington Rd N, Houns.
   TW4 50 C1
Wellington Rd S, Houns.
   TW4 50 C1
Wellington St SE18 49 D4
Wellington Way, Wey.
   KT13 50 A4
Welling Way SE9; Well.
   DA16 53 E1
Well St E9 48 B3
Wells Way SE5 48 B4
Wembley, Wem. HA0 47 D2
Wembley Park, Wem.
   HA9 47 D2
Wembley Pk Dr, Wem.
   HA9 47 D2
Wemborough Rd, Stan.
   HA7 47 D1
Wendover Way, Well.
   DA16 53 E1
West Acton W3 47 D3
West Barnes, N.Mal. KT3 51 E2
West Barnes La, N.Mal.
   KT3 51 E3
West Barnes La SW20;
   N.Mal. KT3 51 E3
Westbourne Gro W2; W11 47 F3
Westbourne Pk Rd W2;
   W11 47 F3
Westbridge Rd SW11 47 F4
Westbury Av N22 48 A1
West Byfleet, W.Byf. KT14 50 A4
Westcar La, Walt. KT12 50 B4
West Common Rd, Brom.
   BR2; Kes. BR2 53 D3
West Drayton, West Dr.
   UB7 46 A4
West Drayton Rd, Uxb.
   UB8 46 A3
West Drayton Rd
   (Hayes End), Uxb. UB8 46 A3

West Dulwich SE21 52 B1
West End, Esher KT10 50 C3
West End La, Esher KT10 50 C4
West End La NW6 47 F2
West End Rd, Ruis. HA4 46 B2
Westerham Rd, Kes. BR2 53 D4
Western Av W3; W5; Grnf. UB6;
   Nthlt. UB5; Ruis. HA4;
   Uxb. UB9, UB10 47 D3
Western Perimeter Rd,
   Houns. TW6 46 A4
Western Rd SW19; Mitch.
   CR4 51 F2
Western Rd, Sthl. UB2 46 B4
Western Way SE28 49 E4
West Ewell, Epsom KT19 51 E4
Westferry Rd E14 48 C4
West Green N15 48 B1
West Grn Rd N15 48 A1
West Gro, Walt. KT12 50 B3
West Ham E15 48 C2
West Ham La E15 48 C2
West Harrow, Har. HA1 46 C2
West Heath SE2 49 E4
West Heath Rd NW3 47 F2
West Hill SW15; SW18 51 F1
Westhorne Av SE9; SE12 53 D1
Westminster SW1 48 A4
West Molesey, W.Mol.
   KT8 50 C2
Westmoreland Rd, Brom.
   BR1, BR2 52 C3
Westmount Rd SE9 49 D4
West Norwood SE27 52 B2
Weston Av, W.Mol. KT8 50 C2
Weston Dr, Stan. HA7 47 D1
Weston Green, T.Ditt. KT7 50 C3
Weston Grn Rd, Esher KT10;
   T.Ditt. KT7 50 C3
West Side Common
   SW19 51 E2
West St, Cars. SM5 51 F3
West St, Erith DA8 49 F4
Westway W2; W9; W10;
   W12 47 E3
West Wickham, W.Wick.
   BR4 52 C3
Westwood Hill SE26 52 B2
Westwood La, Sid. DA15;
   Well. DA16 53 E1
Weybridge, Wey. KT13 50 A3
Weybridge Rd, Add. KT15;
   Wey. KT13 50 A3
Whalebone La N, Rom.
   RM6 49 F1
Whalebone La S, Dag.
   RM8; Rom. RM6 49 F2
Whipps Cross Rd E11 48 C1
Whitby Rd, Ruis. HA4 46 B2
Whitchurch La, Edg. HA8 47 D1
Whitechapel E1 48 B3
Whitechapel Rd E1 48 B3
Whitefoot La, Brom. BR1 52 C1
White Hart La, Rom. RM7 49 F1

White Hill, Rick. WD3 46 A1
White Horse Hill, Chis.
   BR7 53 D2
Whitehorse La SE25 52 B2
Whitehorse Rd, Croy. CR0 52 B3
Whiteley Village, Walt.
   KT12 50 B4
Whitton, Twick. TW2 50 C1
Whitton Av E, Grnf. UB6 46 C2
Whitton Av W, Grnf. UB6;
   Nthlt. UB5 46 C2
Whitton Dene, Houns.
   TW3; Islw. TW7 50 C1
Whitton Rd, Houns. TW3 50 C1
Whitton Rd, Twick. TW1 50 C1
Wickham Av, Sutt. SM3 51 E3
Wickham Ct Rd, W.Wick.
   BR4 52 C3
Wickham La SE2; Well.
   DA16 49 E4
Wickham Rd, Beck. BR3 52 C2
Wickham Rd, Croy. CR0 52 B3
Wickham Rd SE4 52 C1
Wickham Rd, Beck. BR3 52 C2
Wick Rd E9 48 B2
Wide Way, Mitch. CR4 52 A2
Widmore, Brom. BR1 53 D2
Widmore Rd, Brom. BR1 53 D2
Wightman Rd N4; N8 48 A1
Willersley Av, Sid. DA15 53 E1
Willesden NW10 47 E2
Willesden La NW2; NW6 47 E2
William Barefoot Dr SE9 53 D2
Willoughby La N17 48 B1
Willowbrook Rd SE15 48 B4
Wiltshire La, Pnr. HA5 46 B1
Wimbledon SW19 51 E2
Wimbledon Hill Rd SW19 51 E2
Wimbledon Park SW19 51 F1
Wimbledon Pk Rd SW18;
   SW19 51 F1
Wimbledon Pk Side SW19 51 E1
Winchelsea Rd NW10 47 E3
Winchester Rd E4 48 C1
Winchester St W3 47 E4
Windmill Hill, Ruis. HA4 46 B2
Windmill La, Epsom KT17 51 E4
Windmill La, Islw. TW7;
   Sthl. UB2 46 C4
Windmill La, Mitch. CR4 52 A3
Windmill Rd, Sun. TW16 50 B2
Windmill Rd SW18 51 F1
Windmill Rd W5; Brent.
   TW8 47 D4
Winkworth Rd, Bans. SM7 51 F4
Winn Rd SE12 53 D1
Winston Way, Ilf. IG1 49 D2
Woburn Hill, Add. KT15 50 A3
Woodcock Hill, Har. HA3 47 D1
Woodcote, Pur. CR8 52 A4
Woodcote Rd, Epsom
   KT18 51 E4
Woodcote Valley Rd, Pur.
   CR8 52 A4

Woodfield Rd W5 47 D3
Woodford, Wdf.Grn. IG8 49 D1
Woodford Av, Ilf. IG2,
   IG4; Wdf.Grn. IG8 49 D1
Woodford Bridge,
   Wdf.Grn. IG8 49 D1
Woodford New Rd E17;
   E18; Wdf.Grn. IG8 48 C1
Woodford Rd E18 49 D1
Woodgrange Rd E7 48 C2
Wood Green N22 48 A1
Woodhayes Rd SW19 51 E2
Wood La, Dag. RM8, RM9 49 E2
Wood La, Islw. TW7 46 C4
Wood La NW9 47 E2
Wood La W12 47 E3
Woodmansterne La, Cars.
   SM5; Wall. SM6 52 A4
Woodmansterne Rd, Cars.
   SM5 51 F4
Woodside, Croy. CR0 52 B3
Woodstock La N, Surb.
   KT6 51 D3
Woodstock La S, Chess.
   KT9; Esher KT10 51 D3
Wood St, Kings.T. KT1 51 D2
Wood St E17 48 C1
Woodthorpe Rd, Ashf.
   TW15 50 A2
Wood Vale SE23 52 B1
Woodward Rd, Dag. RM9 49 E2
Woolstone Rd SE23 52 C1
Woolwich SE18 49 D4
Woolwich Ch St SE18 49 D4
Woolwich High St SE18 49 D4
Woolwich Manor Way E6;
   E16 49 D3
Woolwich Rd SE2; Belv.
   DA17 49 E4
Woolwich Rd SE7 49 D4
Worcester Park, Wor.Pk.
   KT4 51 E3
Worcester Pk Rd, Wor.Pk.
   KT4 51 E3
Worple Rd, Stai. TW18 50 A2
Worple Rd SW19; SW20 51 E2
Worship St EC2 48 B3
Worton Rd, Islw. TW7 50 C1
Wrythe, The, Cars. SM5 51 F3
Wrythe La, Cars. SM5 51 F3
Wyndham Rd SE5 48 A4
Yarnton Way SE2; Erith
   DA18 49 E4
Yeading, Hayes UB4 46 B3
Yeading Gdns, Hayes UB4 46 B3
Yeading La, Hayes UB4;
   Nthlt. UB5 46 B3
Yiewsley, West Dr. UB7 46 A3
York Rd SW11; SW18 51 F1
York St, Twick. TW1 51 D1
York Way N1; N7 48 A3

LONDON CENTRAL pages 54 to 61

Abbey Orchard St
   SW1 59 N6
Abbey St SE1 61 N6
Abbots La SE1 61 N3
Abbots Manor Est
   SW1 59 H9
Abchurch La EC4 57 L10
Abchurch Yd EC4 57 K10
Aberdour St SE1 61 M8
Abingdon St SW1 59 P6
Achilles Way W1 58 G3
Acton St WC1 56 B3
Adam & Eve Ct W1 55 L8
Adams Ct EC2 57 L8
Adams Row W1 58 G1
Adam St WC2 60 A1
Addington St SE1 60 C5
Addle Hill EC4 56 G10
Addle St EC2 57 J7
Adelaide St WC2 59 P1
Adeline Pl WC1 55 N7
Adelphi Ter WC2 60 A1
Affleck St N1 56 C1
Agar St WC2 59 P1
Agdon St EC1 56 F4
Air St W1 59 L1
Alaska St SE1 60 D3
Albany W1 59 K1
Albany Ctyd W1 59 L1
Albemarle St W1 59 J1
Albemarle Way EC1 56 F5
Alberta Est SE17 60 G10
Alberta St SE17 60 F10
Albert Gate SW1 58 E4
Albion Cl W2 54 C10
Albion Ms W2 54 C9
Albion Pl EC1 56 F6

Albion St W2 54 C9
Albion Way EC1 57 H7
Aldbridge St SE17 61 N10
Aldburgh Ms W1 54 G8
Aldenham St NW1 55 L1
Aldermanbury EC2 57 J8
Aldermanbury Sq
   EC2 57 J7
Alderman's Wk EC2 57 M7
Alderney Ms SE1 61 K6
Alderney St SW1 59 J10
Aldersgate St EC1 57 H8
Aldford St W1 58 F2
Aldgate EC3 57 P9
Aldgate Av E1 57 P8
Aldgate High St EC3 57 P9
Aldwych WC2 56 B10
Alexander Pl SW7 58 B8
Alexander Sq SW3 58 B8
Alford Pl N1 57 J1
Alfred Ms W1 55 M6
Alfred Pl WC1 55 M6
Alice St SE1 61 M7
Allhallows La EC4 61 K1
Allington St SW1 59 K7
Allitsen Rd NW8 54 B1
Allsop Pl NW1 54 E5
All Souls Pl W1 55 J7
Alpha Cl NW1 54 C3
Alsace Rd SE17 61 M10
Alscot Way SE1 61 P8
Alvey Est SE17 61 M9
Alvey St SE17 61 M10
Ambassador's Ct
   SW1 59 L3
Ambergate St SE17 60 G10
Ambrosden Av SW1 59 L7

Amelia St SE17 60 G10
Amen Cor EC4 56 G9
Amen Ct EC4 56 G8
America Sq EC3 57 P10
America St SE1 61 H3
Ampthill Sq NW1 55 L1
Ampton Pl WC1 56 B3
Ampton St WC1 56 B3
Amwell St EC1 56 D2
Anchor Yd EC1 57 J4
Anderson St SW3 58 D10
Andrew Borde St
   WC2 55 N8
Andrewes Ho EC2 57 J7
Andrews Crosse WC2 56 D9
Angel Ct EC2 57 L8
Angel Ct SW1 59 L3
Angel Gate EC1 56 G2
Angel Ms N1 56 E1
Angel Pas EC4 57 K1
Angel Pl SE1 61 K4
Angel Sq EC1 56 E1
Angel St EC1 57 H8
Anning St EC2 57 N4
Ann's Cl SW1 58 E5
Ann's Pl E1 57 P7
Apothecary St EC4 56 F9
Apple Tree Yd SW1 59 L2
Appold St EC2 57 M6
Apsley Way W1 58 G4
Aquinas St SE1 60 E3
Arcade, The EC2 57 M7
Archer St W1 55 M10
Archery Cl W2 54 C9
Arches, The WC2 60 A2
Archibald Ms W1 58 G1
Archie St SE1 61 N5

Arch St SE1 61 H7
Arden Est N1 57 M1
Argyle Sq WC1 56 A2
Argyle St WC1 55 P2
Argyle Wk WC1 56 A3
Argyll St W1 55 K9
Arlington St SW1 59 K2
Arlington Way EC1 56 E2
Arne St WC2 56 A9
Arneway St SW1 59 N7
Arnold Circ E2 57 P3
Arthur St EC4 61 L1
Artillery La E1 57 N7
Artillery Pas E1 57 N7
Artillery Pl SW1 59 M7
Artillery Row SW1 59 M7
Artizan St E1 57 N8
Arundel Gt Ct WC2 56 C10
Arundel St WC2 56 C10
Ashbridge St NW8 54 B5
Ashby Ct EC1 56 G3
Ashby St EC1 56 F2
Ashentree Ct EC4 56 E9
Ashford St N1 57 M2
Ashland Pl W1 54 F6
Ashley Gdns SW1 59 L7
Ashley Pl SW1 59 K7
Ashmill St NW1 54 B6
Aske St N1 57 M2
Asolando Dr SE17 61 J9
Astell St SW3 58 C10
Atterbury St SW1 59 N9
Attneave St WC1 56 D3
Audley Sq W1 58 G2
Augustus St NW1 55 J1
Austin Friars EC2 57 L8
Austin Friars Pas EC2 57 L8
Austin Friars Sq EC2 57 L8

Austin St E2 57 P3
Austral St SE11 60 F8
Aveline St SE11 60 D10
Ave Maria La EC4 56 G9
Avery Fm Row SW1 58 G9
Avery Row W1 55 H10
Avonmouth St SE1 61 H6
Avon Pl SE1 61 J5
Aybrook St W1 54 F7
Aylesbury St EC1 56 F5
Aylesford St SW1 59 M10
Aylwyn Est SE1 61 P6
Ayres St SE1 61 J4
Babmaes St SW1 59 L1
Bacchus Wk N1 57 M1
Baches St N1 57 L3
Backhouse Pl SE17 61 N9
Bacon Gro SE1 61 P7
Baden Pl SE1 61 K4
Bainbridge St WC1 55 N8
Baird St EC1 57 J4
Bakers Hall Ct EC3 61 N1
Baker's Ms W1 54 F8
Baker's Rents E2 57 P3
Baker's Row EC1 56 D5
Baker St NW1 54 E6
Baker St W1 54 E6
Balcombe St NW1 54 D5
Balderton St W1 54 G9
Baldwin's Gdns EC1 56 D6
Baldwin St EC1 57 K3
Balfe St N1 56 A1
Balfour Ms W1 58 G2
Balfour Pl W1 58 G1
Balfour St SE17 61 K8
Balniel Gate SW1 59 N10

Baltic St E EC1 57 H5
Baltic St W EC1 57 H5
Banbury Ct WC2 55 P10
Bank End SE1 61 J2
Bankside SE1 61 H1
Banner St EC1 57 J5
Barbican EC2 57 H7
Barbon Cl WC1 56 B6
Barge Ho St SE1 60 E2
Barkham Ter SE1 60 E6
Barley Mow Pas EC1 56 G7
Barlow Pl W1 59 J1
Barlow St SE17 61 L9
Barnard's Inn EC1 56 E8
Barnby St NW1 55 L1
Barnham St SE1 61 N4
Barons Pl SE1 60 E5
Barrett St W1 54 G9
Barrow Hill Rd NW8 54 B1
Barter St WC1 56 A7
Bartholomew Cl EC1 57 H7
Bartholomew La EC2 57 L9
Bartholomew Pl EC1 57 H7
Bartholomew Sq EC1 57 J4
Bartholomew St SE1 61 K7
Bartlett Ct EC4 56 E8
Bartletts Pas EC4 56 E8
Barton St SW1 59 P6
Basil St SW3 58 D6
Basinghall Av EC2 57 K7
Basinghall St EC2 57 K8
Basing Ho Yd E2 57 N2
Basing Pl E2 57 N2
Bastwick St EC1 57 H4
Bateman's Bldgs W1 55 M9
Bateman's Row EC2 57 N4
Bateman St W1 55 M9
Bath Ct EC1 56 D5
Bath Pl EC2 57 M3
Bath St EC1 57 J3
Bath Ter SE1 61 H7
Battle Br La SE1 61 M3
Battle Br Rd NW1 55 P1
Bayley St WC1 55 M7
Baylis Rd SE1 60 D5
Bayswater Rd W2 54 A10
Beak St W1 55 L10
Bear All EC4 56 F8
Bear Gdns SE1 61 H2
Bear La SE1 60 G2
Bear St WC2 55 N10
Beauchamp Pl SW3 58 C6
Beauchamp St EC1 56 D7
Beaufort Gdns SW3 58 C6
Beaufoy Wk SE11 60 C9
Beaumont Ms W1 54 G6
Beaumont Pl W1 55 L4
Beaumont St W1 54 G6
Becket St SE1 61 K6
Beckway St SE17 61 L9
Bedale St SE1 61 K3
Bedford Av WC1 55 N7
Bedfordbury WC2 55 P10
Bedford Ct WC2 59 P1
Bedford Pl WC1 55 P6
Bedford Row WC1 56 C6
Bedford Sq WC1 55 N7
Bedford St WC2 55 P10
Bedford Way WC1 55 N5
Bedlam Ms SE11 60 C8
Beech St EC2 57 H6
Beehive Pas EC3 57 M9
Beeston Pl SW1 59 J7
Belgrave Ms N SW1 58 F5
Belgrave Ms S SW1 58 G6
Belgrave Ms W SW1 58 F6
Belgrave Pl SW1 58 G6
Belgrave Rd SW1 59 K9
Belgrave Sq SW1 58 F6
Belgrave Yd SW1 59 H7
Belgravia SW1 58 F7
Belgrove St WC1 55 P2
Bell Inn Yd EC3 57 L9
Bell La E1 57 P7
Bell St NW1 54 B6
Bell Wf La EC4 57 J10
Bell Yd WC2 56 D8
Belvedere Bldgs SE1 60 G5
Belvedere Pl SE1 60 G5
Belvedere Rd SE1 60 C4
Bendall Ms NW1 54 C6
Benjamin St EC1 56 F6
Bennet's Hill EC4 56 G10
Bennett St SW1 59 K2
Bennetts Yd SW1 59 N7
Bentinck Ms W1 54 G8
Bentinck St W1 54 G8
Berkeley Ms W1 54 E8
Berkeley Sq W1 59 J1
Berkeley St W1 59 J1
Bermondsey SE1 61 P7
Bermondsey Sq SE1 61 N6
Bermondsey St SE1 61 M3
Bernard St WC1 55 P5
Berners Ms W1 55 L7
Berners Pl W1 55 L8
Berners St W1 55 L7
Bernhardt Cres NW8 54 B4
Berryfield Rd SE17 60 G10
Berry Pl EC1 56 G3
Berry St EC1 56 G4
Berwick St W1 55 M9
Bessborough Gdns SW1 59 N10
Bessborough Pl SW1 59 M10
Bessborough St SW1 59 M10
Bethnal Grn Rd E1 57 P4
Bethnal Grn Rd E2 57 P4
Betterton St WC2 55 P9
Bevenden St N1 57 L2
Beverley Ho NW8 54 B3
Beverston Ms W1 54 D7
Bevin Way WC1 56 D2
Bevis Marks EC3 57 N8
Bickenhall St W1 54 E6
Bidborough St WC1 55 P3
Billiter Sq EC3 57 N10
Billiter St EC3 57 N9
Bingham Pl W1 54 F6
Binney St W1 54 G10
Birchin La EC3 57 L9
Birdcage Wk SW1 59 L5
Bird St W1 54 G9
Birkenhead St WC1 56 A2
Bishop's Ct EC4 56 F8
Bishop's Ct WC2 56 D8
Bishopsgate EC2 57 M9
Bishopsgate Arc EC2 57 N7
Bishopsgate Chyd EC2 57 M7
Bishops Ter SE11 60 E8
Bittern St SE1 61 H5
Blackall St EC2 57 M4
Blackburne's Ms W1 54 F10
Blackfriars Br EC4 56 F10
Blackfriars Br SE1 56 F10
Blackfriars Ct EC4 56 F10
Black Friars La EC4 56 F10
Blackfriars Pas EC4 56 F10
Blackfriars Rd SE1 60 F5
Black Horse Ct SE1 61 L6
Blacklands Ter SW3 58 D9
Black Prince Rd SE1 60 B9
Black Prince Rd SE11 60 C9
Black Swan Yd SE1 61 N4
Blackwood St SE17 61 K10
Blandford Sq NW1 54 C5
Blandford St W1 54 E8
Bleeding Heart Yd EC1 56 E7
Blenheim St W1 55 H9
Bletchley Ct N1 57 K1
Bletchley St N1 57 J1
Blomfield St EC2 57 L7
Bloomburg St SW1 59 L9
Bloomfield Pl W1 55 J10
Bloomfield Ter SW1 58 G10
Bloomsbury WC1 55 N7
Bloomsbury Ct WC1 56 A7
Bloomsbury Pl WC1 56 A6
Bloomsbury Sq WC1 56 A7
Bloomsbury St WC1 55 N7
Bloomsbury Way WC1 55 P8
Blore Ct W1 55 M9
Blossom St E1 57 N6
Blue Ball Yd SW1 59 K3
Bluelion Pl SE1 61 M6
Bolney Gate SW7 58 B5
Bolsover St W1 55 J5
Bolt Ct EC4 56 E9
Bolton St W1 59 J2
Bond Ct EC4 57 K9
Bonhill St EC2 57 L5
Book Ms WC2 55 N9
Booth's Pl W1 55 L7
Boot St N1 57 M3
Boreas Wk N1 56 G1
Borough, The SE1 61 H5
Borough High St SE1 61 H5
Borough Rd SE1 60 F6
Borough Sq SE1 61 H5
Boscobel Pl SW1 58 G8
Boscobel St NW8 54 A5
Boss Ho SE1 61 P4
Boss St SE1 61 P4
Boston Pl NW1 54 D5
Boswell Ct WC1 56 A6
Boswell St WC1 56 A6
Botolph All EC3 57 M10
Botolph La EC3 57 M10
Boundary Pas E2 57 P4
Boundary Row SE1 60 F4
Boundary St E2 57 P3
Bourchier St W1 55 M10
Bourdon Pl W1 55 J10
Bourdon St W1 55 J10
Bourlet Cl W1 55 K7
Bourne Est EC1 56 D6
Bourne St SW1 58 F9
Bouverie Pl W2 54 A8
Bouverie St EC4 56 E9
Bow Chyd EC4 57 J9
Bowland Yd SW1 58 E5
Bow La EC4 57 J9
Bowl Ct EC2 57 N5
Bowling Grn La EC1 56 E4
Bowling Grn Pl SE1 61 K4
Bowling Grn Wk N1 57 M2
Bow St WC2 56 A9
Boyce St SE1 60 C3
Boyfield St SE1 60 G5
Boyle St W1 55 K10
Brabant Ct EC3 57 M10
Brackley St EC1 57 H6
Brad St SE1 60 E3
Braganza St SE17 60 F10
Braidwood St SE1 61 M3
Brandon St SE17 61 H9
Bray Pl SW3 58 D9
Bread St EC4 57 J9
Bream's Bldgs EC4 56 D8
Brendon St W1 54 C8
Bressenden Pl SW1 59 J6
Brewer's Grn SW1 59 M6
Brewers Hall Gdns EC2 57 J7
Brewer St W1 55 L10
Brewery Sq EC1 56 G4
Brewhouse Yd EC1 56 G4
Brick Ct EC4 56 D9
Bricklayer's Arms Distribution Cen SE1 61 N9
Bricklayer's Arms Roundabout SE1 61 K8
Brick St W1 59 H3
Bride Ct EC4 56 F9
Bride La EC4 56 F9
Bridewain St SE1 61 P6
Bridewell Pl EC4 56 F9
Bridford Ms W1 55 J6
Bridgeman St NW8 54 B1
Bridge Pl SW1 59 J8
Bridge St SW1 59 P5
Bridgewater Sq EC2 57 H6
Bridgewater St EC2 57 H6
Bridgeway St NW1 55 M1
Bridge Yd SE1 61 L2
Bridle La W1 55 L10
Brill Pl NW1 55 N1
Brinton Wk SE1 60 F3
Briset St EC1 56 F6
Britannia St WC1 56 B2
Britannia Wk N1 57 K2
Britton St EC1 56 F5
Broadbent St W1 55 H10
Broad Ct WC2 56 A9
Broadgate EC2 57 L6
Broadgate Circle EC2 57 M6
Broad La EC2 57 M6
Broadley St NW8 54 A6
Broadley Ter NW1 54 C5
Broadmayne SE17 61 K10
Broad Sanctuary SW1 59 N5
Broadstone Pl W1 54 F7
Broad St Av EC2 57 M7
Broad St Pl EC2 57 L7
Broad Wk NW1 55 H3
Broad Wk W1 58 F2
Broadwall SE1 60 E2
Broadway SW1 59 M6
Broadwick St W1 55 L10
Broad Yd EC1 56 F5
Brockham St SE1 61 J6
Broken Wf EC4 57 H10
Bromley Pl W1 55 K6
Brompton SW3 58 B7
Brompton Arc SW3 58 D5
Brompton Pl SW3 58 C6
Brompton Rd SW1 58 C6
Brompton Rd SW3 58 B8
Brompton Rd SW7 58 C6
Brompton Sq SW3 58 B6
Brook Dr SE11 60 E7
Brooke's Ct EC1 56 D6
Brookes Mkt EC1 56 E6
Brooke St EC1 56 D7
Brook Gate W1 58 E1
Brook's Ms W1 55 H10
Brook St W1 54 G10
Brook St W2 54 A10
Brown Hart Gdns W1 54 G10
Browning Ms W1 55 H7
Browning St SE17 61 J10
Brownlow Ms WC1 56 C5
Brownlow St WC1 56 C7
Brown's Bldgs EC3 57 N9
Brown St W1 54 D8
Brune St E1 57 P7
Brunswick Ct SE1 61 N5
Brunswick Ms W1 54 E8
Brunswick Pl N1 57 L3
Brunswick Pl NW1 54 G4
Brunswick Shop Cen WC1 55 P4
Brunswick Sq WC1 56 A5
Brushfield St E1 57 N7
Bruton La W1 59 J1
Bruton Pl W1 59 J1
Bruton St W1 59 J1
Bryanston Ms E W1 54 D7
Bryanston Ms W W1 54 D7
Bryanston Pl W1 54 D7
Bryanston Sq W1 54 D7
Bryanston St W1 54 D9
Brydges Pl WC2 59 P1
Buck Hill Wk W2 58 A1
Buckingham Arc WC2 60 A1
Buckingham Gate SW1 59 K5
Buckingham Ms SW1 59 K6
Buckingham Palace Rd SW1 59 H9
Buckingham Pl SW1 59 K6
Buckingham St WC2 60 A1
Buckland St N1 57 L1
Bucklersbury EC4 57 K9
Bucklersbury Pas EC4 57 K9
Bucknall St WC2 55 N8
Budge Row EC4 57 K10
Bulinga St SW1 59 N9
Bullied Way SW1 59 J9
Bull Inn Ct WC2 60 A1
Bulls Gdns SW3 58 C8
Bull's Head Pas EC3 57 M9
Bulstrode Pl W1 54 G7
Bulstrode St W1 54 G8
Bunhill Row EC1 57 K4
Bunhouse Pl SW1 58 F10
Buonaparte Ms SW1 59 M10
Burbage Cl SE1 61 K7
Burdett St SE1 60 D6
Burge St SE1 61 L7
Burgon St EC4 56 G9
Burleigh St WC2 56 B10
Burlington Arc W1 59 K1
Burlington Gdns W1 59 K1
Burne St NW1 54 B6
Burnsall St SW3 58 C10
Burrell St SE1 60 F2
Burrows Ms SE1 60 F4
Burton Ms SW1 58 G9
Burton Pl WC1 55 N3
Burton St WC1 55 N3
Burwash Ho SE1 61 L5
Burwood Pl W2 54 C8
Bury Ct EC3 57 N8
Bury Pl WC1 55 P7
Bury St EC3 57 N9
Bury St SW1 59 K2
Bury Wk SW3 58 B9
Bushbaby Cl SE1 61 M7
Bush La EC4 57 K10
Butler Pl SW1 59 M6
Buttermere Cl SE1 61 P8
Buttesland St N1 57 L2
Buxton Ct N1 57 J2
Byng Pl WC1 55 M5
Byward St EC3 61 N1
Bywater St SW3 58 D10
Bywell Pl W1 55 K7
Cabbell St NW1 54 B7
Cadogan Gdns SW3 58 E8
Cadogan Gate SW1 58 E8
Cadogan La SW1 58 F7
Cadogan Pl SW1 58 E6
Cadogan Sq SW1 58 E7
Cadogan St SW3 58 D9
Cahill St EC1 57 J5
Caleb St SE1 61 H4
Caledonian Rd N1 56 A1
Caledonia St N1 56 A1
Cale St SW3 58 B10
Calthorpe St WC1 56 C4
Calvert Av E2 57 N3
Calvert's Bldgs SE1 61 K3
Calvin St E1 57 P5
Cambridge Circ WC2 55 N9
Cambridge Gate NW1 55 J3
Cambridge Gate Ms NW1 55 J3
Cambridge Sq W2 54 B8
Cambridge St SW1 59 J9
Cambridge Ter NW1 55 J3
Cambridge Ter Ms NW1 55 J3
Camlet St E2 57 P4
Camomile St EC3 57 M8
Canal Way NW1 54 C2
Canal Way NW8 54 B3
Candover St W1 55 K7
Cannon St EC4 57 H9
Canon Row SW1 59 P5
Canterbury Pl SE17 60 G9
Canvey St SE1 60 G2
Capel Ct EC2 57 L9
Capener's Cl SW1 58 F5
Capland St NW8 54 A4
Capper St WC1 55 L5
Carburton St W1 55 J6
Cardigan St SE11 60 D10
Cardinal Bourne St SE1 61 L7
Cardington St NW1 55 K2
Carey La EC2 57 H8
Carey Pl SW1 59 M9
Carey St WC2 56 C9
Carlisle Av EC3 57 N9
Carlisle La SE1 60 C7
Carlisle Ms NW8 54 A6
Carlisle Pl SW1 59 K7
Carlisle St W1 55 M9
Carlos Pl W1 58 G1
Carlton Gdns SW1 59 M3
Carlton Ho Ter SW1 59 M3
Carlton St SW1 59 M1
Carlton Twr Pl SW1 58 E6
Carmelite St EC4 56 E10
Carnaby St W1 55 K9
Caroline Ter SW1 58 F9
Carpenter St W1 59 H1
Carrington St W1 59 H3
Carteret St SW1 59 M5
Carter La EC4 56 G9
Carthusian St EC1 57 H6
Carting La WC2 60 A1
Carton St W1 54 E8
Cartwright Gdns WC1 55 P3
Casey Cl NW8 54 B3
Castle Baynard St EC4 56 G10
Castlebrook Cl SE11 60 F8
Castle Ct EC3 57 L9
Castle La SW1 59 L6
Castlereagh St W1 54 D8
Castle Yd SE1 60 G2
Catesby St SE17 61 L9
Cathedral Piazza SW1 59 K7
Cathedral St SE1 61 K2
Catherine Griffiths Ct EC1 56 E4
Catherine Pl SW1 59 K6
Catherine St WC2 56 B10
Catherine Wheel All E1 57 N7
Catherine Wheel Yd SW1 59 K3
Cato St W1 54 C7
Catton St WC1 56 B7
Causton St SW1 59 N9
Cavendish Av NW8 54 A1
Cavendish Cl NW8 54 A2
Cavendish Ct EC3 57 N8
Cavendish Ms N W1 55 J6
Cavendish Ms S W1 55 J7
Cavendish Pl W1 55 J8
Cavendish Sq W1 55 J8
Cavendish St N1 57 K1
Caxton St SW1 59 L6
Cayton Pl EC1 57 K3
Cayton St EC1 57 K3
Cecil Ct WC2 59 N1
Centaur St SE1 60 C6
Central St EC1 57 H3
Centre at the Circ W1 59 L1
Centrepoint WC1 55 N8
Chadwell St EC1 56 E2
Chadwick St SW1 59 N7
Chagford St NW1 54 D5
Chaloner Ct SE1 61 K4
Chalton St NW1 55 N2
Chancel St SE1 60 F2
Chancery La WC2 56 D8
Chance St E1 57 P4
Chance St E2 57 P4
Chandos Pl WC2 59 P1
Chandos St W1 55 J7
Change All EC3 57 L9
Chapel Ct SE1 61 K4
Chapel Pl EC2 57 M3
Chapel Pl W1 55 H9
Chapel St NW1 54 B7
Chapel St SW1 58 G6
Chaplin Cl SE1 60 E4
Chapone Pl W1 55 M9
Chapter Ho Ct EC4 57 H9
Chapter St SW1 59 M9
Charing Cross SW1 59 P2
Charing Cross Rd WC2 55 N8
Charles La NW8 54 A1
Charles Pl NW1 55 L3
Charles II St SW1 59 M2
Charles Sq N1 57 L3
Charles St W1 59 H2
Charleston St SE17 61 J9
Charles Townsend Ho EC1 56 E3
Charlotte Ms W1 55 L6
Charlotte Pl SW1 59 K9
Charlotte Pl W1 55 L7
Charlotte Rd EC2 57 M4
Charlotte St W1 55 L6
Charlwood Pl SW1 59 L9
Charlwood St SW1 59 L9
Charterhouse Bldgs EC1 56 G5
Charterhouse Ms EC1 56 G6
Charterhouse Sq EC1 56 G6
Charterhouse St EC1 56 E7
Chart St N1 57 L2
Chatham St SE17 61 K8
Cheapside EC2 57 J9
Chelsea Br Rd SW1 58 F10

Name	Page	Grid
Chelsea Sq SW3	58	A10
Cheltenham Ter SW3	58	E10
Chenies Ms WC1	55	M5
Chenies St WC1	55	M6
Chequer St EC1	57	J5
Cherbury Ct N1	57	L1
Cherbury St N1	57	L1
Cherry Tree Wk EC1	57	J5
Chesham Cl SW1	58	F7
Chesham Ms SW1	58	F6
Chesham Pl SW1	58	F7
Chesham St SW1	58	F7
Cheshire Ct EC4	56	E9
Chester Cl SW1	58	G5
Chester Cl N NW1	55	J2
Chester Cl S NW1	55	J3
Chester Cotts SW1	58	F9
Chester Ct NW1	55	J2
Chesterfield Gdns W1	59	H2
Chesterfield Hill W1	59	H1
Chesterfield St W1	59	H2
Chester Gate NW1	55	H3
Chester Ms SW1	59	H6
Chester Pl NW1	55	H2
Chester Rd NW1	54	G3
Chester Row SW1	58	F9
Chester Sq SW1	59	H8
Chester Sq Ms SW1	59	H7
Chester St SW1	58	G6
Chester Ter NW1	55	H2
Chester Way SE11	60	E9
Chettle Cl SE1	61	K6
Cheval Pl SW7	58	C6
Chicheley St SE1	60	C4
Chichester Rents WC2	56	D8
Chiltern St W1	54	F6
Ching Ct WC2	55	P9
Chiswell St EC1	57	J6
Chitty St W1	55	L6
Christ Ch Pas EC1	56	G8
Christina St EC2	57	M4
Christopher Pl NW1	55	N3
Christopher St EC2	57	L5
Church Entry EC4	56	G9
Church Pl SW1	59	L1
Church St NW8	54	A6
Church St W2	54	A6
Church St Est NW8	54	A5
Churchway NW1	55	N2
Churchyard Row SE11	60	G8
Churton Pl SW1	59	L9
Churton St SW1	59	L9
Circle, The SE1	61	P4
Circus Ms W1	54	D6
Circus Pl EC2	57	L7
Citadel Pl SE11	60	B10
City Forum EC1	57	H2
City Gdn Row N1	56	G1
City Pt EC2	57	K6
City Rd EC1	56	F1
Clabon Ms SW1	58	D7
Clare Mkt WC2	56	B9
Claremont Cl N1	56	E1
Claremont Sq N1	56	D1
Clarence Gdns NW1	55	J3
Clarence Ter NW1	54	E4
Clarendon Cl W2	54	B10
Clarendon Gro NW1	55	M2
Clarendon Ms W2	54	B9
Clarendon Pl W2	54	B10
Clarges Ms W1	59	H2
Clarges St W1	59	J2
Clarke's Ms W1	54	G6
Clarkson Row NW1	55	K1
Clarks Pl EC2	57	M8
Clay St W1	54	E7
Cleaver Sq SE11	60	E10
Cleaver St SE11	60	E10
Clement's Inn WC2	56	C9
Clement's Inn Pas WC2	56	C9
Clements La EC4	57	L10
Clennam St SE1	61	J4
Clenston Ms W1	54	D8
Clere St EC2	57	L4
Clerkenwell EC1	56	F5
Clerkenwell Cl EC1	56	E4
Clerkenwell Grn EC1	56	E5
Clerkenwell Rd EC1	56	D5
Cleveland Ms W1	55	K6
Cleveland Pl SW1	59	L2
Cleveland Row SW1	59	K3
Cleveland St W1	55	K5
Clifford's Inn Pas EC4	56	D9
Clifford St W1	59	K1
Clifton Pl W2	54	A10
Clifton St EC2	57	M6
Clink St SE1	61	J2
Clipstone Ms W1	55	K5
Clipstone St W1	55	J6
Cliveden Pl SW1	58	F8
Cloak La EC4	57	J10
Cloth Ct EC1	56	G7
Cloth Fair EC1	56	G7
Clothier St E1	57	N8
Cloth St EC1	57	H6
Club Row E1	57	P4
Club Row E2	57	P4
Clunbury St N1	57	L1
Cluny Est SE1	61	M6
Cluny Pl SE1	61	M6
Coach & Horses Yd W1	55	J10
Coach Ho Ms SE1	61	M6
Cobb St E1	57	P7
Cobourg St NW1	55	L3
Coburg Cl SW1	59	L8
Cochrane Ms NW8	54	A1
Cochrane St NW8	54	A1
Cock Hill E1	57	N7
Cock La EC1	56	F7
Cockpit Steps SW1	59	N5
Cockpit Yd WC1	56	C6
Cockspur Ct SW1	59	N2
Cockspur St SW1	59	N2
Coin St SE1	60	D2
Coldbath Sq EC1	56	D4
Cole St SE1	61	J5
Coley St WC1	56	C5
College Hill EC4	57	J10
College Ms SW1	59	P6
College St EC4	57	J10
Collier St N1	56	B1
Collinson St SE1	61	H5
Collinson Wk SE1	61	H5
Colnbrook St SE1	60	F7
Colombo St SE1	60	F3
Colonnade WC1	55	P5
Colonnade Wk SW1	59	H9
Columbia Rd E2	57	P2
Colville Pl W1	55	L7
Colworth Gro SE17	61	J9
Commercial St E1	57	P5
Compton Cl NW1	55	J3
Compton Pas EC1	56	G4
Compton Pl WC1	55	P4
Compton St EC1	56	F4
Comus Pl SE17	61	M9
Concert Hall App SE1	60	C3
Conduit Ct WC2	55	P10
Conduit St W1	55	J10
Congreve St SE17	61	M8
Connaught Cl W2	54	B9
Connaught Pl W2	54	D10
Connaught Sq W2	54	D9
Connaught St W2	54	B9
Cons St SE1	60	E4
Constitution Hill SW1	59	H4
Content St SE17	61	J9
Conway Ms W1	55	K5
Conway St W1	55	K5
Coombs St N1	56	G1
Cooper Cl SE1	60	E5
Cooper's Row EC3	57	P10
Copperfield St SE1	60	G4
Copper Row SE1	61	P3
Copthall Av EC2	57	L8
Copthall Bldgs EC2	57	K8
Copthall Cl EC2	57	K8
Coptic St WC1	55	P7
Coral St SE1	60	E5
Coram St WC1	55	P5
Corbet Ct EC3	57	L9
Corbet Pl E1	57	P6
Cork St W1	59	K1
Cork St Ms W1	59	K1
Corlett St NW1	54	B6
Corner Ho St WC2	59	P2
Cornhill EC3	57	L9
Cornwall Rd SE1	60	D2
Cornwall Sq SE11	60	F10
Cornwall Ter NW1	54	E5
Cornwall Ter Ms NW1	54	E5
Coronet St N1	57	M3
Corporation Row EC1	56	E4
Corsham St N1	57	L3
Cosmo Pl WC1	56	A6
Cosser St SE1	60	D6
Cosway St NW1	54	C6
Cotham St SE17	61	J9
Cotswold Ct EC1	57	H4
Cottage Pl SW3	58	B6
Cottesloe Ms SE1	60	E6
Cottington St SE11	60	E10
Cottons Gdns E2	57	N2
Cottons La SE1	61	L2
Coulson St SW3	58	D10
Counter St SE1	61	M3
County St SE1	61	J7
Courtenay St SE11	60	D10
Cousin La EC4	61	K1
Coventry St W1	59	M1
Cowcross St EC1	56	F6
Cowley St SW1	59	P6
Cowper St EC2	57	L4
Coxson Way SE1	61	P5
Crabtree Cl E2	57	P1
Craig's Ct SW1	59	P2
Crail Row SE17	61	L9
Cramer St W1	54	G7
Crampton St SE17	61	H9
Cranbourn All WC2	55	N10
Cranbourn St WC2	55	N10
Crane Ct EC4	56	E9
Cranfield Row SE1	60	E6
Cranleigh St NW1	55	L1
Cranmer Ct SW3	58	C9
Cranston Est N1	57	L1
Cranwood St EC1	57	K3
Craven Pas WC2	59	P2
Craven St WC2	59	P2
Crawford Ms W1	54	D7
Crawford Pas EC1	56	D5
Crawford Pl W1	54	C8
Crawford St W1	54	D7
Creasy Est SE1	61	M7
Creechurch La EC3	57	N9
Creechurch Pl EC3	57	N9
Creed La EC4	56	G9
Cremer St E2	57	P1
Crescent EC3	57	P10
Crescent Pl SW3	58	B8
Crescent Row EC1	57	H5
Crestfield St WC1	56	A2
Cricketers Ct SE11	60	F9
Crimscott St SE1	61	N7
Cripplegate St EC2	57	H6
Crispin St E1	57	P7
Cromer St WC1	56	A3
Cromwell Gdns SW7	58	A7
Cromwell Ms SW7	58	A8
Cromwell Pl SW7	58	A8
Cromwell Twr EC2	57	J6
Crondall Ct N1	57	M1
Crondall St N1	57	L1
Crosby Ct SE1	61	K4
Crosby Row SE1	61	K5
Crosby Sq EC3	57	M9
Cross Keys Cl W1	54	G7
Cross Keys Sq EC1	57	H7
Cross La EC3	61	M1
Crosslet St SE17	61	L8
Crosswall EC3	57	P10
Crown Ct EC2	57	J9
Crown Ct WC2	56	A9
Crown Office Row EC4	56	D10
Crown Pas SW1	59	L3
Crown Pl EC2	57	M6
Crucifix La SE1	61	M4
Cruikshank St WC1	56	D2
Crutched Friars EC3	57	N10
Cubitt St WC1	56	B3
Cubitts Yd WC2	56	A10
Cuff Pt E2	57	P2
Culford Gdns SW3	58	E9
Cullum St EC3	57	M10
Culross St W1	58	F1
Culworth St NW8	54	B1
Cumberland Gdns WC1	56	C2
Cumberland Gate W1	54	D10
Cumberland Mkt NW1	55	J2
Cumberland Mkt Est NW1	55	J2
Cumberland Pl NW1	55	H2
Cumberland St SW1	59	J10
Cumberland Ter NW1	55	H1
Cumberland Ter Ms NW1	55	H1
Cumming St N1	56	B1
Cunard Pl EC3	57	N9
Cundy St SW1	58	G9
Cundy St Est SW1	58	G9
Cureton St SW1	59	N9
Curlew St SE1	61	P4
Cursitor St EC4	56	D8
Curtain Rd EC2	57	M5
Curtis St SE1	61	P8
Curtis Way SE1	61	P8
Curzon Gate W1	58	G3
Curzon Sq W1	58	G3
Curzon St W1	58	G3
Custom Ho Wk EC3	61	M1
Cut, The SE1	60	E4
Cutlers Gdns E1	57	N8
Cutler St E1	57	N8
Cynthia St N1	56	C1
Cypress Pl W1	55	L5
Cyrus St EC1	56	G4
Dacre St SW1	59	M6
Dalehead NW1	55	K1
Dallington St EC1	56	G4
Dane St WC1	56	B7
Dansey Pl W1	55	M10
Dante Pl SE11	60	G8
Dante Rd SE11	60	F8
Danube St SW3	58	C10
D'Arblay St W1	55	L9
Dartmouth St SW1	59	M5
Darwin St SE17	61	L8
Daventry St NW1	54	B6
Davidge St SE1	60	F5
David Ms W1	54	E6
Davies Ms W1	55	H10
Davies St W1	55	H10
Dawes Ho SE17	61	L9
Dawes St SE17	61	L10
Deacon Way SE17	61	H8
Dean Bradley St SW1	59	P7
Deanery Ms W1	58	G2
Deanery St W1	58	G2
Dean Farrar St SW1	59	M6
Dean Ryle St SW1	59	P8
Deans Bldgs SE17	61	K9
Deans Ct EC4	56	G9
Deans Ms W1	55	J8
Dean Stanley St SW1	59	P7
Dean St W1	55	M8
Dean's Yd SW1	59	N6
Dean Trench St SW1	59	P7
Decima St SE1	61	M6
Defoe Ho EC2	57	J6
Dell's Ms SW1	59	L9
Denbigh Ms SW1	59	K9
Denbigh Pl SW1	59	K10
Denbigh St SW1	59	K9
Denman St W1	59	M1
Denmark Pl WC2	55	N8
Denmark St WC2	55	N9
Denny Cres SE11	60	E9
Denny St SE11	60	E10
Denyer St SW3	58	C9
Derby Gate SW1	59	P4
Derby St W1	58	G3
Dereham Pl EC2	57	N3
Dering St W1	55	H9
Deverell St SE1	61	K7
Devereux Ct WC2	56	D9
Devonshire Cl W1	55	H6
Devonshire Ms N W1	55	H6
Devonshire Ms S W1	55	H6
Devonshire Ms W W1	55	H5
Devonshire Pl W1	54	G5
Devonshire Pl Ms W1	54	G5
Devonshire Row EC2	57	N7
Devonshire Row Ms W1	55	J5
Devonshire Sq EC2	57	N8
Devonshire St W1	54	G6
De Walden St W1	54	G7
Diadem Ct W1	55	M9
Dickens Sq SE1	61	J6
Dingley Pl EC1	57	J3
Dingley Rd EC1	57	H3
Disney Pl SE1	61	J4
Disney St SE1	61	J4
Diss St E2	57	P2
Distaff La EC4	57	H10
Distin St SE11	60	D9
Doby Ct EC4	57	P9
Dodson St SE1	60	E5
Dolben St SE1	60	F3
Dombey St WC1	56	B6
Dominion St EC2	57	L6
Donegal St N1	56	C1
Donne Pl SW3	58	C8
Doon St SE1	60	D3
Doric Way NW1	55	M2
Dorrington St EC1	56	D6
Dorrit St SE1	61	J4
Dorset Bldgs EC4	56	F9
Dorset Cl NW1	54	D6
Dorset Ms SW1	59	H6
Dorset Ri EC4	56	F9
Dorset Sq NW1	54	D5
Dorset St W1	54	E7
Doughty Ms WC1	56	B5
Doughty St WC1	56	B4
Douglas St SW1	59	M9
Dove Ct EC2	57	K9
Dovehouse St SW3	58	B10
Dover St W1	59	J1
Dover Yd W1	59	K2
Dove Wk SW1	58	F10
Dowgate Hill EC4	57	K10
Downing St SW1	59	P4
Down St W1	59	H3
Down St Ms W1	59	H3
Doyce St SE1	61	H4
D'Oyley St SW1	58	F8
Drake St WC1	56	B7
Draycott Av SW3	58	C8
Draycott Pl SW3	58	D9
Draycott Ter SW3	58	E8
Druid St SE1	61	N4
Drummond Cres NW1	55	M2
Drummond Gate SW1	59	N10
Drummond St NW1	55	K4
Drury La WC2	56	A9
Dryden Ct SE11	60	E9
Dryden St WC2	56	A9
Drysdale Pl N1	57	N2
Drysdale St N1	57	N3
Duchess Ms W1	55	J7
Duchess St W1	55	J7
Duchy St SE1	60	E2
Duck La W1	55	M9
Dudmaston Ms SW3	58	A10
Dufferin Av EC1	57	K5
Dufferin St EC1	57	J5
Dufour's Pl W1	55	L9
Dugard Way SE11	60	F8
Duke of Wellington Pl SW1	58	G4
Duke of York Sq SW3	58	E9
Duke of York St SW1	59	L2
Duke's Ms W1	54	G8
Dukes Pl EC3	57	N9
Duke's Rd WC1	55	N3
Duke St SW1	59	L2
Duke St W1	54	G8
Duke St Hill SE1	61	L2
Duke's Yd W1	54	G10
Duncannon St WC2	59	P1
Duncan Ter N1	56	F1
Dunloe St E2	57	P1
Dunmore Pt E2	57	P3
Dunns Pas WC1	56	A8
Dunraven St W1	54	E10
Dunstable Ms W1	54	G6
Dunster Ct EC3	57	M10
Dunsterville Way SE1	61	L5
Dunton Rd SE1	61	P10
Duplex Ride SW1	58	E5
Durham Ho St WC2	60	A1
Durweston Ms W1	54	E6
Durweston St W1	54	E6
Dyer's Bldgs EC1	56	D7
Dyott St WC1	55	P8
Dysart St EC2	57	M5
Eagle Ct EC1	56	F6
Eagle Pl SW1	59	L1
Eagle St WC1	56	B7
Earlham St WC2	55	N9
Earlstoke St EC1	56	F2
Earl St EC2	57	M6
Earnshaw St WC2	55	N8
Easley's Ms W1	54	G8
Eastcastle St W1	55	K8
Eastcheap EC3	57	L10
East Harding St EC4	56	E8
Easton St WC1	56	D3
East Pas EC1	56	G6
East Poultry Av EC1	56	F7
East Rd N1	57	K3
East St SE17	61	J10
Eaton Cl SW1	58	F9
Eaton Gate SW1	58	F8
Eaton La SW1	59	J7
Eaton Ms N SW1	58	F8
Eaton Ms S SW1	58	G8
Eaton Ms W SW1	58	G8
Eaton Pl SW1	58	F7
Eaton Row SW1	59	H7
Eaton Sq SW1	59	H6
Eaton Ter SW1	58	F8
Eaton Ter Ms SW1	58	F8
Ebenezer Ho SE11	60	E9
Ebenezer St N1	57	K2
Ebor St E1	57	P4
Ebury Br SW1	59	H10
Ebury Br Est SW1	59	H10
Ebury Ms SW1	58	G8
Ebury Ms E SW1	59	H8
Ebury Sq SW1	58	G9
Ebury St SW1	59	H8
Eccleston Br SW1	59	J8
Eccleston Ms SW1	58	G7
Eccleston Pl SW1	59	H8
Eccleston Sq SW1	59	J9
Eccleston Sq Ms SW1	59	K9
Eccleston St SW1	59	H7
Edgware Rd W2	54	C8
Edinburgh Gate SW1	58	D4
Edward Ms NW1	55	J1
Edwards Ms W1	54	F9
Egerton Cres SW3	58	C8
Egerton Gdns SW3	58	B7
Egerton Gdns Ms SW3	58	C7
Egerton Pl SW3	58	C7
Egerton Ter SW3	58	C7
Elba Pl SE17	61	J8
Elder St E1	57	P6
Eldon Ct EC2	57	L7
Elephant & Castle SE1	60	G7
Elephant Rd SE17	61	H8
Elia Ms N1	56	F1
Elia St N1	56	F1
Elim Est SE1	61	M6
Elizabeth Br SW1	59	H9
Elizabeth Ct SW1	59	N7
Elizabeth St SW1	58	G8
Elliotts Row SE11	60	F8
Ellis St SW1	58	E8
Elm Ct EC4	56	D10
Elm St WC1	56	C5
Elsted St SE17	61	L9
Elverton St SW1	59	M8
Ely Ct EC1	56	E7
Ely Pl EC1	56	E7
Elystan Pl SW3	58	C10
Elystan St SW3	58	B9
Embankment Pl WC2	60	A2
Emerald St WC1	56	B6
Emerson St SE1	61	H2
Emery Hill St SW1	59	L7
Emery St SE1	60	E6
Endell St WC2	55	P8
Endsleigh Gdns WC1	55	M4
Endsleigh Pl WC1	55	N4

Name	Page	Grid
Endsleigh St WC1	55	M4
Enford St W1	54	D6
English Grds SE1	61	M3
Ennismore Gdns SW7	58	B5
Ennismore Gdns Ms SW7	58	B6
Ennismore Ms SW7	58	B6
Ennismore St SW7	58	B6
Epworth St EC2	57	L5
Erasmus St SW1	59	N9
Errol St EC1	57	J5
Essex Ct EC4	56	D9
Essex St WC2	56	D10
Esterbrooke St SW1	59	M9
Ethel St SE17	61	H9
Europa Pl EC1	57	H3
Euston Gro NW1	55	M3
Euston Rd N1	55	P2
Euston Rd NW1	55	J5
Euston Sq NW1	55	M3
Euston Sta Colonnade NW1	55	M3
Euston St NW1	55	L4
Euston Twr NW1	55	K4
Evelyn Ct N1	57	K1
Evelyn Wk N1	57	K1
Evelyn Yd W1	55	M8
Everton Bldgs NW1	55	K3
Ewer St SE1	61	H3
Excel Ct WC2	59	N1
Exchange Arc EC2	57	N6
Exchange Ct WC2	60	A1
Exchange Pl EC2	57	M6
Exchange Sq EC2	57	M6
Exeter St WC2	56	A10
Exhibition Rd SW7	58	A5
Exmouth Mkt EC1	56	D4
Exmouth Ms NW1	55	L3
Exon St SE17	61	M10
Exton St SE1	60	D3
Eyre St Hill EC1	56	D5
Fairchild Pl EC2	57	N5
Fairchild St EC2	57	N5
Fairford Ho SE11	60	E9
Fairholt St SW7	58	C6
Fair St SE1	61	N4
Falconberg Ct W1	55	N8
Falconberg Ms W1	55	M8
Falcon Cl SE1	60	G2
Falcon Ct EC4	56	D9
Falkirk St N1	57	N1
Falmouth Rd SE1	61	J6
Fann St EC1	57	H5
Fann St EC2	57	H5
Fanshaw St N1	57	M2
Fareham St W1	55	M8
Farm St W1	59	H1
Farnham Pl SE1	60	G3
Farringdon La EC1	56	E5
Farringdon Rd EC1	56	D4
Farringdon St EC4	56	F8
Fashion St E1	57	P7
Faulkner's All EC1	56	F6
Featherstone St EC1	57	K4
Fellmongers Path SE1	61	N5
Fellows Ct E2	57	P1
Fenchurch Av EC3	57	M9
Fenchurch Bldgs EC3	57	N9
Fenchurch Pl EC3	57	N10
Fenchurch St EC3	57	M10
Fen Ct EC3	57	M10
Fendall St SE1	61	N7
Fenning St SE1	61	M4
Fernsbury St WC1	56	D3
Fetter La EC4	56	E9
Field Ct WC1	56	C7
Field St WC1	56	B2
Finch La EC3	57	L9
Finsbury Cir EC2	57	L6
Finsbury Av EC2	57	L7
Finsbury Av Sq EC2	57	L7
Finsbury Circ EC2	57	L7
Finsbury Est EC1	56	F3
Finsbury Mkt EC2	57	M5
Finsbury Pavement EC2	57	L6
Finsbury Sq EC2	57	L6
Finsbury St EC2	57	K6
Finsbury Twr EC1	57	K5
First St SW3	58	C8
Fisher St WC1	56	A7
Fish St Hill EC3	57	L10
Fitzalan St SE11	60	D8
Fitzhardinge St W1	54	F8
Fitzmaurice Pl W1	59	J2
Fitzroy Ct W1	55	L5
Fitzroy Ms W1	55	K5
Fitzroy Sq W1	55	K5
Fitzroy St W1	55	K5
Fives Ct SE11	60	E7
Flaxman Ct W1	55	M9
Flaxman Ter WC1	55	N3
Fleet Sq WC1	56	B3
Fleet St EC4	56	D9
Fleur de Lis St E1	57	N5
Flinton St SE17	61	N10
Flint St SE17	61	L9
Flitcroft St WC2	55	N8
Floral St WC2	55	P10
Foley St W1	55	K7
Folgate St E1	57	N6
Fore St EC2	57	J7
Fore St Av EC2	57	K7
Forset St W1	54	C8
Fort St E1	57	N7
Fortune St EC1	57	J5
Forum Magnum Sq SE1	60	B4
Foster La EC2	57	H8
Foubert's Pl W1	55	K9
Foulis Ter SW7	58	A10
Founders Ct EC2	57	K8
Foundry Ms NW1	55	L4
Fountain Ct EC4	56	D10
Fountain Sq SW1	59	H8
Fournier St E1	57	P6
Fox & Knot St EC1	56	G6
Francis St SW1	59	K8
Franklin's Row SW3	58	E10
Frazier St SE1	60	D5
Frederick Cl W2	54	D10
Frederick's Pl EC2	57	K9
Frederick's Row EC1	56	F2
Frederick St WC1	56	B3
Frederic Ms SW1	58	E5
Freemantle St SE17	61	M10
French Pl E1	57	N4
French Ordinary Ct EC3	57	N10
Friars Cl SE1	60	G3
Friar St EC4	56	G9
Friary Ct SW1	59	L3
Friday St EC4	57	H9
Friend St EC1	56	F2
Frith St W1	55	M9
Frying Pan All E1	57	P7
Fullwoods Ms N1	57	L2
Fulwood Pl WC1	56	C7
Furnival St EC4	56	D8
Fynes St SW1	59	M8
Gabriel's Wf SE1	60	D2
Gage St WC1	56	A6
Gainsford St SE1	61	P4
Galen Pl WC1	56	A7
Galway St EC1	57	J3
Gambia St SE1	60	G3
Garbutt Pl W1	54	G6
Garden Ct EC4	56	D10
Garden Row SE1	60	F7
Garden Ter SW1	59	M10
Garden Wk EC2	57	M3
Gard St EC1	56	G2
Garlick Hill EC4	57	J10
Garnault Ms EC1	56	E3
Garnault Pl EC1	56	E3
Garrett St EC1	57	J4
Garrick St WC2	55	P10
Gascoigne Pl E2	57	P3
Gateforth St NW8	54	B5
Gatesborough St EC2	57	M4
Gate St WC2	56	B8
Gateways, The SW3	58	C9
Gaunt St SE1	60	G6
Gavel St SE17	61	L8
Gayfere St SW1	59	P7
Gaywood Est SE1	60	G7
Gaywood St SE1	60	G7
Gees Ct W1	54	G9
Gee St EC1	57	H4
Geffrye Ct N1	57	N1
George Ct WC2	60	A1
George Inn Yd SE1	61	K3
George Mathers Rd SE11	60	F8
George Ms NW1	55	K3
George St W1	54	E8
George Yd EC3	57	L9
George Yd W1	54	G10
Geraldine St SE11	60	F7
Gerald Ms SW1	58	G8
Gerald Rd SW1	58	G8
Gerrard Pl W1	55	N10
Gerrard St W1	55	M10
Gerridge St SE1	60	E5
Gibson Rd SE11	60	C9
Gilbert Pl WC1	55	P7
Gilbert Rd SE11	60	E9
Gilbert St W1	54	G9
Gildea St W1	55	J7
Gillfoot NW1	55	K1
Gillingham Ms SW1	59	K8
Gillingham Row SW1	59	K8
Gillingham St SW1	59	J8
Giltspur St EC1	56	G8
Gladstone St SE1	60	F6
Glasshill St SE1	60	G4
Glasshouse St W1	59	L1
Glasshouse Wk SE11	60	A10
Glasshouse Yd EC1	57	H5
Glentworth St NW1	54	E5
Globe St SE1	61	J6
Globe Yd W1	55	H9
Gloucester Ct EC3	61	N1
Gloucester Pl NW1	54	D4
Gloucester Pl W1	54	E6
Gloucester Pl Ms W1	54	E7
Gloucester Sq W2	54	A9
Gloucester Way EC1	56	E3
Glynde St SE1	58	C7
Godfrey St SW3	58	C10
Godliman St EC4	57	H9
Golden Jubilee Br SE1	60	B3
Golden Jubilee Br WC2	60	B2
Golden La EC1	57	H5
Golden La Est EC1	57	H5
Golden Sq W1	55	L10
Goldsmith St EC2	57	J8
Goodge Pl W1	55	L7
Goodge St W1	55	L7
Goodmans Ct E1	57	P10
Goodmans Yd E1	57	P10
Goodwins Ct WC2	55	P10
Gophir La EC4	57	K10
Gordon Sq WC1	55	N5
Gordon St WC1	55	M4
Goring St EC3	57	N8
Gorsuch Pl E2	57	P2
Gorsuch St E2	57	P2
Gosfield St W1	55	K6
Goslett Yd WC2	55	N9
Goswell Rd EC1	57	H5
Gough Sq EC4	56	E8
Gough St WC1	56	C4
Goulston St E1	57	P8
Gower Ct WC1	55	M4
Gower Ms WC1	55	M7
Gower Pl WC1	55	L4
Gower St WC1	55	L4
Gracechurch St EC3	57	L10
Grafton Ms W1	55	K5
Grafton Pl NW1	55	M3
Grafton St W1	59	J1
Grafton Way W1	55	K5
Grafton Way WC1	55	K5
Graham St N1	56	G1
Graham Ter SW1	58	F9
Granby Pl SE1	60	D5
Granby Ter NW1	55	K1
Grand Av EC1	56	G6
Grand Junct Wf N1	57	H1
Grange, The SE1	61	P6
Grange Ct WC2	56	C9
Grange Rd SE1	61	N6
Grange Wk SE1	61	N6
Grange Yd SE1	61	P7
Grant's Quay Wf EC3	61	L1
Granville Pl W1	54	F9
Granville Sq WC1	56	C3
Granville St WC1	56	C3
Grape St WC2	55	P8
Graphite Sq SE11	60	B10
Gravel La E1	57	P8
Gray's Inn Pl WC1	56	C7
Gray's Inn Rd WC1	56	B3
Gray's Inn Sq WC1	56	D6
Gray St SE1	60	E5
Gray's Yd W1	54	G9
Great Bell All EC2	57	K8
Great Castle St W1	55	J8
Great Cen St NW1	54	D6
Great Chapel St W1	55	M8
Great Coll St SW1	59	P6
Great Cumberland Ms W1	54	D9
Great Cumberland Pl W1	54	D8
Great Dover St SE1	61	J5
Great Eastern St EC2	57	M3
Great Eastern Wk EC2	57	N7
Great George St SW1	59	N5
Great Guildford St SE1	61	H2
Great James St WC1	56	B5
Great Marlborough St W1	55	K9
Great Maze Pond SE1	61	L4
Great New St EC4	56	E8
Great Ormond St WC1	56	A6
Great Percy St WC1	56	C2
Great Peter St SW1	59	M7
Great Portland St W1	55	J6
Great Pulteney St W1	55	L10
Great Queen St WC2	56	A9
Great Russell St WC1	55	N8
Great St. Helens EC3	57	M8
Great St. Thomas Apostle EC4	57	J10
Great Scotland Yd SW1	59	P3
Great Smith St SW1	59	N6
Great Suffolk St SE1	60	G3
Great Sutton St EC1	56	G5
Great Swan All EC2	57	K8
Great Titchfield St W1	55	K8
Great Twr St EC3	57	M10
Great Trinity La EC4	57	J10
Great Turnstile WC1	56	C7
Great Winchester St EC2	57	L8
Great Windmill St W1	55	M10
Great Yd SE1	61	N4
Greek Ct W1	55	N9
Greek St W1	55	N9
Greek Yd WC2	55	P10
Green Arbour Ct EC1	56	F8
Greenberry St NW8	54	B1
Greencoat Pl SW1	59	L8
Greencoat Row SW1	59	L7
Green Dragon Ct SE1	61	K2
Greenham Cl SE1	60	D5
Greenhill's Rents EC1	56	G6
Green's Ct W1	55	M10
Green St W1	54	E10
Green Ter EC1	56	E3
Green Wk SE1	61	M7
Greenwell St W1	55	J5
Greenwood Ct SW1	59	K10
Greet St SE1	60	E3
Grendon St NW8	54	B4
Grenville St WC1	56	A5
Gresham St EC2	57	H8
Gresse St W1	55	M7
Greville St EC1	56	E7
Greycoat Pl SW1	59	M7
Greycoat St SW1	59	M7
Grey Eagle St E1	57	P6
Greyfriars Pas EC1	56	G8
Greystoke Pl EC4	56	D8
Griggs Pl SE1	61	N7
Grindal St SE1	60	D5
Grocer's Hall Ct EC2	57	K9
Groom Pl SW1	58	G6
Grosvenor Cotts SW1	58	F8
Grosvenor Cres SW1	58	G5
Grosvenor Cres Ms SW1	58	F5
Grosvenor Est SW1	59	N8
Grosvenor Gdns SW1	59	H6
Grosvenor Gdns Ms E SW1	59	J6
Grosvenor Gdns Ms N SW1	59	H7
Grosvenor Gdns Ms S SW1	59	J7
Grosvenor Gate W1	58	E1
Grosvenor Hill W1	55	H10
Grosvenor Pl SW1	58	G5
Grosvenor Sq W1	54	G10
Grosvenor St W1	55	H10
Grotto Pas W1	54	G6
Grove Gdns NW8	54	C3
Groveland Ct EC4	57	J9
Guildhall Yd EC2	57	K8
Guildhouse St SW1	59	K8
Guilford Pl WC1	56	B5
Guilford St WC1	56	A5
Guinness Sq SE1	61	M8
Guinness Trust Bldgs SE11	60	G10
Guinness Trust Bldgs SW3	58	D9
Gulston Wk SW3	58	E9
Gunpowder Sq EC4	56	E8
Gun St E1	57	P7
Guthrie St SW3	58	B10
Gutter La EC2	57	J8
Guy St SE1	61	L4
Gwynne Pl WC1	56	C3
Haberdasher Pl N1	57	L2
Haberdasher St N1	57	L2
Hackney Rd E2	57	P3
Half Moon Ct EC1	57	H7
Half Moon St W1	59	J2
Halkin Arc SW1	58	F6
Halkin Ms SW1	58	F6
Halkin Pl SW1	58	F6
Halkin St SW1	58	G5
Hallam Ms W1	55	J6
Hallam St W1	55	J5
Hall St EC1	56	G2
Hall Twr W2	54	A6
Halpin Pl SE17	61	L9
Halsey Ms SW3	58	D8
Halsey St SW3	58	D8
Halstead Ct N1	57	L1
Hamilton Ms W1	59	H4
Hamilton Pl W1	58	G3
Hamilton Sq SE1	61	L4
Hammett St EC3	57	P10
Hampden Cl NW1	55	N1
Hampden Gurney St W1	54	D9
Hampton St SE1	60	G9
Hampton St SE17	60	G9
Ham Yd W1	55	M10
Hanbury St E1	57	P6
Hand Ct WC1	56	C7
Handel St WC1	55	P4
Hanging Sword All EC4	56	E9
Hankey Pl SE1	61	L5
Hanover Gate NW1	54	C3
Hanover Gate Mans NW1	54	C4
Hanover Pl WC2	56	A9
Hanover Sq W1	55	J9
Hanover St W1	55	J9
Hanover Ter NW1	54	C3
Hanover Ter Ms NW1	54	C3
Hans Cres SW1	58	D6
Hanson St W1	55	K6
Hans Pl SW1	58	E6
Hans Rd SW3	58	D6
Hans St SW1	58	E7
Hanway Pl W1	55	M8
Hanway St W1	55	M8
Harbet Rd W2	54	A7
Harcourt St W1	54	C7
Hardwicke Ms WC1	56	C3
Hardwick St EC1	56	E3
Hardwidge St SE1	61	M4
Hare Ct EC4	56	D9
Hare Pl EC4	56	E9
Hare Wk N1	57	N1
Harewood Av NW1	54	C5
Harewood Pl W1	55	J9
Harewood Row NW1	54	C6
Harley Pl W1	55	H7
Harley St W1	55	H7
Harmsworth Ms SE11	60	F7
Harold Est SE1	61	N7
Harold Laski Ho EC1	56	F3
Harp All EC4	56	F8
Harper Rd SE1	61	H6
Harp La EC3	61	M1
Harpur Ms WC1	56	B6
Harpur St WC1	56	B6
Harriet St SW1	58	E5
Harriet Wk SW1	58	E5
Harrington Sq NW1	55	K1
Harrington St NW1	55	K2
Harrison St WC1	56	A3
Harrowby St W1	54	C8
Harrow Pl E1	57	N8
Hartshorn All EC3	57	N9
Hart St EC3	57	N10
Hasker St SW3	58	C8
Hastings St WC1	55	P3
Hat & Mitre Ct EC1	56	G5
Hatchers Ms SE1	61	N5
Hatfields SE1	60	E2
Hatherley St SW1	59	L8
Hatton Gdn EC1	56	E6
Hatton Pl EC1	56	E5
Hatton Row NW8	54	A5
Hatton St NW8	54	A5
Hatton Wall EC1	56	D6
Haunch of Venison Yd W1	55	H9
Haverstock St N1	56	G1
Haydon St EC3	57	P10
Hayes Pl NW1	54	C5
Hay Hill W1	59	J1
Hayles St SE11	60	F8
Haymarket SW1	59	M1
Haymarket Arc SW1	59	M1
Hayne St EC1	56	G6
Hay's La SE1	61	M3
Hay's Ms W1	59	H1
Hayward's Pl EC1	56	F5
Hazel Way SE1	61	P8
Headfort Pl SW1	58	G5
Hearn's Bldgs SE17	61	L9
Hearn St EC2	57	N5
Heathcote St WC1	56	B4
Heddon St W1	55	K10
Hedger St SE11	60	F8
Helmet Row EC1	57	J4
Hemp Wk SE17	61	L8
Hendre Rd SE1	61	N9
Heneage La EC3	57	N9
Henrietta Ms WC1	56	A4
Henrietta St WC2	56	A10
Henshaw St SE17	61	K8
Herald's Pl SE11	60	F8
Herbal Hill EC1	56	E5
Herbert Cres SW1	58	E6
Herbrand St WC1	55	P4
Hercules Rd SE1	60	C7
Hermes St N1	56	D1
Hermit St EC1	56	F2
Herrick St SW1	59	N8
Hertford Pl W1	55	K5
Hertford St W1	59	H2
Hewett St EC2	57	N5
Heygate St SE17	61	H9
Hide Pl SW1	59	M9
Hide Twr SW1	59	M9
High Holborn WC1	56	A8
High Timber St EC4	57	H10
Hillery Cl SE17	61	L9
Hills Pl W1	55	K9
Hill St W1	58	G2
Hind Ct EC4	56	E9
Hinde St W1	54	G8
Hobart Pl SW1	59	H6
Hocker St E2	57	P3
Hogarth Ct EC3	57	N10
Holbein Ms SW1	58	F10
Holbein Pl SW1	58	F9
Holborn WC2	56	B8
Holborn EC1	56	D7
Holborn Circ EC1	56	E7
Holborn Pl WC1	56	B7
Holborn Viaduct EC1	56	E7
Holford Ms WC1	56	D1
Holford Pl WC1	56	C2
Holford St WC1	56	D2
Holford Yd WC1	56	D1
Holland St SE1	60	G2

Hollen St W1 55 M8
Holles St W1 55 J8
Holmes Ter SE1 60 D4
Holsworthy Sq WC1 56 C5
Holyoak Rd SE11 60 F8
Holyrood St SE1 61 M3
Holywell La EC2 57 N4
Holywell Row EC2 57 M5
Homefield St N1 57 M1
Homer Row W1 54 C7
Homer St W1 54 C7
Honduras St EC1 57 H4
Honey La EC2 57 J9
Hood Ct EC4 56 E9
Hooper's Ct SW3 58 D5
Hop Gdns WC2 59 P1
Hopkins St W1 55 L9
Hopton Gdns SE1 60 G2
Hopton St SE1 60 G2
Hornbeam Cl SE11 60 D8
Horse & Dolphin Yd W1 55 N10
Horseferry Rd SW1 59 M7
Horse Guards Av SW1 59 P3
Horse Guards Rd SW1 59 N3
Horselydown La SE1 61 P4
Horsemongers Ms SE1 61 J5
Horse Ride SW1 59 L3
Horselydown Old Stairs SE1 61 P3
Hosier La EC1 56 F7
Hotspur St SE11 60 D10
Houghton St WC2 56 C9
Houndsditch EC3 57 N8
Howell Wk SE1 60 G9
Howick Pl SW1 59 L7
Howland Ms E W1 55 L6
Howland St W1 55 K6
Hoxton N1 57 M1
Hoxton Mkt N1 57 M3
Hoxton Sq N1 57 M3
Hoxton St N1 57 N3
Hudson's Pl SW1 59 J8
Huggin Ct EC4 57 J10
Huggin Hill EC4 57 J10
Hugh Ms SW1 59 J9
Hugh St SW1 59 J9
Hull St EC1 57 H3
Hulme Pl SE1 61 J5
Humphrey St SE1 61 P10
Hungerford Br SE1 60 A2
Hungerford Br WC2 60 A2
Hungerford La WC2 59 P2
Hunter Cl SE1 61 L7
Hunter St WC1 56 A4
Huntley St WC1 55 L5
Hunt's Ct WC2 59 N1
Huntsman St SE17 61 L9
Huntsworth Ms NW1 54 D5
Hurley Ho SE11 60 E9
Hutton St EC4 56 E9
Hyde Pk SW7 58 B2
Hyde Pk W1 58 B2
Hyde Pk Cor W1 58 G4
Hyde Pk Cres W2 54 B9
Hyde Pk Gdns W2 54 A10
Hyde Pk Gdns Ms W2 54 A10
Hyde Pk Pl W2 54 C10
Hyde Pk Sq W2 54 B9
Hyde Pk Sq Ms W2 54 B9
Hyde Pk St W2 54 B9
Idol La EC3 61 M1
Iliffe St SE17 60 G10
Iliffe Yd SE17 60 G10
India Pl WC2 56 B10
India St EC3 57 P9
Ingestre Pl W1 55 L9
Inglebert St EC1 56 D2
Ingram Ct SE11 60 C8
Inigo Pl WC2 55 P10
Inner Circle NW1 54 F3
Inner Temple La EC4 56 D9
Invicta Plaza SE1 60 F2
Ireland Yd EC4 56 G9
Ironmonger La EC2 57 K9
Ironmonger Pas EC1 57 J4
Ironmonger Row EC1 57 J3
Irving St WC2 59 N1
Isabella St SE1 60 F3
Islington High St N1 56 E1
Ives St SW3 58 C8
Ivor Pl NW1 54 D5
Ivybridge La WC2 60 A1
Ivychurch La SE17 61 P10
Ixworth Pl SW3 58 B10
Jacob's Well Ms W1 54 G8
James St W1 54 G8
James St WC2 56 A10
Jasper Wk N1 57 K2
Jermyn St SW1 59 K2
Jerome Cres NW8 54 B4
Jerome St E1 57 P6

Jerrard St N1 57 N1
Jerusalem Pas EC1 56 F5
Jervis Ct W1 55 J9
Jewry St EC3 57 P9
Joan St SE1 60 F3
Jockey's Flds WC1 56 C6
Johanna St SE1 60 D5
John Adam St WC2 60 A1
John Carpenter St EC4 56 F10
John Islip St SW1 59 P9
John Maurice Cl SE17 61 K8
John Princes St W1 55 J8
John's Ms WC1 56 C5
John St WC1 56 C5
Joiner St SE1 61 L3
Jonathan St SE11 60 B10
Jones St W1 59 H1
Jubilee Pl SW3 58 C10
Judd St WC1 55 P3
Junction Ms W2 54 B8
Junction Pl W2 54 B8
Juxon St SE11 60 C8
Kean St WC2 56 B9
Keats Cl SE1 61 P9
Keats Pl EC2 57 K7
Keeley St WC2 56 B9
Kell St SE1 60 G6
Kemble St WC2 56 B9
Kemp's Ct W1 55 L9
Kempsford Rd SE11 60 E9
Kendall Pl W1 54 F7
Kendal St W2 54 C9
Kennet Wf La EC4 57 J10
Kennings Way SE11 60 F10
Kennington La SE11 60 E10
Kennington Rd SE1 60 D6
Kennington Rd SE11 60 D7
Kenrick Pl W1 54 F6
Kensington Rd SW7 58 A5
Kentish Bldgs SE1 61 K3
Kenton St WC1 55 P4
Kent Pas NW1 54 D4
Kent Ter NW1 54 C3
Kent Yd SW7 58 C5
Keppel Row SE1 61 H3
Keppel St WC1 55 N6
Kestrel Ho EC1 57 H2
Keyse Rd SE1 61 P7
Keystone Cres N1 56 A1
Keyworth St SE1 60 G6
Kiffen St EC2 57 L4
Kimbolton Row SW3 58 B9
King & Queen St SE17 61 J9
King Charles St SW1 59 N4
King Edward St EC1 57 H8
King Edward Wk SE1 60 E6
Kinghorn St EC1 57 H7
King James Ct SE1 60 G5
King James St SE1 60 G5
King John Ct EC2 57 N4
Kinglake Est SE17 61 N10
Kingly Ct W1 55 K10
Kingly St W1 55 K9
Kings Arms Yd EC2 57 K8
Kings Bench St SE1 60 G4
Kings Bench Wk EC4 56 E9
Kingscote St EC4 56 F10
King's Cross Br N1 56 A2
King's Cross Rd WC1 56 C2
Kings Head Yd SE1 61 K3
Kingsland Rd E2 57 N2
King's Ms WC1 56 C5
Kings Pl SE1 61 H5
King Sq EC1 57 H3
King's Reach Twr SE1 60 E2
King's Rd SW1 58 C10
King's Rd SW3 58 C10
King's Scholars' Pas SW1 59 K8
King St EC2 57 J9
King St SW1 59 L3
King St WC2 55 P10
Kingsway WC2 56 B8
Kingsway Pl EC1 56 E4
King William St EC4 61 L1
Kinnerton Pl N SW1 58 E5
Kinnerton Pl S SW1 58 E5
Kinnerton St SW1 58 F5
Kinnerton Yd SW1 58 E5
Kintore Way SE1 61 P8
Kipling Est SE1 61 L5
Kipling St SE1 61 L5
Kirby Gro SE1 61 M4
Kirby St EC1 56 E6
Kirkman Pl W1 55 M7
Kirk St WC1 56 B5
Knightrider St EC4 57 H10
Knights Arc SW1 58 D5
Knightsbridge SW1 58 E5
Knightsbridge SW7 58 C5
Knightsbridge Grn SW1 58 D5
Knights Wk SE11 60 F9
Knox St W1 54 D6
Lackington St EC2 57 L6
Lafone St SE1 61 P4

Lambeth SE1 60 B6
Lambeth Br SE1 60 A8
Lambeth Br SW1 60 A8
Lambeth High St SE1 60 B9
Lambeth Hill EC4 57 H10
Lambeth Palace Rd SE1 60 B7
Lambeth Rd SE1 60 C7
Lambeth Rd SE11 60 C7
Lambeth Wk SE11 60 C8
Lamb's Bldgs EC1 57 K5
Lambs Conduit Pas WC1 56 B6
Lamb's Conduit St WC1 56 B5
Lamb's Pas EC1 57 K6
Lamb St E1 57 P6
Lamb Wk SE1 61 M5
Lamlash St SE11 60 F8
Lamp Office Ct WC1 56 B5
Lancashire Ct W1 55 J10
Lancaster Pl WC2 56 B10
Lancaster St SE1 60 G5
Lancelot Pl SW7 58 D5
Lancing St NW1 55 M3
Landon Pl SW1 58 D6
Lanesborough Pl SW1 58 G4
Langham Pl W1 55 J7
Langham St W1 55 J7
Langley Ct WC2 55 P10
Langley St WC2 55 P9
Langthorn Ct EC2 57 K8
Langton Cl WC1 56 C3
Lansdowne Pl SE1 61 L7
Lansdowne Row W1 59 J2
Lansdowne Ter WC1 56 A5
Lant St SE1 61 H4
Larcom St SE17 61 J9
Larissa St SE17 61 L10
Lauderdale Twr EC2 57 H6
Laud St SE1 60 B10
Launcelot St SE1 60 D5
Laurence Pountney Hill EC4 57 K10
Laurence Pountney La EC4 57 K10
Lavington St SE1 60 G3
Lawrence La EC2 57 J9
Lawson St SE1 61 K7
Laxton Pl NW1 55 J4
Laystall St EC1 56 D5
Laytons Bldgs SE1 61 J4
Leadenhall Pl EC3 57 M9
Leadenhall St EC3 57 M9
Leake St SE1 60 C4
Leather La EC1 56 E7
Leathermarket Ct SE1 61 M5
Leathermarket St SE1 61 M5
Leeke St WC1 56 B2
Lees Pl W1 54 F10
Leicester Ct WC2 55 N10
Leicester Pl WC2 55 N10
Leicester Sq WC2 59 N1
Leicester St WC2 55 N10
Leigh Hunt St SE1 61 H4
Leigh Pl EC1 56 D6
Leigh St WC1 55 P4
Lennox Gdns SW1 58 D7
Lennox Gdns Ms SW1 58 D7
Leonard St EC2 57 L4
Leopards Ct EC1 56 D6
Leo Yd EC1 56 G5
Leroy St SE1 61 M8
Leverett St SW3 58 C8
Lever St EC1 56 G3
Lewisham St SW1 59 N5
Lexington, The EC1 57 K4
Lexington St W1 55 L9
Leyden St E1 57 P7
Library St SE1 60 F5
Lidlington Pl NW1 55 K1
Ligonier St E2 57 P4
Lilac Pl SE11 60 B9
Lilestone St NW8 54 B4
Lillington Gdns Est SW1 59 L9
Lily Pl EC1 56 E6
Limeburner La EC4 56 F9
Lime St EC3 57 M10
Lime St Pas EC3 57 M9
Lincoln's Inn Flds WC2 56 B8
Lincoln St SW3 58 D9
Lindsay Sq SW1 59 N10
Lindsey St EC1 56 G6
Linhope St NW1 54 D4
Lisle St WC2 55 N10
Lisson Grn Est NW8 54 B3
Lisson Grove NW8 54 A5
Lisson Gro NW1 54 B4
Lisson Gro NW8 54 B4
Lisson St NW1 54 B6
Litchfield St WC2 55 N10
Little Albany St NW1 55 J4
Little Argyll St W1 55 K9
Little Britain EC1 57 H8

Little Chester St SW1 58 G6
Little Coll St SW1 59 P6
Little Dean's Yd SW1 59 P6
Little Dorrit Ct SE1 61 J4
Little Edward St NW1 55 J2
Little Essex St WC2 56 D10
Little George St SW1 59 P5
Little Marlborough St W1 55 K9
Little Newport St WC2 55 N10
Little New St EC4 56 E8
Little Portland St W1 55 K8
Little Russell St WC1 55 P7
Little St. James's St SW1 59 K3
Little Sanctuary SW1 59 N5
Little Smith St SW1 59 N6
Little Somerset St E1 57 P9
Little Titchfield St W1 55 K7
Little Trinity La EC4 57 J10
Little Turnstile WC1 56 B8
Liverpool St EC2 57 M7
Livonia St W1 55 L9
Lizard St EC1 57 J3
Lloyd Baker St WC1 56 C3
Lloyd's Av EC3 57 N9
Lloyd Sq WC1 56 D2
Lloyd's Row EC1 56 E3
Lloyd St WC1 56 D2
Lockyer Est SE1 61 L4
Lockyer St SE1 61 L5
Lodge Rd NW8 54 A3
Lollard St SE11 60 C8
Loman St SE1 60 G4
Lombard Ct EC3 57 L10
Lombard La EC4 56 E9
Lombard St EC3 57 L9
London Br EC4 61 L2
London Br SE1 61 L2
London Br St SE1 61 K3
London Br Wk SE1 61 L2
London Ms W2 54 A9
London Rd SE1 60 F6
London Shop Pav W1 59 M1
London St EC3 57 N10
London Wall EC2 57 J7
London Wall Bldgs EC2 57 L7
Long Acre WC2 55 P10
Longford St NW1 55 J4
Long La EC1 56 G6
Long La SE1 61 K5
Longmoore St SW1 59 K9
Long's Ct WC2 55 M10
Long St E2 57 P2
Longville Rd SE11 60 F8
Long Wk SE1 61 N6
Long Yd WC1 56 B5
Lord N St SW1 59 P7
Lord's Vw NW8 54 A3
Lorenzo St WC1 56 B2
Lorne Cl NW8 54 C3
Lothbury EC2 57 K8
Loughborough St SE11 60 C10
Lovat La EC3 61 M1
Love La EC2 57 J8
Lover's Wk W1 58 F2
Lower Belgrave St SW1 59 H7
Lower Grosvenor Pl SW1 59 H6
Lower James St W1 55 L10
Lower John St W1 55 L10
Lower Marsh SE1 60 D5
Lower Sloane St SW1 58 F9
Lower Thames St EC3 61 L1
Lowndes Cl SW1 58 G7
Lowndes Ct W1 55 K9
Lowndes Pl SW1 58 F7
Lowndes Sq SW1 58 E5
Lowndes St SW1 58 E6
Lowther Gdns SW7 58 A5
Loxham St WC1 56 A3
Lucan Pl SW3 58 B9
Ludgate Bdy EC4 56 F9
Ludgate Circ EC4 56 F9
Ludgate Hill EC4 56 F9
Ludgate Sq EC4 56 G9
Ludlow St EC1 57 H4
Luke St EC2 57 M4
Lulworth SE17 61 K10
Lumley Ct WC2 60 A1
Lumley St W1 54 G9
Lupino Ct SE11 60 C9
Luton St NW8 54 A5
Luxborough St W1 54 F6
Lyall Ms SW1 58 F7
Lyall Ms W SW1 58 F7
Lyall St SW1 58 F7
Lygon Pl SW1 59 H7
Mabledon Pl WC1 55 N3
Macauley Cl SE1 60 D6
Macclesfield Rd EC1 57 H2
Macclesfield St W1 55 N10
McCoid Way SE1 61 H5
Macfarren Pl NW1 54 G5

Mackennal St NW8 54 C1
Macklin St WC2 56 A8
Mackworth St NW1 55 K2
Mac's Pl EC4 56 D8
Maddox St W1 55 J10
Madron St SE17 61 N10
Magdalen St SE1 61 M3
Magpie All EC4 56 E9
Maiden La SE1 61 J2
Maiden La WC2 60 A1
Maidstone Bldgs Ms SE1 61 J3
Makins St SW3 58 C9
Malet Pl WC1 55 M5
Malet St WC1 55 M5
Mall, The SW1 59 L4
Mallory St NW8 54 C4
Mallow St EC1 57 K4
Malta St EC1 56 G4
Maltby St SE1 61 P5
Maltravers St WC2 56 C10
Malvern Ct SW7 58 A9
Manchester Ms W1 54 F7
Manchester Sq W1 54 F7
Manchester St W1 54 F7
Manciple St SE1 61 K5
Mandela Way SE1 61 N8
Mandeville Pl W1 54 G8
Manette St W1 55 N9
Manningford Cl EC1 56 F2
Mansfield Ms W1 55 H7
Mansfield St W1 55 H7
Mansion Ho Pl EC4 57 K9
Mansion Ho St EC4 57 K9
Maple Pl W1 55 L5
Maple St W1 55 K6
Marchmont St WC1 55 P4
Marcia Rd SE1 61 N9
Margaret Ct W1 55 K8
Margaret St W1 55 J8
Margery St WC1 56 D3
Marigold All SE1 60 F1
Market Ct W1 55 K8
Market Ms W1 59 H3
Market Pl W1 55 K8
Market Yd Ms SE1 61 N6
Markham Pl SW3 58 D10
Markham Sq SW3 58 D10
Markham St SW3 58 C10
Mark La EC3 61 N1
Mark Sq EC2 57 M4
Mark St EC2 57 M4
Marlborough SW3 58 C8
Marlborough Cl SE17 60 G9
Marlborough Ct W1 55 K9
Marlborough Rd SW1 59 L3
Marlborough St SW3 58 B9
Marshall St W1 55 L9
Marshalsea Rd SE1 61 J4
Marsham St SW1 59 N7
Martha's Bldgs EC1 57 K4
Martin La EC4 57 L10
Martlett Ct WC2 56 A9
Marylebone NW1 54 D8
Marylebone Flyover NW1 54 A7
Marylebone Flyover W2 54 A7
Marylebone High St W1 54 G6
Marylebone La W1 55 H9
Marylebone Ms W1 55 H7
Marylebone Pas W1 55 L8
Marylebone Rd NW1 54 C6
Marylebone St W1 54 G7
Marylee Way SE11 60 C10
Masons Arms Ms W1 55 J9
Masons Av EC2 57 K8
Mason's Pl EC1 56 G2
Mason St SE17 61 L9
Mason's Yd SW1 59 L2
Massinger St SE17 61 M9
Matthew Parker St SW1 59 N5
Matthews Yd WC2 55 P9
Maunsel St SW1 59 M8
Mayfair W1 59 H1
Mayfair Pl W1 59 J2
Mays Ct WC2 59 P1
Meadow Row SE1 61 H7
Mead Row SE1 60 D6
Meakin Est SE1 61 M6
Meard St W1 55 M9
Mecklenburgh Pl WC1 56 B4
Mecklenburgh Sq WC1 56 B4
Mecklenburgh St WC1 56 B4
Medway St SW1 59 N7
Melbourne Pl WC2 56 C10
Melcombe Pl NW1 54 D6
Melcombe St NW1 54 E5
Melior Pl SE1 61 M4
Melior St SE1 61 M4
Melon Ct SW7 58 A9
Melton St NW1 55 L3
Memel Ct EC1 57 H5
Memel St EC1 57 H5
Mepham St SE1 60 C3

Street	Page	Grid
Mercer St WC2	55	P9
Meredith St EC1	56	F3
Merlin St WC1	56	D3
Mermaid Ct SE1	61	K4
Merrick Sq SE1	61	J6
Merrow Wk SE17	61	L10
Meymott St SE1	60	F3
Micawber St N1	57	J2
Middlesex Pas EC1	56	G7
Middlesex St E1	57	N7
Middle St EC1	57	H6
Middle Temple EC4	56	D10
Middle Temple La EC4	56	D9
Middleton Pl W1	55	K7
Middle Yd SE1	61	L2
Midford St W1	55	L5
Midhope St WC1	56	A3
Midland Rd NW1	55	N1
Milcote St SE1	60	F5
Miles Pl NW1	54	A6
Milford La WC2	56	C10
Milk St EC2	57	J9
Millbank SW1	59	P7
Millbank Twr SW1	59	P9
Miller Wk SE1	60	E3
Millman Ms WC1	56	B5
Millman St WC1	56	B5
Mills Ct EC2	57	N3
Millstream Rd SE1	61	P5
Mill St W1	55	J10
Milner St SW3	58	D8
Milroy Wk SE1	60	F2
Milton Cl SE1	61	P9
Milton Ct EC2	57	K6
Milton St EC2	57	K6
Mincing La EC3	57	M10
Minera Ms SW1	58	G8
Minnow Wk SE17	61	N9
Minories EC3	57	P10
Mint St SE1	61	H4
Mitchell St EC1	57	H4
Mitre Ct EC2	57	J8
Mitre Ct EC4	56	E9
Mitre Rd SE1	60	E4
Mitre Sq EC3	57	N9
Mitre St EC3	57	N9
Molyneux St W1	54	C7
Monck St SW1	59	N7
Moncorvo Cl SW7	58	B5
Monkton St SE11	60	E8
Monkwell Sq EC2	57	J7
Monmouth St WC2	55	P9
Montague Cl SE1	61	K2
Montague Pl WC1	55	N6
Montague St EC1	57	H7
Montague St WC1	55	P6
Montagu Mans W1	54	E6
Montagu Ms N W1	54	E7
Montagu Ms S W1	54	E8
Montagu Ms W W1	54	E8
Montagu Pl W1	54	D7
Montagu Row W1	54	E7
Montagu Sq W1	54	E7
Montagu St W1	54	E8
Montaigne Cl SW1	59	N8
Montclare St E2	57	P3
Montpelier Ms SW7	58	C6
Montpelier Pl SW7	58	C6
Montpelier Sq SW7	58	C5
Montpelier St SW7	58	C5
Montpelier Ter SW7	58	C5
Montpelier Wk SW7	58	C6
Montreal Pl WC2	56	B10
Montrose Ct SW7	58	A5
Montrose Pl SW1	58	G5
Monument St EC3	57	L10
Moore St SW3	58	D8
Moorfields EC2	57	K7
Moorgate EC2	57	K8
Moorgate Pl EC2	57	K8
Moor La EC2	57	K7
Moor Pl EC2	57	K7
Moor St W1	55	N9
Mora St EC1	57	J3
Morecambe St SE17	61	J9
Moreland St EC1	56	G2
Moreton Cl SW1	59	L10
Moreton Pl SW1	59	L10
Moreton St SW1	59	L10
Moreton Ter SW1	59	L10
Moreton Ter Ms N SW1	59	L10
Moreton Ter Ms S SW1	59	L10
Morgans La SE1	61	M3
Morley St SE1	60	E6
Morocco St SE1	61	M5
Morpeth Ter SW1	59	K7
Mortimer Mkt WC1	55	L5
Mortimer St W1	55	K8
Morton Pl SE1	60	D7
Morwell St WC1	55	N7
Mossop St SW3	58	C8
Motcomb St SW1	58	E6
Motley Av EC2	57	M4
Mount Mills EC1	56	G3
Mount Pleasant WC1	56	C5
Mount Row W1	59	H1
Mount St W1	58	G1
Moxon St W1	54	F7
Mozart Ter SW1	58	G9
Mulready St NW8	54	B5
Mulvaney Way SE1	61	L5
Mumford Ct EC2	57	J8
Mundy St N1	57	M2
Munster Sq NW1	55	J3
Munton Rd SE17	61	J8
Murphy St SE1	60	D5
Murray Gro N1	57	J1
Muscovy St EC3	61	N1
Museum St WC1	55	P7
Myddelton Pas EC1	56	E2
Myddelton Sq EC1	56	E2
Myddelton St EC1	56	E3
Mylne St EC1	56	D1
Myrtle Wk N1	57	M1
Nag's Head Ct EC1	57	H5
Nantes Pas E1	57	P6
Naoroji St WC1	56	D3
Napier Gro N1	57	J1
Nash St NW1	55	J3
Nassau St W1	55	K7
Navarre St E2	57	P4
Nazrul St E2	57	P2
Neal St WC2	55	P9
Neal's Yd WC2	55	P9
Neathouse Pl SW1	59	K8
Nebraska St SE1	61	K5
Nelson Pas EC1	57	J3
Nelson Pl N1	56	G1
Nelson Sq SE1	60	F4
Nelson Ter N1	56	G1
Netley St NW1	55	K3
Neville Cl NW1	55	N1
New Bond St W1	55	H9
New Br St EC4	56	F9
New Broad St EC2	57	M7
Newburgh St W1	55	K9
New Burlington Ms W1	55	K10
New Burlington Pl W1	55	K10
New Burlington St W1	55	K10
Newbury St EC1	57	H7
Newcastle Cl EC4	56	F8
Newcastle Pl W2	54	A7
Newcastle Row EC1	56	E4
New Cavendish St W1	55	J6
New Change EC4	57	H9
New Charles St EC1	56	G2
Newcomen St SE1	61	K4
New Compton St WC2	55	N9
New Ct EC4	56	D10
Newcourt St NW8	54	B1
New Fetter La EC4	56	E8
Newgate St EC1	56	G8
New Globe Wk SE1	61	H2
New Goulston St E1	57	P8
Newington SE1	61	H8
Newington Butts SE1	60	G9
Newington Butts SE11	60	G9
Newington Causeway SE1	60	G7
New Inn Bdy EC2	57	N4
New Inn Pas WC2	56	C9
New Inn Sq EC2	57	N4
New Inn St EC2	57	N4
New Inn Yd EC2	57	N4
New Kent Rd SE1	61	H7
New London St EC3	57	N10
Newman Pas W1	55	L7
Newman's Ct EC3	57	L9
Newman's Row WC2	56	C7
Newman St W1	55	L7
Newman Yd W1	55	M8
Newnham Ter SE1	60	D6
New N Pl EC2	57	M5
New N Rd N1	57	L1
New N St WC1	56	B6
New Oxford St WC1	55	N8
Newport Ct WC2	55	N10
Newport Pl WC2	55	N10
Newport St SE11	60	B9
New Quebec St W1	54	E9
New Ride SW7	58	D4
New River Head EC1	56	E2
New Row WC2	55	P10
New Sq WC2	56	C8
New St EC2	57	N7
New St Sq EC4	56	E8
Newton St WC2	56	A8
New Turnstile WC1	56	B7
New Union St EC2	57	K7
Nicholas La EC4	57	L10
Nicholas Pas EC4	57	L10
Nichols Ct E2	57	P1
Nicholson St SE1	60	F3
Nightingale Ms SE11	60	E8
Nile St N1	57	J2
Noble St EC2	57	H8
Noel St W1	55	L9
Norfolk Cres W2	54	C8
Norfolk Pl W2	54	A8
Norfolk Row SE1	60	B8
Norfolk Sq W2	54	A9
Norfolk Sq Ms W2	54	A9
Norman St EC1	57	H3
Norris St SW1	59	M1
Northampton Rd EC1	56	E4
Northampton Row EC1	56	E3
Northampton Sq EC1	56	F3
North Audley St W1	54	F9
North Bk NW8	54	A3
Northburgh St EC1	56	G4
North Carriage Dr W2	54	B10
Northchurch SE17	61	L10
North Cres WC1	55	M6
North Gower St NW1	55	L3
Northington St WC1	56	B5
North Ms WC1	56	C5
North Ride W2	58	B3
North Row W1	54	E10
North Ter SW3	58	B7
Northumberland All EC3	57	N9
Northumberland Av WC2	59	P2
Northumberland St WC2	59	P2
Norton Folgate E1	57	N6
Norwich St EC4	56	D8
Nottingham Ct WC2	55	P9
Nottingham Pl W1	54	F5
Nottingham St W1	54	F6
Nottingham Ter NW1	54	F5
Nun Ct EC2	57	K8
Nursery Row SE17	61	K9
Nutford Pl W1	54	C8
Oakden St SE11	60	E8
Oakey La SE1	60	D6
Oakley Cres EC1	56	G1
Oakley Sq NW1	55	L1
Oak Tree Rd NW8	54	A3
Oat La EC2	57	H8
Occupation Rd SE17	61	H10
Octagon Arc EC2	57	M7
Odhams Wk WC2	56	A9
Ogle St W1	55	K6
Old Bailey EC4	56	G9
Old Barrack Yd SW1	58	F4
Old Bond St W1	59	K1
Old Brewers Yd WC2	55	P9
Old Broad St EC2	57	L9
Old Bldgs WC2	56	D8
Old Burlington St W1	55	K10
Oldbury Pl W1	54	G6
Old Castle St E1	57	P7
Old Cavendish St W1	55	H8
Old Compton St W1	55	M10
Old Fish St Hill EC4	57	H10
Old Fleet La EC4	56	F8
Old Gloucester St WC1	56	A6
Old Jewry EC2	57	K9
Old Kent Rd SE1	61	L7
Old Mkt Sq E2	57	P2
Old Marylebone Rd NW1	54	C7
Old Nichol St E2	57	P4
Old N St WC1	56	B6
Old Palace Yd SW1	59	P6
Old Paradise St SE11	60	B8
Old Pk La W1	58	G3
Old Pye St SW1	59	M6
Old Quebec St W1	54	E9
Old Queen St SW1	59	N5
Old Seacoal La EC4	56	F8
Old St WC2	56	C8
Old St EC1	57	H4
Olivers Yd EC1	57	L4
O'Meara St SE1	61	J3
Omega Pl N1	56	A1
Onslow Sq SW7	58	A8
Onslow St EC1	56	E5
Ontario St SE1	60	G7
Opal St SE11	60	F9
Orange Sq SW1	58	G9
Orange St WC2	59	M1
Orange Yd W1	55	N9
Oratory La SW3	58	A10
Orb St SE17	61	K9
Orchard St W1	54	F9
Orde Hall St WC1	56	B5
Orient St SE11	60	F8
Ormond Cl WC1	56	A6
Ormond Pl SW1	58	F9
Ormond Ms WC1	56	A5
Ormond Yd SW1	59	L2
Orsett St SE11	60	C10
Osbert St SW1	59	M9
Oslo Ct NW8	54	B1
Osnaburgh St NW1	55	J5
Osnaburgh St (north section) NW1	55	J3
Osnaburgh Ter NW1	55	J4
Osric Path N1	57	M1
Ossington Bldgs W1	54	F6
Ossulston St NW1	55	M1
Oswin St SE11	60	G8
Othello Cl SE11	60	F10
Outer Circle NW1	54	F5
Outwich St EC3	57	N8
Ovington Gdns SW3	58	C7
Ovington Ms SW3	58	C7
Ovington Sq SW3	58	C7
Ovington St SW3	58	C7
Owen's Ct EC1	56	F2
Owen's Row EC1	56	F2
Owen St EC1	56	F1
Oxendon St SW1	59	M1
Oxford Circ Av W1	55	K9
Oxford Ct EC4	57	K10
Oxford Dr SE1	61	M3
Oxford Sq W2	54	C9
Oxford St W1	55	L8
Oxo Twr Wf SE1	60	E1
Paddington Grn W2	54	A6
Paddington St W1	54	F6
Pageantmaster Ct EC4	56	F9
Page St SW1	59	N8
Pages Wk SE1	61	M8
Paget St EC1	56	F2
Pakenham St WC1	56	C3
Palace Ms SW1	58	G9
Palace Pl SW1	59	K6
Palace St SW1	59	K6
Palgrave Gdns NW1	54	C4
Palissy St E2	57	P3
Pall Mall SW1	59	L3
Pall Mall E SW1	59	N2
Palmer St SW1	59	M5
Pancras La EC4	57	J9
Panton St SW1	59	M1
Panyer All EC4	57	H9
Paragon Ms SE1	61	L8
Pardoner St SE1	61	L6
Pardon St EC1	56	G4
Paris Gdn SE1	60	F2
Park Cl SW1	58	D5
Park Cres W1	55	H5
Park Cres Ms E W1	55	J5
Park Cres Ms W W1	55	H5
Parker Ms WC2	56	A8
Parker St WC2	56	A8
Park La W1	58	G3
Park Pl SW1	59	K3
Park Rd NW1	54	B2
Park Rd NW8	54	B2
Park Sq E NW1	55	H4
Park Sq Ms NW1	55	H5
Park Sq W NW1	55	H4
Park St SE1	61	H2
Park St W1	54	F10
Park W W2	54	C9
Park W Pl W2	54	C9
Parliament Sq SW1	59	P5
Parliament St SW1	59	P5
Parliament Vw Apartments SE1	60	B8
Parmoor Ct EC1	57	H4
Passing All EC1	56	G5
Passmore St SW1	58	F9
Pastor St SE11	60	G8
Paternoster Row EC4	57	H9
Paternoster Sq EC4	56	G9
Paton St EC1	57	H3
Paul St EC2	57	L5
Paul's Wk EC4	56	G10
Paveley St NW8	54	C4
Pavilion Rd SW1	58	E7
Pavilion St SW1	58	E7
Peabody Av SW1	59	H10
Peabody Dws WC1	55	P4
Peabody Est EC1	57	J5
Peabody Est SE1	60	E3
Peabody Sq SE1	60	F5
Peabody Trust SE1	61	H3
Peacock St SE17	60	G9
Peacock Yd SE17	60	G9
Pearman St SE1	60	D4
Pear Pl SE1	60	D4
Pear Tree Ct EC1	56	E5
Pear Tree St EC1	56	G4
Pecks Yd E1	57	P6
Peerless St EC1	57	K3
Pelham Cres SW7	58	B9
Pelham Pl SW7	58	B9
Pelham St SW7	58	A8
Pelter St E2	57	P2
Pemberton Row EC4	56	E8
Pembroke Cl SW1	58	G5
Penfold Pl NW1	54	A6
Penfold St NW1	54	A5
Penfold St NW8	54	A5
Penhurst Pl SE1	60	C7
Penry St SE1	61	N9
Penton Gro N1	56	D1
Penton Pl SE17	60	G10
Penton Ri WC1	56	C2
Pentonville N1	56	D1
Pentonville Rd N1	56	B1
Pepper St SE1	61	H4
Pepys St EC3	57	N10
Percival St EC1	56	F4
Percy Circ WC1	56	C2
Percy Ms W1	55	M7
Percy Pas W1	55	L7
Percy St W1	55	M7
Percy Yd WC1	56	C2
Peregrine Ho EC1	56	G2
Perkin's Rents SW1	59	M6
Perkins Sq SE1	61	J2
Perrys Pl W1	55	M8
Peters Hill EC4	57	H10
Peter's La EC1	56	G6
Peter St W1	55	L10
Peto Pl NW1	55	J4
Petticoat Sq E1	57	P8
Petty France SW1	59	L6
Petyward SW3	58	C9
Philpot La EC3	57	M10
Phipp's Ms SW1	59	J7
Phipp St EC2	57	M4
Phoenix Pl WC1	56	C4
Phoenix Rd NW1	55	M2
Phoenix St WC2	55	N9
Phoenix Yd WC1	56	C3
Piccadilly W1	59	J3
Piccadilly Arc SW1	59	K2
Piccadilly Circ W1	59	M1
Piccadilly Pl W1	59	L1
Pickard St EC1	56	G2
Pickering Pl SW1	59	L3
Pickfords Wf N1	57	H1
Pickwick St SE1	61	H5
Picton Pl W1	54	G9
Pilgrimage St SE1	61	K5
Pilton Pl SE17	61	J10
Pimlico SW1	59	K10
Pimlico Rd SW1	58	F10
Pimlico Wk N1	57	M2
Pindar St EC2	57	M6
Pineapple Ct SW1	59	K6
Pine St EC1	56	D4
Pitfield Est N1	57	L2
Pitfield St N1	57	M3
Pitt's Head Ms W1	58	G3
Plantain Pl SE1	61	K4
Platina St EC2	57	L4
Playhouse Yd EC4	56	F9
Plaza Shop Cen, The W1	55	L8
Pleydell Ct EC4	56	E9
Pleydell St EC4	56	E9
Plough Ct EC3	57	L10
Plough Pl EC4	56	E8
Plough Yd EC2	57	N5
Plumtree Ct EC4	56	E8
Plympton Pl NW8	54	B5
Plympton St NW8	54	B5
Pocock St SE1	60	F4
Poland St W1	55	L9
Pollen St W1	55	J9
Polperro Ms SE11	60	E8
Polygon Rd NW1	55	M1
Ponsonby Pl SW1	59	N10
Ponsonby Ter SW1	59	N10
Pont St SW1	58	D7
Pont St Ms SW1	58	D7
Pontypool Pl SE1	60	F4
Pooles Bldgs EC1	56	D5
Pope St SE1	61	N5
Poppins Ct EC4	56	F9
Porchester Pl W2	54	C9
Porlock St SE1	61	K4
Porter St SE1	61	J2
Porter St W1	54	E6
Portland Ms W1	55	L9
Portland Pl W1	55	J7
Portland St SE17	61	K10
Portman Cl W1	54	E8
Portman Gate NW1	54	C5
Portman Ms S W1	54	F9
Portman Sq W1	54	E8
Portman St W1	54	F9
Portpool La EC1	56	D6
Portsea Ms W2	54	C9
Portsea Pl W2	54	C9
Portsmouth St WC2	56	B9
Portsoken St E1	57	P10
Portugal St WC2	56	B9
Post Office Ct EC3	57	L9
Potier St SE1	61	L7
Potters Flds SE1	61	N3
Poultry EC2	57	K9
Powis Pl WC1	56	A5
Praed Ms W2	54	A8
Praed St W2	54	B7
Pratt Wk SE11	60	C8
President St EC1	57	H2
Preston Cl SE1	61	M8
Prestwood St N1	57	J1
Price's St SE1	60	G3
Prideaux Pl WC1	56	C2
Priest Ct EC2	57	H8
Primrose Hill EC4	56	E9
Primrose St EC2	57	M6
Prince Albert Rd NW1	54	C1
Prince Albert Rd NW8	54	C1
Prince of Wales Gate SW7	58	B4

Street	Page	Grid
Prince of Wales Pas NW1	55	K3
Prince Regent Ms NW1	55	K3
Prince's Arc SW1	59	L2
Princes Gdns SW7	58	A6
Princes Gate SW7	58	B5
Princes Gate Ct SW7	58	A5
Princes Gate Ms SW7	58	A6
Princes Pl SW1	59	L2
Princess Louise Cl W2	54	A6
Princess St SE1	60	G7
Princes St EC2	57	K8
Princes St W1	55	J9
Princeton St WC1	56	B6
Printers Inn Ct EC4	56	D8
Printer St EC4	56	E8
Printing Ho Yd E2	57	N2
Prioress St SE1	61	L7
Procter St WC1	56	B7
Providence Ct W1	54	G10
Provost Est N1	57	K2
Provost St N1	57	K3
Prudent Pas EC2	57	J8
Pudding La EC3	61	L1
Puddle Dock EC4	56	G10
Puma Ct E1	57	P6
Pump Ct EC4	56	D9
Purbrook Est SE1	61	N5
Purbrook St SE1	61	N6
Quadrangle, The W2	54	B8
Quadrangle Cl SE1	61	M8
Quadrant Arc W1	59	L1
Quaker Ct E1	57	P5
Quaker St E1	57	P5
Quality Ct WC2	56	D8
Quebec Ms W1	54	E9
Queen Anne Ms W1	55	J7
Queen Anne's Gate SW1	59	M5
Queen Anne St W1	55	H8
Queen Elizabeth St SE1	61	N4
Queenhithe EC4	57	J10
Queen's Head Pas EC4	57	H8
Queens Head Yd SE1	61	K3
Queen Sq WC1	56	A5
Queen Sq Pl WC1	56	A5
Queen St EC4	57	J10
Queen St W1	59	H2
Queen St Pl EC4	61	J1
Queen's Wk SE1	60	B3
Queen's Wk SW1	59	K3
Queens Yd WC1	55	L5
Queen Victoria St EC4	56	G10
Quick St N1	56	G1
Quick St Ms N1	56	F1
Quilp St SE1	61	H4
Radcliffe Rd SE1	61	N6
Radnor Ms W2	54	A9
Radnor Pl W2	54	B9
Radnor St EC1	57	J3
Railway App SE1	61	L2
Railway St N1	56	A1
Rainsford St W2	54	B8
Ramillies Pl W1	55	K9
Ramillies St W1	55	K9
Rampayne St SW1	59	M10
Randall Rd SE11	60	B10
Randall Row SE11	60	B9
Ranelagh Gro SW1	58	G10
Rangoon St EC3	57	P9
Ranston St NW1	54	B6
Raphael St SW7	58	D5
Rathbone Pl W1	55	M8
Rathbone St W1	55	L7
Ravey St EC2	57	M4
Rawlings St SW3	58	D8
Rawstorne Pl EC1	56	F2
Rawstorne St EC1	56	F2
Raymond Bldgs WC1	56	C6
Ray St EC1	56	E5
Ray St Br EC1	56	E5
Redchurch St E2	57	P4
Redcross Way SE1	61	J4
Redhill St NW1	55	J2
Red Lion Ct EC4	56	E8
Red Lion Sq WC1	56	B7
Red Lion St WC1	56	B6
Red Lion Yd W1	58	G2
Red Pl W1	54	F10
Redvers St N1	57	N2
Reedworth St SE11	60	E9
Reeves Ms W1	58	F1
Regan Way N1	57	M1
Regency Pl SW1	59	N8
Regency St SW1	59	M8
Regent Pl W1	55	L10
Regent's Park NW1	54	G1
Regent's Pk Est NW1	55	K3
Regent Sq WC1	56	A3
Regent St SW1	59	M1
Regent St W1	55	J8
Regnart Bldgs NW1	55	L4
Reliance Sq EC2	57	N4
Relton Ms SW7	58	C6
Rembrandt Cl SW1	58	F9
Remington St N1	56	G1
Remnant St WC2	56	B8
Renfrew Rd SE11	60	F8
Rennie St SE1	60	F2
Rephidim St SE1	61	M7
Retford St N1	57	N1
Rex Pl W1	58	G1
Richardson's Ms W1	55	K5
Richards Pl SW3	58	C8
Richbell Pl WC1	56	B6
Richmond Bldgs W1	55	M9
Richmond Ms W1	55	M9
Richmond Ter SW1	59	P4
Ridgmount Gdns WC1	55	M5
Ridgmount Pl WC1	55	M6
Ridgmount St WC1	55	M6
Riding Ho St W1	55	K7
Riley Rd SE1	61	N6
Ring, The W2	54	B10
Risborough St SE1	60	G4
Rising Sun Ct EC1	56	G7
River St EC1	56	D2
Rivington Pl EC2	57	N3
Rivington St EC2	57	M3
Robert Adam St W1	54	F8
Roberts Ms SW1	58	F7
Robert's Pl EC1	56	E4
Robert St NW1	55	J3
Robert St WC2	60	A1
Robert Dashwood Way SE17	61	H9
Rochelle St E2	57	P3
Rochester Row SW1	59	L8
Rochester St SW1	59	M7
Rochester Wk SE1	61	K2
Rockingham Est SE1	61	H7
Rockingham St SE1	61	H7
Rocliffe St N1	56	G1
Rodmarton St W1	54	E7
Rodney Pl SE17	61	J8
Rodney Rd SE17	61	J8
Roger St WC1	56	C5
Rolls Bldgs EC4	56	D8
Rolls Pas EC4	56	D8
Romilly St W1	55	M10
Romney Ms W1	54	F6
Romney St SW1	59	N7
Rood La EC3	57	M10
Ropemaker St EC2	57	K6
Roper La SE1	61	N5
Roscoe St EC1	57	J5
Rose All SE1	61	J2
Rose & Crown Ct EC2	57	H8
Rose & Crown Yd SW1	59	L2
Rosebery Av EC1	56	D5
Rosebery Sq EC1	56	D5
Rose Ct E1	57	P7
Rosemoor St SW3	58	D9
Rose Sq SW3	58	A10
Rose St EC4	56	G8
Rose St WC2	55	P10
Rosoman Pl EC1	56	E4
Rosoman St EC1	56	E3
Rossmore Ct NW1	54	D4
Rossmore Rd NW1	54	C5
Rotary St SE1	60	F6
Rotherham Wk SE1	60	F3
Rothsay St SE1	61	M6
Rotten Row SW1	58	F4
Rotten Row SW7	58	B4
Roupell St SE1	60	E3
Rowcross St SE1	61	P10
Royal Arc W1	59	K1
Royal Av SW3	58	D10
Royal Ex Av EC3	57	L9
Royal Ex Bldgs EC3	57	L9
Royal Oak Yd SE1	61	N5
Royal Opera Arc SW1	59	M2
Royal St SE1	60	C6
Royalty Ms W1	55	M9
Rufus St N1	57	M3
Rugby St WC1	56	B5
Rupert Ct W1	55	M10
Rupert St W1	55	M10
Rushworth St SE1	60	G4
Russell Ct SW1	59	L3
Russell Sq WC1	55	P5
Russell St WC2	56	A10
Russia Ct EC2	57	J8
Russia Row EC2	57	J9
Rutherford St SW1	59	M8
Rutland Gdns SW7	58	C5
Rutland Gdns Ms SW7	58	C5
Rutland Gate SW7	58	C5
Rutland Gate Ms SW7	58	B5
Rutland Ms E SW7	58	B6
Rutland Ms S SW7	58	B6
Rutland Pl EC1	57	H5
Rutland St SW7	58	C6
Ryder Ct SW1	59	L2
Ryder St SW1	59	L2
Ryder Yd SW1	59	L2
Rysbrack St SW3	58	D6
Sackville St W1	59	L1
Saddle Yd W1	59	H2
Saffron Hill EC1	56	E5
Saffron St EC1	56	E6
Sage Way WC1	56	B3
Sail St SE11	60	C8
St. Albans Ct EC2	57	J8
St. Albans St SW1	59	M1
St. Alphage Gdns EC2	57	J7
St. Alphage Highwalk EC2	57	K7
St. Andrew's Hill EC4	56	G10
St. Andrews Pl NW1	55	J4
St. Andrew St EC4	56	E7
St. Anne's Ct W1	55	M9
St. Ann's La SW1	59	N6
St. Ann's St SW1	59	N6
St. Anselm's Pl W1	55	H9
St. Barnabas St SW1	58	G10
St. Benet's Pl EC3	57	L10
St. Botolph Row EC3	57	P9
St. Botolph St EC3	57	P9
St. Brides Av EC4	56	F9
St. Bride's Pas EC4	56	F9
St. Bride St EC4	56	F8
St. Catherine's Ms SW3	58	D8
St. Chad's Pl WC1	56	A2
St. Chad's St WC1	56	A2
St. Christopher's Pl W1	54	G8
St. Clare St EC3	57	P9
St. Clement's La WC2	56	C9
St. Cross St EC1	56	E6
St. Dunstan's All EC3	57	M10
St. Dunstan's Hill EC3	61	M1
St. Dunstan's La EC3	61	M1
St. Ermin's Hill SW1	59	M6
St. Georges Circ SE1	60	F6
St. Georges Ct EC4	56	F8
St. George's Dr SW1	59	K10
St. Georges Flds W2	54	C9
St. Georges La EC3	57	M10
St. Georges Ms SE1	60	E6
St. Georges Rd SE1	60	E6
St. George's Sq SW1	59	M10
St. George St W1	55	J9
St. Giles High St WC2	55	N8
St. Giles Pas WC2	55	N9
St. Helena St WC1	56	D3
St. Helen's Pl EC3	57	M8
St. James's SW1	59	L3
St. James's Ct SW1	59	L6
St. James's Mkt SW1	59	M1
St. James's Pas EC3	57	N9
St. James's Pl SW1	59	K3
St. James's Sq SW1	59	L2
St. James's St SW1	59	K2
St. James's Wk EC1	56	F4
St. John's Est N1	57	L1
St. John's Est SE1	61	P4
St. John's La EC1	56	F5
St. John's Path EC1	56	F5
St. John's Pl EC1	56	F5
St. John's Sq EC1	56	F5
St. John St EC1	56	G5
St. John's Wd Ct NW8	54	A3
St. John's Wd High St NW8	54	A1
St. Katherine's Row EC3	57	N9
St. Leonards Ct N1	57	J2
St. Luke's EC1	57	J4
St. Luke's Cl EC1	57	J4
St. Luke's Est EC1	57	K3
St. Luke's St SW3	58	B10
St. Margaret's Ct SE1	61	J3
St. Margaret's St SW1	59	P5
St. Martin's La WC2	55	P10
St. Martin's-le-Grand EC1	57	H8
St. Martin's Ms WC2	59	P1
St. Martin's Pl WC2	59	P1
St. Martin's St WC2	59	N1
St. Mary at Hill EC3	61	M1
St. Mary Axe EC3	57	M9
St. Mary's Gdns SE11	60	E8
St. Mary's Wk SE11	60	E8
St. Matthew St SW1	59	M7
St. Michael's All EC3	57	L9
St. Michaels St W2	54	A8
St. Olaves Ct EC2	57	K9
St. Olave's Est SE1	61	N4
St. Olaves Gdns SE11	60	D8
St. Oswulf St SW1	59	N9
St. Pancras WC1	55	P3
St. Paul's Chyd EC4	56	G9
St. Peter's La EC1	57	L9
St. Saviour's Est SE1	61	P6
St. Stephens Row EC4	57	K9
St. Swithin's La EC4	57	K10
St. Thomas St SE1	61	K3
St. Vincent St W1	54	G7
Salamanca Pl SE1	60	B9
Salamanca St SE1	60	A9
Sale Pl W2	54	B7
Salisbury Cl SE17	61	K8
Salisbury Ct EC4	56	F9
Salisbury Pl W1	54	D6
Salisbury Sq EC4	56	F9
Salisbury St NW8	54	A5
Salters Hall Ct EC4	57	K10
Samford St NW8	54	A5
Samuel Lewis Trust Dws SW3	58	B9
Sancroft St SE11	60	C10
Sanctuary, The SW1	59	N5
Sanctuary St SE1	61	J5
Sandell St SE1	60	D4
Sandland St WC1	56	C7
Sandwich St WC1	55	P3
Sandy's Row E1	57	N7
Sans Wk EC1	56	E4
Saperton Wk SE11	60	C8
Sapperton Ct EC1	57	H4
Saracen's Head Yd EC3	57	N9
Sardinia St WC2	56	B9
Saunders St SE11	60	D8
Savage Gdns EC3	57	N10
Savile Row W1	55	K10
Savoy Bldgs WC2	60	B1
Savoy Ct WC2	60	A1
Savoy Hill WC2	60	B1
Savoy Pl WC2	60	A1
Savoy Row WC2	56	B10
Savoy St WC2	56	B10
Savoy Way WC2	60	B1
Sawyer St SE1	61	H4
Scala St W1	55	L6
Sclater St E1	57	P4
Scoresby St SE1	60	F3
Scotland Pl SW1	59	P2
Scotswood St EC1	56	E4
Scovell Cres SE1	61	H5
Scovell Rd SE1	61	H5
Scrutton St EC2	57	M5
Seaford St WC1	56	A3
Searles Rd SE1	61	L8
Seaton Cl SE11	60	E10
Sebastian St EC1	56	G3
Secker St SE1	60	D3
Sedan Way SE17	61	M10
Sedding St SW1	58	F8
Seddon St WC1	56	C3
Sedley Pl W1	55	H9
Seething La EC3	61	N1
Sekforde St EC1	56	F5
Semley Pl SW1	58	G9
Serjeants Inn EC4	56	E9
Serle St WC2	56	C8
Sermon La EC4	57	H9
Serpentine Rd W2	58	D3
Setchell Rd SE1	61	P8
Setchell Way SE1	61	P8
Seville St SW1	58	E5
Seward St EC1	56	G4
Seymour Ms W1	54	F8
Seymour Pl W1	54	D7
Seymour St W1	54	D9
Seymour St W2	54	D9
Shad Thames SE1	61	P3
Shaftesbury Av W1	55	M10
Shaftesbury Av WC2	55	M10
Shaftesbury St N1	57	J1
Shafto Ms SW1	58	D7
Shakespeare Twr EC2	57	J6
Shand St SE1	61	M4
Shavers Pl SW1	59	M1
Sheffield St WC2	56	B9
Shelton St WC2	55	P9
Shenfield St N1	57	N1
Shepherdess Pl N1	57	J2
Shepherd Mkt W1	59	H2
Shepherd's Pl W1	54	F10
Shepherd St W1	59	H3
Sheraton St W1	55	M9
Sherborne La EC4	57	K10
Sherlock Ms W1	54	F6
Sherwood St W1	55	L10
Shillibeer Pl W1	54	C6
Ship & Mermaid Row SE1	61	L4
Ship Tavern Pas EC3	57	M10
Shipwright Yd SE1	61	M3
Shoe La EC4	56	E8
Shoreditch E1	57	P5
Shoreditch High St E1	57	N5
Shoreditch Ho N1	57	L3
Shorncliffe Rd SE1	61	P10
Shorter St E1	57	P10
Shorts Gdns WC2	55	P9
Short St SE1	60	E4
Shouldham St W1	54	C7
Shropshire Pl WC1	55	L5
Shroton St NW1	54	B6
Sicilian Av WC1	56	A7
Siddons La NW1	54	E5
Sidford Pl SE1	60	C7
Sidmouth St WC1	56	A3
Sidney Gro EC1	56	F1
Silbury St N1	57	K2
Silex St SE1	60	G5
Silk St EC2	57	J6
Silver Pl W1	55	L10
Silvester St SE1	61	J5
Simla Ho SE1	61	L5
Singer St EC2	57	L3
Sise La EC4	57	K9
Skinner Pl SW1	58	F9
Skinners La EC4	57	J10
Skinner St EC1	56	E3
Slingsby Pl WC2	55	P10
Sloane Av SW3	58	B8
Sloane Ct E SW3	58	F10
Sloane Ct W SW3	58	F10
Sloane Gdns SW1	58	F9
Sloane Sq SW1	58	F9
Sloane St SW1	58	E8
Sloane Ter SW1	58	E8
Smart's Pl WC2	56	A8
Smithfield St EC1	56	F7
Smith's Ct W1	55	L10
Smith Sq SW1	59	P7
Smith St SW3	58	D10
Smokehouse Yd EC1	56	G6
Snowden St EC2	57	M5
Snow Hill EC1	56	F7
Snow Hill Ct EC1	56	F7
Snowsfields SE1	61	L4
Soho W1	55	M10
Soho Sq W1	55	M8
Soho St W1	55	M8
Soley Ms WC1	56	D2
Somers Cres W2	54	B9
Somers Ms W2	54	B9
Somers Town NW1	55	N2
Southall Pl SE1	61	K5
Southampton Bldgs WC2	56	D8
Southampton Pl WC1	56	A7
Southampton Row WC1	56	A6
Southampton St WC2	56	A10
South Audley St W1	58	G1
South Carriage Dr SW1	58	D4
South Carriage Dr SW7	58	A5
Southcott Ms NW8	54	B1
South Cres WC1	55	M7
South Eaton Pl SW1	58	G8
South Molton La W1	55	H9
South Molton St W1	55	H9
South Par SW3	58	A10
South Pl EC2	57	L6
South Pl Ms EC2	57	L7
South Sq WC1	56	D7
South St W1	58	G2
South Ter SW7	58	B8
Southwark Br EC4	61	J2
Southwark Br SE1	61	J2
Southwark Br Rd SE1	60	G6
Southwark St SE1	60	G2
Southwick Ms W2	54	A8
Southwick Pl W2	54	B9
Southwick St W2	54	B8
Spafield St EC1	56	D4
Spa Grn Est EC1	56	E2
Spanish Pl W1	54	G8
Spa Rd SE16	61	P8
Speedy Pl WC1	55	P3
Spencer St EC1	56	F3
Spenser St SW1	59	L6
Spital Sq E1	57	N6
Spital Yd E1	57	N6
Sprimont Pl SW3	58	D10
Spring Gdns SW1	59	N2
Spring Ms W1	54	E6
Spurgeon St SE1	61	K7
Spur Rd SE1	60	D4
Spur Rd SW1	59	K5
Stables Way SE11	60	D10
Stable Yd SW1	59	K4
Stable Yd Rd SW1	59	K3
Stacey St WC2	55	N9
Stackhouse St SW3	58	D6
Stafford Pl SW1	59	K6
Stafford St W1	59	K2
Staff St EC1	57	L2
Stag Pl SW1	59	K6
Stainer St SE1	61	L3
Staining La EC2	57	J8
Stalbridge St NW1	54	C6
Stamford St SE1	60	D3
Stamp Pl E2	57	P2
Standard Pl EC2	57	N3
Stanford Pl SE17	61	M9
Stanford St SW1	59	M9
Stanhope Gate W1	58	G2
Stanhope Par NW1	55	K2
Stanhope Pl W2	54	D9
Stanhope Row W1	59	H3
Stanhope St NW1	55	K3
Stanhope Ter W2	54	A10
Stanway Ct N1	57	N1
Stanworth St SE1	61	P5
Staple Inn WC1	56	D7
Staple Inn Bldgs WC1	56	D7
Staple St SE1	61	L5
Star All EC3	57	N10
Starcross St NW1	55	L3
Star St W2	54	A8
Star Yd WC2	56	D8
Station App SE1	60	C3
Stead St SE17	61	J8
Stedham Pl WC1	55	P8
Steedman St SE17	61	H9
Stephen Ms W1	55	M7
Stephenson Way NW1	55	L4
Stephen St W1	55	M7
Sterling St SW7	58	C6
Sterry St SE1	61	K5
Stevens St SE1	61	N6
Steward St E1	57	N7
Stewart's Gro SW3	58	A10
Stew La EC4	57	H10

Street	Map	Grid
Stillington St SW1	59	L8
Stone Bldgs WC2	56	C7
Stonecutter St EC4	56	F8
Stone Ho Ct EC3	57	M8
Stones End St SE1	61	H5
Stoney La E1	57	N8
Stoney St SE1	61	K2
Store St WC1	55	M7
Storey's Gate SW1	59	N5
Stoughton Cl SE11	60	C9
Stourcliffe St W1	54	D9
Strand WC2	55	P10
Strand WC2	59	P1
Strand La WC2	56	C10
Stratford Pl W1	55	H9
Strathearn Pl W2	54	A10
Stratton St W1	59	J2
Streatham St WC1	55	N8
Strouts Pl E2	57	P2
Strutton Grd SW1	59	M6
Strype St E1	57	P7
Studio Pl SW1	58	E5
Studland St SE17	61	K10
Stukeley St WC2	56	A8
Sturge St SE1	61	H4
Sturt St N1	57	J1
Sudeley St N1	56	G1
Sudrey St SE1	61	H5
Suffolk La EC4	57	K10
Suffolk Pl SW1	59	N2
Suffolk St SW1	59	N2
Sugar Quay Wk EC3	61	N1
Sullivan Rd SE11	60	E8
Summer St EC1	56	D5
Sumner St SW7	58	A9
Sumner Pl Ms SW7	58	A9
Sumner St SE1	60	G2
Sun Ct EC3	57	L9
Sun St EC2	57	M7
Sun St Pas EC2	57	M7
Surrey Lo SE1	60	D7
Surrey Row SE1	60	F4
Surrey Sq SE17	61	M10
Surrey St WC2	56	C10
Surrey Ter SE17	61	N10
Sussex Ms E W2	54	A9
Sussex Ms W W2	54	A10
Sussex Pl NW1	54	D3
Sussex Pl W2	54	A9
Sussex Sq W2	54	A10
Sutherland Row SW1	59	J10
Sutherland St SW1	59	H10
Sutton Est SW3	58	C10
Sutton La EC1	56	G5
Sutton Row W1	55	N8
Sutton's Way EC1	57	J3
Sutton Wk SE1	60	C3
Swain St NW8	54	B4
Swallow Pas W1	55	J9
Swallow Pl W1	55	J9
Swallow St W1	59	L1
Swanfield St E2	57	P3
Swan La EC4	61	K1
Swan Mead SE1	61	M7
Swan St SE1	61	J6
Swinton Pl WC1	56	B2
Swinton St WC1	56	B2
Swiss Ct W1	59	N1
Sycamore St EC1	57	H5
Sydney Cl SW3	58	A9
Sydney Ms SW3	58	A9
Sydney Pl SW7	58	A9
Sydney St SW3	58	B10
Symister Ms N1	57	M3
Symons St SW3	58	E9
Tabard Gdn Est SE1	61	L5
Tabard St SE1	61	K5
Tabernacle St EC2	57	L5
Tachbrook Ms SW1	59	K8
Tachbrook St SW1	59	L9
Talbot Ct EC3	57	L10
Talbot Sq W2	54	A9
Talbot Yd SE1	61	K3
Tallis St EC4	56	E10
Tankerton St WC1	56	A3
Tanner St SE1	61	N5
Tanswell Est SE1	60	E5
Tanswell St SE1	60	D5
Taplow St N1	57	J1
Tarn St SE1	61	H7
Tarrant Pl W1	54	D7
Tatum St SE17	61	L9
Taunton Ms NW1	54	D5
Taunton Pl NW1	54	D4
Tavistock Pl WC1	55	N4
Tavistock Sq WC1	55	N4
Tavistock St WC2	56	A10
Taviton St WC1	55	M4
Tavy Cl SE11	60	E10
Telegraph St EC2	57	K8
Temple Av EC4	56	E10
Temple La EC4	56	E9
Temple Pl WC2	56	C10
Temple W Ms SE11	60	F7
Tenison Ct W1	55	K10
Tenison Way SE1	60	D3
Tennis St SE1	61	K4
Tenterden St W1	55	J9
Tenter Grd E1	57	P7
Terminus Pl SW1	59	J7
Thanet St WC1	55	P3
Thavies Inn EC1	56	E8
Thaxted Ct N1	57	K1
Thayer St W1	54	G7
Theed St SE1	60	D3
Theobald's Rd WC1	56	B6
Theobald St SE1	61	K7
Theseus Wk N1	56	G1
Thirleby Rd SW1	59	L7
Thomas Doyle St SE1	60	F6
Thoresby St N1	57	J2
Thorndike St SW1	59	M10
Thorney St SW1	59	P8
Thornhaugh Ms WC1	55	N5
Thornhaugh St WC1	55	N6
Thornton Pl W1	54	E6
Thrale St SE1	61	J3
Threadneedle St EC2	57	L9
Three Barrels Wk EC4	57	J10
Three Cups Yd WC1	56	C7
Three Kings Yd W1	55	H10
Three Oak La SE1	61	P4
Three Quays Wk EC3	61	N1
Throgmorton Av EC2	57	L8
Throgmorton St EC2	57	L8
Thrush St SE17	61	H10
Thurloe Cl SW7	58	B8
Thurloe Pl SW7	58	A8
Thurloe Pl Ms SW7	58	A8
Thurloe Sq SW7	58	B8
Thurloe St SW7	58	A8
Thurlow St SE17	61	L10
Tilney Ct EC1	57	J4
Tilney St W1	58	G2
Timber St EC1	57	H4
Tinworth St SE11	60	A10
Tisdall Pl SE17	61	L9
Titchborne Row W2	54	C9
Tiverton St SE1	61	H7
Tokenhouse Yd EC2	57	K8
Tolmers Sq NW1	55	L4
Tompion St EC1	56	F3
Tonbridge St WC1	55	P2
Took's Ct EC4	56	D8
Tooley St SE1	61	L2
Topham St EC1	56	D4
Torrens St EC1	56	E1
Torrington Pl WC1	55	L6
Torrington Sq WC1	55	N5
Tothill St SW1	59	M5
Tottenham Ct Rd W1	55	L5
Tottenham Ms W1	55	L6
Tottenham St W1	55	L7
Toulmin St SE1	61	H5
Tower 42 EC2	57	M8
Tower Br E1	61	P3
Tower Br SE1	61	P3
Tower Br App E1	61	P2
Tower Br Piazza SE1	61	P3
Tower Br Rd SE1	61	M7
Tower Ct WC2	55	P9
Tower Hill EC3	61	N1
Tower Pl EC3	61	N1
Tower Royal EC4	57	J10
Tower St WC2	55	N9
Townley St SE17	61	K10
Townsend St SE17	61	L9
Toynbee St E1	57	P7
Trafalgar Sq SW1	59	N2
Trafalgar Sq WC2	59	N2
Trafalgar St SE17	61	K10
Transept St NW1	54	B7
Trebeck St W1	59	H2
Tresham Cres NW8	54	B4
Treveris St SE1	60	F3
Trevor Pl SW7	58	C5
Trevor Sq SW7	58	D5
Trevor St SW7	58	C5
Triangle, The EC1	56	G4
Trig La EC4	57	H10
Trinity Ch Sq SE1	61	J6
Trinity Pl EC3	61	P1
Trinity Sq EC3	61	N1
Trinity St SE1	61	J5
Trio Pl SE1	61	J5
Triton Sq NW1	55	K4
Trundle St SE1	61	H4
Tryon St SW3	58	D10
Tudor St EC4	56	E10
Tufton St SW1	59	N6
Turk's Head Yd EC1	56	F6
Turks Row SW3	58	E10
Turnagain La EC4	56	F8
Turnmill St EC1	56	E5
Turnpike Ho EC1	56	G3
Turpentine La SW1	59	J10
Turquand St SE17	61	J9
Turville St E2	57	P4
Tweezer's All WC2	56	D10
Twyford Pl WC2	56	B8
Tyburn Way W1	54	E10
Tyers Est SE1	61	M4
Tyers Gate SE1	61	M4
Tyers St SE11	60	B10
Tyler's Ct W1	55	M9
Tysoe St EC1	56	D3
Udall St SW1	59	L9
Ufford St SE1	60	E4
Ulster Pl NW1	55	H5
Ulster Ter NW1	55	H4
Undershaft EC3	57	M8
Underwood Row N1	57	J2
Underwood St N1	57	J2
Union Ct EC2	57	M8
Union St SE1	60	G3
Union Wk E2	57	N2
Union Wf N1	57	H1
University St WC1	55	L5
Unwin Rd SW7	58	A6
Upnor Way SE17	61	N10
Upper Belgrave St SW1	58	G6
Upper Berkeley St W1	54	D9
Upper Brook St W1	58	F1
Upper Grosvenor St W1	58	F1
Upper Grd SE1	60	D2
Upper James St W1	55	L10
Upper John St W1	55	L10
Upper Marsh SE1	60	C6
Upper Montagu St W1	54	D6
Upper St. Martin's La WC2	55	P10
Upper Tachbrook St SW1	59	K8
Upper Thames St EC4	56	G10
Upper Wimpole St W1	55	H6
Upper Woburn Pl WC1	55	N3
Valentine Pl SE1	60	F4
Valentine Row SE1	60	F5
Vandon Pas SW1	59	L6
Vandon St SW1	59	L6
Vandy St EC2	57	M5
Vane St SW1	59	L8
Varndell St NW1	55	K2
Vauxhall Br Rd SW1	59	L8
Vauxhall Wk SE11	60	B10
Venables St NW8	54	A6
Vere St W1	55	H9
Vernon Pl WC1	56	A7
Vernon Ri WC1	56	C2
Vernon Sq WC1	56	C2
Verulam Bldgs WC1	56	C6
Verulam St WC1	56	D6
Vestry St N1	57	K2
Victoria Av EC2	57	N7
Victoria Embk EC4	60	B1
Victoria Embk SW1	60	A4
Victoria Embk WC2	60	B1
Victoria Pl SW1	59	J8
Victoria Sq SW1	59	J6
Victoria St SW1	59	K7
Victory Pl SE17	61	J8
Vigo St W1	59	K1
Villiers St WC2	59	P1
Vincent Sq SW1	59	L8
Vincent St SW1	59	M8
Vince St EC1	57	L3
Vinegar Yd SE1	61	M4
Vine Hill EC1	56	D5
Vine La SE1	61	N3
Vine St EC3	57	P10
Vine St W1	59	L1
Vine St Br EC1	56	E5
Vine Yd SE1	61	J4
Vineyard Wk EC1	56	D4
Vintners Ct EC4	57	J10
Virgil Pl W1	54	D7
Virgil St SE1	60	C6
Virginia Rd E2	57	P3
Viscount St EC1	57	H5
Wadding St SE17	61	K9
Waithman St EC4	56	F9
Wakefield Ms WC1	56	A3
Wakefield St WC1	56	A4
Wakley St EC1	56	F2
Walbrook EC4	57	K10
Walcorde Av SE17	61	J9
Walcot Sq SE11	60	E8
Walcott St SW1	59	L8
Walkers Ct W1	55	M10
Wallis All SE1	61	J4
Wallside EC2	57	J7
Walmer Pl W1	54	D6
Walmer St W1	54	D6
Walnut Tree Wk SE11	60	D8
Walpole St SW3	58	D10
Walters Cl SE17	61	J9
Walton Pl SW3	58	D6
Walton St SW3	58	C8
Walworth SE17	61	H10
Walworth Rd SE1	61	H8
Wansey St SE17	61	H9
Wardens Gro SE1	61	H3
Wardour Ms W1	55	L9
Wardour St W1	55	M10
Wardrobe Ter EC4	56	G9
Warner St EC1	56	D5
Warner Yd EC1	56	D5
Warren Ms W1	55	K5
Warren St W1	55	J5
Warwick Ct WC1	56	C7
Warwick Ho St SW1	59	N2
Warwick La EC4	56	G9
Warwick Pas EC4	56	G8
Warwick Pl N SW1	59	K9
Warwick Row SW1	59	J6
Warwick Sq EC4	56	G8
Warwick Sq SW1	59	K10
Warwick Sq Ms SW1	59	K9
Warwick St W1	55	L10
Warwick Way SW1	59	K9
Warwick Yd EC1	57	J5
Water Gdns, The W2	54	C8
Watergate EC4	56	F10
Watergate Wk WC2	60	A2
Waterhouse Sq EC1	56	D7
Water La EC3	61	M1
Waterloo Br SE1	60	B1
Waterloo Br WC2	60	B1
Waterloo Pl SW1	59	M2
Waterloo Rd SE1	60	D4
Waterson St E2	57	N2
Water St WC2	56	C10
Watling Ct EC4	57	J9
Watling St EC4	57	H9
Watson's Ms W1	54	C7
Watts Way SW7	58	A6
Waverton St W1	58	G2
Webber Row SE1	60	E6
Webber St SE1	60	E4
Webb St SE1	61	M7
Wedgwood Ms W1	55	N9
Weighhouse St W1	54	G9
Weir's Pas NW1	55	N2
Welbeck St W1	55	H8
Welbeck Way W1	55	H8
Well Ct EC4	57	J9
Weller St SE1	61	H4
Wellesley Pl NW1	55	M3
Wellesley Ter N1	57	J2
Wellington Pl NW8	54	A2
Wellington Sq SW3	58	D10
Wellington St WC2	56	A10
Wells Ms W1	55	L7
Wells Sq WC1	56	B3
Wells St W1	55	K7
Wenlock Ct N1	57	L1
Wenlock St N1	57	J1
Wentworth St E1	57	P8
Werrington St NW1	55	L1
Wesley Cl SE17	60	G9
Wesley St W1	54	G7
West Carriage Dr W2	58	A3
West Cen St WC1	55	P8
West Eaton Pl SW1	58	F8
West Eaton Pl Ms SW1	58	F8
West Gdn Pl W2	54	C9
West Halkin St SW1	58	F6
West Harding St EC4	56	E8
Westland Pl N1	57	K2
West Ms SW1	59	J9
Westminster SW1	59	K6
Westminster Br SE1	60	A5
Westminster Br SW1	60	A5
Westminster Br Rd SE1	60	C5
Westminster Gdns SW1	59	P8
Westmoreland St W1	54	G7
West One Shop Cen W1	54	G9
Weston Ri WC1	56	C1
Weston St SE1	61	L6
West Poultry Av EC1	56	F7
West Smithfield EC1	56	F7
West Sq SE11	60	F7
West St WC2	55	N9
West Warwick Pl SW1	59	K9
Weymouth Ms W1	55	H6
Weymouth St W1	54	G7
Whalebone Ct EC2	57	L8
Wharton St WC1	56	C3
Wheatley St W1	54	G7
Wheler St E1	57	P5
Whetstone Pk WC2	56	B8
Whichcote St SE1	60	D3
Whidborne St WC1	56	A3
Whiskin St EC1	56	F3
Whitby St E1	57	P4
Whitcomb St WC2	59	N1
Whitecross Pl EC2	57	L6
Whitecross St EC1	57	J4
Whitefriars St EC4	56	E9
Whitehall SW1	59	P2
Whitehall Ct SW1	59	P3
Whitehall Gdns SW1	59	P3
Whitehall Pl SW1	59	P3
White Hart St EC4	56	G8
White Hart St SE11	60	E10
White Hart Yd SE1	61	K3
Whitehaven St NW8	54	B5
Whitehead's Gro SW3	58	C10
White Horse All EC1	56	F6
White Horse Ms SE1	60	E6
White Horse St W1	59	H3
White Horse Yd EC2	57	K8
White Kennett St E1	57	N8
White Lion Ct EC3	57	M9
White Lion Hill EC4	56	G10
White Lion St N1	56	D1
Whites Grds SE1	61	N5
Whites Grds Est SE1	61	N4
White's Row E1	57	P7
Whitfield Pl W1	55	K5
Whitfield St W1	55	M7
Whitgift St SE11	60	B8
Whittaker St SW1	58	F9
Whittington Av EC3	57	M9
Whittlesey St SE1	60	D3
Wickham St SE11	60	B10
Wicklow St WC1	56	B2
Widegate St E1	57	N7
Wigmore Pl W1	55	H8
Wigmore St W1	54	F9
Wilbraham Pl SW1	58	E8
Wilcox Pl SW1	59	L7
Wild Ct WC2	56	B8
Wild's Rents SE1	61	M6
Wild St WC2	56	A9
Wilfred St SW1	59	K6
Wilks Pl N1	57	N1
William IV St WC2	59	P1
William Ms SW1	58	E5
William Rd NW1	55	J3
William St SW1	58	E5
Willoughby St WC1	55	P7
Willow Ct EC2	57	M4
Willow Pl SW1	59	L8
Willow St EC2	57	M4
Willow Wk SE1	61	N8
Wilmington Sq WC1	56	D3
Wilmington St WC1	56	D3
Wilson St EC2	57	L6
Wilton Cres SW1	58	F5
Wilton Ms SW1	58	G6
Wilton Pl SW1	58	F5
Wilton Rd SW1	59	J7
Wilton Row SW1	58	F5
Wilton St SW1	59	H6
Wilton Ter SW1	58	F6
Wiltshire Cl SW3	58	D8
Wimpole Ms W1	55	H6
Wimpole St W1	55	H8
Winchester Cl SE17	60	G9
Winchester Sq SE1	61	K2
Winchester St SW1	59	J10
Winchester Wk SE1	61	K2
Wincott St SE11	60	E8
Windmill St W1	55	M7
Windmill Wk SE1	60	E3
Windsor Pl SW1	59	L7
Windsor Ter N1	57	J2
Wine Office Ct EC4	56	E8
Winnett St W1	55	M10
Winsley St W1	55	K8
Woburn Pl WC1	55	N4
Woburn Sq WC1	55	N5
Woburn Wk WC1	55	N3
Wollaston Cl SE1	61	H8
Wolverton SE17	61	L10
Woodbridge St EC1	56	F4
Woods Ms W1	54	E10
Woods Pl SE1	61	N7
Woodstock Ms W1	54	G7
Woodstock St W1	55	H9
Wood St EC2	57	J9
Woolf Ms WC1	55	N4
Wooster Pl SE1	61	L8
Wootton St SE1	60	E4
Wordsworth Rd SE1	61	P9
Worgan St SE11	60	B10
Wormwood St EC2	57	M8
Worship St EC2	57	L5
Wren St WC1	56	C4
Wybert St NW1	55	J4
Wyclif St EC1	56	F3
Wyndham Ms W1	54	D7
Wyndham Pl W1	54	D7
Wyndham St W1	54	D6
Wyndham Yd W1	54	D7
Wynyard Ter SE11	60	C10
Wynyatt St EC1	56	F3
Wythburn Pl W1	54	D9
Yardley St WC1	56	D3
Yarmouth Pl W1	59	H3
Yeoman's Row SW3	58	C7
York Br NW1	54	F4
York Bldgs WC2	60	A1
York Gate NW1	54	F5
York Pl WC2	60	A1
York Rd SE1	60	C4
Yorkshire Grey Yd WC1	56	B7
York St W1	54	E6
York Ter E NW1	54	G5
York Ter W NW1	54	F5
Young's Bldgs EC1	57	J4
Zoar St SE1	61	H2

WEST MIDLANDS URBAN pages 64-65

Entry	Ref	Entry	Ref
Abbey Rd	C3	**Blackheath**	**B3**
Acock's Green	**E3**	**Black Lake**	**C1**
Adams Hill	C3	Black Lake	C1
Addison Rd	D4	Blakedown	A4
Airport Way	F3	**Blakenhall**	**A1**
Albert Rd	E2	Bleakhill Rd	E2
Alcester Rd (Birmingham)	D3	Blindpit La	F1
Alcester Rd (Hollywood)	D4	**Bloomfield**	**B1**
Alcester Rd S	D4	Bloomfield Rd	B1
Alcester St	D3	**Blossomfield**	**E4**
Aldridge Rd	D2	Blossomfield Rd	F4
Alexandra Rd (Halesowen)	B3	**Boldmere**	**E1**
Alexandra Rd (Tipton)	B1	Boldmere Rd	E1
Allen End	**F1**	Booth St	D2
Allens Cft Rd	D4	**Bordesley**	**D3**
All Saints Way	C2	Bordesley Grn	E3
Alum Rock	**E3**	Bosworth Dr	F3
Alum Rock Rd	E2	Boulton Rd	D2
Alvechurch Rd	C4	**Bournbrook**	**D3**
Alwold Rd	C3	**Bournville**	**D4**
Amblecote	**A3**	Bournville La	D4
Amblecote Bank	**A3**	Bower La	A3
Amington Rd	E3	**Bowling Green**	**B3**
Antrobus Rd	E1	Bowyer Rd	E2
Ashes Rd	C2	Brades Rd	B2
Ash Rd	E2	**Brades Village**	**B2**
Ash St	B1	Bradford Rd	F2
Aston	**E2**	**Bradley**	**B1**
Aston Ch Rd	E2	Bradley La	B1
Aston Expressway	D2	Bradley's La	B1
Aston La	D2	**Bramford**	**B1**
Auckland Dr	F2	Brandon Way	C2
Audley Rd	D4	**Brandwood End**	**D4**
Audnam	**A3**	Brandwood Pk Rd	D4
Augustus Rd	D3	Brandwood Rd	D4
Avenue Rd	D4	Brasshouse La	C2
Bacon's End	**F2**	Brays Rd	F3
Bagley St	A3	Brennand Rd	C3
Bagnall St	B1	Brettell La	A3
Balds La	A3	Bridge Rd (Saltley)	E2
Balls Hill	**C1**	Bridge Rd (Tipton)	B1
Balsall Heath	**D3**	Bridge St	C2
Balsall Heath Rd	D3	Bridgnorth Rd	A3
Bank Rd	E4	Bridle La	D1
Banners Gate	**E1**	**Brierley Hill**	**A3**
Baptist End	**B2**	Brierley Hill Rd	A3
Baptist End Rd	B2	Brierley La	B1
Barnes Hill	C3	Brighton Rd	D3
Barn La	F3	**Bristnall Fields**	**C3**
Barr Lakes La	D1	Bristnall Hall Rd	C3
Barrows La	F3	Bristol Rd	D3
Barrs Rd	B3	Bristol Rd S (Northfield)	C4
Bartley Green	**C4**	Bristol Rd S (Rubery)	C4
Bath St	A1	Broad La	D4
Batmanshill Rd	B1	Broad Las	E3
Bearwood	**C3**	Broadway (Oldbury)	C3
Bearwood Rd	C3	Broadway (Walsall)	C1
Beeches Rd	D1	Broadway, The	B2
Belcher's La	E3	Broadway W	C1
Belgrave Rd	D3	Broadwell Rd	C2
Bell End	B3	**Brockmoor**	**A2**
Belle Vale	**B3**	**Bromford**	**E2**
Bell La	C1	Bromford Dr	E2
Bell's La	D4	Bromford La (Birmingham)	E2
Belmont Rd	A3	Bromford La (West Bromwich)	C2
Berry Hall La	F4	Bromford Rd	E2
Berwicks La	F3	**Bromley**	**A2**
Bescot	**C1**	Bromley La	A2
Bescot Cres	C1	Bromsgrove Rd (Hagley)	A4
Bescot Rd	C1	Bromsgrove Rd (Halesowen)	B3
Bickenhill	**F4**	Bromsgrove Rd (Romsley)	B4
Bickenhill Rd	F3	Brooke St	A1
Billesley	**E4**	Brook La	D4
Billesley Common	**D4**	**Broome**	**A4**
Billesley La	D4	Broome La	A4
Bills La	E4	**Brown's Green**	**D2**
Bilston	**B1**	**Buckland End**	**F2**
Bilston Rd	B1	**Buckpool**	**A3**
Bilston St	A1	Buffery Rd	B2
Birches Green	**E2**	Bulls La	F1
Birchfield	**D2**	Bunbury Rd	C4
Birmingham	**D3**	Burney La	E2
Birmingham New Rd	A1	**Burnt Tree**	**B2**
Birmingham Rd (Dudley)	B2	Burton Rd	A2
Birmingham Rd (Hagley)	A4	Cakemore Rd	B3
Birmingham Rd (Rowley Regis)	B2	Caledonia	A3
Birmingham Rd (Sutton Coldfield)	E1	**California**	**C3**
Birmingham Rd (Walsall)	C1	Cape Hill	C2
Birmingham Rd (Water Orton)	F2	Carter's La	C3
Birmingham Rd (West Bromwich)	C2	Cartland Rd	D4
Birmingham St	A3	**Castle Bromwich**	**F2**
Blackford La	E4	Castle Hill	B2
Blackhaynes Rd	C4	Castle Rd	C3
		Castle Vale	**F2**
		Catherine-de-Barnes	**F4**
		Catherine-de-Barnes La	F4

Entry	Ref	Entry	Ref
Catholic La	A1	Cotwall End Rd	A2
Causeway Green	**C2**	Court La	E1
Cemetery Rd	A3	Court Oak Rd	C3
Central Dr	B1	Coventry Rd	E3
Chad Valley	**D3**	Cox's La	B3
Chapelhouse Rd	F3	Crabmill La	D4
Chapel La	D1	**Cradley**	**B3**
Charlemont	**C1**	**Cradley Heath**	**B3**
Charlemont Rd	C1	Cradley Rd (Cradley Heath)	B3
Charles Rd	E3	Cradley Rd (Dudley)	B2
Chelmsley Rd	F3	Cranford St	D2
Chelmsley Wood	**F3**	Crankhall La	C1
Chester Road	**E1**	Cranmore Boul	E4
Chester Rd (Castle Bromwich)	F2	Crockett Rd	D2
Chester Rd (Sutton Coldfield)	E1	Croftdown Rd	C3
Chester Rd N	E1	Cromwell La	C4
Chin Brook Rd	E4	Crook La	D1
Chipperfield Rd	F2	Cross Farms La	C4
Church Br	C2	Crosswells Rd	C2
Churchfield	**C1**	Cuckoo Rd	E2
Church Hill	**C1**	Curdworth La	F1
Church Hill	C4	Dad's La	D4
Church Hill Rd	D2	Daisy St	B1
Churchill Rd	A4	Damson La	F4
Church La (Handsworth)	D2	Damson Parkway	F4
Church La (Kitts Green)	F3	Danford La	E4
Church La (West Bromwich)	C1	Dangerfield La	B1
Church La (Wishaw)	F1	**Darby End**	**B2**
Church Rd (Edgbaston)	D3	**Darby's Hill**	**B2**
Church Rd (Moseley)	D3	Darby's Hill Rd	B2
Church Rd (Northfield)	C4	Dark La (Birmingham)	D4
Church Rd (Sheldon)	F3	Dark La (Romsley)	B4
Church Rd (Sutton Coldfield)	E1	**Darlaston**	**B1**
Church Rd (Yardley)	E3	Darlaston Rd	B1
Church St (Brierley Hill)	A3	**Dayhouse Bank**	**B4**
Church St (Stourbridge)	A3	Delph Rd	A3
Cinder Bk	B2	**Delves, The**	**C1**
Cinder Hill	**A1**	Devonshire Rd	C2
Cinder Rd	A2	Dial La	C1
City Rd (Birmingham)	C3	Dibdale Rd	A2
City Rd (Oldbury)	B2	**Digbeth**	**D3**
Clapgate La	C3	Digbeth	D3
Clatterbach	A4	Dingle La	F4
Clay La	E3	**Dixon's Green**	**B2**
Claypit La	C2	Dixon St	A1
Clements Rd	E3	**Doe Bank**	**E1**
Clent	**A4**	Doe Bk La	D1
Clifton Rd	E1	Doulton Rd	B2
Clifton St	A1	Dovedale Rd	A1
Coalway Rd	A1	Dovehouse La	F4
Cockshot	B3	Downing St	C2
Coldbath Rd	E4	Drews La	E2
Colebrook Rd	E4	**Dudley**	**B2**
Colehall	**F2**	**Dudley Port**	**B2**
Cole Hall La	F2	Dudley Port	B2
Coleshill Rd (Birmingham)	E2	Dudley Rd (Birmingham)	D2
Coleshill Rd (Curdworth)	F1	Dudley Rd (Brierley Hill)	A2
Coleshill Rd (Marston Green)	F3	Dudley Rd (Dudley)	A1
Coleshill Rd (Sutton Coldfield)	E1	Dudley Rd (Halesowen)	B3
Coles La (Sutton Coldfield)	E1	Dudley Rd (Kingswinford)	A2
Coles La (West Bromwich)	C1	Dudley Rd (Oldbury)	B2
Cole Valley Rd	E4	Dudley Rd (Rowley Regis)	B2
Collector Rd	F2	Dudley Rd (Stourbridge)	A3
College Rd (Moseley)	E3	Dudley Rd W	B2
College Rd (Sutton Coldfield)	D1	Dudley Southern Bypass	B2
Colley La	B3	Dudley St	C2
Collis St	A3	**Dudley Wood**	**B3**
Collingwood Dr	D1	Dunn's Bank	A3
Colmore Row	D3	Dunsley Rd	A3
Colton Hills	**A1**	Dunton La	F1
Commonside	A2	Dyas Rd	D1
Cooksey La	D1	Eachelhurst Rd	F2
Coombes Rd	B3	East Meadway	F3
Coombeswood	**B3**	East Tipton Rd	B2
Coopers Bk Rd	A2	East Vw Rd	E1
Coppice La	A3	**Edgbaston**	**D3**
Copt Heath	**F4**	Edgbaston Pk Rd	D3
Corngreaves Rd	B3	Edward Rd	D3
Cornyx La	F4	Egghill La	C4
Coseley	**B1**	Electric Av	E2
Cot La	A2	**Elmdon**	**F3**
Cotteridge	**D4**	**Elmdon Heath**	**F4**
Cotterills La	E2	Enville St	A3
		Erdington	**E2**
		Ettingshall	**B1**
		Ettingshall Park	**A1**
		Ettingshall Rd	B1
		Eve Hill	**A2**
		Eve La	A1
		Expressway, The	C2
		Fairway, The	D4
		Falcon Lodge	**F1**
		Fallings Heath	**C1**
		Farley La	B4
		Farnborough Rd	F2
		Field Ho La	B4

Entry	Ref	Entry	Ref
Field La (Birmingham)	C4	Halesowen Rd (Netherton)	B2
Field La (Solihull)	F4	Halesowen Rd (Quinton)	C3
Finchley Rd	E1	Halford's La	C2
Fordbridge	**F3**	Hallam St	C2
Fordhouse La	D4	**Hall Green**	**E4**
Forge La (Cradley Heath)	B3	Hall Grn Rd	C1
Forge La (West Bromwich)	C1	Ham La (Kingswinford)	A2
Forman's Rd	E3	Ham La (Stourbridge)	A3
Fox Hollies La	F1	Hampton La	F4
Fox Hollies Rd (Stourbridge)	E4	**Hamstead**	**D1**
Fox Hollies Rd (Sutton Coldfield)	F1	Hamstead Hill	D2
Foyle Rd	D4	Hamstead Rd (Great Barr)	D1
Frankley	**C4**	Hamstead Rd (Handsworth)	D2
Frankley Beeches Rd	C4	**Handsworth**	**D2**
Frankley Grn	B4	**Handsworth Wood**	**D2**
Frankley Hill	C4	Handsworth Wd Rd	D2
Frankley La	C4	**Harborne**	**C3**
Friar Park	**C1**	Harborne Rd	D3
Friar Pk Rd	C1	Harbourne Pk Rd	C3
Friary Rd	D2	Harding St	A3
Friday La	F4	**Harvills Hawthorn**	**C1**
Frogmill La	C4	**Hasbury**	**B3**
Furlong La	B3	**Hasluck's Green**	**E4**
Furnace La	B3	Haslucks Grn La	E4
Garrett's Green	**F3**	**Hateley Heath**	**C1**
Garrett's Grn La	F3	Haunch La	D4
Gayhill La	D4	**Hawbush**	**A3**
Genners La	C4	**Hawkesley**	**D4**
George Rd (Oldbury)	E2	**Hawne**	**B3**
George Rd (Stourbridge)	C3	Hawne La	B3
Gibbins Rd	D3	Hawthorn Rd	D1
Gib Heath	**D2**	**Hayes, The**	**A3**
Gigmill	**A3**	Hayes La	A3
Gilbertstone	**F3**	**Hay Mills**	**E3**
Gillhurst Rd	C3	Heathfield Rd	D2
Gillot Rd	D3	Heathfield Way	B3
Gipsy La	E1	Heath La	C1
Glebe Farm	**F2**	Heath Rd	D4
Golden Hillock Rd	E3	Heath St	D2
Golds Green	**C1**	Heath Way	F2
Goldthorn Hill	A1	Heeley Rd	D3
Goldthorn Park	**A1**	Helmswood Dr	F3
Goosemoor La	E1	Henwood La	F4
Gorge Rd	A1	Heybarnes Rd	E3
Gornalwood	**A2**	High Arcal	A2
Gospel End	**A1**	Highbridge Rd	E1
Gospel End Rd	A1	Highfield Rd (Halesowen)	B3
Gospel La	E4	Highfield Rd (Saltley)	E2
Gospel Oak	B1	Highfield Rd (Yardley Wood)	E4
Gough Rd	B1	Highfields Rd	B1
Grafton Rd	C3	**Highgate**	**D3**
Grange La	A3	Highgate Rd (Birmingham)	D3
Grange Rd (Birmingham)	E3	Highgate Rd (Dudley)	A2
Grange Rd (Erdington)	E2	Highlands Rd	E4
Grange Rd (Solihull)	E4	**High Park**	**A3**
Grange Rd (Stourbridge)	A3	High Pk Av	A3
Gravelly Hill	**E2**	High St (Brierley Hill)	A2
Gravelly Hill	E2	High St (Cradley Heath)	B3
Gravelly La	E1	High St (Dudley)	B2
Great Barr	**D1**	High St (Erdington)	E2
Great Br Rd	B1	High St (Harborne)	C3
Great Br St	B1	High St (King's Heath)	D4
Great Stone Rd	C4	High St (Kingswinford)	A2
Green, The	B1	High St (Lye)	A3
Green Holm Rd	D1	High St (Moxley)	B1
Greenlands Rd	F3	High St (Pensnett)	A2
Green La (Castle Bromwich)	F2	High St (Princes End)	B1
Green La (Small Heath)	E3	High St (Quarry Bank)	A3
Green Las	E1	High St (Rowley Regis)	B3
Greets Grn Rd	C2	High St (Saltley)	E2
Grove La (Handsworth)	D2	High St (Sedgley)	A1
Grove La (Smethwick)	C2	High St (Shirley)	E4
Grove La (Sutton Coldfield)	F1	High St (Smethwick)	C2
Grove Rd	D4	High St (Stourbridge)	A3
Grove Vale	**C1**	High St (West Bromwich)	C2
Guns Village	**C2**	High St (Wollaston)	A3
Haden Cross	**B3**	**Highter's Heath**	**D4**
Hagley	**A4**	Highters Heath La	D4
Hagley Causeway	A4	Highwood Avanue	F4
Hagley Rd (Birmingham)	C3	Hillfield Rd	A3
Hagley Rd (Halesowen)	B3	Hillfields Rd	A3
Hagley Rd (Stourbridge)	A3	**Hill Top**	**C1**
Hagley Rd W	C3	Hill Top	C1
Halesowen	**B3**	Himley Rd (Dudley)	A2
Halesowen Rd (Cradley Heath)	B3		

Name	Ref		Name	Ref
Hob Moor Rd	E3		Lodge Hill	C3
Hob's Moat Rd	F3		Lodge Rd	D2
Hobs Rd	C1		Londonderry La	C2
Hockley	**D2**		**London Fields**	**A2**
Hodgehill	**E2**		Long Acre	E2
Hodge Hill Rd	F2		Longbridge La	C4
Hoggs La	C4		Long La	B3
Holbeache La	A2		Longmore Rd	E4
Holder Rd	E3		Long Nuke Rd	C4
Hole La	D4		Lordswood Rd	C3
Holloway	C4		**Lower Bradley**	**B1**
Holloway Bk	C1		**Lower Gornal**	**A2**
Holloway End	**A3**		Loxdale St	B1
Holloway St	A2		**Lozells**	**D2**
Hollybank Rd	D4		Lozells Rd	D2
Hollyfield Rd	F1		Lugtrout La	F4
Hollyhedge Rd	C1		Lunt Rd	B1
Holly La (Erdington)	E2		Lutley La	B3
Holly La (Smethwick)	C2		**Lye**	**A3**
Holly La (Wishaw)	F1		**Lyndon**	**C2**
Holly Rd	D2		**Lyndon Green**	**F3**
Hollywood La	D4		Lyndon Rd	F3
Holt La	B4		Mackadown La	F3
Holy Cross	**A4**		**Major's Green**	**E4**
Holyhead Rd	C2		Manby Rd	F2
Homer Rd	F4		**Maney**	**E1**
Horseley Heath	**B1**		Manor Ho Rd	C1
Howard Rd	D4		Manor La	B3
Hunnington	**B4**		Manor Rd (Smethwick)	C2
Hunters Rd	D2		Manor Rd (Stechford)	E3
Huntingtree Rd	B3		Manor Way	B3
Hurst Green	**C3**		Market St	A2
Hurst Grn Rd	C3		Marriot Rd	B2
Hurst Hill	**B1**		Marshall Lake Rd	E4
Hurst Rd N	F2		Marsh Hill	E2
Hurst Rd (Hurst Hill)	A1		Marsh La (Erdington)	E2
Hurst Rd (Smethwick)	C3		Marsh La (Water Orton)	F2
Hydes Rd	C1		Marsh La (West Bromwich)	C1
Icknield Port Rd	D2		**Marston Green**	**F3**
Icknield St	D2		Mary Vale Rd	D4
Illey	**B4**		Maypole La	D4
Illey La	B4		Meadow La	D4
Jacobean La	F4		Meadway	F3
Jennens Rd	D3		Melton Av	F3
Jiggins La	C4		Merritts Brook La	C4
Jockey Rd	E1		Merritts Hill	C4
John St	A2		**Merry Hill**	**D2**
Kate's Hill	**B2**		**Mesty Croft**	**C1**
Kelvin Way	C2		Metchley La	D3
Kenrick Way	C2		Middlemore Rd	C2
Kent Rd	B3		Middle Pk Rd	C4
Kent St	A1		Middleton Hall Rd	D4
Kineton Green	**E4**		Milking Bk	A2
Kineton Grn Rd	E4		Millfields Rd	B1
Kingsbury Rd (Castle Vale)	F2		Millhouse Rd	E3
Kingsbury Rd (Curdworth)	F1		Mill Rd	E2
Kingsbury Rd (Erdington)	E2		Mill St	A3
King's Heath	**D4**		Mincing La	B3
Kings	**C1**		**Minworth**	**F1**
Kingshurst	**F2**		Moat La (Solihull)	F4
King's Norton	**D4**		Moat La (Yardley)	E3
Kings Rd (Birmingham)	E3		Moat Rd	C2
King's Rd (Kingstanding)	D1		Moden Hill	A1
Kingstanding	**D1**		Mogul La	A3
Kingstanding Rd	D1		Monmouth Dr	E1
King St	B2		Montgomery St	E3
Kingsway	C3		Monument Rd	D3
Kingswinford	**A2**		Monyhull Hall Rd	D4
Kingswinford Rd	C2		Moor End Av	F3
Kitt's Green	**F2**		Moor End La	E2
Kitts Grn Rd	F2		**Moor Green**	**D3**
Kitwell La	C4		Moor Grn La	D4
Knightsbridge Rd	F4		Moor La (Bartley Green)	C4
Knowle, The	**B2**		Moor La (Witton)	D1
Lady Byron La	F4		**Moor Street**	**C3**
Ladypool Rd	E3		Moor St	A3
Ladywood	**D3**		**Moseley**	**D3**
Ladywood Middleway	D3		Moseley Rd	D3
Lake St	E4		Moss Gro	A2
Lakey La	E4		**Mount Pleasant**	**A2**
Lanesfield	**A1**		Mount Pleasant	B1
Langley	**C2**		Mount Rd	A1
Langley Green	**C2**		**Moxley**	**B1**
Lapal	**C3**		Moxley Rd	B1
Lapal La	C3		Mucklow Hill	B3
Leabrook Rd	B1		Muntz St	E3
Lea Hall	**F3**		Myvod Rd	C1
Lea Hall Rd	F3		Narrow La	B3
Lee Bank	**D3**		**Nechells**	**E2**
Lee Bk	D3		Nechell's Parkway	D2
Level St	A2		**Netherend**	**B3**
Leys Rd	A2		**Netherton**	**B2**
Lichfield Rd	D1		Newbury La	A3
Lifford La	D4		New Fm Rd	A3
Lightwoods Hill	C3		New John St W	D2
Lincoln Rd	D1		**New Oscott**	**E1**
Linden Rd	D4		New Rd	B2
Lindridge Rd	F1		New Rowley Rd	B2
Lister Rd	B1		New St	C4
Little Bromwich	**E3**		**Newton**	**C1**
Lode Heath	**F4**		Newton Rd (Great Barr)	B4
Lode La	F4		Newton Rd (Romsley)	C1
Lodgefield Rd	B3			

Name	Ref		Name	Ref
Newtown (Birmingham)	**D2**		Prince Of Wales La	E4
New Town (West Bromwich)	**B2**		**Princes End**	**B1**
New Town Row	D2		Prince's Way	F4
Norfolk Rd	D3		Priory Rd (Dudley)	B2
Norman Rd	C3		Priory Rd (Hall Green)	E4
Northfield	**C4**		Pritchatts Rd	D3
Northfield Rd (Dudley)	B2		Prospect La	E4
Northfield Rd (Harborne)	C3		Putney La	B4
Northfield Rd (Kings Norton)	D4		**Pype Hayes**	**E2**
North Way	A1		**Quarry Bank**	**B3**
Norton Rd	A3		Quarry La	C4
Nursery Rd	D2		Quarry Rd	B3
Oakfield Rd	D3		Queensbridge Rd	D3
Oakham	**B2**		Queens Rd (Smethwick)	C2
Oakham Rd	B2		Queen's Rd (Tipton)	B2
Oak La	A2		Queensway	C3
Oak Rd	C2		**Queslett**	**D1**
Ocker Hill	**B1**		Queslett Rd	D1
Oldbury	**B2**		**Quinton**	**C3**
Oldbury Rd (Rowley Regis)	B3		Quinton Expressway	C3
Oldbury Rd (Smethwick)	C2		Quinton La	C3
Old Ham La	A3		Quinton Rd	C3
Old Hill	**B3**		Quinton Rd W	C3
Old Lode La	F3		Rabone La	C2
Oldnall Rd	A3		Racecourse La	A3
Old Oscott	**D1**		Raddlebarn Rd	D4
Old Pk Rd	C1		Radleys, The	F3
Old Walsall Rd	D1		Ravenhayes La	C4
Olive La	B3		Ravenhurst Rd	C3
Ollerton Rd	F3		Rectory Rd	E1
Olton	**F3**		**Reddicap Heath**	**F1**
Olton Boul E	E3		Reddicap Heath Rd	F1
Olton Boul W	E3		Reddicap Hill	E1
Olton Rd	E4		Redding's La	E3
Orphanage Rd	E1		Redfern Rd	E3
Oscott La	D1		**Redhall**	**A2**
Overend	**B3**		Red Hill	A3
Over Green	**F1**		Redlake Rd	A3
Owen St	B2		Rednal Rd	C4
Oxbarn Av	A1		Redstone Fm Rd	E4
Oxford Rd	D3		Reservoir Rd	E2
Oxford St	B1		Richmond Hill Rd	D3
Oxhill Rd	D2		Richmond Rd	F3
Ox Leys Rd	F1		**Ridgacre**	**C3**
Packington Av	F2		Ridgacre Rd	C3
Palfrey	**C1**		Ridgeway, The	E1
Parkfield	**A1**		Ringway	C2
Parkfield Rd	A1		Robin Hood La	E4
Park Hall	D1		Rocky La (Aston)	E2
Park Hill	D3		Rocky La (Perry Barr)	D1
Park La (Aston)	D2		Rolfe St	C2
Park La (Castle Vale)	F2		**Romsley**	**B4**
Park La (Halesowen)	B3		**Romsley Hill**	**B4**
Park La (Handsworth)	C2		**Rood End**	**C2**
Park La (Wednesbury)	C1		Roodend Rd	C2
Park La E	B2		Rookery Rd	D2
Park La W	B2		**Roseville**	**B1**
Park Rd (Hagley)	A4		**Ross**	**B3**
Park Rd (Halesowen)	A3		**Rotton Park**	**D2**
Park Rd (Hockley)	D2		Rotton Pk Rd	D2
Park Rd (Smethwick)	C3		Rough Rd	D1
Park Rd (Walsall)	D1		**Rounds Green**	**C2**
Parsons Hill	D4		**Rowley Regis**	**B2**
Peartree La	A2		**Rubery**	**C4**
Pedmore La	A3		**Ruiton**	**A2**
Pedmore Rd	A3		Rupert St	D2
Penn	**A1**		Russell Rd	D3
Penn Rd (Sedgley)	A1		**Russell's Hall**	**A2**
Penn Rd (Wolverhampton)	A1		St. Benedicts Rd	E3
Penns La	E1		St. Bernard's Rd	E4
Pennwood La	A1		St. Giles Rd	F3
Pensnett	**A2**		St. James's Rd	B2
Pensnett Rd	A2		St. John's Rd	A3
Percy Rd	E3		St. Kenelm's Rd	B4
Perry	**D1**		St. Margaret's Av	E2
Perry Barr	**D2**		St. Mark's Rd	B1
Perry Barr Expressway	D2		St. Paul's Rd	C2
Perry Beeches	**D1**		St. Peter's Rd	B2
Perry Common	**E1**		Salisbury Rd	D3
Perry Common Rd	E1		Salop St	B2
Pershore Rd	D4		**Saltley**	**E2**
Peterbrook Rd	E4		Saltwell's Rd	B3
Pheasey	**D1**		Sam's La	C2
Phoenix St	C2		Sandon Rd	C3
Pineapple Rd	D4		Sand Pits	D2
Pinfold La (Penn)	A1		**Sandwell**	**C2**
Pinfold La (Walsall)	B1		Sandwell Rd	D2
Plank La	F2		Sandyfields Rd	A1
Portland Rd	C3		Sandy La	A3
Portway	**B2**		Sarehole Rd	E4
Portway Hill	B2		School La	F2
Portway Rd	B2		School Rd (Hall Green)	E4
Pound Rd	C3		School Rd (Moseley)	D4
Powis Av	B1		School Rd (Yardley Wood)	E4
Powke La	B2		Scotland La	C4
Pretoria Rd	E3		**Sedgley**	**A1**
Priestfield	**A1**		Sedgley Rd	A1
Primrose Hill	**B2**		Sedgley Rd W	B1
Primrose Hill	D4		Selby Rd	D3
			Selly Oak	**D3**
			Selly Oak Rd	D4
			Seven Star Rd	D1
			Shady La	D1
			Shaftmoor La	E3
			Shard End	**F2**
			Shard End Cres	F2

Name	Ref		Name	Ref
Sharmans Cross	**F4**		Thicknall La	A4
Sharman's Cross Rd	E4		**Thimble End**	**F1**
Shaw La	B2		Thornbridge Av	D1
Sheaf La	F3		Thornhill Rd	E1
Sheldon	**F3**		Thorns Rd	A3
Sheldon Heath Rd	F3		Throne Rd	B2
Shenley Fields	**C4**		**Tile Cross**	**F3**
Shenley Flds Rd	C4		Tile Cross Rd	F3
Shenley La	C4		Tiled Ho La	A2
Sherlock St	D3		**Tipton**	**B2**
Shirley	**E4**		**Tipton Green**	**B2**
Shirley Heath	**E4**		Tipton Rd (Dudley)	B2
Shirley Rd	E4		Tipton Rd (Sedgley)	B2
Shirley Street	**E4**		**Tividale**	**B2**
Short Heath	**E1**		**Toll End**	**B1**
Short Heath Rd	E1		Toll End Rd	B1
Showell Grn La	E3		**Tower Hill**	**D1**
Signal Hayes Rd	F1		Trinity Rd	D2
Sir Harry's Rd	D3		Trinity Way	C2
Skip La	D1		Trittiford Rd	E4
Sladefield Rd	E2		Trysull Rd	A1
Slade Rd	D2		**Tudor Hill**	**E1**
Small Heath	**E3**		**Turves Green**	**C4**
Small Heath Highway	E3		Turves Grn	C4
Smethwick	**C2**		Two Gates La	B3
Smithy La	A2		**Tyburn**	**E2**
Soho	**D2**		Tyburn Rd	E2
Soho Rd	D2		Tynedale Rd	E3
Soho Way	C2		**Tyseley**	**E3**
Solihull	**F4**		Uffmoor La	B4
Solihull La	E4		Ulleries Rd	F3
Solihull Lodge	**E4**		**Ulverley Green**	**F4**
Solihull Rd	E4		Ulverley Grn Rd	F4
Somerset Rd	D3		Umberslade Rd	D4
Somerville Rd (Birmingham)	E3		Union Rd	A4
Somerville Rd (Sutton Coldfield)	E1		Uplands, The	C2
South Rd (Erdington)	E2		Upper Ch La	B1
South Rd (Stourbridge)	A3		**Upper Gornal**	**A1**
South Yardley	**E3**		Upper High St	B3
Sparkbrook	**E3**		**Upper Witton**	**E2**
Sparkhill	**E3**		**Vauxhall**	**E2**
Spies La	C3		Vauxhall Rd	E2
Spon La	C2		Vicarage Rd (King's Heath)	D4
Spouthouse La	D1		Vicarage Rd (Penn)	A1
Springfield Rd (Moseley)	E4		Vicarage Rd (Stourbridge)	A3
Springfield Rd (Sutton Coldfield)	F1		Vicarage Rd (West Bromwich)	C1
Spring Hill	**E2**		Vicarage Rd (Wollaston)	A3
Spring Hill (Halesowen)	**B3**		Victoria Rd (Aston)	D2
Spring Hill (Wolverhampton)	**A1**		Victoria Rd (Harborne)	C3
Spring La	E2		Victoria Rd (Oldbury)	C2
Stakenbridge Rd	A4		Victoria Rd (Tipton)	D2
Stallings La	A2		Villa Rd	D2
Stambermill	**A3**		Vine La	A4
Stanhope Rd	C3		Vulcan Rd	B1
Stanley Rd	C3		Wagon La	F3
Staple Lo Rd	C4		**Wake Green**	**E4**
Station Rd (Cradley Heath)	B3		Wake Grn Rd	D3
Station Rd (Stechford)	E2		Wakeley Hill	A1
Station Rd (Sutton Coldfield)	E1		Walford Rd	E3
Stechford	**E3**		**Walkers Heath**	**D4**
Stechford Rd	E2		Walkers Heath Rd	D4
Stirchley	**D4**		**Wallbrook**	**B1**
Stockfield Rd	E3		Wallows La	C1
Stone Cross	**C1**		**Walmley**	**F1**
Stonehouse La	C3		Walmley Ash La	F1
Stonehouse Rd	E1		Walmley Ash Rd	F1
Stoney La (Balsall Heath)	E3		Walmley Rd	F1
Stoney La (Yardley)	E3		Walsall Rd (Perry Barr)	D1
Stony La	C2		Walsall Rd (Wednesbury)	B1
Stourbridge	**A3**		Walsall Rd (West Bromwich)	C1
Stourbridge Rd (Dudley)	A2		Walsall St	C1
Stourbridge Rd (Hagley)	A4		Walstead Rd	C1
Stourbridge Rd (Halesowen)	B3		Walton Pool La	A4
Straits, The	A2		**Ward End**	**E2**
Stratford Rd	E3		Wardstreet	B1
Stream Rd	A2		War La	C3
Streetly Rd	E2		**Warley**	**C3**
Streets Brook Rd	E4		Warley Rd	C2
Summer Hill	**B1**		Warren Fm Rd	D1
Summer La	D2		**Warstock**	**E4**
Sutton Coldfield	**E1**		Warstock La	E4
Sutton Oak Rd	D1		Warstock Rd	D4
Sutton Rd	E1		Warstones Rd	A1
Swan La	C1		Warwards La	D2
Swanshurst La	E4		Warwick Rd (Solihull)	F4
Swan Village	**C2**		Warwick Rd (Sparkhill)	E3
Swarthmore Rd	C4		Wash La	E3
Tame Rd	C3		**Washwood Heath**	**E2**
Tamworth La	E4		Washwood Heath Rd	E2
Tangmere Dr	F2		Wassell Gro Rd	A4
Tansey Grn Rd	A2		Waterfall La	B3
Tat Bk Rd	C2		**Water Orton**	**F2**
Taylor Rd	D4		Water Orton La	F2
Tennal Rd	C3		Water Orton Rd	F2
Tessall La	C4		Watton La	F2
			Wattville Rd	C2

Webster Way F1
Wednesbury C1
Wednesbury Oak B1
Wellington Rd (Bilston) B1
Wellington Rd (Dudley) B2
Wellington Rd (Edgbaston) D3
Wellington Rd (Handsworth) D2
Wells Green F3
Weoley Av C3
Weoley Castle C4
Weoley Castle Rd C4
West Boul C3
Westbourne Rd D3
West Bromwich C2
West Bromwich Rd C1
West Bromwich St C2
Western Rd A4
West Hagley A4
West Heath C4
West Heath Rd C4
Westhill Rd D4
Westley Rd E3
Westminster Rd D2
Weston St C1
Westwood Av A3
Wheelers La D4
Wheeler St D2
Wheeleys Rd D3
Wheelwright Rd E2
Whitefields Rd F4
Whitehall Rd B2
Whitehouse Common E1
Whittington Rd A3
Widney La F4
Widney Manor Rd F4
Wiggins Hill Rd F1
Willows Rd D3
Windmill La C2
Windward Way F2
Winson Green D2
Wishaw F1
Wishaw La (Curdworth) F1
Wishaw La (Middleton) F1
Wishaw La (Minworth) F1
Withy Hill Rd F1
Withymoor Village A3
Witton D2
Witton La C1
Witton Lo Rd E1
Witton Rd D2
Wodehouse La A1
Woden Rd C1
Woden Rd E C1
Woden Rd N C1
Wollaston A3
Wollescote A3
Wollescote Rd A3
Wolverhampton Rd (Kingswinford) A2
Wolverhampton Rd (Oldbury) C2
Wolverhampton Rd (Sedgley) A1
Wolverhampton Rd S C3
Wolverhampton St B1
Woodbourn Rd C3
Woodcross St A1
Woodgate C4
Woodgate La C3
Wood Green C1
Wood Grn Rd C1
Wood La (West Bromwich) C2
Wood La (Woodgate) C4
Woods, The C1
Woods Bank B1
Woodsetton B2
Woodside A2
Woods La A3
Worcester La A3
Worcester St A3
Wordsley A3
Worlds End F4
Wrens Nest Rd B2
Wychall La D4
Wychall Rd C4
Wylde Green E1
Wylde Grn Rd E1
Wynall La A3
Wyrley Rd E2
Yardley E3
Yardley Grn Rd E3
Yardley Rd E3
Yardley Wood E4
Yardley Wd Rd E3
Yatesbury Av F2
Yew Tree C1
Yew Tree La C4
York Rd E3

BIRMINGHAM CENTRAL pages 66-67

Abbey St E2
Abbey St N E2
Aberdeen St A4
Acorn Gro F7
Adams St Q3
Adderley St R10
Adelaide St P12
Albert St N8
Albion St G6
Alcester St P13
Aldgate Gro K3
Allcock St R9
Allesley St N2
Allison St P10
All Saints Ind Est E3
All Saints Rd E2
All Saints St E3
Alma Cres U5
Alport Cft U8
Alston St C10
Amiss Gdns U13
Anchor Cl A10
Anderflat Pl V3
Anderton St F7
Angelina St P13
Ansbro Cl B3
Arden Gro E10
Arthur Pl G7
Arthur St U11
Artillery St U8
Ascot Cl B9
Ashted Lock Q5
Ashted Wk T4
Ashton Cft E9
Aston R1
Aston Br P1
Aston Brook St P1
Aston Brook St E Q2
Aston Expressway P3
Aston Rd P4
Aston Science Pk Q5
Aston Seedbed Cen R1
Aston St N6
Attenborough Cl L2
Auckland Rd S14
Augusta St H4
Augustine Gro C1
Austen Pl F13
Autumn Gro J1
Avenue Cl S1
Avenue Rd Q1
Bacchus Rd A1
Bagot St N4
Balcaskie Cl A14
Banbury St P7
Barford Rd A5
Barford St P11
Barnford Cl U11
Barn St Q9
Barrack St S5
Barrow Wk M14
Barr St H2
Bartholomew Row P7
Bartholomew St P8
Barwick St L7
Bath Pas M10
Bath Row G11
Bath St M5
Beak St L9
Beaufort Gdns B1
Beaufort Rd D11
Bedford Rd S11
Beeches, The H13
Belgrave Middleway M14
Bell Barn Rd H12
Bellcroft F9
Bellevue L14
Bellis St B11
Belmont Pas S8
Belmont Row Q6
Benacre Dr Q8
Bennett's Hill L8
Benson Rd B1
Berkley St H9
Berrington Wk N14
Bexhill Gro J12
Birchall St P11
Bishopsgate St G10
Bishop St N13
Bissell St N13
Blews St N3
Bloomsbury St T3
Bloomsbury Wk U2
Blucher St K10
Blyton Cl B6
Boar Hound Cl E5
Bodmin Gro T2
Bolton Rd U12
Bolton St T9
Bond Sq E5
Bond St K5
Bordesley T10
Bordesley Circ T11
Bordesley Middleway S13
Bordesley St P8
Boulton Ind Cen G2
Boulton Middleway G2
Bow St L11
Bowyer St S11
Bracebridge St N1
Bradburn Way S3
Bradford St P10
Branston St H3
Brearley Cl M3
Brearley St L3
Bredon Cft D2
Brewery St N3
Bridge St J9
Bridge St W K2
Brindley Dr H8
Broad St G11
Bromley St R10
Bromsgrove St L11
Brookfield Rd D3
Brook St J6
Brook Vw Cl J1
Broom St R12
Broseley Brook Cl V10
Brough Cl T1
Browning St F9
Brownsea Dr K10
Brunel St K9
Brunswick St G9
Buckingham St K4
Bullock St R3
Bull St M7
Cala Dr F14
Calthorpe Rd E13
Cambridge Rd H8
Camden Dr G6
Camden Gro G6
Camden St F5
Camelot Way V12
Camp Hill S13
Camp Hill Ind Est S14
Camp Hill Middleway R14
Cannon St M8
Capstone Av E4
Cardigan St Q6
Carlisle St A3
Carlyle Rd A10
Caroline St J5
Carpenter Rd E14
Carrs La N8
Carver St F5
Cato St U4
Cato St N V2
Cattell Rd V10
Cawdor Cres C11
Cecil St M4
Cemetery La G3
Chad Rd B13
Chadsmoor Ter T1
Chad Valley A13
Chamberlain Sq K8
Chancellor's Cl A14
Chapel Ho St Q10
Chapman Rd V12
Chapmans Pas K10
Charles Dr U1
Charles Henry St N13
Charlotte Rd H13
Charlotte St J7
Cheapside P11
Chelsea Trd Est S1
Cherry Dr U10
Cherry St M8
Chester St Q2
Chilwell Cft M1
Christchurch Cl A12
Church Rd E14
Church St L6
City Trd Est D7
Civic Cl H8
Clare Dr B13
Clarel Av V7
Clarendon Rd A10
Clark St C8
Claybrook St M11
Clement St G7
Clipper Vw A10
Clissold Cl N14
Clissold St D4
Cliveland St M5
Clyde St R11
Colbrand Gro K13
Coleshill St N7
College St D5
Colmore Circ M6
Colmore Row L8
Commercial St J10
Communication Row H11
Constitution Hill J4
Conybere St N14
Cooksey Rd U12
Cope St D6
Coplow St B6
Cornwall St K7
Corporation St M8
Coveley Gro D2
Coventry Rd S11
Coventry St P9
Cox St K5
Coxwell Gdns C9
Crabtree Rd D3
Cregoe St J11
Crescent, The F1
Crescent Av F1
Cromwell St T2
Crondal Pl G14
Crosby Cl F7
Cumberland St G9
Curzon Circ R6
Curzon St Q7
Daisy Rd B9
Dale End N8
Daley Cl F7
Dalton St N7
Darnel Cft U11
Darnley Rd C9
Dartmouth Circ P2
Dartmouth Middleway P3
Dart St T11
Darwin St P12
Dean St N10
Dearman Rd U14
Deeley Cl H14
Denby Cl T3
Derby St S8
Devonshire Av C1
Devonshire St D1
Devon St V4
Digbeth N9
Digbeth P11
Dixon Rd U13
Dollman St T6
Dorking Gro J11
Dover St D1
Duchess Rd D11
Duddeston Manor Rd S4
Duddeston Mill Rd U4
Dudley St M9
Dymoke Cl P13
East Holme V9
Eastwood Ind Est C5
Edgbaston D14
Edgbaston St M10
Edmund St K7
Edward St G8
Eldon Rd B10
Elkington St N2
Ellen St F4
Ellis St K10
Elvetham Rd H12
Embassy Dr E12
Emily Gdns B6
Emily St P14
Emmeline St U10
Enfield Rd G12
Enterprise Way P4
Ernest St K11
Erskine St T5
Essex St L11
Essington St G10
Estria Rd F14
Ethel St L8
Exeter Pas L11
Exeter St L11
Eyre St D6
Eyton Cft Q14
Farmacre T9
Farm Cft H1
Farm St G1
Fawdry St S8
Fazeley St P8
Felsted Way S5
Ferndale Cres R13
Finstall Cl S5
Five Ways F11
Fleet St J7
Floodgate St Q10
Florence St K11
Ford St F2
Fore St M8
Forster St R6
Foster Gdns C1
Fowler St U1
Fox St P7
Francis Rd D10
Francis St S5
Frankfort St L1
Frederick Rd F13
Frederick St H5
Freeman Rd U2
Freeman St N8
Freeth St C8
Friston Av F11
Fulmer Wk E7
Garland St V7
Garrison Circ S8
Garrison La T8
Garrison St S8
Gas St H9
Gaywood Cft J12
Geach St L1
Gee St L1
George Rd G13
George St H7
George St W E5
Gibb St Q10
Gilby Rd E9
Gilldown Pl G14
Gisborn Cl U12
Glebeland Cl F10
Gloucester St M10
Glover St S9
Gooch St M13
Gooch St N M11
Goode Av E2
Goodman St F7
Goodrick Way U2
Gopsal St Q6
Gough St K10
Grafton Rd T14
Graham St H6
Grant St K12
Granville St H10
Graston Cl E9
Gray St U9
Great Barr St R9
Great Brook St R5
Great Charles St Queensway K7
Great Colmore St J12
Great Hampton Row J4
Great Hampton St H3
Great King St H2
Great King St N J1
Great Lister St Q4
Great Tindal St E8
Greenfield Cres E12
Green La V11
Green St Q11
Greenway St V11
Grenfell Dr B13
Grosvenor St P7
Grosvenor St W F10
Guest Gro H1
Guild Cl D9
Guild Cft L1
Guthrie Cl K1
Hack St R10
Haden Circ R5
Hadfield Cft J3
Hagley Rd A11
Hall St J5
Hampshire Dr A13
Hampton St K4
Hanley St L4
Hanwood Cl P13
Harborne Rd B13
Harford St J4
Harmer St E3
Harold Rd B10
Hartley Pl B12
Hatchett St L2
Hawthorn Cl T10
Hawthorne Rd A14
Heartlands Parkway V2
Heath Mill La Q10
Heath St S C6
Heaton Dr A13
Heaton St G2
Helena St H7
Heneage St Q4
Heneage St W Q5
Henley St S14
Henrietta St L5
Henstead St L12
Herbert Rd U11
Herne Cl E5
Hickman Gdns C10
Highfield Rd D12
Highgate Q14
Highgate St N14
High St N8
Hilden Rd S5
Hill St K8
Hinckley St L10
Hindlow Cl T5
Hindon Sq C13
Hingeston St F4
Hitches La G14
Hobart Cft S3
Hobson Cl D2
Hockley Brook Cl D2
Hockley Cl L1
Hockley Goods Yd F3
Hockley Hill H2
Hockley St H3
Holland St H7
Holliday Pas J10
Holliday St J9
Holloway Circ L10
Holloway Head K11
Holt St P4
Holywell Cl D10
Hooper St C5
Hope St L13
Hospital St L2
Howard St K4
Howe St Q6
Howford Gro T4
Hubert St Q2
Hunter's Vale G1
Huntly Rd D11
Hurdlow Av F3
Hurst St L10
Hylton St G3
Hyssop Cl S3
Icknield Port Rd A5
Icknield Sq D7
Icknield St F6
Inge St L11
Inkerman St T6
Irving St K11
Isbourne Way U8
Islington Row F11
Ivy La S8
Jackson Cl T14
James St J6
James Watt Queensway N6
Jenkins St V13
Jennens Rd P7
Jewellery Quarter G4
Jinnah Cl P13
John Bright St L9
John Kempe Way R14
Keeley St T9
Keer Ct U8
Kellett Rd R4
Kelsall Cft F7
Kelsey Cl T4
Kemble Cft M14
Kendal Rd T14
Kenilworth Ct B12
Kent St M12
Kent St N C2
Kenyon St J5
Ketley Cft P14
Key Hill G3
Key Hill Circ G3
Key Hill Dr G3
Kilby Av F8
King Edwards Rd G8
Kingston Rd T10
Kingston Row H8
Kirby Rd A1
Knightstone Av E4
Kyotts Lake Rd S14
Ladycroft E9
Ladywell Wk M10
Ladywood E8
Ladywood Middleway D9
Ladywood Rd C10
Lancaster Circ N5
Landor St S7
Langdon St T8
Lansdowne St B4
Latimer Gdns K14
Lawden Rd T12
Lawford Cl S6
Lawford Gro N13
Lawley Middleway R5
Ledbury Cl D9
Ledsam St E8
Lee Bank K13
Lee Bk Middleway H12
Lee Cres H13
Lee Mt H13

Street	Ref	Street	Ref	Street	Ref
Lees St	C2	Montgomery St	U14	Pakenham Rd	G14
Legge La	G6	Monument Rd	C9	Palmer St	S9
Legge St	P4	Moore's Row	Q10	Palomino Pl	C8
Lennox St	K1	Moorsom St	M2	Pannel Cft	L1
Leopold St	P13	Moor St		Parade	H7
Leslie Rd	B9	Queensway	N8	Paradise Circ	J8
Leyburn Rd	E10	Moreton St	F5	Paradise St	K8
Lighthorne Av	E8	Morville St	F10	Parker St	B11
Lingard Cl	U2	Mosborough Cres	J2	Parkfield Cl	H14
Link Rd	A6	Moseley Rd	R12	Park Rd	E1
Lionel St	J7	Moseley St	P11	Park Rd S	F2
Lister St	P5	Moss Ho Cl	G11	Park St	N9
Little Ann St	Q9	Mostyn Rd	B9	Parkway Ind Cen	R5
Little Barr St	S8	Mott St	J4	Paxton Rd	E3
Little Broom St	R12	Mount Pleasant	U11	Peel St	A3
Little Edward St	S9	Mowbray St	M13	Pemberton St	G4
Little Francis Grn	T3	Murrell Cl	L14	Penn St	R6
Little Hall Rd	U4	Musgrave Rd	B2	Pershore St	M10
Little Shadwell St	M5	Myddleton St	D5	Phillips St Ind Est	P1
Liverpool St	R9	Navigation St	K9	Phoenix Business Pk	S1
Livery St	L6	**Nechells**	V1	Pickford St	Q9
Locke Pl	S7	Nechells Pk Rd	U1	Pinfold St	K8
Lodge Rd	F2	Nechells Parkway	R5	Pinto Cl	C9
Lombard St	P12	Nechells Pl	U1	Pitsford St	E3
Lord St	Q4	Needless All	L8	Pitt St	R6
Louisa St	H7	Nelson St	G7	Plough &	
Loveday St	M5	New Bartholomew		Harrow Rd	C11
Love La	P4	St	P8	Pool St	P1
Lower Dartmouth St	T8	Newbold Cft	T2	Pope St	F5
Lower Essex St	M11	New Bond St	T10	Port Hope Rd	S14
Lower Loveday St	L4	New Canal St	P8	Powell St	G6
Lower Severn St	L9	Newhall Hill	H6	Power Cres	E10
Lower Temple St	L8	Newhall St	J6	Premier Trd Est	Q4
Lower Twr St	L3	Newhope Cl	L13	Price St	M5
Lower Trinity St	R10	New John St	N3	Princip St	M5
Lowe St	S12	New John St W	J2	Printing Ho St	M6
Lucas Circ	J2	New Mkt St	K7	Priory Queensway,	
Ludgate Hill	K6	New Moseley Rd	R13	The	M7
Lytham Cft	K11	New Spring St	E5	Pritchett St	M3
Macdonald St	N12	New Spring St N	D3	Proctor St	R3
Magreal Trd Est	C7	New St	M8	Queens Hosp Cl	H11
Mainstream Way	V4	New Summer St	L4	Quigley Av	T9
Malcolmson Cl	B13	Newton St	M6	Radnor St	D1
Manchester St	M3	**Newtown**	J1	Rake Way	G10
Margaret St	K7	Newtown Dr	H1	Rann Cl	E10
Mariner Av	A10	Newtown		Ravenhurst St	R12
Marroway St	B6	Middleway	M2	Rawlins St	E10
Marshall St	K10	New Town Row	M2	Rea St	P11
Mary Ann St	K6	Niall Cl	A13	Rea St S	N12
Mary St	J5	Noel Rd	B10	Rea Ter	Q9
Masshouse La	P7	Norman St	A3	Rectory Gro	A1
Maxstoke St	U9	Northampton St	H4	Regent Par	H5
Mearse Cl	E3	Northbrook St	B5	Regent Pk Rd	V12
Mease Cft	U8	North Holme	V9	Regent Pl	H5
Melton Dr	G14	Northumberland St	S6	Regent St	H5
Melvina Rd	U4	Northwood St	H6	Reservoir Retreat	C10
Meredith Pool Cl	B13	Norton St	D2	Reservoir Rd	B9
Meriden St	P10	Nova Scotia St	P7	Richard St	Q3
Merryhill St	B1	Nursery Rd	G1	Rickman Dr	K13
Meyrick Wk	B11	Oak Hill Dr	A14	Ridley St	J11
Middleway Vw	E6	Old Bridge St	G1	Ringway	
Midford Gro	J12	Old Camp Hill	S12	Business Pk	R2
Midland St	V7	Old Smithy Pl	E2	River St	R9
Milford Cft	K3	Old Snow Hill	L5	Rocky La	T1
Milk St	Q10	Old Sq	M7	Rocky La Trd Est	S1
Mill Burn Way	U8	Oliver Rd	C9	Rodney Cl	D8
Mill La	P10	Oliver St	S2	Rosebery St	D4
Mill St	P3	Oozells St	H9	Roseland Way	G11
Milton St	M1	Orchid Dr	K1	Rotton Pk St	C7
Moat La	N9	Orwell Pas	N9	Rupert St	R4
Moland St	N4	Osler St	B9	Ruston St	E10
Montague St	S8	Oxford St	P10	Ryland Rd	H14
		Paddocks Grn	D3	Ryland St	F10

Street	Ref	Street	Ref	Street	Ref
Sadlers Wk	D10	Spring Hill Pas	E6	Victor Rd	A1
St. Andrew's Rd	T8	Spring St	K13	Vittoria St	H5
St. Andrew's St	U9	Stainsby Av	H2	Vyse St	H5
St. Chad's Circ	L6	Stanhope Rd	P14	Walter St	T1
St. Chad's		Staniforth St	N4	Wardlow Rd	S3
Queensway	M5	Star Hill	G13	Ward St	M4
St. Clements Rd	V1	Station St	L10	Warner St	R12
St. Georges Cl	D14	Steelhouse La	M6	Warstone La	F5
St. Georges St	K4	Stephenson Pl	M9	Warstone Par E	G4
St. Helen's Pas	H6	Stephenson St	L9	Warwick Pas	M8
St. James Pl	S6	Steward St	D6	Warwick St	R11
St. James Rd	F12	Stirling Rd	A11	Washington St	J10
St. Jude's Pas	L10	Stoke Way	H10	Waterloo St	K8
St. Lukes Rd	M14	Stone Rd	K14	Waterside	U8
St. Marks Cres	E7	Stone Yd	Q10	Waterside Vw	D3
St. Marks St	F6	Stour St	D6	Water St	K6
St. Martin's Circ		Stratford Pl	R13	Waterworks Rd	B10
Queensway	M9	Stratford Rd	S13	Watery La	
St. Martin's St	G11	Stratford St N	S13	Middleway	S8
St. Mary's Row	M6	Suffolk St		Weaman St	M6
St. Paul's Sq	K6	Queensway	K9	Well La	P9
St. Phillips Pl	L7	Sugden Gro	M12	Well St	H3
St. Stephen's St	M1	Summer Cft	L1	Westbourne Cres	E13
St. Vincent St	F8	Summerfield Rd	A6	Westbourne Gdns	D14
St. Vincent St W	D9	Summer Hill Rd	F6	Westbourne Rd	B14
Salop St	Q13	Summer Hill St	G7	Western Rd	C5
Saltley Rd	U2	Summer Hill Ter	G6	West Grn Cl	G13
Saltley Viaduct	V2	Summer La	L5	West Holme	V9
Sampson Rd	T14	Summer Rd	J14	Westhorpe Gro	J2
Sampson Rd N	T12	Summer Row	J7	Westley St	S9
Sandfields Av	U12	Sutton St	K11	Wharf La	E2
Sand Pits	F6	Swallow St	K9	Wharf St	D1
Sandy Way	G10	Sydney Rd	V9	Wheeler St	K1
Sarah St	U9	Talbot St	B1	Wheeley's La	H12
Scotland St	H7	Templefield Gdns	V10	Whitehouse St	Q1
Sefton Rd	B9	Temple Pas	L8	Whitfield Gro	K13
Severn St	K10	Temple Row	L8	Whitmore St	F2
Shadwell St	M5	Temple Row W	L7	Whittall St	M6
Shawbury Gro	Q13	Temple St	L8	Wiggin St	B7
Shaw's Pas	P8	Tenby St	G5	William Booth La	L5
Sheepcote St	G10	Tenby St N	G5	William Henry St	S1
Shefford Rd	P2	Tennant St	G11	William St	H11
Shepherds Gdns	G11	Theatre App	M10	William St N	L4
Sherborne Gro	E7	Theresa Rd	T14	Willow Gdns	B5
Sherborne St	F9	Thomas St	P1	Windmill St	L11
Sheringham	A12	Thorp St	L11	Windsor Ind Est	S2
Sherlock St	M13	Tilton Rd	V9	Windsor St	Q3
Shetland Cl	C9	Tower St	L3	Windsor St S	R5
Shillcock Gro	M3	Townsend Way	G7	**Winson Green**	**B2**
Shire Cl	B8	Trent St	Q9	Witton St	T8
Shyltons Cft	E9	Trinity Ter	S12	Wolseley St	U8
Skinner La	N11	Unett St	J2	Woodcock St	P5
Skipton Rd	D10	Union Pas	M8	Woodcote Way	D4
Sloane St	H7	Union St	M8	Woodview Dr	J14
Smallbrook		Upper Dean St	M10	Wrentham St	L12
Queensway	M9	Upper Gough St	K11	Wrottesley St	M10
Small Heath Br	U14	Upper Marshall St	K10	Wyndham Rd	B11
Small Heath		Upper Trinity St	R10	Wynn St	K12
Highway	U13	Uxbridge St	K2	Yew Tree Rd	H12
Smith St	H2	Vann Cl	V13		
Snow Hill		Vaughton St	P13		
Queensway	L6	Vaughton St S	N14		
Soho Pool Way	D1	Vauxhall Gro	T5		
Southacre Av	M12	Vauxhall Rd	S6		
South Holme	V9	Vauxhall Trd Est	U4		
South Rd	T14	Venetia Rd	V9		
Spencer St	H4	Venture Way	Q4		
Spooner Cft	M13	Verbena Gdns	S3		
Springbank Rd	J14	Vere St	L13		
Springfield St	D7	Vernolds Cft	M12		
Spring Gro Gdns	B1	Vesey St	M5		
Spring Hill	D5	Viaduct St	S7		
Spring Hill Ind Pk	D6	Vicarage Rd	C12		

COVENTRY URBAN page 68

Street	Ref	Street	Ref	Street	Ref	Street	Ref
Abbey Hill	A3	**Brandon**	**C2**	**Corley Ash**	**A1**	Earlsdon Av S	B2
Albany Rd	B2	Brandon La	C3	**Corley Moor**	**A1**	**Eathorpe**	**C4**
Alderman's Green	**B1**	Brandon Rd	C2	**Coundon**	**A1**	Eburne Rd	B1
Alderman's Grn Rd	B1	Bredon Av	C2	**Court House Green**	**B2**	**Edgewick**	**B1**
Allard Way	B2	Bridle Brook La	A1	**Coventry**	**B2**	Exhall Rd	B1
Allesley	**A1**	Broad La	A2	Coventry Airport	B3	Farmer Ward Rd	A3
Allesley Old Rd	B2	**Brownshill Green**	**A1**	Coventry Eastern		Fieldgate La	A3
Ansty	**C1**	Brown's La	A1	Bypass	C2	Fineacre La	C3
Ashow	**A4**	**Bubbenhall**	**B3**	Coventry Rd		Fivefield Rd	A1
Avon St	B2	Bulkington Rd	C1	(Baginton)	B3	Fletchamstead	
Baginton	**B3**	**Burton Green**	**A3**	Coventry Rd		Highway	A2
Barnacle	**C1**	**Canley**	**A2**	(Bedworth)	B1	**Foleshill**	**B1**
Beake Av	B1	Cannon Hill Rd	A2	Coventry Rd		Foleshill Rd	B1
Beechwood Av	A2	Castle Rd	A3	(Bulkington)	C1	Fosse Way	C3
Bell Green	**B1**	**Chapel Fields**	**A2**	Coventry Rd		Four Pounds Av	A2
Bell Grn Rd	B1	Charter Av	A2	(Warwick)	A4	**Gibbet Hill**	**A3**
Bennett's Rd N	A1	Chesils, The	B2	**Crackley**	**A3**	Gibbet Hill Rd	A3
Bennett's Rd S	B1	Cheveral Av	B1	Crackley La	A3	**Goodyers End**	**B1**
Bericote Rd	A4	**Cheylesmore**	**B2**	Crew La	A3	Goodyers End La	B1
Binley	**C2**	Church La	A1	Cromwell La	A2	**Gosford Green**	**B2**
Binley Rd	C2	Church Rd	C1	**Cubbington**	**B4**	Grange Rd	B1
Binley Woods	**C2**	Clarendon St	B4	Cubbington Rd	B4	Green La	B3
Birdingbury Rd	C4	Clay La	A1	Dalehouse La	A3	Harnall La E	B2
Blackberry La	B2	Clifford Br Rd	C2	Dunchurch Highway	A2	Harvest Hill La	A1
Blackdown	**B4**	Clinton La	A3	Dyer's La	C3	**Hawkes End**	**A1**
Black Horse Rd	B1	**Corley**	**A1**	Earlsdon Av N	B2	Hawkes Mill La	A1

Street	Ref	Street	Ref	Street	Ref
Hen La	B1	Kirby Cor Rd	A2		
Henley Rd	C1	**Ladyes Hill**	**A3**		
High St	A3	Langbank Av	B2		
Hill Wootton	**A4**	Leamington Rd	B2		
Hill Wootton Rd	A4	Leamington Rd			
Hinckley Rd	C1	(Kenilworth)	A4		
Hipswell Highway	C2	**Leek Wootton**	**A4**		
Hockley	**A2**	Leicester La	B4		
Holbrooks	**B1**	Leicester St	B4		
Hollyfast La	A1	Lenton's La	C1		
Hollyfast Rd	A1	Leyes La	A3		
Holyhead Rd	B2	**Lillington**	**B4**		
Howes La	B3	Lillington Av	A4		
Humber Rd	B2	Lillington La	B4		
Hunningham	**C4**	Lime Av	B4		
Kenilworth	**A3**	Lockhurst La	B1		
Kenilworth Rd	A3	London Rd	B2		
Kenilworth Rd		Longfellow Rd	B2		
(Cubbington)	B4	Longford Rd	B1		
Kenilworth Rd (Royal		Long La	A1		
Leamington Spa)	A4	**Lower Eastern**			
Keresley	**A1**	Green	A2		
Keresley		Lower Rd	C1		
Newland	**B1**	**Lower Stoke**	**B2**		
Kingfield Rd	B2	Lythalls La	B1		
Kirby Corner	**A2**	**Marton**	**C4**		

Marton Rd C4
Mason Av B4
Middle Stoke B2
Mile La B2
Mill Hill B3
Milverton A4
Moorfield, The B2
Moseley Av B2
Neal's Green B1
New Rd B1
Northumberland Rd A4
Oak La A1
Offchurch B4
Old Ch Rd B1
Old Milverton Rd A4
Oxford Rd C3
Park Hill A3
Phoenix Way B2
Pickford A1
Pickford Green A1
Pinkett's Booth A1
Plott La C3
Potter's Green C1
Primrose Hill A4
Princethorpe C4
Princethorpe Way C2
Radford B1
Radford Rd B2
Randall Rd A3
Rotherham Rd B1
Rowley Rd B3
Rowley's Grn La B1
Royal Leamington Spa B4
Rugby Rd (Binley Woods) C2
Rugby Rd (Cubbington) B4
Rugby Rd (Princethorpe) C4
Rugby Rd (Royal Leamington Spa) A4
Rugby Rd (Weston under Wetherley) B4
Ryton-on-Dunsmore C3
St. James La B2
St. Martin's Rd B3
Sandy La (Blackdown) A4
Sandy La (Milverton) A4
School La (Exhall) B1
School La (Stretton-on-Dunsmore) C3
School St C3
Sewall Highway B2
Shakers La C4
Shilton C1
Shilton La (Bulkington) C1
Shilton La (Shilton) C1
Siskin Dr B3
Sky Blue Way B2
Spon End B2
Staircase La A2
Stareton B3
Stivichall B2
Stonebridge Highway B3
Stoneleigh B3
Stoneleigh Hill B3
Stoneleigh Hill B3
Stoney Stanton Rd B2
Stretton-on-Dunsmore C3
Tamworth Rd A1
Telford Av B4
Tile Hill A2
Tile Hill La A2
Tollbar End B3
Top Rd C1
Upper Eastern Green A2
Upper Eastern Grn La A2
Upper Stoke B2
Wall Hill Rd A1
Walsgrave on Sowe C2
Warwick A4
Warwick Pl A4
Warwick Rd B2
Warwick Rd (Kenilworth) A4
Washbrook La A1
Watery La B1
Welsh Rd B4
Westhill Rd B4
Weston La B3
Weston under Wetherley B4
Westwood Heath A2
Westwood Heath Rd A2
Wheelwright La B1
Whitemoor A3
Whitley B2
Whitmore Park B1
Whoberley A2
Wigston Rd A2
Willenhall B2
Willenhall La C2
Willes Rd B4
Windmill Rd B1
Windy Arbour A3
Winsford Av A2
Wolston C3
Wolston La C3
Woodway La C1
Woodway Park C1
Wyken B2
Wyken Cft C2

LEICESTER URBAN page 69

Abbey La B3
Abbey Pk Rd B3
Aikman Av B3
Anstey B3
Anstey La B3
Anstey La (Groby) A3
Anstey La (Thurcaston) B2
Anstey Way B3
Asquith Way B4
Attlee Way B4
Avebury Av B3
Aylestone B4
Aylestone La C4
Aylestone Rd B4
Barkby C2
Barkby La C2
Barkby Rd C3
Barkby Rd (Queniborough) C2
Barkby Rd (Syston) C2
Barkby Thorpe La C2
Barkby Thorpe Rd C3
Barrow Rd (Quorn) B1
Barrow Rd (Sileby) C1
Barrow upon Soar B1
Barry Dr A4
Beacon Rd (Loughborough) A1
Beacon Rd (Woodhouse Eaves) A1
Beaumont Leys B3
Beaumont Leys La B3
Beeby Rd C2
Beggars La A4
Belgrave C3
Belgrave Rd C3
Bennion Rd B3
Benscliffe Rd A2
Berrycott La C1
Big La C1
Birstall C2
Birstall Rd C3
Blaby Rd B4
Bond La B1
Bradgate Hill A2
Bradgate Rd (Anstey) A2
Bradgate Rd (Cropston) B2
Brand Hill A2
Brand La A1
Braunstone B4
Braunstone Av B4
Braunstone La B4
Braunstone La E B4
Braunstone Way B4
Breakback Rd A1
Broad Av C3
Broome La C1
Burleys Way B3
Burnham Dr B3
Carisbrooke Rd C4
Carlton Dr C4
Catherine St C3
Charley Rd A1
Chaveney Rd B1
Chesterfield Rd C4
Church Hill A1
Church Rd (Evington) C4
Church Rd (Thurlaston) A4
Colchester Rd C3
Coleman Rd C3
Copse Cl C4
Cort Cres B4
Cossington C2
Cossington Rd C1
Cropston B2
Cropston Rd B3
Dane Hills B3
Dean's La A1
Desford La A3
Desford Rd (Enderby) A4
Desford Rd (Kirby Muxloe) A3
Desford Rd (Thurlaston) A4
Dominion Rd B3
Dorest Av B4
Downing Dr C4
Duncan Rd B4
Dysart Way C3
East Goscote C2
East Pk Rd C4
Enderby A4
Enderby Rd A4
Ethel Rd C4
Evington C4
Evington La C4
Evington Rd C4
Farley Way B1
Field Head A2
Forest Rd (Loughborough) A1
Forest Rd (Narborough) A4
Forest Rd (Woodhouse) A1
Fosse Rd N B3
Fosse Rd S B4
Fosse Way C2
Frog Island B3
Gartree Rd C4
Gipsy La C3
Glebe Way C2
Gleneagles Av C3
Glenfield B3
Glenfield Frith Dr B3
Glenfield Rd B3
Glenfrith Way B3
Glenhills Way B4
Glen Parva B4
Glen Rd C4
Gooding Av B4
Goodwood Rd C3
Grace Rd B4
Great Cen Rd B1
Greengate La B2
Green La Rd C3
Groby A3
Groby La A2
Groby Rd B3
Groby Rd (Anstey) B3
Groby Rd (Glenfield) A3
Groby Rd (Ratby) A3
Gynsill Lnae B3
Halifax Dr B3
Hallam Cres E B4
Hallfields La B2
Hall Wk A4
Halstead Rd B1
Hamilton C3
Hastings Rd C3
Heacham Dr B3
Henley Rd B3
High St (Barrow upon Soar) B1
High St (Quorn) B1
High St (Syston) C2
Hinckley Rd B4
Holderness Rd B3
Humberstone C3
Humberstone Dr C3
Humberstone Rd C3
Humberstone Rd (Thurmaston) C3
Hungarton Boul C3
Joe Moores La A2
John St A4
Keyham La C3
Keyham La W C3
King Richards Rd B3
King St C2
Kirby Fields A4
Kirby La A4
Kirby Muxloe A3
Kirby Rd A3
Knighton C4
Knighton Gra Rd C4
Knighton La E B4
Knighton Rd C4
Krefeld Way B3
Leicester B4
Leicester Forest East A4
Leicester La (Desford) A4
Leicester La (Enderby) A4
Leicester La (Swithland) B2
Leicester Rd (Glenfield) B3
Leicester Rd (Groby) A3
Leicester Rd (Markfield) A2
Leicester Rd (Mountsorrel) B1
Leicester Rd (Oadby) C4
Leicester Rd (Quorn) B1
Leicester Rd (Thurcaston) B2
Leicester Rd (Wigston) C4
Leicester Western Bypass B3
Liberty Rd B3
Link Rd B2
London Rd C4
Loughborough A1
Loughborough Rd B3
Loughborough Rd (Loughborough) B1
Loughborough Rd (Mountsorrel) B1
Loughborough Rd (Quorn) B1
Lower Keyham La C3
Lubbesthorpe Way B4
Lutterworth Rd B4
Main St B4
Main St (Cossington) C2
Main St (Evington) C4
Main St (Glenfield) A3
Main St (Kirby Muxloe) A3
Main St (Newtown Linford) A2
Main St (Ratby) A3
Main St (Ratcliffe on the Wreake) C1
Main St (Swithland) B2
Main St (Woodhouse Eaves) A1
Manor Rd C4
Maplewell Rd A2
Markfield A2
Markfield La A2
Markfield Rd (Groby) A3
Markfield Rd (Ratby) A3
Meadow Way C4
Melbourne Rd C4
Melton Rd C3
Melton Rd (Barrow upon Soar) B1
Mill Hill A4
Milligan Rd B4
Mountsorrel B1
Mountsorrel La (Rothley) B2
Mountsorrel La (Sileby) B1
Mowmacre Hill B3
Nanpantan A1
Nanpantan Rd A1
Narborough Rd B4
Narborough Rd S B4
Nedham St C3
Netherhall Rd C3
Newark Rd C3
New Ashby Rd A1
New Parks B3
New Parks Way B3
New Romney Cres C3
New St C4
Newtown Linford A2
Newtown Linford La A3
Newtown Unthank A3
North End B1
North Evington C3
North St B1
Oadby C4
Oadby Rd C4
Old Ashby Rd A1
Old Gate Rd C1
Overdale Rd C4
Oxford St B3
Palmerston Way C4
Parker Dr B3
Park Hill La C1
Park Rd A1
Pindar Rd B3
Priory La A2
Queens Rd C4
Queniborough Rd C2
Quorn B1
Quorn - Mountsorrel Bypass B1
Ratby A3
Ratby La (Kirby Muxloe) A3
Ratby La (Markfield) A3
Ratby Rd A3
Ratcliffe on the Wreake C1
Ratcliffe Rd C1
Raw Dykes Rd B4
Red Hill Way B3
Regent Rd C4
Reservoir Rd B2
Ridings, The B2
Roecliffe Rd A2
Rosemead Dr C4
Rothley B2
Rothley Rd B1
Rushey Mead C3
Sacheverell Way A3
Saffron La B4
Saffron Rd B4
St. Margaret's Way B3
St. Saviour's Rd C3
Scraptoft La C3
Scudamore Rd A3
Seagrave C1
Seagrave Rd (Sileby) C1
Seagrave Rd (Thrussington) C1
Seine La A4
Shady La C4
Shanklin Dr C4
Sharpley Hill A2
Shelthorpe A1
Sileby C1
Sileby Rd B1
Slash La B1
Snell's Nook La A1
Soar Rd B1
Soar Valley Way B4
Sparkenhoe St C3
Spencefield La C4
Spinney Hills C3
Stamford St A3
Station Rd (Cropston) B2
Station Rd (Glenfield) A3
Station Rd (Kirby Muxloe) A3
Station Rd (Ratby) A3
Stephenson Dr B3
Stonesby Av B4
Stoneygate C4
Stoughton Dr C4
Stoughton Dr S C4
Stoughton La C4
Stoughton Rd C4
Stoughton Rd (Oadby) C4
Strasbourg Dr B3
Sturdee Rd B4
Swithland B2
Swithland La B2
Syston C2
Syston Rd C2
Thorpe La C2
Thrussington Rd C1
Thurcaston B2
Thurlaston A4
Thurlaston La A4
Thurmaston C2
Thurmaston La C3
Thurnby C4
Thurncourt Rd C3
Troon Way C3
Ulverscroft La A2
Ulverscroft Rd C3
University Rd C4
Uplands Rd C4
Upperton Rd B4
Valley Rd A1
Vaughan Way B3
Victoria Pk Rd C4
Wakerley Rd C4
Walnut St B4
Walton Way B2
Wanlip C2
Wanlip La C2
Wanlip Rd C2
Warren Hill A2
Watergate La B4
Waterloo Way B4
Watermead Way C3
Welford Rd B3
Wembley Rd A3
West Av C4
Westfield La B2
Wicklow Dr C3
Wigston C4
Wigston La B4
Wigston Rd C4
Woodgate B3
Woodhouse B1
Woodhouse Eaves A1
Woodhouse La A1
Woodhouse Rd B1
Wood La B1
Woodthorpe B1

DERBY & NOTTINGHAM URBAN pages 70-71

Abbey Br E2
Abbey Hill A2
Abbey St (Derby) A3
Abbey St (Nottingham) E2
Acorn Bk F3
Acorn Way B3
Adbolton F2
Adbolton La F2
Addison Rd A3
Alfred's La C1
Alfreton Rd (Derby) B2
Alfreton Rd (Nottingham) E2
Allenton B4
Allestree A2
Allestree La A2
Alvaston B3
Ambaston C3
Ambaston La C3
Ambleside F2
Arbour Hill C2
Arleston Dr E2
Arleston La A4
Arnold F1
Arnold La F1
Arnold Rd E1
Arnott Hill Rd F1
Arno Vale Rd F1

Ascot Dr	B3	Cavendish Rd	F1	**Draycott**	**C3**
Ashbourne Rd	A3	**Chaddesden**	**B2**	Draycott Rd	
Aspley	**E1**	Chaddesden La	B3	(Borrowash)	C3
Aspley La	E2	Chaddesden Pk Rd	B3	Draycott Rd	
Aston		**Chaddesden**		(Breaston)	C3
(Chellaston)	B4	**Common**	**B2**	Draycott Rd (Sawley)	D3
Aston La (Shardlow)	C4	Chain La	A3	**Duffield**	**A1**
Aston-on-Trent	**C4**	Chalons Way	D1	**Duffieldbank**	**A1**
Attenborough	**E3**	Chapel St	B1	Duffield Bk	A1
Attenborough La N	E3	**Chellaston**	**B4**	Duffield Rd	
Awsworth	**D1**	Chellaston La	B4	(Allestree)	A2
Awsworth & Cossell		Chellaston Rd	B3	Duffield Rd	
Bypass	D1	**Cherrytree Hill**	**B3**	(Little Eaton)	A2
Awsworth La	D1	Chevin Rd	A1	**Dunkirk**	**E2**
Back La	C4	Chewton St	D1	**Eastwood**	**D1**
Bagnall Rd	E1	**Chilwell**	**E3**	Eastwood Rd	D1
Bakeacre La	A4	Chilwell La	D2	Eaton Bk	A1
Baker Rd	D1	Chilwell Rd	E3	**Edwalton**	**F3**
Baker St	B3	Church Hill	D1	Edwards La	F1
Banks Rd	D3	Church La (Barrow		Elton Rd	A3
Bargate	**B1**	upon Trent)	A4	**Elvaston**	**B3**
Bargate Rd	A1	Church La		Elvaston La	B3
Bar La	E1	(Darley Abbey)	A2	Faraday Rd	E2
Barrow La	B4	Church La (Horsley		**Farnah Green**	**A1**
Barrow upon Trent	**A4**	Woodhouse)	B1	Farnah Grn Rd	A1
Barton in Fabis	E3	Church La		Farnborough Rd	E3
Barton La		(Thrumpton)	D4	Ferrers Way	A2
(Attenborough)	D3	Church Rd		Field, The	C1
Barton La		(Greasley)	D1	Field La	B3
(Barton in Fabis)	F2	Church Rd		Fields Fm Rd	D3
Bassingfield La	F2	(Quarndon)	A2	Firestone	A1
Bath St	F2	Church St (Arnold)	F1	Flawforth La	F3
Beaufort St	B2	Church St		**Flaxholme**	**A1**
Beauvale	**D1**	(Eastwood)	D1	Ford La	A2
Beauvale Dr	C1	Church St (Horsley)	B1	Ford St	A3
Beckside	F3	Church St (Ilkeston)	C1	Forest Rd E	E2
Beechdale Rd	E2	Church St		Forest Rd W	E2
Beech La	C2	(Lockington)	D4	Foxhill Rd Cen	F2
Beeston	**E3**	Church St (Spondon)	B3	Foxhill Rd E	F2
Beeston Rd	E2	Church St		Foxhill Rd W	F2
Bell La	C1	(Stapleford)	D2	Frizams La	A4
Bells La	E1	**Church Wilne**	**C4**	**Gamston**	**F2**
Belper Rd (Bargate)	B1	**Cinderhill**	**E1**	Gamston Lings	
Belper Rd (Stanley		Cinderhill Rd	E1	Bar Rd	F3
Common)	C1	Cleve Av	D3	Gedling Rd	F1
Bestwood	**F1**	**Clifton**	**D3**	Gilt Hill	D1
Bestwood Pk Dr	E1	Clifton Boul	E2	Gin Cl Way	D1
Bestwood Pk Dr W	E1	Clifton La	E3	Glaisdale Dr E	E2
Bestwood Rd	E1	Cole La	C3	Glaisdale Dr W	E2
Bilborough	**E2**	Coleridge St	A3	Godfrey Dr	C2
Bilborough Rd	D2	College St	D3	Goodsmoor Rd	A3
Birchover Way	A2	Colwick Rd	F2	Goodwin's La	A1
Bishop's Dr	B2	Common, The	A2	Gordon Rd	F2
Blagreaves La	A3	Common La	C2	**Gotham**	**E4**
Blenheim Dr	A2	**Common Side**	**C1**	Gotham Rd	D4
Bondgate	C4	Compton Acres	F3	Grampian Way	A4
Borrowash	**C3**	Coppice Rd	F1	**Greasley**	**D1**
Borrowash Bypass	C3	Coronation Rd	D1	Green La	D1
Borrowash Rd	C3	Corporation Rd	D2	Greens La	D1
Boulton	**B3**	**Cossall**	**D1**	Gregory Boul	E2
Boulton La	B3	**Cossall Marsh**	**D1**	Greythorn Dr	F3
Boundary Rd	F3	Cossall Rd	D2	Gypsy La	C3
Boyer St	A3	**Cotmanhay**	**D1**	Hallam Way	C2
Brackley Gate	**B1**	Cotmanhay Rd	D1	Hall Fm Rd	A1
Bradmore	**F4**	Coxbench	B1	Hampshire Rd	B2
Bradmore La	F3	Coxbench Rd	B1	Hand's Rd	C1
Bramcote	**E2**	Crayford Rd	B3	Hardy Barn	C1
Bramcote Av	E3	**Crewton**	**B3**	Hardy St	D1
Bramcote Hills	**E2**	Croft La	B2	Hartley Rd	E2
Bramcote La		Cross St	F1	Harvey Rd	B3
(Beeston)	E3	Cumberhills Rd	A1	Haslam's La	A2
Bramcote La		Dairy Ho Rd	A3	Hassock La N	C1
(Nottingham)	E2	**Dale Abbey**	**C2**	Hassock La S	C1
Breach Rd	C1	**Dale Moor**	**C2**	Havenbaulk La	A3
Breadsall	**B2**	Dale Rd (Dale Abbey)	C2	Haydn Rd	F1
Breadsall Hilltop	**B2**	Dale Rd (Spondon)	B3	**Hazelwood**	**A1**
Breaston	**D3**	Daleside Rd	F2	Hazelwood Hill	A1
Breckhill Rd	F1	**Darley Abbey**	**A2**	Hazelwood Rd	A1
Bridge Rd	E2	Davies St	F2	**Heanor**	**C1**
Bridgford Rd	F2	**Daybrook**	**F1**	**Heanor Gate**	**C1**
Brierley Way	A3	Dead La	D2	Heanor Rd (Ilkeston)	C1
Brighton Rd	B3	Dean St	A3	Heanor Rd (Smalley)	B1
Brisbane Rd	A3	Deep Dale La	A4	**Hemington**	**C4**
Broadgate	E2	**Denby**	**B1**	**Hempshill Vale**	**E1**
Broadway	A2	**Denby Bottles**	**B1**	Hickings La	D2
Broadway (Duffield)	A1	**Derby**	**A3**	Highbury Rd	E1
Brook Hill	**F3**	Derby Rd		**Highbury Vale**	**E1**
Brookside Rd	B2	(Aston-on-Trent)	C4	**High Lane**	**C2**
Broxtowe	**E1**	Derby Rd (Bramcote)	E2	High La Cen	C1
Broxtowe La	E1	Derby Rd		High La E	C2
Bulwell	**E1**	(Chaddesden)	B3	High La W	C2
Bunny	**F4**	Derby Rd (Chellaston)	B4	High Rd (Beeston)	E2
Bunny Hill	**F4**	Derby Rd (Denby)	B1	High Rd (Toton)	D3
Bunny La	F4	Derby Rd (Draycott)	C3	High St (Arnold)	F1
Burley La	A2	Derby Rd (Duffield)	A1	High St (Chellaston)	B4
Burton Rd	A3	Derby Rd (Heanor)	C1	High St (Heanor)	C1
Buxton Av	C1	Derby Rd (Ilkeston)	C2	High St (Long Eaton)	D3
Bye Pass Rd	E3	Derby Rd (Kegworth)	D4	Hillsway	A3
Callow Hill Way	A3	Derby Rd		Hilltop	B2
Camberley Rd	E1	(Long Eaton)	D3	Holborn Dr	A2
Carlton	**F2**	Derby Rd (Milford)	A1	**Holbrook**	**B1**
Carlton Hill	F2	Derby Rd		**Holbrook Moor**	**B1**
Carlton Rd	F2	(Nottingham)	E2	Holbrook Rd	B3
Carrington	**F1**	Derby Rd (Risley)	C3	Hollington Rd	E2
Castle Boul	E2	Derby Rd (Spondon)	B3	Hollow, The	A3
Castle Br Rd	E2	Derby Rd (Stanley)	B2	Holly Brook Way	D1
Castle Donington	**C4**	Derby Rd (Stapleford)	D3	Holly Rd	D1
Cat & Fiddle La	C2	Derwent Par	B2	Hopewell Rd	C3
Catfoot La	F1	Dovecote Rd	D1	**Horsley**	**B1**
Cavendish Bridge	**C4**	Dovedale Av	D3		

Horsley Rd	B1	**Makeney**	**A1**	Nottingham Rd	
Horsley Woodhouse	**B1**	Makeney Rd		(Trowell)	D2
Hucknall La	E1	(Duffield)	A1	**Nuthall**	**D1**
Hucknall Rd	E1	Makeney Rd		Nuthall Rd	E1
Humber Rd	E2	(Holbrook)	B1	**Oakwood**	**B2**
Humber Rd S	E3	Manners Av	C1	**Ockbrook**	**C3**
Huntley Av	B3	**Manor Park**	**F3**	**Old Basford**	**E1**
Ilkeston Rd		Manor Rd (Barton in		**Osmaston**	**B3**
(Bramcote)	D2	Fabis)	E3	Osmaston Pk Rd	A3
Ilkeston Rd (Heanor)	C1	Manor Rd (Derby)	A3	Osmaston Rd	A3
Ilkeston Rd (Ilkeston)	D2	Mansfield Rd		Over La	A1
Ilkeston Rd (Radford)	E2	(Derby)	A2	Oxclose La	F1
Ilkeston Rd (Stanley		Mansfield Rd		Park Hall La	C2
Common)	B1	(Heanor)	C1	Park La (Allestree)	A2
Ilkeston Rd		Mansfield Rd		Park La	
(Stapleford)	D2	(Nottingham)	F2	(Castle Donington)	C4
Ilkeston Rd (Trowell)	D2	Manvers St	F2	Park La (Nottingham)	E1
Ingleby	**A4**	Maple Dr	B4	Park Rd	A1
Ingleby Rd	B4	**Mapperley**		Park Rd (Ilkeston)	D2
Jubilee Rd	B4	**(Derbyshire)**	**C1**	Park St	E3
Kedleston Rd	A2	**Mapperley**		Pasture Rd	D2
Kegworth Rd		**(Nottingham)**	**F1**	**Pastures Hill**	A3
(Gotham)	E4	Mapperley La	C1	**Pear Tree**	**A3**
Kegworth Rd		**Mapperley Park**	**F1**	Perth St	B2
(Kingston on Soar)	D4	Mapperley Plains	F1	Petersham Rd	D3
Keldholme La	B3	Mapperley Rd	F2	Pit La	C1
Keyworth La	F4	Marian Marian Way	F2	Plains Rd	F1
Kilburn	**B1**	**Markeaton**	**A2**	**Plumtree**	**F3**
Killis La	B1	Markeaton La	A2	**Plumtree Park**	**F4**
Kimberley	**D1**	Market St	C1	**Porchester**	**F1**
Kimberley Eastwood		**Marlpool**	**C1**	Porchester Rd	F1
Bypass	E1	Matlock Rd	B2	Porter Rd	A3
Kimberley Rd	D1	Maws La	D1	Portland St	A3
Kings Dr	A3	Max Rd	B2	Port Way	B1
Kingston La	D4	Mayfield Rd	B2	Potato Pit La	C2
Kingston on Soar	**D4**	Meadow La (Chilwell)	E3	**Pride Park**	**B3**
King St	A1	Meadow La		Pride Parkway	B3
Kingsway	A3	(Long Eaton)	D3	Prince Charles Av	A3
Kirk Hallam	**C2**	Meadow Rd	E3	Priorway Av	C3
Kirk La	F3	**Meadows**	**F2**	**Quarndon**	**A2**
Kitchener Av	A3	Meadows Way	F2	Quarry Hill Rd	D2
Lace Market	**F2**	Melbourne Rd	E2	Queen's Bower Rd	F1
Ladywood Rd	C2	Melton Gdns	F3	Queen's Dr	F2
Landmere La	F3	Melton Rd	F3	Queen's Rd	E3
Lane, The	D1	Merlin Way	D2	Queen's Rd E	E2
Langley	**C1**	Merrill Way	B4	Queen's Rd W	E3
Langley Mill	**C1**	**Mickleover**	**A3**	Queensway	A3
Larkfield Rd	D1	**Mickleborough Hill**	**F3**	Racecourse Rd	F2
Leake Rd	E4	**Micklemeadow**	**A3**	Radbourne La	A3
Lenton	**E2**	Middleton Boul	E2	Radcliffe Rd	F2
Lenton Abbey	**E2**	Mileash La	A2	**Radford**	**E2**
Lenton Boul	E2	**Milford**	**A1**	Radford Boul	E2
Lilac Gro	E3	Mill Hill La (Breaston)	D3	Radford Rd	E1
Lime Gro	B3	Mill Hill La (Derby)	A3	Ransom Rd	F1
Lime La	B2	Mill St	E1	Ratcliffe La	A2
Lindon Dr	B3	Milnhay Rd	C1	**Ratcliffe on Soar**	**D4**
Litchurch La	B3	Milward Rd	C1	**Rawson Green**	**B1**
Little Chester	**A2**	Moorbridge La	D2	Raynesway	B3
Little Eaton	**B2**	Moorgreen	D1	Rectory La	B2
Little Hallam Hill	C2	Moor La	B3	Rectory Rd	F2
Little Hallam La	D2	Moor La (Barrow		Redcliffe Rd	F2
Littleover	**A3**	upon Trent)	A4	**Redhill**	**F1**
Littleover La	A3	Moor La		Redhill Rd	F1
Littlewell La	D2	(Dale Abbey)	C2	Red La	A1
Lockington Rd	C4	Moor La (Ockbrook)	C3	Regatta Way	F2
Lock La	D4	Moor Rd	B2	Reginald Rd S	B3
Locko Rd	B3	Moor St	B3	Ridge Way	E1
Lockton Av	C1	Moorway La	A3	Ridings, The	C3
London Rd	A3	**Morley**	**B2**	**Rise Park**	**E1**
London Rd		Morley La		**Risley**	**D3**
(Shardlow)	B4	(Little Eaton)	B2	Risley La	C3
Long Eaton	**D3**	Morley La (Stanley)	C2	Robinettes La	D2
Longfield La	D2	Morley Rd	B2	Robin Hood Way	F2
Long La		Musters Rd	F3	Robins Wd Rd	E2
(Attenborough)	E3	Narrow La	D1	Rolleston Dr	F1
Long La (Kegworth)	D4	**New Basford**	**E1**	Roper Av	C1
Longmoor La		Newdigate Rd	D1	**Rose Hill**	**A3**
(Breaston)	D3	**Newlands**	**C1**	Rose Hill St	A3
Longmoor La		New Rd	E3	**Ruddington**	**F3**
(Stapleford)	D3	**New Sawley**	**D3**	Ruddington La	F3
Longmoor Rd	D3	**Newthorpe**	**D1**	Rugby Rd	F3
Lord St	B3	Newthorpe Common	D1	Rushy La	D3
Loscoe Rd	C1	**New Zealand**	**A3**	Ruskin Av	D3
Loughborough Rd		Nightingale Rd	B3	Russell Dr	E2
(Ruddington)	F3	No Man's La	C2	Rycroft Rd	C4
Loughborough Rd		**Normanton**	**A3**	Rykneld Rd	A3
(West Bridgford)	F3	Normanton Rd	A3	Ryknield Rd	B1
Lower Kilburn	B1	Nottingham Rd		**Rylands**	**E3**
Lower Rd	A2	(Arnold)	F1	St. Alban's Rd	
Lowes La	B4	Nottingham Rd		(Arnold)	F1
Low's La	C2	(Borrowash)	C3	St. Albans Rd	A3
Low Wd Rd	E1	Nottingham Rd		St. Alban's Rd	
Mackworth	**A3**	(Derby)	B3	(Nottingham)	E1
Maine Dr	B3	Nottingham Rd		St. Andrews Vw	B2
Main Rd (Watnall)	D1	(Eastwood)	D1	**St. Ann's**	**F2**
Main Rd (Wilford)	F2	Nottingham Rd		St. Ann's Well Rd	F2
Main St (Ambaston)	C3	(Gotham)	E4	St. Chad's Rd	A3
Main St (Breaston)	C3	Nottingham Rd		St. Norbert Dr	C2
Main St (Bulwell)	E1	(Ilkeston)	D2	St. Peter's St	E2
Main St (Hemington)	C4	Nottingham Rd		St. Wilfred's Rd	C2
Main St (Horsley		(Kimberley)	D1	Sandbed La	B1
Woodhouse)	B1	Nottingham Rd		Sandcroft Rd	B3
Main St (Kimberley)	D1	(Long Eaton)	D3	Sandfield Rd	F1
Main St (Lockington)	D4	Nottingham Rd		**Sandiacre**	**D3**
Main St (Long Eaton)	D3	(Nottingham)	E1	Sandringham Dr	B3
Main St (Mapperley)	C1	Nottingham Rd		Sawley Rd	
Main St (Newthorpe)	D1	(Nuthill)	E1	(Breaston)	D3
Main St (Strelley)	D2	Nottingham Rd			
Main St		(Spondon)	B3		
(Weston-on-Trent)	B4	Nottingham Rd			
		(Stapleford)	D2		

Sawley Rd C3
School La D2
Sellers Wd Dr E1
Shacklecross C3
Shardlow C4
Shardlow Rd (Alvaston) B3
Shardlow Rd (Aston-on-Trent) C4
Sharpley Hill E4
Shaw La A1
Shelton Lock B4
Sherwood F1
Sherwood Ri F1
Shipley Common C1
Shipley La C1
Side Ley D4
Sinfin A4
Sinfin Av B4
Sinfin La A4
Sir Frank Whittle Rd B3
Slack La A3
Slack Rd C1
Smalley B1
Smalley Dr B2
Smalley Mill Rd B1
Smithy Houses B1
Sneinton F2
Snelsmoor La B4
Somersby Rd F1
South Ch Dr E3
South St C1
Spittal C4
Spondon B3
Spring La F1
Springwood Dr B2
Stanley C2
Stanley Common C2
Stanton by Bridge B4
Stanton Gate D2
Stanton Rd D3
Stapleford D3
Stapleford La D3
Stapleford Rd D2
Station Rd (Beeston) E3
Station Rd (Borrowash) C3
Station Rd (Castle Donington) C4
Station Rd (Draycott) C3
Station Rd (Heanor) C1
Station Rd (Ilkeston) D1
Station Rd (Long Eaton) D3
Station Rd (Spondon) B3
Station Rd (Stanley) C2
Station Rd (Sutton Bonington) D4
Station Rd (West Hallam) C2
Stenson A4
Stenson Rd A3
Stockbrook St A3
Stockhill La E1
Stoney La B3
Stores Rd A2
Strelley D2
Strelley Rd E2
Summerfields Way C1
Sunny Gro B3
Sunny Hill A3
Sutton Av B4
Swarkestone B4
Swarkestone Rd (Barrow upon Trent) A4
Swarkestone Rd (Chellaston) B4
Swingate D1
Swingate D1
Talbot St F2
Tamworth Rd C4
Thoresby Rd E2
Thorneywood F2
Thrumpton D4
Thulston B4
Tollerton F3
Tollerton Rd F3
Top Valley E1
Top Valley Dr E1
Toton D3
Toton La D3
Town St (Bramcote) D2
Town St (Duffield) A1
Town St (Sandiacre) D3
Trent Boul F2
Trent Br F2
Trent La (Castle Donington) C4
Trent La (Weston-on-Trent) B4
Trentlock D4
Trent Rd E3
Trevor Rd F3
Trough Rd D1
Trowell D2
Trowell Rd D2
Twyford A4
University Boul E2
Uppermoor Rd B3
Uttoxeter New Rd A3
Uttoxeter Old Rd A3
Uttoxeter Rd A3
Vale Rd F2
Valley Rd (Derby) A3
Valley Rd (Nottingham) E1
Valley Rd (West Bridgford) F3
Vernon Rd E1
Victoria Av C3
Victoria Embk F2
Victory Rd A3
Village Rd E3
Village St (Derby) A3
Village St (West Bridgford) F3
Walbrook Rd A3
Walker St D1
Warren La D4
Warwick Av A3
Watnall D1
Watnall Rd D1
Waverley St F2
Wellin La F3
Wells Rd, The F2
Westbourne Pk A3
West Bridgford F3
Westdale La E F1
Westdale La W F1
Western Boul E2
Western Outer Loop Rd E1
West Hallam C2
West Leake La E4
Weston-on-Trent B4
Weston Rd B4
Whitaker Rd A3
Whitemoor E1
Wigman Rd E2
Wilford F3
Wilford Gro F2
Wilford La F3
Wilford Rd F3
Willson Av A3
Wilmot St C1
Wilne La (Church Wilne) C4
Wilne La (Great Wilne) C4
Wilne Rd C3
Wilne Rd (Sawley) D4
Wilsthorpe D3
Wilsthorpe Rd (Breaston) D3
Wilsthorpe Rd (Long Eaton) D3
Wiltshire Rd B2
Wirksworth Rd A1
Wollaton E2
Wollaton Rd E2
Wollaton Vale D2
Woodborough Rd F2
Woodhouse Rd B1
Woodlands La A2
Woodlands Rd A2
Wood La B1
Wood Rd B2
Woodside B1
Woodside B1
Woodside Rd E2
Woodstock Rd D3
Woodthorpe F1
Woodthorpe Dr F1
Worrall Av F1
Wragley Way A4
Wysall F4
Wyvern Way B3

STOKE-ON-TRENT URBAN page 72

Abbey Hulton C2
Abbey La C2
Abbey Rd C2
Abbots Rd C2
Abbot's Way B2
Acres Nook B1
Acton A3
Adderley Green C2
Allerton Rd B3
Alsager Rd A1
Alsagers Bank A2
Anchor Rd C3
Apedale A1
Apedale Rd A2
Armshead Rd D2
Ash Bank C2
Ash Bk Rd C2
Audley A1
Audley Rd (Newcastle-under-Lyme) A1
Audley Rd (Talke Pits) A1
Avenue, The B2
Baddeley Edge C1
Baddeley Green C1
Baddeley Grn La C1
Bagnall C1
Bagnall Rd C1
Baldwin's Gate A3
Ball Green C1
Ball La C1
Bambury St C2
Bank Top B1
Barlaston Old Rd B3
Barlaston Rd C3
Basford B2
Basfordbridge La D1
Basford Pk Rd B2
Beaconsfield Dr C3
Belgrave Rd C3
Bellerton La C1
Bell's Hollow A1
Bemersley Rd C1
Bent La A3
Berry Hill C2
Beverley Dr C2
Biddulph Rd B1
Bignall End Rd A1
Bignall Hill A1
Birches Head Rd C2
Blackbank Rd A2
Black Bk Rd D1
Blurton C3
Blurton Rd C3
Blythe Bridge D3
Blythe Br Rd D3
Blythe Marsh D3
Boon Hill A1
Boon Hill Rd A1
Boothen B2
Boundary D3
Bradeley B1
Bradwell B1
Bradwell La B1
Brampton Rd B2
Breach Rd C1
Broadfield Rd B1
Broad La C1
Broad Meadow A2
Broad St B2
Brookhouse La C2
Brookwood Dr C3
Brown Edge C1
Brund La D1
Bucknall C2
Bucknall New Rd C2
Burslem B1
Butters Green A1
Butterton A3
Butterton La A3
Campbell Rd B3
Carmountside C1
Castle St A1
Caverswall D3
Caverswall La D3
Caverswall Old Rd D3
Caverswall Rd D3
Caverswell Common D2
Caverswall Rd D3
Cedar Rd A1
Cellarhead D2
Cellarhead Rd D2
Chaplin Rd C3
Cheadle Rd (Cheddleton) D1
Cheadle Rd (Draycott in the Moors) D3
Cheadle Rd (Forsbrook) D3
Cheadle Rd (Leekbrook) D1
Cheddleton D1
Cheddleton Heath D1
Chell Heath B1
Chell Heath Rd B1
Chell St C2
Chelmsford Dr C2
Chesterton B1
Church La (Endon) C1
Church La (Hanford) B3
Church La (Knutton) A2
Church La (Walstanton) B2
Church Rd C3
Church St (Audley) A1
Church St (Brown Edge) C1
City Rd B2
Clay Lake C1
Clayton B3
Clayton La B3
Clayton Rd B3
Clewlows Bk C1
Clough Hall B1
Clough St B2
Coalpitford La D1
Coalpit Hill A1
Cobridge B2
Cocknage Rd C3
College Rd B2
Common, The D3
Congleton Rd A1
Consall D2
Cookshill D3
Crackley A1
Crackley Bk A1
Cresswell D3
Cresswell Old La D3
Cross Heath B2
Cross La A1
Dartmouth Av B2
Davenport St B1
Dawlish Dr C2
Deansgate B2
Dean's La A1
Delphouse Rd D3
Denford D1
Denford Rd D1
Dilhorne D3
Dilhorne La D3
Dilhorne Rd (Dilhorne) D2
Dilhorne Rd (Forsbrook) D3
Dimsdale B2
Dimsdale Par W B2
Dividy Rd C2
Draycott Old Rd D3
Drayton Rd B3
Dresden C3
Drive, The A2
Eardleyend Rd A1
Eaves La C2
Endon C1
Endon Bank C1
Etruria B2
Etruria Rd B2
Etruria Vale Rd B2
Fegg Hayes B1
Fenton C2
Fenton Pk Rd C2
Festival Way B2
Folly, The D1
Folly La D1
Ford Green C1
Ford Grn Rd B1
Ford Hayes La C2
Forsbrook D3
Furlong Rd B1
Godleybarn La D2
Godleybrook D2
Godley La D3
Goldclough La B1
Goldenhill B1
Grange Rd C3
Greasley Rd C2
Great Chell B1
Greatoak Rd A1
Greenbank Rd B1
Greenway Hall Rd C1
Grindley La C3
Halmer End A1
Hanchurch B3
Handley Banks D3
Hanford B3
Hanley B2
Hanley Rd B1
Harpfield Rd B2
Hartshill Rd B2
Heathcote St C2
Heath Rd A3
High Carr B1
High La B1
High La (Alsagers Bank) A2
High La (Brown Edge) C1
High St B1
High St (Boon Hill) A1
High St (Caverswall) D3
High St (Dilhorne) D3
High St (Halmer End) A2
High St (Knutton) A2
High St (May Bank) B2
High St (Silverdale) A2
High St (Talke Pits) A1
High St (Walstanton) B2
Hilderstone Rd C3
Hill Chorlton A3
Hilton Rd B2
Hollybush C3
Hollywall Rd B1
Horse Bridge D1
Hulme C2
Hulme La C2
Hulme Rd C2
Huntley Rd D1
Jack Haye La C1
Keele A2
Keele Rd (Keele) A2
Keele Rd (Newcastle-under-Lyme) A2
Keelings Rd C2
Kidsgrove B1
Kidsgrove Bk B1
Kingsley Rd D2
King St C2
King St (Newcastle-under-Lyme) B2
Knowl Wall B3
Knowsley Rd D1
Knutton A2
Knutton Rd B2
Leek New Rd C1
Leek Rd C2
Leek Rd (Cheddleton) D1
Leek Rd (Endon) C1
Leek Rd (Weston Coyley) D2
Leek Rd (Wetley Rocks) D2
Leycett La A2
Lichfield St C2
Light Oaks C1
Lightwood C3
Lightwood Rd C3
Linley Rd A1
Little Chell B1
Liverpool Rd (Kidsgrove) B1
Liverpool Rd (Newcastle-under-Lyme) B2
London Rd B2
London Rd (Chesterton) A1
London Rd (Newcastle-under-Lyme) B2
Longport B1
Longton C3
Longton Hall Rd C3
Longton Rd (Barlaston) C3
Longton Rd (Trentham) B3
Lower Milehouse La B2
Lower St B2
Lowlands Rd B1
Lysander Rd C3
Madeley Heath A2
Market Pl B1
May Bank B2
Mayne St B3
Meir C3
Meir Heath D3
Merelake Rd A1
Middleport B1
Milehouse La B2
Miles Green A1
Mill La D2
Milton C1
Milton Rd C1
Moorland Rd B1
Mount Pleasant B3
Newcastle La B2
Newcastle Rd B2
Newcastle Rd (Talke) A1
Newcastle St B1
Newcastle-under-Lyme B2
Newfield B1
New Inn La B3
Newport La B1
New Rd (Audley) A1
New Rd (Dilhorne) D3
Newstead C3
Nile St B1
Normacot C3
North La C1
Northwood C2
Northwood (Newcastle-under-Lyme) B3
Northwood La B3
Norton Green C1
Norton-in-the-Moors C1
Oak Hill B3
Ostlers La D1
Oxford B1
Packmoor B1
Paris Av A2
Park End A1
Park Hall Rd C2
Park La (Audley) A1
Park La (Endon) D1
Park Rd (Butterton) B3
Park Rd (Silverdale) A2
Peacock Hay Rd B1
Peacock La B3
Penkhull New Rd B2
Pepper St A2
Pit La A1
Pits Hill B1
Port Hill B2
Porthill Bk B2
Post La C1
Potteries Way C2
Prince's Rd B2
Priory Rd B2
Quarry Bk Rd A2
Queen's Rd B2
Queensway B2
Raven's La A1
Redhills Rd C1
Red Street A1
Riceyman Rd B1
Roe La B3
Rough Close C3
Roughcote La D2
Rownall Rd D2
Ruxley Rd C2
St. Anne's Vale C1
St. Mary's Rd C2
Salters La D2
Sandon Rd C3
Sandyford B1
Sandy La (Baldwin's Gate) A3
Sandy La (Newcastle-under-Lyme) B2
School La D3
School Rd C1
Scot Hay Rd A2
Scotia Rd B1
Scott Hay A2
Seabridge B3
Seabridge La B3
Shaffalong La D1
Shelton New Rd B2
Shraleybrook A1
Silverdale A2
Silverdale Rd A2
Smallthorne B1
Snapehall A3
Sneyd Av B2
Sneyd Green C1
Sneyd St B2
Spring Bk Rd B1
Springfields B2
Square, The D3
Stafford Av B2
Stallington D3
Stallington Rd D3
Stanfield B1
Stanley C1
Stanley Matthews Way B3
Stanley Moor C1

Stanley Rd	C1	Talke Rd (Chesterton)	A1	Trent Vale	B3	Wedgwood	C3	Wetley Rocks	D2	
Station Rd (Cheddleton)	D1	Talke Rd (Red Street)	A1	Trent Valley Rd	B3	Wedgwood Dr	C3	Whitehurst La	D2	
Station Rd (Endon)	C1	Three Mile La	A2	Tunstall	B1	Wellfield Rd	C2	**Whitfield**	C1	
Station Rd (Halmer End)	A2	Tickhill La	D2	**Turnhurst**	B1	**Werrington**	D2	**Whitmore**	A3	Woodpark La C3
Station Rd (Keele)	A2	Tomkin Rd	D1	Turnhurst Rd	B1	Werrington Rd	C2	Whitmore Rd (Hanchurch)	B3	Woodside A3
Stockton Brook	C1	Tongue La	C1	**Ubberley**	C2	West Av	A1	Whitmore Rd		Wood St C3
Stoke-on-Trent	C2	Town Rd	B2	Uttoxeter Rd	C3	**Westbury Park**	B3	(Newcastle-under-Lyme)	A3	Wye Rd B3
Stoke Rd	B2	**Townsend**	C2	Valley Rd	D3	**Westcliffe**	B1	Willfield La	C1	
Stonehouses	D3	**Trentham**	B3	Victoria Pk Rd	B1	**Westlands**	B2	Windmill Hill	C3	
Stone Rd	B3	Trentham Rd	C3	Victoria Rd	C2	**Weston Coyney**	D3	**Withysakes**	D2	
Talke	A1	Trentham Rd (Butterton)	A3	**Walstanton**	B2	Weston Coyney Rd	C3	Woodhouse La	C1	
Talke Pits	A1			**Washerwall**	C2	Weston Rd	C3	**Wood Lane**	A1	
				Waterloo Rd	B1	Westport Rd	B1			
				Waterside Dr	C3	Wetlands Vw	B2			

SHEFFIELD URBAN page 73

Name	Ref	Name	Ref	Name	Ref	Name	Ref	Name	Ref	Name	Ref
Abbeydale	A3	**Charnock Hall**	B3	**Grimesthorpe**	B1	**Lowedges**	A3	Penistone Rd (Sheffield)	A2	Stannington Rd	A2
Abbeydale Park	A3	Chaucer Rd	A1	**Hackenthorpe**	C3	Lowedges Rd	A3	Petre St	B2	Station Rd (Eckington)	C3
Abbeydale Rd	A3	Chesterfield Rd	A3	Hagg La	A2	**Lowfield**	A2	**Pismire Hill**	B1	Station Rd (Halfway)	C3
Abbeydale Rd S	A3	Chesterfield Rd S	A3	**Halfway**	C3	Loxley Rd	A1	**Pitsmoor**	A1	Station Rd (Kiveton Park)	D3
Abbey La	A3	Church St	B1	Halifax Rd	A1	**Lydgate**	A2	Pitsmoor Rd	A2	Station Rd (Woodhouse)	C2
Albert Rd	A2	City Rd	B2	Hallowmoor Rd	A1	Lydgate La	A2	Pleasley Rd	C1	Stockarth La	A1
Arbourthorne	B2	Clarkehouse Rd	A2	**Handsworth**	B2	Main Rd (Ridgeway)	B3	Prince Of Wales Rd	B2	**Stradbroke**	B2
Archer Rd	A3	**Clifton**	C1	**Handsworth Hill**	B2	Main Rd (Sheffield)	B2	Prospect Rd	A3	Stradbroke Rd	B2
Arundel Gate	A2	Clifton La	C1	Handsworth Rd	B2	Main St (Aughton)	C2	Psalter La	A2	Stubbing Ho La	A1
Ash La	B3	**Coal Aston**	B3	Hangingwater Rd	A2	Main St (Grenoside)	A1	Queen's Rd	A2	Stubbin La	B1
Aston	C2	Coleridge Rd	B2	Hanover St	A2	Main St (Rotherham)	C1	Queen St	C3	**Sunnyside**	D1
Aston La	C2	College Rd	C1	Harborough Av	B2	Main St (Sheffield)	C3	Queen Victoria Rd	A3	**Thurcroft**	D2
Attercliffe	B2	Cowper Av	A1	**Harthill**	D3	**Malin Bridge**	A2	**Ranmoor**	A2	Tinker La	A2
Attercliffe Common	B1	**Crabtree**	A1	Hartley Brook Rd	B1	**Manor Estate**	B2	Red Hill	D3	**Tinsley**	B1
Attercliffe Rd	B2	Creswick La	A1	Hastilar Rd	B2	**Manor Park**	B2	Reney Rd	A3	**Todwick**	D3
Aughton	C2	**Crookes**	A2	Hatfield Ho La	B1	Manor La	B2	Retford Rd	C2	Todwick Rd	D2
Aughton Rd	C2	**Crookesmoor**	A2	Hazelhurst La	B3	Manor Rd	D3	Richards Rd	A2	**Totley Brook**	A3
Back La	A2	Crookesmoor Rd	A2	**Heeley**	A2	Mansfield Rd (Sheffield)	B2	**Richmond**	B2	**Totley Rise**	A3
Badsley Moor La	C1	Crookes Rd	A2	**Hellaby**	D1	Mansfield Rd (Swallownest)	C2	**Richmond Park**	B1	**Treeton**	C2
Barnsley Rd	A1	Crowder Rd	A1	**Hemsworth**	B3	Mansfield Rd (Wales Bar)	D3	Richmond Rd	B2	Treeton La	C2
Batemoor	A3	**Dalton**	C1	Hemsworth Rd	A3	**Masbrough**	C1	**Ridgeway**	B3	**Troway**	B3
Bawtry Rd (Brinsworth)	B1	**Dalton Magna**	D1	Herries Dr	A1	Meadowbank Rd	B1	**Ridgeway Moor**	B3	Tullibardine Rd	A3
Bawtry Rd (Rotherham)	C1	**Dalton Parva**	C1	Herries Rd	A1	**Meadow Hall**	B1	Ridgeway Moor	B3	Twentywell La	A3
Beauchief	A3	**Darnall**	B2	**Herringthorpe**	C1	Meadowhall Rd	B1	Ridgeway Rd	B2	Tyler St	B1
Beaver Hill Rd	C2	Darnall Rd	B2	Herringthorpe Valley Rd	C1	**Meadow Head**	A3	Rivelin Valley Rd	A2	**Ulley**	D2
Beighton	C3	Deerlands Av	A1	Highcliffe Rd	A2	Meadow Head	A3	Robin La	C3	Upper Hanover Way	A2
Beighton Rd (Hackenthorpe)	C3	Derbyshire La	A3	**Highfield**	A2	**Meersbrook Bank**	A3	Rod Moor Rd	A3	**Upper Whiston**	C2
Beighton Rd (Woodhouse)	C2	Doncaster Rd	C1	Highfield Spring	C2	Mickley La	A3	**Rotherham**	C1	Upwell St	B1
Bellhouse Rd	B1	Donetsk Way	B3	**Highlane**	B3	Middle La	C1	Rotherham Rd (Eckington)	C3	**Wadsley**	A1
Ben La	A1	**Dore**	A3	High La	B3	Middle La S	C1	Rotherham Rd (Handsworth)	C2	**Wadsley Bridge**	A1
Bents Green	A2	Drakehouse La	C3	High Storrs Rd	A2	Middlewood Rd	A1	Rother Way	C1	Wadsley L Ane	A1
Bents Rd	A3	**Dropping Well**	B1	High St (Ecclesfield)	A1	**Millhouses**	A3	Rural La	A1	**Wales**	D3
Bernard St	B2	Droppingwell Rd	B1	High St (Eckington)	C3	Millhouses La	A2	Rustlings Rd	A2	Wales Rd	D3
Birley Carr	A1	Duke St (Mosborough)	C3	High St (Killamarsh)	C3	Montgomery Rd	A2	Rutland La	A2	**Walkley**	A2
Birley Edge	A1	Duke St (Sheffield)	B2	High St (Mosborough)	C3	Moonshine La	A1	St. Ann's Rd	C1	Walkley Bk Rd	A2
Birley La	B3	Dyche La	A3	High St (Swallownest)	C2	**Moorgate**	C1	St. Mary's Rd	A2	Walkley La	A2
Birley Moor Rd	B3	Dykes Hall Rd	A1	Hill La	A2	Moorgate	C1	**Sandygate**	A2	Washington Rd	A2
Birley Spa La	B3	Dyke Vale Rd	B3	**Hillsborough**	A1	**Morthen**	D2	Sandygate Rd	A2	Water Thorpe Greenway	C3
Blackburn	B1	East Bk Rd	B2	**Hill Top**	B1	**Mosborough**	C3	Savile St	A2	Weedon St	B1
Blackburn Rd	B1	East Bawtry Rd	C1	**Holbrook**	C3	Mosborough Moor	C3	Savile St E	B2	Wellgate	C1
Blackstock Rd	B3	**East Dene**	C1	**Hollins End**	B3	Moss Way	C3	School Rd	D3	Well La	C2
Bochum Parkway	A3	**Eastwood**	C1	Hollinsend Rd	B3	Mowbray St	A2	**Sharrow**	A2	West Bawtry Rd	C1
Bocking La	A3	**Ecclesall**	A2	Hollybank Rd	B2	Nab La	B3	**Sheffield Lane Top**	A1	Westbourne Rd	A2
Bole Hill	C2	Ecclesall Rd	A2	Holme La	A2	Neepsend La	A1	Sheffield Parkway	B2	Westgate	C1
Bole Hill Rd	A2	**Ecclesfield**	A1	**Holmley Common**	A3	**Nether Edge**	A2	Sheffield Rd (Dronfield)	A3	West La	C2
Bolsover St	A2	Ecclesfield Rd	B1	Holmley La	A3	Nether Shire La	B1	Sheffield Rd (Eckington)	C3	West St	C3
Bradgate	C1	**Eckington**	C3	Holywell Rd	B1	Netherthorpe Rd	A2	Sheffield Rd (Hackenthorpe)	B3	Wheel La	A1
Bradway	A3	Eckington Rd	A3	Hopefield La	B3	Newhall Rd	B2	Sheffield Rd (Killamarsh)	C3	**Whirlow**	A3
Bramall La	A2	Eckington Way	C3	Howard Rd	A2	Newman Rd	B1	Sheffield Rd (Rotherham)	C1	Whirlowdale Rd	A3
Bramley	D1	Edge La	A1	Hucklow Rd	B1	**New Totley**	A3	Sheffield Rd (Tinsley)	B1	**Whiston**	C1
Brampton en le Morthen	D2	Effingham Rd	B2	Hutcliffe Wd Rd	A3	New Wortley Rd	C1	Sheffield Rd (Woodhouse)	B2	White Hill La	C1
Bridge St	C3	Effingham St	A2	**Ickles**	C1	Normanton Hill	B2	Sheffield Rd (Woodhouse Mill)	C2	White La	B3
Brightside	B1	Elm La	A1	Infirmary Rd	A2	**Normanton Spring**	B2	Sheldon Rd	A2	Witham Rd	A2
Brightside La	B1	Europa Link	B2	**Intake**	B2	Northern Common	A3	Shepcote La	B1	**Wickersley**	D1
Brincliffe	A2	Eyre St	A2	Ivy Pk Rd	A2	Northfield Rd	A2	**Shirecliffe**	A1	Wickersley Rd	C1
Brinsworth	C1	Far La	C1	**Jordanthorpe**	A3	North Penistone Rd	A1	Shirecliffe Rd	A1	**Wincobank**	B1
Brinsworth La	C1	Fenton Rd	B1	Jordanthorpe Parkway	A3	**Norton**	A3	**Shiregreen**	B1	Woodall La	D3
Brinsworth Rd	C1	Ferham Rd	B1	Junction Rd	A2	Norton Av	B3	Shiregreen La	B1	Woodbourn Rd	B2
Broad Elms La	A3	Firth Pk Rd	B1	**Killamarsh**	C3	Norton Lees La	A3	Sicey Av	B1	**Woodhouse**	C2
Broadfield Rd	A2	Fitzwilliam Rd	C1	**Kimberworth**	B1	**Norton Woodseats**	A3	Skew Hill	A1	Woodhouse La	C2
Broad La	A2	Fitzwilliam St	A2	Kimberworth Rd	B1	**Norwood (Derbyshire)**	D3	Skew Hill La	A1	**Woodhouse Mill**	C2
Brookhouse	D2	Folds La	A3	**Kimberworth Park**	B1	**Norwood (South Yorkshire)**	A1	Sloade La	B3	Woodhouse Rd	B2
Broom	C1	**Ford**	B3	Kiverton La	D3	Nursery St	A2	Smallage La	C2	Wood La (Sheffield)	A2
Broomhill	A2	Ford La	B3	**Kiveton Park**	D3	Occupation La	B3	Snowdon La	B3	Wood La (Treeton)	C2
Broom La	C1	Ford Rd	B3	Knowle La	A2	Old Wortley Rd	B1	Sothall Gro	C2	Wood Rd	A1
Broom Rd	C1	Fox Hill Rd	A1	Langsett Av	A1	**Orgreave**	C2	**South Anston**	D3	Woodseats Rd	A3
Broughton La	B1	**Frecheville**	B3	Langsett Rd	A1	Orgreave La	C2	**Southey Green**	A1	**Woodthorpe**	B2
Burngreave	A2	Front St	C2	Langsett Rd S	A1	Orgreave Rd	C2	Southey Grn Rd	A1	Wordsworth Av	A1
Burngreave Rd	A2	Fulwood Rd	A2	Leighton Rd	B3	Oughtibridge	A1	Southey Hill	A1	Worksop Rd (Sheffield)	B2
Canklow	C1	Gashouse La	C3	Leppings La	A1	**Owlerton**	A1	South Rd	A2	Worksop Rd (Swallownest)	C2
Canklow Rd	C1	Gladstone Rd	A2	Lightwood La	B3	**Owlthorpe**	C3	Spital Hill	A2	Worrall Rd	A1
Carbrook	B1	**Gleadless**	B3	Linley La	B3	Owlthorpe Greenway	C3	Springfield Rd	A3	Worry Goose La	C1
Carlisle St E	B2	Gleadless Rd	A2	**Listerdale**	D1	**Parkhead**	A3	**Springvale**	D1	Wortley Rd	B1
Carr	D1	**Gleadless Townend**	B3	Littlemoor	C3	**Park Hill**	B2	Staniforth Rd	B2	Yew La	A1
Carrfield Rd	A2	Glossop Rd	A2	Lodge La	C2	Parkway Av	B2				
Carter Knowle	A3	Granville Rd	A2	London Rd	A2	**Parkwood Springs**	A2				
Carter Knowle Rd	A2	**Greenhill**	A3	Long La (Sheffield)	A2	**Parson Cross**	A1				
Catcliffe	C2	Greenhill Av	A3	Long La (Treeton)	C2	Penistone Rd (Grenoside)	A1				
Cemetery Rd	A2	Greenhill Parkway	A3	**Longley**	A1						
Centenary Way	C1	**Greenland**	B2	Longley La	A1						
		Greenland Rd	B2								
		Grenoside	A1								
		Greystones	A2								
		Greystones Rd	A2								

MERSEYSIDE URBAN pages 74-75

Place	Ref		Place	Ref		Place	Ref
Abbey Rd	D1		Brimstage La	A3		Crow La E	F1
Acorn St	F1		Brimstage Rd	A4		Crow La W	F1
Aigburth	**B3**		Broad Grn Rd	B2		**Crow Wood**	**E3**
Aigburth Dr	B2		Broad La (Collins Green)	E1		**Croxteth**	**C1**
Aigburth Hall Av	B3		Broad La (Kirkby)	C1		Croxteth Dr	B2
Aigburth Rd	B3		**Broad Oak**	**E1**		Croxteth Hall La	B1
Aigburth Vale	B3		Broad Oak Rd	E1		Croxteth Rd	B2
Aintree Rd	A1		Brodie Av	B3		**Cuerdley Cross**	**E3**
Albert Rd	E3		**Bromborough**	**A3**		Cumber La	D2
Alder La (Burtonwood)	F1		**Bromborough Pool**	**A3**		Cut La	C1
Alder La (Prescot)	D2		Bromborough Rd	A3		Dale St	A2
Alder Rd	B2		Brookfield Dr	B1		**Dallam**	**F2**
Allerton	**C3**		**Brookhurst**	**A4**		Dans Rd	E3
Allerton Rd	B3		Brownlow Hill	A2		**Daresbury**	**F4**
Allport La	A4		Burrows La	D1		Daresbury Expressway	E3
Allport Rd	A4		Burtonhead Rd	E1		Daresbury La	F3
Almonds Grn	B1		**Burtonwood**	**F2**		Delph La (Daresbury)	F3
Anfield	**B1**		Burtonwood Rd	F2		Delph La (Whiston)	D2
Anfield Rd	B1		**Calderstones**	**B3**		**Denton's Green**	**D1**
Appleton	**E3**		Calderstones Rd	B3		Dentons Grn La	D1
Archway Rd	C2		**Callands**	**F2**		Derby La	B2
Ashcroft St	E1		Campbell Dr	C2		Derby Rd (Birkenhead)	A3
Ashton Rd	F1		Canal St	E1		Derby Rd (Bootle)	A1
Ashtons Grn Dr	E1		Carr La	D3		Derby Rd (Widnes)	D2
Astmoor	**E3**		Carr La E	B1		Derby St	D2
Astmoor Rd	E3		Cartbridge La	C3		Deysbrook La	C1
Aston	**F4**		**Castlefields**	**E3**		Dibbinsdale Rd	A4
Aston La	E4		Catchdale Moss La	D1		Dinas La	C2
Back La	F1		Central Expressway	E4		**Dingle**	**B3**
Bailey Dr	B1		Chain La	E1		Dingle La	B3
Balliol Rd	A1		Chapel La (Burtonwood)	F1		Ditchfield Rd	D3
Ball o' Ditton	**D3**		Chapel La (Cronton)	D2		**Ditton**	**D3**
Balls Rd	A2		Chapel La (Rainhill)	D2		Ditton Rd	D3
Bankhall St	A1		Chelwood Av	C2		Dock Rd	A2
Banks Rd	C3		Chester La	E2		**Dog And Gun**	**B1**
Barker's Hollow Rd	F4		Chester Rd (Higher Walton)	F3		Domingo Rd	B1
Barn La	F1		Chester Rd (Preston Brook)	F4		**Dovecot**	**C2**
Barrows Grn La	E3		Chester Rd (Sutton Weaver)	E4		Dovecot Av	C2
Bath St	A2		Chester St	A2		Dragon La	D2
Baxters La	E1		**Childer Thornton**	**B4**		Druids Cross Rd	C2
Beaconsfield Rd	C3		**Childwall**	**B3**		Duke St	E1
Bebington	**A3**		Childwall Abbey Rd	C2		Dundalk Rd	D3
Bebington Rd (Bebington)	A3		Childwall La	C2		Dunrabin Rd	B2
Bebington Rd (Birkenhead)	A3		Childwall Pk Av	C2		Dunriding La	D1
Bedford Rd	A3		Childwall Rd	B2		**Dutton**	**F4**
Beechwood	**E4**		Childwall Valley Rd	C2		Dwerry Ho La	B1
Beechwood Ave	E4		Church Rd (Bebington)	A3		Earle St	F1
Belle Vale	**C2**		Church Rd (Birkenhead)	A3		**Eastham**	**B4**
Belle Vale Rd	C2		Church Rd (Halewood)	C3		Eastham Rake	A4
Bell La	E2		Church Rd (Haydock)	F1		East Lancashire Rd	B1
Belmont Rd	B2		Church Rd (Seaforth)	A1		East Prescot Rd	B2
Belvedere Rd	F1		Church Rd (Wavertree)	B2		Eaton Rd	B2
Bennetts La	E3		Church Rd (Woolton)	C3		Eaves La	E2
Benty Heath La	A4		Church St (Frodsham)	E4		**Eccleston**	**D1**
Berrys La	E1		Church St (Runcorn)	E1		**Eccleston Park**	**D1**
Bewsey	**F2**		City Rd	E1		**Edge Hill**	**B2**
Bewsey Rd	F2		Clatterbridge Rd	A4		Edge La	B2
Birchfield Rd	E2		**Claughton**	**A2**		**Egremont**	**A2**
Birkenhead	**A2**		Clay La (Burtonwood)	F2		Elephant La	D1
Birkenhead Rd	A2		Clay La (Eccleston)	D1		**Ellesmere Port**	**B4**
Bishop Rd	E1		Cleveland St	A2		Ellesmere Rd	F3
Blackbrook	**E1**		Clifton Rd	E4		Elmswood Rd	B3
Blackbrook Rd	E1		Clipsley La	E1		Elton Head Rd	D2
Blakeley Rd	A4		**Clock Face**	**E2**		**Everton**	**B2**
Bleak Hill Rd	D1		Clock Face Rd	E2		Everton Brow	B2
Blind Foot Rd	D1		**Clubmoor**	**B1**		Everton Rd	B2
Blue Bell La	C2		College St	E1		Exmouth St	A2
Blundells La	D2		**Collins Green**	**F1**		**Fairfield**	**B2**
Bold Heath	**E2**		Collins Grn Rd	F1		**Farnworth**	**E3**
Bold La	E1		Commercial Rd (Bromborough)	B3		Farnworth Rd	E3
Bolton Rd	A3		Commercial Rd (Liverpool)	A2		**Fazakerley**	**B1**
Booker Av	B3		Common Rd	F1		Ferry Rd	B4
Bootle	**A1**		Conway St	A2		**Fincham**	**C2**
Borough Rd (Birkenhead)	A3		Coopers La	C1		Finch La (Halewood)	D3
Borough Rd (St. Helens)	D1		Copplehouse La	B1		Finch La (Knotty Ash)	C2
Borough Rd (Wallasey)	A2		Corporation St	E1		Finger Ho La	E2
Boundary Rd	D1		County Rd	B1		Fir Tree La	F1
Boundary St	A2		**Court Hey**	**C2**		Fleet La	E1
Bowring Park	**C2**		Cowley Hill La	E1		Folly La	F2
Bowring Pk Rd	C2		Crank Rd	D1		Forest Rd	E2
Bracken La	A3		Cromwell Av	F2		Fountains Rd	A1
Brasenose Rd	A1		**Cronton**	**D2**		Four Acre La	E2
Breckfield Rd N	B2		Cronton La	D2		Foxes Bk La	D2
Breckfield Rd S	B2		Cronton Rd	D2		**Frodsham Bridge**	**E4**
Breck Rd (Anfield)	B2		Crosby Rd S	A1		Gamble Av	D1
Breck Rd (Everton)	B2		Cross Hillocks La	D3		**Garston**	**B3**
Breeze Hill	A1		Cross La (Bebington)	A3		Garton's La	E2
Brewster St	A1		Cross La (Newton-le-Willows)	F1		Gaskell St	E1
Bridge La	E4		Cross La (Whiston)	D2		**Gateacre**	**C3**
Bridge Rd (Litherland)	A1		Crossley Rd	D1		Gerards La	E1
Bridge Rd (Prescot)	D2					Gerrards La	C3
Bridge St	E3					Gillars La	D1
Bridgewater Expressway	E3					**Gillmoss**	**B1**
Bridle Rd (Bootle)	B1					Golborne Dale Rd	F1
Bridle Rd (Eastham)	B4					Golborne Rd	F1
Brighton St	A2					Gorsey La (Burtonwood)	E2
Brimstage	**A3**					Gorsey La (Widnes)	E3

Place	Ref		Place	Ref		Place	Ref
Grange	**E4**		Kings Dr	C3		Mill La (Winwick)	F2
Grange La	C2		Kings La	A3		Mill St	B2
Grange Park	**D1**		Kings Rd	A3		Mollys La	C1
Grangeway	E4		King St (St. Helens)	E1		**Moore**	**F3**
Grassendale	**B3**		King St (Wallasey)	A2		Moore La	F3
Great Homer St	A2		**Kingsway**	**E3**		Moorfield Rd	E1
Great Howard St	A2		Kingsway (Prescot)	D2		Moorgate Rd	C1
Great Sankey	**F2**		Kingsway (Widnes)	E3		**Moss Bank (St. Helens)**	**E1**
Greenbank La	B2		**Kirkdale**	**A1**		**Moss Bank (Widnes)**	**E3**
Greenfield Rd	D1		Kirkdale Rd	A2		Moss Bk Rd	E3
Green La (Eccleston)	D1		Kitling Rd	C1		Moss La (Bootle)	B1
Green La (Mossley Hill)	B2		**Knotty Ash**	**B2**		Moss La (Moore)	F3
Green La (Stoneycroft)	B2		**Knowsley**	**C1**		Moss La (St. Helens)	D1
Green Leach La	E1		Knowsley La	C1		**Mossley Hill**	**B3**
Greensbridge La	D3		Knowsley Rd (Bootle)	A1		Mossley Hill Dr	B2
Grimsmith La	F4		Knowsley Rd (St. Helens)	D1		Moughland La	E4
Hale	**D4**		Laburnum La	E2		Mount Pleasant Rd	A1
Hale Bank	**D3**		Laf Rd	E1		Mount Rd	A3
Hale Bk Rd	D3		Lancots La	E1		Muirhead Av	B2
Hale Gate Rd	D3		Leach La	E2		Muirhead Av E	B1
Hale Rd (Ditton)	D3		Lea Grn Rd	E2		Naylors Rd	C2
Hale Rd (Hale Bank)	D3		Leathers La	C3		Neill's Rd	E2
Hale Rd (Speke)	C4		Leigh Av	E3		Netherfield Rd N	B2
Hale Rd (Walton)	A1		Lever Causeway	A3		Netherfield Rd S	B2
Halewood	**C3**		Leyfield Rd	B2		**Netherley**	**C2**
Halewood Rd	C3		Lickers La	D2		Netherley Rd	D3
Hall La (Burtonwood)	F1		Lilford Rd	F2		**New Brighton**	**A1**
Hall La (Cronton)	D2		Lime St	A2		New Chester Rd	A3
Hall La (Huyton)	C2		Linacre La	A1		**New Ferry**	**A3**
Hall La (Liverpool)	B2		Linacre Rd	A1		New Islington	B2
Hallwood Link Rd	E4		**Lingley Green**	**F2**		New St	E1
Halton (Runcorn)	**E4**		Lingley Grn Av	E2		Newton La	E1
Halton (Widnes)	**E3**		**Liscard**	**A2**		**Newton-le-Willows**	**F1**
Halton Brook	**E4**		Liscard Rd	A2		Newton Rd (St. Helens)	E1
Halton Brow	E4		**Liverpool**	**B2**		Newton Rd (Winwick)	F1
Halton Lea	**E4**		Liverpool Rd (Huyton)	C2		**Newtown**	**D1**
Halton Rd	E3		Liverpool Rd (Warrington)	E2		Norlands La	E2
Hamlet	**B3**		Liverpool Rd (Widnes)	D3		Norman Rd	E4
Hard La	D1		Lockett Rd	E3		**Norris Green**	**B1**
Hardman St	B2		Lodge La (Liverpool)	B2		North Hill St	B2
Hargrave La	A4		Lodge La (Warrington)	F2		North Rd (Ellesmere Port)	B4
Harlow St	B2		London Rd	B2		North Rd (St. Helens)	E1
Haswell Dr	C1		Long La (Garston)	C3		Northwich Rd	F4
Hatton	**F3**		Long La (Liverpool)	B1		**Norton**	**E4**
Hawthorne Rd	A1		Longmoor La	B1		**Nutgrove**	**D2**
Haydock	**F1**		Longshaw St	F2		Nutgrove Rd	D1
Haydock La	E1		**Longview**	**C2**		Oakfield Rd	B2
Heathfield Rd	B2		Long Vw Dr	C2		Oak La	A3
Heath La	A4		Long Vw La	C2		Okell Dr	C3
Heath Rd (Bebington)	A3		Lorenzo Dr	B1		Old Chester Rd	A3
Heath Rd (Runcorn)	E4		Lovely La	F2		**Old Hall**	**F2**
Heath Rd S	E4		**Lower Bebington**	**A3**		Old Hall St	A2
Hermitage Grn La	F1		Lower Breck Rd	B2		Old La (Prescot)	D2
Heyworth St	B2		Lower Ho La (Liverpool)	B1		Old La (Rainhill)	D2
Higher Bebington	**A3**		Lower Ho La (Widnes)	E3		**Old Swan**	**B2**
Higher La (Dutton)	F4		Lower La	B1		Ormskirk Rd (Aintree)	B1
Higher La (Liverpool)	B1		Lower Rd	D3		Ormskirk Rd (Knowsley)	C1
Higher Rd (Halewood)	C3		**Lower Walton**	**F3**		**Orrell**	**A1**
Higher Rd (Widnes)	D3		Lowfield La	E2		Orrell La	B1
Higher Walton	**F3**		**Lugs Dale**	**E3**		Orrell Rd	A1
High St (Frodsham)	E4		Lugsdale Rd	E3		**Otterspool**	**B3**
High St (Golborne)	F1		Lumber La	F1		Oxford St	E1
High St (Newton-le-Willows)	F1		**Lunts Heath**	**E2**		**Page Moss**	**C2**
High St (Runcorn)	E3		Lunts Heath Rd	E2		Page Moss La	C2
High St (Wavertree)	B2		Lydiate La	C3		Palace Flds Av	E4
High St (Woolton)	C3		Mackets La	C3		Pall Mall	A2
Hillfoot Av	C3		Main St	E4		Parkfield	B2
Hillfoot Rd	C3		Manchester Rd	D2		Park La (Higher Walton)	F3
Hinckley Rd	E1		Manor Rd	A2		Park La (Liverpool)	A2
Hollies Rd	C3		Market St	F1		Park Rd (Birkenhead)	A2
Hollins La	F2		**Marshall's Cross**	**E2**		Park Rd (Great Sankey)	F2
Holloway	E4		Marshalls Cross Rd	E2		Park Rd (St. Helens)	E1
Holt	**D2**		Marsh La (Bootle)	A1		Park Rd (Toxteth)	B2
Honey's Grn Rd	C2		Marsh La (Lower Whitley)	F4		Park Rd E	A2
Hood La	F2		Mather Av	B3		Park Rd N (Birkenhead)	A2
Hooton	**B4**		Meeting La	F2		Park Rd N (Newton-le-Willows)	F1
Hooton Rd	B4		Melling Rd	B1		Park Rd S	A2
Hough Green	**D3**		Melrose Rd	A1		Park Rd W	A1
Hough Grn Rd	D3		Melwood Dr	B1		Parkside Rd	F1
Houghtons La	D1		Menlove Av	C2		**Parr**	**E1**
Howards La	D1		Mersey Rd	B3		Parr Stocks Rd	E1
Hulme	**F2**		Merton Bk Rd	E1		Parr St	E1
Hunts Cross	**C3**		Merton Rd	A1		**Peasley Cross**	**E1**
Huyton	**C2**		Millbank	B2		Peasley Cross La	E1
Huyton La	C2		Millbrook La	D1		Peel Ho La	E3
Huyton Park	**C2**		Mill Brow	D1		**Penketh**	**F2**
Huyton Quarry	**D2**		Millfields	D1		Penketh Rd	F2
Huyton with Roby	**C2**		Mill Grn La	E2		Penkford La	F1
Islands Brow	E1		Mill La (Newton-le-Willows)	F1		Pennington La	E1
Jackson St	E1		Mill La (Old Swan)	B2		Penny La	B2
Jericho La	B3		Mill La (Rainhill)	D2		Penny La (Collins Green)	F1
Jubits La	E2		Mill La (St. Helens)	E1			
Keckwick	**F3**		Mill La (Wallasey)	A2			
Keckwick La	F3		Mill La (West Derby)	B2			
Kemble St	D2		Mill La (Widnes)	E2			
Kensington	B2						
Kiln La	D1						

Name	Ref	Name	Ref
Penny La (Cronton)	D2	Raby	A4
Penny La (Haydock)	F1	Raby Hall Rd	A4
Penrhyn Rd	C1	Raby Mere Rd	A4
Perimeter Rd	C1	Raby Rd	A4
Phipps La	F1	Rainford Rd	D1
Picton Rd	B2	Rainhill	D2
Piele Rd	F1	Rainhill Rd	D2
Pilch La	C2	Rainhill Stoops	D2
Pinehurst Av	B1	Rake La	A2
Plantation Rd	B3	Ramsbrook La	D3
Plymyard Av	A4	Rathbone Rd	B2
Pool La	A3	Ravenhead	E1
Portico	D1	Ravenhead Rd	D1
Portico La	D2	Red Hill Rd	A3
Port Sunlight	A3	Regent Rd	A1
Pottery La	D2	Reginald Rd	E2
Poulton (Wallasey)	A2	Rest Hill Rd	A3
Poulton (Wirral)	A4	Rice La	B1
Poulton Rd (Wallasey)	A2	Rimrose Rd	A1
Poulton Rd (Wirral)	A4	Rivacre Rd	B4
Prenton	A3	Riversdale Rd	B3
Prenton La	A3	Riverview Rd	B3
Prenton Rd E	A3	Riverwood Rd	B4
Prenton Rd W	A3	Rivington Rd	D1
Prescot	D2	Robins La	E1
Prescot Bypass	D2	Rob La	F1
Prescot Rd (Fairfield)	B2	Roby	C2
Prescot Rd (St. Helens)	D1	Roby Ch Rd	C2
Prescot Rd (Tarbock Green)	D2	Roby Rd	C2
Prescot Rd (Widnes)	D3	Rock Ferry	A3
Preston Brook	F4	Rock Ferry Bypass	A3
Preston on the Hill	F4	Rock La W	A3
Price St	A2	Rocksavage Expressway	E4
Priestley St	F2	Rocky La (Anfield)	B2
Primrose Dr	C2	Rocky La (Childwall)	B2
Prince's Av	B2	Rose La	B3
Princes Park	B2	Runcorn	E4
Princess Dr	C1	Runcorn Rd	F3
Priory Rd	B1	Runcorn Spur Rd	E4
Quarry St	C3	Rupert Rd	C2
Queens Dr (Mossley Hill)	B3	St. George St	B2
Queen's Dr (Newton-le-Willows)	F1	St. Helens	E1
Queens Dr Stoneycroft	B2	St. Helens Rd	D1
Queens Dr Walton	B1	St. James La	A2
Queens Dr Wavertree	B2	St. John's Rd	C2
Queens Dr W Derby	B2	St. Michael's	B3
Queensway	E3	Sandy La (Cronton)	D2
		Sandy La (Lingley Green)	E2
		Sandy La (Runcorn)	D4
		Sandy Rd	A1
		Sankey Bridges	F2
		Sankey St	F1
		Sankey Way	F2

Name	Ref	Name	Ref
Scafell Rd	E1	Summer La	F4
Scholes La	D1	Sutton Heath	D1
School La (Bold Heath)	E2	Sutton Leach	E2
School La (Knowsley)	C1	Sutton Manor	E2
School La (Rainhill)	D2	Sutton Oak	E1
School La (Woolton)	C3	Sutton Rd	E1
Score La	C2	Sutton Weaver	E4
Scotchbarn La	D2	Swanside	C2
Scotland Rd	A2	Taggart Av	C2
Seabank Rd	A1	Talbot Rd	A3
Seacombe	A2	Tan Ho La (Burtonwood)	F2
Seaforth	A1	Tan Ho La (Widnes)	E3
Seaforth Rd	A1	Tannery La	E3
Sea Vw Rd	A2	Tarbock Green	D3
Seeds La	B1	Tarbock Rd	C2
Sefton Rd	A1	Thatto Heath	D1
Sefton St	A2	Thermal Rd	A3
Shaw St	B2	Thingwall Rd	B2
Shell Rd	B2	Thomas La	C2
Sherdley Rd	E1	Thornton Common Rd	A4
Sherwoods La	B1	Thornton Hough	A4
Slate Rd	A2	Thornton Rd	A3
Smithdown Rd	B2	Tibbs Cross La	E2
South Boundary Rd	C1	Tithe Barn La	C1
Southdene	C1	Tithebarn St	A2
Southern Expressway	E4	Toll Bar	D1
Southport Rd	B1	Torrington Dr	C3
Southworth Rd	F1	Town End	D2
Speke	C3	Town La (Bebington)	A3
Speke Boul	C3	Town La (Hale)	D4
Speke Hall Av	C3	Town Row	B1
Speke Rd (Garston)	C3	Townsend Av	B1
Speke Rd (Woolton)	C3	Townsend La	B2
Speke-Widnes Link Rd	D3	Toxteth	A2
Spital Rd	A3	Tranmere	A3
Springfield La	D1	Travers Entry	E1
Springwood Av	C3	Tuebrook	B2
Stadium Rd	B3	Tue La	D2
Stafford Rd	D1	Tunnel Rd	B2
Stanley Rd	A1	Twyford La	E2
Stanton Rd	A3	Ullet Rd	B2
Stockbridge La	C2	Union La	E2
Stocks La	F3	Upper Duke St	B2
Stockswell Rd	D3	Upper Parliament St	B2
Stonebridge La	B1	Upper Warwick St	B2
Stoneycroft	B2	Upton La	E2
Stoney La	D2	Utting Av	B1
Storeton	A3	Utting Av E	B1
Storeton Rd	A3	Valley Rd	B1
Strand, The	A2	Vauxhall Rd	A2
Sugar La	C1	Victoria Rd (New Brighton)	A1

Name	Ref	Name	Ref
Victoria Rd (Newton-le-Willows)	F1	Westbrook Way	F2
Victoria Rd (Runcorn)	E3	West Derby Rd	B2
Victoria Rd (Widnes)	E3	West End Rd	E1
Victoria St	A2	Western Av (Huyton)	C2
View Rd	D2	Western Av (Speke)	C3
Village Rd	A3	Weston	E4
Vista Rd	F1	Weston Point	D4
Vulcan Village	F1	Weston Pt Expressway	D4
Walkers La	E2	Weston Rd	E4
Wallasey	A2	West Park	D1
Walton	B1	Wharf Rd	F1
Walton Breck Rd	B1	Wheathill Rd	C2
Walton Hall Av	B1	Wheats Cl	E3
Walton La	B1	Whiston	D2
Walton Lea Rd	F3	Whiston Cross	D2
Walton New Rd	F3	Whiston La	C2
Walton Rd	B1	Whittle Av	F2
Wapping	A2	Widnes	E3
Warbreck Moor	B1	Widnes Rd	E3
Wargrave	F1	Willaston	A4
Wargrave Rd	F1	Willowbrow Rd	A4
Waring Av	E1	Willow La	A4
Warrington	F3	Wilmere La	E2
Warrington Rd (Astmoor)	E3	Wilson Rd	C2
Warrington Rd (Bold Heath)	E2	Windmill Hill Av N	E3
Warrington Rd (Hatton)	F3	Windmill Hill Av S	E3
Warrington Rd (Penketh)	F3	Windy Arbor	D2
Warrington Rd (Rainhill)	D2	Windy Arbour Rd	D2
Warrington Rd (Widnes)	E3	Winwick	F2
Warwick St	A2	Winwick Rd (Newton-le-Willows)	F1
Washway La	E1	Winwick Rd (Warrington)	F2
Water La	D3	Woodchurch Rd	A3
Waterloo Rd (Liverpool)	A2	Woodend	D3
Waterloo Rd (Widnes)	E3	Wood End Av	C3
Waterpark Dr	C1	Woodhey	A3
Waterworks La	F1	Woodlands Rd	E1
Watery La	E1	Wood La	C2
Watson St	A2	Wood Rd	C3
Watts La	A1	Woolfall Heath	C2
Wavertree Av	B2	Woolton	C3
Wavertree Rd	B2	Woolton Hill Rd	C3
Wellington Rd	B2	Woolton Rd (Childwall)	B2
Well La	A3	Woolton Rd (Garston)	C3
West Bank	E3	Wrights La	F2
		Yew Tree La	C2
		Yew Tree Rd	C3

LIVERPOOL CENTRAL pages 76-77

Name	Ref	Name	Ref
Abercromby Sq	L8	Baker St	N3
Abney Cl	Q10	Baker Way	M4
Acorn Ct	K13	Balmoral Rd	S2
Acton Way	R10	Balm St	Q5
Adderley St	Q6	Baltimore St	J9
Addison St	F4	Bannerman St	T10
Addison Way	F4	Barnet St	R10
Adelaide Pl	H1	Basnett St	F7
Adelaide Rd	P7	Bath St	B5
Adele Thompson Dr	M12	Battenberg St	N6
Agnes Way	Q7	Bayhorse La	K5
Aigburth St	P10	Beaconsfield St	N13
Ainsworth St	J7	Beaufort St	H13
Albany Rd	N6	Beaumont St	P11
Albert Edward Rd	N6	Beau St	H2
Albert St	N7	Beckwith St	F10
Alderson Rd	T12	Bective St	S10
Alexandra Cl	P3	Bedford Cl	L10
Alexandra Rd	S10	Bedford St S	L9
Alex Cl	L13	Beech St	S5
Alfred Ms	H11	Benson St	H8
Alfred St	T9	Beresford St	J2
Altcar Av	T11	Berington St	F2
Alt St	P12	Berkley St	K12
Amberley St	M11	Berry St	H10
Amelia St	L4	Berwick Cl	Q2
Amethyst Cl	P1	Berwick St	Q2
Angela St	P10	Bevington Bush	F3
Anglezark Cl	Q5	Bevington Hill	F2
Anglican Ct	J12	Bidder St	J4
Archbishop Warlock Ct	D2	Bigham Rd	R4
Argyle St	F9	Birchfield St	J4
Arley St	E2	Bird St	S11
Arnold Cres	L13	Birkett St	H4
Arnold St	L13	Birstall Rd	P4
Arnside Rd	R7	Birt Cl	P11
Arrad St	K9	Bishop Sheppard Ct	D2
Arundel Cl	N13	Bixteth St	D5
Asbridge St	P13	Blackburne Pl	K10
Ashton St	L6	Blackstock St	E3
Ashwell St	H12	Blair St	J12
Askham Cl	P12	Blenheim St	E1
Aspen Gro	Q13	Bluefields St	K12
Atlantic Pt	F3	Blundell St	F11
Atwell St	N2	Boaler St	N3
Back Colquitt St	H9	Bold Pl	H9
Back Guildford St	L2	Bold St	G8
Back Leeds St	C4	Bolton St	H7
		Bond St	F2

Name	Ref	Name	Ref
Boothwood Cl	Q9	Cambridge St	K8
Boswell St	Q12	Camden St	H5
Botanic Grn	R6	Cameo Cl	P1
Botanic Pl	S6	Cameron St	R5
Botanic Rd	S6	Campbell St	F9
Boundary La	N1	Canada Boul	C7
Boyton Ct	S10	Canning Pl	E8
Bradfield St	R6	Canning St	K10
Brae St	Q6	Canteury St	J4
Brahms Cl	P13	Cantebury Way	K4
Brampton Dr	M10	Cantsfield St	S11
Brassey St	H13	Cardigan St	T10
Breames Cl	R8	Cardigan Way	Q1
Breck Rd	L1	Cardwell St	N9
Bremner Cl	R7	Carlingford Cl	N11
Brick St	G12	Carlton St	B1
Bridge Rd	T9	Carruthers St	D3
Bridgewater St	F12	Carstairs Rd	S2
Bridport St	H6	Carter St	L12
Bright St	M3	Carver St	K4
Brindley St	G13	Caryl St	G13
Britannia Av	T11	Castle St	D7
Britten Cl	Q13	Catharine St	L9
Bronte St	J6	Cathedral Cl	J11
Brook St	C5	Cathedral Gate	J10
Brownlow Hill	H7	Cathedral Wk	J8
Brownlow St	K7	Cawdor St	N13
Brow Side	K2	Cazneau St	G2
Brunswick Rd	L5	Cedar Gro	Q13
Brunswick St	C8	Chadwick St	C3
Bryges St	N8	Chaloner St	F11
Brythen St	F7	Chandos St	Q8
Burlington St	E2	Channell Rd	R3
Burnley Cl	N1	Chapel St	C7
Burroughs Gdns	F2	Chase Way	J2
Burrows Ct	D1	Chatham Pl	P8
Burton Cl	F10	Chatham St	L10
Bute St	H3	Chatsworth Dr	Q10
Bute St (Toxteth)	Q11	Chaucer St	G3
Butler Cres	P4	Cheapside	E5
Butler St	Q3	Chesney Cl	J13
Button St	F7	Chesterfield St	J12
Byrom St	G5	Chester St	J13
Cadogan St	T10	Chestnut St	L8
Caird St	N3	Chichester Cl	T10
Cairns St	N13	Childwall Av	T11
Caledonia St	K9	Chisenhale St	D2
Callander Rd	T3	Chiswell St	R5
Cambria St	Q3	Christian St	G4
Cambridge Ct	K9	Chris Ward Cl	R7

Name	Ref	Name	Ref
Church All	F8	Cropper St	H8
Church Mt	P7	Crosfield Cl	S7
Church St	F7	Crosfield Rd	R8
Churton Ct	M3	Crosshall St	F6
Cicely St	P7	Crown St	L6
Clarence St	J7	Crow St	G13
Claribel St	M13	Crump St	H12
Claughton Cl	R8	Cullen St	R12
Claypole Cl	R10	Cumberland St	E6
Clay St	C1	Cunliffe St	E5
Clearwater Cl	Q5	Custom Ho La	E8
Clegg St	H1	Dale St	D7
Clement Gdns	E2	Daniel Davies Dr	N12
Cleveland Sq	F9	Dansie St	K7
Clifford St	J5	Danube St	R11
Cliff St	R6	Darrel Dr	R11
Clifton Gro	J2	Daulby St	L6
Clint Rd	R7	Davies St	E6
Clint Rd W	R7	Dawber Cl	N1
Clint Way	R7	Dawson St	F7
Coal St	H6	Dean Dillistone Ct	H11
Cobden St	L3	Deane Rd	R5
Cockspur St	D5	Dean Patey Ct	H10
Coleridge St	Q4	Deeley Cl	R8
College La	F8	Dell St	R5
College St N	K4	Denham Dr	R1
College St S	L4	Denham Rd	R1
Colquitt St	H9	Dentdale Dr	J2
Coltart Rd	P13	Devon St	J5
Commutation Row	H6	Dexter St	J13
Compton Rd	N1	Dial St	R6
Comus St	G3	Diamond St	F1
Concert St	G9	Dickson St	B1
Connaught Rd	N6	Dobson St	M1
Contance St	K5	Dorothy St	Q7
Cookson St	H11	Dorset Av	T11
Cook St	E7	Douro St	H2
Copperas Hill	H7	Dovestone Cl	Q9
Corinto St	J12	Dove St	P11
Corney St	R11	Drury La	D7
Cornhill	F10	Dryden St	G1
Cornwallis St	H10	Dublin St	B1
Corsewall St	T10	Duckinfield St	K7
Cotswold St	Q5	Duke St	F9
Cotton St	B1	Duncan St	H11
Covent Gdn	D6	Dunkeld Cl	N3
Cowan St	M1	Dunstan La	R10
Cranborne Rd	T12	Durden St	R11
Craven St	J5	Durning Rd	R6
Cresswell St	L2	Dwerryhouse St	G13

Street	Ref	Street	Ref	Street	Ref	Street	Ref	Street	Ref	Street	Ref
		Great Newton St	K6	Johnson St	F5	Marlborough St	E4	Park La	E9	Roseberry St	M12
		Great Orford St	K8	John St	J3	Marlsford St	R3	Park Pl	J13	Rose Hill	G3
		Great Richmond St	G3	Jordan St	G12	Marmaduke St	P7	Parkside St	L3	Rosemary Cl	N8
Dyke St	M1	Greek St	J6	Jubilee Dr	P6	Marquis St	J6	Park Way	L11	Rose Pl	G3
Earle Rd	Q11	Greenland St	G12	Judges Dr	S2	Marsden St	M4	Parliament Cl	J12	Rothsay Cl	J1
Earle St	D5	Green La	J8	Judges Way	S1	Marsden Way	M4	Parliament St	G12	Rothwell St	N1
East St	D5	Greenleaf St	R12	Juvenal Pl	H2	Marshall Pl	E2	Parr St	G9	Royal Mail St	H7
Eaton St	D4	Greenside	L4	Juvenal St	G3	Martensen St	P7	Parton St	E3	Royston St	P7
Eden St	Q12	Green St	E1	Keble St	N4	Marvin St	N4	Paul McCartney Way	Q4	Rufford Rd	S3
Edgar St	F3	Gregson St	L3	Kelso Rd	S4	Marybone	E5	Paul Orr Ct	D2	Rumford Pl	C6
Edge Hill	**P10**	Grenville St S	G10	Kempston St	J5	Maryland St	J9	Paul St	E3	Rumford St	D6
Edge La	P7	Gresley Cl	S8	Kenley Cl	R1	Mason St	N7	Pavilion Cl	P12	Rupert Dr	M3
Edinburgh Rd	N5	Grierson St	Q12	Kensington	N5	Mathew St	E7	Pear Gro	Q3	Russel Pl	J7
Edmund St	D6	Grinfield St	N8	**Kensington**	**N5**	Maud St	M13	Pearl Way	P1	Russel St	J6
Edward St	J7	Grosvenor St	G2	Kent St	G10	Maxton Rd	R3	Peet St	Q7	Ryedale Cl	P11
Egerton St	K11	Grove Rd	T4	Kilshaw St	N2	Mayfair Cl	Q1	Pembroke Gdns	K6	St. Andrew St	J7
Eldonian Way	D2	Grove St	M11	Kimberley Cl	M11	May Pl	J8	Pembroke Pl	J6	St. Anne St	H3
Eldon Pl	E2	Guelph St	M5	Kinder St	L4	May St	J8	Pembroke St	K7	St. Bride St	L10
Eldon St	E2	Guion St	Q2	Kinglake St	P7	Melda St	L4	Penarth Cl	P10	St. James Pl	H12
Elizabeth St	L6	Gwenfron Rd	P4	Kingsley Rd	N11	Melville Pl	M9	Pendine Cl	R2	St. James Rd	J11
Ellen's Cl	M5	Gwent St	M13	Kings Par	D10	Michael Dragonette		Penlinken Dr	Q1	St. James St	G11
Elliot St	G7	Hackins Hey	D6	Kingsway Ct	F2	Ct	E2	Penvalley Cres	R1	St. John's La	G6
Elm Gro	M7	Haigh St	K4	Kingswell Cl	P8	Midghall St	E4	Peover St	G3	St. Josephs Cres	H4
Elm Vale	T2	Hale St	E6	Kitchen St	F11	Mile End	F1	Pera Cl	N4	St. Martins Ms	H1
Elstree Rd	T3	Hall La	M5	Knight St	H10	Mill La	G5	Percy St	K11	St. Michaels Gro	Q2
Embledon St	P11	Halsbury Rd	R3	Lace St	F5	Mill Rd	M2	Perrygate Cl	P10	St. Nicholas Pl	C7
Emerson St	K12	Hampstead Rd	S3	Ladybower Cl	Q9	Mill St	J13	Perth St	N3	St. Stephen's Pl	F4
Empress Rd	P7	Hampton St	K12	Laggan St	Q6	Millvale St	R2	Peter's La	F8	Salisbury Rd	T12
Epworth St	L5	Hannan Rd	R3	Lairds Pl	F2	Milroy St	Q7	Peter St	F6	Salisbury St	J2
Erskine Ind Est	M4	Hanover St	E9	Lakeland Cl	F9	Milverton St	R2	Phillimore Rd	R4	Salthouse Quay	D9
Erskine St	L5	Harbord St	P8	Lambert Way	J5	Minshull St	M7	Pickop St	E5	Saltney St	B1
Esher Rd	R3	Hardman St	J9	Lance Cl	L1	Minster Ct	M9	Picton Rd	T9	Sandhead St	T10
Eversley St	M13	Hardy St	H11	Langsdale St	J4	Minto Cl	R5	Pilgrim St	J10	Sandino St	J13
Everton Brow	J3	Harewood St	N1	Langton Rd	T12	Minto St	Q5	Pine Ms	J12	Sandon St	L10
Everton Rd	L1	Harker St	H4	Lanyork Rd	C4	Mirfield St	Q3	Pinetop Cl	Q2	Saxon Cl	P1
Every St	P2	Harke St	Q9	Laurel Gro	R13	Molyneux Rd	P4	Pitt St	G10	Saxony Rd	N6
Exchange St E	D6	Harper St	M5	Lavan Cl	M3	Montgomery Way	Q1	Pleasant St	J8	Scholar St	S11
Exchange St W	D6	Harrington St	E7	Lawrence Rd	T11	Moorfields	E6	Plimsoll St	Q7	Schomberg St	N3
Fairclough St	G8	Harrowby Cl	N12	Lawton St	G8	Moor Pl	J6	Plumpton St	L2	School La	F8
Fairfield	**T4**	Harrowby St	M12	Leece St	J9	Moor St	D8	Pomfret St	M13	Scotland Rd	G3
Falkland St	K5	Hartley Quay	D9	Leeds St	C4	Morden St	R2	Pomona St	J8	Seaport Rd	N13
Falkner Sq	M11	Hart St	J6	Leigh St	G7	Moss Gro	Q13	Pond Cl	R2	Seddon St	F9
Falkner St	K10	Hatherley Cl	N12	Leigh St (Edge Hill)	S8	Mount Pleasant	H8	Ponsonby St	N13	Seel St	F8
Fareham Rd	S5	Hatherley St	M13	Lemon Cl	S8	Mount St	J10	Porter St	B2	Sefton St	F12
Farnworth St	P3	Hatton Gdn	E5	Lemon Gro	R13	Mount Vernon Grn	N6	Portland Pl	H1	Selborne Cl	M12
Fazakerley St	C6	Haverston Rd	T3	Leopold Rd	P7	Mount Vernon Rd	M7	Portwood Cl	P10	Selborne St	L12
Fearnside St	S10	Hawdon Ct	S10	Lesseps Rd	R12	Mount Vernon St	M6	Pownall Sq	E5	Selsey Cl	Q10
Fell St	Q6	Hawke St	H7	Lestock St	J12	Mozart Cl	P13	Pownall St	E9	Severs St	N2
Fenwick St	D7	Hawkins St	Q4	Liffey St	P12	Muirhead Av	R2	Prescot Rd	S4	Seymour St	J6
Fern Gro	Q13	Hawthorn Gro	Q7	Lightwood Dr	R10	Mulberry Pl	L9	Prescot St	L5	Shakespeare Cl	N1
Fielding St	N4	Head St	J13	Lightwood St	R10	Mulberry St	L9	Preston St	F6	Shallcross Pl	N1
Field St	J3	Heathcote Cl	R10	Lilley Rd	T4	Mulgrave St	M11	Price St	E9	Shaws All	F10
Finch Pl	K5	Heathfield St	H8	Lilly Vale	T4	Mulliner St	S11	Primrose Hill	F5	Shaw St	K2
Finlay St	R4	Helena St	Q8	Lime Gro	Q13	Myrtle St	K9	Prince Albert Ms	H11	Sheil Rd	R1
Fishguard Cl	L1	Helsby St	N8	Limekiln La	F3	Nash Gro	G3	Prince Edwin St	H2	Shenstone St	P7
Fitzclarence Way	L2	Hendon Rd	T2	Lime St	H7	Naylor St	E4	Princes Av	L12	Sherwood St	C1
Fitzpatrick Ct	D1	Henglers Cl	M4	Lincoln Cl	Q1	Needham Rd	R5	Princes Gdns	E5	Shimmin St	N8
Fitzroy Way	M4	Henry Edward St	F4	Lindley Cl	R10	Nelson Rd	P8	Princes Par	B5	Sidney Pl	N8
Fleet St	G8	Henry St	F9	Lindley St	S10	Nelson St	H10	Princes Rd	L12	Silkstone Cl	Q9
Fleming Ct	D1	Hewitts Pl	E5	Ling St	Q6	Netherfield Rd S	J1	Princes St	E6	Simpson St	F11
Flint St	G12	Highfield St	D5	Lister Cres	S5	Nevin St	M3	Prince William St	H13	Sim St	J4
Fontenoy St	F5	Highgate St	N7	Lister Rd	S4	Nevison St	P8	Prospect St	M5	Sirdar Cl	Q10
Ford St	E3	High St	D6	Little Catherine St	K11	New Bird St	G12	Prussia St	D5	Sir Thomas St	E6
Forrest St	F10	Hilbre St	H7	Little Ct	D1	New Grey Rock Cl	P2	Pudsey St	H6	Skelhorne St	H7
Fowler Cl	R8	Hillside St	L3	Little Hardman St	J9	Newhall St	G12	Pumpfields Rd	D4	Slater St	G9
Fox St	H2	Hill St	H13	Little Howard St	C2	Newington	H8	Pythian Cl	P4	Smithdown La	M7
Fraser St	H5	Hinton St	S4	Little St. Bride St	K10	New Red Rock Vw	P1	Pythian St	M4	Smithdown Rd	Q11
Freedom Cl	N9	Hockenhall All	E6	Little Woolton St	M7	Newsham Dr	R1	Queen Anne St	H4	Smithfield St	E5
Freeman St	S10	Hodson Pl	L1	Liver St	E10	Newstead Rd	R12	Queensland St	P8	Soho Pl	J3
Freemasons' Row	E4	Holborn St	M5	Lloyd Cl	L1	Newton Way	K7	Queens Wf	D12	Soho St	J4
Frost St	R6	Holden St	N10	Lockerby Rd	T4	Noel St	Q11	Quorn St	Q6	Solomon St	Q5
Galloway St	T10	Holdsworth St	Q5	London Rd	H6	Norfolk St	F12	Rachel St	G1	Solway St E	Q12
Gannock St	R6	Holly Rd	S5	Longfellow St	Q12	Norman St	K6	Radstock Rd	S3	Solway St W	P12
Gardenside St	L3	Holmes St	R12	Longstone Wk	P9	Northbrook Cl	N12	Raffles St	H11	South Chester St	J13
Gardners Dr	R2	Holt Rd	R6	Lord Nelson St	H6	North Brook St	M12	Rainford Gdns	F7	South Hunter St	K9
Gardner's Row	F3	Holy Cross Cl	F4	Lord St	E7	Northcote Cl	L1	Rainford Sq	E7	South John St	E8
Garrick St	S11	Homerton Rd	T3	Lorton St	Q11	North John St	E6	Ranelagh St	G8	Sparling St	F10
Gascoyne St	D4	Hood St	F6	Love La	D2	North St	F5	Raymond Pl	F1	Spekeland Rd	R10
Geneva Rd	S3	Hope Pl	J9	Lower Castle St	D7	North Vw	N7	Red Cross St	D8	Spencer St	L2
George Harrison Cl	P4	Hope St	K10	Low Hill	M4	Norton St	H5	Redgrave St	R5	Spindle Cl	L1
Georges Dockway	C8	Hornby Wk	E1	Lowther St	M11	Norwood Gro	Q1	Redmires Cl	Q9	Spofforth Rd	T10
George St	D6	Hotham St	H6	Low Wd St	M5	Nuttall St	Q7	Red Rock St	P1	Sprainger St	C2
Gerard St	G5	Houghton St	G7	Lyceum Pl	G8	Oakes St	K6	Regent St	B2	Springfield	H4
Gibraltar Row	C5	Houlton St	R5	Lydia Ann St	F9	O'Connell Rd	F2	Renfrew St	N5	Squires St	N8
Gibson St	L12	Hughes Cl	S8	Lytton St	L3	Odsey St	R5	Renshaw St	H7	Stafford St	J5
Gilbert St	F9	Hughes St	N2	Maddrell St	C1	Oil St	B2	Reservoir St	M2	Stamford St	R6
Gildarts Gdns	E2	Huntly Rd	S3	Madeleine St	M13	Old Hall St	C5	Reynolds Cl	N1	Standish St	F5
Gildart St	K5	Hurst St	E10	Madeley St	R2	Oldham St	H9	Rialto Cl	L12	Stanhope St	H13
Gilead St	Q5	Huskisson St	K11	Magdala St	R11	Old Leeds St	C5	Rice St	J10	Stanier Way	R8
Gill St	K6	Hutchinson St	N4	Maitland Cl	Q12	Olympia St	N3	Richardson St	S11	Stanley St	E6
Gilroy Rd	Q3	Hutchinson Wk	N4	Malden Rd	R3	Onslow Rd	S3	Richmond Row	H3	Steinberg Ct	D1
Gladstone Rd	P7	Hygeia St	N2	Mallow Rd	R3	Opal Cl	P1	Richmond St	F7	Sterndale Cl	Q9
Gladstone St	E4	Hyslop St	J13	Malt St	P10	Orange Gro	R13	Ridley Rd	R4	Stockdale Cl	E4
Gleave Cres	L2	Iliad St	H1	Malvern Rd	R3	O'Reilly Ct	D1	Rigby St	C5	Stone St	C1
Glegg St	C1	Ingrow Rd	Q4	Manchester St	F6	Oriel Steet	E3	Ringo Starr Dr	Q4	Stowell St	K9
Gloucester Ct	N4	Irvine St	N7	Manesty's La	F8	Ormond St	D6	Ritson St	P13	Strada Way	K4
Gloucester Pl	M5	Irwell St	C8	Manfred St	M5	Orphan St	M9	River Avon St	R11	Strand, The	C7
Gore St	H13	Islington	J5	Mann Island	C8	Orthes St	K8	Roberts St	B4	Strand St	D8
Gower St	D10	Ivatt Way	R8	Mann St	H13	Ottley St	S4	Roderick St	J4	Strathmore Rd	R1
Gradwell St	F8	Jack McBain Ct	D2	Mansell Rd	Q3	Overbury St	P8	Rodney St	J10	Strauss Cl	Q13
Grafton St	G12	Jade St	Q1	Mansfield St	H4	Overton St	P8	Roe St	G6	Suffolk St	G10
Granby St	N12	Jamaica St	G11	Manton Rd	R3	Oxendale Cl	P11	Rokeby Cl	J3	Sugnall St	K9
Granville Rd	T12	James Clarke St	E1	Marathon Cl	L2	Oxford St	K8	Rokeby St	J3	Summer Seat	F2
Grayson St	E10	James St	D8	Marcot Rd	T2	Oxford St E	N8	Rokesmith Av	R10	Surrey St	F10
Great Crosshall St	E5	Janet St	Q7	Margaret St	M1	Paddington	M7	Romer Rd	R4	Sutcliffe St	Q3
Great George Pl	G12	Jasmine Cl	K1	Mariners Wf	E13	Page Wk	J4	Romilly St	N4	Sweeting St	D7
Great George St	H12	Jenkinson St	J3	Maritime Pl	J4	Paisley St	B4	Roscastle Cl	N4	Swindale Cl	P11
Great Howard St	C4	Jet Cl	Q1	Maritime Way	F9	Pall Mall	C3	Roscoe La	H9	Swiss Rd	S3
Great Nelson St	G2	John Lennon Dr	P4			Paradise St	F8	Roscoe St	J9	Tabley St	F11
		John Moores Cl	M9			Parker St	G7	Roscommon St	H1	Tace Cl	L12

Name	Ref	Name	Ref	Name	Ref	Name	Ref	Name	Ref	Name	Ref
Tagus Cl	P13	Tom Mann Cl	G5	Upper Harrington St	H13	Vulcan St	B2	Westbourne St	L4	Windsor Vw	Q12
Tamar Cl	M1	Tordelow Cl	M1	Upper Hill St	J13	Wainwright Cl	R10	West Derby Rd	P3	Winifred St	Q7
Tarleton St	F7	Tower Gdns	C7	Upper Hope Pl	K10	Wakefield St	H4	West Derby St	L6	Winter St	M4
Tatlock St	E1	Trafalgar Way	L4	Upper Mason St	N7	Waldron Cl	E4	Westmorland Dr	E4	Wolstenholme Sq	G9
Tavy Rd	M1	Trowbridge St	J7	Upper Newington	H8	Walker St	M4	Whitcroft Rd	T3	Woodside St	Q8
Teck St	N6	Trueman St	F5	Upper Parliament St	H12	Walsh Cl	E1	Whitechapel	F7	Wood St	G8
Teign Cl	M1	Tudor St	Q3	Upper Pitt St	G11	Wapping	E9	Whitefield Rd	P1	Wordsworth St	Q12
Tempest Hey	D6	Tulloch St	P3	Upper Pownall St	F10	Ward St	H6	Whitefield Way	N1	Wrayburn Cl	R10
Temple Ct	E7	Tunnel Rd	Q10	Upper Stanhope St	J13	Warren St	J7	White Rock Ct	P1	Wrenbury St	R6
Temple La	E6	Tunstall St	S11	Upper William St	C1	Waterloo Quay	B3	White Rock St	P1	Yanwath St	Q11
Tenterden St	F1	Tweed St	R2	Uxbridge St	Q8	Water St	D7	Whithorn St	T10	York St	F9
Thackeray Pl	L13	Twomey Cl	E1	Vandries St	B2	Watkinson St	F12	Whitland Rd	T2		
Thames St	P13	Underley St	S11	Vandyke St	Q12	Watmough St	J2	Whitley St	C2		
Thorburn St	Q7	Union Ct	E7	Vauxhall Rd	E3	Wavertree Boul	T8	Whittier St	R12		
Thornes Rd	P4	Union St	C6	Vernon St	E5	Wavertree Rd	P7	Wightman St	P4		
Tichbourne Way	L4	Upper Baker St	N3	Verulam Cl	N11	Webb Cl	R8	Wilde St	H6		
Tideswell Cl	Q10	Upper Beau St	H2	Victoria St	E7	Webb St	R11	Wilfer Cl	R10		
Timpron St	R10	Upper Bute St	J2	Village St	K2	Webster Rd	T12	William Brown St	G6		
Titchfield St	E1	Upper Duke St	H10	Vincent Ct	G10	Webster St	F5	William Henry St	J3		
Tithebarn St	D6	Upper Frederick St	F10	Virgil St	G1	Wedgwood St	Q6	Williamson St	F7		
Tobin Cl	E1	Upper Hampton St	L12			Wendell St	R12	Wimpole St	Q6		
Toft St	R6					Wentworth Dr	L1	Windsor St	K12		

GREATER MANCHESTER URBAN pages 80–81

Name	Ref	Name	Ref	Name	Ref	Name	Ref	Name	Ref	Name	Ref	Name	Ref
Abbey Hey	E2	Barton upon Irwell	C2	Burford La	A4	Chorlton Rd	D3	Delauney's Rd	D1	Gee Cross	F3		
Abbey Hey La	E2	Bayley St	F2	Burnage	E3	Churchgate	E4	Den La	F1	George St	B1		
Abbey Hills Rd	F1	Bean Leach Rd	F4	Burnage La	E3	Churchill Way	D2	Denton	F3	Gin Pit	A2		
Adelphi St	D2	Beaufort Rd	F2	Burnley La	F1	Church La	E1	Denton La	E1	Glazebrook	A3		
Adswood	E4	Bedford	A2	Burton Rd	D3	Church Rd (Gatley)	D4	Denton Rd	F2	Glazebrook La	A3		
Adswood Rd	E4	Benchill	D4	Bury New Rd	D1	Church Rd (Urmston)	C3	Derbyshire La	C3	Glazebury	A2		
Agecroft Rd	C1	Bennett St	F2	Bury Old Rd	D1	Church St (Altrincham)	C4	Dewsnap La	F2	Glebelands Rd	C3		
Alan Turing Way	E2	Bentinck Rd	C4	Busk	F1	Church St (Eccles)	C2	Dialstone La	F4	Globe La	F2		
Albert Rd (Cheadle Hulme)	E4	Bent La	A4	Butterstile La	D1	Cinder Hill	C1	Dickenson Rd	D3	Glodwick	F1		
Albert Rd (Farnworth)	B1	Besses o' th' Barn	D1	Buxton Rd (Hazel Grove)	F4	City Rd	D2	Didsbury	D3	Glodwick Rd	F1		
Albert Rd (Levenshulme)	E3	Beswick	E2	Buxton Rd (Stockport)	E4	Claremont Rd (Manchester)	D3	Didsbury Rd	E4	Glynne St	B1		
Alder Forest	B2	Birchfield Rd	E3	Cadishead	B3	Claremont Rd (Salford)	C2	Dorchester Rd	C2	Godley	F3		
Alexandra Rd	D3	Birch La	F2	Cadishead Way	B3	Clarence St	F2	Dowson Rd	F3	Godson St	F1		
Alexandra Rd S	D3	Birch St	F2	Cale Green	E4	Clarendon Rd	F3	Droylsden	E2	Gorse Hill	C3		
Alkrington	E1	Birchwood Way	A3	Cambrian Rd	E2	Clayton	E2	Droylsden Rd	F2	Gorsey La	F2		
Alt	F1	Bird Hall La	E4	Camp St	D2	Clayton Bridge	E2	Dukinfield	F2	Gorton	E2		
Alt Hill	F1	Blackfriars Rd	D2	Canal Bk	C2	Cleggs La	B1	Dukinfield Rd	F2	Gorton La	E2		
Alt Hill La	F1	Blackley	E1	Carr Green	B4	Cliff, The	D2	Dumplington	C2	Gorton Rd (Manchester)	E2		
Altrincham	C4	Blackley New Rd	D1	Carrington	B3	Clifton	C1	Dunham Rd	C4	Gorton Rd (Reddish)	E3		
Altrincham Rd	C4	Blackmoor	A2	Carrington La	C3	Clifton Green	C1	Dunham Town	B4	Great Ancoats St	D2		
Amos Av	E2	Black Moss Rd	B4	Carrington Rd (Stockport)	E3	Clifton Junction	C1	Dunham Woodhouses	B4	Great Cheetham St	D2		
Ancoats	D2	Boarshaw Rd	B4	Carrington Rd (Urmston)	B3	Clifton Rd	E3	Eagle Row	A4	Great Clowes St	D2		
Anson Rd	E3	Bolton Rd (Atherton)	A1	Carrington Spur	C3	Clive Rd	E2	East Didsbury	D4	Great Duce St	D2		
Ardwick	E2	Bolton Rd (Kearsley)	B1	Carr Wd Rd	E4	Coal Pit La	F1	East Lancashire Rd	A2	Great Egerton St	E4		
Ardwick Grn St	D2	Bolton Rd (Pendlebury)	C1	Castle Hill	F3	Coalshaw Grn Rd	E1	Eccles	C2	Great Moor	E4		
Ashburton Rd W	C2	Bolton Rd (Salford)	C2	Castle St	E4	Collyhurst	D2	Eccles New Rd	C2	Great Norbury St	F3		
Ashley Heath	C4	Bolton Rd (Worsley)	B2	Cavendish Rd (Altrincham)	C4	Collyhurst Rd	D2	Eccles Old Rd	C2	Great Portwood St	E4		
Ashley Rd	C4	Booth's Hill Rd	A4	Cavendish Rd (Manchester)	D3	Commercial Rd	F4	Edge Fold	A1	Greave	F3		
Ashton La	C3	Boothstown	B2	Centenary Way	C2	Conran St	D2	Edge La (Droylsden)	E2	Greek St	E4		
Ashton New Rd	E2	Bowdon	C4	Central Av	D1	Coppice	F1	Edge La (Stretford)	C3	Greenacres	F1		
Ashton Old Rd	E2	Bowfell Rd	B3	Chadderton	E1	Copster Hill	F1	Edgeley	E4	Greenacres Rd	F1		
Ashton Rd (Bredbury)	F3	Bowgreen	B4	Chadderton Way	F1	Copster Hill Rd	F1	Edgeley Rd	E4	Green End	E3		
Ashton Rd (Denton)	F3	Bowgreen Rd	B4	Chaddock La	B2	Cornwall St	E2	Edward St	F1	Green End Rd	E3		
Ashton Rd (Droylsden)		Boyds Wk	F2	Chadkirk	F4	Corporation Rd	F2	Egerton Rd	D3	Greenheys	B1		
Ashton Rd (Dukinfield)	F2	Bradfield Rd	C3	Chain Bar	E1	Councillor La	E4	Egerton St	F1	Green Hill Rd	D1		
Ashton Rd (Failsworth)	F2	Bradford	E2	Chamber Rd	F1	Cowhill	E1	Elizabeth St	D2	Green La (Eccles)	C2		
Ashton Rd (Oldham)	F1	Bradford Rd	B1	Chapel Field	C1	Cowlishaw Rd	F3	Ellenbrook	B1	Green La (Failsworth)	E2		
Ashton Rd E	E1	Bradford St	E2	Chapel Rd	F1	Cranbourne Rd	F2	Ellenbrook Rd	B2	Greenleach La	B1		
Ashton Rd W	E1	Bramhall La	E4	Chapel St	D2	Crescent	D2	Ellesmere Park	C2	Greenside La	E2		
Ashton St	D2	Bramhall La S	E4	Chapman St	E2	Crescent Rd (Dukinfield)	F2	Elm Rd	F1	Greg St	E3		
Ashton-under-Lyne	F2	Bramhall Moor	F4	Chappell Rd	E2	Crescent Rd (Manchester)	D1	Errwood Rd	E3	Grey Mare La	E2		
Ashton upon Mersey	C3	Bramhall Moor La	E4	Charcoal Rd	B4	Crofts Bank	C3	Etchell Rd	E4	Grimshaw La (Manchester)	E2		
Assheton Rd	E2	Bramhall Park	E4	Charles St	F2	Crofts Bk Rd	C3	Europa Way	C2	Grimshaw La (Middleton)	E1		
Astley	A2	Bramhall Pk Rd	E4	Charlestown (Manchester)	E1	Cromwell Rd (Eccles)	C2	Every St	D2	Guide Bridge	F2		
Astley Green	A2	Bredbury	F3	Charlestown (Salford)	D2	Cromwell Rd (Salford)	D2	Factory La	D1	Guide La	F2		
Astley Rd	B3	Bredbury Green	F4	Charlestown Rd	E1	Cross Acres Rd	D4	Failsworth	E1	Guinness Rd	C2		
Astley St	F2	Bridge St	C1	Chassen Rd	B3	Crossley Rd	E3	Failsworth Rd	F2	Hale	C4		
Atherton	A1	Bridgewater Rd (Mosley Common)	B1	Chatsworth Rd	C3	Cross St	C3	Fairfield	E2	Hale La	E1		
Atlantic St	B4	Bridgewater Rd (Worsley)	B1	Cheadle	E4	Crowhill	F2	Fairfield Rd	E2	Hale Rd	C4		
Audenshaw	F2	Brindle Heath	C2	Cheadle Heath	E4	Crumpsall	D1	Fallowfield	D3	Half Edge La	C2		
Audenshaw Rd	F2	Brinell Dr	B3	Cheadle Hulme	E4	Crumpsall La	D1	Farnworth	B1	Hall La	E3		
Austerlands	F1	Brinksway	E4	Cheadle Rd	E4	Culcheth	A3	Featherstall Rd N	F1	Hall St	E4		
Ayres Rd	D3	Brinnington	F3	Cheadle Royal	E4	Culcheth La	E2	Featherstall Rd S	F1	Harboro Way	C3		
Back O' Th' Low Rd	F1	Brinnington Rd	F3	Cheetham	D2	Cutler Hill Rd	F1	Ferndown Rd	C4	Harper Green	B1		
Baguley	D4	Briscoe La	E2	Cheetham Hill	D1	Dairyhouse La	B4	Fields New Rd	E1	Harpurhey	E1		
Banks La	E4	Broadheath	C4	Cheetham Hill Rd (Dukinfield)	F2	Daisy Nook	F2	Finney La	D4	Harrowby St	B1		
Bank St	E2	Broadoak Rd	F2	Cheetham Hill Rd (Manchester)	D1	Dales Brow	C2	Firs, The	C4	Hart Rd	D3		
Bardsley	F1	Broad Rd	C3	Cheetwood	D2	Dales La	C1	Firs Rd	C3	Hartshead Green	F1		
Barlow Moor	D3	Broadstone Rd	E3	Chequerbent	A1	Dane Bank	E3	Firs Way	C4	Hartshead Pike	F1		
Barlow Moor Rd	D3	Broad St	C2	Cherry La	C4	Dane Rd	C3	Fitzwarren St	C2	Hathersage Rd	D3		
Barlow Rd	E3	Broadway (Cheadle)	D4	Cherry Tree	F4	Daniel Adamson Rd	C2	Flixton	B3	Hathershaw	F1		
Barrington Rd	C4	Broadway (Failsworth)	E1	Chester Gate	E4	Darley St	B1	Flixton Rd	B3	Haughton Green	F3		
Barton Dock Rd	C2	Broadway (Salford)	C2	Chester Rd (Manchester)	D2	Darnton Rd	F2	Flowery Field	F3	Haughton Grn Rd	F3		
Barton La	C2	Brooklands	C4	Chester Rd (Stretford)	C3	Davenport	E4	Foggbrook	F4	Haveswater Rd	C3		
Barton Moss	B2	Brooklands Rd	C4	Chichester Rd	D3	Davenport Green	C4	Fog La	D3	Hawk Green	F4		
Barton Rd (Eccles)	C2	Broomfield La	C4	Chorley Rd	C1	Davyhulme	B3	Folly La	C2	Hazelbottom Rd	D2		
Barton Rd (Stretford)	C3	Broom La	E3	Chorlton-cum-Hardy	D3	Davyhulme Rd (Stretford)	C3	Foundry St	F2	Hazel Grove	F4		
Barton Rd (Urmston)	C3	Broughton Park	D1			Davyhulme Rd (Urmston)	B3	Fowley Common	A3	Hazelhurst (Ashton-under-Lyne)	F2		
Barton Rd (Worsley)	B2	Broughton Rd	D2			Debdale	E3	Frederick Rd	D2	Hazelhurst (Swinton)	B1		
		Brownley Rd	D4					Frederick St	F1	Heald Green	D4		
		Brunswick	D2					Garforth St	F1	Heatley	A4		
		Brunswick St	D2					Garner's La	E4	Heaton Chapel	E3		
		Buckley La	B1					Gatley	D4				
		Bunkers Hill	F4					Gatley Rd	D4				

Name	Ref
Heaton Mersey	E3
Heaton Moor	E3
Heaton Moor Rd	E3
Heaton Norris	E3
Heaviley	E4
Hempshaw La	E4
Henrietta St	F2
Heron St	F1
Heywood Old Rd	D1
Higham La	F3
Higher Blackley	D1
Higher Broughton	D2
Higher Folds	A2
Higher Green	A2
Higher Irlam	B3
Higher La (Lymm)	A4
Higher La (Whitefield)	C1
Higher Rd	C3
Highfield	B1
Highfield Rd	B1
High Lane	F4
High La	D3
High St (Cheadle)	D4
High St (Gorton)	E2
High St (Lees)	F1
High St (Stalybridge)	F2
Hillcrest Rd	F4
Hillgate	E4
Hill Top	B1
Hilton Fold La	E1
Hilton La (Prestwich)	D1
Hilton La (Worsley)	B1
Hilton Park	D1
Hindsford	A1
Holcroft La	A3
Hollins	A1
Hollins Green	A3
Hollins Rd	F1
Hollinwood	E1
Hollinwood Av	E1
Hollyedge Rd	D4
Holts	F1
Honeywell La	F1
Hospital Rd	C1
Howe Bridge	A1
Huddersfield Rd	F1
Hulme	D2
Hulme Hall La	E2
Hulme Hall Rd	E4
Hulmes Rd	E2
Hunt La	E1
Hurst	F2
Hyde	F3
Hyde Rd (Denton)	F3
Hyde Rd (Manchester)	E2
Hyde Rd (Woodley)	F3
Irlam	B3
Irlam Rd	B3
Irlams o' th' Height	C2
Joel La	F3
Joshua La	E1
Joyce St	E1
Katherine St	F2
Kearsley	B1
Kearsley Rd	C1
Kensington Rd	D3
Kenyon La	E1
Kersal	D1
Kersal Vale	D1
King Sreet W	E4
King's Rd (Ashton-under-Lyne)	F2
King's Rd (Old Trafford)	D3
King's Rd (Oldham)	F1
Kingston	F3
King St (Dukinfield)	F2
King St (Farnworth)	B1
Kingsway (Cheadle)	D4
Kingsway (Middleton)	E1
Kingsway (Stretford)	C3
Kingsway S	E4
Kirkhams	D1
Kirkmanshulme La	E3
Kirkway	E1
Knott Lanes	F1
Knott Las	F1
Knowle Av	F2
Knowles La	F1
Laburnum Rd	E3
Ladybarn	E3
Ladybarn La	E3
Ladybridge Rd	E4
Lancashire Hill	E3
Lancaster Rd (Denton)	F3
Lancaster Rd (Salford)	C2
Landsdowne Rd	F1
Lane End	E3
Lanehead Rd	F1
Langley Rd	C1
Langley Rd S	D2
Langworthy Rd	C2
Lansdowne Rd	D1
Lapwing La	D3
Lark Hill (Blackmoor)	A2
Larkhill (Irlam)	B3
Lately Common	A2
Lees	F1
Lees New Rd	F1
Lees Rd	F1
Leicester Rd	D1
Leigh	A2
Leigh Rd	B2
Levenshulme	E3
Ley Hey Park	F4
Lightbowne Rd	E1
Lily La	F1
Limehurst	F2
Lime Side	F1
Limeside Rd	F1
Lingard La	F3
Linnyshaw	B1
Lisburne La	F4
Little Bollington	B4
Little Bolton	C2
Little Hulton	B1
Littlemoss	F2
Littleton Rd	D1
Liverpool Rd	B2
Liverpool St	D2
Lloyd St (Altrincham)	C4
Lloyd St (Manchester)	D3
Lloyd St S	D3
Lodge La	F3
Lomond Rd	D4
London Rd	F4
Long Causeway	B1
Longford Rd W	E3
Long Lane	E4
Longsight	E2
Lord La	E2
Lostock Rd	C3
Lower Bredbury	F3
Lower Broughton	D2
Lower Broughton Rd	D2
Lower Irlam	B3
Lower Kersal	D1
Lowfield Rd	E4
Lumber La	B1
Lumb La (Audenshaw)	F2
Lumb La (Droylsden)	F2
Lumm's La	C1
Lumn Rd	F3
Lymm	A4
Lymm Rd	B4
Mainway	E1
Manchester	D2
Manchester New Rd	E1
Manchester Old Rd	D1
Manchester Rd (Altrincham)	C4
Manchester Rd (Audenshaw)	F2
Manchester Rd (Carrington)	B3
Manchester Rd (Cheadle)	D4
Manchester Rd (Chorlton-cum-Hardy)	D3
Manchester Rd (Clifton)	C1
Manchester Rd (Denton)	E3
Manchester Rd (Droylsden)	E2
Manchester Rd (Oldham)	E1
Manchester Rd (Rixton)	A4
Manchester Rd (Stockport)	E3
Manchester Rd (Swinton)	C1
Manchester Rd (Worsley)	B1
Manchester Rd E	B1
Manchester Rd W	B1
Manchester St	F1
Mancunian Rd	F3
Mancunian Way	D2
Manor Av	C3
Manor Rd (Cheadle Hulme)	E4
Manor Rd (Droylsden)	E2
Margaret St	F2
Market St (Droylsden)	E2
Market St (Farnworth)	B1
Market St (Hyde)	F3
Marple	F4
Marple Dale	F4
Marpleridge	F4
Marple Rd	F4
Marsland Rd	C3
Matthews La	E3
Mauldeth Rd (Manchester)	D3
Mauldeth Rd (Stockport)	E3
Mauldeth Rd W	D3
Medlock Rd	E2
Medlock St	E2
Medlock Vale	E2
Mercian Way	E4
Mersey Rd	E1
Middle Hill Gate	E4
Middleton	E1
Middleton Junction	E1
Middleton Rd (Chadderton)	E1
Middleton Rd (Manchester)	D1
Miles Platting	E2
Millgate La	E1
Mill Hills Rd	E1
Mill La (Denton)	F3
Mill La (Lymm)	A4
Mill St	D2
Monsall Rd	E2
Monsall St	E2
Montague Rd	F2
Monton	C2
Monton Rd	C2
Moor Close	E1
Moorhey	F1
Moorland Rd	E4
Moor La	D1
Moorside	C1
Moorside Rd (Stockport)	E4
Moorside Rd (Swinton)	C1
Moorside Rd (Urmston)	B3
Moorside St	E2
Mort La	B1
Moseley Rd	E3
Mosley Common	B1
Mosley Common Rd	B1
Mosley Rd	C3
Mossbrow	B4
Moss La (Altrincham)	C4
Moss La (Sale)	C3
Moss La E	D3
Moss La W	D3
Mossley Rd	F2
Moss Side (Manchester)	D3
Moss Side (Tyldesley)	A2
Moss Way	F2
Moston	E1
Moston La	E1
Mottram Rd	F3
Mount Rd	E3
Mumps	F1
Nangreave Rd	E4
Navigation Rd	C4
Nell La	D3
Newall Green	D4
New Br La	E4
New Brook Rd	A1
New Bury	B1
Newearth Rd	B1
New La	C2
Newmarket Rd	F2
New Moston	E1
Newton	F2
Newton Heath	E2
Newton St	F3
Newtown	C1
New Zealand Rd	E4
Nimble Nook	E1
Nob End	B1
Norbury Moor	F4
Norris Bank	E4
Norris La	C4
Northenden	D4
Northenden Rd (Gatley)	D4
Northenden Rd (Sale)	C3
Northern Moor	D4
Northmoor Rd	E3
North Reddish	E3
North Rd	E2
Northumberland St	D1
Nuthurst Rd	E1
Oak Bank	D1
Offerton Fold	F4
Offerton Green	F4
Offerton La	F4
Offerton Rd	F4
Ogden La	E2
Old Ch St	E2
Old Clough La	B1
Oldfield Brow	C4
Oldfield La	B4
Oldfield Rd (Altrincham)	C4
Oldfield Rd (Salford)	D2
Old Hall La	D3
Oldham	F1
Oldham Edge	F1
Oldham Rd (Ashton-under-Lyne)	F1
Oldham Rd (Failsworth)	E1
Oldham Rd (Manchester)	D2
Oldham Rd (Middleton)	E1
Oldham Rd (Springhead)	F1
Oldham Way	F1
Old Mkt St	D1
Old Rd (Failsworth)	E1
Old Rd (Hyde)	F3
Old St	F1
Old Trafford	D3
Openshaw	E2
Ordnance Av	A3
Ordsall	D2
Ordsall La	D2
Outwood	C1
Outwood La	D4
Over Hulton	A1
Oxford Rd (Dukinfield)	F2
Oxford Rd (Manchester)	D2
Oxford St	E1
Palatine Rd	D3
Park Bridge	F1
Park Lane	C1
Park Par	F2
Park Rd (Bowdon)	B4
Park Rd (Dukinfield)	F2
Park Rd (Hyde)	F3
Park Rd (Oldham)	F1
Park Rd (Sale)	C4
Park Rd (Stretford)	C3
Park St	C1
Parr Brow	B1
Parrin La	C2
Parrs Wd Rd N	D3
Parrs Wd Rd S	D4
Parsonage Rd	E3
Partington	B3
Patricroft	C2
Peel Green	B2
Peel Grn Rd	C2
Peel Hall	D4
Peel La	B1
Peel St	E1
Pendlebury	C1
Pendleton	D2
Pennine Rd	F3
Penny Meadow	F2
Philips Pk Rd	E2
Pickford La	F2
Piggott St	B1
Pin Mill	D2
Platt La	D3
Plodder La	A1
Plymouth Gro	D2
Pollard St	D2
Portwood	E3
Prestolee	B1
Prestwich	D1
Princess Parkway	D4
Princess Rd	D3
Props Hall Dr	E2
Queen's Rd (Ashton-under-Lyne)	F2
Queens Rd (Manchester)	D2
Queens Way	C1
Rainsough	D1
Rake La	C1
Ravenoak Rd	E4
Raver La	E2
Redclyffe Rd	C2
Reddish	E3
Reddish La	E3
Reddish Rd	E3
Regent Rd	D2
Regent St	C2
Rhodes	D1
Richmond St	F1
Ridge Hill	F2
Ridge Hill La	F2
Ringley	C1
Ringley Rd	C1
Ringley Rd W	C1
River Pk Rd	E2
Rochdale Rd (Manchester)	D2
Rochdale Rd (Oldham)	F1
Rocky La	E2
Roe Green	B1
Roman Rd	E1
Romiley	F3
Roscoe Rd	B3
Rosehill	C4
Rose Hill Rd	F2
Roundthorn	C4
Roundthorn Rd	F1
Rushgreen	A4
Rushgreen Rd	A4
Rusholme	E3
St. Albans Av	F1
St. George's	D2
St. Helens Rd	A1
St. James Rd	D2
St. John St	F1
St. Margaret's Rd	C4
St. Mary's Rd	E1
St. Mary's Way	F1
St. Werburgh's Rd	D3
Sale	C3
Sale Ees	C3
Sale Rd	D4
Salford	C2
Salford Rd	A1
Sandy La (Dukinfield)	F2
Sandy La (Manchester)	D3
Sandy La (Stockport)	E3
Sandy La (Stretford)	C3
Scholes La	D1
School La	B4
Schools Hill	D4
Scotland Hall Rd	E2
Sedgley Park	D1
Seedley	C2
Semple Way	E1
Seymour Gro	D3
Shadow Moss Rd	D4
Shaftesbury Av	C4
Shakerley	A1
Sharston	D4
Shaw Heath	E4
Shaw Heath	E4
Shaw Rd	F1
Sheepfoot La	D1
Sheffield Rd	F3
Shepley Rd	F2
Sibson Rd	C3
Silk St	D2
Simister	D1
Simonsway	D4
Simpson Rd	B2
Sinderland Green	B4
Sinderland La	B4
Singleton Rd	D1
Slack Fold La	A1
Slack Rd	D1
Slade La	E3
Smallshaw	F2
Smedley Rd	D2
South Langworthy Rd	C2
Southmoor Rd	C4
South Reddish	E3
Springfield Rd	B1
Springhead	F1
Spring Hill	F1
Stamford Pk Rd	C4
Stamford Rd (Audenshaw)	F2
Stamford Rd (Bowdon)	C4
Stamford Rd (Lees)	F1
Stamford St	F2
Stand	C1
Stanley Grn	E3
Stanley Rd	E1
Stannybrook Rd	F1
Star La	A4
Statham	A4
Station Rd (Cheadle Hulme)	E4
Station Rd (Swinton)	C1
Stepping Hill	F4
Stockport	E4
Stockport Little Moor	F4
Stockport Rd (Altrincham)	C4
Stockport Rd (Ashton-under-Lyne)	F2
Stockport Rd (Cheadle)	E4
Stockport Rd (Denton)	F3
Stockport Rd (Hyde)	F3
Stockport Rd (Manchester)	E3
Stockport Rd E	F3
Stockport Rd W	F3
Stoneclough	B1
Stoneclough Rd	B1
Stone Rd	D3
Stott La	C2
Strangeways	D2
Stretford	C3
Stretford Rd (Manchester)	D2
Stretford Rd (Urmston)	C3
Styal Rd	D4
Sunnyside Rd	E2
Sussex St	D2
Swinton	C1
Swinton Hall Rd	C1
Swinton Park	C2
Swinton Pk Rd	C2
Talbot Rd (Hyde)	F2
Talbot Rd (Manchester)	D3
Tame St	F2
Taunton	F2
Taunton Rd	F2
Taylor La	C2
Ten Acres La	C2
Tenax Rd	C2
Third Av	C2
Thompson La	E1
Thorley La	D4
Thorpe La	F1
Thorp Rd	E2
Timperley	C4
Tootal Dr	C2
Torkington	F4
Townfield La	A4
Town Lane	A2
Town La	F3
Trafford Park	C2
Trafford Pk Rd	C2
Trafford Rd (Eccles)	C2
Trafford Rd (Salford)	D2
Trafford Wf	C2
Trinity Way	D2
Turf La	E1
Turncroft La	E4
Turves Rd	E4
Twirl Hill Rd	F1
Two Trees La	F3
Tyldesley	A1
Tyldesley Rd	A1
Union Rd	F2
Union St	E1
Upper Brook St	D2
Upper Chorlton Rd	D3
Urmston	C3
Urmston La	C3
Varley St	E2
Victoria Av E	D1
Victoria Rd	F2
Victoria Rd (Chadderton)	F1
Victoria St (Hyde)	F3
Village Way	C2
Vine St	E2
Walkden	B1
Walkden Rd	B1
Wallness	D2
Warburton	A4
Wardley	C1
Warrbruce Rd	C2
Washway Rd	C4
Waterloo	F2
Waterloo Rd	D2
Waterloo St (Manchester)	D1
Waterloo St (Oldham)	F1
Weaste	C2
Weaste La	C2
Well Green	C4
Wellington Rd (Ashton-under-Lyne)	F2
Wellington Rd (Eccles)	C2
Wellington Rd (Timperley)	C4
Wellington Rd N	E3
Wellyhole St	F1
Werneth	F1
Werneth Low	F3
Werneth Low Rd	F3
Werneth Rd	F3
West Didsbury	D3
West Gorton	E2
Westinghouse Rd	C2
Westminster Rd	E1
Whalley Range	D3
Wharfside Way	C2
Wharf St	F2
Whitbarrow Rd	A4
Whiteacre Rd	F2
Whitefield	D1
White Gate	E1
Whitehill St	E3
Whitehouse La	B4
Whitelands Rd	F3
Wilbraham Rd	D3
Wilmslow Rd (Cheadle)	D4
Wilmslow Rd (Heald Green)	D4
Wilmslow Rd (Manchester)	D3
Wilshaw La	F2
Winchester Rd	C3
Windlehurst	F4
Windmill La	E3
Windsor Rd	E3

Winton	B2	Woodhouses (Sale)	C4	Woodley	F3	Worsley Rd (Eccles)	C2	Wythenshawe	D4
Withington	D3	Woodlands Rd		Woodsend Rd	B3	Worsley Rd		Wythenshawe Rd	
Withington Rd	D3	(Altrincham)	C4	Woods Moor	E4	(Farnworth)	B1	(Manchester)	D4
Woodhouse Park	D4	Woodlands Rd		Woodsmoore La	E4	Worsley Rd		Wythenshawe Rd	
Woodhouses		(Manchester)	D1	Wood St	E4	(Worsley)	B2	(Sale)	C3	Yew Tree La	F2
(Failsworth)	E2	Wood La	F2	Worsley	B2	Wrigley Head La	E1	Yew Tree	F2	Yew Tree Rd	D3

MANCHESTER CENTRAL pages 82-83

Abingdon St	K8	Barrhill Cl	F11	Brotherton Cl	D11	Cheapside	J6	Cunard Cl	P12	Epping St	J12
Acton Sq	A5	Barrow St	D6	Brotherton Dr	E4	Cheetham Hill Rd	K3	Cygnus Av	C2	Epsley Cl	K13
Adair St	P8	Barton St	G9	Browfield Av	A10	Cheetwood St	G1	Cyrus St	S5	Epworth St	Q7
Addington St	M4	Beamish Cl	P12	Brown Cross St	F6	Chepstow St	J9	Dainton St	S10	Errington Dr	D1
Addison Cl	P13	Beattock St	E11	Browning St	D13	Cherryton Wk	P13	Daintry Cl	H12	Erskine St	E13
Adelphi St	D5	Beaufort St	F9	Browning St		Chesshyre Av	S6	Dalberg St	R11	Essex St	J7
Aden Cl	S8	Beaver St	K9	(Salford)	E5	Chester Rd	C12	Dale St	M6	Essex Way	E13
Adlington St	R9	Bednal Av	S1	Brown St	J7	Chester St	J11	Dalley Av	D1	Evans St	G3
Adstone Cl	S6	Beechcroft Cl	Q3	Brunel Av	A6	Chevassut St	F12	Dalton Ct	N1	Everard St	C10
Adswood St	T5	Belfort Dr	A9	Brunswick	P13	Cheviot St	J2	Dalton St	N1	Every St	R8
Airton Cl	Q2	Bendix St	M4	Brunswick St	M13	Chevril Cl	K12	Damask Av	D4	Exford Cl	R3
Aked Cl	S13	Bengal St	N4	Brydon Av	Q10	Chiffon Way	D3	Danebank Wk	N11	Fairbrother St	B11
Albion Pl	B5	Bennett St	T12	Buckfield Av	A10	China La	M7	Danson St	T3	Fairfield St	N9
Albion St	H10	Bentinck St	D11	Bugle St	G10	Chippenham Rd	Q5	Dantzic St	K5	Fair St	P7
Albion Way	A5	Bent St	K1	Bunsen St	M6	Chorlton Rd	E13	Dark La	R9	Falkland Av	S1
Alderman Sq	T8	Berkshire Rd	S2	Burnell Cl	Q3	Chorlton St	L7	Dartford Cl	S13	Faraday St	M5
Aldred St	A5	Berry St	N9	Burstock St	M2	Christchurch Av	A5	Darton Av	S3	Farnborough Rd	R2
Alexander Gdns	E1	Beswick Row	K3	Burton St	N1	Churchgate Bldgs	P8	Davy St	N1	Farrell St	F2
Alexandra St	E2	Beswick St	R5	Burton Wk	D4	Church St	L5	Dawson St	D9	Faulkner St	K8
Alfred James Cl	Q3	Betley St	P8	Bury St	F4	Cinder St	P4	Dean Rd	G3	Federation St	K4
Alker Rd	S3	Bevan Cl	T7	Butler La	Q3	Cipher St	P3	Deansgate	H8	Fennel St	J4
Alley St	J6	Bilbrook St	M2	Butler St	Q3	City Rd	E12	Dean St	M6	Fenn St	F13
Almond St	N1	Billing Av	P10	Butter La	H6	City Rd E	H11	Deanwater Cl	N11	Fenwick St	K12
Altair Pl	C1	Binns Pl	N6	Buxton St	N9	Clarence St	J7	Dearden St	G12	Ferdinan St	R1
Amory St	P9	Birchin La	L6	Byrcland Cl	T9	Clarendon St	J12	Dearmans Pl	G5	Fernie St	K2
Anaconda Dr	F3	Birchvale Cl	G12	Byron St	G8	Clare St	N10	Deer St	P8	Fern St	K1
Ancoats	P5	Birt St	R2	Cable St	L4	Clarion St	P3	Denver Av	S2	Ferry St	T8
Ancoats Gro	R7	Bishopsgate	J8	Cabot St	N12	Clayburn Rd	G12	Derby St	K1	Filby Wk	T1
Ancroft St	F13	Blackburn Pl	B7	Cakebread St	P10	Cleminson St	D5	Derwent St	C9	Firbeck Dr	R4
Angela St	E11	Blackburn St	D3	Calder St	C9	Cleworth St	D11	Devine Cl	D4	Firefly Cl	D6
Angel St	L3	Blackfriars Rd	E3	Calico St	D3	Clifford St	M12	Devonshire St	R13	Fire Sta Sq	A5
Angora Cl	D3	Blackfriars St	H5	Cambrian St	S4	Clive St	M3	Devonshire St N	S12	Fir St	R1
Angora Dr	D3	Blackhill Cl	N11	Cambridge St	J10	Cloak St	L10	Dewhurst St	H1	Fitzwilliam St	E1
Anita St	N5	Blacklock St	J1	Cambridge St		Cloughfield Av	A9	Dickinson St	J8	Flora Dr	E1
Anne Nuttall St	D11	Bladon St	M8	(Salford)	F1	Clowes St	G5	Dilston Cl	Q13	Ford St	R12
Anscombe Cl	R2	Blantyre St	E10	Camelford Cl	K13	Cobourg St	M8	Dinsdale Cl	S4	Ford St (Salford)	E5
Antares Av	D2	Blind La	S10	Cameron St	H10	Coburg Av	D1	Dinton St	C11	Foundry La	M5
Apsley Gro	Q12	Blisworth Cl	S6	Camp St	G8	Cockcroft Rd	A4	Dobson Cl	R13	Fountain St	K7
Ardwick	T10	Bloom St	L8	Canal St	L8	Cockspur St	G5	Dolefield	G6	Four Yards	J7
Ardwick Grn N	P10	Blossom St	G4	Cannon St	D4	Coleshill St	T2	Dolphin Pl	Q11	Frances St	N12
Ardwick Grn S	P10	Blossom St		Canon Ct	J5	College Land	H6	Dolphin St	Q11	Francis St	H2
Arlington St	E4	(Ancoats)	N5	Canon Grn Dr	F4	Collier St	G9	Donald St	L9	Frederick St	F5
Artillery St	G8	Blucher St	B7	Carding Gro	F3	Collier St (Salford)	G4	Dorsey St	L5	Freeman Sq	K13
Arundel St	E10	Boad St	N8	Cardroom Rd	P5	Collingham St	L1	Downing St	N10	Freya Gro	B9
Asgard Dr	C9	Bollington Rd	R4	Carey Cl	E1	Collyhurst Rd	N1	Downley Dr	Q5	Frost St	S6
Asgard Grn	C9	Bombay St	L9	Carmel Av	B10	Colman Gdns	A10	Droitwich Rd	R1	Fulmer Dr	Q4
Ashlar Dr	S8	Bond St	P9	Carmel Cl	B9	Colin Murphy Rd	F11	Dryden St	P13	Gaitskell Cl	T7
Ashley St	M3	Bonsall St	H13	Carnarvon St	J1	Comet St	N7	Dryhurst Wk	K13	Galgate Cl	E11
Ashton New Rd	S6	Boond St	G4	Caroline St	F1	Commercial St	G10	Ducie St	M7	Garden La	H6
Ashton Old Rd	R9	Boond St (Ancoats)	R6	Carpenters La	L5	Comus St	B8	Duke Pl	F9	Garden St	G4
Aspin La	L3	Booth St	J7	Carruthers St	R5	Concert La	K7	Duke St	F9	Garden Wall Cl	B9
Atherton St	F8	Booth St (Salford)	H5	Cassidy Cl	N4	Congou St	P8	Duke St (Salford)	H4	Garforth Av	Q4
Atkinson St	G7	Booth St E	L12	Castlefield Urban		Cooper St	J7	Dulwich St	M2	Gartside St	G7
Atwood St	K9	Booth St W	K13	Heritage Pk	E9	Coop St	M5	Duncan St	B8	Garwood St	G11
Auburn St	M7	Bootle St	H7	Castle St	F9	Copeman Cl	P13	Dun Cl	D5	Gateaton St	J5
Audlem Cl	S4	Bothwell Rd	P3	Caterham St	S7	Copperas St	L5	Dunham St	G13	Gaythorn St	C6
Augustus St	K1	Boundary La	K12	Cathedral App	J4	Coral St	P11	Dunlop St	H6	George Leigh St	M5
Aytoun St	L7	Boundary St E	L11	Cathedral Gates	J5	Cork St	S8	Durant St	M3	George Parr Rd	H13
Back Acton St	M8	Boundary St W	L12	Cathedral St	J5	Cornbrook	C11	Durling Av	Q11	George St	K8
Back Ashley St	M3	Bourdon St	S3	Cathedral Yd	J5	Cornbrook	C11	Dutton St	J2	Georgette Dr	G3
Back Bk St	L1	Bow La	J7	Catlow La	L5	Cornbrook Ct	D13	Dyche St	L4	Gibbs St	D6
Back Br St	H6	Bow St	H7	Catlow St	G1	Cornbrook Pk Rd	C12	Dyer St	B10	Gibson Pl	K2
Back China La	M7	Brackley Av	D11	Cavalier St	S5	Cornell St	N4	Eagle St	L4	Girton St	F1
Back Coll Land	H6	Bradford Rd	R5	Cavanagh Cl	R13	Coronation Sq	Q9	Eastburn Av	Q2	Glasshouse St	P3
Back George St	K7	Bradleys Ct	M6	Cavell St	M6	Coronation St	A8	Eastfield Av	T3	Gleden St	T4
Back Hampson St	R1	Braley St	N10	Cavendish St	K12	Corporation St	J5	Eastleigh Dr	R2	Glenbarry Cl	N13
Back Hulme St	C6	Bramble Av	B10	Cawdor St	D11	Cottenham La	F1	East Mkt St	E5	Glenbarry St	S9
Back Junct St	N7	Bramwell Dr	P12	Caxton St	G5	Cottenham St	N12	East Newton St	Q3	Gloucester St	J10
Back Piccadilly	L6	Brancaster Rd	L10	Caygill St	G4	Cotter St	P10	Eastnor Cl	D13	Gloucester St	
Back Pool Fold	J6	Branson St	S5	Cedar Pl	C1	Cottingham Rd	T13	East Ordsall La	D7	(Salford)	B9
Back Red Bk	L2	Brazennose St	H7	Central St	J8	Cotton St	N5	Eastpark Cl	Q12	Goadsby St	L4
Back St. George's		Brazil St	L9	Century St	G9	County St	J7	East Philip St	G2	Gold St	L7
Rd	N3	Brewer St	M6	Chadderton St	M4	Coupland St	J8	East Union St	C13	Gordon St	E1
Back S Par	H6	Brian Redhead Ct	F11	Chain St	K7	Coupland St E	L13	Ebden St	M8	Gore St	M7
Back Thomas St	L5	Brickley St	K2	Chancel Av	B9	Coverdale Cres	R12	Ebenezer St	J11	Gore St (Salford)	F6
Back Turner St	L5	Brick St	L5	Chancellor La	R9	Cowan St	S5	Echo St	M9	Gorton St	H4
Badby Cl	S6	Briddon St	H2	Chancery La	J7	Cowburn St	J2	Eden Cl	J13	Goulden St	M4
Bainbridge Cl	S13	Bridgeford St	L13	Change Way	F3	Cow La	C7	Edgehill St	L5	Gould St	M2
Baird St	N8	Bridge St	G6	Chapelfield Rd	Q9	Crabbe St	L2	Edge St	L5	Granby Row	L9
Bale St	J8	Bridge St W	G6	Chapel St	F5	Cranbourne St	A7	Edward St	G1	Granshaw St	T3
Balloon St	K4	Bridgewater Pl	K6	Chapeltown St	N8	Crane St	Q9	Egerton Rd	E10	Gratrix Av	A11
Balmforth St	E10	Bridgewater St	G9	Chapel Walks	J6	Cranfield Cl	S4	Egerton St	E6	Gravell La	H4
Balsam Cl	P11	Bridgewater St		Chapel Wf	G6	Craven St	C7	Elbe St	Q9	Grear Ducie St	J4
Bankmill Cl	N11	(Salford)	F2	Charles St	K10	Crediton Cl	J13	Eliza St	F12	Great Ancoates St	M5
Bank Pl	D5	Bridgewater		Charley Av	D1	Cresbury St	R10	Ellesmere St	D11	Great Bridgewater	
Bank St	D5	Viaduct	G10	Charlotte St	K7	Crescent, The	A4	Ellis St	G13	St	J9
Baptist St	M3	Briggs St	E3	Charlton Pl	N10	Crossley Ct	S6	Elsworth St	K2	Great Clowes St	E2
Barbeck Cl	T4	Brighton Pl	M13	Charnley Cl	T3	Cross St	J7	Elton St	E2	Great Ducie St	H1
Baring St	N9	Brighton St	L2	Charnock St	H2	Cross St (Salford)	G5	Elton's Yd	E2	Great George St	D5
Barker St	H1	Brindle Pl	K13	Charter St	L3	Crown La	L3	Empire St	J1	Great Jackson St	F10
Barlow Pl	N11	Brocade Cl	D3	Chase St	L2	Crown St	F10	Empress Business		Great John St	F8
Barlow's Cft	G5	Brock St	N6	Chatford Cl	F1	Crown St (Salford)	F4	Cen	C13	Great Marlborough	
Barnett Dr	E4	Bromley St	M2	Chatham St	M7	Cumberland St	D1	Empress St	B13	St	K10
Barrack St	D11	Brook St	L10	Chatley St	J1	Cumbrian Cl	N12	Encombe Pl	D5	Greek St	M11

Green Gate H4
Greengate W F3
Grenham Av D12
Griffiths Cl E1
Groom St M11
Grosvenor Gdns E1
Grosvenor Sq E1
Grosvenor St M11
Guide Post Sq R13
Gunson St Q3
Gun St N5
Gurner Av A11
Gurney St S6
Hackleton Cl S6
Hadfield St C13
Half St G3
Hall St J8
Halmore Rd R4
Halsbury Cl T13
Halston St G13
Hamerton Rd P1
Hampson St R1
Hamsell Rd P11
Handsworth St S10
Hanging Ditch J5
Hanover St K4
Hanworth Cl N11
Harding St R6
Harding St (Salford) H4
Hardman St G7
Hardshaw Cl N12
Harehill Cl N10
Hare St L5
Hargreave's St L2
Harkness St Q11
Harold St C13
Harriett St Q4
Harrison St R7
Harrison St (Salford) E1
Harris St G1
Harry Hall Gdns C1
Harter St K8
Hartfield Cl P12
Hart St L8
Hatter St M4
Hatton Av D2
Haverlock Dr D2
Heath Av C1
Helga St R1
Hellidon Cl R12
Helmet St Q9
Henry St M5
Hewitt St G10
Heyrod St P8
Higher Ardwick Q11
Higher Cambridge St K12
Higher Chatham St K12
Higher Ormond St L11
Higher Oswald St L4
Higher York St L12
High St K6
Hillcourt St L11
Hillkirk St T6
Hilton St L5
Hinton St N3
Hodson St F4
Holkham Cl Q5
Holland St R4
Holly Bk Cl C12
Holly St T8
Holt Town S6
Honey St L1
Hood St N5
Hooper St S9
Hope St L7
Hope St (Salford) B6
Hornby St H1
Hornchurch St F13
Horne Dr Q5
Houldsworth St M5
Hoyle St Q9
Huddart Cl A9
Hughes St T9
Hull Sq D4
Hulme H13
Hulme Ct E11
Hulme Hall Rd D10
Hulme Pl C6
Hulme St H11
Hulme St (Salford) C6
Humberstone Av G11
Hunmanby Av H11
Hunt's Bk J4
Hyde Rd Q11
Inchley Rd M12
Ionas St F2
Irk St L2
Iron St T3
Irwell Pl B5
Irwell St G1
Irwell St (Salford) F6
Islington Way D6
Jackson Cres F12
Jackson's Row H7
James Henry Av A8
James St S2
James St (Salford) D6
Jenkinson St L12
Jersey St N5
Jerusalem Pl H8
Jessamine Av D1
Jessel Cl P12
Joddrell St G7
John Clynes Av Q2
John Dalton St H6
Johnson Sq R1
Johnson St D13
Johnson St (Salford) F5
John St L5
John St (Lower Broughton) E1
John St (Salford) G4
Joiner St L6
Jordan St G10
Joynson Av D1
Julia St H2
Jury St H1
Justin Cl M11
Jutland St N7
Kale St N11
Kays Gdns E5
Keele Wk Q2
Kelling Wk E11
Kelvin St L5
Kennedy St J7
Kenwright St L4
Kincardine Rd M11
King Edward St A9
Kingham Dr Q4
Kingsfold Av Q1
Kingsland Cl R2
King St J6
King St (Salford) G4
King St W H6
Kirkgate Cl Q3
Kirkhaven Sq T1
Kirkstall Sq P13
Kirkwood Dr Q1
Lackford Dr Q2
Lamb La F5
Lamport Cl M10
Lanchester St T3
Landos Rd Q3
Langholme Cl E11
Langport Av T13
Langston St H2
Lanstead Dr T4
Lauderdale Cres Q13
Laystall St N6
Layton St S4
Leaf St H12
Leak St C12
Ledburn Ct E12
Left Bk F7
Lena St M7
Leslie Hough Way A1
Lever St L6
Lewis St S2
Leycroft St N8
Lidbrook Wk T13
Lime Bk St S9
Limekiln La R9
Linby St F11
Lind St S5
Linen Ct D3
Linsley St G4
Linton Cl R8
Litcham Cl M10
Little Ancoats St M5
Little Holme St S6
Little John St F8
Little Lever St M6
Little Nelson St L3
Little Peter St G10
Little Pit St N6
Little Quay St G7
Liverpool Rd E8
Livesey St N2
Lizard St M6
Lloyd St J7
Lockett St G1
Lockton Cl N10
Lomax St P6
London Rd M8
Longacre St P8
Long Millgate J4
Longworth St G8
Loom St N5
Lordsmead St E11
Lord St J1
Lostock St R3
Lowcock St F1
Lower Brook St M8
Lower Byrom St F8
Lower Chatham St J10
Lower Hardman St F7
Lower Mosley St J8
Lower Moss La E11
Lower Ormond St K10
Lower Vickers St S3
Lowndes Wk P12
Loxford St J12
Lucy St D13
Ludgate Hill M3
Ludgate St L3
Luna street M5
Lund St B13
Lupton St E5
Lyceum Pl K11
Maidford Cl S6
Major St K8
Makin St K9
Mallard St K10
Mallow St F12
Malta St R6
Malt St D11
Malvern St D13
Mancunian Way N10
Mangle St Street M6
Manor St P10
Manson Av D11
Maplin Cl P11
Marble St K6
Marcer Rd R4
Marchmont Cl R13
Market St K6
Markham Cl T8
Marsden St J6
Marshall St M4
Marshall St (Ardwick) Q12
Marsworth Dr Q5
Mary France St F12
Mary St G2
Mason St M4
Mason St (Salford) E6
Massey St C6
Mayan Av D4
Mayes St K4
Mayo St R9
Mays St L4
Meadow Rd C2
Medlock St H10
Melbourne St F11
Mellor St R4
Melville St E5
Merrill St R6
Middlewood St C7
Midland St S10
Miles Platting S2
Milk St K6
Millbank St P7
Millbeck St K12
Miller St K3
Mill Grn St R9
Millhead Av T4
Millow St K3
Milnrow Cl M10
Milton St F1
Mincing St L3
Minshull St L7
Minshull St S M8
Mistletoe Grn E3
Moorhead St N3
Morbourne Cl T13
Mosley St K7
Mosscott Wk N10
Mosshall Cl E13
Moulton St G1
Mouncey St K10
Mount Carmel Cres B10
Mount St J8
Mount St (Salford) E4
Mozart Cl Q4
Mullberry St H7
Munday St R6
Munster St K3
Murrey St N5
Museum St J8
Muslin St C7
Myrtle Pl B1
Nancy St D12
Nansen St T9
Naples St L3
Nash St F13
Nathan Dr F4
Naval St P5
Naylor St Q2
Neild St N9
Neill St F1
Nelson St S1
Nether St P9
New Allen St P3
Newbeck St L4
New Br St H4
Newcastle St J11
New Cath St J6
Newcombe St J2
New Elm St E8
New Islington Q5
New Mkt J6
New Mkt St J6
New Mt St L3
New Quay St F7
Newton St M6
New Union St P5
New Vine St H12
New Wakefield St K10
New Welcome St H12
New Windsor B6
Nicholas St K7
Nine Acre Dr A11
Niven St P10
North Bailey St F5
Northdown Av D12
North George St D3
North Hill St E3
North Phoebe St A8
North Star Dr D6
North Western St P9
Norton St H4
Norway St T8
Nuneaton Dr R2
Oakford Av P2
Oak St L5
Old Bk St J6
Old Birley St H13
Oldbury Cl R3
Old Elm St P12
Oldfield Rd B10
Oldham Rd M5
Oldham St L6
Old Medlock St E8
Old Mill St P6
Old Mt St L3
Old Trafford B13
Old York St F12
Oliver St L13
Ordsall Dr A11
Ordsall La B10
Oregon Cl P12
Orion Pl C1
Orsett Cl Q2
Osborne St P1
Oswald St K3
Oswald St (Ancoats) R7
Overbridge Rd G1
Oxford Rd K9
Oxford St J8
Paddock St P10
Palfrey Pl Q11
Pall Mall J7
Palmerston St R8
Parish Vw A8
Parker St L6
Park Pl K2
Park St J2
Park St (Salford) D6
Parsonage H6
Parsonage La H5
Parsonage Way B9
Paton St M7
Pattishall Cl S7
Peak St N6
Peary St N2
Peel Mt A2
Pegasus Sq C2
Pembroke Cl R13
Penfield Cl M10
Percy Dr A11
Percy St E13
Peru St D4
Peter St H8
Phoenix St K6
Piccadilly L6
Pickford St N5
Picton Cl F4
Picton St E2
Piercy Av D1
Piercy St R6
Pigeon St N6
Pimblett St J2
Pine St K7
Pin Mill Brow R9
Pittbrook St S10
Plant St M7
Plymouth Gro P13
Plymouth Vw P13
Pochin St T2
Poland St P4
Polebrook Av R13
Police St H6
Pollard St Q7
Pollard St E R6
Polygon Av Q13
Polygon St P11
Pomona Strand B12
Poplar St T9
Poplin Dr G3
Portland St K9
Portsmouth St N13
Port St M6
Portugal St P4
Portugal St E P8
Postal St N6
Postbridge Cl Q13
Potato Wf E9
Poynton St J12
Price St S6
Primrose St N4
Prince's Br E8
Princess Rd H11
Princess St J7
Princess St (Cornbrook) C12
Pritchard St L9
Providence St R7
Pryme St F10
Pump St T5
Purslow Cl T6
Quay St F7
Quay St (Salford) G5
Queen St H7
Queen St (Salford) G4
Quenby St E12
Quendon Av F1
Rachel St Q10
Radium St N4
Ralli Cts F6
Randerson St P10
Raven St Q9
Reather Wk Q2
Red Bk K3
Redfern St K4
Redhill St N6
Red Lion St L5
Regent Sq A9
Reilly St H12
Reservoir St G3
Reyner St K8
Rial Pl K13
Ribston St F13
Rice St F9
Richmond St L8
Richmond St (Salford) F3
Ridgefield H6
Ridgeway St E R5
Ridgway St R5
Riga St L4
Rigel Pl C2
Rigel St Q3
Rimworth Dr Q2
Ringstead Dr P1
Ripley Cl R8
River Pl G10
Riverside C3
River St (Ardwick) Q9
River St (Deansgate) H11
Robert St J2
Roby St M7
Rochdale Rd L4
Rockdove Av H11
Rocket Way E5
Rockingham Cl S13
Rodney St Q4
Rodney St (Salford) E6
Roe St P3
Roger St L2
Rolla St G4
Rolleston Av R4
Rolls Cres F13
Roman St L5
Rome Rd P3
Rondin Cl T9
Rondin Rd T9
Rope Wk G3
Rosamond Dr E5
Rosamond St W K12
Rosewell Cl S1
Rostron Av T12
Rowendale St H9
Royce Rd F12
Roydale St T3
Ruby St K13
Rudcroft Cl N12
Rudman Dr B9
Rugby St G1
Runcorn St C11
Sackville St K8
Sagar St H1
St. Andrew's Sq Q8
St. Andrew's St P8
St. Ann's Sq J6
St. Ann St H6
St. Bartholomew's Dr B8
St. Chad's St K1
St. Clement's Dr A10
St. George's D12
St. Ignatius Wk A9
St. James's Sq J7
St. James St K7
St. John St G8
St. Mary's Gate J5
St. Mary's Parsonage G6
St. Mary's St E5
St. Michael's Sq L3
St. Nicholas Rd F11
St. Philip's St D5
St. Simon St E2
St. Stephen St E5
St. Thomas St L1
St. Vincent St Q5
St. Wilfrids St F12
Salford A7
Salford App H5
Salmon St L5
Saltford Av Q5
Salutation St J13
Samouth Cl R3
Samuel Ogden St L9
Sanctuary, The G13
Sandal St T3
Sandford St F2
Sand St P1
Sawley Rd S2
Scarsdale St A2
School Ct P5
School St L3
School St (Salford) F1
Scotland K3
Scotporth Cl E11
Sefton Cl N12
Senior St G3
Sharp St M3
Shaw Cres J3
Shawgreen Cl E12
Shawheath Cl E12
Sheffield St N8
Shepley St M8
Sherborne St H1
Sherbourne St W G2
Sherratt St N4
Shetland Rd R2
Shilford Dr N3
Shortcroft St H10
Short St L6
Short St (Salford) F2
Shudehill L5
Sidney St (Salford) E5
Sidney St (off Deansgate) H7
Sidney St (off Oxford Road) L11
Silkin Cl M11
Silk St N4
Silk St (Salford) D3
Silvercroft St F10
Silver St L7
Simeon St M3
Simms Cl D5
Simpson St L3
Sirius Pl D2
Skerry Cl N11
Skip Pl K2
Slate Av Q6
Sleaford Cl R2
Smallridge Cl R3
Smith St B12
Smithy La H6
Snell St R7
Soar St L5
Sorrel St F12
Southall St H8
Southall St (Strangeways) H2
Southend Av D13
Southern St G9
Southgate H6
South Hall St C9
South King St H6
Southmill St J7
South Pump St M8
Sparkle St N7
Spaw St F5
Spear St L6
Spectator St R5
Springfield H7
Springfield Business Cen G3
Springfield La G3
Spring Gdns K7
Spruce St F13
Stalham Cl R2
Stanley St L1
Stanley St (Salford) F6
Stansby Gdns T13
Station App (for Oxford Road Station) K10
Station App (for Piccadilly Station) M7
Staverton Cl P12
Stephen St J2
Stevenson Pl M6
Stevenson Sq M6
Stevenson St D6
Stockland Cl M11
Stockport Rd Q11
Stocks St K2
Stocks St E K2
Stonall Av E12
Stonelow Cl J12
Stone St F9
Store St M8
Stracey St T3
Strawberry Hill A2
Stretford Rd H12
Style St L3
Sudell St N3
Sussex St D2
Swan St L4
Swiftsure Av D6
Syndall Av R12
Syndall St R12
Talgarth Rd P1
Tamar Ct D13
Tame St R7
Tariff St M6
Tasle All H7
Tatton St D12
Tatton St (Salford) A9
Taunton St S6
Tavery Cl Q5
Tebutt St N3

Teer St	S5	Trafford Ct	E11	Varley St	S1	Watkin Cl	N13	Whittle's Cft	N7	
Temperance St	P9	Trafford Pl	D13	Vauxhall St	N1	Watkin St	E2	Whittle St	M5	
Tewkesbury Rd	S3	Trafford St	G9	Velour Cl	D2	Watson St	H9	Whitworth St	L9	
Thirsk St	P10	Travis St	N9	Vesta St	Q6	Weald Cl	P12	Whitworth St W	H9	Woollam Pl	E8
Thomas St	L5	Trentham St	C11	Viaduct St	S7	Welland Cl	D13	Wilfred St	G1	Worrall St	B10
Thompson St	M3	Trinity Way	F5	Viaduct St (Salford)	G4	Wellington Grn	E13	William Chadwick		Worsley St	D10
Thompson St		Tristam Cl	P11	Vickers St	T2	Wellington St	E4	Cl	Q2	Worsley St	
(Strangeways)	H2	Troutbeck Av	Q5	Victoria Br St	H5	Well St	K5	Williamson St	M2	(Salford)	G6
Thomson St	Q13	Trumpet St	H9	Victoria Sta App	J4	West Bk St	B8	William St	R9	Wroe St	D6
Thor Grn	C9	Tudbury Way	E4	Victoria St	J5	West Charles St	A6	Wilmott St	J10	Wyatt Av	A10
Thornage Dr	Q1	Tuer St	L13	Victor St	P1	West Crown Av	A8	Wilson St	Q13	Wynne St	A1
Thorncross Cl	C11	Turner St	L5	Victor St (Salford)	E5	West Hope St	A6	Wilton Pl	D5	Wyre St	N9
Thornden Rd	S1	Turner St		Virgil St	C12	West King St	F4	Wilton St	M12	Yorkshire St	G5
Thornley Brow	K4	(Old Trafford)	B12	Wadeford Cl	P3	Westminster St	C11	Winder Dr	Q6	York St	K6
Thornton St	Q1	Tutbury St	R7	Wadeson Rd	N10	West Mosley St	K7	Windmill Av	A10	York St (Hulme)	F11
Tib La	J7	Twillbrook Dr	G3	Wadlow Cl	F3	Weston St	S5	Windmill St	H8	York St (off Charles	
Tib St	L6	Union St	L5	Walker's Cft	J4	West Pk St	A10	Winfell Dr	S3	Street)	K10
Tideswell Av	R3	Union St		Wallness	A2	Weybridge Rd	Q5	Winscombe Dr	Q1	York St E	L11
Tidworth Av	Q5	(Ardwick)	Q10	Wallness La	A1	Whalley St	R4	Winser St	K9	Young St	G7
Tinsley Cl	T4	University Rd	A4	Warde St	F13	Wheater's Cres	C1	Winstanley Rd	R3	Zion Cres	G13
Tivoli St	G7	University Rd W	A5	Wardle St	T3	Wheater's St	C1	Withy Gro	K5		
Todd St	K4	Upper Brook St	M11	Warford St	M1	Wheater's Ter	D1	Woden's Av	B9		
Tomlinson St	G13	Upper Cyrus St	T5	Warmington Dr	T13	Whimberry Cl	B10	Woden St	C10		
Tonge St	S10	Upper Helena St	T4	Warwick St	M5	Whitchurch St	G2	Woodlark Cl	D6		
Tonman St	G8	Upper Kirby St	Q6	Waterloo St	K8	Whitekirk Cl	N12	Wood St	G7		
Towcester Cl	S6	Upper Moss La	F13	Water St	E8	White St	D13	Woodward Pl	Q5		
Town Hall La	J6	Upper Wf St	C6	Water St (Ardwick)	Q9	Whitfield St	K2	Woodward St	Q5		

LEEDS & BRADFORD URBAN pages 84-85

Aachen Way	B3	**Birkby**	**C4**	Britannia Rd	E3	**Clifton**	**C3**	**East Ardsley**	**F3**	**Great Horton**	**C2**
Abbey La	A3	Birkby Hall Rd	C4	**Broad Carr**	**B4**	Clough La	A2	**East Bierley**	**D2**	Great Horton Rd	C2
Abbey Rd	E1	Birkby La	C3	Broad Carr La	B4	Coal Hill La	D1	Easterly Rd	F1	**Greengates**	**D1**
Abb Scott La	C2	Birkby Rd	B4	Broad La (Bowling)	D2	**Cockersdale**	**D2**	Eastgate	F1	Green Hill Rd	E1
Acre St	B4	**Birkenshaw**	**D2**	Broad La (Moorside)	E1	Cock Hill La	B2	East Pk Par	F1	Green La	
Adwalton	**E2**	**Birkenshaw**		Broadstone Way	D2	Cockin La	B2	East St		(Greetland)	B4
Akroydon	**B3**	**Bottoms**	**D2**	Broadway	D1	Cold Edge Rd	A2	(Birchencliffe)	B4	Green La	
Alandale Rd	C4	**Birkhouse**	**C3**	**Brookfoot**	**C3**	**Coley**	**C3**	East St (Leeds)	F1	(Shibden Head)	B2
Albert Rd (Halifax)	A3	**Birstall**	**D3**	**Brookhouse**	**A2**	Coley Rd	B3	Easy Rd	F1	Green La (Thornton)	B2
Albert Rd		Blacker Rd	C4	Brook La	B2	Colne Br Rd	C4	**Eccleshill**	**D1**	Green La	
(New Brighton)	E2	**Blackley**	**B4**	Brow La	B2	**Combs**	**E4**	Edgerton	C4	(Wyke Common)	C3
Albert Rd		Blackley Rd	B4	**Bruntcliffe**	**E3**	Commercial Rd	E1	**Elland**	**B4**	Greenside	D2
(Queensbury)	B2	Blenheim Wk	F1	Bruntcliffe La	E2	Cooper Br Rd	C4	**Elland Lower Edge**	**B4**	**Greetland**	**B4**
Albion Rd	D1	Bog Grn La	D4	Bruntcliffe Rd	E3	Cooper La	C2	Elland Rd (Beeston)	F2	Greetland Rd	A4
Aldams Rd	E4	Bolton St		Burdock Way	B3	**Copley Hill**	**E3**	Elland Rd (Churwell)	E2	Grimescar Rd	B4
Allerton	**B1**	(Bradford)	C1	**Burley**	**E1**	Coplowe La	B1	Elland Rd (Elland)	B4	Guy Rd	B2
Allerton La	B1	Bolton Rd		Burley Rd	E1	Corporation St	E2	Elland Rd		**Haigh Moor**	**F3**
Allerton Rd	B1	(Eccleshill)	C1	**Burmantofts**	**F1**	**Cottingley**	**B1**	(Ripponden)	A4	Haley Hill	B3
Alverthorpe	**F4**	Bond St	F4	Burnley Rd	A3	Cottingley Cliffe Rd	B1	Emm La	C1	Half Mile La	D1
Alverthorpe Rd	F4	**Booth**	**A3**	Butcher Hill	E1	Cottingley Moor Rd	B1	Exley La	B4	**Halifax**	**B3**
Amberton Rd	F1	**Boothroyd**	**E4**	**Buttershaw**	**C2**	Cottingley New Rd	B1	**Fagley**	**D1**	Halifax Old Rd	C4
Ambler Thorn	**B2**	Boothroyd La	E4	Butt La	E2	Cousin La	A2	Fagley Rd	D1	Halifax Rd	
Apperley Bridge	**D1**	**Boothtown**	**B3**	Buttress La	A3	Cow Hill La	A2	Fair Rd	C2	(Birchencliffe)	B4
Ardsley Common	F3	Boothtown Rd	B3	Butts Grn La	A3	Crack La	B1	Farfield Av	C2	Halifax Rd	
Armley	**E1**	Bow La	B3	Cain La	B3	Crag La	A2	**Farnley**	**E2**	(Hipperholme)	B3
Armley Ridge Rd	E1	**Bowling**	**C2**	Calderdale Way	B4	Crag Rd	C1	Farnley Ring Rd	E1	Halifax Rd	
Armley Rd	E1	Bowling Back La	C2	**Calverley**	**D1**	Croft St	C2	Farrar Mill La	B3	(Liversedge)	D3
Asdale Rd	F4	Bowling Hall Rd	C2	Calverley La	D1	**Cromwell Bottom**	**B3**	**Far Royds**	**E2**	Halifax Rd (Odsal)	C2
Ash Brow Rd	C4	**Brackenhall**	**C4**	Canal Rd (Armley)	E1	Crosland Rd	B4	**Farsley**	**D1**	Halifax Rd	
Asquith Av	E2	Bradford &		Canal Rd (Bradford)	C1	**Cross Green**	**F2**	Farsley Beck		(Queensbury)	B2
Avenue, The	B2	Wakefield Rd	D2	Canterbury Av	C2	Cross Grn La	F1	**Bottom**	**D1**	Halifax Rd	
Back Clough	B3	Bradford Old Rd	B2	Cardigan Rd	F1	Cross La		**Fartown**	**C4**	(Staincliffe)	D3
Backhold La	B3	Bradford Rd		**Carlinghow**	**D3**	(Little Horton)	C2	Fartown	D2	Hall La	B3
Back La (Dean Lane		(Birkenshaw)	D2	Carlisle Rd		Cross La		Fenby Av	D2	Hall La (Bradford)	C2
Head)	B1	Bradford Rd		(Bradford)	C1	(Pepper Hill)	B2	Field Head La	D3	Hall La (Farnley)	E2
Back La		(Brighouse)	C3	Carlisle Rd (Pudsey)	D1	**Crossley**	**D4**	Fixby Rd	C4	**Hanging Heaton**	**E3**
(Moor Head)	E2	Bradford Rd		**Carr Gate**	**F3**	**Crossley Hall**	**C1**	**Flanshaw**	**F4**	**Harehills**	**F1**
Back La		(Cleckheaton)	C3	Carr Ho La	C2	Crown Pt Rd	F1	Fleet La	B2	Harehills La	F1
(Old Dolphin)	B2	Bradford Rd		Carr La	C1	**Cullingworth**	**A1**	**Flushdyke**	**F4**	Harehills Rd	F1
Back La (Thornton)	B1	(Dewsbury)	E3	Carr Rd	D1	Cutler Hts La	D2	Ford Hill	B2	Harrogate Rd	D1
Bagley	**D1**	Bradford Rd		**Carr Syke**	**C1**	**Daisy Hill (Bradford)**	**B1**	Fountain St	E3	**Hartshead**	**D4**
Bagley La	D1	(Eccleshill)	C1	**Catherine Slack**	**B2**	**Daisy Hill (Leeds)**	**E2**	**Four Lane Ends**	**C1**	**Hartshead**	
Bailey Hall Rd	B3	Bradford Rd		Cemetery Rd	C1	Dalton Bk Rd	C4	Free Sch La	B3	**Moor Top**	**C3**
Bailiff Bridge	**C3**	(Farsley)	D1	**Chapel Allerton**	**F1**	Dean La	B1	**Frizinghall**	**C1**	**Hawksworth**	**E1**
Baldwin La	B2	Bradford Rd		Chapel La	E2	**Dean Lane Head**	**B1**	**Fulneck**	**D2**	Hawksworth Rd	E1
Balkram Edge Rd	A2	(Huddersfield)	C4	**Chapeltown**	**D1**	Deanstones La	B2	Gain La	D1	**Haworth**	**A1**
Balm Rd	F2	Bradford Rd		Chapeltown Rd	F1	**Deighton**	**C4**	**Gaisby**	**C1**	Haworth Rd	B1
Bank Top		(Northowram)	B3	Charlestown Rd	B3	Deighton Rd	C4	Gaisby La	C1	**Headingley**	**F1**
(Bradford)	**D1**	Bradford Rd		**Chat Hill**	**B1**	Denby Dale Rd	F4	**Gamble Hill**	**E1**	Headingley La	F1
Bank Top (Halifax)	**B3**	(Stone Chair)	B2	Chat Hill Rd	B2	**Denholme**	**A1**	Gamble La	E1	Headley La	B2
Bantam Grove	**E2**	Bradford Rd		**Chickenley**	**E4**	**Denholme Clough**	**A1**	Gate La	A2	**Healey (Dewsbury)**	**D3**
Barkerend Rd	C1	(Tingley)	F3	**Chidswell**	**E3**	**Dewsbury**	**E3**	**Gawthorpe**	**E4**	**Healey (Horbury)**	**E4**
Barkisland	**A4**	Bradford Rd		Church La		**Dewsbury Moor**	**E4**	Gaythorne Rd	C2	Heath Hill Rd	A3
Batley	**E3**	(Wakefield)	F4	(Chapeltown)	D1	Dewsbury Rd		Gelderd Rd	E2	Heathy La	B2
Batley Carr	**E3**	**Bradley**	**C4**	Church La		(Beeston Hill)	F2	Gelderd Rd		**Heaton**	**C1**
Battyeford	**D4**	**Bradley Mills**	**C4**	(Popeley Fields)	D3	Dewsbury Rd		(Copley Hill)	E3	Heaton Rd	C1
Beacon Hill Rd	B3	Bradley Mills Rd	C4	Church La		(Elland)	B4	Gibbet St	A3	**Heaton Royds**	**C1**
Beacon Rd	C2	Bradley Rd	C4	(Southowram)	B3	Dewsbury Rd		Gibb La	A3	**Heaton Shay**	**C1**
Beckett St	F1	**Bradshaw**	**B2**	Church St (Halifax)	B3	(Gomersal)	D3	**Gildersome**	**E2**	Hebble La	B3
Beckside Rd	C2	Bradshaw La	B2	Church St (Hunslet)	F2	Dewsbury Rd		Gildersome La	E2	**Heckmondwike**	**D3**
Beeston	**F2**	**Bramley**	**E1**	**Churwell**	**E2**	(Middleton)	F3	**Gildersome Street**	**E2**	Henconner La	E1
Beeston Hill	**F2**	Bramley La	B3	Claremont Rd	B3	Dewsbury Rd		Gilead Rd	B4	High Bk La	B1
Beeston Park Side	**F2**	Bramley Ring Rd	E1	Clarendon Rd	F1	(Wakefield)	F4	Giles Hill La	B2	Highfield Rd	C1
Beeston Ring Rd	E2	Bridge St (Bradford)	C1	**Clayton**	**B2**	Dick La	D2	**Girlington**	**C1**	Highgate	C1
Beeston Rd	F2	Bridge St (Morley)	E3	Clayton La	B2	Dirkhill St	C2	Girlington Rd	C1	Highgate Rd	B2
Beggarington Hill	**E3**	**Brighouse**	**C3**	Clayton Rd	B2	Dixon La	E2	**Gledhow**	**F1**	High Moor Rd	C3
Belle Isle	F2	Brighouse &		**Cleckheaton**	**D3**	**Drighlington**	**E2**	Gledhow La	F1	High Rd	
Belle Isle Rd	F2	Denholmegate Rd	B2	Cleckheaton Rd	C2	Drub La	D3	Gledhow Wd Rd	F1	(Earlsheaton)	E4
Bierley	**D2**	Brighouse Rd		**Clerk Green**	**E3**	Duckworth La	C1	Godley La	B3	High Rd	
Bierley La	C2	(Hipperholme)	B3	Cliffe La	D3	**Dudley Hill**	**D2**	**Gomersal**	**D3**	(Warley Town)	A3
Bingley Rd	C1	Brighouse Rd		Cliffe Rd	C1	Dudwell La	B3	Gomersal La	D3	High St (Birstall)	D3
Birchencliffe	**B4**	(Low Moor)	C2	Cliff Hollins La	D2	**Earlsheaton**	**E4**			High St (Odsal)	C2

High St (Queensbury) B2
Hightown D3
Hightown Heights C3
Hightown Rd D3
Hill End La B2
Hillfoot D1
Hill Top (Thornton) B1
Hill Top (Upper Armley) E1
Hipperholme C3
Holbeck F1
Holdsworth B2
Hollingwood La C2
Hollybank Rd C2
Holme La D2
Holme Shay D2
Holmewood Rd D2
Holmfield A2
Holywell Green B4
Horbury F4
Horbury Bridge F4
Horbury Junction F4
Horbury Rd F4
Horsforth Woodside E1
Horton Gra Rd C1
Horton Pk Av C2
Horton St B3
Houghside Rd E1
Hove Edge C3
Howden Clough Rd E3
Howes La B3
Huddersfield Rd (Birstall) D3
Huddersfield Rd (Dewsbury) E4
Huddersfield Rd (Elland) B4
Huddersfield Rd (Low Moor) C2
Huddersfield Rd (Lower Wyke) C3
Huddersfield Rd (Roberttown) D4
Huddersfield Rd (Siddal) B3
Huddersfield Rd (Woodhouse) C4
Hudson Av C2
Hullenedge Rd B4
Hunslet F2
Hunslet Rd F1
Hunsworth D3
Hunsworth La (East Bierley) D2
Hunsworth La (Merchant Fields) D3
Hyde Pk Rd F1
Idle D1
Idle Moor C1
Idle Rd C1
Illingworth A2
Ingham La A2
Ingleby Rd C1
Ings Rd F4
Inner Ring Rd F1
Jagger La C4
Jaw Hill F3
Keighley Rd (Bradford) C1
Keighley Rd (Illingworth) A2
Keldregate C4
Kell La B3
Kent Rd E1
Killinghall Rd D1
Kings Rd D2
King St D2
Kirkgate C1
Kirkhamgate F3
Kirkheaton D4
Kirkstall E1
Kirkstall Hill E1
Kirkstall La E1
Kirkstall Rd E1
Knowles La D2
Laisterdyke D1
Lands Head La B2
Lane Side B2
Laund Rd B4
Law La B3
Lawns La E2
Leadwell La F3
Lea Fm Rd E1
Leeds & Bradford Rd E1
Leeds Old Rd D1
Leeds Rd (Bradford) C1
Leeds Rd (Bradley) C4
Leeds Rd (Dewsbury) E4
Leeds Rd (Fagley) D1
Leeds Rd (Heckmondwike) D3
Leeds Rd (Hipperholme) C3

Leeds Rd (Huddersfield) C4
Leeds Rd (Northowram) B3
Leeds Rd (Wakefield) F4
Lee La (Boothtown) B3
Lee La (Cottingley) B1
Leeming A1
Lee Mount B3
Legrams La C2
Leylands La C1
Lidget Green C1
Lidget St B4
Lightcliffe C3
Lightridge Rd C4
Lilycroft Rd C1
Lindley B4
Lindley Moor Rd B4
Lindley Rd B4
Lindwell B4
Listerhills Rd C1
Little Horton C2
Little Horton La C2
Littlemoor Rd D1
Littletown D3
Liversedge D3
Long La (Heaton Shay) C1
Long La (Ovenden) A3
Long La (Queensbury) B2
Longside La C1
Lovell Pk Rd F1
Lower Edge Rd B4
Lower Grange B1
Lower Hopton D4
Lower La D2
Lower Town St E1
Lower Wortley Rd E2
Lower Wyke C3
Lower Wyke La C3
Low La (Birstall) D3
Low La (Chat Hill) B2
Low Moor C2
Low Rd F2
Lowtown D1
Luddenden A3
Luddenden Foot A3
Lumb La C1
Lupset F4
Lupton Av F1
Main St B1
Manchester Rd C2
Manningham C1
Manningham La C1
Manor Row C1
Market St B1
Marsh A1
Marsh La F1
Mayo Av C2
Meanwood Rd F1
Merchant Fields D3
Middleton F2
Middleton Gro F2
Middleton La F3
Middleton Pk Av F2
Middleton Pk Ring Rd F2
Middleton Rd (Belle Isle) F2
Middleton Rd (Morley) E3
Midgley A3
Mill Bank A4
Mill Bk Rd A4
Mill Carr Hill Rd C2
Mill La A2
Mill Shaw F2
Mill St E4
Mirfield D4
Mirfield Moor D4
Mixenden A2
Moore Av C2
Moor End A2
Moor End Rd (Moor End) A2
Moor End Rd (Mount Pellon) A3
Moor Fields D2
Moor Head (Gildersome) E2
Moorhead (Shipley) C1
Moorhead La C1
Moorlands Rd E4
Moor Rd F2
Moor Side C2
Moorside (Birstall) D2
Moorside (Horsforth) E1
Moorside Rd (Eccleshill) D1
Moorside Rd (Moorside) D2
Moor Top D4
Morley E3
Morley St C2
Morris La E1
Mount B4

Mountain B2
Mount Pellon A3
Mount Pleasant E3
Mount St C1
Mount Tabor A2
Mount Tabor Rd A2
Muffit La D3
Nab Hill C4
Nab Wood C1
Ned Hill Rd A2
Ned La D2
Netherlands Av C2
Netheroyd Hill C4
Neville Rd D2
New Bk B3
New Brighton E2
New Cross St C2
New Farnley E2
New Hey Rd (Huddersfield) B4
New Hey Rd (Rastrick) B4
Newlands Rd A3
New La D2
Newlay Wood E1
New N Rd C4
New Pk Rd B2
New Rd (Kirkheaton) D4
New Rd (Scholes) C3
New Rd (Sowood) B4
New Rd Side E1
New Wks Rd C2
New York Rd F1
Noon Nick B1
Norland A4
Norman Av D1
Norman La C1
Norr B1
Norristhorpe D3
North Bk Rd B1
Northedge La B3
Northgate (Dewsbury) E4
Northgate (Huddersfield) C4
North Moor D4
Northorpe D4
Northowram B3
Northowram Grn B2
North St F1
Norwood Green C3
Nursery La A3
Oakenshaw C2
Oak La C1
Oakwell D3
Oakwood F1
Oakwood La F1
Odsal C2
Odsal Rd C2
Ogden A2
Old Dolphin B2
Oldfield La E1
Old La F2
Old Lindley Rd B4
Old Pk Rd F1
Old Rd (Farsley) D1
Old Rd (Great Horton) C2
Old Rd (Thornton) B1
Osmondthorpe F1
Ossett F4
Ossett Spa F4
Otley Rd (Bradford) C1
Otley Rd (Shipley) C1
Otley Rd (Weetwood) E1
Outlane A4
Outwood La E1
Ovenden B3
Ovenden Rd B3
Ovenden Way B3
Ovenden Wd Rd A3
Overthorpe E4
Oxenhope A1
Oxford La B3
Oxford Rd D3
Park Av F1
Park La (Leeds) F1
Park La (Queensbury) B2
Park La (Siddal) B4
Park Rd B4
Parry La D2
Pasture La B2
Pavement La A2
Pearson La C1
Pellon La B3
Pepper Hill B2
Pepper Rd F2
Per La A2
Piece Hall B3
Pit La B2
Pollard La (Bradford) C1
Pollard La (Whitecote) E1
Pontefract La F1
Pontefract Rd F2
Popeley Fields D3
Potternewton F1

Potternewton La F1
Priesthorpe D1
Priestley Green C3
Prince Royd B4
Prune Pk La B1
Pudsey E1
Pudsey Rd E1
Pule Hill B3
Pullan Av D1
Queensbury B2
Queensbury Rd B3
Queens Rd (Bradford) C1
Queen's Rd (Halifax) B3
Queens Wd Dr E1
Raikes La (Birstall) D3
Raikes La (East Bierley) D2
Raikes La (Holme Shay) D2
Ramsden St A3
Rastrick C4
Ravenscliffe D1
Ravensthorpe D4
Raw End Rd A3
Reevy Rd C2
Regent Treet F1
Rein Rd E3
Rhodesway B1
Richardshaw La D1
Riley La B2
Ring Rd (Farsley) D1
Ring Rd (Pudsey) E1
Ring Rd Beeston Pk F2
Ring Rd Middleton F2
Ripley St C2
Ripponden A4
Rishworth A4
Roberttown D4
Robin Hood F2
Robin La D1
Rochdale Rd A3
Rocks La A2
Rodley D1
Rodley La D1
Roils Head Rd A3
Roker Av E2
Roker La E2
Rookes La C3
Rook La D2
Rooley Av C2
Rooley La C2
Roper La B2
Roseville Rd F1
Roundhay Rd F1
Royds Hall La C2
Saddleworth Rd A4
St. Enoch's Rd C2
St. John's Rd C4
St. Paul's Av C2
St. Peg La D3
Saints Rd C2
Salendine Nook B4
Sandy Lane B1
Savile Rd B4
Savile Town E4
Savil Rd E4
Scholemoor C2
Scholes C3
Scholes La C3
School Green B1
School La B2
Score Hill B2
Scott Hall Rd F1
Sharp La F2
Shay Gate B1
Shay La (Frizinghall) C1
Shay La (Holmfield) B3
Shay La (Wilsden) B1
Sheepridge C4
Shelf B2
Shelf Hall La B2
Shetcliffe La D2
Shibden Hall Rd B3
Shibden Head B2
Shipley C1
Shroggs Rd B3
Siddal B3
Siddal New Rd B3
Skircoat Moor Rd B3
Skircoat Rd B3
Smithies Moor La D3
Smith La C1
Snow Hill F3
Snow Lee B4
Soaper Ho La B3
Soaper La B2
South Accommodation Rd F2
Southfield La C2
Southfield Rd C2
South La (Elland) B4
South La (Shelf) B2
South Ossett F4
Southowram B3
Sowerby A3
Sowerby Bridge A3
Sowood B4

Soyland Town A4
Spaines Rd C4
Spen D3
Spencer Rd C2
Spen La (Gomersal) D3
Spen La (West Park) E1
Spring Hall La A3
Squire La C1
Stainbeck La F1
Stainbeck Rd F1
Staincliffe E3
Stainland A4
Stainland Rd B4
Staithgate La C2
Stanhope Rd F3
Stanningley D1
Stanningley Rd E1
Station La (Thorpe on the Hill) F3
Station La (Westgate Hill) D2
Station Rd (Clayton) B2
Station Rd (Moorside) D2
Station Rd (Norwood Green) C3
Steps La A3
Sticker La D2
Stock La A3
Stock's La A3
Stonebridge La E2
Stone Chair B2
Stonegate Rd F1
Stoney Ridge Rd B1
Stony La B1
Stourton F2
Straight La A2
Stump Cross B3
Sunbridge Rd C1
Swain House C1
Swain Ho Rd C1
Swinnow La E1
Swinnow Moor D1
Swinnow Rd E1
Syke La C3
Thornbury D1
Thornes F4
Thornhill E4
Thornhill Edge E4
Thornhill Lees E4
Thornhill Rd (Calverley) D1
Thornhill Rd (Edgerton) B4
Thornhill Rd (Savile Town) E4
Thornhills C3
Thornton B1
Thornton La C2
Thornton Rd (Bradford) C1
Thornton Rd (Queensbury) B2
Thornton Rd (Thornton) B1
Thorpe La F3
Thorpe Lwr La F3
Thorpe on the Hill F3
Thorpe Rd F3
Tingley F3
Toftshaw D2
Toftshaw La D2
Toller La C1
Tong D2
Tong La D2
Tong Rd (Gamble Hill) E1
Tong Rd (Pudsey) E2
Tong Street D2
Tong St D2
Toothill C4
Toothill C4
Topcliffe E3
Towngate (Calverley) D1
Towngate (Wyke Common) C3
Town St (Armley) E1
Town St (Belle Isle) F2
Town St (Farsley) D1
Town St (Mill Shaw) F2
Town St (Rodley) D1
Town St (Stanningley) D1
Triangle A4
Trinity St C2
Troydale La E1
Turnsteads Av D3
Tyresal D1
Tyresal La D2
Undercliffe C1
Union La A2
Upper Armley E1
Upper Batley La E3
Upper Brockholes A2

Upper Green F3
Upper Heaton D4
Upper Heaton La D4
Upper Hopton D4
Upper La (Northowram) B3
Upper La (Popeley Fields) D3
Upper Moor D1
Uppermoor D1
Upper Moor Side E2
Upper Town St E1
Upper Wortley Rd E1
Valley Rd (Bradford) C1
Valley Rd (Pudsey) D1
Valley Rd (Shipley) C1
Victoria Rd (Eccleshill) D1
Victoria Rd (Elland) B4
Victoria Rd (Headingley) F1
Victoria Rd (New Brighton) E2
Village St C3
Wadehouse Rd B2
Wainstalls A2
Wainstalls La A2
Wainstalls Rd A2
Wakefield F4
Wakefield Rd (Adwalton) E2
Wakefield Rd (Bradford) C2
Wakefield Rd (Bradley) C4
Wakefield Rd (Dewsbury) E4
Wakefield Rd (Gildersome Street) E2
Wakefield Rd (Halifax) A3
Wakefield Rd (Hipperholme) C3
Wakefield Rd (Stourton) F2
Warley Rd A3
Warley Town A3
Warley Town La A3
Waterloo Rd D1
Weather Hill Rd B4
Weetwood E1
Wellington Rd F1
Wellington St F1
Well La A3
Wentworth St F4
West Bowling C2
West End B2
Westercroft La B3
Western Rd F3
Westfield D3
Westfield La (Shipley) C1
West Fld La (Wyke) C3
Westgate (Bradford) C1
Westgate (Cleckheaton) D3
Westgate (Wakefield) F4
Westgate End F4
Westgate Hill D2
Westgate Hill St D2
West La B3
West Park E1
West Pk Rd C1
West Royd C1
West Scholes B2
West St B4
Whetley Hill C1
Whetley La C1
Whingate E1
Whitcliffe Rd D3
White Abbey Rd C1
Whitechapel La D3
Whitechapel Rd C3
Whitecote E1
Whitehall Rd (Cockersdale) D2
Whitehall Rd (Leeds) F1
Whitehall Rd (New Farnley) E2
Whitehall Rd (Wyke Common) C3
Whitehall Rd E C2
Whitehall Rd W D3
Whitehill Rd A2
Whitley Lower D4
Wibsey C2
Wibsey Pk Av C2
Wide La E2
Willow La C4
Wilsden B1
Wilsden Rd B1

Windhill C1	**Woodhall Hills** D1	Woodhouse Hill C4	Wood La A3	Wortley Ring Rd E2
Windybank La	Woodhall La D1	Woodhouse La	Woodside Rd C3	**Wrenthorpe** F3
(Liversedge) B2	Woodhall Rd D1	(Leeds) F1	Workhouse La	Wrigley Hill A2
Windy Bk La	Woodhead Rd C1	Woodhouse La	(Kirkheaton) D4	Wrose Rd C1
(Queensbury) C3	**Woodhouse**	(Woodhouse) C4	Workhouse La	**Wyke** C3
Winrose Dr F2	**(Brighouse)** C4	Woodhouse St F1	(Warley Town) A3	**Wyke Common** C3
Winterburn La A3	**Woodhouse (Leeds)** F1	**Woodkirk** E3	**Wortley** E1	Wyke La C3

Yewtree Rd B4	York Rd F1

LEEDS CENTRAL pages 86-87

Abbey St E5
Abbott Ct A6
Abbott Rd A7
Abbott Vw A6
Admiral St K13
Aire St H7
Albion Pl K6
Albion St K6
Alexander St J5
Alexandra Gro C2
Alexandra Rd B2
Alma St Q3
Anderson Av Q1
Anderson Mt Q1
Apex Business Pk L12
Apex Vw J11
Apex Way K11
Appleton Cl S5
Appleton Ct S5
Appleton Sq S5
Appleton Way S6
Archery Pl H1
Archery Rd H1
Archery St J2
Archery Ter J2
Armley Rd B6
Armouries Rd N10
Artist St C7
Ascot Ter S8
Ashley Av T1
Ashley Rd S1
Ashley Ter T1
Ashton Av S1
Ashton Gro S1
Ashton Mt S1
Ashton Pl S1
Ashton Ter S1
Ashton Vw S1
Ashville Vw B1
Assembly St L7
Atkinson St P11
Autumn Av C2
Autumn Gro C2
Autumn Pl C2
Autumn St C2
Autumn Ter C2
Avenue, The P7
Aysgarth Cl S7
Aysgarth Dr S7
Aysgarth Pl S7
Aysgarth Wk S7
Back Ashville Av A1
Back Hyde Ter F3
Back Row J9
Balm Pl F11
Balm Wk E11
Bank St K7
Barclay St M3
Barrack St L1
Barran Ct R1
Bath Rd G10
Bayswater Vw R1
Beamsley Gro B1
Beamsley Mt B1
Beamsley Pl B1
Beamsley Ter B1
Beckett St Q5
Bedford St J6
Beech Gro Ter G2
Belgrave St K5
Belle Vue Rd D3
Bell St N5
Belmont Gro G4
Benson St M2
Benyon Pk Way A13
Berking Av S6
Bertrand St F12
Bexley Av R1
Bexley Gro S1
Bexley Mt R1
Bexley Pl R1
Bexley Rd S1
Bexley Ter S1
Bingley St E6
Bishopgate St J7
Black Bull St M10
Blackman La J2
Blandford Gdns H2
Blandford Gro H2
Blayds St R7
Blayd's Yd K8
Blenheim Av J1
Blenheim Ct J2

Blenheim Cres J1
Blenheim Gro J2
Blenheim Sq J1
Blenheim Vw H1
Blenheim Wk H1
Blundell St H4
Boar La J7
Bodley Ter A3
Bond St J6
Boundary Pl P1
Boundary St P1
Bowling Grn Ter H11
Bowman La M8
Bow St P8
Bracken Ct B12
Brancepeth Pl C7
Brandon Rd F4
Brandon St D7
Branksome Pl C2
Brick St N7
Bridge Ct F10
Bridge End K8
Bridge Rd F10
Bridge St M6
Bridgewater Rd Q11
Briggate K7
Brignall Garth S4
Brignall Way R4
Bristol St N3
Britannia St H7
Brookfield St N11
Brown Av C13
Brown La E D12
Brown La W B12
Brown Pl C13
Brown Rd C13
Bruce Gdns C8
Bruce Lawn C8
Brunswick Ct M5
Brunswick Ter K4
Brussels St N7
Burley A1
Burley Lo Rd B2
Burley Lo St C3
Burley Lo Ter C2
Burley Pl A4
Burley Rd D4
Burley St E5
Burmantofts R5
Burmantofts St P5
Burton Way T3
Butterfield St R7
Butterley St L11
Butts Ct K6
Byron St M4
Cain Cl R8
Call La L8
Calls, The L7
Calverley St H4
Cambrian St G13
Cambrian Ter G13
Canal Pl D7
Canal St B6
Canal Wf H8
Carberry Pl B2
Carberry Rd B2
Carlisle Rd N10
Carlton Carr K2
Carlton Ct B13
Carlton Gdns K1
Carlton Gate K2
Carlton Gro K1
Carlton Hill K2
Carlton Pl K1
Carlton Ri K2
Carlton Twrs L2
Carlton Vw K1
Castle St G6
Castleton Cl D7
Castleton Rd B5
Cautley Rd S10
Cavalier App R10
Cavalier Cl R10
Cavalier Ct R9
Cavalier Gdns R10
Cavalier Gate R10
Cavalier Ms R10
Cavalier Vw R9
Cavendish Rd H2
Cavendish St E5
Cemetery Rd F13
Central Rd L7

Central St H6
Chadwick St M9
Chadwick St S N10
Chantrell Ct M7
Charles Av S9
Charlton Gro T8
Charlton Pl T8
Charlton Rd T8
Charlton St T8
Cherry Row P4
Chesney Av M13
Chiswick St B3
Chorley La G4
Churchill Gdns J2
Church La M7
City Sq J7
Claremont Av F4
Claremont Gro F4
Claremont Vw F4
Clarence Rd M8
Clarendon Pl F2
Clarendon Rd F2
Clarendon Way G4
Clark Av S8
Clark Cres S8
Clark Gro S9
Clark La R9
Clark Mt S8
Clark Rd S9
Clark Row S9
Clark Ter S8
Clark Vw S9
Clay Pit La K4
Cleveleys Rd E13
Cleveleys St E13
Cloberry St F2
Close, The P7
Cloth Hall St L7
Clyde App B9
Clyde Gdns C9
Clyde Vw B9
Coleman St D9
Colenso Gdns E13
Colenso Mt E13
Colenso Pl E13
Colenso Rd E13
Colenso Ter E13
Commercial St K6
Compton Av T2
Compton Cres T2
Compton Gro T1
Compton Mt T1
Compton Pl T2
Compton Rd T2
Compton St T1
Compton Ter T2
Compton Vw T2
Concordia St K8
Concord St M4
Consort St E4
Consort Ter E4
Consort Vw D3
Consort Wk E4
Cookridge St J5
Copley Hill B9
Copley Hill Way B11
Copley St B9
Copperfield Av S10
Copperfield Cres S10
Copperfield Gro S10
Copperfield Mt T9
Copperfield Pl S10
Copperfield Row S10
Copperfield Ter S9
Copperfield Vw S10
Copperfield Wk S10
Copperfiield Dr S10
Cotton St N7
Cowper Av T1
Cowper Cres T1
Cowper Rd T1
Cromer Pl F2
Cromer Rd F2
Cromer St F2
Cromer Ter F3
Cromwell Mt P4
Cromwell St P5
Crosby Pl F12
Crosby Rd F13
Crosby St E12
Crosby Ter F12
Crosby Vw F12
Cross Aysgarth Mt R7

Cross Belgrave St L5
Cross Catherine St Q7
Cross Green T11
Cross Grn App T12
Cross Grn Av R10
Cross Grn Cl T11
Cross Grn Cres R10
Cross Grn Dr T11
Cross Grn Garth T12
Cross Grn La Q9
Cross Grn Ri T11
Cross Grn Way T12
Cross Ingram Rd E11
Cross Kelso Rd E3
Cross Mitford Rd A7
Cross Stamford St N3
Cross York St M7
Crown Pt Rd L9
Crown St L7
Croydon St D10
Cudbear St M10
Czar St F10
Danby Wk R7
David St H10
Dene Ho Ct J1
Denison Rd F5
Dent St R8
Derwent Pl G10
Devon Cl H1
Devon Rd H1
Dewsbury Rd K11
Dial St R9
Dock St L8
Dolly La P3
Dolphin Ct Q7
Dolphin St Q7
Domestic Rd C11
Domestic St E10
Donisthorpe St P11
Drive, The P8
Driver Ter C9
Duke St M6
Duncan St K7
Duncombe St F6
Duxbury Ri J1
Dyer St M6
East Fld St Q7
Eastgate L6
East King St P8
East Par J6
East Pk Dr S7
East Pk Gro T8
East Pk Mt T8
East Pk Par T8
East Pk Pl T8
East Pk Rd S8
East Pk St T8
East Pk Ter T8
East Pk Vw T7
East St N7
Easy Rd Q10
Ebor Mt D1
Ebor Pl D1
Ebor St D1
Edgware Av R1
Edgware Gro R1
Edgware Mt R1
Edgware Pl R1
Edgware Row R1
Edgware Ter R1
Edgware Vw Q1
Edward St L5
Edwin Rd D1
Eighth Av A9
Elland Ter H11
Ellerby La Q9
Ellerby Rd P8
Elmtree La N13
Elmwood La L3
Elmwood Rd K3
Elsworth St A7
Enfield Av P1
Enfield St N2
Enfield Ter P1
Euston Gro D13
Everleigh St T6
Far Cft Ter A9
Fewston Av R10
Fewston Ct S9
Finsbury Rd H3
First Av A8
Firth St N3

Firth Ter P3
Fish St L6
Flax Pl P8
Florence Av T1
Florence Gro T1
Florence Mt T1
Florence Pl T1
Florence Sq T1
Forster St P12
Foundry St
 (Holbeck) H9
Foundry St
 (Quarry Hill) P7
Fountain St G6
Fourteenth Av A9
Fourth Ct F10
Fox Way Q12
Fraser St S4
Frederick Av T9
Front Row H9
Front St H9
Gargrave App R5
Gargrave Pl R4
Garth, The P7
Garton Av T8
Garton Gro T8
Garton Rd T8
Garton Ter T8
Garton Vw T8
Gelderd Pl C10
Gelderd Rd C10
Gelderd Trd Est C12
George St L6
Gilpin Pl A9
Gilpin St A9
Gilpin Ter A9
Gilpin Vw A9
Glasshouse St N12
Gledhow Mt Q1
Gledhow Pl Q1
Gledhow Rd Q2
Gledhow Ter Q1
Glencoe Vw S10
Glensdale Gro S8
Glensdale Mt S8
Glensdale Rd S8
Glensdale St S7
Glensdale Ter T8
Glenthorpe Av T6
Glenthorpe Cres T6
Glenthorpe Ter T6
Globe Rd F8
Gloucester Ter B7
Goodman St P12
Gotts Rd E7
Gower St M5
Grace St G6
Grafton St L3
Grange Cl N13
Grange Rd N13
Grant Av P1
Granville Rd Q3
Grape St M13
Grasmere Cl A9
Grassmere Rd A9
Great George St G5
Great Wilson St J9
Greek St J6
Greenfield Rd Q7
Green La
 (Cross Green) S10
Green La (Wortley) B9
Grosvenor Hill K1
Hall Gro D1
Hall La A7
Hall Pl R7
Hanover Av E4
Hanover La G5
Hanover Mt E4
Hanover Sq F5
Hanover Wk F5
Harewood St L6
Harold Av B1
Harold Gro B1
Harold Mt B1
Harold Pl B1
Harold Rd B1
Harold St B1
Harold Ter B1
Harold Vw B1
Harold Wk B1
Harper St M7
Harrison St L5

Hartwell Rd C2
Haslewood Cl Q6
Haslewood Ct R6
Haslewood Dene Q6
Haslewood Dr Q5
Haslewood Ms S6
Haslewood Pl R6
Haslewood Sq R6
Hawkins Dr K1
Headrow, The K5
Heaton's Ct K8
Hedley Chase B7
Hedley Gdns B7
Hedley Grn B8
Henbury St N3
High P13
High Ct M7
High Ct La M7
Hillary Pl H2
Hilidge Rd M13
Hillidge Sq M13
Hill Top Pl D2
Hill Top St D2
Hirst's Yd L7
Holbeck G10
Holbeck La E10
Holbeck Moor Rd F12
Holdforth Cl B8
Holdforth Gdns B8
Holdforth Grn B9
Holdforth Pl B8
Holmes St K10
Holroyd St N2
Hope Rd N5
Howden Gdns C2
Howden Pl C1
Hudson Rd T2
Hudswell Rd M13
Hunslet Grn Way M13
Hunslet Hall Rd H13
Hunslet La L9
Hunslet Rd L8
Hyde Pk Cl D1
Hyde Pk Rd D2
Hyde Pl F4
Hyde St F4
Hyde Ter F3
Infirmary St J6
Ingram Cl E11
Ingram Cres D13
Ingram Gdns E11
Ingram Row J10
Ingram St J10
Ingram Vw E12
Inner Ring Rd J3
Ivory St L11
Jack La H11
Jenkinson Cl G11
Jenkinson Lawn G12
Joseph St P13
Junction St L10
Keeton St Q6
Kelsall Av C2
Kelsall Gro C3
Kelsall Pl C2
Kelsall Rd C2
Kelsall Ter C2
Kelso Gdns E2
Kelso Rd E2
Kelso St E3
Kendal Bk E4
Kendal Cl E4
Kendal Gro F4
Kendal La E4
Kendell St L8
Kenneth St D11
Kepler Gro Q1
Kepler Mt Q1
Kepler Ter Q1
Kidacre St L10
Kildare Ter C9
King Charles St K6
King Edward St L6
Kings Av C3
King's Rd C2
Kingston Ter H1
King St H7
Kippax Pl R8
Kirkgate L6
Kirkstall Rd B4
Kitson Rd N12
Kitson St R8
Knowsthorpe Cres R10

Street	Ref	Street	Ref	Street	Ref
Knowsthorpe La	S12	Milford Pl	A4	Park Sq W	H6
Ladybeck Cl	M5	Millgarth St	M6	Park St	H5
Lady La	L6	Mill Grn	D10	Park Vw Rd	A1
Lands La	K6	Mill Hill	K7	Pearson St	M11
Lane, The	P8	Mill St	N7	Pilot St	P3
Larchfield Rd	P12	Millwright St	N4	Pitt Row	K8
Laura St	E9	Milner Gdns	R9	Place's Rd	Q8
Lavender Wk	R7	Milnes St	C9	Plaid Row	Q6
Leathley Rd	L12	Mitford Rd	A8	Pleasant Mt	F11
Leeds City Office Pk	K10	Mitford Vw	A7	Pleasant Pl	F11
Leicester	J1	Moor Cres Chase	K13	Pleasant Ter	F11
Leicester Gro	J1	Moorland Av	D1	Pontefract Av	S8
Leicester Pl	H1	Moorland Rd	D1	Pontefract La	R6
Leighton St	G5	Moor Vw	G12	Pontefract La Cl	R7
Leodis Ct	H10	Moorvile Cl	H13	Pontefract St	R8
Leylands Rd	N4	Moorville Ct	G13	Portland Cres	J5
Lifton Pl	F2	Moorville Gro	G13	Portland Gate	J4
Lincoln Grn Rd	P4	Moorville Rd	H13	Portland St	H5
Lincoln Rd	P3	Mount Preston St	F3	Portland Way	J4
Lindsey Ct	Q4	Mullins Ct	R9	Pottery Rd	M13
Lindsey Gdns	Q4	Mushroom St	N3	Prosper St	P13
Lindsey Rd	Q4	Naseby Garth	P4	Providence Pl	K3
Lisbon St	G6	Naseby Ter	Q5	Pym St	N12
Little King St	J7	National Rd	Q12	**Quarry Hill**	**N6**
Little Queen St	G7	Navigation Wk	L8	Quebec St	H6
Little Woodhouse St	G4	Neptune St	N8	Queen Sq	K4
Livinia Gro	J1	Neville St	J8	Queens Rd	C2
Lodge St	H3	New Briggate	L5	Queen St	G7
Lofthouse Pl	J2	New Craven Gate	L12	Radnor St	C9
Londesboro Gro	T7	New La	J9	Railway St	P7
Long Causeway	R11	New Mkt St	L7	Raincliffe Gro	T6
Long Cl La	R8	New Princess St	H12	Raincliffe Rd	T6
Lord St	E9	New Sta St	J7	Raincliffe St	T6
Lord Ter	D9	New York Rd	N5	Recreation Cres	E13
Lovell Pk Cl	M3	New York St	L7	Recreation Gro	E13
Lovell Pk Gate	L3	Nickleby Rd	T6	Recreation Mt	E13
Lovell Pk Hill	L3	Nile St	M5	Recreation Pl	E13
Lovell Pk Rd	L4	Nineveh Gdns	G11	Recreation Row	E13
Lovell Pk Vw	M3	Nineveh Par	G12	Recreation St	E13
Lower Basinghall St	J6	Nineveh Rd	F11	Recreation Ter	E13
Lower Brunswick St	M4	Nippet La	Q5	Recreation Vw	E13
Low Flds Rd	A13	Normanton Gro	F13	Rectory St	Q3
Low Flds Way	C13	Normanton Pl	G13	Redshaw Rd	A9
Low Fold	P9	Nortech Cl	N2	Regent St	N5
Low Rd	P13	Northcote Cres	J13	Regent Ter	D1
Low Whitehouse Row	N12	Northcote Dr	H13	Rhodes Ter	B9
Ludgate Hill	L6	Northcote Grn	H13	Richmond Hill App	Q8
Lyddon Ter	F2	North Ct	L5	Richmond Hill Cl	Q8
Lydgate	S3	Northern St	G7	Richmond St	P8
Lydia St	M5	North St	L5	Rickard St	E9
Mabgate	N5	Oak Rd	B8	Rider St	P5
Mabgate Grn	N5	Oatland Cl	L1	Rigton App	Q5
Macaulay St	P5	Oatland Ct	L2	Rigton Cl	R5
Maitland Pl	G13	Oatland Dr	L2	Rigton Dr	Q5
Manor Rd	H10	Oatland Gdns	L2	Rigton Grn	Q5
Manor St	N2	Oatland Grn	L1	Rigton Lawn	Q5
Mark La	K5	Oatland Hts	M2	Rigton Ms	Q5
Marlborough Gdns	H2	Oatland La	K1	Rillbank La	D3
Marlborough Gro	H2	Oatland Rd	K1	Rosebank Gdns	D3
Marlborough St	H5	Oatland Twrs	L2	Rosebank Rd	D3
Marlborough Twrs	F5	O'Grady Sq	R8	Rosebud Wk	P1
Marshall St	G9	Oval, The	N13	Roseville Rd	P2
Marsh La	N7	Oxford Pl	H5	Roseville St	Q1
Maude St	M8	Oxford Row	H5	Rossington St	J5
Meadowcroft Ms	Q8	Oxley St	S8	Roundhay Rd	N1
Meadow La	K9	Oxton Mt	S5	Roxby Cl	Q4
Meadow Rd	J11	Oxton Way	S6	Royal Pk Av	D1
Melbourne St	M4	Parade, The	P8	Royal Pk Gro	D1
Merrion Pl	L5	Park Cross St	H6	Royal Pk Rd	B1
Merrion St	K5	Parkfield St	K12	Royal Pk Ter	D1
Merrion Way	K4	Park La	E5	Ruby St	P3
Meynell App	F12	Park Par	T9	Runswick Av	E12
Middleton Av	S4	Park Pl	G6	Runswick Pl	F12
		Park Row	J5	Runswick St	E12
		Park Sq E	H6	Runswick Ter	F12
		Park Sq N	H5	Russell St	J6
		Park Sq S	H6	Rydall Pl	E12

Street	Ref	Street	Ref	Street	Ref
Rydall St	E12	Springfield Mt	F3	Wade La	K5
Rydall Ter	E12	Spring Gro Vw	C2	Walford Gro	T6
Sackville St	L1	Spring Gro Wk	B2	Walford Rd	T6
St. Andrew's St	E5	Springwell Ct	E9	Walford Ter	T6
St. Ann St	J5	Springwell Rd	E9	Walter Cres	R8
St. Barnabas Rd	J10	Springwell St	E9	Walter St	A3
St. Georges Rd	G4	Springwell Vw	F10	Walton St	G10
St. Helen's St	N12	Stafford St	P13	Washington St	C5
St. Hilda's Av	S10	Stanley Av	S1	Water La	H9
St. Hilda's Cres	R10	Stanley Pl	T1	Waterloo St	L8
St. Hilda's Mt	S10	Stanley Rd	S1	Weaver St	A4
St. Hilda's Pl	S10	Stanley Ter	S1	Welbeck Rd	T7
St. Hilda's Rd	S10	Stocks Hill	F11	Well Cl Ri	K2
St. John's Av	E2	Stoney Rock Gro	S4	Wellington Br St	E6
St. John's Cl	D2	Stoney Rock La	R4	Wellington Rd	D8
St. John's Gro	D1	Stott St	A7	Wellington Rd Ind Est	D7
St. John's Rd	D3	Studio Rd	C4	Wellington St	G7
St. Luke's Cres	G13	Sutton St	E9	Wesley Pl	Q7
St. Mark's Av	G1	Sweet St	H10	Westfield Cres	D3
St. Mark's Rd	H1	Sweet St W	G10	Westfield Rd	C3
St. Mark's St	G1	Swinegate	K8	Westfield Ter	D3
St. Mary's Cl	A9	Sydenham Rd	D10	Westgate	H5
St. Mary's St	N5	Sydenham St	D10	Westlock Av	S3
St. Matthew's St	F12	Telephone Pl	N3	West St	E5
St. Matthias St	A2	Templar La	M6	West Vale	B12
St. Matthias Ter	A2	Templar Pl	M6	Wharf St	M7
St. Paul's St	G6	Templar St	L5	Whitehall Rd	D9
St. Peter's Pl	N6	Temple Vw Gro	T7	Whitehouse St	N13
St. Peter's Sq	N6	Temple Vw Pl	S8	Whitelock St	M3
St. Stephen's Ct	R5	Temple Vw Rd	S6	Whitfield Gdns	P13
St. Stephen's Rd	R5	Temple Vw Ter	S8	Whitfield Way	P13
Sandlewood Cl	G12	Thealby Cl	P5	Willis St	Q8
Sandlewood Grn	G12	Thealby Lawn	P4	Willoughby Ter	E12
Sardinia St	M12	Thealby Pl	P5	Willow App	B3
Saville Grn	S6	Third Av	A9	Willow Av	B3
Saxton La	N7	Thirsk Row	H7	Willow Cl	C3
Sayner La	N10	Thoresby Pl	H5	Willow Garth	B3
Sayner Rd	M10	Thornleigh Gdns	S9	Willow Rd	B3
Scargill Cl	R4	Thornleigh Gro	S9	Willow Ter Rd	G3
Scarth Av	T1	Thornleigh Mt	S9	Winchester St	A7
Scotch Pk Trd Est	A5	Thornleigh St	S9	Winfield Gro	J1
Second Av	B8	Thornleigh Vw	S9	Winfield Pl	J1
Seminary St	G3	Thornville Pl	C1	Winfield Ter	J1
Shafton La	E12	Thornville Rd	B2	Wintoun St	M3
Shafton Pl	E12	Thornville Row	C1	Wolseley Rd	A2
Shafton St	F12	Thornville St	C2	Woodhouse La	J4
Shafton Vw	E12	Thornville Vw	C1	Woodhouse Sq	G5
Shakespeare App	R3	Tilbury Rd	E13	Woodsley Grn	D2
Shakespeare Av	R3	Tong Rd	B9	Woodsley Rd	C3
Shakespeare Cl	S3	Top Moor Side	F12	Wormald Row	K5
Shakespeare Gdns	S3	Torre Cl	T5	Wortley La	D10
Shakespeare Lawn	R3	Torre Dr	T4	Wortley Pk	B10
Shakespeare St	S2	Torre Rd	R5	Yarn St	Q12
Shannon Rd	Q6	Tower Ho St	L4	York Pl	G6
Shannon St	P6	Trafalgar St	L5	York Rd	Q6
Sheaf St	M9	Trent Rd	S5	York St	M7
Sheepscar Gro	M3	Trent St	H11		
Sheepscar St N	M1	Triumph Cl	F10		
Sheepscar St S	N2	Union Pl	G10		
Siddal St	H10	Union St	L6		
Sidney St	L6	University Rd	F2		
Skinner La	M3	Upper Accommodation Rd	Q6		
Skinner St	F6	Upper Basinghall St	J6		
Somers St	G6	Upper N St	J4		
South Accommodation Rd	N11	Upper Westlock Av	T3		
South Par	J6	Vernon Rd	H3		
Sovereign St	J8	Vernon St	J4		
Spence La	D9	Vicar La	L6		
Spenceley St	G1	Victoria Rd	J9		
Spinney, The	Q8	Victoria St	E4		
Spinneyfield Ct	Q8	Victoria Ter	E4		
Spring Cl Av	R9	Village Ter	A1		
Spring Cl Gdns	R9	Vinery Mt	T7		
Spring Cl St	Q9	Vinery Pl	T7		
Spring Cl Wk	R9	Vinery St	T6		
		Vinery Ter	T7		

NEWCASTLE UPON TYNE URBAN page 88

Street	Ref	Street	Ref	Street	Ref
Abingdon Way	C2	Benton Bk	B1	**Boldon Colliery**	**C2**
Addison Rd	C2	Benton La	B1	Boldon La (Cleadon)	D2
Albion Rd	C1	Benton Pk Rd	A1	Boldon La (West Harton)	D2
Albion St	B2	Benton Rd (Newcastle upon Tyne)	B1	Brighton Gro	A2
Allendale Rd	B2	Benton Rd (South Shields)	D2	Broadway	D1
Archer St	C1	**Benton Square**	**B1**	Broadway W	A1
Arthur's Hill	**A2**	Bents Pk Rd	D1	Broom La	A2
Askew Rd	A2	**Benwell**	**A2**	Brunton La	A1
Atkinson Rd	A2	Benwell La	A2	Brunton Rd	A1
Baring St	D1	Bewicke St	C1	Buddle St	B2
Barston	**C3**	**Bill Quay**	**B2**	Burdon Rd	D3
Battle Hill	**B1**	**Billy Mill**	**C1**	**Byker**	**B2**
Battle Hill Dr	C1	Billy Mill Av	C1	Byker Br	B2
Beach Rd	C1	Billy Mill La	C1	**Carley Hill**	**D3**
Beacon Lough Rd	B3	**Birtley**	**B3**	Carlisle St	B2
Bell Vue Bk	A3	**Blackfell**	**B3**	**Carr Hill**	**B2**
Benfield Rd	B1	**Blakelaw**	**A1**	Carr Hill Rd	B2
Bensham	**A2**	Boker La	D2	**Castletown**	**C3**
Bensham Rd	A2	**Boldon**	**C2**	Cedar Rd	A2
Bentinck Rd	A2			Cemetery Rd	B2
Benton	**B1**				

Street	Ref	Street	Ref	Street	Ref
Centenary Av	D2	Cleadon La (East Boldon)	D2	**Coxlodge**	**A1**
Chester Rd	D3	**Cleadon Park**	**D2**	Cragside	B1
Cheviot Rd	D2	Coach La (Newcastle upon Tyne)	B1	Crossgate	D1
Chichester Rd	D1	Coach La (North Shields)	C1	**Cullercoats**	**D1**
Chillingham Rd	B1	Coast Rd	D2	Dame Dorothy St	D3
Chirton	**C1**	Coast Rd, The	C1	**Deckham**	**B2**
Chowdene	**A3**	Coatsworth Rd	A2	**Donwell**	**B3**
Chowdene Bk	A3	Coble Dene	C1	Dovedale Rd	D3
Church Av	A1	Coldwell La	C2	**Downhill**	**C3**
Church Bk	C2	Colegate	B2	Downhill La	C3
Churchill St	C1	Commercial Rd	C1	Drive, The	B2
Church Rd (Gateshead)	B3	Condercum Rd	A2	**Dunston**	**A2**
Church St (Gosforth)	A1	Consett Rd	A3	Dunston Bk	A2
City Rd	A2	Cotemede	B3	**Dunston Hill**	**A2**
Claremont Rd	A2	Cotswold La	C2	Dunston Rd	A2
Clayton Rd	A2	Coutts Rd	B2	Durham Rd	B2
Cleadon	**D2**	**Cowgate**	**A2**	Easedale Gdns	B3
Cleadon La (Cleadon)	D2			**East Boldon**	**D2**
				East Brunton	**A1**
				Eastern Av	A3
				Edgefield Av	A1

EDINBURGH URBAN page 89

Name	Ref
Kingston Av	C2
Kirkbrae	C2
Kirkgate	A3
Lanark Rd	A2
Lanark Rd W	A3
Lang Ln	C3
Lasswade	**C3**
Lasswade Rd (Dalkeith)	D3
Lasswade Rd (Gracemount)	C2
Lauder Rd	D3
Lauriston Pl	B2
Leith	**B1**
Leith Wk	B1
Levenhall	D2
Liberton	**C2**
Liberton Brae	C2
Liberton Dr	C2
Liberton Gdns	C2
Lindsay Rd	B1
Linkfield Rd	D2
Links Gdns	C1
Links Pl	C1
Loan, The	C3
Loanhead	**C3**
Lochend Rd	C1
London Rd	B1
Long Hermiston	**A2**
Longstone	**A2**
Longstone Rd	A2
Lothianbridge	**D3**
Lothian Rd	B1
Lower Granton Rd	B1
Macbeth Moir Rd	D2
Main St (Davidson's Mains)	A1
Main St (Newtongrange)	D3
Main St (Roslin)	C3
Malleny Mills	**A3**
Mansfield Rd	A3
Marine Dr	A1
Market St	D2
Maybury Dr	A1
Maybury Rd	A1
Mayfield	**D3**
Mayfield Rd	C2
Melville Dr	B2
Melville Dykes	C3
Merchiston	**B2**
Middle Kinleith	**A3**
Millerhill	**D2**
Millerhill Rd	C2
Milton Rd E	C2
Monktonhall	**D2**
Moredun	**C2**
Moredun Pk Rd	C2
Moredunvale Rd	C2
Morningside	**B2**
Morningside Dr	B2
Morningside Rd	B2
Mountcastle Dr N	C1
Mountcastle Dr S	C2
Mount Vernon Rd	C2
Muirhouse	**A1**
Muirhouse Parkway	A1
Murderdean Rd	D3
Murrayfield	**A1**
Murrayfield Rd	B1
Musselburgh	**D1**
Musselburgh Rd (Dalkeith)	D3
Musselburgh Rd (Edinburgh)	D1
Newbattle	**D3**
Newbattle Rd	D3
Newcraighall	**D2**
Newcraighall Rd	D2
Newhailes	**D2**
Newhailes Rd	D2
Newhaven	**B1**
Newhaven Rd	B1
Newington	**B2**
Newmills Rd	D3
Newtoft St	C2
Newton	**C2**
Newton Ch Rd	C2
Newtongrange	**D3**
New Town	**B1**
Niddrie	**C2**
Niddrie Mains Rd	C2
Niven's Knowe Rd	C3
North Fld	C1
North Gyle	**A2**
North High St	D2
North Leith	**B1**
Old Craighall Rd	D2
Old Dalkeith Rd	C2
Old Town	**B2**
Oxgangs	**B2**
Oxgangs Av	B2
Oxgangs Rd	B2
Oxgangs Rd N	B2
Palmerston Pl	B1
Peffermill Rd	C2
Penicuik	B3
Pennywell Gdns	A1
Pennywell Rd	B1
Pentland Rd	B3
Pilrig St	B1
Pilton	**B1**
Pleasance	B2
Polton	**C3**
Polton Av Rd	C3
Polton Bk	C3
Polton Rd	C3
Polwarth Ter	B2
Portobello	**C1**
Portobello High St	C1
Portobello Rd	C1
Prestonfield	**C2**
Princes St	B1
Queen's Dr	C2
Queensferry Rd	A1
Queen St	B1
Ravelston	**B1**
Ravelston Dykes	B1
Ravelston Dykes Rd	B1
Ravenshaugh Rd	D2
Redford Rd	B2
Regent Rd	B1
Restalrig	**C1**
Restalrig Rd	C1
Restalrig Rd S	C1
Riccarton Mains Rd	A2
Roseburn St	B2
Rosewell	**C3**
Roslin	**C3**
Rostbank St	B1
St. Andrew's St	D3
St. John's Rd	A2
Salamander St	C1
Salter's Rd (Dalkeith)	D2
Salter's Rd (Wallyford)	D2
Saughton Rd	A2
Saughton Rd N	A2
Seacarr St	B1
Seafield	**B3**
Seafield Moor Rd	B3
Seafield Rd	C1
Shandwick Pl	B1
Shawfair Rd	C2
Sighthill	**A2**
Silverknowes	**A1**
Silverknowes Rd	A1
Slateford Rd	B2
Sleigh Dr	C1
South Gyle	**A2**
South Gyle Bdy	A2
South Gyle Rd	A2
South Leith	**C1**
Spylawbank Rd	A2
Stenhouse	**A2**
Stenhouse Dr	A2
Stevenson Dr	B2
Stobhill Rd	D3
Straiton	**C3**
Strathearn Rd	B2
Street Leonard's St	B2
Suttieslea Rd	D3
Swanston	**B3**
Swanston Rd	B3
Telford Rd	B1
Torphin	**A3**
Torphin Rd	A3
Trinity	**B1**
Turnhouse	**A1**
Turnhouse Rd	A2
Wakefield Av	C1
Warriston	**B1**
Warriston Rd	A2
West App Rd	B2
Wester Hailes	**A2**
Wester Hailes Rd	A2
Wester Kinleith	**A3**
West Granton Rd	B1
West Harbour Rd	B1
Westhouses	D3
West Mains Rd	B1
West Milton Rd	C2
West Pier	B1
West Pilton	**B1**
West Saville Ter	B2
West Shore Rd	B1
Whitecraig	**D2**
Whitecraig Rd	D2
Whitehill	**D3**
Whitehouse Rd	A1
Willowbrae Rd	C1
Wisp, The	C2
Woodhall Rd	A2

GLASGOW URBAN pages 90-91

Name	Ref
Abbotsinch Rd	A2
Aikenhead Rd	C3
Airbles Rd	F4
Airdrie	**F2**
Aitchison St	F2
Aitkenhead Rd	E3
Alderman Rd	B2
Alexandra Par	C2
Allanton	**F4**
Almada St	E4
Amulree St	D3
Angus Av	D1
Annathill	**F1**
Anniesland	**B2**
Anniesland Rd	B2
Archerhill Rd	B2
Arden	**B3**
Ardencraig Rd	C4
Argyle St	C2
Argyll Rd	A1
Arkleston Rd	A3
Arrochar St	C1
Ashfield St	C2
Ashgill Rd	C2
Auchengeich Rd	E1
Auchenhowie Rd	B1
Auchentibber	**E4**
Auchinairn	**C2**
Auchinairn Rd	C2
Auchindavie Rd	E1
Auchinlea Rd	D2
Auchinloch	**D1**
Auchinloch Rd	D1
Aurs Rd	A4
Avenue End Rd	D2
Avenuehead Rd	E1
Ayr Rd	B4
Baillieston	**E2**
Baillieston Rd (Baillieston)	D3
Baillieston Rd (Broomhouse)	E3
Baldernock Rd	B1
Balgrayhill Rd	C2
Baljaffray Rd	B1
Ballater St	C3
Balloch Loop Rd	F1
Balmore	**C1**
Balmore Rd	C1
Balmuildy Rd	C1
Balornock	**C2**
Bankhead Rd (King's Park)	C3
Bankhead Rd (Kirkintilloch)	E1
Bank St	F2
Bardowie	**C1**
Bardykes Rd	E4
Bargeddie	**E2**
Barlanark	**D2**
Barmulloch	**D2**
Barnhill	**E4**
Barnsford Rd	A2
Barrachnie	**D3**
Barrachnie Rd	D3
Barrhead	**A4**
Barrhead Rd (Paisley)	A3
Barrhead Rd (Pollok)	A3
Bartiebeith Rd	D2
Battlefield	**C3**
Bearsden	**B1**
Bearsden Rd	B2
Bellshill	**F3**
Bellshill Rd (Motherwell)	F4
Bellshill Rd (Uddingston)	E3
Bent Rd	E4
Bilsland Dr	C2
Birkenshaw	**E3**
Bishopbriggs	**C1**
Blackbyers Rd	A3
Blackhall	**A3**
Blackhill Rd	C1
Blairbeth Rd	C3
Blairlinn	**F1**
Blair Rd	F2
Blantyre	**E4**
Blantyre Fm Rd	E3
Boclair Rd	B1
Boghall Rd	E3
Boghead Rd	D1
Boness Rd	F3
Bothwell	**E4**
Bothwell Rd (Hamilton)	
Bothwell Rd (Uddingston)	E3
Boydstone Rd	B3
Braehead	**C4**
Braid Craft Rd	B3
Braidfauld	**D3**
Braidfauld St	D3
Braidholm Rd	B3
Brandon St	F4
Bridgend	**E1**
Bridgeton	**C3**
Broadwood	**E1**
Broom	**B4**
Brockburn Rd	B3
Broomfield Rd	C2
Broomhouse	**D3**
Broomlands St	A3
Broomloan Rd	B2
Brownside Rd	D3
Buckhey	**C1**
Burnbank	**E4**
Burnbank Rd	E4
Burnbank St	E4
Burnbrae Rd	D1
Burnfield Rd	B3
Burnside	**D3**
Burnside Rd	D3
Busby	**C4**
Byres Rd	B2
Cadder	**C1**
Cadzow St	F4
Cairnhill Rd	F2
Calderbank	**F3**
Caldercuilt Rd	B1
Calderside Rd	D4
Calder St (Coatbridge)	F2
Calder St (Govanhill)	C3
Calderwood	**D4**
Calderwood (East Kilbride)	D4
Calderwood Rd (Rutherglen)	D3
Calfmuir Rd	E1
Calside	A3
Cambuslang	**D3**
Cambuslang Rd	D3
Camphill Av	C3
Campsie Rd (Kirkintilloch)	D1
Campsie Rd (Torrance)	D1
Canal St	A3
Canniesburn Rd	B1
Capelrig Rd	B4
Caplethill Rd	A3
Carbrain	**F1**
Cardonald	**B3**
Cardowan Rd (Carntyne)	D2
Cardowan Rd (Craigmuir)	D2
Carlisle Rd (Airdrie)	F2
Carlisle Rd (Hamilton)	F4
Carmunnock	**C4**
Carmunnock Rd	C3
Carmyle	**D3**
Carmyle Av	D3
Carnbroe	**F3**
Carntyne	**D2**
Carntynehall Rd	D2
Carntyne Rd	D2
Carnwardric	**B3**
Carrick Dr	D3
Castle Av	E3
Castlebay St	C1
Castlehead	**A3**
Castlemilk	**C4**
Castlemilk Dr	C3
Castlemilk Rd	C3
Cathcart	**C3**
Cathcart Rd (Govanhill)	C3
Cathcart Rd (Rutherglen)	C3
Cathkin By-pass	D3
Cathkin Rd	D3
Causeway Side St	D3
Central Way	F1
Chanting Hall Rd	E4
Chapelton Rd	F1
Charleston	**A3**
Chryston	**E1**
Chryston Rd	E1
Clarence Dr	B2
Clarkston	**C4**
Clarkston Rd	C4
Clark St	F2
Cleekhimin	**F4**
Cleveden Rd	B2
Clober Rd	B1
Clydebank	**A2**
Clydesford Rd	D3
Clydeside Expressway	C2
Clydesmill Rd	D3
Coal Rd	D1
Coatbank St	F2
Coatbridge	**E2**
Coatbridge Rd (Bargeddie)	E2
Coatbridge Rd (Gartcosh)	E2
Coatbridge Rd (Glenmavis)	F2
Coatdyke	**F2**
Cochno Rd	A1
Cockels Ln	A2
Coltswood Rd	F2
Commonhead Rd	E2
Condorrat	**F1**
Condorrat Rd	F2
Copland Rd	B2
Corkerhill Rd	B3
Corsebar Rd	A3
Cowgate	D1
Craigdhu Rd	B1
Craigendmuir	**D2**
Craigneuk	**F4**
Craigton	**B3**
Craigton Rd	B2
Croftfoot	**C3**
Croftfoot Rd	C3
Crookfur	**B4**
Crookston	**B3**
Crookston Rd	B3
Crosshill	**E3**
Crosshill Rd	D1
Crossmyloof	**C3**
Crowhill	**C1**
Crow Rd	B2
Cumbernauld	**F1**
Cumbernauld Rd	D2
Curtis Av	C3
Dalmarnock Rd	C3
Dalmuir	**A1**
Dalton	**D4**
Danes Dr	B2
Darnley	**B3**
Darnley Rd	C3
Dean Park	**A2**
Dean Pk Rd	A2
Deedes St	F2
Deer Dykes Rd	E1
Dennistoun	**C2**
Donaldswood Rd	A3
Dorchester Av	B2
Dougrie Rd	C4
Dowanhill	**B2**
Dowan Rd	C1
Drakemire Dr	C4
Drumcavel Rd	E2
Drumchapel	**B1**
Drumchapel Rd	B1
Drumry	**A1**
Drumry Rd	A1
Drymen Rd	B1
Dukes Rd	D3
Duke St	C2
Dumbarton Rd (Dalmuir)	A1
Dumbarton Rd (Duntocher)	A1
Dumbarton Rd (Scotstoun)	A2
Dumbreck	**B3**
Dumbreck Rd	B3
Dunbeth Rd	F2
Dundyvan Rd	F2
Duntocher	**A1**
Duntocher Rd (Bearsden)	A2
Duntocher Rd (Dalmuir)	A1
Dykehead Rd	F2
Dyke Rd	B2
Eaglesham Rd (Clarkston)	C4
Eaglesham Rd (Newton Mearns)	B4
Earnock	**E4**
Earnock Rd	E4
Easterhouse	**E2**
Eastfield	**D3**
East Greenlees Rd	D3
East Hallhill Rd	E2
East Kilbride	**D4**
East Kilbride Rd	D3
East Mains	**D4**
East Mains Rd	D4
Eastwoodmains Rd	B4
Edinburgh Rd	D2
Edmiston Dr	B2
Eglinton St	C3
Faifley	**A1**
Fairway Av	A3
Fallside	**E3**
Fallside Rd	E3
Falside Rd	A3
Fenwick Rd	B4
Fernhill Rd	D3
Ferniegair	**F4**
Ferry Rd	A2
Finnieston	**C2**
Flemington	**D3**
Flemington Rd	D4
Flenders Rd	B4
Forgewood	**F4**
Freeland	**A2**
Fullarton Rd	D3
Fulton St	B2
Gallowgate	C2
Gallowhill (East Dunbartonshire)	**D1**
Gallowhill (Renfrewshire)	**A2**
Gallowhill Rd (Gallowhill)	D1
Gallowhill Rd (Paisley)	A3
Garliston Rd	F2
Garngaber Ave	D1
Garnieland	A2
Garnkirk	**E2**
Garrowhill	**E3**
Garscadden Rd	B1
Garscube Rd	C2
Gartcosh	**E2**
Gartcraig Rd	D2
Gartferry Rd	E1
Gartgill	**E2**
Garthamlock	**D2**
Gartlea	**F2**
Gartloch Rd	D2
Gartsherrie	**E2**
Gartsherrie Rd	F2
Gartshore Rd	E1
George St	A3
Giffnock	**C4**
Gilbertfield Rd	D3
Gilshochill	**B2**
Glasgow Rd (Baillieston)	D3
Glasgow Rd (Clydebank)	A1
Glasgow Rd (Coatbridge)	E2
Glasgow Rd (Cumbernauld)	F1
Glasgow Rd (East Kilbride)	D4
Glasgow Rd (Hamilton)	E4
Glasgow Rd (Hardgate)	A1
Glasgow Rd (Kirkintilloch)	D1
Glasgow Rd (Milngavie)	B1
Glasgow Rd (Paisley)	A3
Glasgow Rd (Renfrew)	A2
Glasgow Rd (Rutherglen)	C3
Glasgow Rd (Waterfoot)	C4
Glebe St	A2
Glenboig	**F2**
Glenburn	**A3**
Glenburn Rd (East Kilbride)	C4
Glenburn Rd (Paisley)	A3
Glenmavis	**F2**
Glenmavis Rd	F2
Gorbals St	C3
Govan	**B2**
Govanhill	**C3**
Govan Rd	B2
Grahamston Rd	A3
Grampian Way	B1
Great Western Rd	A1
Greenend	**F2**
Greenfaulds	**F1**
Greenfaulds Rd	F1
Greenfoot	**F1**
Greenlees Rd	D4

Street	Ref
Greenock Rd	A2
Hallhill Rd	D2
Hallside	**E3**
Hallside Rd	E3
Hamilton	**E4**
Hamilton Rd (East Kilbride)	D4
Hamilton Rd (Motherwell)	F4
Hamilton Rd (Mount Vernon)	D3
Hardgate	**A1**
Harestanes	**D1**
Hawkhead	**A3**
Hawkhead Rd	A3
Hawthorn St	C2
Helen St	B2
High Blantyre	**E4**
High Blantyre Rd	E4
High Crosshill	**D3**
High St (Airdrie)	F2
High St (Glasgow)	C2
High St (Kirkintilloch)	D1
High St (Paisley)	A3
High St (Renfrew)	A2
Hillhead Rd	D1
Hillhouse	**E4**
Hillhouse Rd	E4
Hillingdon	**A3**
Hillington Rd	B2
Hilton Rd	C1
Holehills	**F2**
Holmbrae Rd	E3
Holmlea Rd	C3
Holytown	**F3**
Holytown Rd	F3
Hunter Rd	B1
Hunthill Rd	E4
Hurlet	**B3**
Hurlet Rd	A3
Hyndland Rd	B2
Ibrox	**B2**
Inchinnan	**A2**
Inchinnan Rd (Paisley)	A2
Inchinnan Rd (Renfrew)	A2
Inner Ring Rd	C2
Inveresk St	D2
Jane's Brae	F1
Jerviston Rd	F3
Johnston Rd	E2
Kelso St	A2
Kelvindale	**B2**
Kelvindale Rd	B2
Kelvinside	**B2**
Kenmure	**C1**
Kennishead Rd	B3
Keppochhill Rd	C2
Kilbowie	**A1**
Kilbowie Rd	A1
Killin St	D3
Kilmardinny Av	B1
Kilmarnock Rd	C3
Kilnside Rd	A3
Kilsyth Rd	D1
Kinfauns Dr	A1
King's Inch Rd	A2
King's Park	**C3**
King's Pk Av	C3
Kingston Rd	A4
King St (Coatbridge)	F2
King St (Paisley)	A3
Kingsway	D4
Kirkfield	**E4**
Kirkhill Rd	B4
Kirkintilloch	**D1**
Kirkintilloch Rd (Bishopbriggs)	C1
Kirkintilloch Rd (Lenzie)	D1
Kirklee Rd	B2
Kirkshaws	**F3**
Kirkshaws Rd	F3
Kirkwood	**E3**
Knightswood	**B1**
Knightswood Rd	B2
Kylepark	**E3**
Laighstonehall	**E4**
Lainshaw Dr	C4
Lambhill	**C2**
Langlands Rd	B2
Langmuirhead Rd	D1
Langmuir Rd	E1
Langside	**C3**
Langside Rd	C3
Ledard Rd	C3
Ledi Dr	B1
Lenzie	**D1**
Lenziemill	**F1**
Lenziemill Rd	F1
Lenzie Rd	D1
Letham Dr	D1
Levern Rd	A3
Liberty Rd	F3
Liddesdale Rd	C2
Lincoln Av	B2
Lindsaybeg Rd	D1
Linthaugh Rd	B3
Loaning, The	F4
Lochdochart Rd	E2
Lochend Rd (Easterhouse)	E2
Lochend Rd (Gartcosh)	E2
Lochfield Rd	A3
Lochwood	**E2**
Locks St	F2
London Rd	C3
Lounsdale Rd	A3
Love St	A2
Low Blantyre	**E4**
Low Waters	**F4**
Low Waters Rd	E4
Luggiebank	**F1**
Main Rd	F1
Main St (Bellshill)	F3
Main St (Calderbank)	F3
Main St (Cambuslang)	D3
Main St (Coatbridge)	F2
Main St (East Kilbride)	D4
Main St (High Blantyre)	E4
Main St (Holytown)	F3
Main St (Milngavie)	B1
Main St (Rutherglen)	D3
Main St (Thornliebank)	B3
Main St (Uddingston)	E3
Manor Av	D4
Manse Rd	B1
Mansewood	**B3**
Market Hill Rd	D4
Marnock	**E2**
Maryhill	**B2**
Maryhill Rd	B1
Maukin Fauld Rd	D3
Maxwell Av	B1
Maxwellton Rd	D4
Mearns	**B4**
Mearns Rd	B4
Menock Rd	C3
Menteith	F4
Merkland Dr	D1
Merrylee	**C3**
Merrylee Rd	C3
Merry St	F4
Millerston	**D2**
Mill Rd (Cambuslang)	D3
Mill Rd (Hamilton)	E4
Mill St (Paisley)	A3
Mill St (Rutherglen)	C3
Milngavie Rd	B1
Milton	**C1**
Mitchell St	E3
Mollinsburn	**E1**
Mollins Rd	E1
Monkland Motorway	D2
Moodiesburn	**E1**
Moorpark	**A2**
Mossend	**F3**
Mosspark	**B3**
Mosspark Boul	B3
Mosspark Dr	B3
Motherwell	**F4**
Mountblow	**A1**
Mountblow Rd	A1
Mount Florida	**C3**
Mount Vernon	**D3**
Mt Vernon Av	D3
Muckcroft Rd	E1
Muirend	**C3**
Muirhead (Glasgow)	**E3**
Muirhead (North Lanarkshire)	**E2**
Muirhead Rd	E3
Muirhouse	**F4**
Muir St	F4
Muiryfauld Dr	D3
Neilsland Rd	E4
Neilston	**A4**
Neilston Rd	A3
Nerston	**D4**
Netherhouse Rd	E2
Netherlee	**C4**
Netherlee Rd	C3
Netherplace	**B4**
New Edinburgh Rd	E3
Newhouse West	**F3**
Newlands	**C3**
Newlands Rd	C3
New Stevenson	**F3**
Newton	**D3**
Newton Mearns	**B4**
Nithsdale Rd	B3
Nitshill	**B3**
Nitshill Rd	B3
North Carbrain Rd	F1
North Motherwell	**F4**
North Rd (Bellshill)	F3
North Rd (Broadwood)	F1
Oatlands	**C3**
Old Coach Rd	D4
Old Edinburgh Rd	E3
Oldhall	A3
Old Monkland	**F3**
Old Monkland Rd	F3
Orchard Pk	B3
Orchardton Rd	E1
Overton Rd	D3
Oxgang	**D1**
Paisley	**A3**
Paisley Rd (Barrhead)	A3
Paisley Rd (Renfrew)	A2
Paisley Rd W	B3
Palacerigg Rd	F1
Parkhall	**A1**
Parkhead	**C3**
Parkhouse Rd	B3
Park Mains	**A1**
Parkneuk Rd	E4
Park Rd	A3
Partick	**B2**
Peat Rd	B3
Peel Glen Rd	B1
Pendicle Rd	B1
Penilee Rd	A2
Petershill Rd	C2
Pinkston Rd	C2
Pollok	**B3**
Pollokshaws	**B3**
Pollokshaws Rd	B3
Pollokshields	**C3**
Polmadie	**C3**
Polmadie Rd	C3
Possilpark	**C2**
Possil Rd	C2
Priesthill	**B3**
Prospecthill Rd	C3
Provanmill	**D2**
Quarry St	E4
Queen Elizabeth Av	A2
Queensway	D4
Radnor Park	**A1**
Raebog Rd	F2
Ralston	**A3**
Rawyards	**F2**
Redbrae Rd	D1
Red Rd	C2
Renfrew	**A2**
Renfrew Rd (Paisley)	A3
Renfrew Rd (Renfrew)	B2
Riddrie	**D2**
Riddrie Knowes	D2
Riggend	**F1**
Righead	**F2**
Robroyston Rd	D2
Rogerton	**D4**
Roman Rd	B1
Rosehall	**F3**
Rouken Glen Rd	B4
Rowan St	A3
Royston	**C2**
Royston Rd	C2
Ruchazie	**D2**
Rutherglen	**C3**
Rutherglen Rd	C3
St. Andrews Dr	B3
St. Andrews Rd	C3
St. Leonards	**D4**
St. Leonards Rd	D4
Sandyhills Rd	D3
Sandy Rd	A2
Saracen St	C2
Sauchenhall Rd	E1
Sauchiehall	C2
School St	F3
Scotstoun	**B2**
Scotstounhill	**B2**
Seafar Rd	F1
Second Av	A1
Seedhill Rd	A3
Shawhead	**F3**
Shawlands	**B3**
Sheddens	**C4**
Sheildmuir	**F4**
Sherry Dr	E4
Shettleston	**D3**
Shettleston Rd	D2
Shieldhall	**B2**
Shields Rd	F4
Shortroods	**A2**
Silvertonhill	**F4**
Southbrae Dr	B2
South Carbrain Rd	F1
South St	B2
Springboig	**D2**
Springboig Rd	D2
Springburn	**C2**
Springburn Rd	C2
Springfield Rd (Neilston)	A4
Springfield Rd (Parkhead)	C3
Springwells	**E4**
Stamperland	**C4**
Stand	**F2**
Standburn Rd	D2
Stanely Rd	A3
Station Rd	B1
Stepps	**D2**
Stepps Rd	D2
Stewartfield	**D4**
Stewartfield Way	D4
Stewarton Rd	B4
Stirling Rd	F1
Stonefield Rd	E4
Stonelaw Rd	D3
Stoneymeadow Rd	D4
Summerston	**B1**
Swinton	**E2**
Switchback Rd	B1
Tannochside	**E3**
Temple	**B2**
Temple Rd	B2
Thorniewood	**E3**
Thornliebank	**B4**
Thornliebank Rd	B3
Thornly Park	**A3**
Thorntonhall	**C4**
Thrashbush	**F2**
Titwood	B3
Tollcross Rd	D3
Torrance	**C1**
Torrance Rd	C1
Townhead	**E2**
Townhead	D1
Townhead Rd	E2
Tresta Rd	C1
Turnlaw Rd	D4
Uddingston	**E3**
Uddingston Rd	E3
Union St	E4
University Av	B2
Victoria Rd	C3
Viewfield Rd	E3
Viewpark	**E3**
Wallacewell Rd	D2
Waterfoot	**C4**
Waterfoot Rd	B4
Waterside	**E1**
Waterside Rd	D1
Wattston	**F1**
Wellhall Rd	E4
Wellhouse Rd	D2
Wellshot Rd	D3
Westburn Dr	D3
Westburn Rd	D3
Wester Cleddens Rd	C1
Westerhill Rd	D1
Westerhouse Rd	E2
Wester Rd	D3
Westfield	**F1**
Westfield Rd	F1
West Mains	**D4**
West Mains Rd	D4
Westmuir St	D3
Whifflet	**F2**
Whifflet St	F3
Whistleberry Rd	E4
Whitecraigs	**B4**
Whitecrook	**A1**
Whitehill	**E4**
Whitehill Rd	D1
Whiteinch	**B2**
Williamwood	**B4**
Woodfoot Rd	E4
Woodhill	**D1**
Woodhill Rd	D1
Woodilee Rd	D1
Woodlands	**E3**
Woodlands Rd	C2
Yoker	**A2**
Yoker Mill Rd	A2

GLASGOW CENTRAL pages 92–93

Street	Ref
Abbotsford Pl	K12
Abercromby Dr	T10
Abercromby Sq	T10
Abercromby St	S12
Academy Pk	A13
Adams Ct La	L9
Adelphi St	M11
Admiral St	E11
Aird's La	N10
Albert Br	N11
Albion Gate	P8
Albion St	P8
Alexander Cres	L13
Alexandra Par	S5
Allen Glen Pl	P6
Anchor La	M7
Anderston	**J7**
Anderston Quay	H9
Anson St	T12
Anthony St	H7
Arcadia Pl	S12
Arcadia St	S12
Argyle St	L8
Argyll Arc	M8
Ark La	T7
Arlington St	G3
Armour St	S9
Arthur St	B4
Ashley La	G3
Ashley St	G3
Ashton La	B1
Ashton Rd	B1
Auchentoshan Ter	S1
Bain St	R10
Baird St	Q4
Balaclava St	H8
Baliol La	G4
Baliol St	G4
Ballantrae Ct	G7
Ballater Pl	P13
Ballater St	M11
Bank St	D2
Barrack St	S9
Barrington Dr	F2
Bath La	L6
Bath St	L6
Beaumont Gate	A1
Bedford La	L12
Bedford St	K11
Bell St	P8
Beltane St	G5
Benny Lynch Ct	N12
Bentinck St	D4
Berkeley St	E5
Berkeley Ter La	F5
Binnie Pl	R12
Bishop St	H7
Blackburn St	C10
Blackfriars St	P8
Blackie St	C5
Black St	Q4
Blantyre St	B4
Blythswoodhill	**J6**
Blythswood Sq	J6
Blythswood St	K6
Bothwell La	J7
Bothwell La (Hillhead)	E1
Bothwell St	J7
Braid Sq	J2
Braid St	J1
Breadalbane St	F6
Brechin St	E5
Bridgegate	M10
Bridge St	K11
Bridgeton Cross	T12
Bright St	T3
Broadford St	N1
Broomielaw	**J8**
Broomielaw	J9
Broompark Dr	T7
Brown St	J9
Brunswick St	N8
Buccleuch La	J4
Buccleuch St	H4
Buchanan St	M6
Bunhouse Rd	A3
Burnbank Gdns	G1
Burnbank La	G1
Burnbank Pl	G1
Burnbank Ter	G2
Burns St	K1
Bute Gdns	C1
Bute La	C1
Cadogan St	J7
Cadzow St	H8
Caledonian Cres	E1
Caledon La	A1
Caledon St	A1
Calgary St	N4
Cambridge St	K5
Canal St	N3
Candleriggs	P9
Carfrae St	F2
Carlton Ct	K10
Carlton Pl	L10
Carnarvon St	G3
Carnoustie Pl	G12
Carnoustie St	G10
Carrick St	J9
Carrington St	G2
Castle St	R7
Cathcart Rd	L13
Cathedral Sq	R7
Cathedral St	M6
Cavendish Pl	K13
Cavendish St	K13
Cecil St	C1
Cedar Ct	J1
Cedar St	J1
Centre St	K10
Cessnock	**A10**
Chalmers St	S10
Charles St	S3
Charlotte St	Q10
Cheapside St	G9
Chisolm St	P9
Church St	A3
Circus Dr	T7
Citizen La	M7
Civic St	K3
Clairmont Gdns	E4
Claremont Pl	F4
Claremont St	E5
Claremont Ter	E4
Claremont Ter La	E4
Clarendon Pl	H2
Clarendon St	H2
Clayslaps Rd	C4
Claythorn Av	R11
Claythorn Circ	R10
Claythorn Pk	R11
Claythorn St	S10
Claythorn Ter	S10
Cleland La	L12
Cleland St	M12
Cleveland La	G5
Cleveland St	G5
Clifford La	C11
Clifford Pl	B11
Clifford St	B11
Cliff Rd	F2
Clifton Pl	E5
Clifton St	E4
Clutha St	B11
Clyde Pl	K10
Clydeside Expressway	D7
Clyde St	L9
Cobden Rd	T1
Coburg St	L11
Cochrane St	N7
College La	Q7
College St	P8
Collins St	R7
Commerce St	K10
Commercial Ct	P12
Commercial Rd	N13
Congress Rd	C7
Congress Way	D7
Cook St	J11
Cooperage Pl	A5
Corn St	K2
Cornwall St S	C13

Street	Ref	Street	Ref	Street	Ref	Street	Ref	Street	Ref	Street	Ref
Corunna St	D5	Gladstone St	H2	Lancefield Quay	E8	North Claremount St	E4	Royal Ex Ct	M8	Thistle Ter	L13
Couper Pl	P4	Glasgow Br	L10	Lancefield St	F8	North Ct	M7	Royal Ex Sq	M7	Thornbank St	A5
Couper St	P4	Glassford St	N8	Landressy Pl	S13	North Ct La	M7	Royal Ter	D4	Thurso St	A3
Cowan La	E1	Glebe Ct	Q5	Landressy St	T13	North Dr	L8	Royal Ter La	D4	Tobago Pl	T10
Cowan St	D1	Glebe St	Q4	Langshot St	B11	North Frederick Path	N6	Royston	T4	Tobago St	S12
Cowcaddens	M4	Glenbarr St	S3	Lansdowne Cres	F1	North Frederick St	N7	Roystonhill	S4	Toll La	E10
Cowcaddens Rd	K4	Glenfarg St	H2	Lansdowne Cres La	F1	North Gower St	A11	Royston Rd	S4	Tontine La	P9
Cownwall St	C11	Glenmavis St	K3	Larbert St	L4	North Hanover St	N7	Royston Sq	S3	Torness St	A2
Cragmaddie Ter La	D4	Gloucester St	G11	Laurieston	L12	North Portland St	P7	Rupert St	G2	Tower St	D11
Craighall Business		Goosedubbs	N10	Laurieston Rd	L13	North St	G4	Rutland Ct	E10	Townhead	P4
Pk	M1	Gorbals	N13	Lendel Pl	B11	North Wallace St	P4	Rutland Cres	E10	Townsend St	M3
Craighall Rd	L1	Gorbals St	L13	Lilybank Gdns	B1	Oakfield Av	D2	Rutland Pl	D10	Tradeston	J11
Craigiehall Pl	C9	Gordon La	L7	Lilybank Gdns La	B1	Oakfield La	D2	St. Andrews Cres	E13	Tradeston St	J10
Craigiehall St	C10	Gordon St	K7	Lilybank Ter	C1	Oak St	H8	St. Andrew's La	P9	Trongate	N9
Cranston Hill	F6	Govan Rd	D9	Lister St	Q4	Old Dumbarton Rd	B4	St. Andrews Sq	P10	Tullis Ct	S13
Cranston St	E7	Grace St	F7	Little Dovehill	Q9	Old Rutherglen Rd	M11	St. Andrews St	P9	Tunnel St	D8
Cressnock St	A10	Grafton Pl	N5	Little St	F7	Old Wynd	N9	St. Clair St	G1	Tureen St	S10
Crimea St	H8	Graham Sq	T10	London Rd	P9	Orr St	T12	St. Enoch	M9	Turnbull St	P10
Cromwell La	H2	Graignestock St	S11	Lorne St	C10	Osborne St	M9	St. Enoch Sq	L8	Tyndrum St	M3
Cromwell St	H2	Granby La	C1	Lumsden St	B5	Oswald St	K9	St. Francis Rigg	N13	Union Pl	L7
Crownpoint Rd	T11	Grant St	G3	Lymburn St	C4	Otago La	E1	St. Georges Rd	H3	Union St	L8
Crown St	N12	Granville St	G5	Lynedoch Cres	F3	Otago La N	E1	St. James Rd	P5	Unity Pl	J2
Cumberland St	K12	Gray St	C5	Lynedoch Cres La	F3	Otago St	D2	St. Josephs Vw	T4	University Av	B1
Dalhouse St	J5	Great Dovehill	Q9	Lynedoch Pl	F4	Overnewton Pl	C5	St. Luke's Pl	M12	University Gdns	B1
Dalhousie La	J4	Great George St	D1	Lynedoch St	F4	Overnewton Sq	B5	St. Luke's Ter	M12	University Pl	A1
Dalintober St	H11	Green, The	S13	Lynedoch Ter	G4	Overnewton St	B4	St. Margaret's Pl	N10	Vermont St	C12
Dalmarnock Rd	T13	Greendyke St	P10	Mcalpine St	H9	Oxford La	L11	St. Marys La	L7	Victoria Br	M10
Dalnair St	A4	Greenhead St	S12	McAslin Ct	Q5	Oxford St	K10	St. Mungo Av	N5	Viewfield La	D2
Derby St	D5	Green St	S11	Mcaslin St	R5	Pacific Dr	A9	St. Mungo Pl	Q5	Vinter St	M1
Devon St	K13	Grovepark Ct	H1	Mcfarlane St	R10	Pacific Quay	B8	St. Ninian Ter	N12	Virginia Pl	N8
Dixon St	L9	Grovepark Gdns	H1	McIntosh Ct	T8	Paisley Rd	H10	St. Peters La	J7	Virginia St	N8
Dobbies Ln	N4	Hanover St	M7	McIntosh St	T8	Paisley Rd W	E10	St. Peters St	J3	Waddell Ct	P12
Dobbie's Ln Pl	P5	Harley St	A11	Mcintyre St	G7	Palmerston Pl	C5	St. Rollox Brae	S1	Waddell St	P13
Dornoch St	T11	Harvey St	M1	MacKeith St	T13	Parine St	N9	St. Valentine Ter	P13	Wallace St	J11
Dorset St	F6	Harvie St	C10	Maclean Sq	D9	Park Av	F2	St. Vincent Cres	C5	Walls St	P8
Douglas La	J6	Hastie St	B4	Maclean St	C10	Park Circ	E3	St. Vincent Cres La	C5	Walmer Cres	A11
Douglas St	J5	Haugh Rd	B5	Maclennan St	A12	Park Circ La	E3	St. Vincent La	L7	Warnock St	S6
Dover St	E6	Hayfield Ct	P13	Macleod St	R7	Park Circ Pl	F3	St. Vincent Pl	M7	Warroch St	G9
Drake St	S11	Hayfield St	P13	McNeil Gdns	Q13	Park Dr	E2	St. Vincent St	K6	Washington St	H9
Drury La	L7	Herbertson St	K11	McPhail St	S13	Park Gdns	E4	St. Vincent Ter	F6	Waterloo La	K7
Drygate	R7	High Craighall Rd	L2	McPhater St	L4	Park Gdns La	E4	Salisbury La	L13	Waterloo St	J7
Duke St	Q7	High St	P9	Mair St	D10	Park Gate	E3	Salisbury St	L13	Waterside Pl	Q13
Dunblane St	L4	Hillhead St	C1	Maitland St	L3	Parkgrove Ter	D4	Salkeld St	J13	Watson St	P9
Dunchattan Pl	T9	Hill St	H4	Manresa Pl	K2	Parkgrove Ter La	D4	Saltmarket	N10	Watt St	F11
Dunchattan St	T7	Holland St	H6	Marine Cres	E10	Park Quad	E3	Sandiefield Rd	M13	Weaver St	Q7
Dundashill	L2	Holm St	J8	Marine Gdns	F10	Park Rd	E2	Sandyford Pl La	E5	Wellcroft Pl	K13
Dundas La	M6	Holyrood Cres	F1	Marlow St	E13	Park St S	E3	Sandyford St	A5	Wellington La	J7
Dundas St	M7	Holyrood Quad	G1	Martha St	N6	Park Ter	E3	Sauchiehall La	K5	Wellington St	K8
Dunearn St	G2	Hopehill Rd	H1	Mart St	N10	Park Ter E La	E3	Sauchiehall St	K5	Wellpark St	S8
Dunlop St	M9	Hope St	L7	Mary St	L2	Park Terrrace La	E3	Sawmillfield St	K1	Westbank La	D2
Durham St	C12	Houldsworth La	E6	Mauchline St	J13	Parsonage Row	Q8	Scotland St	F12	Westbank Quad	D2
Eaglesham Ct	D10	Houldsworth St	E6	Mavisbank Gdns	D9	Parsonage Sq	Q8	Scotland St W	C11	West Campbell St	J8
Eaglesham Pl	C10	Houston Pl	F10	Maxwell Dr	B13	Parson St	R5	Scott St	J5	West End Pk St	F3
Eagle St	L1	Houston St	F11	Maxwell Gdns	B13	Paterson St	H10	Seamore St	G1	West George La	L7
Earlston Av	T4	Howard St	L9	Maxwell Grn	C13	Payne St	M2	Seaward La	F10	West George St	K6
Earlston Pl	S4	Hunter St	R9	Maxwell St	M9	Pembroke St	F6	Seaward Pl	E12	West Graham St	J3
East Bath La	M6	Huntingdon Rd	R1	Megan Gate	T13	Percy St	A11	Seaward St	F11	West Greenhill Pl	D6
East Campbell St	R10	Huntingdon Sq	R1	Megan St	T13	Perth St	G7	Shaftesbury St	G6	West Nile St	L7
Edington St	K1	Hutcheson St	N9	Melbourne St	T9	Piccadilly St	G8	Shamrock St	J3	West Prince's La	E1
Edwin St	C11	Hutchinson Town		Melrose St	H2	Pine Pl	N13	Shields La	F11	West Princes St	F2
Eglinton Ct	K12	Ct	N13	Merchant City	P8	Pinkston Dr	Q3	Shipbank La	N10	West Regent La	K6
Elcho St	S10	Hydepark St	F9	Merchant La	N10	Pinkston Rd	Q2	Shuttle St	P8	West Regent St	K6
Elderslie St	F4	India St	H6	Metropole La	M10	Pitt St	J7	Sighthill	R2	West St	H12
Eldon St	E2	Ingram St	M7	Middlesex Gdns	D11	Plantation Pk Gdns	C11	Silvergrove St	S12	Whitehall St	G8
Elie St	A2	Jamaica St	L9	Middlesex St	D12	Plantation Sq	D10	Somerset Pl Ms	E4	William St	G6
Elliot Pl	E7	James Morrison St	P10	Middleton St	A10	Port Dundas	M2	South Ex Ct	M8	Willowbank Cres	F2
Elliot St	E7	James Nisbet St	S5	Midwharf St	M2	Port Dundas		South Frederick St	N7	Willowbank St	F3
Elmbank Cres	H5	James St	S13	Miller St	M8	Business Pk	K1	Southpark Av	C2	Wilson St	N8
Elmbank St	H6	James Watt St	J9	Millroad Dr	S10	Port Dundas La	M5	Southpark La	D1	Windsor St	H1
Elmbank St La	H6	Jocelyn Sq	N10	Millroad Gdns	T10	Port Dundas Rd	L3	South Portland St	L10	Windsor Ter	H1
Errol Gdns	M12	John Knox St	S8	Millroad St	R10	Port Eglinton	H13	Southside Cres	L13	Wishart St	S7
Esmond St	A4	John St	N7	Milnpark Gdns	C11	Portman St	E11	South Woodside		Woodlands Dr	F2
Eton La	D1	Kelvingrove	D3	Milnpark St	D11	Port St	F6	Rd	F1	Woodlands Gate	F3
Exchange Pl	M7	Kelvingrove St	D5	Milton St	M4	Portugal St	L12	Spiers Wf	L2	Woodlands Rd	E1
Falfield St	J13	Kelvinhaugh	A5	Minerva St	D6	Possil Rd	K1	Spoutmouth	Q9	Woodlands Ter	E4
Farnell St	K1	Kelvinhaugh Gate	B5	Minerva Way	C6	Professors Sq	C2	Springburn Rd	S4	Woodrow Circ	B13
Finnieston	D6	Kelvinhaugh Pl	C5	Mitchell La	L7	Provanhill St	T3	Springfield Ct	M8	Woodrow Pl	A13
Finnieston Quay	D8	Kelvinhaugh St	A5	Mitchell St	L8	Queen Elizabeth		Springfield Quay	F9	Woodside Cres	G4
Finnieston Sq	E6	Kelvin Way	C4	Moir St	Q10	Gdns	N13	Spring Wynd	N13	Woodside Pl	F4
Finnieston St	E7	Kennedy Path	P5	Molendinar St	Q9	Queens Cres	G2	Stafford St	N4	Woodside Pl La	F4
Firpark St	T5	Kennedy St	N5	Moncur St	R10	Queen St	M8	Stanley St	E11	Woodside Ter	F4
Firpark Ter	T7	Kent Rd	F5	Montague St	F2	Radnor St	C4	Stanley St La	E11	Woodside Ter La	F4
Fitzroy La	D5	Kent St	R10	Monteith Pl	R11	Raglan St	J2	Steel St	P10	Yorkhill	C4
Florence St	N12	Keppochhill Pl	P1	Monteith Row	Q10	Regent Moray St	B4	Stevenson St	R10	Yorkhill Par	A4
Forbes Dr	T11	Keppochhill Way	P1	Montrose St	P8	Renfield La	K7	Stewart St	L3	Yorkhill St	B5
Forbes St	T10	Kerr Dr	T12	Moore St	T9	Renfield St	L7	Stirlingfauld Pl	L13	York St	J9
Fountainwell Av	Q1	Kerr Pl	T12	Morrison Ct	L8	Renfrew Ct	M5	Stirling Rd	Q6		
Fountainwell Dr	Q1	Kerr St	T12	Morrison St	H10	Renfrew La	L5	Stobcross Rd	B6		
Fountainwell Pl	Q1	Kilbarchan St	K12	Mosque Av	M11	Renfrew St	H4	Stobcross St	E7		
Fountainwell Rd	Q1	Kilbirnie Pl	H13	Nairn St	B4	Renton St	M3	Stobcross Wynd	A6		
Fountainwell Sq	R1	Kilbirnie St	J13	Napiershall La	G1	Rhymer St	T4	Stockwell Pl	M9		
Fountainwell Ter	R1	Killermont St	M5	Napiershall Pl	G1	Richmond St	P7	Stockwell St	M10		
Fox St	L9	King George V Br	K9	Napiershall St	G1	Ritchie St	J13	Stromness St	J13		
Francis St	J13	King's Br	Q13	Nelson Mandela Pl	M7	Riverview Dr	H10	Suffolk St	Q10		
Gadshill St	T3	Kingston	G12	Nelson St	J10	Riverview Gdns	J9	Surrey St	L13		
Gallowgate	P9	Kingston St	J10	Netherby Dr	B13	Riverview Pl	H10	Sussex St	D11		
Garnethill	J4	King St	N10	New City Rd	K3	Robertson La	J8	Sutherland La	A1		
Garnethill St	J4	Kinning Park	D12	Newton St	G4	Robertson St	K9	Swan St	N3		
Garnet St	H5	Kinning St	G11	Newton Ter La	F5	Rodney St	K1	Sydney St	S9		
Garscube Rd	K4	La Belle Allee	E4	New Wynd	N9	Ropework La	M10	Taylor Pl	Q6		
Garth St	N8	La Belle Pl	E4	Nicholas St	Q7	Rose St	K5	Taylor St	Q7		
George Sq	M7	Ladywell St	S7	Nicholson St	L11	Ross St	Q10	Templeton Business			
George St	N7	Laidlaw St	H10	Norfolk Ct	L11	Rottenrow	P6	Cen	S12		
Gibson St	R10	Lambhill Quad	C11	Norfolk St	L11	Rottenrow E	Q7	Templeton St	S12		
Gibson St (Hillhead)	D1	Lambhill St	C11	North Canal Bk	N2	Royal Bk Pl	M7	Teviot St	A5		
Gilbert St	A5	Lanark St	Q10	North Canal Bk St	L2	Royal Cres	D5	Thistle St	N11		

Distances between two selected towns in this table are shown in miles and kilometres. In general, distances are based on the shortest routes by classified roads.

DISTANCE IN KILOMETRES

DISTANCE IN MILES

For further information on motorway services providers:
Moto www.moto-way.com   RoadChef www.roadchef.com   Welcome Break www.welcomebreak.co.uk

Motorway	Junction	Service Provider	Service Name	On-site Services
A1(M)	1	Welcome Break	South Mimms	
	10	Extra	Baldock	
	17	Extra	Peterborough	
	34	Moto	Blyth	
	61	RoadChef	Durham	
	64	Moto	Washington	
A74(M)	16	RoadChef	Annandale Water	
	22	Welcome Break	Gretna Green	
M1	2–4	Welcome Break	London Gateway	
	11–12	Moto	Toddington	
	14–15	Welcome Break	Newport Pagnell	
	15A	RoadChef	Northampton	
	16–17	RoadChef	Watford Gap	
	21–21A	Welcome Break	Leicester Forest East	
	22	Moto	Leicester	
	23A	Moto	Donington Park	
	25–26	Moto	Trowell	
	28–29	RoadChef	Tibshelf	
	30–31	Welcome Break	Woodall	
	38–39	Moto	Woolley Edge	
M2	4–5	Moto	Medway	
M3	4A–5	Welcome Break	Fleet	
	8–9	RoadChef	Winchester	
M4	3	Moto	Heston	
	11–12	Moto	Reading	
	13	Moto	Chieveley	
	14–15	Welcome Break	Membury	
	17–18	Moto	Leigh Delamere	
	23A	First Motorway	Magor	
	30	Travel Rest	Cardiff Gate	
	33	Moto	Cardiff West	
	36	Welcome Break	Sarn Park	
	47	Moto	Swansea	
	49	RoadChef	Pont Abraham	
M5	3–4	Moto	Frankley	
	8	RoadChef	Strensham (South)	
	8	RoadChef	Strensham (North)	
	13–14	Welcome Break	Michael Wood	
	19	Welcome Break	Gordano	
	21–22	RoadChef	Sedgemoor (South)	
	21–22	Welcome Break	Sedgemoor (North)	
	24	Moto	Bridgwater	
	25–26	RoadChef	Taunton Deane	
	28	Extra	Cullompton	
	29–30	Moto	Exeter	

On-site Services:

- ⛽ Fuel
- £ Service shops
- ₤ₓ Other shops
- ♿ Disabled facilities
- ℹ Information
- 👥 Conference facilities
- 🍴 Food
- 🛏 Accommodation
- 🚿 Showers

All motorway service areas must provide fuel, free toilets and free short term parking 24 hours a day

Motorway	Junction	Service Provider	Service Name	Fuel	Disabled	Food	Service shops	Information	Accommodation	Other shops	Conference	Showers
M6	3–4	Welcome Break	Corley	●	●	●	●	●	●			●
	10–11	Moto	Hilton Park	●	●	●	●	●	●	●		●
	14–15	RoadChef	Stafford (South)	●	●	●	●		●	●	●	
	14–15	Moto	Stafford (North)	●	●	●	●	●	●	●	●	
	15–16	Welcome Break	Keele	●	●	●	●	●				●
	16–17	RoadChef	Sandbach	●	●	●	●		●			●
	18–19	Moto	Knutsford	●	●	●	●	●	●	●		●
	27–28	Welcome Break	Charnock Richard	●	●	●	●	●	●		●	●
	32–33	Moto	Lancaster	●	●	●	●	●	●	●		●
	35A–36	Moto	Burton-in-Kendal (North)	●	●	●	●	●				●
	36–37	RoadChef	Killington Lake (South)	●	●	●	●	●	●			
	38–39	Westmorland	Tebay	●	●	●	●		●		●	●
	41–42	Moto	Southwaite	●	●	●	●	●	●	●		●
M6 Toll	T6–T7	RoadChef	Norton Canes	●	●	●	●		●	●	●	●
M8	4–5	RoadChef	Harthill	●	●	●	●					●
M9	9	Moto	Stirling	●	●	●	●	●	●			
M11	8	Welcome Break	Birchanger Green	●	●	●	●	●	●		●	●
M18	5	Moto	Doncaster North	●	●	●	●	●	●	●		●
M20	8	RoadChef	Maidstone	●	●	●	●	●	●	●	●	●
M23	11	Moto	Pease Pottage	●	●	●	●	●				●
M25	5–6	RoadChef	Clacket Lane	●	●	●	●	●	●	●	●	●
	23	Welcome Break	South Mimms	●	●	●	●	●	●	●	●	
	30	Moto	Thurrock	●	●	●	●	●	●			●
M27	3–4	RoadChef	Rownhams	●	●	●	●		●	●	●	
M40	8	Welcome Break	Oxford	●	●	●	●	●	●		●	●
	10	Moto	Cherwell Valley	●	●	●	●	●	●	●	●	●
	12–13	Welcome Break	Warwick	●	●	●	●	●	●		●	●
M42	2	Welcome Break	Hopwood Park	●	●	●	●	●		●		●
	10	Moto	Tamworth	●	●	●	●	●	●	●	●	●
M48	1	Moto	Severn View	●	●	●	●	●	●			
M50	4	Welcome Break	Ross Spur	●	●	●	●					●
M54	4	Welcome Break	Telford	●	●	●	●	●	●		●	●
M56	14	RoadChef	Chester	●	●	●	●	●	●			
M61	6–7	First Motorway	Bolton West	●	●	●	●		●		●	●
M62	7–9	Welcome Break	Burtonwood	●	●	●	●	●	●			●
	18–19	Moto	Birch	●	●	●	●	●	●	●	●	●
	25–26	Welcome Break	Hartshead Moor	●	●	●	●	●	●		●	●
	33	Moto	Ferrybridge	●	●	●	●		●	●		●
M65	4	Extra	Blackburn with Darwen	●	●	●	●		●			
M74	4–5	RoadChef	Bothwell (South)	●	●	●	●					●
	5–6	RoadChef	Hamilton (North)	●	●	●	●	●	●		●	●
	11–12	Cairn Lodge	Happendon	●	●	●	●				●	●
	12–13	Welcome Break	Abington	●	●	●	●	●	●		●	
M90	6	Moto	Kinross Sevices	●	●	●	●	●	●			●

MOTORING INFORMATION

ROUTE PLANNING

UK and Continental route-planning services offered through:

The AA
www.theaa.com/travelwatch/planner_main.jsp

The RAC
rp.rac.co.uk/routeplanner

For planning door to door trips across Europe:

Via Michelin
www.viamichelin.com

Address searches to provide online road and street maps.

Multimap
www.multimap.co.uk

Streetmap
www.streetmap.co.uk

WEATHER

UK national and regional weather reports are available from:

BBC Weather
www.bbc.co.uk/weather

The Met Office
www.met-office.gov.uk

TRAFFIC NEWS

The latest traffic news can be obtained from:

AA Roadwatch
www.theaa.com/travelwatch/travel_news.jsp

RAC Traffic News
www.rac.co.uk/travelservices/traffic

Travel information for Wales
www.traffic-wales.com

Travel information for Scotland
www.nadics.org.uk

FERRIES

For information about times, availability, cost and booking:

Brittany Ferries (for France and Spain)
www.brittany-ferries.co.uk

Caledonian MacBrayne (for Scottish Islands)
www.calmac.co.uk

Condor Ferries (for the Channel Islands and St. Malo)
www.condorferries.co.uk

DFDS Seaways (for Holland and Scandinavia)
www.dfdsseaways.co.uk

Emeraude Lines (Channel Islands to France)
www.emeraude.co.uk

Fjord Line (for Norway)
www.fjordline.co.uk

Hoverspeed (for cross-channel services)
www.hoverspeed.co.uk

Irish Ferries (for Ireland)
www.irishferries.com

Norfolk Line (for Dunkirk)
www.norfolkline.com

Norse Merchant Ferries (for Ireland)
www.norsemerchant.com

NorthLink Ferries (for Orkney and Shetland)
www.northlinkferries.co.uk

Orkney Ferries (for Orkney Islands)
www.orkneyferries.co.uk

P & O Ferries
  (for Ireland, France, Belgium, Holland and Spain)
www.poferries.com

Pentland Ferries (for Orkney Islands)
www.pentlandferries.com

Red Funnel (for Isle of Wight)
www.redfunnel.co.uk

SeaCat/Isle of Man Steam Packet Company
  (for Great Britain, Isle of Man and Ireland)
www.steam-packet.com

SeaFrance (for Dover and Calais)
www.seafrance.com

Shetland Island Council (for Shetland Islands)
www.shetland.gov.uk/ferryinfo/ferry.htm

Smyril Line (for Norway, Faroe Islands and Iceland)
www.smyril-line.com/uk

Speed Ferries (for cross-channel services)
www.speedferries.com

Stena Line
  (for Great Britain, Republic of Ireland and Holland)
www.stenaline.co.uk

Superfast Ferries (Scotland to Belgium)
www.superfast.com

Swansea Cork ferries (for southern Ireland)
www.swanseacorkferries.com

Wightlink (for Isle of Wight)
www.wightlink.co.uk

MOTORWAY SERVICES

Moto
www.moto-way.co.uk

RoadChef
www.roadchef.com

Welcome Break
www.welcomebreak.co.uk

TOURIST INFORMATION

BRITAIN

British Tourist Authority
www.visitbritain.com

@ UK (UK travel and tourist guide)
www.atuk.co.uk

Information Britain
www.information-britain.co.uk

The National Trust
www.nationaltrust.org.uk

Good Beach Guide
www.goodbeachguide.co.uk

British Waterways
www.britishwaterways.co.uk

The Forestry Commission
www.forestry.gov.uk

The National Virtual Museum
www.24hourmuseum.org.uk

ENGLAND

English Tourist Board
www.visitengland.com

English Nature
www.english-nature.org.uk

The Countryside Agency
www.countryside.gov.uk

English Heritage
www.english-heritage.org.uk

WALES

Welsh Tourist Board
www.visitwales.com

Countryside Council for Wales
www.ccw.gov.uk

Castles of Wales
www.castlewales.com/home.html

National Museums and Galleries of Wales
www.nmgw.ac.uk

SCOTLAND

Scottish Tourist Board
www.visitscotland.com

Scottish Natural Heritage
www.snh.org.uk

The National Trust for Scotland
www.nts.org.uk

Historic Scotland
www.historic-scotland.gov.uk

National Museums of Scotland
www.nms.ac.uk

VENUES

Earls Court & Olympia, London
www.eco.co.uk

ExCeL, London
www.excel-london.co.uk

G-Mex Centre, Manchester
www.g-mex.co.uk

MEN Arena, Manchester
www.men-arena.com

Metro Radio Arena, Newcastle
www.telewestarena.co.uk

National Exhibition Centre (NEC), Birmingham
www.necgroup.co.uk/nec

Scottish Exhibition and Conference Centre (SECC), Glasgow
www.secc.co.uk

Wembley Complex, London
www.wembley.co.uk/venues

DRIVING HELP AND ADVICE

MOTORING ORGANISATIONS

The following organisations provide specialist motoring services and travel information, plus a vehicle recovery service in the event of a breakdown or road accident.

The Automobile Association (AA)
www.theaa.com

The Royal Automobile Club (RAC)
www.rac.co.uk

Greenflag
www.greenflag.co.uk

europ assistance
www.europ-assistance.co.uk

Direct Line
www.directline.com

DRIVING IN BRITAIN

Information on driving, road signs, rules and regulations are contained in the following sites:

Department for Transport
For news, items and views concerning roads and road safety.
www.dft.gov.uk

Disabled Persons Transport Advisory Committee
An organisation providing advice on transport needs for disabled people and information on the Blue Badge Scheme.
www.dptac.gov.uk

Driver and Vehicle Licensing Agency
Deals with all aspects of driving licence and vehicle registration.
www.dvla.gov.uk

Driving Standards Agency
Responsible for conducting driving tests, and maintaining a register of Approved Driving Instructors.
www.dsa.gov.uk

Highways Agency
Responsible for managing, maintaining and improving England's motorways and trunk roads.
www.highways.gov.uk

Highway Code
Shows the latest version of the Highway Code.
www.highwaycode.gov.uk

The Institute of Advanced Motorists
An organisation which promotes road safety through its advanced driving guidance courses and the IAM Advanced Driving Test.
www.iam.org.uk

National Travelwise Association
This is an initiative which aims to make people more aware of alternative forms of transport and ultimately change their attitude to the use of their cars.
www.travelwise.org.uk

Pass Plus
A scheme backed by the Driving Standards Agency and insurers to encourage newly qualified drivers to improve their driving skills.
www.passplus.org.uk

The Royal Society for the Prevention of Accidents
This association encourages an active interest in road safety by improving driving standards and encouraging members to pass its advanced driving test.
www.rospa.com

The Think! Road Safety Website
Information and advice about the Government's Think! road safety campaigns.
www.thinkroadsafety.gov.uk

Transport for London
The organisation responsible for the management of an integrated transport system in London.
www.londontransport.co.uk

Vehicle and Operator Services Agency (VOSA)
This is the agency responsible for ensuring that all vehicles are maintained to a minimum standard as laid down by law through the MOT examination scheme.
www.vosa.gov.uk